T0212978

# Lecture Notes in Computer Science 10453

More information about this series at http://www.springer.com/series/7410

Marc Dacier · Michael Bailey
Michalis Polychronakis · Manos Antonakakis (Eds.)

# Research in Attacks, Intrusions, and Defenses

## 20th International Symposium, RAID 2017
## Atlanta, GA, USA, September 18–20, 2017
## Proceedings

Springer

*Editors*
Marc Dacier
Qatar Computing Research Institute
Doha
Qatar

Michael Bailey
University of Illinois at Urbana Champaign
Champaign, IL
USA

Michalis Polychronakis
Stony Brook University
Stony Brook, NY
USA

Manos Antonakakis
Georgia Institute of Technology
Georgia
USA

ISSN 0302-9743 ISSN 1611-3349 (electronic)
Lecture Notes in Computer Science
ISBN 978-3-319-66331-9 ISBN 978-3-319-66332-6 (eBook)
DOI 10.1007/978-3-319-66332-6

Library of Congress Control Number: 2017952320

LNCS Sublibrary: SL4 – Security and Cryptology



Printed on acid-free paper

This Springer imprint is published by Springer Nature
The registered company is Springer International Publishing AG
The registered company address is: Gewerbestrasse 11, 6330 Cham, Switzerland

# Preface

The International Symposium on Research in Attacks, Intrusion, and Defenses (RAID) is celebrating its 20th anniversary this year! You have the proceedings of this event in your hands and we hope you will enjoy it.

RAID was created to offer a venue for researchers looking at the emerging field of intrusion detection. It was the follow up to the CMAD workshop (future directions in Computer Misuse and Anomaly Detection), which was held for the fourth and last time in 1996. CMAD was initiated by Becky Bace, who sadly passed away in 2017, and had approached intrusion detection from both an operational as well as from an "intelligence" point of view. RAID has grown in much the same spirit, expanding its scope beyond the sole intrusion detection area, encouraging research on real-world problems, fostering sound, thorough, and reproducible experiments, and building bridges to other communities (e.g., measurement, networking, systems) that share these same values. Twenty years later, RAID is a well-established international conference that enjoys truly worldwide recognition. Hosted every year in a different location, it has alternated between Europe and the USA with a few notable exceptions, including Australia (2007), Saint Lucia (2013), and Japan (2015).

This year, RAID 2017 received 105 admissible submissions of which 21 were accepted (20% acceptance rate). Each paper received at least 3 reviews and 43 papers (41%) received two additional reviews to settle disagreements between the first three reviewers, to answer questions raised during the online discussion phase, or to address issues brought forth by the authors' rebuttal. As in previous years, a double blind reviewing process was used to ensure that the reviewers remained unaware of the authors' names and affiliations during the discussion. The final decision for each paper was made during a face-to-face PC meeting following the IEEE Symposium on Security and Privacy in San Jose (CA), in May 2017. More than two thirds of the PC members attended that meeting.

The quality, diversity, and commitment of the Program Committee is paramount to the success of any conference and, with RAID, we have striven to broaden the pool of reviewers. Over the last ten years, an average of 50% of the members of the PC were changed from year to year. Furthermore, this year, nearly a third of the new PC members had never served on the RAID PC before, ensuring the healthy development of the community by reaching out to external experienced reviewers. It is also worth noting that RAID always tries to maintain a balance between industry and academia within its PC members, as well as between the various geographies. This year, around 75% of the PC members came from academia and 25% from industry. Approximately half of the members work in the USA, a bit less than a third in Europe, and the rest, 15%, were from the rest of the world, mostly Asia.

We endeavor to provide quality reviews to those who submit a paper to RAID and we try to provide constructive feedback when a paper is unfortunately rejected. In order to improve transparency, accepted papers are accompanied by a public summary, which is available within the online proceedings as supplementary material. It briefly explains the reasons why a given paper has been accepted but also, sometimes, acknowledges some reservations expressed by members of the PC. We hope that these open summaries will encourage future researchers to address the limitations identified by the PC members and consider new directions for research.

In 2012, for the 15th anniversary of RAID, we began the process of awarding, every five years, an "influential paper" award to a previously published paper at RAID that has had a major influence on the community. This year's award was given to the 2004 RAID paper by K. Wang and S.J. Stolfo, entitled "Anomalous Payload-Based network intrusion detection." That paper has been cited 869 times since its publication, which is an average of 67 times per year, every year, since its publication, the highest yearly average for every paper published at RAID since its creation.

RAID wouldn't exist without the dedication of the reviewers, who play a special role and spend a great deal of time reviewing papers, discussing them online, attending the PC meeting, shepherding papers, etc. To express our gratitude to them, every year RAID awards an "Outstanding Reviewer" prize. The winner is selected based on a number of factors: the quality of the reviews as judged by the other reviewers (usefulness, technical depth, etc.), timeliness of the reviews, participation in the online discussion and the face-to-face meeting, and the willingness to defend papers as opposed to quickly discard them. While we had a difficult time identifying a winner amongst so many excellent reviewers, it is with great pleasure that we announce that this year the award goes to Jon Giffin, from Hewlett Packard Enterprise.

RAID only exists because of the community that supports it. Indeed, RAID is completely self-funded. Every organizer independently shoulders the financial risks associated with its organization. The sponsors, therefore, play a very important role and ensure that the registration fees remain very reasonable. Therefore, we want to take this opportunity to thank Spamhaus and Comcast for their generous sponsorships of RAID 2017. We, of course, are very grateful to the general chair, Manos Antonakakis, from Georgia Tech, and his assembled team for ensuring that the conference ran smoothly. Special thanks go to the local arrangement chair, Roberto Perdisci, University of Georgia; to the publication chair, Michalis Polychronakis, from Stony Brook University; to the publicity chair, Nick Nikiforakis, from Stony Brook University; to the sponsor chair, Yacin Nadji, from Georgia Tech; to the local infrastructure chair, William R. Garrison, from Georgia Tech; and to the poster chair and webmaster, Chaz Lever, from Georgia Tech.

Happy Birthday, RAID. We all look forward for many more years to come.

September 2017

Marc Dacier
Michael Bailey

# Organization

## Organizing Committee

### General Chair

Manos Antonakakis — Georgia Tech, USA

### Program Committee Chair

Marc Dacier — QCRI/HBKU, Qatar

### Program Committee Co-chair

Michael Bailey — University of Illinois at Urbana Champaign, USA

### Publication Chair

Michalis Polychronakis — Stony Brook University, USA

### Publicity Chair

Nick Nikiforakis — Stony Brook University, USA

### Sponsor Chair

Yacin Nadji — Georgia Tech, USA

### Local Arrangement Chair

Roberto Perdisci — University of Georgia, USA

### Local Infrastructure Chair

William R. Garrison — Georgia Tech, USA

### Poster Chair and Webmaster

Chaz Lever — Georgia Tech, USA

## Program Committee

| | |
|---|---|
| Magnus Almgren | Chalmers University of Technology, Sweden |
| Johanna Amann | ICSI, USA |
| Leyla Bilge | Symantec Research Labs, France |
| Lorenzo Cavallaro | Royal Holloway, University of London, UK |
| Mihai Christodorescu | Qualcomm Research, USA |
| Hervé Debar | Télécom SudParis, France |
| Manuel Egele | Boston University, USA |

| | |
|---|---|
| Sandro Ettale | Technical University Eindhoven, The Netherlands |
| Aurélien Francillon | Eurecom, France |
| Jon Giffin | HPE Fortify, USA |
| Virgil Gligor | Carnegie Mellon University, USA |
| Guofei Gu | Texas A&M University, USA |
| Sotiris Ioannidis | FORTH, Greece |
| Yongdae Kim | Korea Advanced Institute of Science and Technology, South Korea |
| Andrea Lanzi | University of Milan, Italy |
| Wenke Lee | Georgia Tech, USA |
| Corrado Leita | Lastline, UK |
| David Naccache | ENS Paris, France |
| Roberto Perdisci | University of Georgia, USA |
| Jason Polakis | University of Illinois at Chicago, USA |
| Bill Sanders | University of Illinois at Urbana-Champaign, USA |
| Kevin Snow | Zeropoint, USA |
| Angelos Stavrou | George Mason University, USA |
| Sal Stolfo | Columbia University, USA |
| Purui Su | Institute of Software/CAS, China |
| Mark Tehranipoor | University of Florida, USA |
| Al Valdes | University of Illinois at Urbana Champaign, USA |
| X. Sean Wang | Fudan University, China |
| Xiaogang (Cliff) Wang | US Army Research Office and adjunct with NC State University, USA |
| Ting Fang Yen | DataVisor, Inc., USA |
| Kehuan Zhang | Chinese University of Hong Kong, China |

## External Reviewers

| | |
|---|---|
| Ali Abbasi | University of Twente, The Netherlands |
| Mahdi Alizadeh | University of Eindhoven, The Netherlands |
| Luca Allodi | University of Eindhoven, The Netherlands |
| Wissam Aoudi | Chalmers University of Technology, Sweden |
| Grégory Blanc | Télécom SudParis, France |
| Nicole Borrelli | Google, USA |
| Bram Cappers | University of Eindhoven, The Netherlands |
| Jiongyi Chen | Chinese University of Hong Kong, China |
| Phakpoom Chinprutthiwong | Texas A&M University, USA |
| Aisling Connolly | ENS, France |
| Nassim Corteggiani | Maxim Integrated, France |
| Andrei Costin | Jyväskylä University, Finland |
| Wenrui Diao | Chinese University of Hong Kong, China |
| Shuaike Dong | Chinese University of Hong Kong, China |
| Mohamed Elsabagh | George Mason University, USA |
| Houda Ferradi | NTT, France |

| | |
|---|---|
| Remi Geraud | ENS, France |
| Thomas Hayes | Eurecom, France |
| Weili Han | Fudan University, China |
| Kevin Hong | Texas A&M University, USA |
| Panagiotis Ilia | FORTH, Greece |
| Mikel Iturbe | Mondragon University, Spain |
| Ryan Johnson | George Mason University, USA |
| Yuan Kang | Columbia University, USA |
| Aljoscha Lautenbach | Chalmers University of Technology, Sweden |
| Florian Lugou | Télécom ParisTech, France |
| Clémentine Maurice | TU Graz, Austria |
| Abner Mendoza | Texas A&M University, USA |
| Soo-Jin Moon | Carnegie Mellon University, USA |
| Marus Muench | Eurecom, France |
| Boel Nelson | Chalmers University of Technology, Sweden |
| Dario Nisi | Eurecom, France |
| Nasser Nowdehi | Volvo Car Corporation and Chalmers University of Technology, Sweden |
| Melek Önen | Eurecom, France |
| Thomas Rosenstatter | Chalmers University of Technology, Sweden |
| Vyas Sekar | Carnegie Mellon University, USA |
| Boris Skoric | University of Eindhoven, The Netherlands |
| Saumya Solanki | University of Illinois at Chicago, USA |
| Charalampos Stylianopoulos | Chalmers University of Technology, Sweden |
| Adrian Tang | Columbia University, USA |
| Di Tang | Chinese University of Hong Kong, China |
| Stefan Thaler | University of Eindhoven, The Netherlands |
| Haopei Wang | Texas A&M University, USA |
| Yunfeng Xi | DataVisor, Inc., USA |
| Fenghao Xu | Chinese University of Hong Kong, China |
| Lei Xu | Texas A&M University, USA |
| Min Yang | Fudan University, China |
| Zhemin Yang | Fudan University, China |
| Emmanuele Zambon | SecurityMatters, The Netherlands |
| Yuan Zhang | Fudan University, China |
| Yunlei Zhao | Fudan University, China |
| Zhe Zhou | Chinese University of Hong Kong, China |

## Steering Committee

| | |
|---|---|
| Davide Balzarotti | Eurecom, France |
| Herbert Bos | Vrije Universiteit Amsterdam, The Netherlands |
| Herve Debar | Télécom SudParis, France |
| Deborah Frincke | NSA Research, USA |
| Ming-Yuh Huang | Northwest Security Institute, USA |

| | |
|---|---|
| Somesh Jha | University of Wisconsin, USA |
| Erland Jonsson | Chalmers University of Technology, Sweden |
| Engin Kirda | Northeastern University, USA |
| Christopher Kruegel | UC Santa Barbara, USA |
| Wenke Lee | Georgia Tech, USA |
| Richard Lippmann | MIT Lincoln Laboratory, USA |
| Ludovic Me | CentraleSupélec, France |
| Robin Sommer | ICSI/LBNL, USA |
| Angelos Stavrou | George Mason University, USA |
| Sal Stolfo | Columbia University, USA |
| Alfonso Valdes | University of Illinois at Urbana Champaign, USA |
| Giovanni Vigna | UC Santa Barbara, USA |
| Andreas Wespi | IBM Research, Switzerland |
| S. Felix Wu | UC Davis, USA |
| Diego Zamboni | Swisscom, Switzerland |

## Sponsors

Spamhaus
Comcast

# Contents

## Software Security



## Intrusion Detection



## Android Security

## Systems Security



## Cybercrime



## Cloud Security



## Network Security

# Software Security

# VDF: Targeted Evolutionary Fuzz Testing of Virtual Devices

Andrew Henderson[1(✉)], Heng Yin[2], Guang Jin[1], Hao Han[1], and Hongmei Deng[1]

[1] Intelligent Automation, Inc., Rockville, MD 20855, USA
hendersa@icculus.org, {gjin,hhan,hdeng}@i-a-i.com
[2] University of California, Riverside, CA 92521, USA
heng@cs.ucr.edu

**Abstract.** As cloud computing becomes more and more prevalent, there is increased interest in mitigating attacks that target hypervisors from within the virtualized guest environments that they host. We present VDF, a targeted evolutionary fuzzing framework for discovering bugs within the software-based virtual devices implemented as part of a hypervisor. To achieve this, VDF selectively instruments the code of a given virtual device, and performs record and replay of memory-mapped I/O (MMIO) activity specific to the virtual device. We evaluate VDF by performing cloud-based parallel fuzz testing of eighteen virtual devices implemented within the QEMU hypervisor, executing over two billion test cases and revealing over one thousand unique crashes or hangs in one third of the tested devices. Our custom test case minimization algorithm further reduces the erroneous test cases into only 18.57% of the original sizes on average.

**Keywords:** Virtualization · Fuzzing · Device testing · Security

## 1 Introduction

As cloud computing becomes more prevalent, the usage of virtualized guest systems for rapid and scalable deployment of computing resources is increasing. Major cloud service providers, such as Amazon Web Services (AWS), Microsoft Azure, and IBM SoftLayer, continue to grow as demand for cloud computing resources increases. Amazon, the current market leader in cloud computing, reported that AWS's net sales exceeded *7.88 billion USD* in 2015 [2], which demonstrates a strong market need for virtualization technology.

This popularity has led to an increased interest in mitigating attacks that target hypervisors from within the virtualized guest environments that they host.

This document has been approved for public release: 88ABW-2016-3973.

**Electronic supplementary material** The online version of this chapter (doi:10.1007/978-3-319-66332-6_1) contains supplementary material, which is available to authorized users.


M. Dacier et al. (Eds.): RAID 2017, LNCS 10453, pp. 3–25, 2017.
DOI: 10.1007/978-3-319-66332-6_1

Unfortunately, hypervisors are complex pieces of software that are difficult to test under every possible set of guest runtime conditions. *Virtual hardware devices* used by guests, which are hardware peripherals emulated in software (rather than directly mapping to physical devices on the host system), are particularly complex and a source of numerous bugs [3–6]. This has led to the ongoing discovery of vulnerabilities that exploit these virtual devices to access the host.

Because virtual devices are so closely associated with the hypervisor, if not integrated directly into it, they execute at a higher level of privilege than any code executing within the guest environment. They are not part of the guest environment, per se, but they are privileged subsystems that the guest environment directly interacts with. Under no circumstances should activity originating from within the guest be able to attack and compromise the hypervisor, so effectively identifying potential vulnerabilities in these virtual devices is a difficult, but valuable, problem to consider. However, these virtual devices are written by a number of different authors, and the most complex virtual devices are implemented using thousands of lines of code. Therefore, it is desirable to discover an effective and efficient method to test these devices in a scalable and automated fashion without requiring expert knowledge of each virtual device's state machine and internal details.

Such issues have led to a strong interest in effectively testing virtual device code [9,28] to discover bugs or other behaviors that may lead to vulnerabilities. However, this is a non-trivial task as virtual devices are often tightly coupled to the hypervisor codebase and may need to pass through a number of device initialization states (i.e. BIOS and guest kernel initialization of the device) before representing the device's state within a running guest system.

Evolutionary fuzzing techniques (e.g., AFL [38]) has gained its popularity recently for its effectiveness in discovering crashes and hangs. It is widely used in industry, and most finalists in the DARPA Cyber Grand Challenge used it for vulnerability discovery. Several academic research papers soon appeared to further improve the effectiveness of evolutionary fuzzing, such as AFLFast [21], VUzzer [33], Driller [35], and DeepFuzz [22]. While these efforts greatly improve the state-of-the-art, they aim at finding defects within the entire user-level program, and cannot be directly applied to find bugs in virtual devices, for several reasons. First of all, the fuzz testing must be targeted at specific virtual device code, which is a rather small portion of the entire hypervisor code base. It must be *in-situ* as well, as virtual devices frequently interact with the rest of the hypervisor code. Last but not least, it must be stateful, since virtual devices need to be properly initialized and reach certain states to trigger defects.

To address these unique challenges, we propose Virtual Device Fuzzer (*VDF*), a novel fuzz testing framework that provides targeted fuzz testing of interesting subsystems (virtual devices) within complex programs. VDF enables the testing of virtual devices within the context of a running hypervisor. It utilizes *record and replay* of virtual device memory-mapped I/O (MMIO) activity to create fuzz testing seed inputs that are guaranteed to reach states of interest and initialize each virtual device to a known good state from which to begin each test. Providing proper seed test cases to the fuzzer is important for effective exploring the branches of a program [25,34], as a good starting seed will focus the fuzzer's efforts in areas of interest within the program. VDF mutates these seed inputs to generate and replay fuzzed MMIO activity to exercise additional branches of interest.

As a proof of concept, we utilize VDF to test a representative set of eighteen virtual devices implemented within the QEMU whole-system emulator [19], a popular type-2 hypervisor that uses a virtualized device model. Whether QEMU completely emulates the guest CPU or uses another hypervisor, such as KVM [10] or Xen [18], to execute guest CPU instructions, hardware devices made available to the guest are software-based devices implemented within QEMU.

In summary, this paper makes the following contributions:

- We propose and develop a targeted, in-situ fuzz testing framework for virtual devices.
- We evaluate VDF by testing eighteen QEMU virtual devices, executing over 2.28 billion test cases in several parallel VDF instances within a cloud environment. This testing discovered a total of 348 crashes and 666 hangs within six of the tested virtual devices. Bug reports and CVEs have been reported to the QEMU maintainers where applicable.
- We devise a testcase minimization algorithm to reduce each crash/hang test case to a minimal test case that still reproduces the same bug. The average test case is reduced to only 18.57% of its original size, greatly simplifying the analysis of discovered bugs and discovering duplicate test cases that reproduce the same bug. We also automatically generate source code suitable for reproducing the activity of each test case to aid in the analysis of each discovered bug.
- We analyze the discovered bugs and organize them into four categories: excess host resource usage, invalid data transfers, debugging asserts, and multi-threaded race conditions.

## 2 Background

Within QEMU, virtual device code registers callback functions with QEMU's virtual memory management unit (MMU). These callback functions expose virtual device functionality to the guest environment and are called when specific memory addresses within the guest memory space are read or written. QEMU uses this mechanism to implement memory-mapped I/O (MMIO), mimicking the MMIO mechanism of physical hardware.

We have identified a model for guest activity that attempts to attack these virtual devices:

1. The virtual device is correctly instantiated by the hypervisor and made available to the guest environment.
2. The virtual device is correctly initialized via the guest's BIOS and OS kernel and is brought to a stable state during the guest boot process. Any needed guest kernel device drivers have been loaded and initialized.

3. Once the guest boots, the attacker acquires privileged access within the guest and attempts to attack the virtual devices via memory reads/writes to the MMIO address(es) belonging to these virtual devices.

Unfortunately, it is non-trivial to perform large-scale testing of virtual devices in a manner analogous to this model. The read/write activity would originate from within the guest environment, requiring the guest to completely boot and initialize prior to performing a test[1]. Because any read/write to a virtual device control register may change the internal state of the device, the device must be returned to a known good "just initialized" state prior to the start of each test.

While utilizing virtual machine (VM) state snapshots to save and restore the state of the guest is a potential solution, the time required to continually restore the state of the guest to a known good state makes this approach inefficient for large-scale testing. Consider the megabytes of system state data (guest RAM, CPU state, and device state and internal cache storage) required to restore a running VM to a known state. Even when ignoring the time required to retrieve such state information from secondary storage, megabytes of data within the snapshot must still be unserialized and placed into hypervisor data structures prior to the start of each test.

## 2.1 Understanding Guest Access of Virtual Devices

The flow of activity for virtual device access from within QEMU is shown in Fig. 1. This figure shows a KVM-accelerated QEMU hypervisor configuration. The guest environment executes within QEMU, and the virtual devices are provided to the guest by QEMU. CPU instruction execution and memory accesses, however, are serviced by the KVM hypervisor running within the host system's Linux kernel. A request is made from a guest process (a) and the guest kernel accesses the device on the process's behalf (b). This request is passed through QEMU's KVM interface to the KVM kernel module in the host's kernel. KVM then forwards the request to a QEMU virtual device (c). The virtual device responds (d) and the result is provided to the guest kernel (e). Finally, the guest process receives a response from the guest kernel (f).

Unlike the standard 0–3 ring-based protection scheme used by x86 platforms, virtualized systems contain two sets of rings: rings 0 through 3 on the host, and rings 0' through 3' on the guest. The rings within the guest are analogous to their counterparts on the host with one exception: the highest priority guest ring (ring 0') is at a lower priority than the lowest priority ring on the host (ring 3). While a guest environment may be compromised by malicious software, it is still safely contained within a virtualized environment. However, if malware were to compromise the hypervisor and gain host ring 3 privileges, it would effectively "break out" of the virtualization and gain the opportunity to attack the host.

[1] QEMU provides the *qtest* framework to perform arbitrary read/write activity without the guest. We discuss qtest, and its limitations when fuzz testing, in Sect. 3.

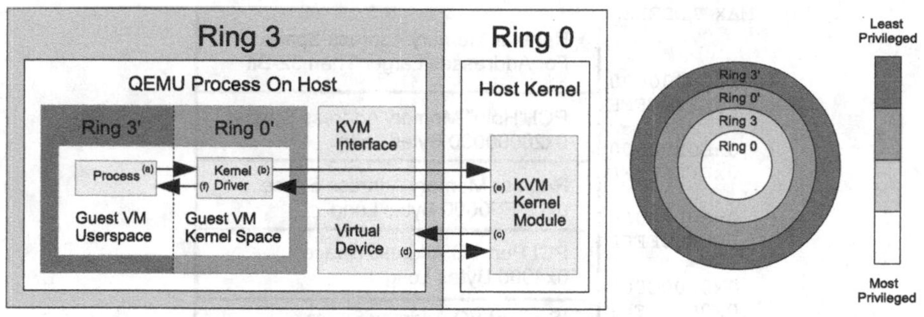


**Fig. 1.** Device access process for a device request originating from inside of a QEMU/KVM guest. Note that the highest level of privilege in the guest (ring 0') is still lower than that of the QEMU process (ring 3).

## 2.2 Understanding Memory Mapped I/O

Both physical and virtual peripherals provide one or more registers that control their behavior. By accessing these control registers, the hardware is instructed to perform tasks and provide information about the current state of the device. Each device's control registers are organized into one or more *register banks*. Each register bank is mapped to a contiguous range of guest physical memory locations that begin at a particular *base address*. To simplify interaction with these control registers, the registers are accessed via normal memory bus activity. From a software point of view, hardware control registers are accessed via reads and writes to specific physical memory addresses.

The x86 family of processors is unique because it also provides port I/O-specific memory (all memory addresses below `0x10000`) that cannot be accessed via standard memory reads and writes [29]. Instead, the x86 instruction set provides two special I/O-specific instructions, `IN` and `OUT`, to perform 1, 2, or 4 byte accesses to port I/O memory. Other common architectures, such as Alpha, ARM, MIPS, and SPARC, do not have this port I/O memory region and treat all control register accesses as regular memory-mapped I/O. For simplicity in our discussion, we use port-mapped I/O (PMIO) and memory-mapped I/O interchangeably throughout this paper.

Figure 2 shows where MMIO devices are mapped in guest physical memory on x86-based systems. PCI-based PMIO mappings occur in the addresses ranging from `0xC000` through `0xFFFF`, with ISA-based devices mapped into the sub-`0xC000` range. PCI devices may also expose control registers or banks of device RAM or ROM in the PCI "hole" memory range `0xE0000000-0xFFFFFFFF`.

While some ISA devices are historically mapped to specific addresses (for example, `0x3F8` for the COM1 serial port), other ISA devices can be configured to use one or more of a small set of selectable base addresses to avoid conflicts with other devices. PCI devices are far more flexible in the selection of their address mapping. At boot, the BIOS queries the PCI bus to enumerate all PCI devices connected to the bus. The number and sizes of the control register banks

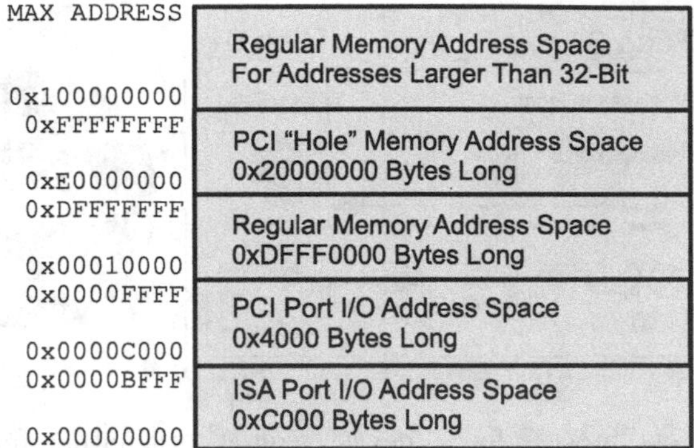


**Fig. 2.** The x86 address space layout for port- and memory-mapped I/O.

needed by each PCI device are reported to the BIOS. The BIOS then determines a memory-mapping for each register bank that satisfies the MMIO needs of all PCI devices without any overlap. Finally, the BIOS instructs the PCI bus to map specific base addresses to each device's register banks using the PCI base address registers (BARs) of each device.

However, PCI makes the task of virtual device testing more difficult. By default, the BARs for each device contain invalid addresses. Until the BARs are initialized by the BIOS, PCI devices are unusable. The PCI host controller provides two 32-bit registers in the ISA MMIO/PMIO address space for configuring each PCI device BAR[2]. Until the proper read/write sequence is made to these two registers, PCI devices remain unconfigured and inaccessible to the guest environment. Therefore, configuring a virtual PCI-based device involves initializing both the state of the PCI bus and the virtual device.

## 3 Fuzzing Virtual Devices

### 3.1 Evolutionary Fuzzing

Fuzzing mutates seed input to generate new test case inputs which execute new paths within a program. Simple fuzzers naively mutate seed inputs without any knowledge of the program under test, treating the program as a "black box". In comparison, evolutionary fuzzing, such as AFL [38] can insert compile-time instrumentation into the program under test. This instrumentation, placed at every branch and label within the instrumented program, tracks which branches have been taken when specific inputs are supplied. Such evolutionary fuzzing is much more effective at exploring new branches.

If AFL generates a test case that covers new branches, that test case becomes a new seed input. As AFL continues to generate new seeds, more and more states of the program are exercised. Unfortunately, all branches are considered to be of

[2] `CONFIG_ADDRESS` at `0xCF8` and `CONFIG_DATA` at `0xCFC` [11].

equal priority during exploration, so uninteresting states are explored as readily as interesting states are. This leads to a large number of wasted testing cycles as uninteresting states are unnecessarily explored. Therefore, VDF modifies AFL to only instrument the portions of the hypervisor source code that belong to the virtual device currently being tested. This effectively makes AFL ignore the remainder of the hypervisor codebase when selectively mutating seed inputs.

AFL maintains a "fuzz bitmap", with each byte within the bitmap representing a count of the number of times a particular branch within the fuzzed program has been taken. AFL does not perform a one-to-one mapping between a particular branch and a byte within the bitmap. Instead, AFL's embedded instrumentation places a random two-byte constant ID into each branch. Whenever execution reaches an instrumented branch, AFL performs an `XOR` of the new branch's ID and the last branch ID seen prior to arriving at the new branch. This captures both the current branch and the unique path taken to reach it (such as when the same function is called from multiple locations in the code). AFL then applies a hashing function to the `XOR`'d value to determine which entry in the bitmap represents that branch combination. Whenever a particular branch combination is exercised, the appropriate byte is incremented within the bitmap.

VDF modifies AFL to use a much simpler block coverage mechanism that provides a one-to-one mapping between a particular instrumented branch and a single entry in the bitmap. Because VDF selectively instruments *only* the branches within a virtual device, the bitmap contains more than enough entries to dedicate an entry to each instrumented branch[3]. VDF's modifications do away with the `XOR`ing of IDs and AFL's hash function. Instead, IDs are assigned linearly, simplifiying the ground truth determination of whether a particular branch has been reached during testing while guaranteeing that no IDs are duplicated.

Thus, AFL takes a general purpose approach towards fuzzing/exploring all branches within a program. VDF's modified AFL takes a more focused approach that constrains fuzzing to only the branches of interest in a program. VDF's approach eliminates the possibility of ambiguous branch coverage, which is still possible to experience with an unmodified AFL.

### 3.2 VDF Workflow

Figure 3 shows the three-step flow used by VDF when testing a virtual device. In the first step, virtual device activity is recorded while the device is being exercised. This log of activity includes any initialization of PCI BARs for the virtual device via the PCI host controller (if needed), initialization of any internal device registers, and any MMIO activity that exercises the virtual device. This log is saved to disk and becomes the seed input for the fuzzer. This collection of seed input is described further in Sect. 3.3.

In the second step, the collected virtual device read/write activity is then provided as seed data to AFL. Multiple AFL instances can be launched in parallel, with one required master instance and one or more optional slave instances. The

[3] VDF still uses a two-byte branch ID, allowing for 65536 unique branches to be instrumented. In practice, this is more than adequate for virtual device testing.

Step 1: Record read/write activity of a virtual device by using our instrumented QEMU and generate a device activity seed test case.

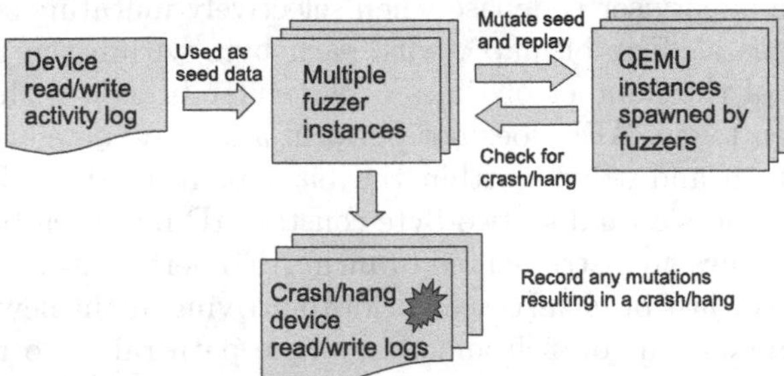


Step 2: Execute multiple fuzzer instances in parallel to repeatedly mutate the seed, launch QEMU instances to replay the mutated seed, and discover any crashes or hangs.

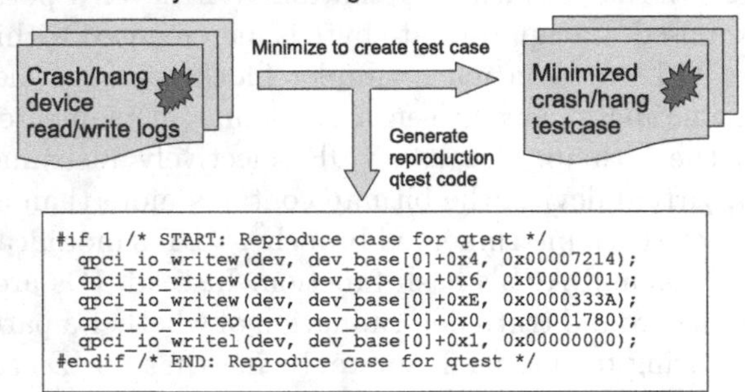


Step 3: Minimize crash/hang tests to simplify analysis and generate qtest code for future reproduction of each discovered crash or hang.

**Fig. 3.** VDF's process for performing fuzz testing of QEMU virtual devices.

primary difference between master and slave instances is that the master uses a series of sophisticated mutation strategies (bit/byte swapping, setting bytes to specific values like 0x00 and 0xFF, etc.) to explore the program under test. Slave instances only perform random bit flips throughout the seed data.

Once the seed input has been mutated into a new test case, a new QEMU instance is spawned by AFL. VDF replays the test case in the new QEMU instance and observes whether the mutated data has caused QEMU to crash or hang. VDF does not blindly replay events, but rather performs strict filtering on the mutated seed input during replay. The filter discards malformed events, events describing a read/write outside the range of the current register bank, events referencing an invalid register bank, etc. This prevents mutated data from potentially exercising memory locations unrelated to the virtual device under test. If a test case causes a crash or hang, the test case is logged to disk.

Finally, in the third step, each of the collected crash and hang test cases is reduced to a minimal test case capable of reproducing the bug. Both a minimized test case and source code to reproduce the bug are generated. The minimization of test cases is described further in Sect. 3.5.

### 3.3 Virtual Device Record and Replay

Fuzzing virtual devices is difficult because they are *stateful*. It is necessary to traverse an arbitrarily large number of states within both the virtual device and the remainder of the hypervisor prior to reaching a desired state within the virtual device. Because each virtual device must be initialized to a known good start state prior to each test, VDF uses *record and replay* of previous virtual device activity to prepare the device for test and then perform the test itself.

First, VDF records any guest reads or writes made to the virtual device's control registers when the device is initialized during guest OS boot[4]. This captures the setup performed by the BIOS (such as PCI BAR configuration), device driver initialization in the kernel, and any guest userspace process interaction with the device's kernel driver. Table 1 shows the different sources of initialization activity used by VDF when recording device activity during our testing.

**Table 1.** QEMU virtual devices seed data sources.

| Device class | Device | Seed data source |
|---|---|---|
| Audio | AC97 | Linux guest boot with ALSA [1] `speaker-test` |
| | CS4231a | |
| | ES1370 | |
| | Intel-HDA | |
| | SoundBlaster 16 | |
| Block | Floppy | qtest test case |
| Char | Parallel | Linux guest boot with directed console output |
| | Serial | |
| IDE | IDE Core | qtest test case |
| Network | EEPro100 (i82550) | Linux guest boot with `ping` of IP address |
| | E1000 (82544GC) | |
| | NE2000 (PCI) | |
| | PCNET (PCI) | |
| | RTL8139 | qtest test case |
| SD Card | SD HCI | Linux guest boot with mounted SDHCI volume |
| TPM | TPM | Linux guest boot with TrouSerS test suite [16] |
| Watchdog | IB700 | qtest test case |
| | 16300ESB | Linux guest boot |

[4] If only a minimal amount of recorded activity is required, VDF can capture initialization activity via executing a QEMU qtest test case.

Second, the recorded startup activity is partitioned into two sets: an *init* set and a *seed* set. The init set contains any seed input required to initialize the device for testing, such as PCI BAR setup, and the activity in this set will never be mutated by the fuzzer. VDF plays back the init set at the start of each test to return the device to a known, repeatable state. The seed set contains the seed input that will be mutated by the fuzzer. It can be any read/write sequence that exercises the device, and it usually originates from user space activity that exercises the device (playing an audio file, pinging an IP address, etc.).

Even with no guest OS booted or present, a replay of these two sets returns the virtual device to the same state that it was in immediately after the register activity was originally recorded. While the data in the sets could include timestamps to ensure that the replay occurs at the correct time intervals, VDF does not do this. Instead, VDF takes the simpler approach of advancing the virtual clock one microsecond for each read or write performed. The difficulty with including timestamps within the seed input is that the value of the timestamp is too easily mutated into very long virtual delays between events. While it is true that some virtual device branches may only be reachable when a larger virtual time interval has passed (such as interrupts that are raised when a device has completed performing some physical event), our observation is that performing a fixed increment of virtual time on each read or write is a reasonable approach.

**Event Record Format.** VDF event records contain three fields: a header field, base offset field, and data written field. This format captures all data needed to replay an MMIO event and represents this information in a compact format requiring only 3–8 bytes per event. The compactness of each record is an important factor because using a smaller record size decreases the number of bits that can potentially be mutated.

The header is a single byte that captures whether the event is a read or write event, the size of the event (1, 2, or 4 bytes), and which virtual device register bank the event takes place in. The base offset field is one to three bytes in size and holds the offset from the base address. The size of this field will vary from device to device, as some devices have small register bank ranges (requiring only one byte to represent an offset into the register bank) and other devices map much larger register banks and device RAM address ranges (requiring two or three bytes to specify an offset). The data field is one or four bytes in size and holds the data written to a memory location when the header field specifies a write operation. Some devices, such as the floppy disk controller and the serial port, only accept single byte writes. Most devices accept writes of 1, 2, or 4 bytes, requiring a 4 byte field for those devices to represent the data. For read operations, the data field is ignored.

While VDF's record and replay of MMIO activity captures the interaction of the guest environment with virtual devices, some devices may make use of interrupts and DMA. However, we argue that such hardware events are not necessary to recreate the behavior of most devices for fuzz testing. Interrupts are typically *produced* by a virtual device, rather than *consumed*, to alert the guest environment that some hardware event has completed. Typically, another read or write event would be initiated by the guest in reaction to an interrupt, but since we record all this read/write activity, the guest's response to the interrupt is captured without explicitly capturing the interrupt.

DMA events copy data between guest and device RAM. DMA copies typically occur when buffers of data must be copied and the CPU isn't needed to copy this data byte-by-byte. Our observation is that if we are only copying data to be processed, it is not actually necessary to place legitimate data at the correct location within guest RAM and then copy it into the virtual device. It is enough to say that the data has been copied and then move onto the next event. While the size of data and alignment of the data may have some impact on the behavior of the virtual device, such details are outside the scope of this paper.

**Recording Virtual Device Activity.** Almost every interaction between the guest environment and virtual devices occurs via virtual device callback functions. These functions are registered with QEMU's MMU and are triggered by MMIO activity from the guest. Such callback functions are an ideal location to record the virtual device's activity. Rather than attempt to capture the usage of each device by reconstructing the semantics of the guest's kernel and memory space, we capture device activity at the point of the hardware interface that is provided to software. In fact, we have no immediate need to understand the details of the guest environment as the virtual devices execute at a level above that of even the guest's BIOS or kernel. By placing recording logic in these callback functions, VDF is able to instrument each virtual device by manually adding only 3–5 LOC of recording logic to each MMIO callback function.

**Playback of Virtual Device Activity.** Once VDF has recorded a stream of read/write events for a virtual device, it must replay these events within the context of a running QEMU. Because QEMU traverses a large number of branches before all virtual devices are instantiated and testing can proceed, it isn't possible to provide the event data to QEMU via the command line. The events must originate from within the guest environment in the form of memory read/write activity. Therefore, QEMU must be initialized before performing event replay.

QEMU provides *qtest*, which is a lightweight framework for testing virtual devices. qtest is a QEMU *accelerator*, or type of execution engine. Common accelerators for QEMU are *TCG* (for the usage of QEMU TCG IR) and *KVM* (for using the host kernel's KVM for hardware accelerated execution of guest CPU instructions). The qtest framework works by using a test driver process to spawn a separate QEMU process which uses the qtest accelerator. The qtest accelerator within QEMU communicates with the test driver process via IPC. The test driver remotely controls QEMU's qtest accelerator to perform guest memory read/write instructions to virtual devices exposed via MMIO. Once the test is complete, the test driver terminates the QEMU process.

While the qtest accelerator is convenient, it is inadequate for fuzz testing for two reasons. First, the throughput and timing of the test is slowed because of QEMU start-up and the serialization, deserialization, and transfer time of the

IPC protocol. Commands are sent between the test driver and QEMU as plain-text messages, requiring time to parse each string. While this is not a concern for the virtual clock of QEMU, wall clock-related issues (such as thread race conditions) are less likely to be exposed.

Second, qtest does not provide control over QEMU beyond spawning the new QEMU instance and sending control messages. It is unable to determine exactly where a hung QEMU process has become stuck. A hung QEMU also hangs the qtest test driver process, as the test driver will continue to wait for input from the non-responsive QEMU. If QEMU crashes, qtest will respond with the feedback that the test failed. Reproducing the test which triggers the crash may repeat the crash, but the analyst still has to attach a debugger to the spawned QEMU instance prior to the crash to understand the crash.

VDF seeks to automate the discovery of any combination of virtual device MMIO activity that triggers a hang or crash in either the virtual device or some portion of the hypervisor. qtest excels at running known-good, hard-coded tests on QEMU virtual devices for repeatable regression testing. But, it becomes less useful when searching for unknown vulnerabilities, which requires automatically generating new test cases that cover as many execution paths as possible.

To address these shortcomings, we have developed a new *fuzzer* QEMU accelerator, based upon qtest, for VDF's event playback. This new accelerator adds approximately 850 LOC to the QEMU codebase. It combines the functionality of the qtest test driver process and the qtest accelerator within QEMU, eliminating the need for a separate test driver process and the IPC between QEMU and the test driver. More importantly, it allows VDF to directly replay read/write events as if the event came directly from within a complete guest environment.

### 3.4 Selective Branch Instrumentation

Fuzz testing must explore as many branches of interest as possible, so determining the *coverage* of those branches during testing is a metric for measuring the thoroughness of each testing session. While the code within any branch may host a particular bug, execution of the branch must be performed to trigger the bug. Thus, reaching more branches of interest increases the chances that a bug will be discovered. However, if the fuzzer attempts to explore *every* branch it discovers, it can potentially waste millions of tests exploring uninteresting branches.

To address this issue, VDF leverages the instrumentation capabilities of AFL to selectively place instrumentation in only the branches of interest (those belonging to a virtual device). By default, the compiler toolchain supplied with AFL instruments programs built using it. VDF modifies AFL to selectively instrument only code of interest within the target program. A special compile-time option has been added to AFL's toolchain, and only branches in source files compiled with this flag are instrumented. Other files will have uninstrumented branches that are ignored by the fuzzer as they are seen as (very long) basic blocks of instructions that occur between instrumented branches.

Prior to the start of each testing session, VDF dumps and examines all function and label symbols found in the instrumented hypervisor. If a symbol is found that maps to an instrumented branch belonging to the current virtual device under test, the name, address, and AFL branch ID (embedded in the symbol name) of the symbol are stored and mapped to the symbol's location in the fuzz bitmap. At any point during testing, the AFL fuzz bitmap can be dumped using VDF to provide ground truth of exactly which branches have been covered.

```
static void voice_set_active (AC97LinkState *s, int bm_index, int on) {
    switch (bm_index) {
    case PI_INDEX:
        AUD_set_active_in (s->voice_pi, on);
        break;
    case PO_INDEX:
        AUD_set_active_out (s->voice_po, on);
        break;
    case MC_INDEX:
        AUD_set_active_in (s->voice_mc, on);
        break;
    default:
        AUD_log ("ac97",
            "invalid bm_index(%d) in voice_set_active",
            bm_index);
        break;
    }
}
ID: COVERED: ADDRESS: SYMBOL:                             LINE:
--- -------- -------- -------                             -----
00c COVER    002e92e0 voice_set_active                    296
00d COVER    002e9324 REF_LABEL__tmp_ccBGk9PX_s__27_39 296
00e COVER    002e9368 REF_LABEL__tmp_ccBGk9PX_s__28_40 296
00f UNCOVER  002e93a4 REF_LABEL__tmp_ccBGk9PX_s__29_41 296
```

**Fig. 4.** A sample of the branch coverage data for the AC97 virtual device.

Figure 4 shows an example of the coverage information report that VDF provides. This example shows both the original source code for a function in the AC97 audio virtual device (top) and the generated branch coverage report for that function (bottom). The report provides two pieces of important information. The first is the ground truth of which branches are instrumented, including their address within the binary, the symbol associated with the branch (inserted by the modified AFL), and the original source file line number where the branch's code is located. The second is whether a particular branch has been visited yet.

The four branches listed in the report are associated with the four cases in the switch statement of the `voice_set_active()` function, which is located on line 296 in the source file. An analyst familiar with the internals of the AC97 virtual device could review this report and then devise new seed inputs to trigger any unexplored branches. Thus, such reports are useful for not only an understanding of *which* branches have been reached, but they also providing insight into *how* unexplored virtual device branches might be reached.

### 3.5 Creation of Minimal Test Cases

Once VDF detects either a crash or a hang in a virtual device, the test case that produced the issue is saved for later examination. This test case may contain a large amount of test data that is not needed to reproduce the discovered issue, so it is desirable to reduce this test case to the absolute minimum number of records needed to still trigger the bug. Such a minimal test case simplifies the job of the analyst when using the test case to debug the underlying cause.

AFL provides a test case minimization utility called `afl-tmin`. `afl-tmin` seeks to make the test case input smaller while still following the same path of execution through the binary. Unfortunately, this will not be useful for reducing the test cases recorded by VDF, which is only interested in reaching the state in which a crash/hang occurs. It has no interest in reaching every state in the test case, but only the states necessary to reach the crash/hang state. Therefore, VDF performs a three-step test case post-processing, seen in Fig. 5, to produce a minimal test case which passes through a minimimal number of states from any test case shown to reproduce an issue.

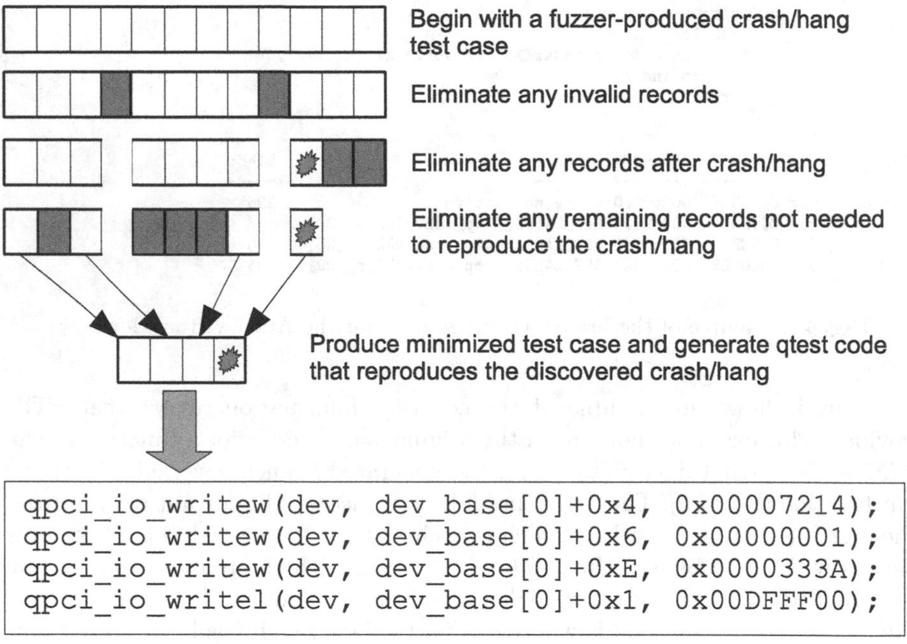
Begin with a fuzzer-produced crash/hang test case
Eliminate any invalid records
Eliminate any records after crash/hang
Eliminate any remaining records not needed to reproduce the crash/hang
Produce minimized test case and generate qtest code that reproduces the discovered crash/hang
qpci_io_writew(dev, dev_base[0]+0x4, 0x00007214);
qpci_io_writew(dev, dev_base[0]+0x6, 0x00000001);
qpci_io_writew(dev, dev_base[0]+0xE, 0x0000333A);
qpci_io_writel(dev, dev_base[0]+0x1, 0x00DFFF00);

**Fig. 5.** The test case minimization process.

First, the test case file is read into memory and any valid test records in the test case are placed into an ordered dataset in the order in which they appear within the test case. Because the fuzzer lacks semantic understanding of the fields within these records, it produces many records via mutation that contain invalid garbage data. Such invalid records may contain an invalid header field, describe a base offset to a register outside of the register bank for the device, or simply be a truncated record at the end of the test case. After this filtering step, only valid test records remain.

Second, VDF eliminates all records in the dataset that are located after the point in the test case where the issue is triggered. To do this, it generates a new test case using all but the last record of the dataset and then attempts to trigger the issue using this truncated test case. If the issue is still triggered, the last record is then removed from the dataset and another new truncated test case is generated in the same fashion. This process is repeated until a truncated test case is created that no longer triggers the issue, indicating that all dataset records located after the issue being triggered are now removed.

Third, VDF eliminates any remaining records in the dataset that are not necessary to trigger the issue. Beginning with the first record in the dataset, VDF iterates through each dataset record, generating a new test case using all but the current record. It then attempts to trigger the issue using this generated test case. If the issue is still triggered, the current record is not needed to trigger the issue and is removed from the dataset. Once each dataset record has been visited and the unnecessary records removed, the dataset is written out to disk as the final, minimized test case. In addition, source code is generated that is suitable for reproducing the minimized dataset as a qtest testcase.

While simple, VDF's test case minimization is very effective. The 1014 crash and hang test cases produced by the fuzzer during our testing have an average size of 2563.5 bytes each. After reducing these test cases to a minimal state, the average test case size becomes only 476 bytes, a mere 18.57% of the original test case size. On average, each minimal test case is able to trigger an issue by performing approximately 13 read/write operations. This average is misleadingly high due to some outliers, however, as over 92.3% of the minimized test cases perform fewer than six MMIO read/write operations.

## 4 Evaluation

The configuration used for all evaluations is a cloud-based 8-core 2.0 GHz Intel Xeon E5-2650 CPU instance with 8 GB of RAM. Each instance uses a minimal server installation of Ubuntu 14.04 Linux as its OS. Eight cloud instances were utilized in parallel. Each device was fuzzed within a single cloud instance, with one master fuzzer process and five slave fuzzer processes performing the testing. A similar configuration was used for test case minimization: each cloud instance ran six minimizer processes in parallel to reduce each crash/hang test case.

We selected a set of eighteen virtual devices, shown in Table 2, for our evaluation of VDF. These virtual devices utilize a wide variety of hardware features, such as timers, interrupts, and DMA. Each of these devices provides one or more MMIO interfaces to their control registers, which VDF's fuzzing accelerator interacts with. All devices were evaluated using QEMU v2.5.0[5], with the exception of the TPM device. The TPM was evaluated using QEMU v2.2.50 with an applied patchset that provides a libtpms emulation [20] of the TPM

[5] US government approval for the engineering and public release of the research shown in this paper required a time frame of approximately one year. The versions of QEMU identified for this study were originally selected at the start of that process.

**Table 2.** QEMU virtual devices tested with VDF.

| Device class | Device | Branches of interest | Initial coverage | Final coverage | Crashes found | Hangs found | Tests per instance | Test duration |
|---|---|---|---|---|---|---|---|---|
| Audio | AC97 | 164 | 43.9% | 53.0% | 87 | 0 | 24.0 M | 59d 18 h |
| | CS4231a | 109 | 5.5% | 56.0% | 0 | 0 | 29.3 M | 65d 12 h |
| | ES1370 | 165 | 50.9% | 72.7% | 0 | 0 | 30.8 M | 69d 18 h |
| | Intel-HDA | 273 | 43.6% | 58.6% | 238 | 0 | 23.1 M | 59d 12 h |
| | SoundBlaster 16 | 311 | 26.7% | 81.0% | 0 | 0 | 26.7 M | 58d 13 h |
| Block | Floppy | 370 | 44.9% | 70.5% | 0 | 0 | 21.0 M | 57d 15 h |
| Char | Parallel | 91 | 30.8% | 42.9% | 0 | 0 | 14.6 M | 25d 12 h |
| | Serial | 213 | 2.3% | 44.6% | 0 | 0 | 33.0 M | 62d 12 h |
| IDE | IDE Core | 524 | 13.9% | 27.5% | 0 | 0 | 24.9 M | 65d 6 h |
| Network | EEPro100 (i82550) | 240 | 15.8% | 75.4% | 0 | 0 | 25.7 M | 62d 12 h |
| | E1000 (82544GC) | 332 | 13.9% | 81.6% | 0 | 384 | 23.9 M | 61d |
| | NE2000 (PCI) | 145 | 39.3% | 71.7% | 0 | 0 | 25.2 M | 58d 13 h |
| | PCNET (PCI) | 487 | 11.5% | 36.1% | 0 | 0 | 25.0 M | 58d 13 h |
| | RTL8139 | 349 | 12.9% | 63.0% | 0 | 6 | 24.2 M | 58d 12 h |
| SD Card | SD HCI | 486 | 18.3% | 90.5% | 14 | 265 | 24.0 M | 62d |
| TPM | TPM | 238 | 26.1% | 67.3% | 9 | 11 | 2.1M | 36d 12 h |
| Watchdog | IB700 | 16 | 87.5% | 100.0% | 0 | 0 | 0.3 M | 8 h |
| | I6300ESB | 76 | 43.4% | 68.4% | 0 | 0 | 2.1 M | 26 h |

hardware device [23]. Fewer than 1000 LOC were added to each of these two QEMU codebases to implement both the fuzzer accelerator and any recording instrumentation necessary within each tested virtual device.

VDF discovered *noteworthy bugs in six virtual devices* within the evaluation set, including a known denial-of-service CVE [7] and a new, previously undiscovered denial-of-service CVE [8]. Additional bugs were discovered relating to memory management and thread-race conditions, underscoring VDF's ability to discover bugs of a variety of natures utilizing the same techniques and principles.

### 4.1 Virtual Device Coverage and Bug Discovery

During our testing with VDF, we collected four metrics to aid in our understanding of both the speed and magnitude of VDF's coverage. These metrics are (1) the number of branches covered by the initial seed test case; (2) the total number of branches in the virtual device; (3) the current total number of branches covered (updated at one minute intervals); and (4) the percentage of total bugs discovered during each cumulative day of testing. Taken together, these metrics describe not only the total amount of coverage provided by VDF, but also the speed at which coverage improves via fuzzing and how quickly it discovers crash/hangs.

Figure 6 shows the average percentage of covered branches over cumulative testing time. Of the eighteen tested virtual devices, 30.15% of the total branches were covered by the initial seed test cases. After nine cumulative days of testing (36 h of parallel testing with one master and five slave fuzzing instances),

62.32% of the total branches were covered. The largest increase in average coverage was seen during the first six cumulative hours of testing, where coverage increased from the initial 30.15% to 52.84%. After 2.25 days of cumulative testing, average coverage slows considerably and only 0.43% more of the total branches are discovered during the next 6.75 cumulative days of testing. While eleven of the eighteen tested devices stopped discovering new branches after only one day of cumulative testing, six of the seven remaining devices continued to discover additional branches until 6.5 cumulative days had elapsed. Only in the serial device were additional branches discovered after nine cumulative days.

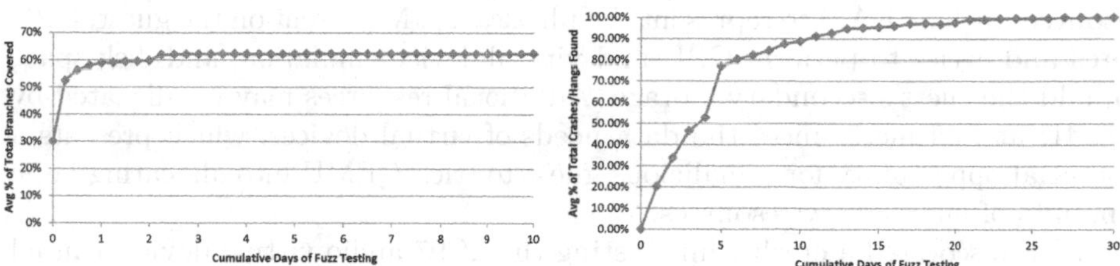


**Fig. 6.** Average percentage of branches covered (left) and average percentage of total bugs discovered (right) over time during fuzz testing.

Table 2 presents some insightful statistics about coverage. The smallest improvement in the percentage of coverage was seen in the AC97 virtual device (9.1% increase), and the largest improvement in coverage was seen in the SDHCI virtual device (72.2% increase). The smallest percentage of coverage for any virtual device with discovered crashes/hangs was 53.0% (AC97), but eight others had a greater level of coverage than 53.0% with no discovered crashes/hangs.

Figure 6 also shows the average percentage of discovered hangs/crashes over cumulative testing time. As shown in Table 2, a total of 1014 crashes and hangs were discovered in six virtual devices. These 1014 test cases were all discovered within 27 days of cumulative testing for each device, with no additional test cases being discovered after that point. Approximately 50% of all test cases were discovered after four days of cumulative testing, with approximately 80% of all test cases discovered after five days of cumulative testing.

One interesting insight is that even though the number of branches covered is very close to its maximum after approximately 2.5 cumulative days of testing, only approximately 25% of all crash/hang test cases were discovered at that point in time. This shows that it is not necessarily an *increase in branch coverage* that leads to the discovery of bugs, but rather the *repeated fuzz testing of those discovered branches*.

## 4.2 Classification of All Discovered Virtual Device Bugs

While it is straightforward to count the number of discovered crash/hang test cases generated by VDF, it is non-trivial to map these test cases to their underlying cause without a full understanding of the virtual device under test.

Our proposed test case minimization greatly simplifies this process, as many unique bugs identified by VDF minimize to the same set of read/write operations. The ordering of these operations may differ, but the final read/write that triggers the bug remains the same. Each discovered virtual device bug falls into one of four categories: Excess resource usage (AC97), invalid data transfers (E1000, RTL8139, SDHCI), debugging asserts (Intel-HDA), and thread race conditions (TPM).

**Excess Host Resource Usage.** Host system resources must be allocated to QEMU to represent the resources belonging to the guest environment. Such resources include RAM to represent the physical RAM present on the guest, CPU cores and cycles to perform CPU and virtual device emulation, and disk space to hold the guest's secondary storage. Additional resources may be allocated by QEMU at runtime to meet the data needs of virtual devices, which presents a potential opportunity for a malicious guest to trick QEMU into allocating large amounts of unnecessary resources.

VDF discovered a crash while testing the AC97 audio virtual device, caused by QEMU allocating approximately 500 MB of additional host memory when the control register for `AC97_MIC_ADC_Rate` is set to an invalid, non-zero value. An important observation on this type of resource bug is that it will easily remain hidden unless the resource usage of the QEMU process is strictly monitored and enforced. For example, using the Linux `ulimit` command to place a limit on the virtual memory allocated to QEMU will discover this bug when the specified memory limit is exceeded. VDF enforces such a limitation during its testing, restricting the amount of virtual memory allocated to each QEMU instance. Once this limit is exceeded, a `SIGTRAP` signal is raised and a crash occurs.

Allocating excessive resources for a single guest instance is typically not a concern, but the potential impact increases greatly when considering a scenario with large numbers of instances deployed within a cloud environment. Discovering and correcting such bugs can have a measurable impact on the resource usage of hosts implementing cloud environments. Cloud service providers must allocate some amount of host hardware RAM and secondary storage to each VM hosted on that hardware. Thus, each VM must have a resource quota that is determined by the service provider and enforced by the host and hypervisor. However, if this quota does not take into account the resources used by the hypervisor itself, an excess host resource usage bug can potentially consume considerable host resources. Therefore, we reported this as a bug to the QEMU maintainers.

**Invalid Data Transfers.** Many virtual devices transfer blocks of data. Such transfers are used to move data to and from secondary storage and guest physical memory via DMA. However, invalid data transfers can cause virtual devices to hang in an infinite loop. This type of bug can be difficult to deal with in production systems as the QEMU process is still running while the guest's virtual clock is in a "paused" state. If queried, the QEMU process appears to be running and responsive. The guest remains frozen, causing a denial of service of any processes running inside of the guest.

VDF discovered test cases that trigger invalid data transfer bugs in the E1000 and RTL8139 virtual network devices and the SDHCI virtual block device. In each case, a transfer was initiated with either a block size of zero or an invalid transfer size, leaving each device in a loop that either never terminates or executes for an arbitrarily long period of time.

For the E1000 virtual device, the guest sets the device's `E1000_TDH` and `E1000_TDT` registers (TX descriptor head and tail, respectively) with offsets into guest memory that designate the current position into a buffer containing transfer operation descriptors. The guest then initiates a transfer using the `E1000_TCTL` register (TX control). However, if the values placed into the `E1000_TDH/TDL` registers are too large, then the transfer logic enters an infinite loop. A review of reported CVEs has shown that this issue was already discovered in January 2016 [7] and patched [14].

For the RTL8139 virtual device, the guest resets the device via the `ChipCmd` (chip control) register. Then, the `TxAddr0` (transfer address), `CpCmd` ("C+" mode command), and `TxPoll` (check transfer descriptors) registers are set to initiate a DMA transfer in the RTL8139's "C+" mode. However, if an invalid address is supplied to the `TxAddr0` register, QEMU becomes trapped in an endless loop of DMA lookups. This was an undiscovered bug, which has been patched and assigned CVE-2016-8910 [8] as a denial of service exploit.

For the SDHCI virtual device, the guest sets the device's `SDHC_CMDREG` register bit for "data is present" and sets the block size to transfer to zero in the `SDHC_BLKSIZE` register. The `switch` case for `SDHC_BLKSIZE` in the `sdhci_write()` MMIO callback function in `hw/sd/sdhci.c` performs a check to determine whether the block size exceeds the maximum allowable block size, but it does not perform a check for a block size of zero. Once the transfer begins, the device becomes stuck in a loop, and the guest environment becomes unresponsive. Luckily, fixes for this issue were integrated into mainline QEMU [12] in December 2015.

**Debugging Asserts.** While using an `assert` is a commonly-used debugging technique in mature software codebases, `asserts` are used to catch a particular case that should "never happen". If that impossible case actually *can* happen as a result of untrusted input, proper error-handling logic should be added to the code to address it. Within the Intel-HDA audio device, the `intel_hda_reg_write()` function in `hw/audio/intel-hda.c` uses an `assert` call to trigger a `SIGABRT` when a write is made to an address offset of 0 from the MMIO register base address. VDF was able to trigger this assert, which we have reported as a bug to the QEMU maintainers.

**Thread Race Conditions.** The virtual TPM in mainline QEMU is a pass-through device to the host's hardware TPM device. It is possible to implement a TPM emulated in software using libtpms [20] and then have QEMU pass TPM activity through to the emulated hardware. QEMU interacts with the separate process implementing the TPM via RPC. However, it is also possible to integrate libtpms directly into QEMU by applying a patchset provided by IBM [23]. This allows each QEMU instance to "own" its own TPM instance and directly control the start-up and shutdown of the TPM via a TPM backend in QEMU.

VDF discovered a hang that is the result of the TPM backend thread pool shutdown occurring before the tasks allocated to the thread pool have all been completed. Without an adequately long call to `sleep()` or `usleep()` prior to the thread pool shutdown to force a context switch and allow the thread pool worker threads to complete, the thread pool will hang on shutdown. Because the shutdown of the TPM backend is registered to be called at `exit()` via an `atexit()` call, any premature `exit()` prior to the necessary `sleep()` or `usleep()` call will trigger this issue. QEMU's signal handlers are never unregistered, so using a `SIGTERM` signal to kill QEMU is unsuccessful.

Note that this thread pool is part of the TPM backend design in QEMU, and is not part of the libtpms library that implements the actual TPM emulator. Most likely this design decision was made to avoid any noticeable slowdown in QEMU's execution by making the TPM virtual device run in an asynchronous manner to avoid any performance impact caused by performing expensive operations in the software TPM. Other newer TPM pass-through options, such as the Character in User Space (CUSE) device interface to a stand-alone TPM emulator using libtpms [13], should not experience this particular issue.

## 5 Related Work

Fuzzing has been a well-explored research topic for a number of years. The original fuzzing paper [32] used random program inputs as seed data for testing Unix utilities. Later studies on the selection of proper fuzzing seeds [25,34] and the use of concolic fuzzing to discover software vulnerabilities [17] have both been used to improve the coverage and discovery of bugs in programs undergoing fuzz testing. By relying on the record and replay of virtual device activity, VDF provides proper seed input that is known to execute branches of interest.

Frameworks for testing virtual devices are a fairly recent development. qtest [9] was the first framework to approach the idea of flexible low-level testing of virtual devices. VDF leverages qtest, but has improved on the approach to better improve test case throughput and test automation. Tang and Li proposed an approach [36] using a custom BIOS within the guest environment that listened on a virtual serial port to drive testing. VDF's approach relies upon no software executing within the guest environment (BIOS, kernel, etc.), and performs device-specific BIOS-level initialization as part of its init set.

A number of tools utilize record and replay. ReVirt [31] records system events to replay the activity of compromised guest systems to better analyze the nature of the attack. Aftersight [27] records selected system events and then offloads those events to another system for replay and analysis. Its primary contribution of decoupled analysis demonstrates that record and replay facilitates repeated heavyweight analysis after the moment that the event of interest originally occurred. PANDA [30], a much more recent work in this area, uses a modified

QEMU to record non-deterministic guest events that occur system-wide. These events are then replayed through increasingly heavier-weight analysis plugins to reverse engineer the purpose and behavior of arbitrary portions of the guest.

Symbolic execution of complex programs is also a common technique to calculate the path predicates and conditionals needed to exercise branches of interest. KLEE [24] performs symbolic execution at the process level. Selective Symbolic Execution (S2E) [26] executes a complete guest environment under QEMU and performs symbolic execution at the whole-system level. The approach proposed by Cong et al. [28] attempts to extract the code for five network virtual devices from QEMU, stub out key QEMU datatypes, and then perform symbolic execution on the resulting code. VDF is capable of performing its testing and analysis of a much larger set of virtual devices within the context of QEMU. However, the techniques laid out in [28] can complement VDF by generating new seed test cases designed to augment VDF's ability to reach new branches of interest.

Driller [35] uses both white box fuzzing and symbolic execution to discover vulnerabilities within programs. Unlike VDF, which is interested in exploring only branches of interest, Driller seeks to explore all branches within a program. It switches between symbolic execution and fuzzing when fuzzing gets "stuck" and can no longer discover data values that explore new branches. VDF focuses on executing large numbers of fuzzing test cases without using expensive symbolic execution to create new seeds.

The discovery of vulnerable code is a difficult and ongoing process, and there is interest in research work orthogonal to our effort that seeks to protect the host system and harden hypervisors. DeHype [37] reduces the privileged attack surface of KVM by deprivileging 93.2% of the KVM hypervisor code from kernel space to user space on the host. The Qubes OS project [15] compartmentalizes software into a variety of VMs, allowing the isolation of trusted activities from trusted ones within the OS. Qubes relies upon the bare-metal Xen hypervisor, which is much harder to exploit than a hypervisor executing under the host OS.

## 6 Conclusion

In this paper, we presented VDF, a system for performing fuzz testing on virtual devices, within the context of a running hypervisor, using record/replay of memory-mapped I/O events. We used VDF to fuzz test eighteen virtual devices, generating 1014 crash or hang test cases that reveal bugs in six of the tested devices. Over 80% of the crashes and hangs were discovered within the first day of testing. VDF covered an average of 62.32% of virtual device branches during testing, and the average test case was minimized to 18.57% of its original size.

**Acknowledgment.** The authors would like to thank the staff of the Griffiss Institute in Rome, New York for generously allowing the use of their cloud computing resources. This material is based upon research sponsored by the Air Force Research Lab, Rome Research Site under agreement number FA8750-15-C-0190.

## References


1. Advanced Linux Sound Architecture (ALSA). http://www.alsa-project.org
2. Amazon.com, Inc., Form 10-K 2015. http://www.sec.gov/edgar.shtml
3. CVE-2014-2894: Off-by-one error in the cmd start function in smart self test in IDE core. https://cve.mitre.org/cgi-bin/cvename.cgi?name=CVE-2014-2894
4. CVE-2015-3456: Floppy disk controller (FDC) allows guest users to cause denial of service. https://cve.mitre.org/cgi-bin/cvename.cgi?name=CVE-2015-3456
5. CVE-2015-5279: Heap-based buffer overflow in NE2000 virtual device. https://cve.mitre.org/cgi-bin/cvename.cgi?name=CVE-2015-5279
6. CVE-2015-6855: IDE core does not properly restrict commands. http://cve.mitre.org/cgi-bin/cvename.cgi?name=CVE-2015-6855
7. CVE-2016-1981: Reserved. https://cve.mitre.org/cgi-bin/cvename.cgi?name=CVE-2016-1981
8. CVE-2016-8910: Qemu: net: rtl8139: infinite loop while transmit in C+ mode. https://cve.mitre.org/cgi-bin/cvename.cgi?name=CVE-2016-8910
9. Features/QTest. http://wiki.qemu.org/Features/QTest
10. Kernel-Based Virtual Machine. http://www.linux-kvm.org/
11. PCI - OSDev Wiki. http://wiki.osdev.org/PCI
12. [Qemu-devel] [PATCH 1/2] hw/sd: implement CMD23 (SET_BLOCK_COUNT) for MMC compatibility. https://lists.gnu.org/archive/html/qemu-devel/2015-12/msg00948.html
13. [Qemu-devel] [PATCH 1/5] Provide support for the CUSE TPM. https://lists.nongnu.org/archive/html/qemu-devel/2015-04/msg01792.html
14. [Qemu-devel] [PATCH] e1000: eliminate infinite loops on out-of-bounds transfer start. https://lists.gnu.org/archive/html/qemu-devel/2016-01/msg03454.html
15. Qubes OS Project. https://www.qubes-os.org/
16. TrouSerS - The open-source TCG software stack. http://trousers.sourceforge.net
17. Avgerinos, T., Cha, S.K., Lim, B., Hao, T., Brumley, D.: AEG: automatic exploit generation. In: Proceedings of Network and Distributed System Security Symposium (NDSS) (2011)
18. Barham, P., Dragovic, B., Fraser, K., Hand, S., Harris, T., Ho, A., Neugebauer, R., Pratt, I., Warfield, A.: Xen and the art of virtualization. ACM SIGOPS Operating Syst. Rev. **37**(5), 164 (2003)
19. Bellard, F.: QEMU, a fast and portable dynamic translator. In: USENIX Annual Technical Conference, Freenix Track, pp. 41–46 (2005)
20. Berger, S.: libtpms library. https://github.com/stefanberger/libtpms
21. Böhme, M., Pham, V.T., Roychoudhury, A.: Coverage-based greybox fuzzing as markov chain. In: Proceedings of the 2016 ACM SIGSAC Conference on Computer and Communications Security, CCS 2016 (2016)
22. Böttinger, K., Eckert, C.: Deepfuzz: triggering vulnerabilities deeply hidden in binaries. In: Proceedings of the 13th International Conference on Detection of Intrusions and Malware, and Vulnerability Assessment, DIMVA 2016 (2016)
23. Bryant, C.: [1/4] tpm: Add TPM NVRAM Implementation (2013). https://patchwork.ozlabs.org/patch/288936/
24. Cadar, C., Dunbar, D., Engler, D.: KLEE: unassisted and automatic generation of high-coverage tests for complex systems programs. In: Proceedings of the 8th Symposium on Operating Systems Design and Implementation, pp. 209–224. USENIX Association (2008)

25. Cha, S.K., Avgerinos, T., Rebert, A., Brumley, D.: Unleashing mayhem on binary code. In: 2012 IEEE Symposium on Security and Privacy, pp. 380–394. IEEE, May 2012
26. Chipounov, V., Georgescu, V., Zamfir, C., Candea, G.: Selective symbolic execution. In: Proceedings of Fifth Workshop on Hot Topics in System Dependability, June, Lisbon, Portugal (2009)
27. Chow, J., Garfinkel, T., Chen, P.M.: Decoupling dynamic program analysis from execution in virtual environments. In: USENIX Annual Technical Conference, pp. 1–14 (2008)
28. Cong, K., Xie, F., Lei, L.: Symbolic execution of virtual devices. In: 2013 13th International Conference on Quality Software, pp. 1–10. IEEE, July 2013
29. Corbet, J., Rubini, A., Kroah-Hartman, G.: Linux Device Drivers, 3rd edn. O' Reilly Media Inc., Sebastopol (2005)
30. Dolan-Gavitt, B., Hodosh, J., Hulin, P., Leek, T., Whelan, R.: Repeatable Reverse Engineering for the Greater Good with PANDA. Technical report, Columbia University, MIT Lincoln Laboratory, TR CUCS-023-14 (2014)
31. Dunlap, G.W., King, S.T., Cinar, S., Basrai, M.A., Chen, P.M.: ReVirt: enabling intrusion analysis through virtual-machine logging and replay. ACM SIGOPS Operating Syst. Rev. **36**(SI), 211–224 (2002)
32. Miller, B.P., Fredriksen, L., So, B.: An empirical study of the reliability of UNIX utilities. Commun. ACM **33**(12), 32–44 (1990)
33. Rawat, S., Jain, V., Kumar, A., Cojocar, L., Giuffrida, C., Bos, H.: VUzzer: application-aware evolutionary fuzzing. In: NDSS, February 2017
34. Rebert, A., Cha, S.K., Avgerinos, T., Foote, J., Warren, D., Grieco, G., Brumley, D.: Optimizing seed selection for fuzzing. In: 23rd USENIX Security Symposium (2014)
35. Stephens, N., Grosen, J., Salls, C., Dutcher, A., Wang, R., Corbetta, J., Shoshitaishvili, Y., Kruegel, C., Vigna, G.: Driller: augmenting fuzzing through selective symbolic execution. In: Proceedings of NDSS 2016, February 2016
36. Tang, J., Li, M.: When virtualization encounter AFL. In: Black Hat Europe (2016)
37. Wu, C., Wang, Z., Jiang, X.: Taming hosted hypervisors with (mostly) deprivileged execution. In: Network and Distributed System Security Symposium (2013)
38. Zalewski, M.: American Fuzzy Lop Fuzzer. http://lcamtuf.coredump.cx/afl/

# Static Program Analysis as a Fuzzing Aid

Bhargava Shastry[1(✉)], Markus Leutner[1], Tobias Fiebig[1], Kashyap Thimmaraju[1], Fabian Yamaguchi[2], Konrad Rieck[2], Stefan Schmid[3], Jean-Pierre Seifert[1], and Anja Feldmann[1]

[1] TU Berlin, Berlin, Germany
bshastry@sec.t-labs.tu-berlin.de
[2] TU Braunschweig, Braunschweig, Germany
[3] Aalborg University, Aalborg, Denmark

**Abstract.** Fuzz testing is an effective and scalable technique to perform software security assessments. Yet, contemporary fuzzers fall short of thoroughly testing applications with a high degree of control-flow diversity, such as firewalls and network packet analyzers. In this paper, we demonstrate how static program analysis can guide fuzzing by augmenting existing program models maintained by the fuzzer. Based on the insight that code patterns reflect the data format of inputs processed by a program, we automatically construct an *input dictionary* by statically analyzing program control and data flow. Our analysis is performed before fuzzing commences, and the input dictionary is supplied to an off-the-shelf fuzzer to influence input generation. Evaluations show that our technique not only increases test coverage by 10–15% over baseline fuzzers such as *afl* but also reduces the time required to expose vulnerabilities by up to an order of magnitude. As a case study, we have evaluated our approach on two classes of network applications: nDPI, a deep packet inspection library, and tcpdump, a network packet analyzer. Using our approach, we have uncovered 15 zero-day vulnerabilities in the evaluated software that were not found by stand-alone fuzzers. Our work not only provides a practical method to conduct security evaluations more effectively but also demonstrates that the synergy between program analysis and testing can be exploited for a better outcome.

**Keywords:** Program analysis · Fuzzing · Protocol parsers

## 1 Introduction

Software has grown in both complexity and dynamism over the years. For example, the Chromium browser receives over 100 commits every day. Evidently, the scale of present-day software development puts an enormous pressure on program testing. Evaluating the security of large applications that are under active

**Electronic supplementary material** The online version of this chapter (doi:10.1007/978-3-319-66332-6_2) contains supplementary material, which is available to authorized users.


M. Dacier et al. (Eds.): RAID 2017, LNCS 10453, pp. 26–47, 2017.
DOI: 10.1007/978-3-319-66332-6_2

development is a daunting task. Fuzz testing is one of the few techniques that not only scale up to large programs but are also effective at discovering program vulnerabilities.

Unfortunately, contemporary fuzzers are less effective at testing complex network applications that handle diverse yet highly structured input. Examples of such applications are protocol analyzers, deep packet inspection modules, and firewalls. These applications process input in multiple stages: The input is first tokenized, then parsed syntactically, and finally analyzed semantically. The application logic (e.g., intrusion detection, network monitoring etc.) usually resides in the final stage. There are two problems that these applications pose. First, the highly structured nature of program input begets a vast number of control flow paths in the portion of application code where packet parsing takes place. Coping with diverse program paths in the early stages of the packet processing pipeline, and exploring the depths of program code where the core application logic resides is taxing even for state-of-the-art fuzzers. Second, the diversity of program input not only amplifies the number of control flows but also demands tests *in breadth*. For example, the deep packet inspection library, nDPI, analyzes close to 200 different network protocols [27]. In the face of such diversity, generating inputs that efficiently test application logic is a hard problem.

Although prior work on grammar-based fuzzing [13,16,29] partly address the problem of fuzz testing parser applications, they cannot be applied to testing complex third-party network software for two reasons. First, existing grammar-based fuzzers rely on a user-supplied *data model* or *language grammar* specification that describes the input data format. A fundamental problem with a specification-based approach to fuzzing is that the formal grammar of program input might not be available to begin with. Indeed, few network protocols have a readily usable formal specification. Therefore, grammar-based fuzzing at present, is contingent upon a data model that is—most often—manually created by an expert. Although proposals such as Prospex [7] that automatically create grammar specifications from network traces are promising, they are designed with a single protocol in mind. Automatic specification generation for diverse grammars has not been attempted. A second problem with certain grammar-based approaches that use whitebox testing is that they require significant software alterations, and rely on implementation knowledge. For example, to conduct grammar-based whitebox testing, parsing functions must be manually identified in source code, and detokenization functions must be written. Although *manual fallbacks* may be inevitable in the face of implementation diversity, prior approaches demand significant software revisions, making them ill-suited for security evaluation of *third-party* software.

In this paper, we demonstrate how the stated challenges can be addressed by augmenting fuzzing with static program analysis. Being program centric, static analysis can examine control flow throughout an application's codebase, permitting it to analyze parsing code in its entirety. This design choice makes our approach well-suited for testing complex network applications. Our approach has two key steps. First, we automatically generate a dictionary of protocol message constructs and their conjunctions by analyzing application source code. Our key insight is that code patterns signal the use of program input, and therefore sufficient cues about program input may be gathered by analyzing the source code. To this end, we develop a static analyzer that performs data and control-flow analysis to obtain a dictionary of input constructs. Second, the dictionary obtained from the first step is supplied to an off-the-shelf fuzzer. The fuzzer uses the message fragments (constructs and conjunctions) present in the supplied dictionary toward input generation. Although anecdotal evidence suggests that a carefully constructed dictionary can dramatically improve a fuzzer's effectiveness [35], program dictionaries at present are created by a domain-specific expert. To make our analysis and test framework easily deployable on real-world code, we have developed a plugin to the Clang/LLVM compiler that can (i) Be automatically invoked at code compilation time, and (ii) Produce input dictionaries that are readily usable with off-the-shelf fuzzers such as afl. Indeed, our work makes security evaluations accessible to non-domain-experts e.g., audit of third-party code in the government sector.

We have prototyped our approach in a tool that we call Orthrus, and evaluated it in both controlled and uncontrolled environments. We find that our analysis helps reduce the time to vulnerability exposure by an order of magnitude for the `libxml2` benchmark of the fuzzer test suite [15]. Furthermore, we use Orthrus to conduct security evaluations of nDPI (deep packet inspection library), and tcpdump (network packet analyzer). Input dictionaries generated via static code analysis increase test coverage in nDPI, and tcpdump by 15%, and 10% respectively. More significantly, input dictionaries have helped uncover 15 zero-day vulnerabilities in the packet processing code of 14 different protocols in the evaluated applications that were not found by stand-alone fuzzers such as afl, and the Peach fuzzer. These results lend credence to the efficacy of our approach in carrying out security evaluations of complex third-party network software. Our prototype, Orthrus, is available at https://www.github.com/test-pipeline/Orthrus.

**Contributions**

- To address the challenges of fuzzing complex network software, we propose a static analysis framework to infer the data format of program inputs from source code.
- We propose a novel approach—the use of static program analysis—to augment fuzzing. To this end, we couple our analysis framework with an off-the-shelf fuzzer.
- Finally, we prototype our approach and extensively evaluate its impact. Our prototype achieves an improvement of up to 15% in test coverage over state-of-the-art fuzzers such as afl, expedites vulnerability discovery by an order of magnitude, and exposes 15 zero-day vulnerabilities in popular networking software[1]. These results validate our proposition that static analysis can serve as a useful fuzzing aid.

[1] Ethical Considerations: Vulnerabilities found during our case studies have been responsibly disclosed to the concerned vendors who have subsequently patched them.

## 2 Background

In this section, we provide a brief overview of static analysis, and fuzz testing that is relevant to our work.

**Static Analysis.** Our application of static analysis is closer to the notion of static analysis as a program-centric *checker* [10]: Tools that encapsulate a notion of program behavior and check that the implementation conforms to this notion. Historically, static analysis tools aimed at finding programming errors encode a description of correct (error-free) program behavior and check if the analyzed software meets this description. In contrast, our analyses encode input-processing properties of a program in order to extract features of the input message format.

Static analysis helps in analyzing the breadth of a program without concrete test inputs. However, because static analysis usually encapsulates an approximate view of the program, its analysis output (bugs) has to be manually validated. The analysis logic of a static analyzer may be catered to different use cases, such as finding insecure API usages, erroneous code patterns etc. This analysis logic is usually encoded as a set of rules (*checking* rules), while the analysis itself is carried out by a static analyzer's core engine.

Static program analysis includes, among other types of analyses, program data-flow and control-flow analyses [1]. Data-flow analysis inspects the flow of data between program variables; likewise control-flow analysis inspects the flow of control in the program. While data-flow analysis may be used to understand how program input interacts with program variables, control-flow analysis may be used to understand how control is transferred from one program routine to another. In practice, both data and control flow analyses are essential components of a static analyzer.

Program data and control-flow may be analyzed at different program abstractions. In our work, we focus on syntactic as well as semantic analysis, using the program abstract syntax tree (AST), and control flow graph (CFG) respectively. At the syntactic level, our analysis is performed on the program's AST, and at the semantic level, on the program's CFG. A program's AST representation comprises syntactic elements of a program, such as the `If, For, While` statements, program variables and their data types etc. Each syntactic element is represented as an AST node. All AST nodes, with the exception of the root and the leaf nodes, are connected by edges that denote a parent-child relationship. The CFG of a program unit represents its semantic elements, such as the control flow between blocks of program statements. The CFG nodes are basic blocks: Group of program statements without a branching instruction. The CFG edges connect basic blocks that comprise a possible program path. The infrastructure to obtain program AST, CFG, and perform analysis on them is available in modern compiler toolchains.

**Fuzz Testing.** Fuzzing is one of the most common dynamic analysis techniques used in security assessments. It was introduced by Miller et al. to evaluate the robustness of UNIX utilities [22]. Ever since, fuzzing has seen widespread adoption owing to its effectiveness in eliciting faulty program behavior. The first fuzzer functioned without any program knowledge: It simply fed random inputs to the program. In other words, it was a blackbox (program agnostic) fuzzer. Blackbox fuzzers paved the way for modern fuzzers that are program aware.

State-of-the-art fuzzers build a model of the analyzed program as it is tested. This model is used to guide testing more optimally, i.e., expend resources for teasing out unexplored program paths. Techniques used to build a model of the program under test may vary from coverage tracing (afl) [34], to constraint solving (SAGE) [14]. Fuzzers may also expect the user to define a grammar underlying the message format being tested. Examples of such fuzzers are the Peach Fuzzer [29] and Sulley [28], both of which generate inputs based on a user specified grammar. Fuzzers such as afl support the use of message constructs for fuzzer guidance. However, unlike Peach, afl does not require a formal grammar specification; it simply uses pre-defined constructs in the input *dictionary* toward input mutation.

## 3 Program Analysis Guided Fuzzing

In this section, we first briefly outline our specific problem scope with regard to protocol specification inference, then provide an overview of our approach, and finally describe our methodology.

**Problem Scope.** An application protocol specification usually comprises a *state machine* that defines valid sequences of protocol messages, and a *message format* that defines the protocol message. In our work, we focus on inferring the protocol message format only, leaving the inference of the state machine for future work. Since file formats are stateless specifications, our work is applicable for conducting security evaluations of file format parsers as well.

**Approach Overview.** We demonstrate how fuzz testing of network applications can be significantly improved by leveraging static analysis for test guidance. It has already been suggested in non-academic circles that a carefully constructed dictionary of parser input can dramatically improve a fuzzer's effectiveness [35]. However, creating input dictionaries still requires domain expertise. We automatically generate input dictionaries by performing static program analysis, supplying it to an off-the-shelf fuzzer toward input generation. Indeed, our prototype builds on legacy fuzzers to demonstrate the effectiveness of our approach.

Figure 1 illustrates our analysis and test workflow. First, we statically analyze application source code and obtain a dictionary of protocol message constructs and conjunctions. Each item in the dictionary is an independent message fragment: It is either a simple message construct, or a conjunction of multiple constructs. For example, a constant string `SIP/2.0` in the source code is inferred as a message *construct*, while usages of another construct, say the constant string `INVITE`, that are contingent on `SIP/2.0` are inferred to be a *conjunction* of the form `INVITE SIP/2.0`. Second, we supply the input dictionary obtained in the first step to a fuzzer toward input generation. The fuzzer uses the supplied dictionary together with an initial set of program inputs (seeds) toward fuzzing

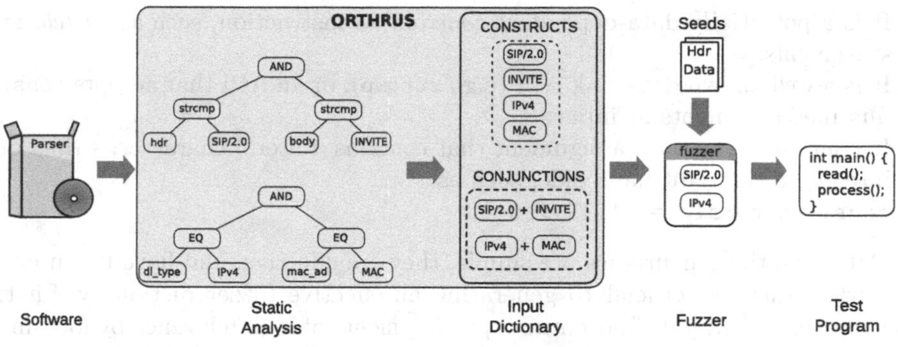


**Fig. 1.** Work-flow for program analysis guided fuzzing.

an application test case. In contrast to prior work, our analysis is automatic, and requires neither a hand-written grammar specification, nor manual software alterations. Furthermore, the input dictionary obtained through our analysis may be supplied *as is* to existing fuzzers such as afl, aflfast, and libFuzzer, making our approach legacy compliant.

### 3.1 Input Dictionary Generation

The use of static program analysis for inferring program properties is a long-standing field of research. However, the main challenge underlying our approach is that our analysis must infer properties of the *program input* from application source code. Although Rice's theorem [17] states that all semantic program properties are undecidable in general, we aim to make an informed judgement.

**Program Slicing.** The first problem we encounter is an instance of the classical forward slicing problem [12]: determining the subset of program statements, or variables that process, or contain program input. Although existing forward slicing techniques obtain precise inter-procedural slices of small programs, they do not scale up to complex network parsers that exhibit a high degree of control as well as data-flow diversity.

As a remedy, we obtain a backward program slice with respect to a pre-determined set of program statements that are deemed to process program input. These program statements are called taint sinks, since program input (taint) flows into them. Since our analysis is localized to a set of taint sinks, it is tractable and scales up to large programs. Naturally, the selection criteria for taint sinks influence analysis precision, and ultimately decide the quality of inferred input fragments. Therefore, we employ useful heuristics and follow reasonable design guidelines so that taint sink selection is not only well-informed by default, but can also benefit from domain expertise when required. We explain our heuristics and design guidelines for taint sink selection in the next paragraph.

**Taint Sinks.** We select a program statement as a taint sink if it satisfies one or more of the following conditions:

1. It is a potentially data-dependent control flow instruction, such as *switch*, `if` statements.
2. It is a well-known data sink API (e.g., `strcmp`), or an API that accepts `const` qualified arguments as input.
3. It contains a constant assignment that contains a literal character, string, or integer on the right hand side, such as
`const char *sip = ''SIP/2.0''`

Although these heuristics are simple, they are effective, and have two useful properties that are crucial to generating an effective fuzzer dictionary. First, they capture a *handful* of potential input fragments of high relevance by focusing on program data and control flow. In contrast, a naïve textual search for string literals in the program will inevitably mix-up interesting and uninteresting use of data, e.g., strings used in print statements will also be returned. Second, although our heuristics are straightforward, they capture a wide array of code patterns that are commonly found in parsing applications. Thus, they constitute a good *default specification* that is applicable to a large class of parsing applications. The defaults that are built-in to our analysis framework make our solution accessible for conducting security assessments of third-party network software.

Naturally, our heuristics may miss application-specific taint sinks. A prominent example is the use of application specific APIs for input processing. As a remedy, we permit the security analyst to specify additional taint sinks as an analysis parameter. In summary, we facilitate entirely automatic analysis of third-party software using a default taint specification, while opportunistically benefiting from application-specific knowledge where possible. This makes our analysis framework flexible in practice.

**Analysis Queries.** In order to infer protocol message constructs, we need to analyze data and control-flow around taint sinks. To facilitate fast and scalable analysis, we design a query system that is capable of both syntactic and semantic analysis. Fortunately, the infrastructure to obtain program AST, CFG, and perform analysis on them is already available in modern compiler toolchains. Thus, we focus on developing the analysis logic for performing backward program slicing toward obtaining protocol message constructs.

Algorithm 1 illustrates our analysis procedure for generating an input dictionary from source code. We begin by initializing our internal data-structures to an empty set (lines 2–4). Next, we iterate over all compilable source files in the code repository, and obtain their program AST and CFG representations (lines 8–9) using existing compiler routines. Based on our default set of taint sinks, we formulate syntactic and semantic queries (described next) that are designed to elicit input message constructs or their conjunctions in source code (line 6). Using these queries, we obtain a set of input message constructs using syntactic analysis (line 11), and a set of input message conjunctions using semantic analysis (line 13) in each source file. The constructs and conjunctions so obtained are added to the dictionary data structure (line 14–15) and the analysis continues on the next source file.

**Algorithm 1.** Pseudocode for generating an input dictionary.

```
function GENERATE-DICTIONARY(SourceCode, Builder)
    dictionary = ∅
    constructs = ∅
    conjunctions = ∅
    ▷ Queries generated from internal database
    queries = Q
    for each sourcefile in SourceCode do
        ast = frontendParse(sourcefile)
        cfg = semanticParse(ast)
        ▷ Obtain constructs
        constructs = syntactic-analysis(ast, queries)
        ▷ Obtain conjunctions of existing constructs
        conjunctions = semantic-analysis(cfg, constructs)
        ▷ Update dictionary
        dictionary += constructs
        dictionary += conjunctions
    return dictionary
function SYNTACTIC-ANALYSIS(AST, Queries)
    constructs = ∅
    for each query in Q do
        constructs += synQuery(AST, query)
    return constructs
function SYNQUERY(AST, Query)
    matches = ∅
    while T = traverseAST(AST) do
        if Query matches T then
            matches += (T.id, T.value)
    return matches
function SEMANTIC-ANALYSIS(CFG, Constructs)
    conjunctions = ∅
    ▷ Obtain conjunctions in a given calling context
    conjunctions += Context-Sensitive-Analysis(CFG, Constructs)
    ▷ Obtain productions in a given program path
    conjunctions += Path-Sensitive-Analysis(CFG, Constructs)
    return conjunctions
```

**Syntactic Queries.** At the syntactic level, our analysis logic accepts functional queries and returns input message constructs (if any) that match the issued query. These queries are made against the program AST. A functional query is composed of boolean predicates on a program statement or data type. As an example, consider the following query:

`stringLiteral(hasParent(callExpr(hasName(''strcmp'')))).`

The query shown above searches for a program value of type string (`stringLiteral`) whose parent node in the AST is a function call (`callExpr`), and whose declaration name is `strcmp`. Thus, a functional query is essentially compositional in nature and operates on properties of the program AST. There are two key benefits of functional queries. First, their processing time is very low allowing them to scale up to large codebases (see Sect. 4.1). Second, since large parsing applications use a recurring pattern of code to parse input messages of different formats, even simple queries can be efficient at building a multi-protocol input dictionary.

Syntactic queries are useful for obtaining a list of simple input message constructs such as constant protocol keywords. However, these queries do not analyze the context in which constructs appear in the program. Analyzing the context brings us a deeper understanding of the input message format. As an example, we may know which two constructs are used in conjunction with each other, or if there is a partial order between grammar production rules involving these constructs. Deeper analysis of message constructs may infer complex message fragments, allowing the fuzzer to explore intricate parsing routines. To facilitate such context-sensitive analyses, we write context and path-sensitive checkers that enable semantic queries.

**Semantic Queries.** At the semantic level, a query accepts a list of input message constructs as input, and returns conjunctions (if any) of constructs as output. Semantic queries are made against a context-sensitive inter-procedural graph [30] constructed on a program's CFG. Each query is written as a checker routine that returns the set of conjunctions that can be validated in the calling context where the input construct appeared. As an example, consider the parsing code snippet shown in Listing 1.1.

**Listing 1.1.** Sample parser code.

```
int parse(const char *token1, const char *token2) {
  if (token1 == "INVITE")
    if (strcmp(token2, "SIP/2.0"))
      do_something();
}
```

The `parse` function takes two string tokens as input and performs an operation only when the first token is `INVITE` and the second token is `SIP/2.0`. From this code, we can infer that there is a dependency between the two tokens, namely, that `INVITE` is potentially followed by the `SIP/2.0` string. While syntactic queries can only identify simple message constructs, semantic queries can be used to make an inference about such message conjunctions. Together, syntactic and semantic queries may be used to build a dictionary of the input message format.

**Implementation.** We have implemented our approach in a research prototype, that we call Orthrus. Our query system is composed of tooling based on the libASTMatchers, and the libTooling infrastructure in Clang (syntactic queries), and checkers to the Clang Static Analyzer [20] (semantic queries).

### 3.2 Dictionary Based Fuzzing

An input dictionary can improve the effectiveness of fuzzing by augmenting the program representation maintained by the fuzzer for test guidance. The input fragments in the supplied dictionary enable input mutations that are well-informed, and in some cases more effective at discovering new program paths than purely random mutations. Contemporary fuzzers offer an interface to plug in an application-specific dictionary. We use this interface to supply the input fragments inferred by our analysis framework to the fuzzer.

**Algorithm 2.** Pseudocode for dictionary-based fuzzing.

```
1: function DICTIONARY-FUZZ(input, Dictionary, deterministic)
2:     dictToken = Random(Dictionary)
3:     if deterministic then
4:         for each byteoffset in input do
5:             fuzz-token-offset(input, dictToken, byteoffset)
6:     else
7:         byteoffset = Random(sizeOf(input))
8:         fuzz-token-offset(input, dictToken, byteoffset)
9:
10: function FUZZ-TOKEN-OFFSET(input, dictToken, byteoffset)
11:     ▷ Token overwrites input byte
12:     input[byteoffset] = dictToken
13:     Program(input)
14:     ▷ Token inserted into input
15:     InsertToken(input, byteoffset, dictToken)
16:     Program(input)
```

Algorithm 2 presents the pseudocode for dictionary based fuzzing employed by most present-day fuzzers. Dictionary based mutations may be performed either deterministically (at all byte offsets in the input stream, line 4–5), or non-deterministically (at a random byte offset, line 7–8). There are two kinds of dictionary based mutations used by fuzzers: overwrite, and insert. In an overwrite operation, the chosen dictionary token is used to overwrite a portion of a program input in the fuzzer queue (line 12–13). In an insert operation, the chosen token is inserted into the queued input at the specified offset (line 15–16). Typically, fuzzers perform both mutations on a chosen token.

Fuzzers bound the runtime allocated to dictionary-based fuzzing routines. In practice, fuzzers either use up to a certain threshold (typically a few hundred) of supplied dictionary tokens deterministically, while using the rest probabilistically, or pick each token at random. Thus, it is important that the size of the supplied dictionary is small, and the relevance of the tokens is high. Our use of demand-driven queries, and analyses of varying precision ensures that we supply such a dictionary to the fuzzer.

## 4 Evaluation

In this section, we present our evaluation of Orthrus in both controlled and uncontrolled environments. First, we (i) Quantitatively evaluate our analysis run time towards dictionary generation, and (ii) Qualitatively evaluate the generated dictionary tokens, for the codebases under test (Sect. 4.1). Second, we measure the time to uncover vulnerabilities using Orthrus generated dictionaries in a set of fuzzer benchmarks (Sect. 4.2). Third, we measure the test coverage achieved and examine the vulnerabilities exposed by fuzzing production code with the aid of Orthrus generated dictionaries (Sect. 4.3). We conclude this section with a discussion of factors that may limit the validity of our approach and how we address them.

**Table 1.** Dictionary generation run time relative to code compilation time. Timing measurements have been averaged over ten runs and are presented in minutes (m) and seconds (s).

| Software | Source lines of code | Compilation | Dictionary generation | | |
|---|---|---|---|---|---|
| | | | Syntactic | Semantic | Total |
| c-ares | 97 k | 2.11 s | 0.43 s | 20.14 s | 20.57 s |
| libxml2 | 196 k | 17.95 s | 1.48 s | 23.09 s | 24.57 s |
| openssl | 278 k | 20.02 s | 6.45 s | 5 m 37.24 s | 5 m 43.69 s |
| nDPI | 27 k | 7.16 s | 2.14 s | 42.84 s | 44.98 s |
| tcpdump | 75 k | 2.99 s | 0.32 s | 9.04 s | 9.36 s |
| woff2 | 39 k | 3.20 s | 3.58 s | 11.58 s | 15.16 s |

**Table 2.** A sample of string input fragments extracted from the source code of libxml2, and nDPI using syntactic queries. Extracted fragments are comma separated.

| Software | Taint sink | Query | Input fragments |
|---|---|---|---|
| libxml2 | xmlBufferWriteChar(), xmlOutputBufferWrite() | Obtain constant argument | xml:lang=", <!DOCTYPE, <! [CDATA[, xmlns |
| nDPI | memcmp(), strcmp() | Obtain constant argument | snort, America Online Inc., last message |

**Measurement Infrastructure.** All measurements presented in this section were performed on a 64-bit machine with 80 CPU threads (Intel Xeon E7-4870) clocked at 2.4 GHz, and 512 GB RAM.

### 4.1 Analysis Run Time and Effectiveness

Table 1 presents the run times of static analysis (both syntactic and semantic) performed for dictionary generation for each of the code bases evaluated in this paper. To put the run times in perspective, the run time of code compilation for each code base is presented in the third column. Since semantic analysis is computationally more expensive than syntactic analysis, it dominates the dictionary generation run time. However, in relation to fuzzing run time that is usually in the order of days, the time required for dictionary generation (at most a few minutes across our data-set) is negligible.

Table 2 presents a sample of input fragments (constructs) extracted from the source code for libxml2, and nDPI for which dictionary-based fuzzing showed substantial improvement in test coverage and outcome. In the interest of space and visual clarity, we have excluded fragments extracted from tcpdump since they mainly comprise binary input. Listing 1.2 shows one of the syntactic queries applied to the nDPI, and libxml2 codebases that resulted in the sample fragments presented in Table 2. Our analysis heuristics have helped build an XML input dictionary that is similar in content to the manually created XML dictionary for afl. Moreover, using backward slicing from familiar taint sinks such as `memcmp`, we have been able to extract protocol fragments (such as the string literal `America Online Inc.` used by nDPI to fingerprint instant messaging traffic) that have been instrumental in increasing test coverage.

**Listing 1.2.** Syntactic query issued on nDPI and libxml2 codebases. The query returns string literals passed as arguments to taint sinks such as `strcmp`.

```
// Obtain string literals passed to POSIX APIs "strcmp", and
// "memcmp", and libxml2 APIs "xmlBufferWriteChar", and
// "xmlOutputBufferWrite".
StatementMatcher StringMatcher =
  stringLiteral(
                hasAncestor(
                            declRefExpr(
                                to(namedDecl(
                                  anyOf(hasName("strcmp"),
                                        hasName("memcmp"),
                                        hasName("xmlBufferWriteChar"),
                                        hasName("xmlOutputBufferWrite")
                                       )
                                    )
                                 )
                            )
                )
  ).bind("construct");
```

### 4.2 Benchmarks: Time to Vulnerability Exposure

To enable independent reproduction, we briefly document our evaluation methodology.

**Fuzzer Test Suite.** In order to measure the time required to expose program vulnerabilities, we used the fuzzer test suite [15]. The fuzzer test suite is well-suited for this purpose because it provides a controlled environment in which timing measurements can be done, and contains test cases for several known high-profile vulnerabilities. Indeed, the test suite has been used for benchmarking the LLVM libFuzzer [21], that we use as a baseline in our evaluation. The specific vulnerabilities in the test suite that feature in our evaluation are: CVE-2014-0160 [23] (OpenSSL Heartbleed), CVE-2016-5180 [25] (buffer overflow in the c-ares dns library), CVE-2015-8317 [24] (buffer overflow in libxml2), and a security-critical bug in Google's WoFF2 font parser [6].

**Test Methodology.** For each test case, our evaluation was performed by measuring the time to expose the underlying vulnerability in two scenarios: (i) The baseline fuzzer alone; and (ii) The baseline fuzzer augmented with an Orthrus generated dictionary. Our approach is deemed effective when the time to expose vulnerability reduces in comparison to the baseline, and is ineffective/irrelevant when it increases or remains the same in comparison to the baseline. Timing measurements were done using Unix's `time` utility. In order to reduce the effect of seemingly random vulnerability exposures, we obtained at least 80 timing

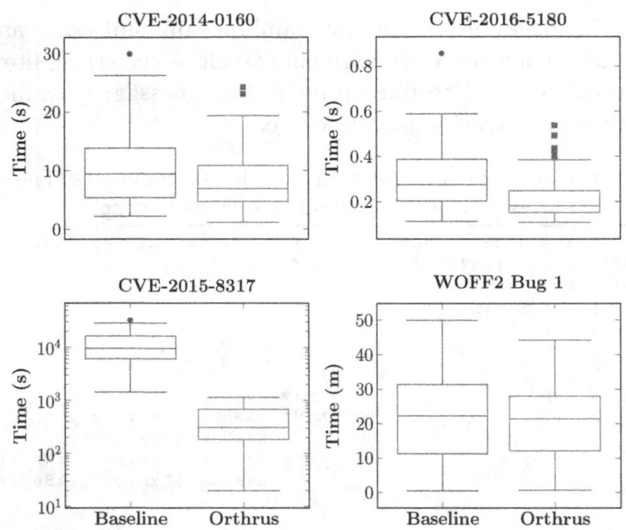


**Fig. 2.** Comparison of time required to expose vulnerability using libFuzzer as the baseline.

measurements for each test case in both scenarios. Measurements for each test case were carried out in parallel, with each experiment being run exclusively on a single core. The input dictionary generated by Orthrus was supplied to libFuzzer via the `-dict` command line argument. Finally, to eliminate the effect of seed corpuses on measurement outcome, we strictly adhered to the selection of seed corpuses as mandated by the fuzzer test suite documentation.

**Results.** Figure 2 presents our test results as box plots. The baseline box plot (libFuzzer) is always on the left of the plot, and results for libFuzzer augmented with Orthrus (Orthrus) on the right. The Orthrus generated input dictionary brought down the time to expose a buffer overflow in the libxml2 library (CVE-2015-8317) by an order of magnitude (from a median value of close to 3 h using the baseline to a median value of 5 min using our approach). For all the other test cases, the median time to expose vulnerability was lower for Orthrus in comparison to libFuzzer. In addition, Orthrus shrunk the range of timing variations in exposing the vulnerability.

To understand the varying impact of the supplied dictionary on the time to vulnerability exposure, we studied each of the tested vulnerabilities to understand their root cause. Our approach consistently brought down the time to exposure for all vulnerabilities that were triggered by a file or protocol message specific to the application under test. Thus, our approach worked well in scenarios where knowledge of the input format was crucial to eliciting the vulnerability. Furthermore, in scenarios where our approach did not substantially lower the time to vulnerability exposure, the time penalty incurred by our approach, owing to the test time dedicated to dictionary mutations, was marginal. In summary, we find that static program analysis can improve bug-finding *efficiency* of fuzzers for those class of bugs that are triggered by highly structured input (commonly found in network applications, and file format parsers), while not imposing a noticeable performance penalty.

### 4.3 Case Study

To investigate the practical utility of Orthrus, we conducted a case study of two popular network applications, namely, nDPI, and tcpdump. These applications were selected because they are not only deployed in security-critical environments but also parse potentially attacker-controlled data. For each application, we conducted multivariate testing using baseline fuzzers such as afl and aflfast [3] with and without an Orthrus generated dictionary.

The chosen applications were also fuzzed using the Peach fuzzer [29], a state-of-the-art fuzzer for protocol security assessments. Since grammar specifications for the set of protocols parsed by tcpdump, and nDPI were not publicly available, we enabled Peach fuzzer's input analyzer mode that automatically infers the input data model. Such an evaluation was aimed at comparing Peach fuzzer with Orthrus in scenarios where a data model specification is not available. However, the community edition of the Peach fuzzer that we had access to, is not geared toward long runs. In our Peach-based experiments, we could not achieve a run time of longer than 24 h. This prevents a fair comparison of the two approaches. Therefore, we document results of our Peach experiments for reference, and not a comparative evaluation.

**Evaluation Methodology.** We evaluated Orthrus using two metrics, namely, test coverage achieved, and the number of program vulnerabilities exposed. Test coverage was measured as the percentage of program branches that were discovered during testing. Since fuzzers often expose identical crashes, making it non-trivial to document unique vulnerabilities, we semi-automatically deduplicated fuzzer crashes in a two-step process. First, we used the concept of fuzzy stack hashes [26] to fingerprint a crash's stack trace using a cryptographic hash function. Second, crashes with a unique hash were manually triaged to determine the number of unique program vulnerabilities. We used two elementary seeds (bare-bone IPv4, and IPv6 packets) to fuzz tcpdump, and nDPI. Tests involving the fuzzers afl and aflfast were conducted in a multi-core setting.

**Fuzzing Duration.** Dictionary based mutations get a fraction of the total fuzz time of a fuzzer. Thus, to fully evaluate our approach, we ran the fuzzer configurations (except Peach) until each unique program input synthesized by the fuzzer was mutated with the supplied dictionary constructs at least once. Owing to the relatively poor execution throughput of the evaluated software (under 100 executions per second), we had to run each fuzzer over a period of

**Table 3.** Test coverage achieved (in %) by different fuzzing configurations.

| Software | afl | afl-orthrus | aflfast | aflfast-orthrus | Peach-analyzer |
|---|---|---|---|---|---|
| tcpdump | 80.56 | 90.23 (+9.67) | 71.35 | 78.82 (+7.47) | 6.25 |
| nDPI | 66.92 | 81.49 (+14.57) | 64.40 | 68.10 (+3.70) | 24.98 |

1 week in which time the supplied dictionary was utilized at least once for each unique input.

**Utilities.** CERT's `exploitable` [11] utility was used for crash deduplication. We used AddressSanitizer [2] as a debugging aid; this expedited the bug reporting process.

**Evaluated Software.** We evaluated nDPI revision f51fef6 (November 2016), and tcpdump trunk (March 2017).

**Test Coverage.** Our test coverage measurements present the fraction of all program branches (edges) covered by test cases generated by a fuzzer configuration. We have evaluated Orthrus against two baselines, namely, afl, and aflfast. Therefore, our measurements have been obtained for afl, afl augmented with Orthrus-generated input dictionary (afl-Orthrus), aflfast, aflfast augmented with Orthrus-generated input dictionary (aflfast-Orthrus), and the Peach fuzzer with a binary analyzer data model. Table 3 shows the test coverage achieved by different fuzzer combinations for tcpdump, and nDPI, while Fig. 3 visualizes code coverage over time. Program coverage was measured when there was a change in its magnitude. Due to the relatively short running duration of the Peach fuzzer, we have excluded its coverage visualization.

As shown in Fig. 3, the obtained coverage measurements for tcpdump, and nDPI, approach a saturation point asymptotically. For both tcpdump, and nDPI, the growth rate in test coverage is higher initially, tapering off asymptotically to zero. The test coverage curves for afl-Orthrus and aflfast-Orthrus have a higher initial growth rate compared to their respective baselines, namely, afl, and aflfast. This results in a consistent increase in overall test coverage achieved by Orthrus in comparison to the baseline fuzzers, as shown in Table 3. For nDPI, Orthrus' input dictionary increases test coverage by 14.57% over the afl fuzzer. In the case of tcpdump, this increase in test coverage is 9.67%. Orthrus' enhancements in test coverage over aflfast for nDPI, and tcpdump are 3.7%, and 7.47% respectively. Although aflfast is a fork of afl, the supplied input dictionary has a lesser effect on the former than the latter. To understand this anomaly, we examined the source code of afl, and aflfast. afl performs dictionary-based mutations on *all* inputs in the fuzzer queue at least once. However, aflfast performs dictionary-based mutations on a given input in the queue, only when the input's *performance score* (computed by the aflfast algorithm) is above a certain threshold. We determined that the threshold used by aflfast is too aggressive, resulting in too few inputs in the fuzzer queue undergoing dictionary mutations.

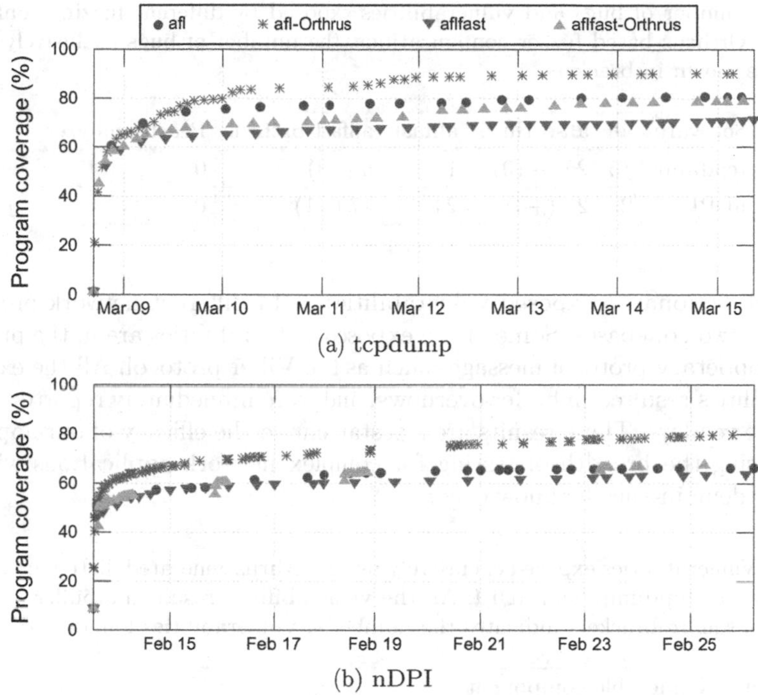


(a) tcpdump

(b) nDPI

**Fig. 3.** Test coverage as a function of time for tcpdump (a), and nDPI (b), for different fuzzing configurations. Program coverage measurements were made only when there was a change in its magnitude.

**Vulnerabilities Exposed.** Table 4 shows the number of vulnerabilities exposed in nDPI, and tcpdump, across all fuzzing configurations. In the case of tcpdump, the positive impact of the Orthrus generated dictionary is evident. afl, and afl-Orthrus, exposed 15, and 26 unique vulnerabilities respectively. 10 out of the 11 additional vulnerabilities exposed by afl-Orthrus, were exclusively found by it, i.e., it exposed 10 vulnerabilities in tcpdump not found by stand-alone afl. aflfast, and aflfast-Orthrus configurations exposed 1 and 5 vulnerabilities respectively. aflfast-Orthrus exposed 4 vulnerabilities that were not exposed by stand-alone aflfast. In the case of nDPI, afl-Orthrus exposed 4 vulnerabilities that were not found by stand-alone afl, while aflfast-Orthrus exposed 1 such vulnerability. For both nDPI, and tcpdump, aflfast-Orthrus finds fewer number of vulnerabilities overall in comparison to its baseline. We conjecture that the fuzz schedule alterations carried out in aflfast [3] influence the scheduling of dictionary-mutations, resulting in the observed drop.

Table 5 documents those vulnerabilities found using Orthrus generated dictionaries that were not found by stand-alone fuzzing of tcpdump, and nDPI. The number of exposed vulnerabilities that may be exclusively attributed to Orthrus are 10, and 5, for tcpdump, and nDPI respectively. Overall, Orthrus

**Table 4.** Number of bugs and vulnerabilities exposed by different fuzzing configurations. For Orthrus-based fuzzer configurations, the number of bugs exclusively found by them is shown in brackets.

| Software | afl | afl-orthrus | aflfast | aflfast-orthrus | Peach-analyzer |
|---|---|---|---|---|---|
| tcpdump | 15 | 26 (+10) | 1 | 5 (+4) | 0 |
| nDPI | 26 | 27 (+4) | 24 | 17 (+1) | 0 |

generated dictionaries exposed vulnerabilities in 14 different network protocols across the two codebases. Some of the exposed vulnerabilities are in the processing of proprietary protocol messages such as the Viber protocol. All the exposed vulnerabilities resulted in buffer overflows, and were immediately reported to the respective vendors. These results are a testament to the efficacy of our approach in increasing the breadth of testing for complex network applications without requiring domain-specific knowledge.

**Table 5.** Vulnerabilities exposed exclusively using Orthrus generated dictionaries in afl, and aflfast, for tcpdump, and nDPI. All the vulnerabilities result in a buffer overflow. Number in square brackets indicates the number of vulnerabilities found.

| Software | Vulnerable component |
|---|---|
| tcpdump | IPv6 DHCP packet printer |
| | IPv6 Open Shortest Path First (OSPFv3) packet printer |
| | IEEE 802.1ab Link Layer Discovery Protocol (LLDP) packet printer |
| | ISO CLNS, ESIS, and ISIS packet printers [**2**] |
| | IP packet printer |
| | ISA and Key Management Protocol (ISAKMP) printer |
| | IPv6 Internet Control Message Protocol (ICMPv6) printer |
| | Point to Point Protocol (PPP) printer |
| | White Board Protocol printer |
| nDPI | ZeroMQ Message Transport Protocol processor |
| | Viber protocol processor |
| | Syslog protocol processor |
| | Ubiquity UBNT AirControl 2 protocol processor |
| | HTTP protocol processor |

**Preliminary Results for Snort++.** We used Orthrus to perform dictionary-based fuzzing of `snort++`, a `C++` implementation of the popular snort IDS. Baseline fuzzing with afl-fuzz helped find a single vulnerability (CVE-2017-6658) in the `snort++` decoder implementation. In contrast, the Orthrus generated dictionary has helped find an additional vulnerability (CVE-2017-6657) in the LLC packet decoder implementation of `snort++` [31].

### 4.4 Limitations

Although our evaluations show that static analysis guided fuzzing is beneficial, our positive results may not generalize to other parsing applications. However, our evaluation comprising six different parser implementations provides strong evidence that our approach can make fuzz testing more effective. Automatically generated parsers (e.g., yacc-based parsers) may contain code that is structurally different than hand-written parsers that we have evaluated. We believe that their analysis may be carried out at the specification level than at the source code level. Furthermore, we make use of simple heuristics to infer input message fragments from source code. Thus, our analysis may miss legitimate input fragments (false negatives), and/or add irrelevant tokens to the input dictionary (false positives). However, we take practical measures to keep the number of false positives/negatives low. For example, our design incorporates practical security advice given by reputed institutes such as CERT [5] that have been compiled over years of source code audits. In our case study, we make use of a small (yet relevant) seed set to bootstrap fuzzing. It is possible that a diverse seed set improves the performance of our baseline fuzzers. Having said that, we have carefully analyzed the additional coverage achieved solely through the use of the supplied dictionary to ensure that the presented increments can be attributed to our method. In addition, we have manually triaged all vulnerabilities found exclusively using dictionary-based fuzzing to ensure causality, i.e., they were ultimately exposed due to the use of specific tokens in the supplied dictionary.

## 5 Related Work

Multiple techniques have been proposed to improve the effectiveness of fuzzing. For our discussion of related work, we focus on approaches that infer the protocol specification, use grammar-based fuzzing, or query-driven static analysis approaches.

**Inferring Protocol Specification.** There are two problems underlying protocol specification inference: Inferring the protocol (i) Message format; and (ii) State machine. Prior work, with the exception of Prospex [7] has focused solely on the message format inference problem. Broadly, two approaches have been proposed to automatically infer the protocol specification. The first approach relies entirely on network traces for performing the inference, exemplified by the tool Discoverer [8]. As other researchers have noted, the main problem with this approach is that network traces contain little semantic information, such as the relation between fields in a message. Therefore, inference based entirely on network traces is often limited to a simple description of the message format that is an under-approximation of the original specification. The second approach, also a pre-dominant one, is to employ dynamic program analysis in a setting where the network application processes sample messages, in order to infer the protocol specification. Proposals such as Polyglot [4], Tupni [9], Autoformat [19], Prospex [7], and the tool by Wondracek et al. [32] fall into this category. In comparison to our work, these proposals have two shortcomings. First, they require dynamic instrumentation systems that are often proprietary or simply inaccessible. Dynamic instrumentation and analysis often requires software expertise, making it challenging for auditing third-party code. In contrast, we show that our analysis can be bundled into an existing compiler toolchain so that performing protocol inference is as simple as compiling the underlying source code. Second, prior work with the exception of Prospex, have not specifically evaluated the impact of their inference on the effectiveness of fuzz testing. Although Comparetti et al. [7] evaluate their tool Prospex in conjunction with the Peach fuzzer, their evaluation is limited to finding known vulnerabilities in controlled scenarios. In contrast to these studies, we extensively evaluate the impact our inference on the effectiveness of fuzzing, both quantitatively in terms of test coverage achieved, and time to vulnerability exposure, and qualitatively in terms of an analysis of vulnerabilities exclusively exposed using our inference in real-world code.

**Grammar-Based Fuzzing.** Godefroid et al. [13] design a software testing tool in which symbolic execution is applied to generate grammar-aware test inputs. The authors evaluate their tool against the IE7 JavaScript interpreter and find that grammar-based testing increases test coverage from 53% to 81%. Although their techniques are promising, their work suffers from three practical difficulties. First, a manual grammar specification is required for their technique to be applied. Second, the infrastructure to perform symbolic execution at their scale is not publicly available, rendering their techniques inapplicable to third-party code. Third, their approach requires non-trivial code annotations, requiring a close co-operation between testers and developers, something that might not always be feasible. In contrast, we solve these challenges by automatically inferring input data formats from the source code. Indeed, we show that more lightweight analysis techniques can substantially benefit modern fuzzers. Langfuzz [16] uses a grammar specification of the JavaScript and PHP languages to effectively conduct security assessments on the respective interpreters. Like Godefroid et al., the authors of Langfuzz demonstrate that, in scenarios where a grammar specification can be obtained, specification based fuzzing is superior to random testing. However, creating such grammar specifications for complex network applications manually is a daunting task. Indeed, network protocol specifications (unlike computing languages) are specified only semi-formally, requiring protocol implementors to hand-write parsers instead of generating them from a parser generator. Such practical difficulties make grammar (specification) based fuzzing challenging for network applications.

**Query Based Program Analysis.** Our static analysis approach is inspired by prior work on the use of queries to conduct specific program analyses by Lam et al. [18], and automatic inference of search patterns for discovering taint-style vulnerabilities from source code by Yamaguchi et al. [33]. At their core, both these works use a notion of program queries to elicit vulnerable code patterns from source code. While Lam et al. leverage datalog queries for analysis, Yamaguchi et al. employ so called *graph traversals*. In contrast to their work, we leverage query-driven analysis toward supporting a fuzzer instead of attempting static vulnerability discovery.

## 6 Conclusions and Future Work

In this paper, we demonstrate how static analysis guided fuzzing can improve the effectiveness of modern off-the-shelf fuzzers, especially for networking applications. Code patterns indicate how user input is processed by the program. We leverage this insight for gathering input fragments directly from source code. To this end, we couple a static analyzer to a fuzzer via an existing interface. Using input dictionaries derived from semantic and syntactic program analysis queries, we are able to not only increase the test coverage of applications by 10–15%, but also reduce the time needed to expose vulnerabilities by an order of magnitude in comparison to fuzzers not supplied with an input dictionary. We leverage our research prototype to fuzz two high-profile network applications, namely, nDPI, a deep packet inspection library, and tcpdump, a network packet analyzer. We find 10 zero-day vulnerabilities in tcpdump, and 5 zero-day vulnerabilities in nDPI that were missed by stand-alone fuzzers. These results show that our approach holds promise for making security assessments more effective.

Our work highlights the need for a stronger interaction between program analysis and testing. Although our study describes one way in which program analysis can enhance fuzzing, exploiting their reciprocal nature poses some interesting problems such as directing static analysis on code portions that have not been fuzzed. This is one avenue for future work. A logical follow up of our work will be to infer the protocol state machine in addition to its message format, and leverage the additional insight for conducting stateful fuzzing. Leveraging our inference algorithm toward conducting large-scale analysis of open-source C/C++ parser implementations is another avenue for future work that will shed light on the security dimension of an important software component. Indeed, targeting our analysis at the binary level will help us evaluate its efficacy against closed source applications.

**Acknowledgements.** We would like to thank Julian Fietkau for helping customize the Peach fuzzer for our experiments. This work was supported by the following awards and grants: Bundesministerium für Bildung und Forschung (BMBF) under Award No. KIS1DSD032 (Project Enzevalos), Leibniz Prize project by the German Research Foundation (DFG) under Award No. FKZ FE 570/4-1, the Helmholtz Research School in Security Technologies scholarship, and the Danish Villum project ReNet. The opinions, views, and conclusions contained herein are those of the author(s) and should not be interpreted as necessarily representing the official policies or endorsements, either expressed or implied, of BMBF, DFG, or, any other funding body involved.

## References


1. Aho, A.V., Sethi, R., Ullman, J.D.: Compilers, Principles, Techniques. Addison-Wesley, Boston (1986)
2. Address Sanitizer. https://clang.llvm.org/docs/AddressSanitizer.html. Accessed 27 Mar 2017
3. Böhme, M., Pham, V.T., Roychoudhury, A.: Coverage-based greybox fuzzing as Markov chain. In: Proceedings of the ACM Conference on Computer and Communications Security (CCS), pp. 1032–1043. ACM (2016)
4. Caballero, J., Yin, H., Liang, Z., Song, D.: Polyglot: automatic extraction of protocol message format using dynamic binary analysis. In: Proceedings of the ACM Conference on Computer and Communications Security (CCS), pp. 317–329 (2007)
5. Cert Secure Coding Standards. https://www.securecoding.cert.org/confluence/display/seccode/SEI+CERT+Coding+Standards. Accessed 01 June 2017
6. Clusterfuzzer: Heap-buffer-overflow in read. https://bugs.chromium.org/p/chromium/issues/detail?id=609042. Accessed 23 Mar 2017
7. Comparetti, P.M., Wondracek, G., Kruegel, C., Kirda, E.: Prospex: Protocol specification extraction. In: Proceedings of the IEEE Security & Privacy, pp. 110–125 (2009)
8. Cui, W., Kannan, J., Wang, H.J.: Discoverer: automatic protocol reverse engineering from network traces. In: Proceedings of the USENIX Security Symposium, vol. 158 (2007)
9. Cui, W., Peinado, M., Chen, K., Wang, H.J., Irun-Briz, L.: Tupni: automatic reverse engineering of input formats. In: Proceedings of the ACM Conference on Computer and Communications Security (CCS), pp. 391–402 (2008)
10. Engler, D., Chelf, B., Chou, A., Hallem, S.: Checking system rules using system-specific, programmer-written compiler extensions. In: Proceedings of the OSDI (2000)
11. Foote, J.: The exploitable GDB plugin (2015). https://github.com/jfoote/exploitable. Accessed 23 Mar 2017
12. Gallagher, K.B., Lyle, J.R.: Using program slicing in software maintenance. IEEE Trans. Softw. Eng. **17**(8), 751–761 (1991)
13. Godefroid, P., Kiezun, A., Levin, M.Y.: Grammar-based whitebox fuzzing. ACM SIGPLAN Not. **43**, 206–215 (2008)
14. Godefroid, P., Levin, M.Y., Molnar, D.: Sage: whitebox fuzzing for security testing. ACM Queue **10**(1), 20 (2012)
15. Google Inc.: Fuzzer test suite. https://github.com/google/fuzzer-test-suite. Accessed 23 Mar 2017
16. Holler, C., Herzig, K., Zeller, A.: Fuzzing with code fragments. In: Proceedings of the USENIX Security Symposium, pp. 445–458 (2012)
17. Hopcroft, J.E., Motwani, R., Ullman, J.D.: Introduction to Automata Theory, Languages, and Computation, 3rd edn. Addison-Wesley, Reading (2006)
18. Lam, M.S., Whaley, J., Livshits, V.B., Martin, M.C., Avots, D., Carbin, M., Unkel, C.: Context-sensitive program analysis as database queries. In: Proceedings of the ACM Symposium on Principles of Database Systems, pp. 1–12 (2005)
19. Lin, Z., Jiang, X., Xu, D., Zhang, X.: Automatic protocol format reverse engineering through context-aware monitored execution. In: Proceedings of Symposium on Network and Distributed System Security (NDSS), pp. 1–15 (2008)
20. LLVM Compiler Infrastructure: Clang static analyzer. http://clang-analyzer.llvm.org/. Accessed 23 Mar 2017

21. LLVM Compiler Infrastructure: libFuzzer: a library for coverage-guided fuzz testing. http://llvm.org/docs/LibFuzzer.html. Accessed 23 Mar 2017
22. Miller, B.P., Fredriksen, L., So, B.: An empirical study of the reliability of UNIX utilities. Commun. ACM **33**(12), 32–44 (1990)
23. MITRE.org: CVE-2014-0160: The Heartbleed Bug. https://cve.mitre.org/cgi-bin/cvename.cgi?name=CVE-2014-0160. Accessed 23 Mar 2017
24. MITRE.org: CVE-2015-8317: Libxml2: several out of bounds reads. https://cve.mitre.org/cgi-bin/cvename.cgi?name=CVE-2015-8317. Accessed 23 Mar 2017
25. MITRE.org: CVE-2016-5180: Project c-ares security advisory. https://cve.mitre.org/cgi-bin/cvename.cgi?name=CVE-2016-5180. Accessed 23 Mar 2017
26. Molnar, D., Li, X.C., Wagner, D.: Dynamic test generation to find integer bugs in x86 binary Linux programs. In: Proceedings of the USENIX Security Symposium, vol. 9, pp. 67–82 (2009)
27. nDPI: Open and Extensible LGPLv3 Deep Packet Inspection Library. http://www.ntop.org/products/deep-packet-inspection/ndpi/. Accessed 23 Mar 2017
28. OpenRCE: Sulley. https://github.com/OpenRCE/sulley. Accessed 23 Mar 2017
29. Peach Fuzzer. http://www.peachfuzzer.com/. Accessed 23 Mar 2017
30. Reps, T., Horwitz, S., Sagiv, M.: Precise interprocedural dataflow analysis via graph reachability. In: Proceedings of the ACM SIGPLAN-SIGACT Symposium on Principles of Programming Languages, pp. 49–61 (1995)
31. Snort++ vulnerabilities found. http://blog.snort.org/2017/05/snort-vulnerabilities-found.html. Accessed 05 June 2017
32. Wondracek, G., Comparetti, P.M., Kruegel, C., Kirda, E.: Automatic network protocol analysis. In: Proceedings of the Symposium on Network and Distributed System Security (NDSS) (2008)
33. Yamaguchi, F., Maier, A., Gascon, H., Rieck, K.: Automatic inference of search patterns for taint-style vulnerabilities. In: Proceedings of the IEEE Security & Privacy, pp. 797–812 (2015)
34. Zalewski, M.: American fuzzy lop. http://lcamtuf.coredump.cx/afl/. Accessed 23 Mar 2017
35. Zalewski, M.: afl-fuzz: making up grammar with a dictionary in hand (2015). https://lcamtuf.blogspot.de/2015/01/afl-fuzz-making-up-grammar-with.html. Accessed 23 Mar 2017

# Breaking Fitness Records Without Moving: Reverse Engineering and Spoofing Fitbit

Hossein Fereidooni[1(✉)], Jiska Classen[2], Tom Spink[3], Paul Patras[3], Markus Miettinen[2], Ahmad-Reza Sadeghi[2], Matthias Hollick[2], and Mauro Conti[1]

[1] University of Padua, Padua, Italy
{hossein,conti}@math.unipd.it

[2] Technische Universität Darmstadt, Darmstadt, Germany
{jclassen,mhollick}@seemoo.de,
{markus.miettinen,ahmad.sadeghi}@trust.tu-darmstadt.de

[3] University of Edinburgh, Edinburgh, UK
{tspink,ppatras}@inf.ed.ac.uk

**Abstract.** Tens of millions of wearable fitness trackers are shipped yearly to consumers who routinely collect information about their exercising patterns. Smartphones push this health-related data to vendors' cloud platforms, enabling users to analyze summary statistics on-line and adjust their habits. Third-parties including health insurance providers now offer discounts and financial rewards in exchange for such private information and evidence of healthy lifestyles. Given the associated monetary value, the authenticity and correctness of the activity data collected becomes imperative. In this paper, we provide an in-depth security analysis of the operation of fitness trackers commercialized by Fitbit, the wearables market leader. We reveal an intricate security through obscurity approach implemented by the user activity synchronization protocol running on the devices we analyze. Although non-trivial to interpret, we reverse engineer the message semantics, demonstrate how falsified user activity reports can be injected, and argue that based on our discoveries, such attacks can be performed at scale to obtain financial gains. We further document a hardware attack vector that enables circumvention of the end-to-end protocol encryption present in the latest Fitbit firmware, leading to the spoofing of valid encrypted fitness data. Finally, we give guidelines for avoiding similar vulnerabilities in future system designs.

**Keywords:** Fitness trackers · Reverse engineering · Spoofing · Fitbit

## 1 Introduction

Market forecasts indicate 274 million wrist-based fitness trackers and smartwatches will be sold worldwide by 2020 [1]. Such devices already enable users

**Electronic supplementary material** The online version of this chapter (doi:10.1007/978-3-319-66332-6_3) contains supplementary material, which is available to authorized users.


M. Dacier et al. (Eds.): RAID 2017, LNCS 10453, pp. 48–69, 2017.
DOI: 10.1007/978-3-319-66332-6_3

and healthcare professionals to monitor individual activity and sleep habits, and underpin reward schemes that incentivize regular physical exercise. Fitbit maintains the lead in the wearables market, having shipped more units in 2016 than its biggest competitors Apple, Garmin, and Samsung combined [2].

Fitness trackers collect extensive information which enables infering the users' health state and may reveal particularly sensitive personal circumstances. For instance, one individual recently discovered his wife was pregnant after examining her Fitbit data [3]. Police and attorneys start recognizing wearables as "black boxes" of the human body and use statistics gathered by activity trackers as admissible evidence in court [4,5]. These developments highlight the critical importance of both preserving data privacy throughout the collection process, and ensuring correctness and authenticity of the records stored. The emergence of third-party services offering rewards to users who share personal health information further strengthens the significance of protecting wearables data integrity. These include health insurance companies that provide discounts to customers who demonstrate physical activity through their fitness tracker logs [6], websites that financially compensate active users consenting to fitness monitoring [7], and platforms where players bet on reaching activity goals to win money [8]. Unfortunately, such on-line services also bring *strong incentives for malicious users to manipulate tracking data, in order to fraudulently gain monetary benefits.*

Given the value fitness data has towards litigation and income, researchers have analyzed potential security and privacy vulnerabilities specific to activity trackers [9–12]. Following a survey of 17 different fitness trackers available on the European market in Q1 2016 [15], recent investigations into the security of Fitbit devices (e.g. [12]), and the work we present herein, we found that in comparison to other vendors, Fitbit employs the most effective security mechanisms in their products. Such competitive advantage, giving users the ability to share statistics with friends, and the company's overall market leadership make Fitbit one of the most attractive vendors to third parties running fitness-based financial reward programs. At the same time it motivates us to choose Fitbit trackers as the target of our security study, in the hope that understanding their underlying security architecture can be used to inform the security and privacy of future fitness tracker system designs. Rahman *et al.* have investigated the communication protocols used by early Fitbit wearables when synchronizing with web servers and possible attacks against this [9]. Cyr *et al.* [10] studied the different layers of the Fitbit Flex ecosystem and argued correlation and man-in-the-middle (MITM) attacks are feasible. Recent work documents firmware vulnerabilities found in Fitbit trackers [11], and the reverse engineering of cryptographic primitives and authentication protocols [12]. However, as rapid innovation is the primary business objective, security considerations remain an afterthought rather than embedded into product design. Therefore, wider adoption of wearable technology is hindered by distrust [13,14].

**Contributions:** We undertake an in-depth security analysis of the Fitbit Flex and Fitbit One fitness trackers and reveal serious security and privacy vulnerabilities present in these devices which, although difficult to uncover, are reproducible and **can be exploited at scale** once identified. Specifically, we reverse engineer the primitives governing the communication between trackers and cloud-based services, implement an open-source tool to extract sensitive personal information in human-readable format, and demonstrate that malicious users can inject fabricated activity records to obtain personal benefits. To circumvent end-to-end protocol encryption implemented in the latest firmware, we perform hardware-based reverse engineering (RE) and document successful injection of falsified data that appears legitimate to the Fitbit cloud. The weaknesses we uncover, as well as the design guidelines we provide to ensure data integrity, authenticity and confidentiality, build foundations for more secure hardware and software development, including code and build management, automated testing, and software update mechanisms. Our insights provide valuable information to researchers and practitioners about the detailed way in which Fitbit operates their fitness tracking devices and associated services. These may help IoT manufacturers in general to improve their product design and business processes, towards developing rigorously secured devices and services.

**Responsible Disclosure:** We have contacted Fitbit prior to submitting our work, and informed the company about the security vulnerabilities we discovered. We disclosed these vulnerabilities to allow sufficient time for them to fix the identified problems before the publication of our findings. At the time of writing, we are aware that the vendor is in the process of evaluating the disclosed vulnerabilities and formulating an effective response to them.

## 2 Adversary Model

To retrieve the statistics that trackers collect, users predominantly rely on smartphone or tablet applications that extract activity records stored by the devices, and push these onto cloud servers. We consider the adversarial settings depicted in Fig. 1, in which users are potentially dishonest, whilst the server is provably trustworthy. We assume an active adversary model in which the wristband user

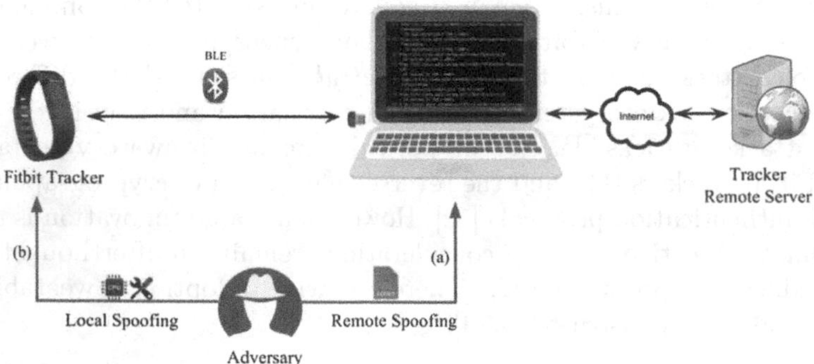


**Fig. 1.** Adversary model considered for (a) devices not implementing encryption and (b) trackers using encryption.

is the primary adversary, who has both the means and motive to compromise the system. Specifically, the attacker (a) views and seeks to manipulate the data uploaded to the server without direct physical control over the device, or (b) inspects and alters the data stored in memory prior to synchronization, having full hardware control of the device. The adversary's motivation is rooted in the potential to obtain financial gains by injecting fabricated fitness data to the remote server. Smartphone and cloud platform security issues are outside the of scope of this paper, therefore not considered in our analysis.

### 2.1 Target Fitbit Devices

The adversary's target devices are the *Fitbit Flex* and *Fitbit One* wrist-based fitness trackers, which record user step counts, distance traveled, calories burned, floors climbed (Fitbit One), active minutes, and sleep duration. These particular trackers have been on the market for a number of years, they are affordable and their security and privacy has been scrutinized by other researchers. Thus, both consumers and the vendor would expect they are not subject to vulnerabilities.

We subsequently found that other Fitbit models (e.g. Zip and Charge) implement the same communication protocol, therefore may be subject to the same vulnerabilities we identify in this work.

### 2.2 End-to-End Communication Paradigms

Following initial pairing, we discover Fitbit trackers are shipped with one of two different firmwares; namely, the latest version (Flex 7.81) which by default encrypts activity records prior to synchronization using the XTEA algorithm and a pre-installed encryption key; and, respectively, an earlier firmware version (Flex 7.64) that by default operates in plaintext mode, but is able to activate message encryption after being instructed to do so by the Fitbit server. If enabled, *encryption is end-to-end* between the tracker and the server, whilst the smartphone app is unaware of the actual contents pushed from tracker to the server. The app merely embeds encrypted records retrieved from the tracker into JSON messages, forwards them to the Fitbit servers, and relays responses back to the tracker. The same functionality can be achieved through software running on a computer equipped with a USB Bluetooth LE dongle, including the open-source Galileo tool, which does not require user authentication [16].

Even though only the tracker and the server know the encryption key, upon synchronization the smartphone app also receives statistic summaries from the server in human readable format over an HTTPS connection. As such, and following authentication, the app and authorized third parties can connect to a user account via the Fitbit API and retrieve activity digests—without physical access to the tracker. We also note that, despite newer firmware enforcing end-to-end encryption, the Fitbit server continues to accept and respond to unencrypted activity records from trackers that only optionally employ encryption, thereby enabling an attacker to successfully modify the plaintext activity records sent to the server.

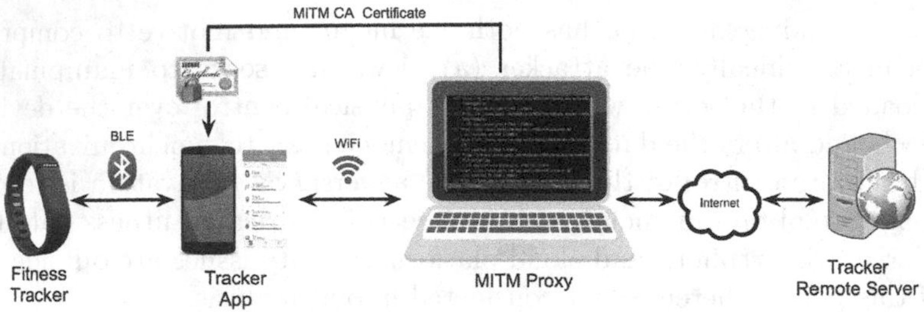


**Fig. 2.** Schematic illustration of the testbed used for protocol reverse engineering. Linux-based laptop used as wireless Internet gateway and running MITM proxy.

## 3 Protocol Reverse Engineering

In this section, we reverse engineer the communication protocol used by the Fitbit trackers studied, uncovering an intricate security through obscurity approach in its implementation. Once we understand the message semantics, we show that detailed personal information can be extracted and fake activity reports can be created and remotely injected, using an approach that scales, as documented in Sect. 4.

### 3.1 MITM Setup

To intercept the communication between the tracker and the remote server, we deploy an MITM proxy on a Linux-based laptop acting as a wireless Internet gateway, as illustrated in Fig. 2. We install a fake CA certificate on an Android phone and trigger tracker synchronization manually, using an unmodified Fitbit application. The application synchronizes the tracker over Bluetooth LE and forwards data between the tracker and the server over the Wi-Fi connection, encapsulating the information into JSON messages sent over an HTTPS connection. This procedure resembles typical user engagement with the tracker, however the MITM proxy allows us to intercept all communications between the tracker and the server, as well as between the smartphone and the server. In the absence of end-to-end encryption, we can both capture and modify messages generated by the tracker. Even with end-to-end encryption enabled, we can still read the activity digests that the server provides to logged-in users, which are displayed by the app running on their smartphones.

### 3.2 Wireshark Plugin Development and Packet Analysis

To simplify the analysis process and ensure repeatability, we develop a custom frame dissector as stand-alone plugin programmed in C for the Wireshark network analyzer [17].[1] Developing this dissector involves cross-correlating the raw

[1] The source code of our plug in is available at https://seemoo.de/fitbit-wireshark.

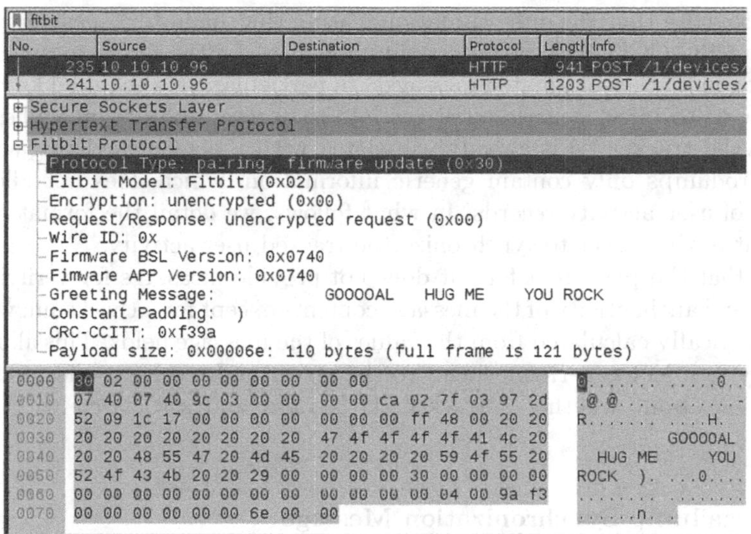


**Fig. 3.** Generic microdump in plain-text, as displayed by the wireshark dissector we implement. Note the ability to filter by 'fitbit' protocol type in the analyzer.

messages sent by the tracker with the server's JSON responses to the client application. After repeated experiments, we infer the many protocol fields that are present in tracker-originated messages and that are encoded in different formats as detailed next. We use the knowledge gained to present these fields in a human-readable format in the protocol analyzer.

There are two types of tracker-originated messages we have observed during our analysis, which will be further described in the following sections:

1. **Microdumps:** A summary of the tracker status and configuration.
2. **Megadumps:** A summary of user activity data from the tracker.

### 3.3 Microdump

Depending on the action being performed by the user (e.g. authentication and pairing, synchronizing activity records), the smartphone app makes HTTPS requests to the server using specific URLs, e.g. `POST` https://<fitbit_server_ip>/1/devices/client/.../validate.json?btle_Name=Flex&secret=null&btAddress=<6Byte_tracker_ID> for initial authentication. Each basic action is accompanied by a so-called *microdump*, which is required to identify the tracker, and to obtain its state (e.g. its current firmware version). Irrespective of whether or not the tracker implements protocol encryption, the microdump header includes the tracker ID and firmware version, and is sent in plain-text. Figure 3 illustrates a microdump sent along with a firmware update request, as interpreted by our Wireshark dissector.

We also note that the only validation feature that plain-text messages implement is a CRC-CCITT checksum, presumably used by the server to detect data corruption in tracker-originated messages. In particular, this acquired knowledge will allow us to inject generic messages into the server and obtain replies, even when a valid tracker ID is already associated with a person's existing account. Yet, microdumps only contain generic information, which does not allow the spoofing of user activity records. In what follows, we detail the format of messages sent to the server to synchronize the tracked user activity.

Note that the plain-text format does not provide measures for verifying the integrity and authenticity of the message contents except for a checksum, which is deterministically calculated from the values of the message fields. This allows the adversary to inject generic messages to the server and receive replies, including information about whether a tracker ID is valid and associated with a user account.

### 3.4 Megadump Synchronization Message

Step counts and other statistics are transmitted by the tracker in the form of a so-called *megadump*. Independent of encrypted or plain-text mode, neither the Fitbit smartphone application nor the Galileo synchronization tool are aware of the exact meaning of this payload. The megadump is simply forwarded to the server, which in turn parses the message and responds with a reply. This reply is then forwarded (by the corresponding application) back to the tracker, confirming to the tracker that the data was synchronized with the server successfully.

Despite this behavior, the Fitbit smartphone application—in contrast to Galileo—is aware of the user's statistics. However, this is due to the application making requests to the Fitbit Web API. Once authenticated, this API can be used to retrieve user information from the server in JSON format. The Fitbit smartphone application periodically synchronizes its display via the Fitbit Web API, allowing the user to see the latest information that was uploaded by the most recent tracker megadump. A plain-text example of this is shown in Fig. 4. Note that the Fitbit Web API separates data by type, such that not all information transmitted within one megadump is contained within one JSON response. From the megadump a total distance of 522720 mm can be extracted, which equals to the 0.52 km from the JSON.

We use this information to reverse engineer and validate the megadump packet format, and have identified that each megadump is split into the following sections: a header, one or more *data sections*, and a footer. These sections start with a *section start* sequence of bytes: `c0 cd db dc`; and end with a *section terminator* byte: `c0`. If the byte `c0` is required to be used within a data section, it is escaped in a manner similar to RFC 1055.[2]

**Message Header.** The megadump header is very similar to the microdump header, but contains a few differences. Figure 5 shows how this header is structured.

[2] A Non-standard for transmission of IP Data-grams over Serial Lines: SLIP.

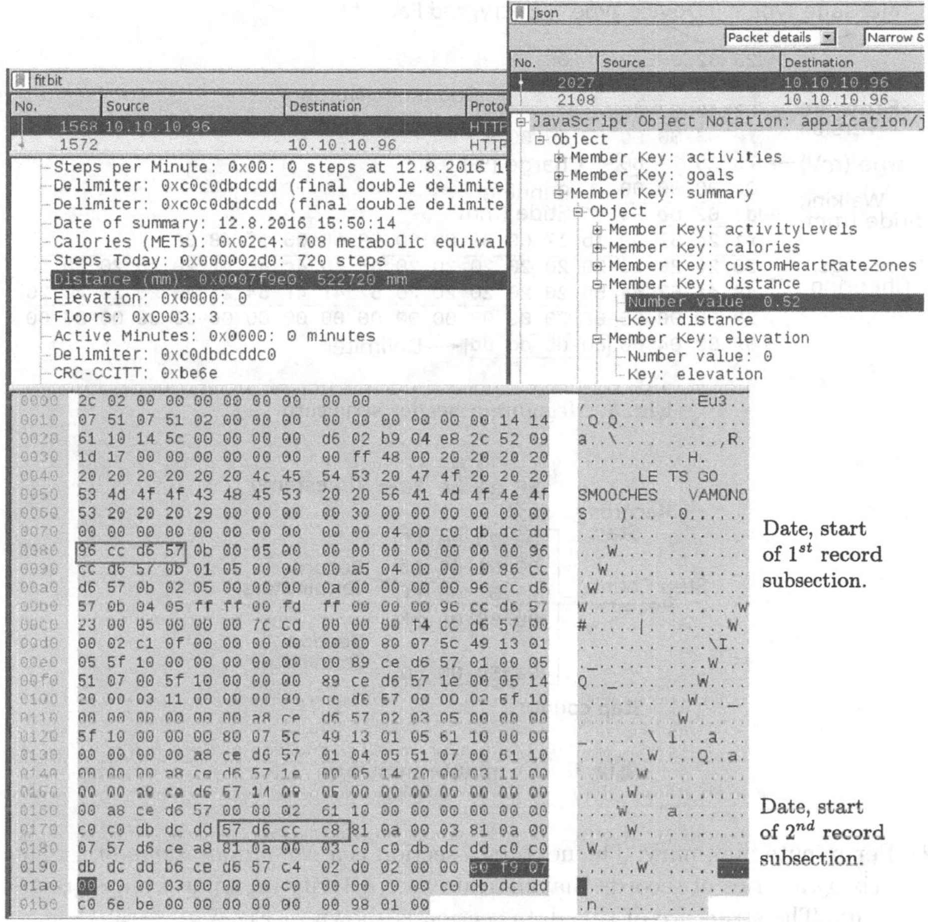


**Fig. 4.** Megadump frame in plain-text format as transmitted to the Fitbit server (main window) and the human-readable JSON status response by the Fitbit Web API (top right).

**Data Sections.** Following the header are one or more *data sections*. Each *data section* contains various statistics in a particular format, and may even be blank. As previously mentioned, each data sections start with c0 cd db dc, and are terminated by a single c0 character. Therefore, the data sections are of variable length. From the packets we have analyzed, it has been observed that there are typically four data sections, which all appear in the following order, and have the following format:

(1) Daily Summary: The first data section contains activity information across a number of different absolute timestamps. This section contains a series of fixed-length records that begin with a little-endian timestamp, and end with a section terminator byte (c0).

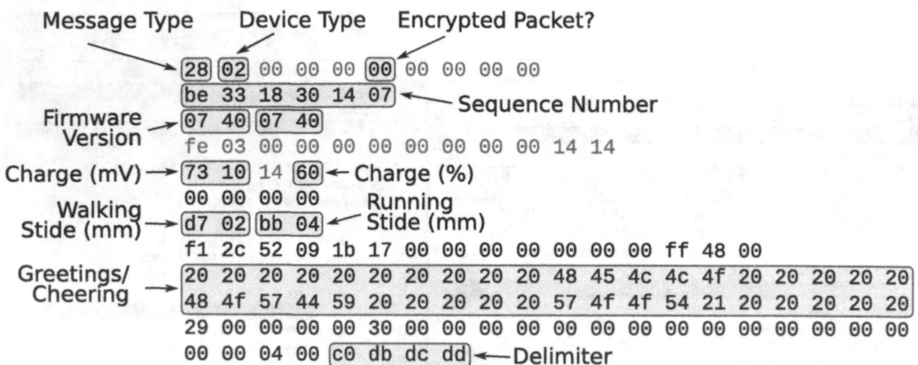


**Fig. 5.** Megadump header structure

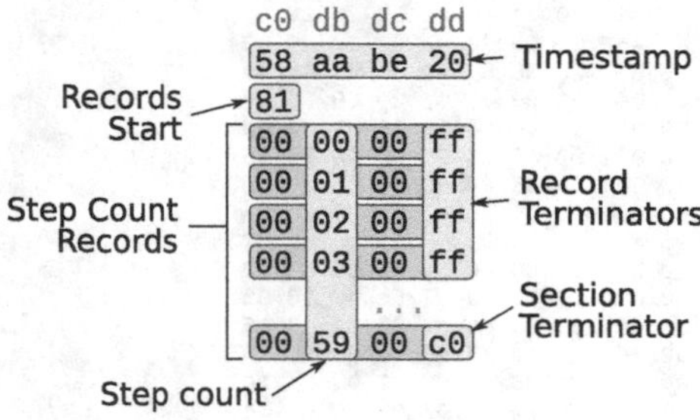


**Fig. 6.** Per-minute summary

(2) Per-minute Summary: The next data section is a *per-minute summary*, comprising a series of records that indicate user activity on a per-minute granularity. The structure of this data section is shown in Fig. 6.

The section begins with a timestamp (unlike other timestamps, this field is big-endian), which acts as the *base* time for this sequence of step counts. Each step count record is then an increment of a time period (typically two minutes), from this base time. Following the timestamp is a byte indicating the start of the step count records. The full meaning of this byte is unclear, but we believe it indicates the time period between each step count record. Following this, a series of records consisting of four bytes state the number of steps taken per-time period. The second byte indicates the number of steps taken, and the fourth byte is either `ff` to indicate another record follows, or `c0` (for the last record) to terminate the data section.

(3) Overall Summary: This data section contains a summary of the previous records, although as will be demonstrated later it is not validated against "per-minute" or "per-day" data. The format of this section is shown in Fig. 7.

This section starts with a timestamp, indicating the base time for this summary data. Following this timestamp is a 16-bit value that holds the number of

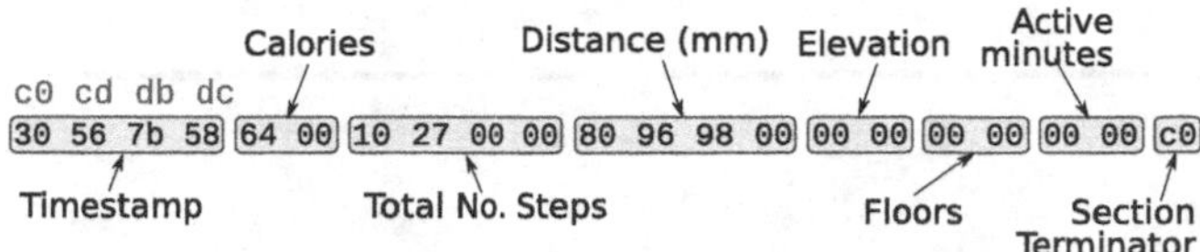


**Fig. 7.** Megadump summary fields

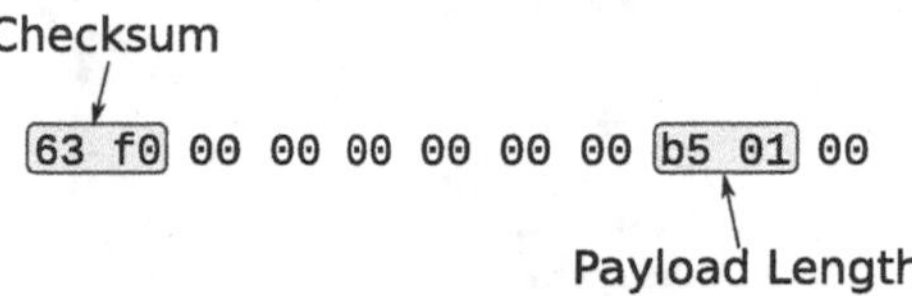


**Fig. 8.** Megadump footer fields

calories burned. Following on from this is a 32-bit value containing the number of steps taken, and a 32-bit value containing the distance travelled in millimeters. Finally, the summary ends with elevation, floors climbed and active minutes—all 16-bit values.

(4) Alarms: The final data section contains information about what alarms are currently set on the tracker, and is typically empty unless the user has instructed the tracker to create an alarm.

**Message Footer.** The megadump footer contains a checksum and the size of the payload, as shown in Fig. 8.

## 4 Protocol-Based Remote Spoofing

This section shows that the construction of a megadump packet containing fake information and the subsequent transmission to the Fitbit server is a viable approach for inserting fake step data into a user's exercise profile. This attack does not actually require the possession of a physical tracker, but merely a known tracker ID to be associated with the user's Fitbit account. This means that one can fabricate fake data for any known and actively used tracker having a firmware version susceptible to this vulnerability. In order to construct a forged packet, however, the format of the message must be decoded and analyzed to determine the fields that must be populated.

### 4.1 Submission of Fake Data

The Fitbit server has an HTTPS endpoint that accepts raw messages from trackers, wrapped in an XML description. The raw message from the tracker is Base64 encoded, and contains various fields that describe the tracker's activity over a period of time.

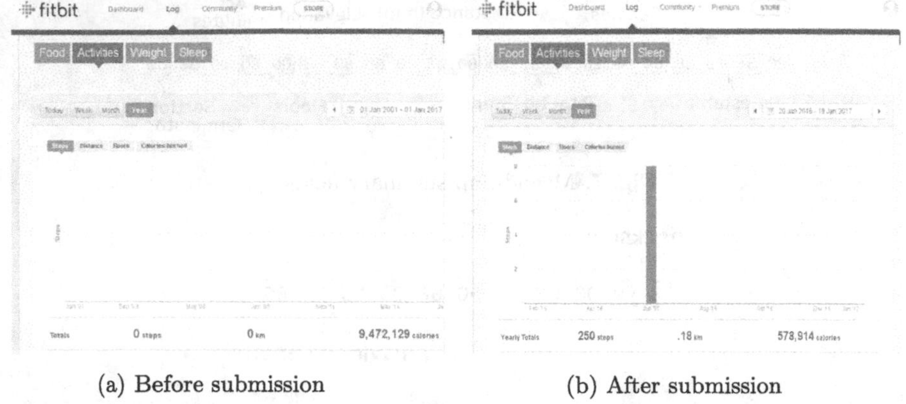


(a) Before submission (b) After submission

**Fig. 9.** The result of replaying data from another Fitbit tracker to a different tracker ID. (a) shows the Fitbit user activity screen before the replay attack, and (b) shows the results after the message is formed by changing the tracker ID, and submitted to the server.

The raw messages of the studied trackers may or may not be encrypted, but the remote server will accept either. Even though the encryption key for a particular tracker is unknown, it is possible to construct an unencrypted frame and submit it to the server for processing, associating it with an arbitrary tracker ID. Provided that all of the fields in the payload are valid and the checksum is correct, the remote server will accept the payload and update the activity log accordingly. In order to form such a message, the raw Fitbit frame must be Base64 encoded and placed within an XML wrapper as shown in Listing 1.1:

**Listing 1.1.** Fitbit frame within an XML wrapper

```
<?xml version="1.0"?>
<galileo-client version="2.0">
 <client-info>
 <client-id>
    6de4df71-17f9-43ea-9854-67f842021e05
 </client-id>
 <client-version>1.0.0.2292</client-version>
 <client-mode>sync</client-mode>
 <dongle-version major="2" minor="5"/>
 </client-info>
 <tracker tracker-id="F0609A12B0C0">
   <data>*** BASE64 PACKET DATA ***</data>
 </tracker>
</galileo-client>
```

The fabricated frame can be stored in a file, e.g. `payload`, and then submitted with the help of an HTTP `POST` request to the remote server as shown in Listing 1.2, after which the server will respond with a confirmation message.

**Listing 1.2.** Submitting fake payload to the server

```
$ curl -i -X POST https://client.fitbit.com/tracker/client/message
-H"Content-Type: text/xml"
--data-binary @payload
```

**Impersonation Attack:** In order to test the susceptibility of the server to this attack, a frame from a particular tracker was captured and re-submitted to the server with a *different* tracker ID. The different tracker ID was associated with a *different* Fitbit user account. The remote server accepted the payload, and updated the Fitbit user profile in question with identical information as for the genuine profile, confirming that simply altering the tracker ID in the submission message allowed arbitrary unencrypted payloads to be accepted. Figure 9 shows the Fitbit user activity logs before and after performing the impersonation attack. The fact that we are able to inject a data report associated to any of the studied trackers' IDs reveals both a severe DoS risk and the potential for a paid rogue service that would manipulate records on demand. Specifically, an attacker could arbitrarily modify the activity records of random users, or manipulate the data recorded by the device of a target victim, as tracker IDs are listed on the packaging. Likewise, a selfish user may pay for a service that exploits this vulnerability to manipulate activity records on demand, and subsequently gain rewards.

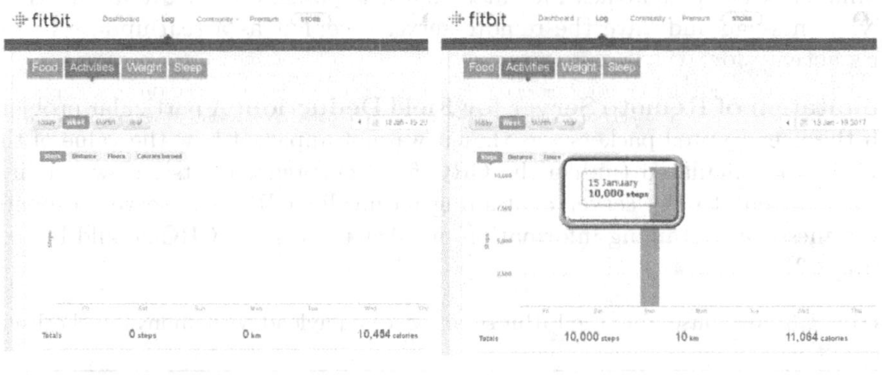


(a) Before submission

(b) After submission

**Fig. 10.** a shows the Fitbit user activity screen before fake data were submitted, and b shows the screen after the attack. In this example, 10000 steps and 10 km were injected for the date of Sunday, January 15th, 2017 by fabricating a message containing the data shown in Table 1.

**Fabrication of Activity Data:** Using the information gained during the protocol analysis phase (see Sect. 3), we constructed a message containing a frame with fake activity data and submitted it to the server, as discussed above. To do this, the payload of a genuine message was used as a *skeleton*, and each data section within the payload was cleared by removing all data bytes between the delimiters. Then, the summary section was populated with fake data. Using only the summary section was enough to update the Fitbit user profile with fabricated step count and distance traveled information. The format of the summary section is shown in Table 1, along with the fake data used to form the fabricated message.

**Table 1.** Data inserted into the packet summary section

| Range | Usage | Value | |
|---|---|---|---|
| 00-03 | Timestamp | 30 56 7b 58 | 15/01/17 |
| 04-05 | Calories | 64 00 | 100 |
| 06-09 | Number of Steps | 10 27 00 00 | 10000 |
| 0A-0D | Distance in mm | 80 96 98 00 | 10000000 |
| 0E-0F | Elevation | 00 00 00 00 | 0 |

Fig. 10 again shows a before and after view of the Fitbit user activity screen, when the fake message is submitted. In this example, the packet is constructed so that 10000 steps and a distance traveled of 10 km were registered for the 15th of January 2017. This attack indicates that it is possible to create an arbitrary activity message and have the remote server accept it as a real update to the user's activity log.

**Exploitation of Remote Server for Field Deduction:** A particular problem with the unencrypted packets was that it was not apparent how the value of the CRC field is calculated (unlike the CRC for encrypted packets). However, if a message is sent to the server containing an invalid CRC, the server responds with a message containing information on what the correct CRC should be (see Listing 1.3).

**Listing 1.3.** Response from the Fitbit server when a payload with an invalid checksum is submitted.

```
$ curl -i -X POST <target-url> --data-binary @payload
<?xml version="1.0"encoding="UTF-8"standalone="yes"?>
<galileo-server version="2.0">
  <error>INVALID_DEVICE_DATA:com.fitbit.protocol.serializer.
     DataProcessingException: Parsing field
  [signature] of the object of type CHECKSUM. IO error -&gt;
     Remote checksum [2246|0x8c6] and local
  checksum [60441|0xec19] do not match.</error>
</galileo-server>
```

This information can be used to reconstruct the packet with a valid CRC. Such an exploit must be used sparingly, however, as the remote server will refuse to process further messages if an error threshold is met, until a lengthy timeout (on the order of hours) expires.

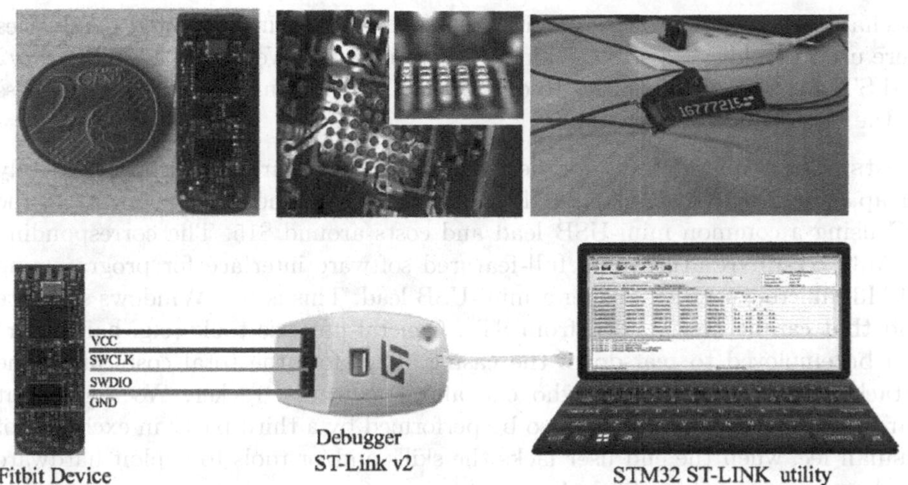


**Fig. 11.** Fitbit tear-down and connecting Fitbit micro-controller to the debugger.

## 5 Hardware-Based Local Spoofing

We now demonstrate the feasibility of hardware-based spoofing attacks focusing on Fitbit Flex and Fitbit One devices. We first conducted an analysis of the Fitbit protocol as previously described in Sect. 3. However, since the newest firmware (Fitbit 7.81) uses end-to-end encryption with a device-specific key, the data cannot be manipulated using MITM attacks, as described in the previous section. Therefore, we resort to a physical attack on the tracker's hardware. We reverse engineered the hardware layout of the devices to gain memory access, which enabled us to inject arbitrary stepcount values into memory, which the tracker would send as valid encrypted frames to the server.

### 5.1 Device Tear-Down

In order to understand how to perform the hardware attack, we needed to tear down the devices. In the following section, we give an overview of the tools required for this process.

**Tools:** The tools to perform the hardware attack were relatively inexpensive and easy to purchase. To accomplish the attack, we used (i) a digital multimeter, (ii) a soldering iron, thin gauge wire, flux (iii) tweezers, (iv) a soldering heat gun, (v) the ST-LINK/v2 in circuit debugger/programmer, and (vi) the STM32 ST-LINK utility.

The digital multimeter was used to locate the testing pins associated with the debug interface of the microcontroller. However, attackers performing the attack would not require a multimeter, as long as the layout of the testing pins is known. The soldering heat gun and tweezers were utilized to perform the mechanical tear-down of the device casing. The soldering iron and accessories were used to solder wires to the identified testing pins. We used the ST-LINK/v2 and STM32 ST-LINK utilities to connect to the device in order to obtain access to the device's memory.

**Costs:** The required tools for performing the hardware attack are relatively cheap. The STLINK/v2 is a small debugger/programmer that connects to the PC using a common mini-USB lead and costs around $15. The corresponding STM32 ST-LINK utility is a full-featured software interface for programming STM32 microcontrollers, using a mini-USB lead. This is free Windows software and that can be downloaded from ST[3]. General-purpose tools (e.g. hair dryer) can be employed to tear-down the casing. Therefore the total costs make the attack accessible to anyone who can afford a fitness tracker. We argue that hardware modifications could also be performed by a third party in exchange of a small fee, when the end user lacks the skills and/or tools to exploit hardware weaknesses in order to obtain financial gains.

**Tear-Down Findings:** According to our tear-down of the Fitbit trackers (Fitbit Flex and Fitbit One), as shown in Fig. 11, the main chip on the motherboard is an ARM Cortex-M3 processor. This processor is an ultra-low-power 32-bit MCU, with different memory banks such as 256 KB flash, 32 KB SRAM and 8 KB EEPROM. The chip used for Fitbit Flex is *STM32L151UC WLCSP63* and for Fitbit One *STM32L152VC UFBGA100*. The package technology used in both micro-controllers is ball grid array (BGA) which is a surface-mount package with no leads and a grid array of solder balls underneath the integrated circuit. Since the required specifications of the micro-controller used in Fitbit trackers are freely available, we were able to perform hardware reverse-engineering (RE).

### 5.2 Hardware RE to Hunt Debug Ports

We discovered a number of testing points at the back of the device's main board. Our main goal was to identify the testing points connected to debug interfaces. According to the IC's datasheet, there are two debug interfaces available for *STM32L*: (i) serial wire debug (SWD) and (ii) joint test action group (JTAG).

| ST-LINK/V2 | SWD Pins | Description |
|---|---|---|
| Pin 1 | Vcc | Target board Vcc |
| Pin 7 | SWDIO | The SWD Data Signal |
| Pin 8 | GND | Ground |
| Pin 9 | SWCLK | The SWD Clock Signal |
| Pin 15 | RESET | System Reset |

**Fig. 12.** Connecting the tracker to the debugger.

[3] http://www.st.com/en/embedded-software/stsw-link004.html.

We found that the Fitbit trackers were using the SWD interface. However, the SWD pins were obfuscated by placing them among several other testing points without the silkscreen identifying them as testing points. SWD technology provides a 2-pin debug port, a low pin count and high-performance alternative to JTAG. The SWD replaces the JTAG port with a clock and single bidirectional data pin, providing test functionality and real-time access to system memory. We selected a straightforward approach to find the debug ports (other tools that can be exploited include *Arduino+JTAGEnum* and *Jtagulator*). We removed the micro-controller from the device printed circuit boards (PCBs). Afterward, using the IC's datasheet and a multimeter with continuity tester functionality, we traced the debug ports on the device board, identifying the testing points connected to them.

### 5.3 Connecting Devices to the Debugger

After discovering the SWD debug pins and their location on the PCB, we soldered wires to the debug pins. We connected the debug ports to ST-LINK v2 pin header, according to Fig. 12.

**Dumping the Firmware:** After connecting to the device micro-controller, we were able to communicate with MCU as shown in Fig. 11. We extracted the entire firmware image since memory readout protection was not activated. There are three levels of memory protection in the STM32L micro-controller: (i) level 0: *no readout protection*, (ii) level 1: *memory readout protection*, the Flash memory cannot be read from or written to, and (iii) level 2: *chip readout protection*, debug features and boot in RAM selection are disabled (JTAG fuse). We discovered that in the Fitbit Flex and the Fitbit One, memory protection was set to *level 0*, which means there is no memory readout protection. This enabled us to extract the contents of the different memory banks (e.g., FLASH, SRAM, ROM, EEPROM) for further analysis.

Note that it is also possible to extract the complete firmware via the MITM setup during an upgrade process (if the tracker firmware does not use encryption). In general, sniffing is easier to perform, but does not reveal the memory layout and temporal storage contents. Moreover, hardware access allows us to change memory contents at runtime.

**Device Key Extraction:** We initially sniffed communications between the Fitbit tracker and the Fitbit server to see whether a key exchange protocol is performed, which was not the case. Therefore, we expected pre-shared keys on the Fitbit trackers we connected to, including two different Fitbit One and three different Fitbit Flex devices. We read out their EEPROM and discovered that the device encryption key is stored in their EEPROM. Exploring the memory content, we found the exact memory addresses where the 6-byte serial ID and 16-byte encryption key are stored, as shown in Fig. 13. We confirm that each device has a *device-specific key* which likely is programmed into the device during manufacturing [12].

**Disabling the Device Encryption:** By analyzing the device memory content, we discovered that by flipping one byte at a particular address in EEPROM, we were able to force the tracker to operate in unencrypted mode and disable the encryption. Even trackers previously communicating in encrypted mode switched to plaintext after modifying the encryption flag (byte). Figure 13 illustrates how to flip the byte, such that the tracker sends all sync messages in plaintext format (Base64 encoded) disabling encryption.

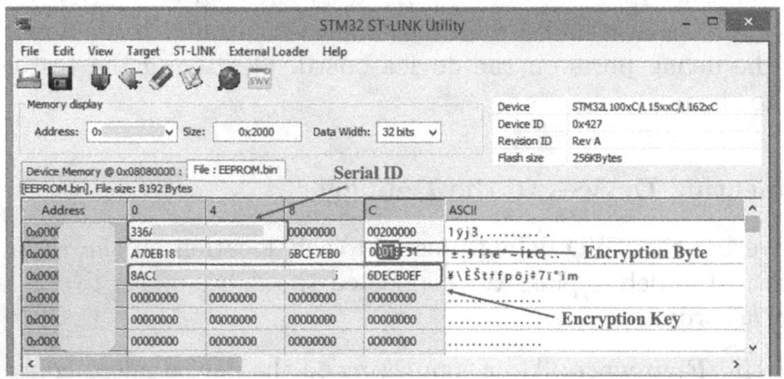


**Fig. 13.** Device key extraction and disabling encryption.

**Injecting Fabricated Data Activities:** We investigated the EEPROM and SRAM content to find the exact memory addresses where the total step count and other data fields are stored. Based on our packet format knowledge and previously sniffed megadumps, we found that the activity records were stored in the EEPROM in the same format. Even encrypted frames are generated based on the EEPROM plaintext records. Therefore, oblivious falsified data can be injected, even with the newest firmware having encryption enabled. As it can be seen in Fig. 14a and b, we managed to successfully inject `0X00FFFFFF` steps equal to 16 777 215 in decimal into Fitbit server by modifying the corresponding address field in the EEPROM and subsequently synchronising the tracker with the server.

## 6 Discussion

In this section we give a set of implementation guidelines for fitness trackers. While Fitbit is currently the only manufacturer that puts effort into securing trackers [15], our guidelines also apply to other health-related IoT devices. We intend to transfer the lessons learned into open security and privacy standards that are being developed.[4]

[4] See https://www.thedigitalstandard.org.

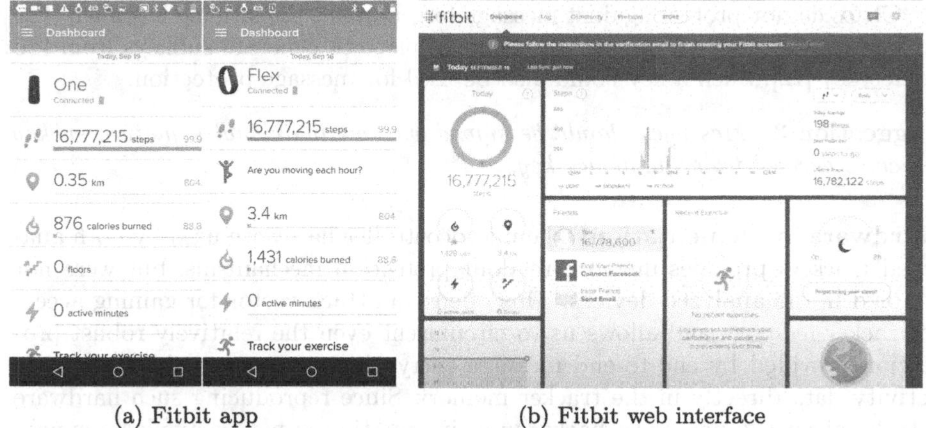


(a) Fitbit app (b) Fitbit web interface

**Fig. 14.** The results of injecting fabricated data. (a) shows the Fitbit app screenshot, and (b) demonstrates the Fitbit web interface.

False data injection as described in the previous sections is made possible by a combination of some of the design choices in the implementation of the Fitbit trackers and in the communication protocol utilized between the trackers and Fitbit application servers. These design choices relate to how encryption techniques have been applied, the design of the protocol messages, and the implementation of the hardware itself. To overcome such weaknesses in future system designs, we propose the following mitigation techniques.

**Application of encryption techniques:** The examined trackers support full end-to-end encryption, but do not enforce its use consistently.[5] This allows us to perform an in-depth analysis of the data synchronization protocol and ultimately fabricate messages with false activity data, which were accepted as genuine by the Fitbit servers.

**Suggestion 1.** *End-to-end encryption between trackers and remote servers should be consistently enforced, if supported by device firmware.*

**Protocol message design:** Generating valid protocol messages (without a clear understanding of the CRC in use) is enabled by the fact that the server responds to invalid messages with information about the expected CRC values, instead of a simple "invalid CRC", or a more general "invalid message" response.

**Suggestion 2.** *Error and status notifications should not include additional information related to the contents of actual protocol messages.*

[5] During discussions we had with Fitbit, the company stressed that models launched after 2015 consistently enforce encryption in the communications between the tracker and server.

CRCs do not protect against message forgery, once the scheme is known. For authentication, there is already a scheme in place to generate subkeys from the device key [12]. Such a key could also be used for message protection.

**Suggestion 3.** *Messages should be signed with an individual signature subkey which is derived from the device key.*

**Hardware implementation:** The microcontroller hardware used by both analyzed trackers provides memory readout protection mechanisms, but were not enabled in the analyzed devices. This opens an attack vector for gaining access to tracker memory and allows us to circumvent even the relatively robust protection provided by end-to-end message encryption as we were able to modify activity data directly in the tracker memory. Since reproducing such hardware attacks given the necessary background information is not particularly expensive, the available hardware-supported memory protection measures should be applied by default.

**Suggestion 4.** *Hardware-supported memory readout protection should be applied.*

Specifically, on the MCUs of the investigated tracking devices, the memory of the hardware should be protected by enabling chip readout protection level 2.

**Fraud detection measures:** In our experiments we were able to inject fabricated activity data with clearly unreasonably high performance values (e.g. more than 16 million steps during a single day). This suggests that data should be monitored more closely by the servers before accepting activity updates.

**Suggestion 5.** *Fraud detection measures should be applied in order to screen for data resulting from malicious modifications or malfunctioning hardware.*

For example, accounts with unusual or abnormal activity profiles should be flagged and potentially disqualified, if obvious irregularities are detected.

## 7 Related Work

Researchers at the University of Toronto [18] have investigated transmission security, data integrity, and Bluetooth privacy of eight fitness trackers including Fitbit Charge HR. They focused on transmission security, specifically at whether or not personal data is encrypted when transmitted over the Internet in order to protect confidentiality. They also examined data integrity concentrating on whether or not fitness data can be considered authentic records of activity that have not been tampered with. They did not attempt to reverse engineer the proprietary encoding or encryption used for transmitting data.

In 2013, Rahman *et al.* [9] studied the communication between Fitbit Ultra and its base station as well as the associated web servers. According to Rahman *et al.*, Fitbit users could readily upload sensor data from their Fitbit device onto the web server, which could then be viewed by others online. They observed two critical vulnerabilities in the communication between the Fitbit device's base station, and the web server. They claimed that these vulnerabilities could be used to violate the security and privacy of the user. Specifically, the identified vulnerabilities consisted of the use of plaintext login information and plaintext HTTP data processing. Rahman *et al.* then proposed FitLock as a solution to the identified vulnerabilities. These vulnerabilities have been patched by Fitbit and no longer exist on contemporary Fitbit devices. Zhou *et al.* [20] followed up on Rahman's work by identifying shortcomings in their proposed approach named FitLock, but did not mention countermeasures to mitigate the vulnerabilities that they found. In 2014, Rahman *et al.* published another paper detailing weaknesses in Fitbit's communication protocol, enabling them to inject falsified data to both the remote web server and the fitness tracker. The authors proposed SensCrypt, a protocol for securing and managing low power fitness trackers [21]. Note that Fitbit's communication paradigm has changed considerably since Fitbit Ultra, which uses ANT instead of Bluetooth, and is not supported by smartphone applications, but only by a Windows program last updated in 2013. Neither the ANT-based firewalls FitLock nor SensCrypt would work on recent Fitbit devices. Transferring their concept to a Bluetooth-based firewall would not help against the attacks demonstrated in this paper, since hardware attacks are one level below such firewalls, while our protocol attacks directly target the Fitbit servers.

Cyr *et al.* [10] analyzed the Fitbit Flex ecosystem. They attempted to do a hardware analysis of the Fitbit device but because of the difficulties associated with debugging the device they decided to focus on other parts such as Bluetooth LE, the associated Android app and network analysis. The authors explained the data collected by Fitbit from its users, the data Fitbit provided to Fitbit users, and methods of recovering data not made available to device owners.

In the report released by AV TEST [19], the authors tested nine fitness trackers including Fitbit Charge and evaluated their security and privacy. The authors tried to find out how easy it is to get the fitness data from the fitness band through Bluetooth or by sniffing the connection to the cloud during the synchronization process.

AV TEST reported some security issues in Fitbit Charge [11]. They discovered that Fitbit Charge with firmware version 106 and lower allows non-authenticated smartphones to be treated as authenticated if an authenticated smartphone is in range or has been in range recently. Also, the firmware version allowed attackers to replay the tracker synchronization process. Both issues have been now fixed by Fitbit.

In [12], the authors captured the firmware image of the Fitbit Charge HR during a firmware update. They reversed engineer the cryptographic primitives used by the Fitbit Charge HR activity tracker and recovered the authentication protocol. Moreover, they obtained the cryptographic key that is used in the authentication protocol from the Fitbit Android application. The authors found a backdoor in previous firmware versions and exploiting this backdoor they extracted the device specific encryption key from the memory of the tracker using Bluetooth interface. Memory readout has been fixed in recent firmware versions.

Principled understanding of the Fitbit protocol remains open to investigation as the open-source community continues to reverse-engineer message semantics and server responses [16].

## 8 Conclusion

Trusting the authenticity and integrity of the data that fitness trackers generate is paramount, as the records they collect are being increasingly utilized as evidence in critical scenarios such as court trials and the adjustment of healthcare insurance premiums. In this paper, we conducted an in-depth security analysis of two models of popular activity trackers commercialized by `Fitbit`, the market leader, and we revealed serious security and privacy vulnerabilities present in these devices. Additionally, we reverse engineered the primitives governing the communication between these devices and cloud-based services, implemented an open-source tool to extract sensitive personal information in human-readable format and demonstrated that malicious users could inject spoofed activity records to obtain personal benefits. To circumvent the end-to-end protocol encryption mechanism present on the latest firmware, we performed hardware-based RE and documented successful injection of falsified data that appears legitimate to the Fitbit cloud. We believe more rigorous security controls should be enforced by manufacturers to verify the authenticity of fitness data. To this end, we provided a set of guidelines to be followed to address the vulnerabilities identified.

**Acknowledgments.** Hossein Fereidooni is supported by the Deutsche Akademische Austauschdienst (DAAD). Mauro Conti is supported by the EU TagItSmart! Project (agreement H2020-ICT30-2015-688061) and IT-CNR/Taiwan-MOST 2016-17 "Verifiable Data Structure Streaming". This work has been co-funded by the DFG as part of projects S1 and S2 within the CRC 1119 CROSSING, and by the BMBF within CRISP. Paul Patras has been partially supported by the Scottish Informatics and Computer Science Alliance (SICSA) through a PECE grant.

We thank the Fitbit Security Team for their professional collaboration with us, and their availability to discuss our findings and address the vulnerabilities we identified.

## References

1. Forbes. Wearable tech market to be worth $34 billion by 2020, February 2016. https://www.forbes.com/sites/paullamkin/2016/02/17/wearable-tech-market-to-be-worth-34-billion-by-2020
2. International Data Corporation. Worldwide quarterly wearable device tracker, March 2017. https://www.idc.com/tracker/showproductinfo.jsp?prod_id=962
3. Mashable. Husband learns wife is pregnant from her Fitbit data, February 2016. http://mashable.com/2016/02/10/fitbit-pregnant/
4. The Wall Street Journal. Prosecutors say Fitbit device exposed fibbing in rape case, April 2016. http://blogs.wsj.com/law/2016/04/21/prosecutors-say-fitbit-device-exposed-fibbing-in-rape-case/

5. The Guardian. Court sets legal precedent with evidence from Fitbit health tracker, November 2014. https://www.theguardian.com/technology/2014/nov/18/court-accepts-data-fitbit-health-tracker
6. VitalityHealth. https://www.vitality.co.uk/rewards/partners/activity-tracking/
7. AchieveMint. https://www.achievemint.com
8. StepBet. https://www.stepbet.com/
9. Rahman, M., Carbunar, B., Banik, M.: Fit and vulnerable: attacks and defenses for a health monitoring device. In: Proceedings of the Privacy Enhancing Technologies Symposium (PETS), Bloomington, IN, USA (2013)
10. Cyr, B., Horn, W., Miao, D., Specter, M.: Security Analysis of Wearable Fitness Devices (Fitbit) (2014). https://courses.csail.mit.edu/6.857/2014/files/17-cyrbritt-webbhorn-specter-dmiao-hacking-fitbit.pdf
11. Clausing, E., Schiefer, M., Morgenstern, M.: AV TEST Analysis of Fitbit Vulnerabilities (2016). https://www.av-test.org/fileadmin/pdf/avtest_2016-04_fitbit_vulnerabilities.pdf
12. Schellevis, M., Jacobs, B., Meijer, C.: Security/privacy of wearable fitness tracking IoT devices. Radboud niversity. Bachelor thesis: Getting access to your own Fitbit data, August 2016
13. Accenture. Digital trust in the IoT era (2015)
14. PwC 2016: Use of wearables in the workplace is halted by lack of trust. http://www.pwc.co.uk/who-we-are/regional-sites/northern-ireland/press-releases/use-of-wearables-in-the-workplace-is-halted-by-lack-of-trust-pwc-research.html
15. Fereidooni, H., Frassetto, T., Miettinen, M., Sadeghi, A.-R., Conti, M.: Fitness Trackers: Fit for health but unfit for security and privacy. In: Proceedings of the IEEE International Workshop on Safe, Energy-Aware, & Reliable Connected Health (CHASE workshop: SEARCH 2017), in press, Philadelphia, Pennsylvania, USA, July 17–19 (2017)
16. Galileo project. https://bitbucket.org/benallard/galileo/
17. Wireshark network protocol analyzer. https://www.wireshark.org/
18. Hilts, A., Parsons, C., Knockel, J.: Every Step You Fake: A Comparative Analysis of Fitness Tracker Privacy and Security. Open Effect Report (2016). https://openeffect.ca/reports/Every_Step_You_Fake.pdf
19. Clausing, E., Schiefer, M., Morgenstern, M.: Internet of Things: Security Evaluation of nine Fitness Trackers. AV TEST, The Independent IT-Security institute, Magdeburg, Germany (2015)
20. Zhou, W., Piramuthu, S.: Security/privacy of wearable fitness tracking IoT devices. In: IEEE Iberian Conference on Information Systems and Technologies (2014)
21. Rahman, M., Carbunar, B., Topkara, U.: Secure management of low power fitness trackers. Published IEEE Trans. Mob. Comput. **15**(2), 447–459 (2016)

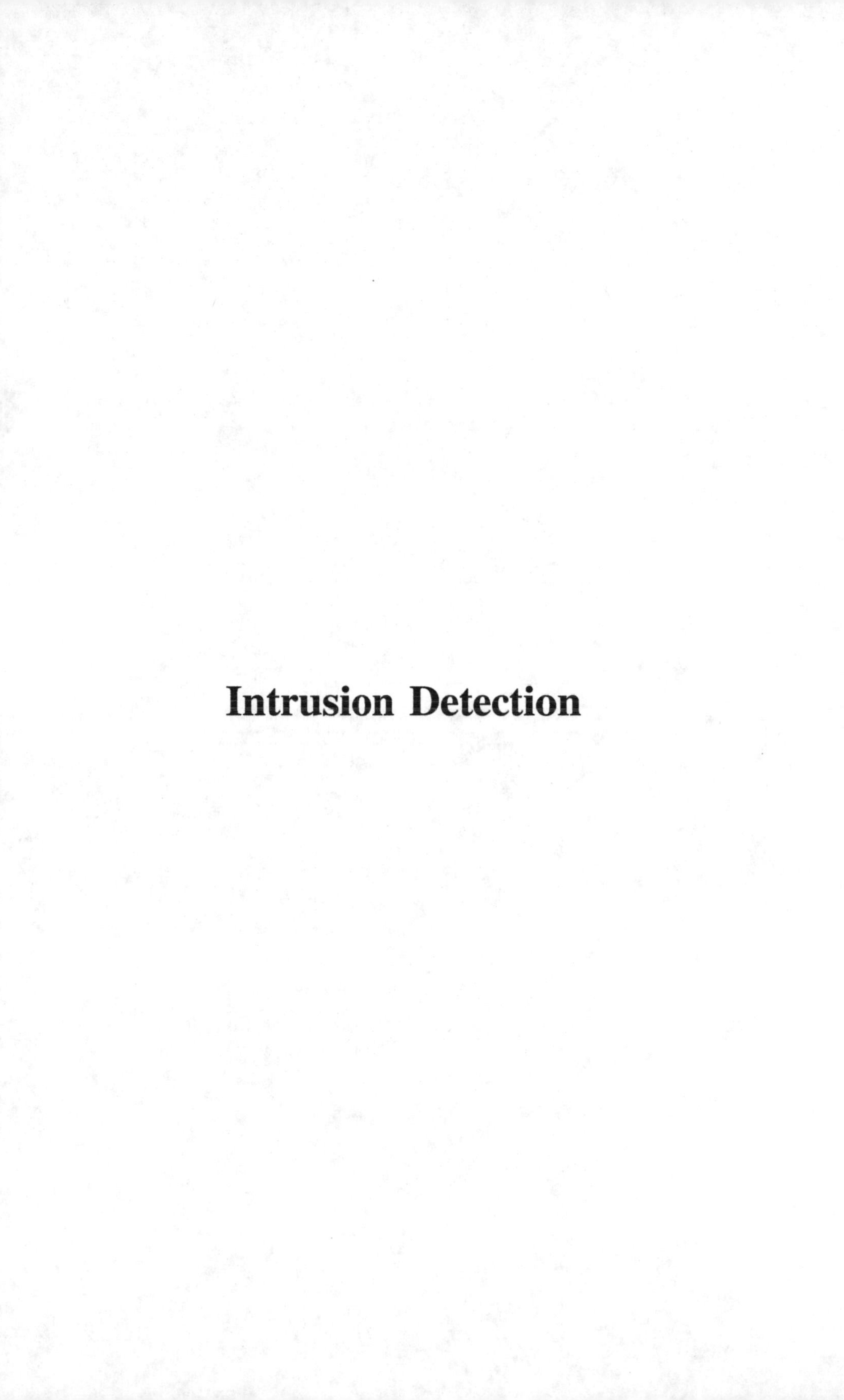

# Intrusion Detection

# Lens on the Endpoint: Hunting for Malicious Software Through Endpoint Data Analysis

Ahmet Salih Buyukkayhan[1](✉), Alina Oprea[1], Zhou Li[2], and William Robertson[1]

[1] Northeastern University, Boston, MA, USA
{bkayhan,wkr}@ccs.neu.edu, a.oprea@northeastern.edu
[2] RSA Laboratories, Bedford, MA, USA
zhou.li@rsa.com

**Abstract.** Organizations are facing an increasing number of criminal threats ranging from opportunistic malware to more advanced targeted attacks. While various security technologies are available to protect organizations' perimeters, still many breaches lead to undesired consequences such as loss of proprietary information, financial burden, and reputation defacing. Recently, endpoint monitoring agents that inspect system-level activities on user machines started to gain traction and be deployed in the industry as an additional defense layer. Their application, though, in most cases is only for forensic investigation to determine the root cause of an incident.

In this paper, we demonstrate how endpoint monitoring can be proactively used for detecting and prioritizing suspicious software modules overlooked by other defenses. Compared to other environments in which host-based detection proved successful, our setting of a large enterprise introduces unique challenges, including the heterogeneous environment (users installing software of their choice), limited ground truth (small number of malicious software available for training), and coarse-grained data collection (strict requirements are imposed on agents' performance overhead). Through applications of clustering and outlier detection algorithms, we develop techniques to identify modules with known malicious behavior, as well as modules impersonating popular benign applications. We leverage a large number of static, behavioral and contextual features in our algorithms, and new feature weighting methods that are resilient against missing attributes. The large majority of our findings are confirmed as malicious by anti-virus tools and manual investigation by experienced security analysts.

**Keywords:** Endpoint data analysis · Enterprise malware detection · Software impersonation · Security analytics · Outlier detection

---

**Electronic supplementary material** The online version of this chapter (doi:10.1007/978-3-319-66332-6_4) contains supplementary material, which is available to authorized users.


M. Dacier et al. (Eds.): RAID 2017, LNCS 10453, pp. 73–97, 2017.
DOI: 10.1007/978-3-319-66332-6_4

## 1 Introduction

Malicious activities on the Internet are increasing at a staggering pace. The 2015 Verizon DBIR report [36] highlighted that in 2015 alone 70 million pieces of malware were observed across 10,000 organizations with a total estimated financial loss of 400 million dollars. Enterprises deploy firewalls, intrusion-detection systems, and other security technologies on premise to prevent breaches. However, most of these protections are only in effect within the organization perimeter. When users travel or work remotely, their devices lack the network-level protections offered within the organization and are subject to additional threats.

Recently, many organizations started to deploy endpoint monitoring agents [34] on user machines with the goal of protecting them even outside the enterprise perimeter. Mandiant [24] reports that in a set of 4 million surveyed hosts, 2.8 million hosts have endpoint instrumentation installed. These agents record various activities related to downloaded files, installed applications, running processes, active services, scheduled tasks, network connections, user authentication and other events of interest, and send the collected data to a centralized server for analysis. Since stringent requirements are imposed on the performance of these tools, they are usually lightweight and collect coarse-grained information. Today, this data is used mainly for forensic investigation, once an alert is triggered by other sources.

We believe that endpoint monitoring offers a huge opportunity for detection and mitigation of many malicious activities that escape current network-side defenses. Endpoint agents get visibility into different types of events such as registry changes and creation of executable files, which do not appear in network traffic. Moreover, existing research in host-based detection methods (e.g., [1,2,12,19,27,31]) confirms our insight that endpoint monitoring can be used successfully for proactive breach detection. Nevertheless, to the best of our knowledge, endpoint monitoring technologies have not yet been used for this goal, as a number of challenges need to be overcome. Most accurate host-based detection technologies rely on much finer-grained data (e.g., system calls or process execution) than what is collected by endpoint agents. Additionally, production environments in large organizations need to handle up to hundreds of thousands of machines, with heterogeneous software configurations and millions of software variants. Ground truth is inherently limited in this setting, since we aim to detect malware that is already running on enterprise hosts, and as such has bypassed the security protections already deployed within the enterprise.

In this paper, we analyze endpoint data collected from a large, geographically distributed organization (including 36K Windows machines), and demonstrate how it can be used for detecting hundreds of suspicious modules (executables or DLLs) overlooked by other security controls. Our dataset includes a variety of attributes for 1.8 million distinct Windows modules installed on these machines. The enterprise of our study uses multiple tools to partially label the modules as *whitelisted* (signed by reputable vendors), *blacklisted* (confirmed malicious by manual investigation), *graylisted* (related to adware), or *unknown*. Interestingly, only 6.5% of modules are whitelisted, very small number (534) are blacklisted, while the large majority (above 90%) have unknown status. As the ground truth of malicious modules in our dataset in very limited, well-known techniques for malware detection such as supervised learning are ineffective.

We use several insights to make the application of machine learning successful in our setting. We first leverage the set of behaviors observed in blacklisted modules to identify other modules with similar characteristics. Towards that goal, we define a similarity distance metric on more than 50 static, behavioral and contextual features, and use a density-based clustering algorithm to detect new modules with suspicious behavior. Second, while enterprise hosts have relatively heterogeneous software configuration, it turns out that popular Windows executables or system processes have a large user base. We exploit the homogeneity of these whitelisted applications for detecting an emerging threat, that of *software impersonation* attacks [26]. We detect a class of attacks impersonating static attributes of well-known files by a novel outlier-detection method. In both settings we use new dynamic feature weighting methods resilient to missing attributes and limited ground truth.

In summary, our contributions are highlighted below.

**Endpoint-data analysis for malware detection.** We are the first to analyze endpoint data collected from a realistic deployment within a large enterprise with the goal of proactively detecting suspicious modules on users' machines. We overcome challenges related to (1) lightweight instrumentation resulting in coarse-grained event capturing; (2) the heterogeneous environment; (3) limited ground truth; (4) missing attributes in the dataset.

**Prioritization of suspicious modules.** We propose a density clustering algorithm for prioritizing the most suspicious modules with similar behavior as the blacklisted modules. Our algorithm reaches a precision of 90.8% and recall of 86.7% (resulting in F1 score of 88.7%) relative to manually-labeled ground truth. Among a set of 388K modules with unknown status, we identified 327 executable and 637 DLL modules with anomalous behavior and the false positive rates are as low as 0.11% and 0.0284% respectively. Through manual investigation, we confirmed as malicious 94.2% of the top ranked 69 executables and 100% of the top 20 DLL modules. Among these, 69 malicious modules were new findings confirmed malicious by manual investigation, but not detected by VirusTotal.

**Software impersonation.** We propose an outlier-detection algorithm to identify malware impersonating popular software. Our algorithm detected 44 outlying modules in a set of 7K unknown modules with similar characteristics as popular whitelisted modules, with precision of 84.09%. Among them, 12 modules are our new findings considered malicious by manual investigation, but not detected by VirusTotal.

**Novel feature weighting methods.** To account for missing attributes and limited ground truth, we propose new feature weighting methods taking into account the data distribution. We compare them with other well-known feature weighting methods and demonstrate better accuracy across multiple metrics of interest.

## 2 Background and Overview

In this section we first describe the problem definition, adversarial model, and challenges we encountered. We then give an overview of our system, provide details on the dataset we used for analysis, and mention ethical considerations.

### 2.1 Problem Statement

Organizations deploy network-perimeter defenses such as firewalls, anti-virus software, and intrusion detection systems to protect machines within their network. To obtain better visibility into user activities and offer protection outside of enterprise perimeter, organizations started to deploy endpoint agents on user machines [34]. These agents monitor processes running on end hosts, binaries downloaded from the web, modifications to system configuration or registries through lightweight instrumentation, and report a variety of recorded events to a centralized server for analysis.

In the organization of our study, machines are instrumented with host agents that perform regular and on-demand scans, collect aggregate behavioral events, and send them to a centralized server. We address the problem of discovering highly risky and suspicious modules installed on Windows machines through analysis of this realistic, large-scale dataset. Specifically, we are looking for two common types of malicious behavior:

- Starting from a set of *blacklisted* modules vetted by security experts, we are interested in discovering other modules with similar characteristics. With the availability of malware building kits [7], attackers can easily generate slightly different malware variants to evade signature detection tools. We leverage the insight that malicious variants produced by these toolkits share significant similarity in their behavior and other characteristics.
- Starting from a set of *whitelisted* modules considered legitimate, we look for malicious files impersonating them. System process impersonation has been used by Advanced Persistent Threats (APT) campaigns for evasion [25,26]. Detecting this in isolation is difficult, but here we exploit the homogeneity of whitelisted files in an enterprise setting. These files have a large user base and should have similar behavior across different machines they are installed on. Our main insight is that malicious files impersonating these popular modules are significantly different in their behavior and contextual attributes.

**Adversarial model.** We assume that endpoint machines are subject to compromise through various attack vectors. An infection could happen either inside the enterprise network or outside when users travel or take their machines home. In modern attacks there are multiple stages in the campaign lifecycle, e.g., a piece of malware is delivered through email followed by download of second-stage malware that initiates communication with its command-and-control center and updates its code [23]. We assume that before attackers have complete control of the machine, the endpoint agent is able to collect and upload information to the centralized server. Of course, we cannot make any assumptions about agents once a machine is completely subverted by attackers. However, our goal is to detect infection early, before it leads to more serious consequences such as data leakage or compromise of administrator credentials.

We assume that the server storing the endpoint data is protected within the enterprise perimeter. Breaches involving a compromise of monitoring tools or servers are much more serious and can be detected through additional defenses, but they are not our focus. Here we aim to detect and remediate endpoint compromise to prevent a number of more serious threats.

**Challenges.** A number of unique challenges arise in our setting. Our dataset is collected from a heterogeneous environment with 1.8 million distinct modules installed on 36K machines. Most users have administrative rights on their machines and can install software of their choice. Second, we have limited ground truth with less then 10% of modules labeled as whitelisted, blacklisted or graylisted and the majority having unknown status. Third, a number of attributes are missing due to machine reboots or disconnection from corporate network. Lastly, the monitoring agents collect lightweight information to minimize their overhead.

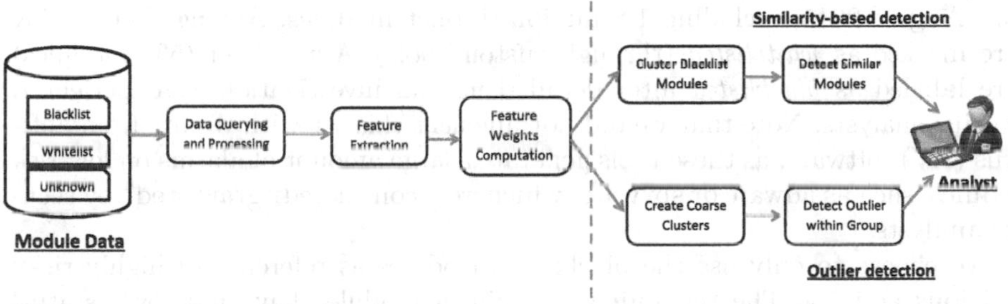


**Fig. 1.** System diagram.

## 2.2 System Overview

Our system analyzes data collected from endpoint agents deployed in a large enterprise. Our goal is to identify among the large set of modules with unknown status those with suspicious behavior and prioritize them by their risk. In particular, we are looking for two types of malicious modules: (1) those with *similar behavior* as known blacklisted modules; and (2) those *impersonating* popular, legitimate whitelisted software. For our analysis, we employ a large number of features from three categories: *static* (extracted from the module's PE headers), *behavioral* (capturing file access patterns, process creation and network access events); and *contextual* (related to module location on the machines it is installed).

Our system architecture is illustrated in Fig. 1. After we query the raw data from the server, we apply some data transformation and aggregation in the processing phase and extract features from these three categories. We define a module distance metric that assigns different feature weights for the two scenarios of interest. In case of similarity detection, high-entropy features are given higher weight and we adapt the DBSCAN algorithm to account for custom-defined distance metric and missing features. For software impersonation we favor features that distinguish malicious from benign files best, and design a novel two-stage outlier detection process. A detailed description of our techniques follows in Sect. 3.

### 2.3 Dataset

The dataset is collected by endpoint agents deployed on 36,872 Windows machines. Agents monitor executable and DLL modules, and perform scheduled scans at intervals of three days. Analysts could also request scans on demand. Data generated by agents is sent to a centralized server. We had access to a snapshot of the database from August 2015, including 1.8 million distinct modules. Among them, 117K were marked as *whitelisted* (through custom tools). A small set (534 modules) were labeled as *blacklisted* after detailed manual investigation by experienced security analysts. Note that we did not augment this set with results from antivirus (AV) software, as these tools generate a large amount of alarms on low-risk modules, such as adware or spyware, which were considered "graylisted" by security analysts.

**Table 1.** Total number of modules in each category (BL – blacklisted, WL – whitelisted, UL – unknown), and those with missing description, company name and signature fields.

| Status | #Total | #Description | #Company Name | #Signature |
|---|---|---|---|---|
| BL | 534 | 440 | 445 | 520 |
| WL | 117,128 | 19,881 | 13,070 | 2,430 |
| UL | 1,692,157 | 1,304,557 | 1,314,780 | 1,503,449 |

We choose to only use the blacklisted modules as reference of highly risky malicious activity. The remaining 1.7 million modules have unknown status, including lesser-known applications and variants of known applications. In total, there are 301K distinct file names in our dataset.

To illustrate the noisy aspect of our dataset, Table 1 lists the total number of modules, as well as the number of modules without description, company name or signature in each category (BL – blacklisted, WL – whitelisted, UL – unknown). As seen in the table, the large majority of blacklisted modules do not include these fields, but also a fair number of unknown and whitelisted modules miss them.

To illustrate the heterogeneity of the environment, the left graph in Fig. 2 shows the CDF for the number of hosts installing the same file name. The large majority of file names are installed on few hosts relative to the population. Even among whitelisted file names, 95% of them are installed on less than 100 hosts. 95% of the blacklisted files are installed on less than 20 hosts. Only a small percentage of files are extremely popular and these are mostly Windows executables and system processes or libraries (e.g., whitelisted `svchost.exe` and unknown `presentationcore.ni.dll` are installed on 36K and 29K machines, respectively).

The right graph in Fig. 2 shows the CDF for the number of file variants with same name but distinct SHA256 hashes. Whitelisted and unknown file names include more variants than blacklisted ones. For instance, whitelisted `setup.exe` has 1300 variants, unknown `microsoft.visualstudio~.dll` has 26K variants, while the maximum number of blacklisted variants is 25. This is due to the limited set of blacklisted modules, as well as the evasive nature of malware changing file name in different variants.

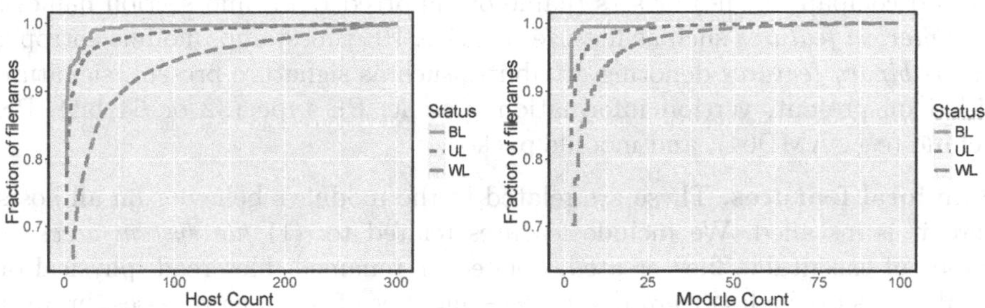


**Fig. 2.** CDFs of hosts (left) and modules (right) sharing same filename.

### 2.4 Ethical Considerations

The enterprise's IT department consented to give us access to a snapshot of the data for the purpose of this study. We had access to data only within the premises of the enterprise and were only allowed to export the results presented in the paper. Our dataset did not include any personal identifying information (e.g., username and source IP of employee's machine) that put users' privacy at risk. We also took measures to prevent potential information leakage: for instance, the behavior and contextual features were aggregated across hosts installing the same module.

## 3 System Design

We provide here details on our system design and implementation. Our first goal is prioritizing the most suspicious unknown modules with similar behavior as known blacklisted modules. Our second goal is detecting malware impersonating popular file names (e.g., system processes) through a novel outlier-detection algorithm. Both techniques can be used to detect suspicious unknown modules, and enlarge the set of blacklisted modules manually labeled by analysts. They both utilize the same set of 52 (*static*, *behavioral*, and *contextual*) features extracted from the dataset (see Sect. 3.1). However feature weights and parameters are customized for the two algorithms, as discussed in Sects. 3.2 and 3.3.

### 3.1 Feature Selection

For each module we extract a multi-dimensional feature vector, with features capturing the module's attributes according to three distinct categories: static, behavioral and contextual. Table 7 in Appendix A provides a comprehensive list of all features.

**Static features.** These are mainly extracted from the module's PE header and include: (1) *descriptive features* represented as either string values (description and company name) or sets (name of imported DLLs and section names); (2) *numerical features* such as file size, PE size, PE timestamp, module entropy; and (3) *binary features* denoting attributes such as signature present, signature valid, icon present, version information present, PE type (32 or 64 bit), PE machine (e.g., AMD64), and module packed.

**Behavioral features.** These are related to the module's behavior on all hosts where it is installed. We include features related to: (1) *file system access* – number of executable files created, deleted or renamed, files read, physical or logical drives opened; (2) *process access* – number of regular processes, browser or OS processes opened, processes or remote threads created; and (3) *network connections* such as set of domains and IP addresses the module connects to. These events are stored cumulatively at the server since the time the module was first observed on the network. Since a module might exist on many machines, we compute average number of events per machine for file system and process access features.

**Contextual features.** The endpoint agents collect information about the time when a module is initially installed on a machine, its full file system path, the user account that created the module and the full path of all files and processes captured by the behavior events initiated by the module. We parse the file path and match it to different categories such as Windows, Systems, ProgramFiles, ProgramData, or AppDataLocal. Additionally, the agents monitor if modules have auto-start functionality and categorizes that into different types (e.g., logon, services, startup, scheduled task). We also have access to the user category owning the module (admin, trusted installer or regular user).

From this information, we extract a number of contextual features related to: (1) *file system path* – number of directory levels, the path category, number of executable and non-executable files in the same folder, and number of sub-folders in the path; (2) *path of destination events* – the path category of destination files, and number of events created by the module in the same and in different paths; (3) *file's metadata* – file owner, hidden attributes, and days from creation; (4) *auto-start functionality* – type of auto-start if enabled. We took the average values across all hosts installing the module.

**Final set of features.** We initially considered a larger set of 70 features, but we reduced the list to 52 features that are available in at least 10 blacklisted modules. Some features related to registry modifications, process and I/O activity were not encountered in our dataset of blacklisted modules, but could be applicable to an enlarged set of malicious modules. The final list of features we used is given in Table 7 in Appendix A.

## 3.2 Prioritizing Suspicious Modules

For detecting modules with similar behavior as known blacklisted modules, we first cluster the set of blacklisted modules, and then identify other unknown modules in these clusters. We prioritize unknown modules according to their distance to the blacklisted modules. We describe our definition of module similarity and distance metric, as well as our feature weighting method that is resilient against missing features.

**Clustering.** Many clustering algorithms are available in the literature, and we choose the DBSCAN [9] algorithm for clustering the blacklisted modules on the set of 52 features. Its advantages are that it does not require the number of clusters be specified in advance, can find arbitrarily-shaped clusters, and can scale to large datasets. DBSCAN creates clusters starting from *core samples*, points that have at least *min_sample* points in their neighborhood, and proceeds iteratively by expanding the clusters with points within distance $\epsilon$ (called *neighborhood radius*).

We use standard distance metrics for each feature, according to the feature's type: L1 distance for integer and real values; binary distance for binary values ($d(x,y) = 0$ if $x = y$, and $d(x,y) = 1$, otherwise); edit distance for strings; Jaccard distance for sets. The distance between two modules $M_1 = (x_1, \ldots, x_n)$ and $M_2 = (y_1, \ldots, y_n)$ is a weighted sum of distances for individual features: $d(M_1, M_2) = \sum_{i=1}^{n} w_i d(x_i, y_i)$, where $\sum_{i=1}^{n} w_i = 1$ [14].

**Feature weights.** One of our main observation is that features should contribute differently to overall modules similarity. While there are many established methods for feature selection and weighting in supervised settings [8,15], the problem is less studied in unsupervised settings like ours.

We tested two methods for setting feature weights. Assume that we have $n$ features in our dataset $X = (X_1, \ldots, X_n)$. First, a simple method is to set weights uniformly across all features, $w_i = 1/n$, for $i \in [1, n]$. In the second novel method we introduce, we choose feature weights *proportional to the feature's entropy* computed from the dataset. If feature $i$ is categorical and has $m$ possible values $v_1, \ldots, v_m$, we define $p_{ij}$ as the probability that feature $i$ takes value $v_j$, for $j \in [1, m]$. If feature $i$ is numerical, we need to define a number $m$ of bins $b_1, \ldots, b_m$ so that the probability of feature $i$ belonging to bin $b_j$ is $p_{ij}$, for $j \in [1, m]$. Then, the entropy for feature $i$ is $H(X_i) = -\sum_{j=1}^{m} p_{ij} \log(p_{ij})$. We assign normalized feature weights proportional to their entropy, according to our intuition that *features with higher variability should contribute more towards module similarity.*

Our algorithms need to be resilient against missing features since a large fraction of behavior features are not available (as machines are offline for extended periods of time, or machines are sometimes rebooted before sending behavior events to the server). When computing the distance between two missing values, rather than setting it at 0 we choose a fixed, *penalty value* which is a parameter of our algorithm (the distance between a missing value and any other existing value is set at the maximum value of 1). Higher penalty results in lower similarity when computing the distance metric, thus the value of the penalty needs to be carefully calibrated. We elaborate more on optimal parameter selection in Sect. 4.

**Prioritizing unknown modules.** After clustering blacklisted modules with DBSCAN and the distance metric described above, our next goal is to identify unknown modules that belong to these clusters. The algorithm is run on 388K unknown modules and assigns some of them to blacklisted clusters according to their distance to cluster points. To prioritize the most suspicious ones, we order the unknown modules that belong to a blacklisted cluster based on their minimum distance to known blacklisted modules. We describe our results in Sect. 4.1.

### 3.3 Impersonation of Popular Software

For detecting malware impersonating popular, legitimate software, we leverage the large machine base in our dataset to determine a set of popular modules and their common characteristics across machines. While it is relatively easy for malware to inherit some of the static features of popular modules to appear legitimate, in order to implement its functionality malware will exhibit differences in its behavioral and contextual features. We leverage this observation to detect a set of modules impersonating popular file names (e.g., system processes or software installers).

Our algorithm proceeds in two steps. First, we generate a set of "coarse" clusters whose large majority of modules are popular whitelisted files. Second, we identify a set of outliers in these clusters whose distance to other whitelisted modules is larger than the typical distance between legitimate modules in the cluster. The list of detected outliers is prioritized by the largest distance from legitimate ones. We elaborate on weight selection, distance computation, and our outlier detection algorithm below.

**Weights and distance computation.** As described in Sect. 3.2, the distance between modules is a sum of feature distances adjusted by weights. However, feature weights are computed differently in this case since we would like to give higher weights to features distinguishing benign and malicious modules. Towards this goal, we compute the information gain of the whole set of features over all whitelisted and blacklisted modules and define *static weights* proportional to the feature's information gain.

Assume that $X = (X_1, \ldots, X_n, y)$ is our dataset with $n$ features and label $y$ (blacklisted or whitelisted). Assume that feature $i$ takes $m$ values $v_1, \ldots, v_m$ and let $S_{ij}$ be the set of records having $X_i = v_j$. The information gain for feature $i$ in dataset $X$ is:

$$IG(X, X_i) = H(X) - \sum_{j \in \{1, \cdots, m\}} \frac{|S_{ij}|}{|X|} H(S_{ij})$$

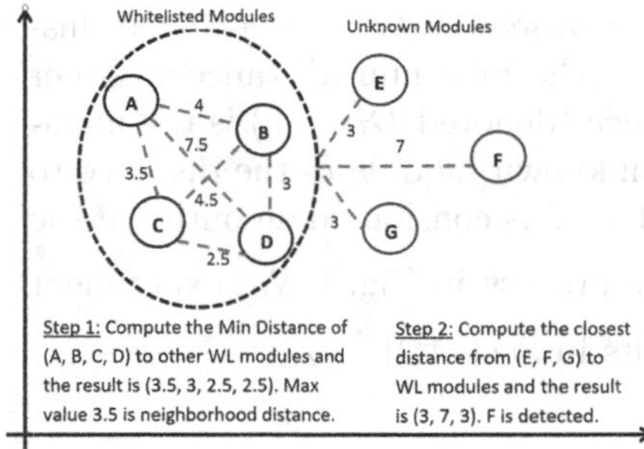

**Fig. 3.** Outlier detection example.

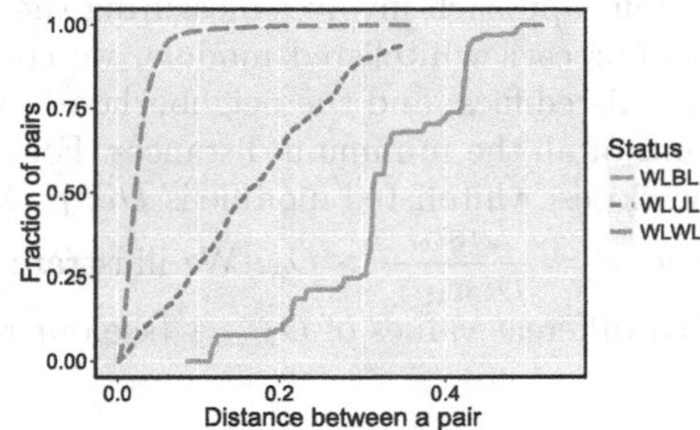


**Fig. 4.** Distance CDF from whitelisted to whitelisted (WLWL), unknown (WLUL) and blacklisted (WLBL) modules.

Here the entropy values $H(X)$ and $H(S_{ij})$ are computed from two bins (malicious and benign). We further refine our method to increase the weights of features with relative stability within the set of whitelisted modules in a cluster. In particular, we compute the average distance for feature $i$ for all pairs of whitelisted modules (denoted $Avg_i$) per cluster and use $1/Avg_i$ as a factor proportional to feature $i$'s stability. We set $Min(1/Avg_i, Max_W)$ as *dynamic weights* ($Max_W$ is a threshold that limits the maximum weight – set at 20). The final feature weights for a cluster are defined as the product of static (global) and dynamic (cluster-specific) weights and normalized to sum up to 1. For missing values, we use a penalty value as in Sect. 3.2.

**Coarse cluster selection.** We create clusters of modules with popular file names. We select file names present on a large number of machines (more than a parameter $O_\gamma$). We enforce that our coarse clusters include sufficient benign samples through two conditions: (1) the clusters include minimum $O_\alpha$ whitelisted modules; and (2) the ratio of whitelisted modules to all modules in a cluster is at least a threshold $O_\beta$. Coarse clusters should also include at least one unknown (or blacklisted) module for being considered.

To account for generic file names (e.g., `setup.exe` or `update.exe`) with variable behavior, we compute the average distance of all pairs of whitelisted modules in a cluster (denoted $Avg_{wdist}$) and remove the clusters with $Avg_{wdist}$ larger than a threshold $O_\theta$. We also remove the modules developed by the company providing us the dataset, as most of the internal builds exhibit diverse behavior.

**Detecting outliers.** Figure 4 shows distance CDFs between whitelisted modules, as well as between whitelisted and blacklisted, and whitelisted and unknown modules in the coarse clusters. This confirms that blacklisted modules impersonating legitimate file names are at a larger distance from other whitelisted modules compared to the typical distance between legitimate modules. Based on this insight, our goal is to identify unknown modules substantially different from whitelisted ones in the coarse clusters.

Our approach involves measuring the *neighborhood distance* in a coarse cluster. For each whitelisted module, we compute the minimum distance to other whitelisted files, and the neighborhood distance (denoted $Dist_{WL}$) is the maximum of all the minimum distances. For an unknown module $U$ the distance to the closest whitelisted module is $Dist_U$. Module $U$ is considered an outlier if the ratio $R = \frac{Dist_U}{Dist_{WL}} > O_\lambda$. We illustrate this process in Fig. 3. We experiment with different values of $O_\lambda \geq 1$ (see our results in Sect. 4.2).

# 4 Evaluation

We evaluated the effectiveness of our system using a snapshot of data from August 2015. Our dataset includes information about 534 blacklisted, 117K whitelisted and 1.7 million unknown modules installed on 36K Windows machines.

For prioritizing modules with known malicious behavior, we use 367 blacklisted modules whose static features have been correctly extracted. These modules were labeled by security experts with the corresponding malware family and we use them as ground truth to evaluate our clustering-based algorithm. Next, we selected a set of 388K unknown modules (79K executable and 309K DLL) installed on at most 100 machines (popular modules have lower chance of being malicious) and identified those that belong to the clusters generated by our algorithm. For validating the new findings, we used external intelligence (VirusTotal), internal AV scan results, as well as manual investigation by tier 3 security analysts. The results are presented in Sect. 4.1.

For validating our software impersonation detection algorithm, we used two datasets. First, we extracted all coarse-clusters with at least one whitelisted and one blacklisted module, and tested the effectiveness in identifying the blacklisted modules. This dataset (referred as `DS-Outlier-Black`) contains 15 clusters and 2K whitelisted, 19 blacklisted, and 2K unknown modules. Second, for higher coverage, we extracted all popular coarse-clusters (file names installed on more than 10K machines) that had at least one whitelisted and one unknown module. This dataset (`DS-Outlier-Unknown`) contains 314 clusters and a total of 11K whitelisted, 14 blacklisted, and 5K unknown modules. Unknown modules at large minimum distance from other whitelisted modules in these clusters were detected as outliers. The results are presented in Sect. 4.2.

Finally, both approaches are able to detect malicious modules ahead of off-the-shelf anti-virus tools. Initially only 25 out of 327 unknown executables and 463 out of 637 unknown DLLs were flagged by VirusTotal but eight months later (in May 2016), we uploaded the hashes of detected modules to VirusTotal again and noticed that 2 executables and 23 DLLs were detected in addition to previous findings (from August 2015). We identified a total of 81 modules (69 by clustering and 12 by outlier detection) confirmed malicious through manual investigation, but still not flagged by VirusTotal.

### 4.1 Results on Prioritizing Malicious Modules

**Results on Blacklisted Modules.** We use the 367 blacklisted modules as ground truth to select optimal values of the *penalty* and $\epsilon$ parameter in DBSCAN (we set $min\_sample = 2$ since we observed clusters with 2 malware samples). Our goal is to optimize a metric called *F1 score* that is a weighted average of precision and recall, but we also consider other metrics (precision, recall, false positives, false negatives). In our ground truth dataset, 147 modules are labeled as noise (they do not belong to any cluster). To account for these, we measure *coverage*, defined as the percentage of blacklisted modules (excluding the ones in the noise set) that belong to a cluster of size at least $min\_sample$.

**Table 2.** Parameters in DBSCAN clustering.

| | |
|---|---|
| Number of modules | 367 Blacklisted (273 EXE, 94 DLL) |
| Features | Static only, All Features |
| Feature weights | Uniform, Entropy-based |
| Missing features | $penalty \in [0.1, 0.8]$ |
| DBSCAN Parameters | $min\_sample = 2$ $\epsilon \in [0.05, 0.3]$ |

We experiment with different parameters in DBSCAN, as detailed in Table 2. We vary $\epsilon$ in DBSCAN between 0.05 and 0.3 and the penalty of missing features in the [0.1,0.8] range at intervals of 0.01. We consider and compare four models: (1) Static-Unif: static features with uniform weights; (2) Static-Ent: static features with entropy weights; (3) All-Unif: all features with uniform weights; (4) All-Ent: all features with entropy weights. Most of the features with highest entropy are static features but some context (time since creation, path-related features) and behavior features (set of contacted IP addresses and created processes) are also highly ranked. We used bins of 7 days for *PE timestamp* and *Days since creation*, and bins of 64 KB for *File Size* and *PE Size*.

**Penalty choice.** We first fix the value of $\epsilon$ and show various tradeoffs in our metrics depending on *penalty* (the distance between a missing feature and any other feature value). Figure 5 (left) shows the dependence on *penalty* for three different metrics (precision, recall and coverage) for the Static-Unif model when $\epsilon$ is set at 0.1. As we increase the *penalty*, the distance between dissimilar modules increases and the coverage decreases as more modules are classified as noise. Also, smaller clusters are created and the overall number of clusters increases,

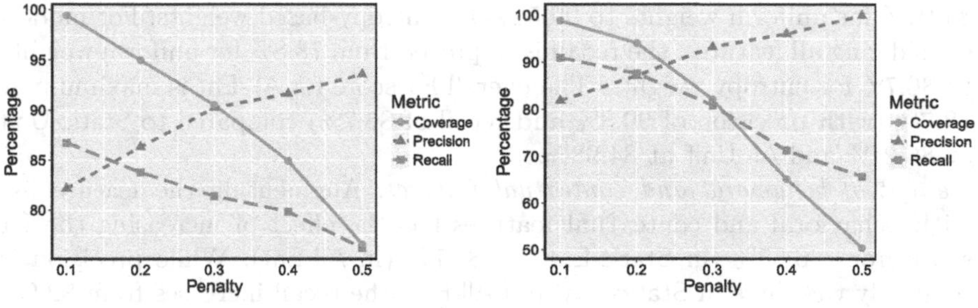


**Fig. 5.** Penalty dependence for Static-Unif with $\epsilon = 0.1$ (left) and All-Ent with $\epsilon = 0.2$ (right).

**Table 3.** Optimal performance metrics for 4 models.

| Model | Penalty | $\epsilon$ | Clusters | Single clusters | FP | FN | Precision | Recall | Coverage | F1 |
|---|---|---|---|---|---|---|---|---|---|---|
| Static-Unif | 0.3 | 0.13 | 50 | 150 | 55 | 42 | 84.67 | 87.86 | 99.16 | 86.24 |
| Static-Ent | 0.3 | 0.15 | 59 | 173 | 34 | 67 | 90.52 | 82.9 | 92.75 | 86.55 |
| All-Unif | 0.2 | 0.17 | 37 | 215 | 28 | 89 | 92.2 | 78.8 | 81.05 | 84.98 |
| All-Ent | 0.1 | 0.16 | 49 | 172 | 33 | 50 | 90.8 | 86.7 | 93.03 | 88.7 |

resulting in higher precision and lower recall. In Fig. 5 the increase in precision is faster than the decrease in recall until *penalty* reaches 0.3, which gives the optimal F1 score for the Static-Unif model.

As we include more features in our models (in the All-Unif and All-Ent models), the *penalty* contribution should be lower as it intuitively should be inversely proportional to the space dimension (particularly as a large number of behavior features are missing). Figure 5 (right) shows how *penalty* choice affects our metrics in the All-Ent model for $\epsilon$ fixed at 0.2. Similar trends as in Static-Unif are observed, but a *penalty* of 0.1 achieves optimal F1 score. In both cases, results are consistent for different values of $\epsilon$.

**Choice of $\epsilon$.** For optimal penalty values as described above, the graph in Fig. 6 shows the F1 score as a function of the neighborhood size in DBSCAN ($\epsilon$) for the four models considered. The optimal $\epsilon$ value is slightly larger in models with all features (0.16 for All-Unif and 0.17 for All-Ent) compared to models using static features only (0.13 for Static-Unif and 0.15 for Static-Ent). When more features are used, naturally the value of the neighborhood size in a cluster needs to be enlarged to account for larger distances between modules and more noise in the feature vectors.

**Model comparison.** Table 3 gives all metrics of interest for the four models with choice of $\epsilon$ and penalty parameters achieving optimal F1 score. Several observations based on Table 3 and Fig. 6 are described below:

- *Feature weights make a difference.* Choosing feature weights proportional to the feature's entropy in the blacklisted set improves our metrics compared to choosing weights uniformly. For static models, precision is increased from 84.97% for uniform weights to 90.52% for entropy-based weights. For models considering all features, the recall is improved from 78.8% for uniform weights to 86.7% for entropy weights. The overall F1 score for All-Ent is maximum at 88.7% (with precision of 90.8% and recall of 86.7%) compared to Static-Unif at 86.24% and All-Unif at 84.98%.
- *Benefit of behavioral and contextual features.* Augmenting the feature list with behavioral and contextual features has the effect of increasing the F1 score from 86.55% (in Static-Ent) to 88.7% (in All-Ent). While precision is relatively the same in Static-Ent and All-Ent, the recall increases from 82.9% in Static-Ent to 86.7% in All-Ent. An additional benefit of using behavioral and contextual features (which we can not though quantify in our dataset) is the increased resilience to malware evasion of the static feature list.

- *Coverage and noise calibration.* The coverage for the optimal All-Ent model is relatively high at 93.03%, but interestingly the maximum coverage of 99.16% was achieved by the Static-Unif model (most likely due to the smaller dimension of the feature space). The model All-Unif performs worse in terms of noise (as 215 single clusters are generated) and coverage (at 81.05%). This shows the need for feature weight adjustment particularly in settings of larger dimensions when missing features are common.

**Results on unknown modules.** We empirically created the blacklisted clusters with All-Ent for optimal parameters $\epsilon = 0.16$ and *penalty*$= 0.1$. We now compare the list of 388K unknown modules to all blacklisted modules. As an optimization, we first compute the distance between blacklisted and unknown modules using only static features and filter out the ones with distance larger than $\epsilon$, leaving 1741 executables and 2391 DLLs. Then, we compute the distance between the remaining unknown and blacklisted modules using all features. If an unknown module is within the distance threshold $\epsilon$ to one blacklisted module, we consider it similar but continue to find the closest blacklisted module. The detected modules are prioritized based on their minimum distance to a blacklisted module. In the end, 327 executables and 637 DLLs were detected.

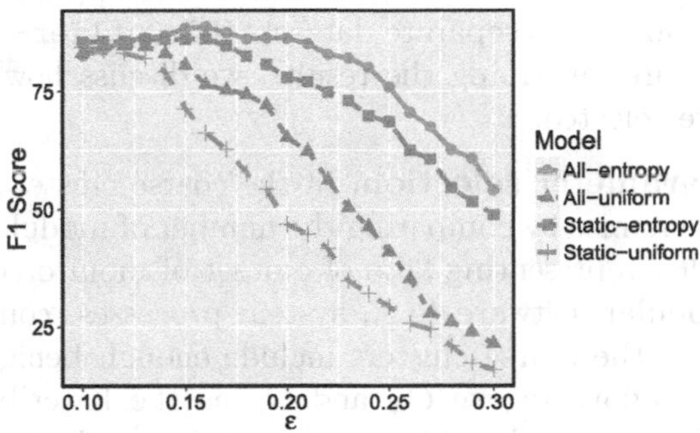


**Fig. 6.** F1 score as a function of $\epsilon$ for four models.

For verification, we uploaded the hashes of these modules to VirusTotal in August 2015 and 25 out of 327 unknown executables and 463 out of 637 unknown DLLs were flagged by at least one anti-virus engine. The reason for such low match on executable files is that most of them were not available in VirusTotal and company policies did not allow us to submit binary files to VirusTotal. When combining VirusTotal with the results from internal AV scan, we identified 239 out of 327 unknown executable and 549 out of 637 DLLs as suspicious, corresponding to a precision of 73% and 86%, respectively. Among the set of 79K executable and 309K DLLs, there were 88 executable and 88 DLL legitimate modules detected by our algorithm, corresponding to a false positive rate of 0.11% and 0.0284%, respectively.

To further confirm our findings, we selected a number of 89 modules with highest score (69 executables and 20 DLLs) and validated them with the help of a tier 3 security analyst. The analyst confirmed 65 out of 69 executables and all 20 DLL modules as malicious, resulting in a precision of 94.2% on executables and 100% on DLLs. Another interesting finding is that our techniques detected new malicious modules confirmed by the security analyst, but not flagged by VirusTotal. In total 60 executables and 9 DLLs from the set of 89 investigated modules were confirmed malicious by the security analyst, but not detected by VirusTotal. These new findings demonstrate the ability of our techniques to complement existing anti-virus detection technologies, and add another protection layer on endpoints.

### 4.2 Results of Outlier Detection

We evaluated the effectiveness of our approach in detecting software impersonation on two separate datasets (`DS-Outlier-Black` and `DS-Outlier-Unknown`). Before describing the results, we discuss how the parameters of the algorithm are selected.

**Parameter selection.** In the coarse cluster selection stage, we select popular file names by comparing the number of module installations to $O_\gamma$. We set $O_\gamma$ to 10K, representing 25% of our set of monitored machines. This setting captures popular software (e.g., system processes, common browsers, Java). To ensure that the coarse clusters include enough benign samples for learning legitimate behavior, we use $O_\alpha$ and $O_\beta$ as the lower-bounds for the number and ratio of whitelisted modules. We set $O_\alpha = 5, O_\beta = 0.2$ in `DS-Outlier-Black` for larger coverage and $O_\alpha = 10, O_\beta = 0.1$ in `DS-Outlier-Unknown`. As illustrated in Fig. 4, the pairwise distances between whitelisted modules are usually small (below 0.05 for $\geq$95% pairs), while distances from whitelisted to unknown and blacklisted modules are much larger. Hence, we only include stable clusters whose $Avg_{wdist}$ is smaller than the threshold $O_\theta$ set at 0.05.

**Results on `DS-Outlier-Black`.** We examined the 15 clusters in `DS-Outlier-Black` (including at least one blacklisted module) and inspected the 19 blacklisted and 2K unknown modules in these clusters. We found most filenames targeted by malware being Windows system files, such as `svchost.exe`, `lsass.exe`, `dwm.exe`, `services.exe` and `explorer.exe`. Malware impersonates these files to avoid causing suspicion as these processes are always present in Windows Task Manager. Additionally, file names belonging to popular software, including `wmplayer.exe` (Windows Media Player), `reader_sl.exe` (Adobe Acrobat SpeedLauncher) and `GoogleUpdate.exe` (Google Installer), are also targets for impersonation.

After coarse cluster selection, we obtained 5 clusters that met our selection criteria. These include 12 blacklisted and 12 unknown modules. We first evaluate the coverage of our algorithm in detecting blacklisted modules. To this end, our outlier detection algorithm captures all 12 blacklisted modules in these 5 clusters, as their distance from whitelisted modules is above 4, much larger than the threshold $O_\lambda$ set at 1 (see Sect. 3.3). Among the 12 unknown modules, 8 modules in 4 clusters are alarmed and are all confirmed to be either malicious (flagged by VirusTotal) or suspicious (experiences unusual behavior, but is not yet confirmed as malicious by domain experts). In particular, a malicious module impersonating `services.exe` is detected one week ahead of VirusTotal, but

**Table 4.** Summary of modules detected as outliers.

| Dataset | #FileName | #Blacklisted | #Malicious | #Suspicious | #Unknown | #Modules | Precision% |
|---|---|---|---|---|---|---|---|
| DS-Outlier-Black | 5 | 12 | 1 | 7 | 0 | 20 | 100 |
| DS-Outlier-Unknown | 10 | 0 | 5 | 12 | 7 | 24 | 70.8 |

other instances of this file are also suspicious (one of them is the ZeroAccess rootkit [26]). The summary of our results is in Table 4.

**Results on DS-Outlier-Unknown.** We use the data from DS-Outlier-Unknown to evaluate our approach on a larger set of clusters including at least one unknown module, but not necessarily any blacklisted modules. DS-Outlier-Unknown includes 314 clusters with 5K unknown modules, and we show that our approach can still achieve high precision in this larger dataset.

**Table 5.** Detection results based on different $O_\lambda$.

| Dataset | Count | $O_\lambda$ | | | |
|---|---|---|---|---|---|
| | | 1 | 4 | 7 | 10 |
| DS-Outlier-Black | Confirmed | 20 | 18 | 8 | 4 |
| | Unknown | 0 | 0 | 0 | 0 |
| DS-Outlier-Unknown | Confirmed | 17 | 13 | 5 | 4 |
| | Unknown | 7 | 4 | 3 | 2 |

After applying our filtering steps, 14 clusters (with 30 unknown and no blacklisted modules) were handed to the outlier detection algorithm. New system processes (e.g., mpcmdrun.exe) and new applications (e.g., installflash player.exe) were identified in this dataset. Among the 30 unknown modules, 24 were flagged as outliers based on their distance to the closest whitelisted module. Among them, 17 were confirmed malicious, but only 5 were detected by VirusTotal. Thus, our outlier detection technique identified 12 modules not detected by VirusTotal as malicious.We did not find enough information to validate the remaining 7 modules and we labeled them as unknown. By considering the malicious and suspicious instances as true positives, the overall precision is 70.8%. In total, 44 modules were detected (combining the results on DS-Outlier-Black) with an overall precision of 84.09%. We summarize our findings in Table 4, provide more details on the detected modules in Table 6, and present a case study in Appendix B.

We also assess the impact of the threshold $O_\lambda$ on the result. We increase $O_\lambda$ incrementally from 1 to 10 and measure the number of confirmed (malicious and suspicious) and unknown modules for both datasets. The results shown in Table 5 suggest that setting $O_\lambda$ to 1 achieves both high accuracy and good coverage.

## 5 Limitations

An adversary with knowledge of the set of features employed by our algorithms might attempt to evade our detection. Most static features (e.g., description, size) can be modified easily. Even if the attacker is successful in evading a subset of static features, our dynamic feature weighting method still provides resilience against this attack. Since feature weights are adaptively adjusted in our case, other features (behavior and contextual) get higher weights, and static features become less significant.

**Table 6.** Summary of the modules alarmed by outlier detection algorithm.

| Dataset | FileName | #Blacklisted | #Malicious | #Suspicious | #Unknown | Anomalous features |
|---|---|---|---|---|---|---|
| DS-Outlier-Black | services.exe | 2 | 1 | 2 | 0 | Unsigned, path, DLLs |
| | svchost.exe | 4 | 0 | 0 | 0 | Unsigned, path, DLLs, size, description, company name, Auto_Logon, hidden attribute |
| | googleupdate.exe | 1 | 0 | 1 | 0 | Invalid signature, DLLs, newly created, ssdeep similar |
| | dwm.exe | 4 | 0 | 1 | 0 | Unsigned, path, DLLs |
| | wmplayer.exe | 1 | 0 | 3 | 0 | Unsigned, description, DLLs, ssdeep similar to malware |
| DS-Outlier-Unknown | udaterui.exe | 0 | 0 | 0 | 1 | Invalid signature |
| | googleupdatesetup.exe | 0 | 0 | 3 | 0 | Unsigned, path, version info, similar to malicious by ssdeep |
| | installflashplayer.exe | 0 | 5 | 5 | 0 | 5 Confirmed by VirusTotal, similar to malicious by ssdeep |
| | intelcphecisvc.exe | 0 | 0 | 1 | 0 | Unsigned, size, entropy, ssdeep similar to malware |
| | mpcmdrun.exe | 0 | 0 | 1 | 0 | Unsigned, size, network connections, ssdeep similar to malware |
| | pwmewsvc.exe | 0 | 0 | 0 | 1 | Unsigned, no version info, size, compile time |
| | tphkload.exe | 0 | 0 | 2 | 0 | Invalid signature, size, compile time, creates remote thread |
| | flashplayerupdateservice.exe | 0 | 0 | 0 | 3 | Invalid signature |
| | vpnagent.exe | 0 | 0 | 0 | 1 | Invalid signature |
| | vstskmgr.exe | 0 | 0 | 0 | 1 | Invalid signature |

To evade the behavior and contextual features, malware authors need to adjust multiple functionalities like processes creation, file access and communications which could incur high cost in the malware development process. For example, we consider abnormal remote IPs as one behavior feature and evading this requires changes to the attacker's or target's network infrastructure. At the same time, most contextual features (e.g., file path, number of executables in the same folder, auto-start functionality) are dependent on the organization's configuration, typically not known by attackers.

Another concern is that behavior-based techniques could be vulnerable to mimicry attacks [5], in which malware simulates system call sequences of legitimate software to avoid detection. We argue that mimicry attacks are less likely to succeed in our setting as we collect a more diverse set of behavioral and contextual features.

Advanced attackers could suppress events generated by the monitors or even inject fake events for evasion. Approaches that protect the agent integrity, like PillarBox [4], could be deployed to defeat against these attacks.

## 6 Related Work

**Malware clustering.** To automatically detect malware variants and reduce the security analysts' workload, malware clustering techniques (e.g., [1,2,17,18, 27,29,31,37]) were proposed by the security community. These techniques perform static and dynamic analysis by running known malware samples in controlled environments. They extract fine-grained features related to file system access, registry modification, OS activities, and network connections. Our work differs from these approaches in the following aspects. First, our features are extracted from data collected by agents installed on a large set of user machines in an enterprise network. Second, we only have access to coarse-grained aggregated behavioral events as stringent performance constraints are imposed on the agents. Moreover, our ground truth is limited with the large majority of modules (more than 90%) having unknown status. Lastly, we introduce a new set of contextual features (e.g., location of files on user machines, file metadata, auto-start functionality) that leverage the large, homogeneous user base in enterprise settings.

**Host-based anomaly detection.** Many previous works proposed algorithms for detection of unusual program behavior based on runtime information collected from hosts. So far, system calls [11,16,21,22,32], return addresses from call stack [10], system state changes [1], memory dumps [3], and access activities on files and registries [20] have been used to detect suspicious behavior. We used a more comprehensive set of features, extracted from a much larger realistic deployment.

Recently, researchers proposed malware detection systems based on data collected from a large number of endpoints (e.g., Polonimum [6], AESOP [35], MASTINO [30]). These approaches rely on file-to-machine and file-to-file affinities, and cannot detect isolated infections. In contrast, our approach is exempted from such restrictions. Gu et. al. [13] developed a detection system against camouflaged attacks (malicious code injected in legitimate applications at runtime). Our system covers camouflage attacks as part of software impersonation, but addresses a larger set of attacks. A recent trend in this area is to combine network and host-based behavioral features for anomaly detection [33,40].

**Enterprise security analytics.** Previous research showed that security logs collected in a large enterprise, such as web proxy, Windows authentication, VPN, and DHCP, can be leveraged to detect host outliers [39], predict host infection [38], and detect malicious communications in multi-stage campaigns initiated by advanced persistent threats [28]. We focus here on analyzing a different source of data (collected by monitoring agents deployed on Windows machines) with the goal of identifying suspicious modules installed on user machines. We believe that combining endpoint and network-based monitoring data is most promising for identifying increasingly sophisticated threats in the future.

## 7 Conclusions

In this paper, we present the first study analyzing endpoint data collected from Windows monitoring agents deployed across 36K machines in a large organization with the goal of identifying malicious modules. We had to address some unforeseen challenges encountered in a large-scale realistic deployment as ours. Using a large set of static, behavioral and contextual features, we propose algorithms to identify modules similar to known blacklisted modules, as well as modules impersonating popular whitelisted software applications. Our validation based on internal AV scanning, VirusTotal and manual investigation by security experts confirms a large number of detected modules as malicious, and results in high precision and low number of false positives. In future work, we plan to extend our techniques to obtain higher coverage and identify other types of suspicious activities in this environment.

**Acknowledgement.** We are grateful to the enterprise who permitted us access to their endpoint data for our analysis. We would like to thank Justin Lamarre, Robin Norris, Todd Leetham, and Christopher Harrington for their help with system design and evaluation of our findings, as well as Kevin Bowers and Martin Rosa for comments and suggestions on our paper. We thank our shepherd Alfonso Valdes and anonymous reviewers for their feedback on drafts of this paper. This work was supported by the National Science Foundation (NSF) under grant CNS-1409738, and Secure Business Austria.

## A Feature Set

Our feature set includes features with different types, such as string, set, binary, and numerical attributes. Table 7 displays the full set of features used for our analysis, as well as their category and type.

## B Case Studies

In this section, we present several detailed case studies of our findings. First, we detail two clusters of similar modules we identified, one with executable modules and another with DLLs, and we highlight the features that our new findings share

**Table 7.** Final list of features. To note, all contextual features and numerical behavior features are computed by averaging the corresponding values across all hosts including the module.

| Category | Sub-category | Feature | Description | Type |
|---|---|---|---|---|
| Static | Descriptive | Description | File description | String |
| | | Company name | Name of company | String |
| | | Imported DLLs | Name of all imported DLLs | Set |
| | | Section names | Name of all section names | Set |
| | Numerical | File size | Size of module | Integer |
| | | PE size | Size from PE header | Integer |
| | | PE timestamp | Time when PE file was created | Date |
| | | Entropy | Module code entropy | Real |
| | | DLL count | Number of imported DLLs | Integer |
| | Attributes | Icon present | Is icon present? | Binary |
| | | Version information present | Is version information present? | Binary |
| | | PE type | Type of PE (32 or 64 bit) | Binary |
| | | PE machine | Type of targeted CPU (Intel 386, AMD64 etc.) | Categorical |
| | | Packed | Is module obfuscated by a packer? | Binary |
| | | .NET | Is it built with .NET? | Binary |
| | | Signature | Signature name | String |
| | | Signature valid | Is signing certificate issued by a trusted authority? | Binary |
| Behavior | File-system access | Written/Renamed executables | Avg. number of executables written/renamed | Real |
| | Process access | Created processes | Avg. number of created processes | Real |
| | | Opened processes | Avg. number of opened processes | Real |
| | Network connections | Set of domains | Set of domain names connected to | Set |
| | | Set of IPs | Set of IP addresses connected to | Set |
| Context | Module path | Path level | Avg. number of levels in path | Real |
| | | Path_System | Is located in System folder? | Real |
| | | Path_Windows | Is located in Windows folder? | Real |
| | | Path_ProgramFiles | Is located in ProgramFiles folder? | Real |
| | | Path_ProgramData | Is located in ProgramData folder? | Real |
| | | Path_AppDataLocal | Is located in AppDataLocal folder? | Real |
| | | Path_AppDataRoaming | Is located in AppDataRoaming folder? | Real |
| | | Path_User | Is located in user-specific folder? | Real |
| | | Number executables | Avg. number of executables in same folder | Real |
| | | Number executables same company | Avg. number of executables with same company in same folder | Real |
| | | Number non-executables | Avg. number of non-executables in same folder | Real |
| | | Number sub-folders | Avg. number of sub-folders in same folder | Real |
| | | Machine count | Number of installations | Integer |
| | Destination path | Dest_SamePath | Is destination path same as the module path? | Real |
| | | Dest_DifferentPath | Is destination path different than the module path? | Real |
| | | Dest_System | Is destination in System(syswow64/system32) folder? | Real |
| | | Dest_Windows | Is destination in Windows folder? | Real |
| | | Dest_ProgramFiles | Is destination in ProgramFiles folder? | Real |
| | | Dest_ProgramData | Is destination in ProgramData folder? | Real |
| | | Dest_AppDataLocal | Is destination in AppDataLocal folder? | Real |
| | | Dest_AppDataRoaming | Is destination in AppDataRoaming folder? | Real |
| | | Dest_User | Is destination in user-specific folder? | Real |
| | | Dest_Temp | Is destination in Temp folder? | Real |
| | Metadata | Administrator | Does owner have administrator privileges? | Real |
| | | Hidden attribute | Does file have hidden attribute set? | Real |
| | | Days since creation | Avg. days since first observed on hosts | Real |
| | Auto-start | Auto_Services | Does the module have auto-start for services? | Real |
| | | Auto_ServiceDLL | Does the module have auto-start for service DLL? | Real |
| | | Auto_Logon | Does the module have auto-start for logon? | Real |
| | | Auto_ScheduledTasks | Does the module have auto-start for scheduled tasks? | Real |

with blacklisted modules. Second, we give more details on some of the detected outliers and emphasize the difference from the legitimate whitelisted modules they impersonate.

## B.1 Similarity

We found 12 unknown modules all with different file names, but similar to a blacklisted module `house of cards s03e01~.exe`. These modules impersonate popular movie or application names such as `Fifty Shades of Grey~.exe` and VCE Exam Simulator∼.exe to deceive users. They all imported a single DLL (KERNEL32.dll) and used the same very common section names (.text, .rdata, .data, .rsrc, .reloc). One of them is even signed with a rogue certificate. Interestingly, these modules could not be grouped together only based on their static features, as these are common among other modules. However, when we consider the behavioral and contextual features, they are similar in some unusual ways. For instance, these modules write executables to a temp directory under AppData and create processes from that location. Moreover, they used the same autostart method (AutoLogon) to be persistent in the system and they reside in the same path under the ProgramData folder.

Another DLL cluster including 15 unknown and 1 blacklisted modules is intriguing as they have randomized 14-character file names (e.g. oXFV21bFU7dgHY.x64.dll). The modules are almost identical in their features except for slightly different entropy values and creation dates. VirusTotal reported 10 of them, but different modules were detected by different number of AVs. One of them was not detected initially, but when we queried VirusTotal later the module was detected by 29 AVs. After eight months, the remaining 5 modules have not yet been detected by any AVs in VirusTotal but confirmed manually by the security analysts.

### B.2 Outlier Detection

Our system identified 2 blacklisted and 3 unknown modules of services.exe as outliers. We found out that one of them was infected by ZeroAccess [26], a Trojan horse that steals personal information, replaces search results, downloads, and executes additional files. This module was confirmed by VirusTotal one week later after our detection. For the remaining two, we performed manual analysis. One of the modules has a description in Korean without a company name and signature. It has additional section names .itext, .bss, .edata, .tls compared to the legitimate process. The module imports some common DLLs such as kernel32 .dll, user32.dll, oleaut32.dll, but also imports shell32.dll and wsock32.dll, which is unusual for benign variants of services.exe modules. In addition, the module size is ∼1 MB whereas other whitelisted modules have sizes between 110 KB to 417 KB. Unfortunately, no behavior features were captured in this module but it has several suspicious contextual features. The module is installed in only a single machine with hidden attributes and it is located in C:\Windows\winservice instead of C:\Windows\System32. The second detected services.exe module is missing the signature field and imports different set of DLLs. Even though the module is 32 bit, the DLLs it imports are usually included in 64-bit versions of benign services.exe. It also has some suspicious contextual features since it is installed only in a single machine relatively recently and its file system path is ∼\Download\ffadecffa baffc instead of the usual C:\Windows\System32. Both of these modules were confirmed as malicious by security experts in the organization.

## References


1. Bailey, M., Oberheide, J., Andersen, J., Mao, Z.M., Jahanian, F., Nazario, J.: Automated classification and analysis of internet malware. In: Kruegel, C., Lippmann, R., Clark, A. (eds.) RAID 2007. LNCS, vol. 4637, pp. 178–197. Springer, Heidelberg (2007). doi:10.1007/978-3-540-74320-0_10
2. Bayer, U., Comparetti, P.M., Hlauschek, C., Kruegel, C., Kirda, E.: Scalable, behavior-based malware clustering. In: Proceedings of Network and Distributed System Security Symposium, NDSS, vol. 9, pp. 8–11 (2009)
3. Bianchi, A., Shoshitaishvili, Y., Kruegel, C., Vigna, G.: Blacksheep: detecting compromised hosts in homogeneous crowds. In: Proceedings of ACM Conference on Computer and Communications Security, CCS, pp. 341–352. ACM (2012)
4. Bowers, K.D., Hart, C., Juels, A., Triandopoulos, N.: PillarBox: combating next-generation malware with fast forward-secure logging. In: Stavrou, A., Bos, H., Portokalidis, G. (eds.) RAID 2014. LNCS, vol. 8688, pp. 46–67. Springer, Cham (2014). doi:10.1007/978-3-319-11379-1_3
5. Canali, D., Lanzi, A., Balzarotti, D., Kruegel, C., Christodorescu, M., Kirda, E.: A quantitative study of accuracy in system call-based malware detection. In: Proceedings of International Symposium on Software Testing and Analysis, pp. 122–132. ACM (2012)
6. Chau, D.H., Nachenberg, C., Wilhelm, J., Wright, A., Faloutsos, C.: Polonium: tera-scale graph mining and inference for malware detection. In: Proceedings of SIAM International Conference on Data Mining, SDM, SIAM (2011)
7. Damballa: first zeus, now spyeye. look at the source code now! (2011). https://www.damballa.com/first-zeus-now-spyeye-look-the-source-code-now/
8. Dash, M., Choi, K., Scheuermann, P., Liu, H.: Feature selection for clustering - a filter solution. In: Proceedings of International Conference on Data Mining, ICDM, pp. 115–122. IEEE (2002)
9. Ester, M., Kriegel, H.P., Sander, J., Xu, X.: A density-based algorithm for discovering clusters in large spatial databases with noise. In: Proceedings of 2nd ACM SIGKDD Conference on Knowledge Discovery and Data Mining, KDD, pp. 226–231. ACM (1996)
10. Feng, H.H., Kolesnikov, O.M., Fogla, P., Lee, W., Gong, W.: Anomaly detection using call stack information. In: Proceedings of IEEE Symposium on Security and Privacy, S&P, pp. 62–75. IEEE (2003)
11. Gao, D., Reiter, M.K., Song, D.: Gray-box extraction of execution graphs for anomaly detection. In: Proceedings of ACM Conference on Computer and Communications Security, CCS, pp. 318–329. ACM (2004)
12. Gu, G., Porras, P., Yegneswaran, V., Fong, M., Lee, W.: BotHunter: detecting malware infection through IDS-driven dialog correlation. In: Proceedings of USENIX Security Symposium, SECURITY, pp. 12:1–12:16. USENIX Association (2007)
13. Gu, Z., Pei, K., Wang, Q., Si, L., Zhang, X., Xu, D.: LEAPS: detecting camouflaged attacks with statistical learning guided by program analysis. In: Proceedings of International Conference on Dependable Systems and Networks, DSN, pp. 57–68. IEEE/IFIP (2015)
14. Hastie, T., Tibshirani, R., Friedman, J.: The Elements of Statistical Learning: Data Mining, Inference, and Prediction. Springer, New York (2009). doi:10.1007/978-0-387-84858-7
15. He, X., Cai, D., Niyogi, P.: Laplacian score for feature selection. In: Proceedings of Advances in Neural Information Processing Systems, NIPS, pp. 507–514 (2005)

16. Hofmeyr, S.A., Forrest, S., Somayaji, A.: Intrusion detection using sequences of system calls. J. Comput. Secur. **6**(3), 151–180 (1998)
17. Hu, X., Shin, K.G.: DUET: integration of dynamic and static analyses for malware clustering with cluster ensembles. In: Proceedings of 29th Annual Computer Security Applications Conference, ACSAC, pp. 79–88 (2013)
18. Hu, X., Shin, K.G., Bhatkar, S., Griffin, K.: MutantX-S: scalable malware clustering based on static features. In: Proceedings of USENIX Annual Technical Conference, ATC, pp. 187–198. USENIX Association (2013)
19. Kolbitsch, C., Comparetti, P.M., Kruegel, C., Kirda, E., Zhou, X., Wang, X.: Effective and efficient malware detection at the end host. In: Proceedings of USENIX Security Symposium, SECURITY, pp. 351–366. USENIX Association (2009)
20. Lanzi, A., Balzarotti, D., Kruegel, C., Christodorescu, M., Kirda, E.: AccessMiner: using system-centric models for malware protection. In: Proceedings of ACM Conference on Computer and Communications Security, CCS, pp. 399–412. ACM (2010)
21. Lee, W., Stolfo, S.J.: Data mining approaches for intrusion detection. In: Proceedings of USENIX Security Symposium, SECURITY. USENIX Association (1998)
22. Lee, W., Stolfo, S.J., Chan, P.K.: Learning patterns from UNIX process execution traces for intrusion detection. In: Proceedings of AAAI Workshop on AI Approaches to Fraud Detection and Risk Management, pp. 50–56. AAAI (1997)
23. MANDIANT: APT1: Exposing one of China's cyber espionage units. Report available from (2013). www.mandiant.com
24. Mandiant Consulting: M-TRENDS 2016 (2016). https://www2.fireeye.com/rs/848-DID-242/images/Mtrends2016.pdf
25. McAfee Labs: Diary of a "RAT" (Remote Access Tool) (2011). https://kc.mcafee.com/resources/sites/MCAFEE/content/live/PRODUCT_DOCUMENTATION/23000/PD23258/en_US/Diary_of_a_RAT_datasheet.pdf
26. McAfee Labs: ZeroAccess Rootkit. (2013). https://kc.mcafee.com/resources/sites/MCAFEE/content/live/PRODUCT_DOCUMENTATION/23000/PD23412/en_US/McAfee
27. Neugschwandtner, M., Comparetti, P.M., Jacob, G., Kruegel, C.: Forecast: skimming off the malware cream. In: Proceedings of 27th Annual Computer Security Applications Conference, ACSAC, pp. 11–20 (2011)
28. Oprea, A., Li, Z., Yen, T., Chin, S.H., Alrwais, S.A.: Detection of early-stage enterprise infection by mining large-scale log data. In: Proceedings of 45th Annual International Conference on Dependable Systems and Networks, DSN, pp. 45–56. IEEE/IFIP (2015)
29. Perdisci, R., Lee, W., Feamster, N.: Behavioral clustering of HTTP-based malware and signature generation using malicious network traces. In: Proceedings of Symposium on Networked Systems Design and Implementation, NSDI, pp. 391–404. USENIX Association (2010)
30. Rahbarinia, B., Balduzzi, M., Perdisci, R.: Real-time detection of malware downloads via large-scale URL → file → machine graph mining. In: Proceedings of ACM Asia Conference on Computer and Communications Security, AsiaCCS, pp. 1117–1130. ACM (2016)
31. Rieck, K., Trinius, P., Willems, C., Holz, T.: Automatic analysis of malware behavior using machine learning. J. Comput. Secur. **19**(4), 639–668 (2011)
32. Sekar, R., Bendre, M., Dhurjati, D., Bollineni, P.: A fast automaton-based method for detecting anomalous program behaviors. In: Proceedings of IEEE Symposium on Security and Privacy, S&P, pp. 144–155. IEEE (2001)

33. Shin, S., Xu, Z., Gu, G.: EFFORT: a new host-network cooperated framework for efficient and effective bot malware detection. Comput. Networks (Elsevier) **57**(13), 2628–2642 (2013)
34. Symantec: The Rebirth Of Endpoint Security. http://www.darkreading.com/endpoint/the-rebirth-of-endpoint-security/d/d-id/1322775
35. Tamersoy, A., Roundy, K., Chau, D.H.: Guilt by association: large scale malware detection by mining file-relation graphs. In: Proceedings of ACM SIGKDD Conference on Knowledge Discovery and Data Mining, KDD, pp. 1524–1533. ACM (2014)
36. Verizon: 2015 data breach investigations report (2015). http://www.verizonenterprise.com/DBIR/2015/
37. Wicherski, G.: peHash: a novel approach to fast malware clustering. In: 2nd Workshop on Large-Scale Exploits and Emergent Threats. LEET, USENIX Association (2009)
38. Yen, T.F., Heorhiadi, V., Oprea, A., Reiter, M.K., Juels, A.: An epidemiological study of malware encounters in a large enterprise. In: Proceedings of ACM Conference on Computer and Communications Security, CCS, pp. 1117–1130. ACM (2014)
39. Yen, T.F., Oprea, A., Onarlioglu, K., Leetham, T., Robertson, W., Juels, A., Kirda, E.: Beehive: large-scale log analysis for detecting suspicious activity in enterprise networks. In: Proceedings of 29th Annual Computer Security Applications Conference, ACSAC, pp. 199–208 (2013)
40. Zeng, Y., Hu, X., Shin, K.G.: Detection of botnets using combined host- and network-level information. In: Proceedings of International Conference on Dependable Systems and Networks, DSN, pp. 291–300. IEEE/IFIP (2010)

# Redemption: Real-Time Protection Against Ransomware at End-Hosts

Amin Kharraz(✉) and Engin Kirda

Northeastern University, Boston, USA
{mkharraz,ek}@ccs.neu.edu

**Abstract.** Ransomware is a form of extortion-based attack that locks the victim's digital resources and requests money to release them. The recent resurgence of high-profile ransomware attacks, particularly in critical sectors such as the health care industry, has highlighted the pressing need for effective defenses. While users are always advised to have a reliable backup strategy, the growing number of paying victims in recent years suggests that an endpoint defense that is able to stop and recover from ransomware's destructive behavior is needed.

In this paper, we introduce REDEMPTION, a novel defense that makes the operating system more resilient to ransomware attacks. Our approach requires minimal modification of the operating system to maintain a transparent buffer for all storage I/O. At the same time, our system monitors the I/O request patterns of applications on a per-process basis for signs of ransomware-like behavior. If I/O request patterns are observed that indicate possible ransomware activity, the offending processes can be terminated and the data restored.

Our evaluation demonstrates that REDEMPTION can ensure zero data loss against current ransomware families without detracting from the user experience or inducing alarm fatigue. In addition, we show that REDEMPTION incurs modest overhead, averaging 2.6% for realistic workloads.

## 1 Introduction

Ransomware continues to be one of the most important security threats on the Internet. While ransomware is not a new concept (such attacks have been in the wild since the last decade), the growing number of high-profile ransomware attacks [8,13,14,19] has resulted in increasing concerns on how to defend against this class of malware. In 2016, several public and private sectors including the healthcare industry were impacted by ransomware [9,11,35]. Recently, US officials have also expressed their concerns about ransomware [16,20], and even asked the U.S. government to focus on fighting ransomware under the Cybersecurity National Action Plan [20].

In response to the increasing ransomware threat, users are often advised to create backups of their critical data. Certainly, having a reliable data backup

**Electronic supplementary material** The online version of this chapter (doi:10.1007/978-3-319-66332-6_5) contains supplementary material, which is available to authorized users.


M. Dacier et al. (Eds.): RAID 2017, LNCS 10453, pp. 98–119, 2017.
DOI: 10.1007/978-3-319-66332-6_5

policy minimizes the potential costs of being infected with ransomware, and is an important part of the IT management process. However, the growing number of paying victims [10,17,29] suggests that unsophisticated users – who are the main target of these attacks – do not follow these recommendations, and easily become a paying victim of ransomware. Hence, ransomware authors continue to create new attacks and evolve their creations as evidenced by the emergence of more sophisticated ransomware every day [7,32–34].

Law enforcement agencies and security firms have recently launched a program to assist ransomware victims in retrieving their data without paying ransom fees to cybercriminals [30]. The main idea behind this partnership is that reverse engineers analyze the cryptosystems used by the malware to extract secret keys or find design flaws in the way the sample encrypts or deletes files. While there are ransomware families that are infamous for using weak cryptography [12,22,24], newer ransomware variants, unfortunately, have learned from past mistakes by relying on strong cryptographic primitives provided by standard cryptographic libraries. In response to the increasing number of ransomware attacks, a desirable and complementary defense would be to augment the operating system with transparent techniques that would make the operating system resistant against ransomware-like behavior. However, an endpoint approach to defend against unknown ransomware attacks would need to immediately stop attacks once the ransomware starts destroying files, and should be able to recover any lost data.

This paper presents a generic, real-time ransomware protection approach to overcome the limitations of existing approaches with regard to detecting ransomware. Our technique is based on two main components: First, an abstract characterization of the behavior of a large class of current ransomware attacks is constructed. More precisely, our technique applies the results of a long-term dynamic analysis to binary objects to determine if a process matches the abstract model. A process is labeled as *malicious* if it exhibits behaviors that match the abstract model. Second, REDEMPTION employs a high-performance, high-integrity mechanism to protect and restore all attacked files by utilizing a transparent data buffer to redirect access requests while tracking the write contents.

In this paper, we demonstrate that by augmenting the operating system with a set of lightweight and generic techniques, which we collectively call REDEMPTION, it is possible to stop modern ransomware attacks without changing the semantics of the underlying file system's functionality, or performing significant changes in the architecture of the operating system. Our experiments on 29 contemporary ransomware families show that our approach can be successfully applied in an application-transparent manner, and can significantly enhance the current protection capabilities against ransomware (achieving a true positive [TP] rate of 100% at 0.8% false positives [FPs]). Finally, we show that this goal can be achieved without a discernible performance impact, or other changes to the way users interact with standard operating systems. To summarize, we make the following contributions.

- We present a general approach to defending against unknown ransomware attacks in a transparent manner. In this approach, access to user files is mediated, and privileged requests are redirected to a protected area, maintaining the consistent state of user data.
- We show that efficient ransomware protection with zero data loss is possible.
- We present a prototype implementation for Windows, and evaluate it with real users to show that the system is able to protect user files during an unknown ransomware attack while imposing no discernible performance overhead.

The rest of the paper is structured as follows. Section 2 presents related work. In Sect. 3, we present the threat model. In Sect. 4, we elaborate on the architecture of REDEMPTION. In Sect. 6, we provide more details about the implementation of the system. In Sect. 7, we present the evaluation results. Limitations of the approach are discussed in Sect. 8. Finally, Sect. 9 concludes the paper.

## 2 Related Work

The first scientific study on ransomware was performed by Gazet [18] where he analyzed three ransomware families and concluded that the incorporated techniques in those samples did not fulfill the basic requirements for mass extortion. The recent resurgence of ransomware attacks has attracted the attention of several researchers once more. Kharraz et al. [22] analyzed 15 ransomware families including desktop locker and cryptographic ransomware, and provided an evolution-based study on ransomware attacks. The authors concluded that a significant number of ransomware in the wild has a very similar strategy to attack user files, and can be recognized from benign processes. In another work, Kharraz et al. [21] proposed Unveil, a dynamic analysis system, that is specifically designed to assist reverse engineers to analyze the intrinsic behavior of an arbitrary ransomware sample. Unveil is *not* an end-point solution and no real end-user interaction was involved in their test. REDEMPTION is an end-point solution that aims differentiate between benign and malicious ransomware-like access requests to the file system.

Scaife et al. [31] proposed CryptoDrop which is built upon the premise that the malicious process aggressively encrypts user files. In the paper, as a limitation of CryptoDrop, the authors state that the tool *does not provide any recovery or minimal data loss guarantees.* Their approach is able to detect a ransomware attack after a median of ten file losses. REDEMPTION does not have this limitation as it is designed to protect the consistent state of the original files by providing *full data recovery* if an attack occurs. Hence, unlike CryptoDrop, REDEMPTION guarantees minimal data loss and is resistant to most of realistic evasion techniques that malware authors may use in future.

Very recently, Continella et al. [15], and Kolodenker et al. [23] *concurrently* and *independently* proposed protection schemes to detect ransomware. Continella et al. [15] proposed ShieldFS which has a similar goal to us.

The authors also look at the file system layer to find typical ransomware activity. While ShieldFS is a significant improvement over the status quo, it would be desirable to complement it with a more generic approach which is also resistant to unknown cryptographic functions. Unlike ShieldFS, REDEMPTION does not rely on cryptographic primitive identification which can result in false positive cases. More importantly, this was a conscious design choice to minimize the interference with the normal operation of processes, minimize the risk of process crashes and avoid intrusive pop-up prompts which can have noticeable usability side-effects.

Kolodenker et al. [23] proposed PayBreak which securely stores cryptographic encryption keys in a key vault that is used to decrypt affected files after a ransomware attack. In fact, KeyBreak intercepts calls to functions that provide cryptographic operations, encrypts symmetric encryption keys, and stores the results in the key vault. After a ransomware attack, the user can decrypt the key vault with his private key and decrypt the files without making any payments. The performance evaluation of the system also shows that PayBreak imposes negligible overhead compared to a reference platform. Similar to ShieldFS, PayBreak relies on identifying functions that implement cryptographic primitives. As mentioned earlier, REDEMPTION does not depend on any hooking technique to identify cryptographic functions. Furthermore, the detection accuracy of REDEMPTION is not impacted by the type of packer a ransomware family may use to evade common anti-malware systems. This makes REDEMPTION a more generic solution to the same problem space.

The evaluation of REDEMPTION covers a significantly larger number of ransomware families compared to [15,31] and shows it can successfully identify unseen ransomware attacks after observing a median of five exposed files without any data loss. Indeed, REDEMPTION shares some similarity with CryptoDrop, ShieldFS, and PayBreak due to the common characteristics of ransomware attacks. However, extracting such behavior of ransomware is not the main contribution of the paper as they have been comprehensively discussed in several security reports. Rather, REDEMPTION is the introduction of a high performance, data loss free end-user protection framework against ransomware that protects the consistent state of the entire user space and can be used as an augmented service to the operating system. We are not aware of any other scientific work on the protection against ransomware attacks.

## 3 Threat Model

In this paper, we assume that ransomware can employ any standard, popular techniques to attack machines similar to other types of malware. That is, ransomware can employ several strategies to evade the detection phase, compromise vulnerable machines, and attack the user files. For example, a ransomware instance could be directly started by the user, delivered by a drive-by download attack, or installed via a simple dropper or a malicious email attachment.

We also assume that the malicious process can employ any techniques to generate the encryption key, use arbitrary encryption key lengths, or in general, utilize any customized or standard cryptosystems to lock the files. Ransomware can access sensitive resources by generating new processes, or by injecting code into benign processes (i.e., similarly to other classes of malware). Furthermore, we assume that a user can install and run programs from arbitrary untrusted sources, and therefore, that malicious code can execute with the privileges of the user. This can happen in several scenarios. For instance, a user may install, execute and grant privileges to a malicious application that claims to be a well-known legitimate application, but in fact, delivers malicious payloads – including ransomware.

In addition, in this work, we also assume that the trusted computing base includes the display module, OS kernel, and underlying software and hardware stack. Therefore, we can safely assume that these components of the system are free of malicious code, and that normal user-based access control prevents attackers from running malicious code with superuser privileges. This is a fair assumption considering the fact that ransomware attacks mainly occur in the user-mode.

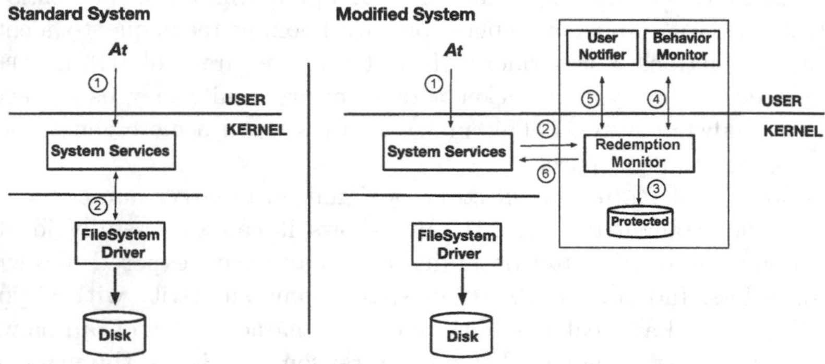


**Fig. 1.** REDEMPTION mediates the access to the file system and redirects each write request on the user files to a protected area without changing the status of the original file. Reading the user files, creating and writing on *new* files follow the standard 2-step procedure since they do not introduce any risk with regard to ransomware attacks on user data.

## 4 Design Overview

In this section, we provide our design goals for REDEMPTION. We refer the reader to Sect. 6 for details of our prototype implementation. REDEMPTION has two main components. First, a lightweight kernel module that intercepts process interactions and stores the event, and manages the changes in a protected area. Second, a user-mode daemon, called behavioral monitor and notification module, that assigns a malice score to a process, and is used to notify the user about the potential malicious behavior of a process.

**Intercepting Access Requests.** In order to implement a reliable dynamic access control mechanism over user data, this part of the system should be implemented in the kernel, and be able to mediate the access to the file system. The prototype redirects each write access request to the user files to a protected area without changing the status of the original file. We explain more details on how we implemented the write redirection semantics in Sect. 6.

Figure 1 presents an example that illustrates how access requests are processed. In an unmodified system, the request would succeed if the corresponding file exists, and as long as the process holds the permission. The system introduces the following changes. (1) REDEMPTION receives the request $A$ from the application $X$ to access the file $F$ at the time $t$, (2) if $A_t$ requests access with write or delete privilege to the file $F$, and the file $F$ resides in a user defined path, the REDEMPTION's monitor is called, (3) REDEMPTION creates a corresponding file in the protected area, called *reflected* file, and handles the write requests. These changes are periodically flushed to the storage to ensure that they are physically available on the disk. The meta-data entry of the corresponding file is updated with the offset and length of the data buffer in the I/O request after a successful data write at Step 3. (4) the malice score of the process is updated, and is compared to a pre-configured threshold $\alpha$. (5) the REDEMPTION monitor sends a notification to the display monitor to alert the user depending on the calculated malice score. (6) a success/failure notification is generated, and is sent to the system service manager.

**Data Consistency.** An important requirement for REDEMPTION is to be able to guarantee data consistency during the interaction of applications with the file system. A natural question that arises here is what happens if the end user confirms that the suspicious operations on the file that was detected by the system are in fact benign. In this case, having a consistency model is essential to protect the benign changes to the user files without on-disk data corruption. The implementation of the consistency policy should maintain the integrity properties the applications desire from the file system. Failure to do so can lead to corrupted application states and catastrophic data loss. For this reason, the system does not change the file system semantics that may affect the crash guarantees that the file system provides. To this end, REDEMPTION operates in three steps: (1) it reads the meta-data generated for the reflected file, and creates write requests based on the changed data blocks, and changes the status of these blocks to *committed*, (2) upon receiving the confirmation notification, the system updates the meta-data of the reflected file from *committed* to *confirmed*, and (3) the reflected file is deleted from the protected area.

Another question that arises here is how the system protects the consistency of the original file during the above-mentioned three-steps procedure if a system crash occurs. In case of a crash, the system works as follows: (1) if data is committed (Step 1), but the corresponding meta-data is not updated (Step 2), the system treats the change as incomplete, and discards the change as a rollback of an incomplete change. This operation means that Step 2 is partially completed before a crash, so the system repeats the Step 1, (2) If the meta-data of the reflected file is updated to confirmed, it means that the benign changes to the file has been successfully committed to the original file. In this case, the reflected file is removed from the protected area. Note that a malicious process may attack the Malice Score Calculation (MSC) function by trying to keep the malice score of the process low while performing destructive changes. We elaborate more on these scenarios in Sect. 8.

**User Notification.** The trusted output that REDEMPTION utilizes is a visual alert shown whenever a malicious process is detected. We have designed the alert messages to be displayed at the top of the screen to be easily noticeable. Since benign applications usually require sophisticated inputs (i.e., clicking on specific buttons, filling out the path prompt) from the user before performing any sensitive operation on the files, the user is highly likely to be present and interacting with the computer, making it difficult for her to miss an alert.

# 5 Detection Approach

As mentioned earlier, an important component of REDEMPTION is to perform system-wide application monitoring. For each process that requires privileged access to user files, we assign a *malice score*. The malice score of a process represents the risk that the process exhibits ransomware behavior. That is, the malice score determines whether the REDEMPTION monitor should allow the process to access the files, or notify the user. In the following, we explain the features we used to calculate the malice score of a process. The features mainly target content-based (i.e., changes in the content of each file) and behavior-based (i.e., cross-file behavior of a process) characteristics of ransomware attacks.

## 5.1 Content-Based Features

**Entropy Ratio of Data Blocks.** For every read and write request to a file, REDEMPTION computes the entropy [25] of the corresponding data buffers in the I/O traces similar to [21]. Comparing the entropy of read and write requests to and from the same file offset serves as an excellent indicator of ransomware behavior. This is due to the popular strategy of reading in the original file data, encrypting it, and writing the encrypted version.

**File Content Overwrite.** REDEMPTION monitors how a process requests write access to data blocks. In a typical ransomware attack, in order to minimize the chance of recovering files, the malicious process overwrites the content of the user files with random data. Our system increases the malice score of a process as the process requests write access to different parts of a file. In fact, a process is assigned a higher malice score if it overwrites all the content of the files.

**Delete Operation.** If a process requests to delete a file that belongs to the end-user, it receives a higher malice score. Ransomware samples may not overwrite the data block of the user files directly, but rather generate an encrypted version of the file, and delete the original file.

### 5.2 Behavior-Based Features

**Directory Traversal.** During an attack, the malicious process often arbitrarily lists user files, and starts encrypting the files with an encryption key. A process receives a higher malice score if it is iterating over files in a given directory. Note that a typical benign encryption or compression program may also iterate over the files in a directory. However, the generated requests are usually for reading the content of the files, and the encrypted or compressed version of the file is written in a different path. The intuition here is that the ransomware usually intends to lock as many files as possible to force the victim to pay.

**Converting to a Specific File Type.** A process receives a higher malice score if it converts files of differing types and extensions to a single known or unknown file type. The intuition here is that in many ransomware attacks, unlike most of the benign applications that are specifically designed to operate on specific types of files, the malicious process targets all kinds of user files. To this end, Redemption logs if a process requests access to widely varying classes of files (i.e., videos, images, documents). Note that accessing multiple files with different extensions is not necessarily malicious. Representative examples include the media player to play `.mp3` files (audio) as well as `.avi` (video) files. However, such applications typically open the files with read permission, and more importantly, only generate one request in a short period of time since the application requires specific inputs from the user. Hence, the key insight is that a malicious ransomware process would overwrite or delete the original files.

**Access Frequency.** If a process frequently generates write requests to user files, we would give this process a higher malice score. We monitor $\delta$ – the time between two consequent write access requests on two different user files. Our intuition is that ransomware attacks programmatically list the files and request access to files. Therefore, the $\delta$ between two write operations on two different files is not very long – unlike benign applications that usually require some input from the user first in order to perform the required operation.

### 5.3 Evaluating the Feature Set

Indeed, the assumption that all the features are equally important hardly holds true in real world scenarios. Therefore, we performed a set of measurements to relax this assumption. We used *Recursive Feature Elimination* (RFE) approach to determine the significance of each feature. To this end, the analysis started by incorporating all the features and measuring the FP and TP rates. Then, in each step, a feature with the minimum weight was removed and the FP and TP rates were calculated by performing 10 fold cross-validation to quantify the contribution of each feature. The assigned weights were then used as the coefficient of the feature in the formula 1 in Sect. 5.4.

Our experiments on several combinations of features shows that the highest false positive rate is 5.9%, and is produced when Redemption only incorporates content-based features ($F_1$). The reason for this is that file compression applications, when configured to delete the original files, are reported as false positives. During our experiments, we also found out that in document editing programs such as Microsoft Powerpoint or Microsoft Paint, if the user inserts a large image in the editing area, the content-based features that monitor content traversal or payload entropy falsely report the application as being anomalous. However, when behavior-based features were incorporated, such programs do not receive a high anomaly score since there is no cross-file activities with write privilege similar to ransomware attacks. When all the features are combined (i.e., $F_{12}$), the minimum false positive rate (0.5% FP with 100% TPs) is produced on labeled dataset. Hence, we use the combination of all the features in our system.

### 5.4 Malice Score Calculation (MSC) Function

The MSC function allows the system to identify the suspicious process and notify the user when the process matches the abstract model. Given a process $X$, we assign a malice score $S$ to the process each time it requests privileged access to a user file. If the malice score $S$ exceeds a pre-defined malice threshold $\alpha$, it means that the process exhibits abnormal behaviors. Hence, we suspend the process and inform the user to confirm the suspicious action. In the following, we provide more details on how we determine the malice score for each process that requests privileged operations on user files:

**($r_1$):** The process that changes the entropy of the data blocks between a read and a write request to a higher value receives a higher malice score. The required value is calculated as an additive inverse of the entropy value of read and write ratio, and resides on [0,1], meaning that the higher the value of entropy in the write operation, the closer the value of the entropy to 1. If the entropy of the data block in write is smaller than the read operation, we assign the value 0 to this feature.

**($r_2$):** If a process iterates over the content of a file with write privilege, it will receive a higher malice score. If the size of the file $A$ is $s_A$, and $y_A$ is the total size of the data blocks modified by the process, the feature is calculated as $\frac{y_A}{s_A}$ where the higher the number of data blocks modified by the process, the closer the value is to 1.

**($r_3$):** If a process requests to delete a file, this behavior is marked as being suspicious. If a process exhibits such I/O activities, the value 1 is assigned to $r_3$.

**($r_4$):** Redemption monitors if the process traverses over the user files with write privilege, and computes the additive inverse of the number of privileged accesses to unique files in a given path. The output of the function resides on [0,1]. Given a process $X$, the function assigns a higher malice score as $X$ generates more write requests to access files in a given path. Here, $write(X, f_i)$ is the $i^{th}$ independent write request generated by the process $X$ on a given file $f_i$.

**($r_5$):** Given a set of document classes, Redemption monitors whether the process requests *write* access to files that belong to different document classes.

The file $A$ and file $B$ belong to two different document classes if the program that opens file $A$ cannot take file $B$ as a valid input. For example, a `docx` and a `pdf` file belong to two different document classes since a `docx` file cannot be opened via a PDF editor program. We assign the score 1 if the process performs cross-document access requests similar to ransomware.

**($r_6$):** The system computes the elapsed time ($\delta$) between two subsequent write requests generated by a single process to access two different files. $\frac{1}{\delta}$ represents the access frequency. As the elapsed time between two write requests increases, the access frequency decreases.

We define the overall malice score of a process at time $t$ by applying the weights of individual features:

$$MSC(r) = \frac{\sum_{i=1}^{k} w_i \times r_i}{\sum_{i=1}^{k} w_i} \tag{1}$$

where $w_i$ is the predefined weight for the feature $i$ in the MSC function. The value of $w_i$ is based on the experiment discussed in Sect. 5.3. The weights we used in (1) are $w_1 = 0.9, w_2 = 1.0, w_3 = 0.6, w_4 = 1.0, w_5 = 0.7, w_6 = 1.0$.

Note that when REDEMPTION is active, even when using all the combined features, file encryption or secure deletion applications are typically reported as being suspicious. As mentioned earlier, such applications generate very similar requests to access user files as a ransomware does. For example, in a secure deletion application, the process iterates over the entire content of the given file with write privileges, and writes random payloads on the contents. The same procedure is repeated over the other files in the path. Hence, such cases are reported to the user as violations, or other inappropriate uses of their critical resources.

## 6 Implementation

In this section, we provide the implementation details of REDEMPTION. Note that our design is sufficiently general to be applied to any OS that is a potential target for ransomware. However, we built our prototype for the Windows environment which is the main target of current ransomware attacks today.

**Monitoring Access Requests.** REDEMPTION must interpose on all privileged accesses to sensitive files. The implementation of the system is based on the Windows Kernel Development framework without any modifications on the underlying file system semantics. To this end, it suffices on Windows to monitor the write or delete requests from the I/O system to the base file system driver. Furthermore, to guarantee minimal data loss, REDEMPTION redirects the write requests from the user files to the corresponding reflected files. The reflected files are implemented via *sparse files* on NTFS. In fact, the NTFS file system does not allocate hard disk drive space to reflected files except in regions where they contain non-zero data. When a process requests to open a user file, a sparse file with the same name is created/opened in the protected area. The sparse files are created by calling the function `FltFsControlFile` with the control code `FSCTL_SET_SPARSE`. The size of the file is then set by calling `FltSetInformationFile` that contains the size of the original file.

Redemption updates the `FileName` field in the file object of the create request with the sparse file. By doing this, the system redirects the operation to the reflected file, and the corresponding handle is returned to the requesting process. The write request is executed on the file handle of the reflected file which has been returned to the process at the opening of the file. Each write request contains the offset and the length of the data block that the process wishes to write the data to.

If the write request is successfully performed by the system, the corresponding meta-data of the reflected file (which is the offset and the length of the modified regions of the original file) is marked in the write requests. In our prototype, the meta-data entry to represent the modified regions is implemented via *Reparse Points* provided by Microsoft – which is a collection of application-specific data – and is interpreted by Redemption that sets the tags. When the system sets a reparse point, a unique reparse tag is associated with it which is then used to identify the offset and the length of every change. The reparse point is set by calling `FltTagFile` when the file is created by Redemption. On subsequent accesses to the file in the protected area, the reparse data is parsed via `FltFsControlFile` with the appropriate control code (i.e., `FSCTL_GET_REPARSE_POINT`). Hence, the redirection is achieved by intercepting the original write request, performing the write, and completing the original request while tracking the write contents.

The consistency of the data redirected to the sparse files is an important design requirement of the system. Therefore, it is required to perform frequent flushing to avoid potential user data loss. Indeed, this approach is not without a cost as multiple write requests are required to ensure critical data is written to persistent media. To this end, we use the Microsoft recommended approach by opening sparse files for *unbuffered I/O* upon creation and enabling write-through caching via `FILE_FLAG_NO_BUFFERING` and `FILE_FLAG_WRITE_THROUGH` flags. In fact, with write-through caching enabled, data is still written into the cache, but cache manager writes the data immediately to disk rather than incurring a delay by using the lazy writer. Windows recommends this approach as replacement for calling the `FlushFileBuffer` function after each write which usually causes unnecessary performance penalties in such applications.

**Behavioral Detection and Notification Module.** We implemented this module as a user-mode service. This was a conscious design choice similar to the design of most anti-malware solutions. Note that Microsoft officially supports the concept of protected services, called Early Launch Anti-Malware (ELAM), to allow anti-malware user-mode services to be launched as protected services. In fact, after the service is launched as a protected service, Windows uses code integrity to only allow trusted code to load into a protected service. Windows also protects these processes from code injection and other attacks from admin processes [28]. If REDEMPTION identifies the existence of a malicious process, it automatically terminates the malicious process.

## 7 Evaluation

The prototype of the REDEMPTION supports all Windows platforms. In our experiments, we used Windows 7 by simply attaching REDEMPTION to the file system. We took popular anti-evasion measures similar to our experiments in Sect. 3. The remainder of this section discusses how benign and malicious dataset were collected, and how we conducted the experiments to evaluate the effectiveness of our approach.

### 7.1 Dataset

The ground truth dataset consists of file system traces of manually confirmed ransomware samples as well as more than 230 GB of data which contains the interaction of benign processes with file system on multiple machines. We used this dataset to verify the effectiveness of REDEMPTION, and to determine the best threshold value to label a suspicious process.

**Collecting Ransomware Samples.** We collected ransomware samples from public repositories [1,3] that are updated on a daily basis, and online forums that share malware samples [2,26]. In total, we collected 9,432 recent samples, and we confirmed 1174 of them to be active ransomware from 29 contemporary ransomware families. We used 504 of the samples from 12 families in our training dataset. Table 2 describes the dataset we used in this experiment.

**Collecting Benign Applications.** One of the challenges to test REDEMPTION was to collect sufficient amount of benign data, which can represent the realistic use of file system, for model training purposes. To test the proposed approach with realistic workloads, we deployed a version of REDEMPTION on five separate Windows 7 machines in two different time slots each for seven days collecting more that 230 GB of data. The users of the machines were advised to perform their daily activities on their machines. REDEMPTION operated in the monitoring mode, and did not collect any sensitive user information such as credentials, browsing history or personal data. The collected information only included the interaction of processes with the file system which was required to model benign interaction with the file system. All the extracted data was anonymized before performing any further experiments. Based on the collected dataset, we created a pool of application traces that consisted of 65 benign executables including applications that exhibit ransomware-like behavior such as secure deletion, encryption, and compression. The application pool consisted of document editors (e.g., Microsoft Word), audio/video editors (e.g., Microsoft Live Movie Maker, Movavi Video Editor), file compression tools (e.g., Zip, WinRAR), file encryption tools (e.g., AxCrypt, AESCrypt), and popular web browsers (e.g., Firefox, Chrome). Due to space limitation, we provided a sub set of benign applications we used in our analysis in Table 1.

### 7.2 Detection Results

As discussed in Sect. 4, one of the design requirements of the system is to produce low false positives, and to minimize the number of unnecessary notifications for the user. To this end, the system employs a threshold value to determine when an end-user should be notified about the suspicious behavior of a process.

We tested a large set of benign as well as ransomware samples on a REDEMPTION enabled machine. As depicted in Tables 1 and 2, the median score of benign applications is significantly lower than ransomware samples. For file encryption programs such as AxCrypt which are specifically designed to protect the privacy of the users, the original file is overwritten with random data once the encrypted version is generated. In this case, REDEMPTION reports the action as being malicious – which, in fact, is a false positive. Unfortunately, such false positive cases are inevitable since these programs are exhibiting the exact behavior that a typical ransomware exhibits. In such cases, REDEMPTION informs the end-user and asks for a manual confirmation. Given these corner cases, we select the malice score as $\alpha = 0.12$ where the system achieves the best detection and false positive rates (FPs = 0.5% at a TP = 100%). Figure 2 represents the false positive and true positive rates as a function of the malice score on the labeled dataset. This malice threshold is still significantly lower than the minimum malice score of all the ransomware families in the dataset as provided in Table 2. The table also shows the median file recovery rate. As depicted, REDEMPTION detects a malicious process and successfully recovers encrypted data after observing on average four files. Our experiment on the dataset also showed that 7 GB storage is sufficiently large for the protected area in order to enforce the data consistency policy.

**Testing with Known/Unknown Samples.** In addition to the 10-fold cross validation on 504 samples, we also tested REDEMPTION with unknown benign and malicious dataset. *The tests included 29 ransomware families which 57% of them were not presented in the training dataset.* We also incorporated the file system traces of benign processes in the second time slot as discussed in Sect. 7.1 as the unseen benign dataset in this test. Table 3 represents the list of ransomware families we used in our experiments. This table also shows the datasets that were used in prior work [15,23,31]. In this experiment, we used the malice threshold $\alpha = 0.12$ similar to the previous experiment and manually checked the detection results to measure the FP and TP rates. The detection results in this set of experiments is (TPs = 100% at 0.8% FPs). Note that the number of FP cases depends on the value of malice threshold. We selected this conservative value to be able to detect all the possible ransomware behaviors. Indeed, observing realistic work loads on a larger group of machines can lead to a more comprehensive model, more accurate malice threshold calibration, and ultimately lower FP rates. However, our experiments on 677 ransomware samples from 29 ransomware families show that REDEMPTION is able to detect the malicious process in *all* the 29 families by observing a median of 5 files. We suspect the difference in the number of files is due to difference in the size of the files being attacked. In fact, this is a very promising result since the detection

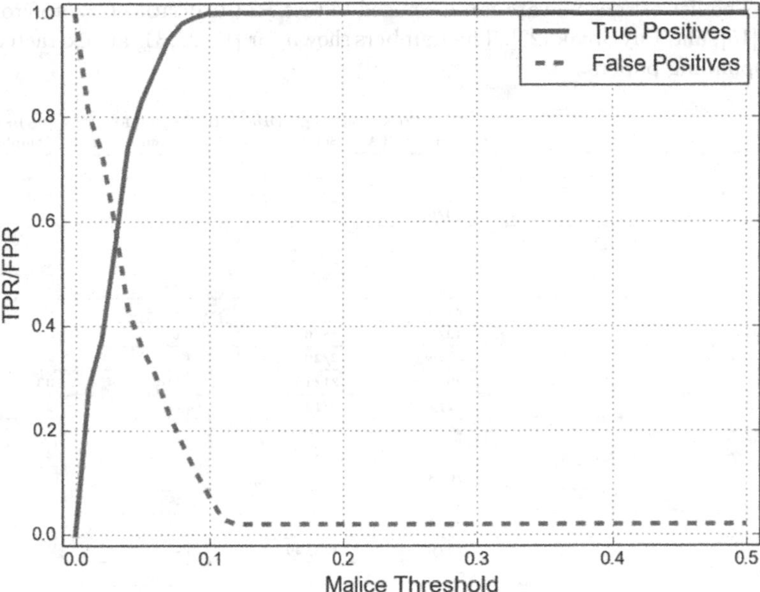


**Fig. 2.** TP/FP analysis of REDEMPTION. The threshold value $\alpha = 0.12$ gives the best detection and false positive rates (FPs = 0.5% at a TP = 100%).

**Table 1.** A list of Benign application and their malice scores.

| Program | Min. Score | Max. Score |
|---|---|---|
| Adobe Photoshop | 0.032 | 0.088 |
| AESCrypt | 0.37 | 0.72 |
| AxCrypt | 0.31 | 0.75 |
| Adobe PDF reader | 0.0 | 0.0 |
| Adobe PDF Pro | 0.031 | 0.039 |
| Google Chrome | 0.037 | 0.044 |
| Internet Explorer | 0.035 | 0.045 |
| Matlab | 0.038 | 0.92 |
| MS Words | 0.041 | 0.089 |
| MS PowerPoint | 0.025 | 0.102 |
| MS Excel | 0.017 | 0.019 |
| VLC Player | 0.0 | 0.0 |
| Vera Crypt | 0.33 | 0.71 |
| WinRAR | 0.0 | 0.16 |
| Windows Backup | 0.0 | 0.0 |
| Windows paintit | 0.029 | 0.083 |
| SDelete | 0.283 | 0.638 |
| Skype | 0.011 | 0.013 |
| Spotify | 0.01 | 0.011 |
| Sumatra PDF | 0.022 | 0.041 |
| Zip | 0.0 | 0.16 |
| **Malice Score Median** | 0.027 | 0.0885 |

**Table 2.** A list of ransomware families and their malice scores.

| Family | Samples | Min. Score | Max. Score | File Recovery |
|---|---|---|---|---|
| Cerber | 33 | 0.41 | 0.73 | 5 |
| Cryptolocker | 50 | 0.36 | 0.77 | 4 |
| CryptoWall3 | 39 | 0.4 | 0.79 | 6 |
| CryptXXX | 46 | 0.49 | 0.71 | 3 |
| CTB-Locker | 53 | 0.38 | 0.75 | 7 |
| CrypVault | 36 | 0.53 | 0.73 | 3 |
| CoinVault | 39 | 0.42 | 0.69 | 4 |
| Filecoder | 54 | 0.52 | 0.66 | 5 |
| GpCode | 45 | 0.52 | 0.76 | 2 |
| TeslaCrypt | 37 | 0.43 | 0.79 | 4 |
| Virlock | 29 | 0.51 | 0.72 | 3 |
| SilentCrypt | 43 | 0.31 | 0.59 | 9 |
| **Total Samples** | **504** | - | - | - |
| **Score Median** | - | **0.43** | **0.73** | - |
| **File Recovery Median** | - | - | - | 4 |

rate of the system did not change by adding unknown ransomware families which do not necessarily follow the same attack techniques (i.e., using different cryptosystems). *The results of this experiment also shows that the number of exposed files to ransomware does not change significantly if* REDEMPTION *is not trained with unseen ransomware families.* This result clearly implies that the system can detect a significant number of *unseen* ransomware attacks.

**Table 3.** The list of ransomware families used to test Redemption, CryptoDrop [31], ShieldFS [15], and PayBreak [23]. The numbers shown for [15,23,31] are extracted from the corresponding papers.

| Family | Redemption Samples/FA | CryptoDrop [31] Samples/FA | ShieldFS [15] Samples | PayBreak [23] Samples |
|---|---|---|---|---|
| Almalocker | - | - | - | 1 |
| Androm | - | - | - | 2 |
| Cerber | 30/6 | - | - | 1 |
| Chimera | - | - | - | 1 |
| CoinVault | 19/5 | - | - | - |
| Critroni | 16/6 | - | 17 | - |
| Crowti | 22/8 | - | - | - |
| CryptoDefense | 42/7 | 18/6.5 | 6 | - |
| CryptoLocker(copycat) | - | 2/20 | - | - |
| Cryptolocker | 29/4 | 31/10 | 20 | 33 |
| CryptoFortess | 12/7 | 2/14 | - | 2 |
| CryptoWall | 29/5 | 8/10 | 8 | 7 |
| CrypWall | - | - | - | 4 |
| CrypVault | 26/3 | - | - | - |
| CryptXXX | 45/3 | - | - | - |
| CryptMIC | 7/3 | - | - | - |
| CTB-Locker | 33/6 | 122/29 | - | - |
| DirtyDecrypt | 8/3 | - | 3 | - |
| DXXD | - | - | - | 2 |
| Filecoder | 34/5 | 72/10 | - | - |
| GpCode | 45/3 | 13/22 | - | 2 |
| HDDCryptor | 13/5 | - | - | - |
| Jigsaw | 12/4 | - | - | - |
| Locky | 21/2 | - | 154 | 7 |
| MarsJokes | - | - | - | 1 |
| MBL Advisory | 12/4 | 1/9 | - | - |
| Petya | 32/5 | - | - | - |
| PayCrypt | - | - | 3 | - |
| PokemonGo | - | - | - | 1 |
| PoshCoder | 17/4 | 1/10 | - | - |
| TeslaCrypt | 39/6 | 149/10 | 73 | 4 |
| Thor Locky | - | - | - | 1 |
| TorrentLocker | 21/6 | 1/3 | 12 | - |
| Tox | 15/7 | - | - | 9 |
| Troldesh | - | - | - | 5 |
| Virlock | 29/7 | 20/8 | - | 4 |
| Razy | - | - | - | 3 |
| SamSam | - | - | - | 4 |
| SilentCrypt | 43/8 | - | - | - |
| Xorist | 14/7 | 51/3 | - | - |
| Ransom-FUE | - | 1/19 | - | - |
| WannaCry | 7/5 | - | - | - |
| ZeroLocker | 5/8 | - | 1 | - |
| **Total Samples (Families)** | **677(29)** | **492(15)** | **305(11)** | **107(20)** |
| **File Attacked/Recovered(FA/FR) Median** | **5/5** | **10/0** | - | - |

## 7.3 Disk I/O and File System Benchmarks

In order to evaluate the disk I/O and file system performance of Redemption, we used IOzone [6], a well-known file system benchmark tool for Windows. To this end, we first generated $100 \times 512$ MB files to test the throughput of block write, rewrite, and read operations. Next, we tested the standard file system operations by creating and accessing 50,200 files, each containing 1 MB of data in multiple directories. We ran IOzone as a normal process. Then, for having a comparison, we repeated all the experiments 10 times, and calculated the average scores to get the final results. We wrote a script in AutoIt [5] to automate the tasks.The results of our findings are summarized in Table 4.

The experiments show that REDEMPTION performs well when issuing heavy reads and writes, and imposes an overhead of 2.8% and 3.4%, respectively. However, rewrite and create operations can experience slowdowns ranging from 7% to 9% when dealing with a large number of small files. In fact, creating the reflected files and redirecting the write requests to the protected area are the main reasons of this performance hit under high workloads. These results also suggest that REDEMPTION might not be suitable for workloads involving many small files such as compiling large software projects. However, note that such heavy workloads do not represent the deployment cases REDEMPTION is designed to target (i.e., protecting the end host of a typical user that surfs the web and engages in productivity activities such as writing text and sending emails).

Another important question that arises here is that how many files should be maintained in the protected area when REDEMPTION is active. In fact, as the protected area is sufficiently large, the system can maintain several files without committing them to the disk and updating the original files. However, this approach may not be desirable in scenarios where several read operations may occur immediately after write operations (i.e., database). More specifically, in these scenarios, REDEMPTION, in addition to write requests, REDEMPTION should also redirect read operations to the protected area which is not ideal from usability perspective. To this end, we also performed an I/O benchmarking on the protected area by requesting write access to files, updating the files, and committing the changes to the protected area without updating the original files. We created a script to immediately generate read requests to access updated files. The I/O benchmark on the protected area shows that the performance overhead for read operations is less than 3.1% when 100 files with median file size of 17.4 MB are maintained in the protected area. This number of files is significantly larger than the maximum number of files REDEMPTION needs to observe to identify the suspicious process. Note that we consider the scenarios where read operations are requested immediately after write operations to exercise the redirection mechanism under high loads. Based on this performance benchmarking, we conclude that read redirection mechanism does not impose a significant overhead as we first expected. In the following, we demonstrate that REDEMPTION incurs minimal performance overhead when executing more realistic workloads for our target audience.

### 7.4 Real-World Application Testing

To obtain measurable performance indicators to characterize the overhead of REDEMPTION, we created micro-benchmarks that exercise the critical performance paths of REDEMPTION. Note that developing benchmarks and custom test cases requires careful consideration of factors that might impact the runtime

**Table 4.** Disk I/O performance in a standard and a REDEMPTION-protected host.

| Operation | Original | REDEMPTION | |
|---|---|---|---|
| | Performance | Performance | Overhead (%) |
| Write | 112,456.25 KB/s | 110094.67KB/s | 3.4 |
| Rewrite | 68,457.57 KB/s | 62501.76 KB/s | 8.7 |
| Read | 114,124.78 KB/s | 112070.53 KB/s | 2.8 |
| Create | 12,785 files/s | 11,852 files/s | 7.3 |

**Table 5.** Runtime overhead of REDEMPTION on a set of end-point applications

| Application | Original (s) | REDEMPTION (s) | Overhead (%) |
|---|---|---|---|
| AESCrypt | 165.55 | 173.28 | 4.67 |
| AxCrypt | 182.4 | 191.72 | 5.11 |
| Chrome | 66.19 | 67.02 | 1.25 |
| IE | 68.58 | 69.73 | 1.67 |
| Media Player | 118.2 | 118.78 | 0.49 |
| MS Paint | 134.5 | 138.91 | 3.28 |
| MS Word | 182.17 | 187.84 | 3.11 |
| SDelete | 219.4 | 231.0 | 5.29 |
| Vera Crypt | 187.5 | 196.46 | 4.78 |
| Winzip | 139.7 | 141.39 | 1.21 |
| WinRAR | 160.8 | 163.12 | 1.44 |
| zip | 127.8 | 129.32 | 1.19 |
| Average | - | - | 2.6 |

measurements. For example, a major challenge we had to tackle was automating the testing of desktop applications with graphical user interfaces. In order to perform the tests as identical as possible on the standard and REDEMPTION-enabled machines, we wrote scripts in AutoIt to interact with each application while monitoring their performance impact. To this end, we called the application within the script, and waited for 5 s for the program window to appear. We then automatically checked whether the GUI of the application is the active window. The script forced the control's window of the application to be on top. We then started interacting with the edit control and other parts of the programs to exercise the core features of the applications using the handle returned by the AutoIt script. Similarly to the previous experiment, we repeated each test 10 times. We present the average runtimes in Table 5.

In our experiments, the overhead of protecting a system from ransomware was under 6% in every test case, and, on average, running applications took only 2.6% longer to complete their tasks. These results demonstrate that REDEMPTION is efficient, and that it should not detract from the user experience. These experiments also support that REDEMPTION can provide real time protection against ransomware without a significant performance impact. We must stress that if REDEMPTION is deployed on machines with a primarily I/O bound workload, lower performance should be expected as indicated by the benchmark in Sect. 7.3.

### 7.5 Usability Experiments

We performed a user study experiment with 28 participants to test the usability of REDEMPTION. We submitted and received IRB waiver for our usability experiments from the office of Human Subject Research Protection (HSRP). The goal of the usability test is to determine whether the system provides transparent monitoring, and also to evaluate how end-users deal with our visual alerts. The participants were from different majors at the authors' institution. Participants were recruited by asking for volunteers to help test a security tool. In order to avoid the effects of priming, the participants were not informed about the key functionality of REDEMPTION. The recruitment requirement was that the participants are familiar with text editors and web browsers so that they could perform the given tasks correctly. All the experiments were conducted using two identical Windows 7 virtual machines enabled with REDEMPTION on two laptops. The virtual machines were provided a controlled Internet access as described in Sect. 7. REDEMPTION was configured to be in the protection mode on the entire data space generated for the test user account. A ransomware sample was automatically started at a random time to observe how the user interacts with REDEMPTION during a ransomware attack. After each experiment, the virtual machines were rolled back to the default state. No personal information was collected from the participants at *any* point of the experiments.

We asked the participants to perform three tasks to evaluate different aspects of the system. The first task was to work with an instance of Microsoft Word and PowerPoint on the test machines running REDEMPTION. The experiment observer asked the participants to compare this process with their previous experience of using Microsoft Word and PowerPoint and rate the difficulty involved in interacting with the test setup on a 5-point Likert scale.

In the second task, the participants were asked to encrypt a folder containing multiple files with AxCrypt on the REDEMPTION-enabled machine. This action caused a visual alert to be displayed to the participant that the operation is suspended, and ask the user to confirm or deny the action. The participants were asked to explain why they confirmed or denied the action and the reason behind their decision.

In the last task, the participants were asked to perform a specific search on the Internet. While they were pre-occupied with the task, the ransomware sample was automatically started. This action was blocked by REDEMPTION and caused another visual alert to be displayed. Similar to the second task, the experiment observer monitored how participants handled the alert.

At the end of the first phase of the experiment, all 28 participants found the experience to be identical to using Microsoft Word and PowerPoint on their own machines. This finding empirically confirms that REDEMPTION is transparent to the users. In the second experiment, 26 participants confirmed the action. Another 2 noticed the alert, but denied the operation so no file was encrypted. In the third phase, all the 28 participants noticed the visual alert, and none of the users confirmed the operation. The participants explained that they were not sure why they received this visual alert, and could not verify the operation. These results confirm that REDEMPTION visual alerts are able to draw all participants' attention while they are occupied with other tasks, and are effective in protecting the user data. Furthermore, the experiments clearly imply that end-users are more likely to recognize the presence of suspicious operations on their sensitive data using REDEMPTION indicators. To confirm statistical significance, we performed a hypothesis test where the null hypothesis is that REDEMPTION's indicators do not assist in identifying suspicious operations during ransomware attacks, while the alternative hypothesis is that REDEMPTION's ransomware indicators do assist in identifying such destructive actions. Using a paired t-test, we obtain a p-value of $4.9491 \times 10^{-7}$, sufficient to reject the null hypothesis at a 1% significance level.

## 8 Discussion and Limitations

Unfortunately, malware research is an arms race. Therefore, there is always the possibility that malware developers find heuristics to bypass the detection on the analysis systems, or on end-user machines. In the following, we discuss possible evasion scenarios that can be used by malware authors, and how Redemption addresses them.

**Attacking Redemption Monitor.** Note that the interaction of any user-mode process as well as kernel mode drivers with the file system is managed by Windows I/O manager which is responsible for generating appropriate I/O requests. Since every access in any form should be first submitted to the I/O manager, and Redemption registers callbacks to all the I/O requests, bypassing Redemption's monitor is not possible in the user-mode. Furthermore, note that direct access to the disk or volume is prohibited by Windows from Windows Vista [27] for user-mode applications in order to protect file system's integrity. Therefore, any other form of requests to access the files is not possible in the user-mode, and is guaranteed by the operating system.

Attackers may be able to use social engineering techniques and frustrate users by creating fake alert messages – accusing a browser to be a ransomware – and forcing the user to turn off Redemption. We believe these scenarios are possible. However, note that such social engineering attacks are well-known security problems and target *all* end-point security solutions including our tool. Defending against such attacks depends more on the security awareness of users and is out of scope of this work.

**Attacking the Malice Score Calculation Function.** An attacker may also target the malice calculation function, and try to keep the malice score of the process lower than the threshold. For example, an attacker can generate code that performs *selective* content overwrite, use a low entropy payload for content overwrite, or launch periodic file destruction. If an attacker employs any one of these techniques *by itself*, the malice score becomes lower, but the malicious action would still be distinguishable. For example, if the file content is overwritten with low entropy payload, the process receives a lower malice score. However, since the process overwrites all the content of a file with a low-entropy payload, it is itself suspicious, and would be reported to the user.

We believe that the worst case scenario would be if an attacker employs all the three techniques simultaneously to bypass the malice score calculation function. This is a fair assumption since developing such a malware is straightforward. However, note that in order to launch a successful ransomware attack, and force the victim to pay the ransom fee, the malicious program needs to attack more than a file – preferably all the files on the system. Hence, even if the malicious program employs all of the bypassing techniques, it requires some sort of *iteration* with write permission over the user files. This action would still be seen and captured by Redemption. In this particular case, a malicious program can successfully encrypt a *single* user file, but the subsequent write attempt on another file would be reported to the user for the confirmation if the write request occurs within a pre-defined six hour period after the first attempt. This means a ransomware can successfully encrypt a user file every six hours. We should stress that, in this particular scenario, the system cannot guarantee zero data loss. However, the system significantly decreases the effectiveness of the attack since the number of files encrypted per day is very small.

Furthermore, since these approaches incur a considerable delay to launch a successful attack, they also increase the risk of being detected by AV scanners on the end-point before encrypting a large number of files, and forcing the user to pay. Consequently, developing such *stealthy* ransomware may not be as profitable as current ransomware attack strategies where the entire point of the attack is to encrypt as many files as possible in a short period of time and request money. An attacker may also avoid performing user file encryption, and only lock the desktop once installed. This approach can make the end-user machine inaccessible. However, such changes are not persistent, and regaining access to the machine is significantly easier, and is out of the scope of this paper.

## 9 Conclusions

In this paper, we proposed a generic approach, called REDEMPTION, to defend against ransomware on the end-host. We show that by incorporating the prototype of REDEMPTION as an augmented service to the operating system, it is possible to successfully stop ransomware attacks on end-user machines. We showed that the system incurs modest overhead, averaging 2.6% for realistic workloads. Furthermore, REDEMPTION does not require explicit application support or any other preconditions to actively protect users against unknown ransomware attacks. We provide an anonymous video of REDEMPTION in action in [4], and hope that the concepts we propose will be useful for end-point protection providers.

**Acknowledgements.** This work was supported by the National Science Foundation (NSF) under grant CNS-1409738, and Secure Business Austria.

## References

1. Minotaur Analysis - Malware Repository. minotauranalysis.com/
2. Malware Tips - Your Security Advisor. http://malwaretips.com/forums/virus-exchange.104/
3. MalwareBlackList - Online Repository of Malicious URLs. http://www.malwareblacklist.com
4. A brief demo on how Redemption operates (2016). https://www.youtube.com/watch?v=iuEgFVz7a7g
5. AutoIt (2016). https://www.autoitscript.com/site/autoit/
6. IOzone Filesystem Benchmark (2016). www.iozone.org
7. Ajjan, A.: Ransomware: Next-Generation Fake Antivirus (2013). http://www.sophos.com/en-us/medialibrary/PDFs/technicalpapers/SophosRansomwareFakeAntivirus.pdf

8. Hern, A.: Major sites including New York Times and BBC hit By Ransomware Malvertising (2016). https://www.theguardian.com/technology/2016/mar/16/major-sites-new-york-times-bbc-ransomware-malvertising
9. Hern, A.: Ransomware threat on the rise as almost 40 percent of bussinesses attacked (2016). https://www.theguardian.com/technology/2016/aug/03/ransomware-threat-on-the-rise-as-40-of-businesses-attacked
10. Dalton, A.: Hospital paid 17K ransom to hackers of its computer network (2016). http://bigstory.ap.org/article/d89e63ffea8b46d98583bfe06cf2c5af/hospital-paid-17k-ransom-hackers-its-computer-network
11. BBC News. University pays 20,000 Dollars to ransomware hackers (2016). http://www.bbc.com/news/technology-36478650
12. Osborne, C.: Researchers launch another salvo at CryptXXX ransomware (2016). http://www.zdnet.com/article/researchers-launch-another-salvo-at-cryptxxx-ransomware/
13. Francescani, C.: Ransomware Hackers Blackmail U.S. Police Departments (2016). http://www.cnbc.com/2016/04/26/ransomware-hackers-blackmail-us-police-departments.html
14. Mannion, C.: Three U.S. Hospitals Hit in String of Ransomware Attacks (2016). http://www.nbcnews.com/tech/security/three-u-s-hospitals-hit-string-ransomware-attacks-n544366
15. Continella, A., Guagnelli, A., Zingaro, G., De Pasquale, G., Barenghi, A., Zanero, S., Maggi, F.: ShieldFS: a self-healing, ransomware-aware filesystem. In: Proceedings of the 32nd Annual Conference on Computer Security Applications, pp. 336–347. ACM (2016)
16. Whitcomb, D.: California lawmakers take step toward outlawing ransomware (2016). http://www.reuters.com/article/us-california-ransomware-idUSKCN0X92PA
17. Dell SecureWorks. University of Calgary paid 20K in ransomware attack (2016). http://www.cbc.ca/news/canada/calgary/university-calgary-ransomware-cyberattack-1.3620979
18. Gazet, A.: Comparative analysis of various ransomware virii. J. Comput. Virol. **6**, 77–90 (2010)
19. Wolf, G.: 8 High Profile Ransomware Attacks You May Not Have Heard Of (2016). https://www.linkedin.com/pulse/8-high-profile-ransomware-attacks-you-may-have-heard-gregory-wolf
20. Zremski, J.: New York Senator Seeks to Combat Ransomware (2016). http://www.govtech.com/security/New-York-Senator-Seeks-to-Combat-Ransomware.html
21. Kharraz, A., Arshad, S., Mulliner, C., Robertson, W., Kirda, E.: A large-scale, automated approach to detecting ransomware. In: 25th USENIX Security Symposium (2016)
22. Kharraz, A., Robertson, W., Balzarotti, D., Bilge, L., Kirda, E.: Cutting the Gordian Knot: a look under the hood of ransomware attacks. In: Almgren, M., Gulisano, V., Maggi, F. (eds.) DIMVA 2015. LNCS, vol. 9148, pp. 3–24. Springer, Cham (2015). doi:10.1007/978-3-319-20550-2_1
23. Kolodenker, E., Koch, W., Stringhini, G., Egele, M.: PayBreak: defense against cryptographic ransomware. In: Proceedings of the 2017 ACM on Asia Conference on Computer and Communications Security, ASIA CCS 2017, pp. 599–611. ACM, New York (2017)
24. Abrams, L.: TeslaCrypt Decrypted: flaw in TeslaCrypt allows Victim's to Recover their Files (2016). http://www.bleepingcomputer.com/news/security/teslacrypt-decrypted-flaw-in-teslacrypt-allows-victims-to-recover-their-files/

25. Lin, J.: Divergence measures based on the shannon entropy. IEEE Trans. Inform. Theory **37**, 145–151 (1991)
26. Malware Don't Need Coffee. Guess who's back again? Cryptowall 3.0 (2015). http://malware.dontneedcoffee.com/2015/01/guess-whos-back-again-cryptowall-30.html
27. Microsoft, Inc. Blocking Direct Write Operations to Volumes and Disks. https://msdn.microsoft.com/en-us/library/windows/hardware/ff551353(v=vs.85).aspx
28. Microsoft, Inc. Protecting Anti-Malware Services (2016). https://msdn.microsoft.com/en-us/library/windows/desktop/dn313124(v=vs.85).aspx
29. Ms. Smith. Kansas Heart Hospital hit with ransomware; attackers demand two ransoms (2016). http://www.networkworld.com/article/3073495/security/kansas-heart-hospital-hit-with-ransomware-paid-but-attackers-demanded-2nd-ransom.html
30. No-More-Ransomware Project. No More Ransomware! (2016). https://www.nomoreransom.org/about-the-project.html
31. Scaife, N., Carter, H., Traynor, P., Butler, K.R.: CryptoLock (and Drop It): stopping ransomware attacks on user data. In: IEEE International Conference on Distributed Computing Systems (ICDCS) (2016)
32. O'Gorman, G., McDonald, G.: Ransomware: A Growing Menance (2012). http://www.symantec.com/connect/blogs/ransomware-growing-menace
33. Symantec, Inc. Internet Security Threat Report (2014). http://www.symantec.com/security_response/publications/threatreport.jsp
34. TrendLabs. An Onslaught of Online Banking Malware and Ransomware (2013). http://apac.trendmicro.com/cloud-content/apac/pdfs/security-intelligence/reports/rpt-cashing-in-on-digital-information.pdf
35. WIRED Magazine. Why Hospitals Are the Perfect Targets for Ransomware (2016). https://www.wired.com/2016/03/ransomware-why-hospitals-are-the-perfect-targets/

# ILAB: An Interactive Labelling Strategy for Intrusion Detection

Anaël Beaugnon[1,2(✉)], Pierre Chifflier[1], and Francis Bach[2]

[1] French Network Security Agency (ANSSI), Paris, France
{anael.beaugnon,pierre.chifflier}@ssi.gouv.fr
[2] INRIA, École Normale Supérieure, Paris, France
francis.bach@ens.fr

**Abstract.** Acquiring a representative labelled dataset is a hurdle that has to be overcome to learn a supervised detection model. Labelling a dataset is particularly expensive in computer security as expert knowledge is required to perform the annotations. In this paper, we introduce ILAB, a novel interactive labelling strategy that helps experts label large datasets for intrusion detection with a reduced workload. First, we compare ILAB with two state-of-the-art labelling strategies on public labelled datasets and demonstrate it is both an effective and a scalable solution. Second, we show ILAB is workable with a real-world annotation project carried out on a large unlabelled NetFlow dataset originating from a production environment. We provide an open source implementation (https://github.com/ANSSI-FR/SecuML/) to allow security experts to label their own datasets and researchers to compare labelling strategies.

**Keywords:** Intrusion detection · Active learning · Rare category detection

## 1 Introduction

Supervised learning is adapted to intrusion detection and has been successfully applied to various detection problems: Android applications [11], PDF files [7,35], botnets [2,5], Windows audit logs [4], portable executable files [19]. However, supervised detection models must be trained on representative labelled datasets which are particularly expensive to build in computer security. Expert knowledge is required to annotate and data are often confidential. As a result, crowd-sourcing [37] cannot be applied as in computer vision or natural language processing to acquire labelled datasets at low cost. Some labelled datasets related to computer security are public (Malicia project [22], KDD99 [41], kyoto2006 [39], etc.) but they are quickly outdated and they often do not account for the idiosyncrasies of each deployment context.

**Electronic supplementary material** The online version of this chapter (doi:10.1007/978-3-319-66332-6_6) contains supplementary material, which is available to authorized users.


M. Dacier et al. (Eds.): RAID 2017, LNCS 10453, pp. 120–140, 2017.
DOI: 10.1007/978-3-319-66332-6_6

Experts are essential for annotating but they are an expensive resource, that is why the labelling process must use expert time efficiently. Active learning methods have been proposed to reduce the labelling cost by asking the expert to annotate only the most informative examples [32]. However, classical active learning methods often suffer from sampling bias [29,34]: a family (a group of similar malicious or benign examples) may be completely overlooked by the annotation queries as the expert is asked to annotate only the most informative examples. Sampling bias is a significant issue in intrusion detection: it may lead to missing a malicious family during the labelling process, and being unable to detect it thereafter. Moreover, the labelling strategy must scale to large datasets to be workable on real-world annotation projects.

Finally, active learning is an interactive process which must ensure a good expert-model interaction, i.e. a good interaction between the expert who annotates and the detection model [33,43]. The expert annotations improve not only the detection model but also the relevance of the following annotation queries. A low execution time is thus required to allow frequent updates of the detection model with the expert feedback. A labelling strategy with a high execution time would alter the expert-model interaction and is unlikely to be accepted by experts.

In this paper, we introduce ILAB, a novel interactive labelling strategy that helps an expert acquire a representative labelled dataset with a reduced workload. ILAB relies on a new hierarchical active learning method with binary labels (malicious vs. benign) and user-defined malicious and benign families. It avoids the sampling bias issue encountered by classical active learning as it is designed to discover the different malicious and benign families. Moreover, the scalable algorithms used in ILAB make it workable on large datasets and guarantee a low expert waiting time for a good expert-model interaction.

Our paper makes the following contributions:

- We present a novel active learning method called ILAB designed to avoid sampling bias. It has a low computation cost to ensure a good expert-model interaction, and it is scalable to large datasets.
- We compare ILAB with two state-of-the-art active learning methods for intrusion detection [14,40] on two detection problems. We demonstrate that ILAB improves the scalability without reducing the effectiveness. Up to our knowledge, [14,40] have never been compared. We provide an open source implementation of ILAB and of these two labelling strategies to foster comparison in future research works.
- We show that ILAB is a workable labelling strategy that scales to large real-world datasets with an annotation project on NetFlow data originating from a production environment. We provide an open source implementation of the graphical user interface deployed during the annotation project to allow security experts to label their own datasets.

The rest of the paper is organized as follows. Section 2 presents the sampling bias issue in active learning and related works. The problem being addressed and the notations are detailed in Sect. 3. Section 4 explains ILAB labelling strategy.

Finally, Sect. 5 compares ILAB with state-of-the-art labelling strategies through simulations run on public fully labelled datasets, and Sect. 6 presents a real-world annotation project carried out with ILAB on a large unlabelled NetFlow dataset.

## 2 Background and Related Work

*Active Learning.* Active learning [32] methods have been developed in the machine learning community to reduce the labelling cost. A labelling strategy asks the expert to annotate only the most informative instances, i.e. the ones that lead to the best detection model. Active learning methods rely on an interactive process where the expert is asked to annotate some instances from a large unlabelled pool to improve the current detection model and the relevance of the future annotation queries (see Fig. 1). However, annotating only the most informative instances may cause a family of observations to be completely missed by the labelling process (see [8,29] for theoretical examples) and, therefore, may have a negative impact on the performance of the detection model.

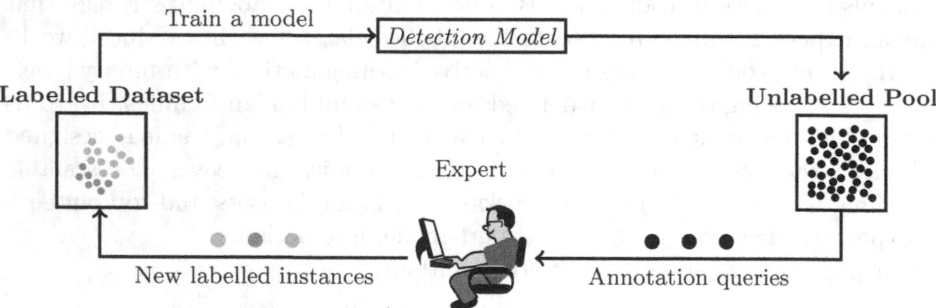


**Fig. 1.** Active learning: an interactive process

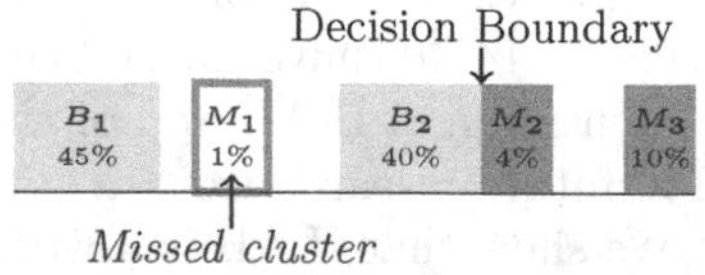


**Fig. 2.** Sampling bias example

*Sampling Bias.* Figure 2 provides an example of sampling bias in one dimension with uncertainty sampling [20] which queries the closest instances to the decision boundary. Each block represents a malicious or a benign family. With this data distribution, instances from the family $M_1$ are unlikely to be part of the initial training dataset, and so the initial decision boundary is likely to lie between the families $B_2$ and $M_3$. As active learning proceeds, the classifier will gradually converge to the decision boundary between the families $B_2$ and $M_2$ and will only ask the expert to annotate instances from these two families to refine the decision boundary. The malicious family $M_1$ on the left is completely overlooked by the query algorithm as the classifier is mistakenly confident that the entire family is benign. As the malicious family $M_1$ is on the wrong side of the decision boundary, the classifier will not be able to detect this malicious family thereafter.

Sampling bias is a significant problem for intrusion detection that may lead to malicious families remaining completely undetected. Besides, the risk of sampling bias is even higher for intrusion detection than for other application domains because the initial labels are not uniformly distributed. Uniform random sampling cannot be used to acquire the initial labelled instances as the malicious class is too under-represented. The signatures widely deployed in detection systems can provide initial labels but they likely all belong to the same family or to a small number of families.

*Related Work.* Online active learning [21,30,31,44,45] is well-suited to follow the evolution of the threats: experts perform annotations over time to update the detection model that is already deployed. In this setting, the detection model in production has been initially trained on a labelled dataset representative of the deployment environment. In our case, such a representative labelled dataset is unavailable and the objective is to acquire it offline to train the initial detection model.

Some works focus on offline active learning to build a labelled dataset for intrusion detection. First, Almgren et al. [1] have applied plain uncertainty sampling [20] to intrusion detection before the sampling bias issue has been discovered. Then, Aladin [40] and Görnitz et al. [14] have proposed new labelling strategies for intrusion detection that intend to discover the different malicious families. Aladin applies rare category detection [26] on top of active learning to foster the discovery of the different families, and Görnitz et al. use a $k$-nearest neighbour approach to detect yet unknown malicious families. However, both [14,40] deal with sampling bias at the expense of the expert-model interaction. These labelling strategies require heavy computations to generate the annotation queries that cause long waiting-periods that cannot be exploited by the expert. ILAB relies on rare category detection to avoid sampling bias, as Aladin, but with a divide and conquer approach to ensure a good expert-model interaction. Aladin [40] and Görnitz et al. [14] labelling strategies have never been compared to our knowledge. We compare ILAB with these two labelling strategies in the simulations presented in Sect. 5 and we provide open source implementations in order to foster comparison in future research works.

Finally, active learning is an interactive process where a user interface is required for the expert to annotate. Almgren et al. and Görnitz et al. have only run simulations on fully labelled datasets with an oracle answering the annotation queries and they have not mentioned any user interface. Aladin has a corresponding graphical user interface, but [40] provides no detail about it. As an ergonomic user interface can definitely reduce the expert effort [9,33], ILAB comes up with an open source graphical user interface briefly described in Sect. 6.

## 3 Problem Statement

Our goal is to acquire a representative labelled dataset from a pool of unlabelled instances with a reduced human effort. Both the number of annotations asked from the expert and the computation time for generating the annotation queries must be minimized to reduce the workload and ensure a good expert-model interaction. We assume that there is no adversary attempting to mislead the labelling strategy as it is performed offline before the detection model is deployed in production.

*Notations.* Let $\mathcal{D} = \{x_i \in \mathbb{R}^m\}_{1 \leq i \leq N}$ be the dataset we want to label partially to learn a supervised detection model $\mathcal{M}$. It contains $N$ instances described by $m$ real-valued features. For example, each instance $x_i$ could represent a PDF file, an Android application, the traffic of an IP address, or the activity of a user. Such unlabelled data are usually easy to acquire from the environment where the detection system is deployed (files, network traffic captures, or logs for example).

To represent an instance with real-valued features the expert must extract discriminating features and transform them into real values. Many research works focus on feature extraction for given detection problems: Android applications [11], PDF files [7,35], Windows audit logs [4], portable executable files [19]. In this paper, we do not address feature extraction and we focus on reducing the cost of building a representative labelled dataset with an effective labelling strategy. Instances are represented by real-valued features regardless of the detection problem thanks to feature extraction. As a result, labelling strategies are generic regarding the detection problems.

Let $\mathcal{L} = \{\texttt{Malicious}, \texttt{Benign}\}$ be the set of labels and $\mathcal{F}_y$ be the set containing the user-defined families of the label $y \in \mathcal{L}$. For example, malicious instances belonging to the same family may exploit the same vulnerability, they may be polymorphic variants of the same malware, or they may be emails coming from the same spam campaign.

Our aim is to create a labelled dataset

$$\mathcal{D}_L \subseteq \{(x, y, z) \mid x \in \mathcal{D},\ y \in \mathcal{L},\ z \in \mathcal{F}_y\}$$

maximizing the accuracy of the detection model $\mathcal{M}$ trained on $\mathcal{D}_L$. $\mathcal{D}_L$ associates a label $y \in \mathcal{L}$ and a family $z \in \mathcal{F}_y$ to each instance $x \in \mathcal{D}$. The labelled dataset $\mathcal{D}_L$ is built with an iterative active learning strategy. At each iteration, a security expert is asked to annotate, with a label and a family, $b \in \mathbb{N}$ instances selected from the pool of remaining unlabelled instances denoted by $\mathcal{D}_U$. During the annotation process, the expert cannot annotate more instances than the annotation budget $B \in \mathbb{N}$.

*Objective.* The objective of the labelling strategy is to build $\mathcal{D}_L$ maximizing the accuracy of the detection model $\mathcal{M}$ while asking the expert to annotate at most $B$ instances. In other words, the labelling strategy aims to ask the expert to annotate the $B$ instances that maximize the performance of the detection model $\mathcal{M}$. Besides, the labelling strategy must be scalable to work on large datasets while keeping a low expert waiting time.

## 4 ILAB Labelling Strategy

ILAB is an iterative annotation process based on active learning [32] and rare category detection [26]. At each iteration, the expert is asked to annotate $b$ instances to improve the current detection model and to discover yet unknown families. Active learning improves the binary classification model raising the alerts while rare category detection fosters the discovery of new families to avoid sampling bias. First, we describe how we initialize the active learning process and then we explain the labelling strategy, i.e. which instances are selected from the unlabelled pool to be annotated by the expert.

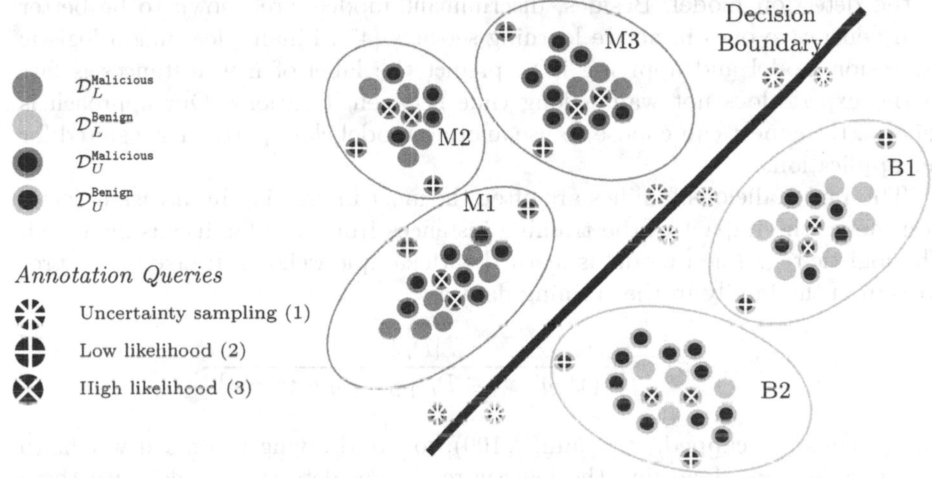


**Fig. 3.** ILAB labelling strategy

*Initial Supervision.* The active learning process needs some initial labelled examples to learn the first supervised detection model. This initial supervision can be difficult to acquire for detection problems. The `Malicious` class is usually too under-represented for uniform random sampling to be effective at collecting a representative labelled dataset.

If a public labelled dataset is available for the detection problem considered, it can be used for the initial supervision. Otherwise, the signatures widely deployed in detection systems can provide `Malicious` examples at low cost, and random sampling can provide `Benign` examples. In both cases, the initial labelled dataset does not contain all the malicious families we want to detect, and it is not representative of the data in the deployment environment. ILAB enriches the initial labelled dataset across the iterations to make it representative of the environment where the detection system is deployed.

The iterations are performed until the annotation budget $B$ has been spent. At each iteration, $b_{\texttt{uncertain}}$ annotation queries are generated with *uncertainty sampling* to improve the detection model and $b_{\texttt{families}} = b - b_{\texttt{uncertain}}$ instances are queried for annotation with *rare category detection* to avoid sampling bias (see Fig. 3).

### 4.1 Uncertainty Sampling

A binary probabilistic detection model $\mathcal{M}$ is learned from the annotated instances in $\mathcal{D}_L$. We use a discriminant linear model, i.e. logistic regression [10]. Linear models are highly valued by computer security experts who do not trust black box detection models [27]. These detection models can be interpreted because the coefficients associated with each feature represent their contribution to the detection model. Besides, discriminant models are known to be better than generative ones in active learning settings [47]. Finally, learning a logistic regression model and applying it to predict the label of new instances is fast so the expert does not wait a long time between iterations. Our approach is generic, the expert can choose to use another model class particularly suited for her application.

The rare malicious families are often the most interesting in intrusion detection, hence the impact of the training instances from rare families is increased. The logistic regression model is learned with sample weights inverse to the proportion of the family in the training dataset:

$$\beta(x, y, z) = \frac{|\mathcal{D}_L|}{|\{(x', y', z') \in \mathcal{D}_L \mid y' = y \wedge z' = z\}|}.$$

The weights are capped, $\hat{\beta} = \min(\beta, 100)$, to avoid giving too much weight to very rare families. Learning the logistic regression detection model with these weights is crucial to ensure a good detection of the rare malicious families.

The model $\mathcal{M}$ is used to compute the probability $p(x)$ that an unlabelled instance $x \in \mathcal{D}_U$ is `Malicious` according to $\mathcal{M}$:

$$\forall x \in \mathcal{D}_U,\ p(x) = P_{\mathcal{M}}(y = \texttt{Malicious} \mid x).$$

*Annotation Queries.* The $b_{\texttt{uncertain}}$ unlabelled instances which are the closest to the decision boundary of $\mathcal{M}$ are annotated by the expert:

$$\underset{x \in \mathcal{D}_U}{\arg\min}\, |p(x) - 1/2|. \tag{1}$$

The detection model is uncertain about the label of these instances, that is why their annotations allow to improve the detection model. This step corresponds to uncertainty sampling [20], a classical active learning method applied in [1]. Uncertainty sampling suffers, however, from sampling bias [29]. We also perform rare category detection to foster the discovery of yet unknown families.

### 4.2 Rare Category Detection

Rare category detection is applied on the instances that are more likely to be `Malicious` and `Benign` (according to the detection model $\mathcal{M}$) separately. Not all families are present in the initial labelled dataset and rare category detection [26] fosters the discovery of yet unknown families to avoid sampling bias. One might think that we could run rare category detection only on the malicious instances since it is the class of interest in intrusion detection. However, a whole malicious family may be on the wrong side of the decision boundary (see the family $M_1$ in Fig. 2), and thus, running rare category detection on the predicted benign instances is necessary. Hereafter, we only detail the rare category detection run on the `Malicious` predictions since the analysis of the `Benign` ones is performed similarly.

Let $\mathcal{D}_U^{\texttt{Malicious}}$ be the set of instances whose predicted label by $\mathcal{M}$ is `Malicious` and $\mathcal{D}_L^{\texttt{Malicious}}$ be the set of malicious instances already annotated by the expert. First, a multi-class logistic regression model is learned from the families specified in $\mathcal{D}_L^{\texttt{Malicious}}$ to predict the family of the instances in $\mathcal{D}_U^{\texttt{Malicious}}$. Let $\mathcal{C}_f$ be the set of instances from $\mathcal{D}_L^{\texttt{Malicious}} \cup \mathcal{D}_U^{\texttt{Malicious}}$ whose family (annotated or predicted) is $f$. Each family $f$ is modelled with a Gaussian distribution $\mathcal{N}(\mu_f, \Sigma_f)$ depicted by an ellipsoid in Fig. 3. The mean $\mu_f$ and the diagonal covariance matrix $\Sigma_f$ are learned with Gaussian Naive Bayes [10]. We denote by $p_{\mathcal{N}(\mu_f,\Sigma_f)}(x)$ the probability that $x$ follows the Gaussian distribution $\mathcal{N}(\mu_f, \Sigma_f)$.

*Annotation Queries.* The family annotation budget $b_{\texttt{families}}$ is evenly distributed among the different families. We now explain which unlabelled instances are queried for annotation from each family.

First, ILAB asks the expert to annotate instances that are likely to belong to a yet unknown family to avoid sampling bias. These instances are located at the edge of the ellipsoid, they have a low likelihood of belonging to the family $f$ [26,40]:

$$\underset{x \in \mathcal{C}_f \setminus \mathcal{D}_L^{\texttt{Malicious}}}{\arg\min} \quad p_{\mathcal{N}(\mu_f,\Sigma_f)}(x). \tag{2}$$

Then, ILAB queries representative examples of each family for annotation. These instances are close to the centre of the ellipsoid, they have a high likelihood of belonging to the family $f$:

$$\underset{x \in \mathcal{C}_f \setminus \mathcal{D}_L^{\texttt{Malicious}}}{\arg\max} \quad p_{\mathcal{N}(\mu_f,\Sigma_f)}(x). \tag{3}$$

Half the budget is allocated to low likelihood instances, and the other half to high likelihood instances. Low likelihood instances are likely to belong to yet unknown families that is why these annotation queries foster the discovery of new families. They are, however, more likely to be outliers that may impair the detection model performance. ILAB also asks the expert to annotate high likelihood instances to get more representative examples of the families in the labelled dataset for a better generalization of the detection model.

## 5 Comparison with State of the Art Labelling Strategies

### 5.1 Datasets

Labelling strategies are generic methods that can be applied to any detection problem once the features have been extracted. We consider a system and a network detection problem: (1) detection of malicious PDF files with the dataset Contagio[1], and (2) network intrusion detection with the dataset NSL-KDD[2]. These datasets cannot be used to train a model intended for production as they are non-representative of real-world data. However, our comparisons are relevant as we are not comparing attack detection models but labelling strategies in order to train attack detection models on new problems.

Contagio is a public dataset composed of 11,101 malicious and 9,000 benign PDF files. We transform each PDF file into 113 numerical features similar to the ones proposed by Smutz and Stavrou [35,36].

NSL-KDD contains 58,630 malicious and 67,343 benign instances. Each instance represents a connection on a network and is described by 7 categorical features and 34 numerical features. The 7 categorical features (e.g. `protocol_type` with the possible values `tcp`, `udp` or `icmp`) are encoded into several binary features corresponding to each value (e.g. `tcp` $\rightarrow [1, 0, 0]$, `udp` $\rightarrow [0, 1, 0]$, `icmp` $\rightarrow [0, 0, 1]$). We end up with 122 features.

**Table 1.** Description of the public datasets

| *Dataset* | #instances | #features | #malicious families | #benign families |
|---|---|---|---|---|
| Contagio_10% | 10,000 | 113 | 16 | 30 |
| NSL-KDD_10% | 74,826 | 122 | 19 | 15 |

The malicious instances in NSL-KDD are annotated with a family but the benign ones are not, and Contagio does not provide any family information. The families are, however, required to run simulations with Aladin and ILAB, and to assess the sampling bias of the different labelling strategies. We have assigned families to the remaining instances with a $k$-means clustering and the number of families $k$ has been selected visually with the silhouette coefficient [28].

Neither dataset has a proportion of malicious instances representative of a typical network (55% for Contagio and 47% for NSL-KDD). We have uniformly sub-sampled the malicious class to get 10% of malicious instances. Table 1 describes the resulting datasets: Contagio_10% and NSL-KDD_10%.

[1] http://contagiodump.blogspot.fr/.

[2] http://www.unb.ca/cic/research/datasets/nsl.html.

### 5.2 Labelling Strategies

We compare ILAB with uncertainty sampling [20], Aladin [40], and Görnitz et al. labelling method [14]. Since there is no open source implementation of these labelling strategies, we have implemented them in Python with the machine learning library scikit-learn [25]. All the implementations are released to ease comparison in future research works. We briefly present each labelling strategy, we provide some details about our implementations and how we set the additional parameters if relevant.

*Uncertainty Sampling* [20]. At each iteration, a binary logistic regression model is trained on the labelled instances, and the expert is asked to annotate the $b$ most uncertain predictions, i.e. the closest to the decision boundary. Uncertainty sampling has no additional parameter.

*Görnitz et al. labelling strategy* [14]. At each iteration, a semi-supervised anomaly detection model is trained on both the labelled and the unlabelled instances. The model relies on an adaptation of an unsupervised anomaly detection model, Support Vector Data Description (SVDD) [42], that takes into account labelled instances. It consists in a sphere defined by a centre $c \in \mathbb{R}^m$ and a radius $r \in \mathbb{R}$: the instances inside are considered benign, and the ones outside malicious. The labelling strategy queries instances that are both close to the decision boundary and have few malicious neighbours to foster the discovery of new malicious families. The nearest neighbours are computed with the Euclidean distance with the scikit-learn ball tree implementation [23] that is effective with a large number of instances in high dimension.

Semi-supervised SVDD has no open source implementation, so we have implemented it for our experiments with the information provided in [12–14]. The parameters $c$, $r$, and the margin $\gamma \in \mathbb{R}$ are determined with the quasi-Newton optimization method BFGS [46] available in scipy [17]. The optimization algorithm requires initial values for $c$, $r$, and $\gamma$ that are not specified in the papers. We initialize $c$ with the mean of the unlabelled and benign instances, $r$ with the average distance of the unlabelled and benign instances to the centre $c$, and $\gamma$ with the default value 1. Moreover, the detection model has three parameters: $\eta_U \in \mathbb{R}$ and $\eta_L \in \mathbb{R}$, the weights of the unlabelled and labelled instances, and $\kappa$ the weight of the margin $\gamma$. The authors provide no information about how to set these parameters. When we set them to the default value 1, numerical instabilities prevent the optimization algorithm from converging properly, and lead to an extremely high execution time and very poor performance (more than 2 hours for training the model on Contagio_10% to get an AUC below 93%). We have thus worked on the setting of these parameters. We have set $\eta_U$ and $\eta_L$ to the inverse of the number of unlabelled and labelled instances, to give as much weight to unlabelled and labelled instances, and to ensure numerical stability. The detection model is trained without any kernel as in the experiments presented in [12–14].

Finally, the labelling strategy requires to set two additional parameters: $k \in \mathbb{N}$ the number of neighbours considered, and $\delta \in [0, 1]$ the trade-off between querying instances close to the decision boundary and instances with few malicious neighbours. We use $k = 10$ as in [14] and the default value $\delta = 0.5$.

*Aladin* [40]. Aladin runs rare category detection on all the data. It asks the expert to annotate uncertain instances lying between two families to refine the decision boundaries, and low likelihood instances to discover yet unknown families. Aladin does not have additional parameters.

This labelling strategy relies on a multi-class logistic regression model and a multi-class Gaussian Naive Bayes model. The logistic regression parameters are selected automatically with a grid search 4-fold cross validation optimizing the AUC [16]. The penalty norm is either $\ell_1$ or $\ell_2$ and the regularization strength is selected among the values $\{0.01, 0.1, 1, 10, 100\}$. The Gaussian Naive Bayes model is trained without any prior.

*ILAB.* ILAB labelling strategy has only an additional parameter: $b_{\texttt{uncertain}}$. It is set to 10% of the number of annotations performed at each iteration, i.e. $b_{\texttt{uncertain}} = 10$ in our case. Some instances near the decision boundary are annotated to help the detection model make a decision about these instances, but not too many since these instances are often harder to annotate for the expert [3,15,33] and they may lead to a sampling bias [29].

The logistic regression and Gaussian Naive Bayes models are trained the same way as for Aladin.

### 5.3 Results

The datasets Contagio_10% and NSL-KDD_10% are split uniformly into two datasets: (1) an active learning dataset (90%) used as a pool to build the labelled dataset $\mathcal{D}_L$, and (2) a validation dataset (10%) to assess the performance of the detection model trained on $\mathcal{D}_L$. The different labelling strategies are compared with simulations where the annotation queries are answered by an oracle providing the ground truth labels and families.

All the strategies are run with $b = 100$ annotations at each iteration. The annotation budget is set to $B = 1000$ for Contagio_10%, and to $B = 2000$ for NSL-KDD_10% as this dataset contains more instances. The initial labelled datasets are composed of instances belonging to the most represented families: 7 malicious instances and 13 benign instances.

All the experiments are run on Linux 3.16 on a dual-socket computer with 64Go RAM. Processors are Intel Xeon E5-5620 CPUs clocked at 2.40 GHz with 4 cores each and 2 threads per core. Each labelling strategy is run 15 times and we report the average performance with the 95% confidence interval.

First, we compare the number of known families across the iterations to assess sampling bias (see Fig. 4a). Then, we compare the performance of the detection models on the validation dataset (see Fig. 4b). Finally, we monitor the execution time of the query generation algorithms to evaluate the expert waiting time between iterations (see Fig. 4c).

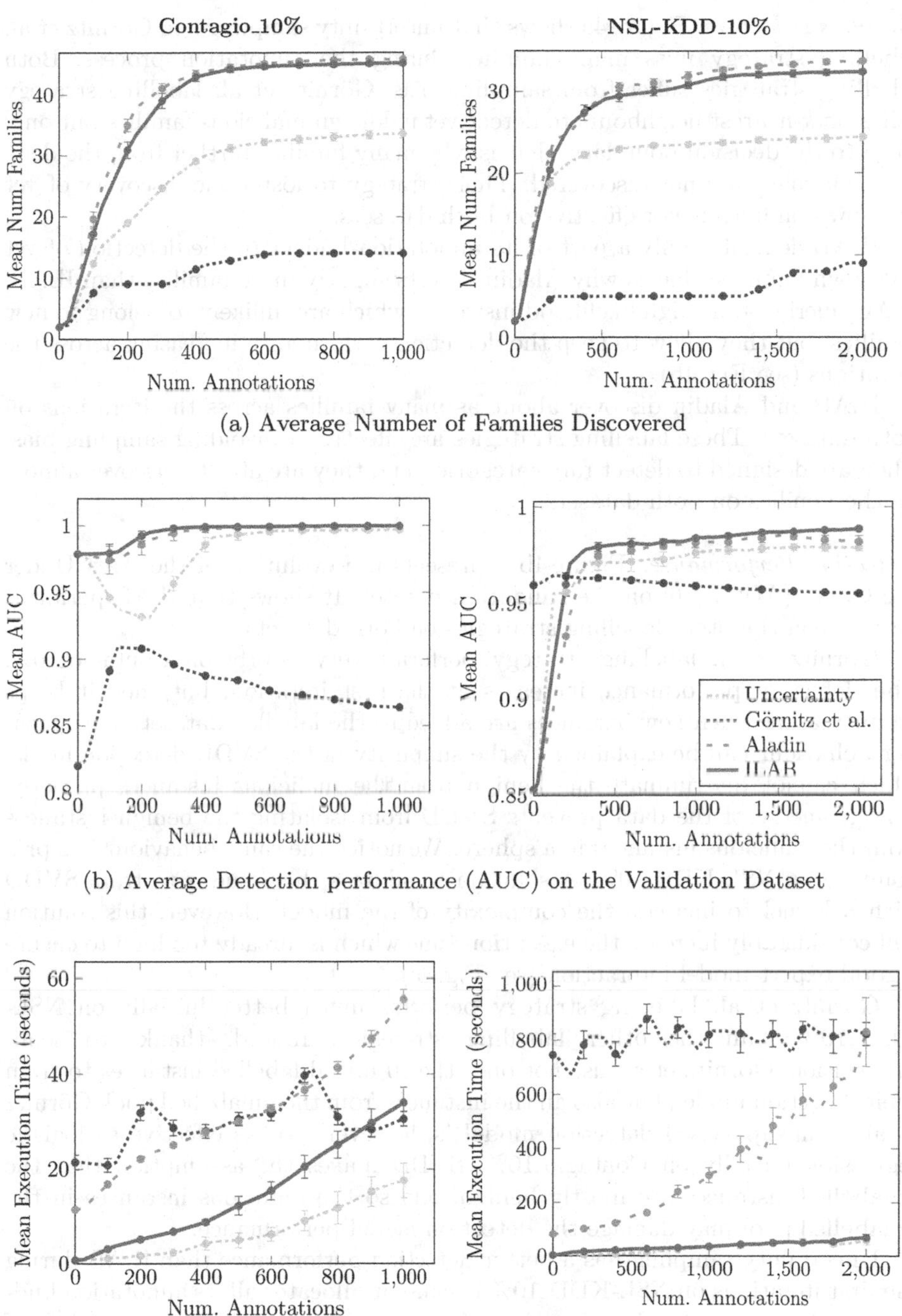


(a) Average Number of Families Discovered

(b) Average Detection performance (AUC) on the Validation Dataset

(c) Average Annotation Queries Generation Execution Time

**Fig. 4.** Comparison of the labelling strategies Contagio_10% (on the left) and NSL-KDD_10% (on the right)

*Families Detection.* Figure 4a shows that uncertainty sampling and Görnitz et al. labelling strategy miss many families during the annotation process. Both labelling strategies suffer from sampling bias. Görnitz et al. labelling strategy relies on $k$-nearest neighbours to detect yet unknown malicious families but only close to the decision boundary, that is why many families further from the decision boundary are not discovered. Their strategy to foster the discovery of yet unknown families is not effective on both datasets.

ILAB dedicates only a part of its annotation budget to the detection of yet unknown families, that is why Aladin detects slightly more families than ILAB. ILAB queries some high likelihood instances which are unlikely to belong to new families, but they allow to keep the detection performance increasing across the iterations (see Fig. 4b).

ILAB and Aladin discover about as many families across the iterations on both datasets. These labelling strategies are effective at avoiding sampling bias. They are designed to detect rare categories, and they are able to discover almost all the families on both datasets.

*Detection Performance.* Figure 4b represents the evolution of the Area Under the Curve (AUC) [16] on the validation dataset. It shows that ILAB performs better than the other labelling strategies on both datasets.

Görnitz et al. labelling strategy performs very poorly on Contagio_10%. The detection performance increases at the first iteration, but then it keeps on decreasing when new instances are added to the labelled dataset. This peculiar behaviour can be explained by the simplicity of the SVDD detection model which cannot discriminate the benign from the malicious instances properly. The geometry of the data prevents SVDD from isolating the benign instances from the malicious instances in a sphere. We notice the same behaviour less pronounced on NSL-KDD_10%. A solution to address this issue is to train SVDD with a kernel to increase the complexity of the model. However, this solution will considerably increase the execution time which is already too high to ensure a good expert-model interaction (see Fig. 4c).

Görnitz et al. labelling strategy performs much better initially on NSL-KDD_10% than the other labelling strategies. Indeed, thanks to semi-supervision, Görnitz et al. use not only the 20 initial labelled instances to train their detection model, but also all the instances from the unlabelled pool. Görnitz et al. semi-supervised detection model is, however, not as effective as logistic regression initially on Contagio_10%. SVDD makes the assumption that the unlabelled instances are mostly benign, and so the malicious instances in the unlabelled pool may damage the detection model performance.

Uncertainty sampling has a better detection performance than ILAB during the first iterations on NSL-KDD_10% because it allocates all its annotation budget to refining the decision boundary. On the contrary, ILAB dedicates 90% of its annotation budget to rare category detection to avoid sampling bias. In the end, uncertainty sampling suffers from sampling bias and converges to a poorer performance.

The detection performance of uncertainty sampling and Aladin decreases during the first iterations on Contagio_10%. This undesirable behaviour is caused by sampling bias: non-representative instances are queried for annotation, added to the training dataset and prevent the detection model from generalizing properly. Uncertainty sampling queries instances close to the decision boundary that are hard to classify for the detection model, but not representative of the malicious or benign behaviours. Aladin queries only uncertain and low likelihood instances which are not necessarily representative of the malicious and benign behaviours either. ILAB addresses this problem by dedicating a part of its annotation budget to high likelihood instances to get representative examples of each family. Therefore, the detection performance keeps on increasing across the iterations.

*Scalability.* Figure 4c depicts the query generation execution time (in seconds) across the iterations. Görnitz et al. query generation algorithm is very slow. For NSL-KDD_10%, the expert waits more than 10 min between each iteration while the labelling strategy computes the annotation queries. A third of the execution time corresponds to the computation of the semi-supervised SVDD model, and the remaining two thirds corresponds to the $k$-nearest neighbour algorithm. The execution time of Görnitz et al. labelling strategy is thus too high to ensure a good expert-model interaction even on a dataset containing fewer than 100,000 instances.

ILAB has an execution time comparable to uncertainty sampling. For NSL-KDD_10%, the expert waits less than 1 min between each iteration. On the contrary, Aladin execution time increases drastically when new instances are added to the labelled dataset and new families are discovered. Aladin runs rare category detection on all the instances, while ILAB runs it on the malicious and the benign instances separately. ILAB divide and conquer approach reduces the execution time as running rare category detection twice on smaller datasets with fewer families is faster than running it on the whole dataset. Aladin's authors were aware of this high execution time. During their experiments, the expert was asked to annotate 1000 instances each day, and the new annotation queries were computed every night. Their solution reduces the expert waiting time, but it significantly damages the expert-model interaction since the expert feedback is integrated only once a day.

In conclusion, uncertainty sampling and Görnitz et al. labelling strategy suffer from sampling bias. Aladin and ILAB are the only labelling strategies able to avoid sampling bias thanks to rare category detection performed at the family level (see Fig. 4a). ILAB main advantage over Aladin is its divide and conquer approach that significantly reduces the execution time (see Fig. 4c) and thus improves the expert-model interaction. Our comparisons show that ILAB is both an effective and a scalable labelling strategy that can be set up on real-world annotation projects.

## 6 Real-World Annotation Project on NetFlow Data

In this section, we deploy ILAB on a large unlabelled NetFlow dataset originating from a production environment.

*NetFlow.* As stated in [5]: "NetFlow is a network protocol proposed and implemented by Cisco [6] for summarizing network traffic as a collection of network flows. A flow is defined as a unidirectional sequence of packets that share specific network properties (e.g. IP source/destination addresses, and TCP or UDP source/destination ports)." Each flow is described by attributes and summary statistics: source and destination IP addresses, source and destination ports, protocol (TCP, UDP, ICMP, ESP, etc.), start and end time stamps, number of bytes, number of packets, and aggregation of the TCP flags for TCP flows.

*Dataset and Features.* The flows are recorded at the border of a defended network. We compute features describing each external IP address communicating with the defended network. from its flows during a given time window. We compute the mean and the variance of the number of bytes and packets sent and received at different levels: globally, for some specific port numbers (80, 443, 53 and 25), and for some specific TCP flags aggregates (`....S`, `.A..S.`, `.AP.SF`, etc.). Besides, we compute other aggregated values: number of contacted IP addresses and ports, number of ports used, entropy according to the contacted IP addresses and according to the contacted ports. In the end, each external IP address is described by 134 features computed from its list of flows.

**Table 2.** NetFlow dataset

| | |
|---|---|
| Num. flows | $1.2 \cdot 10^8$ |
| Num. IP addresses | 463, 913 |
| Num. features | 134 |
| Num. TRW alerts | 70 |

The NetFlow data is recorded during a working day in 2016. The features are computed for each external IP address with a 24-hour time window. The NetFlow dataset is large: it is composed of 463,913 IP addresses represented by 134 real-valued features (see Table 2). A second dataset has been recorded the following day for the validation of the resulting detection model. The results are, however, not reported due to space constraints since the main focus is the deployment of the labelling strategy in an annotation project.

*ILAB Graphical User Interface.* A security expert answers ILAB annotation queries from the graphical user interface depicted in Fig. 5. The top buttons allow the expert to select a type of annotation queries: *Uncertain* for the instances near the decision boundary, *Malicious* and *Benign* for the annotation queries generated by rare category detection. The panel below allows to go through the annotation queries corresponding to each family.

By default, each instance is described only by its features which may be hard to interpret, especially when they are in high dimension. A custom visualization which may point to external tools or information can be displayed to ease the

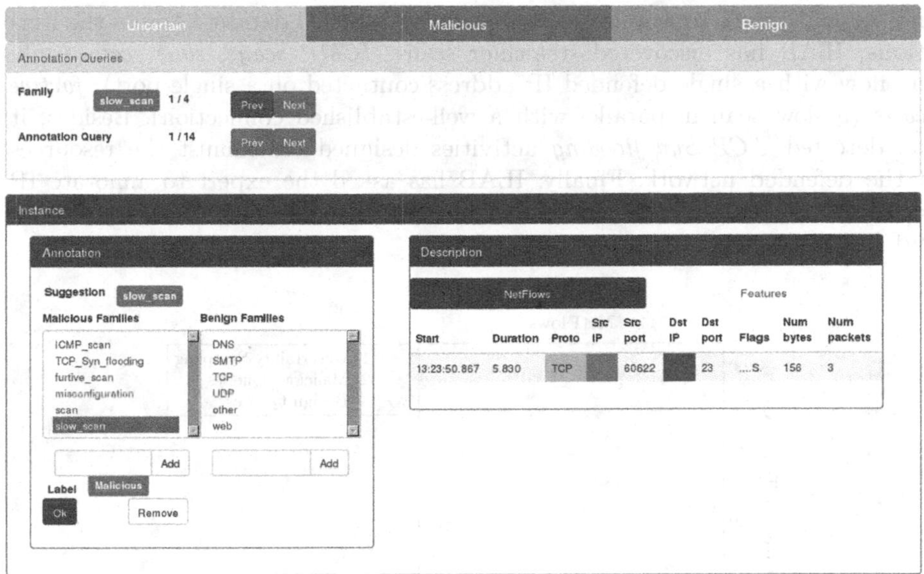


**Fig. 5.** ILAB graphical user interface for annotating

annotations. Figure 5 depicts the custom visualization we have implemented for NetFlow data[3].

Finally, the expert can annotate the selected instance with the *Annotation* panel. For each label, it displays the list of the families already discovered. The expert can pick a family among a list or add a new family. The interface suggests a family for high likelihood queries and pre-selects it. It helps the expert since the model is confident about these predictions. On the contrary, there is no suggestion for the uncertainty sampling and the low likelihood queries. The model is indeed uncertain about the family of these instances and unreliable suggestions may mislead the expert [3].

*ILAB in Practice.* First, we need some labelled instances to initialize the active learning process. The alerts raised by the Threshold Random Walk (TRW) [18] module of Bro [24] provide the initial anomalous examples and the normal examples are drawn randomly. The initial labelled dataset is composed of 70 *obvious scans* detected by TRW, and of 70 normal examples belonging to the *Web*, *SMTP* and *DNS* families. Malicious activities in well-established connections cannot be detected without the payload, which is not available in NetFlow data, that is why we consider the families *Web*, *SMTP* and *DNS* to be normal. All the initial labels are checked individually by the expert to avoid poisoning the model.

This initial labelled dataset is not representative of all the anomalous behaviours we want to detect. We run ILAB with the parameters $B = 1000$, $b = 100$

[3] The IP addresses have been hidden for privacy reasons.

and $b_{\texttt{uncertain}} = 10$ to acquire a representative labelled dataset. Across the iterations, ILAB has discovered stealthier scans: *ICMP scans*, *slow scans* (only one flow with a single defended IP address contacted on a single port), *furtive scans* (a slow scan in parallel with a well-established connection). Besides, it has detected *TCP Syn flooding* activities designed to exhaust the resources of the defended network. Finally, ILAB has asked the expert to annotate IP addresses with anomalous behaviours which are not malicious: *misconfigurations* and *backscatters*.

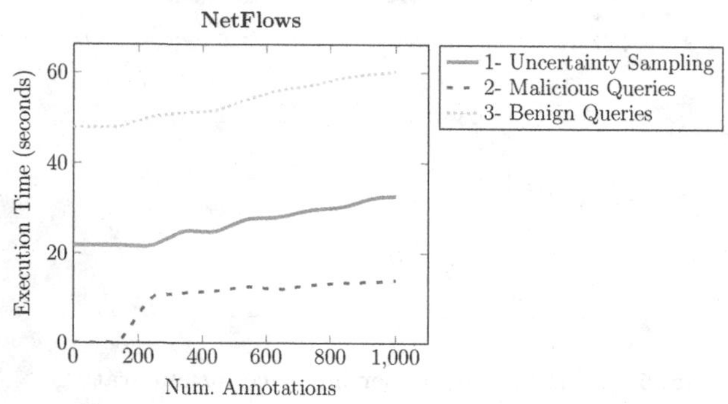


**Fig. 6.** ILAB execution time

*Low Expert Waiting Time.* ILAB divide and conquer approach allows the expert to annotate some instances while the labelling strategy is still computing annotation queries. First, the binary detection model is trained and the uncertainty sampling queries are computed. The binary detection model is indeed required to predict the label of the unlabelled instances to run rare category detection afterwards. Then, rare category detection is performed on the malicious predictions while the expert annotates the uncertain instances. Finally, rare category detection is computed on the benign predictions while the expert annotates the malicious annotation queries. The malicious predictions are analysed before the benign ones, because their number is smaller, so the analysis is faster (see Fig. 6).

In practice, running rare category detection takes less time than the annotations. As a result, the expert must only wait while the uncertain queries are computed (see the orange curve *Uncertainty Sampling* in Fig. 6). During the NetFlow annotation project the expert has waited less than 40 s at each iteration. ILAB low computation cost ensures a good expert-model interaction: the detection model is updated frequently with expert feedback without inducing long waiting-periods.

*Families Benefits.* ILAB and Aladin deal with the sampling bias problem thanks to rare category detection performed at the family level. At first glance, this solution may seem to increase the annotation cost as it requires experts to provide a more precise information than a binary label. However, asking experts to provide a family does not increase the annotation cost in practice: experts place instances in "mental bins" corresponding to families to provide a label [26]. Experts must understand the type of the instance to provide a label, and, therefore, assigning a family does not require an additional effort.

Besides, the clustering of the annotation queries according to families (see Fig. 5) decreases the average annotation cost. Families provide a context that helps the expert answer the queries. Annotation queries related to the same family are likely to share the same label and family, and thus, it reduces the amount of context switching during the annotation process. On the contrary, uncertainty sampling and Görnitz et al. labelling strategy ask the expert to annotate a list of unrelated instances without any context.

Finally, an alert raised by a supervised detection model can be hard to interpret for the security expert. This issue called semantic gap by Sommer et al. [38] is due to the binary output (`Malicious` or `Benign`) of the detection model. The families acquired with ILAB can bridge the semantic gap by enriching the alerts with a malicious family to help the expert supervising the detection system take the necessary actions.

## 7 Conclusion

We introduce ILAB a novel interactive labelling strategy that streamlines annotation projects. It relies on active learning and rare category detection to avoid sampling bias. We demonstrate that ILAB offers a better scalability than two state of the art labelling strategies [14,40] without damaging the effectiveness. Up to our knowledge, [14,40] had never been compared. We provide open source implementations to foster comparison in future research works.

ILAB divide and conquer approach reduces the computation cost, and allows the expert to annotate some instances while the labelling strategy is still computing annotation queries. Thus, ILAB provides a good expert-model interaction: the detection model is updated frequently with expert feedback without inducing long waiting-periods.

The NetFlow annotation project shows that ILAB is a workable labelling strategy that can be applied to a large dataset originating from a production environment. ILAB is a generic labelling strategy that can be applied to other detection problems once the feature extraction task has been performed. It is designed for security experts who deploy intrusion detection systems, and we provide an open source implementation of the graphical user interface to allow them to label their own datasets. For future work, we plan to run broader experiments with independent computer security experts to assess ILAB from an end-user's point of view and to improve its usability from their feedback.

## References

1. Almgren, M., Jonsson, E.: Using active learning in intrusion detection. In: CSFW, pp. 88–98 (2004)
2. Antonakakis, M., Perdisci, R., Nadji, Y., Vasiloglou, N., Abu-Nimeh, S., Lee, W., Dagon, D.: From throw-away traffic to bots: detecting the rise of DGA-based malware. In: USENIX Security, pp. 491–506 (2012)
3. Baldridge, J., Palmer, A.: How well does active learning actually work?: Time-based evaluation of cost-reduction strategies for language documentation. In: EMNLP, pp. 296–305 (2009)
4. Berlin, K., Slater, D., Saxe, J.: Malicious behavior detection using windows audit logs. In: AISEC, pp. 35–44 (2015)
5. Bilge, L., Balzarotti, D., Robertson, W., Kirda, E., Kruegel, C.: Disclosure: detecting botnet command and control servers through large-scale netflow analysis. In: ACSAC, pp. 129–138 (2012)
6. Claise, B.: Cisco systems netflow services export version 9 (2004)
7. Corona, I., Maiorca, D., Ariu, D., Giacinto, G.: Lux0r: detection of malicious PDF-embedded JavaScript code through discriminant analysis of API references. In: AISEC, pp. 47–57 (2014)
8. Dasgupta, S., Hsu, D.: Hierarchical sampling for active learning. In: ICML, pp. 208–215 (2008)
9. Druck, G., Settles, B., McCallum, A.: Active learning by labeling features. In: EMNLP, pp. 81–90 (2009)
10. Friedman, J., Hastie, T., Tibshirani, R.: The Elements of Statistical Learning. Springer Series in Statistics, vol. 1. Springer, Berlin (2001). doi:10.1007/978-0-387-21606-5
11. Gascon, H., Yamaguchi, F., Arp, D., Rieck, K.: Structural detection of android malware using embedded call graphs. In: AISEC, pp. 45–54 (2013)
12. Görnitz, N., Kloft, M., Brefeld, U.: Active and semi-supervised data domain description. In: ECML-PKDD, pp. 407–422 (2009)
13. Görnitz, N., Kloft, M., Rieck, K., Brefeld, U.: Active learning for network intrusion detection. In: AISEC, pp. 47–54 (2009)
14. Görnitz, N., Kloft, M.M., Rieck, K., Brefeld, U.: Toward supervised anomaly detection. JAIR **46**, 235–262 (2013)
15. Hachey, B., Alex, B., Becker, M.: Investigating the effects of selective sampling on the annotation task. In: CoNLL, pp. 144–151 (2005)
16. Hanley, J.A., McNeil, B.J.: The meaning and use of the area under a receiver operating characteristic (ROC) curve. Radiology **143**(1), 29–36 (1982)
17. Jones, E., Oliphant, T., Peterson, P.: SciPy: open source scientific tools for Python (2001). http://www.scipy.org/
18. Jung, J., Paxson, V., Berger, A.W., Balakrishnan, H.: Fast portscan detection using sequential hypothesis testing. In: S&P, pp. 211–225 (2004)
19. Khasawneh, K.N., Ozsoy, M., Donovick, C., Abu-Ghazaleh, N., Ponomarev, D.: Ensemble learning for low-level hardware-supported malware detection. In: Bos, H., Monrose, F., Blanc, G. (eds.) RAID 2015. LNCS, vol. 9404, pp. 3–25. Springer, Cham (2015). doi:10.1007/978-3-319-26362-5_1
20. Lewis, D.D., Gale, W.A.: A sequential algorithm for training text classifiers. In: SIGIR, pp. 3–12 (1994)
21. Miller, B., Kantchelian, A., Afroz, S., Bachwani, R., Dauber, E., Huang, L., Tschantz, M.C., Joseph, A.D., Tygar, J.: Adversarial active learning. In: AISEC, pp. 3–14 (2014)

22. Nappa, A., Rafique, M.Z., Caballero, J.: The MALICIA dataset: identification and analysis of drive-by download operations. IJIS **14**(1), 15–33 (2015)
23. Omohundro, S.M.: Five Balltree Construction Algorithms. International Computer Science Institute, Berkeley (1989)
24. Paxson, V.: Bro: a system for detecting network intruders in real-time. Comput. Netw. **31**(23), 2435–2463 (1999)
25. Pedregosa, F., Varoquaux, G., Gramfort, A., Michel, V., Thirion, B., Grisel, O., Blondel, M., Prettenhofer, P., Weiss, R., Dubourg, V., Vanderplas, J., Passos, A., Cournapeau, D., Brucher, M., Perrot, M., Duchesnay, E.: Scikit-learn: machine learning in Python. JMLR **12**, 2825–2830 (2011)
26. Pelleg, D., Moore, A.W.: Active learning for anomaly and rare-category detection. In: NIPS, pp. 1073–1080 (2004)
27. Rieck, K.: Computer security and machine learning: worst enemies or best friends? In: SysSec, pp. 107–110 (2011)
28. Rousseeuw, P.J.: Silhouettes: a graphical aid to the interpretation and validation of cluster analysis. J. Comput. Appl. Math. **20**, 53–65 (1987)
29. Schütze, H., Velipasaoglu, E., Pedersen, J.O.: Performance thresholding in practical text classification. In: CIKM, pp. 662–671 (2006)
30. Sculley, D.: Online active learning methods for fast label-efficient spam filtering. In: CEAS, pp. 1–4 (2007)
31. Sculley, D., Otey, M.E., Pohl, M., Spitznagel, B., Hainsworth, J., Zhou, Y.: Detecting adversarial advertisements in the wild. In: KDD, pp. 274–282 (2011)
32. Settles, B.: Active learning literature survey. Univ. Wisconsin Madison **52**(55–66), 11 (2010)
33. Settles, B.: From theories to queries: active learning in practice. JMLR **16**, 1–18 (2011)
34. Settles, B.: Active learning. Synth. Lect. Artif. Intell. Mach. Learn. **6**(1), 1–114 (2012)
35. Smutz, C., Stavrou, A.: Malicious PDF detection using metadata and structural features. In: ACSAC, pp. 239–248 (2012)
36. Smutz, C., Stavrou, A.: Malicious PDF detection using metadata and structural features. In: Technical report. George Mason University (2012)
37. Snow, R., O'Connor, B., Jurafsky, D., Ng, A.Y.: Cheap and fast–but is it good?: Evaluating non-expert annotations for natural language tasks. In: EMNLP. pp. 254–263 (2008)
38. Sommer, R., Paxson, V.: Outside the closed world: On using machine learning for network intrusion detection. In: S&P, pp. 305–316 (2010)
39. Song, J., Takakura, H., Okabe, Y., Eto, M., Inoue, D., Nakao, K.: Statistical analysis of honeypot data and building of kyoto 2006+ dataset for NIDS evaluation. In: BADGERS, pp. 29–36 (2011)
40. Stokes, J.W., Platt, J.C., Kravis, J., Shilman, M.: Aladin: active learning of anomalies to detect intrusions. Technical report. Microsoft Network Security Redmond, WA (2008)
41. Tavallaee, M., Bagheri, E., Lu, W., Ghorbani, A.A.: A detailed analysis of the KDD CUP 99 data set. In: CISDA (2009)
42. Tax, D.M., Duin, R.P.: Support vector data description. Mach. Learn. **54**(1), 45–66 (2004)
43. Tomanek, K., Olsson, F.: A web survey on the use of active learning to support annotation of text data. In: ALNLP, pp. 45–48 (2009)
44. Veeramachaneni, K., Arnaldo, I.: AI2: training a big data machine to defend. In: DataSec, pp. 49–54 (2016)

45. Whittaker, C., Ryner, B., Nazif, M.: Large-scale automatic classification of phishing pages. In: NDSS, vol. 10 (2010)
46. Wright, S., Nocedal, J.: Numerical optimization. Springer Sci. **35**, 67–68 (1999)
47. Zhang, T., Oles, F.: The value of unlabeled data for classification problems. In: ICML, pp. 1191–1198 (2000)

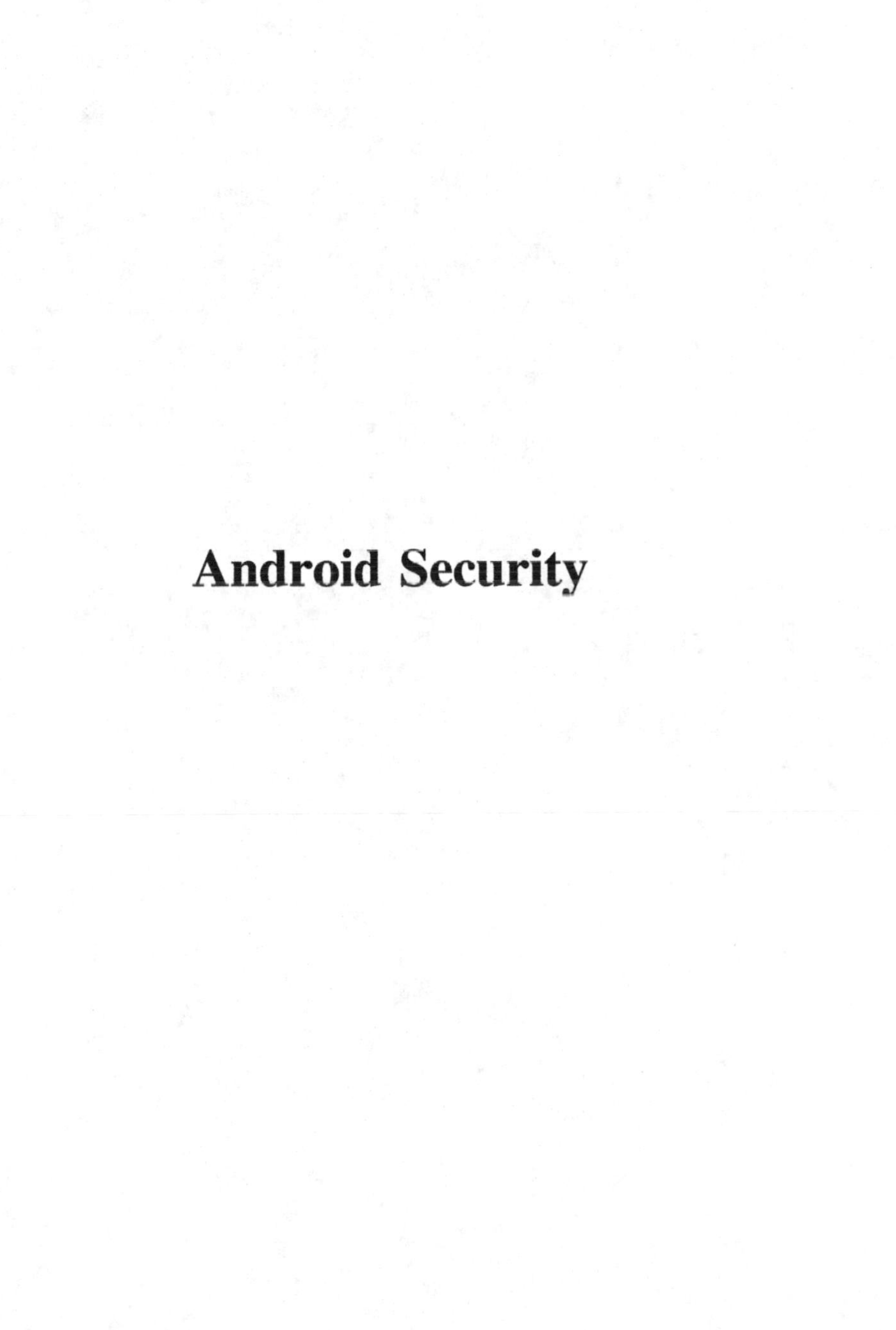

# Android Security

# Precisely and Scalably Vetting JavaScript Bridge in Android Hybrid Apps

Guangliang Yang(✉), Abner Mendoza, Jialong Zhang, and Guofei Gu

SUCCESS LAB, Texas A&M University, College Station, USA
{ygl,abmendoza}@tamu.edu, {jialong,guofei}@cse.tamu.edu

**Abstract.** In this paper, we propose a novel system, named BridgeScope, for precise and scalable vetting of JavaScript Bridge security issues in Android hybrid apps. BridgeScope is flexible and can be leveraged to analyze a diverse set of WebView implementations, such as Android's default WebView, and Mozilla's Rhino-based WebView. Furthermore, BridgeScope can automatically generate test exploit code to further confirm any discovered JavaScript Bridge vulnerability.

We evaluated BridgeScope to demonstrate that it is precise and effective in finding JavaScript Bridge vulnerabilities. On average, it can vet an app within seven seconds with a low false positive rate. A large scale evaluation identified hundreds of potentially vulnerable real-world popular apps that could lead to critical exploitation. Furthermore, we also demonstrate that BridgeScope can discover malicious functionalities that leverage JavaScript Bridge in real-world malicious apps, even when the associated malicious severs were unavailable.

**Keywords:** Android security · WebView security · Javascript Bridge

## 1 Introduction

Android apps (i.e., hybrid apps) increasingly integrate the embedded web browser component, "WebView", to render web pages and run JavaScript code within the app for seamless user experience. App developers can select from a variety of WebView implementations, such as Android's default WebView[1], Mozilla's rhino-based WebView[2], Intel's XWalkView[3], and Chromeview[4].

The power of WebView extends beyond the basic browser-like functionality by enabling rich interactions between web (e.g., JavaScript) and native (e.g., Java for Android) code within an app through a special interface known as

[1] https://developer.android.com/reference/android/webkit/WebView.html.
[2] https://developer.mozilla.org/en-US/docs/Mozilla/Projects/Rhino.
[3] https://crosswalk-project.org/.
[4] https://github.com/pwnall/chromeview.

**Electronic supplementary material** The online version of this chapter (doi:10.1007/978-3-319-66332-6_7) contains supplementary material, which is available to authorized users.


M. Dacier et al. (Eds.): RAID 2017, LNCS 10453, pp. 143–166, 2017.
DOI: 10.1007/978-3-319-66332-6_7

a *"JavaScript Bridge"* [8,14,22,23,26,27,31,32]. The JavaScript Bridge feature eases the development of hybrid apps. However, it also introduces critical security risks, such as sensitive information leakage, and local resource access (Sect. 2.2). Recent research work [8,14,22,23] has highlighted the problems rooted in the use of JavaScript Bridge. However, an automated and fine-grained solution that can precisely and scalably detect JavaScript Bridge security issues is still missing.

In this paper, we present a precise and scalable static detection framework named *"BridgeScope"*. BridgeScope can automatically vet JavaScript Bridge usage in Android hybrid apps, and generate test exploit code to validate problematic JavaScript Bridge usage. Our approach is four-fold. First, BridgeScope fills the semantic gap between different core WebView implementations using a generalized WebView model. Second, using the generalized code, BridgeScope is able to precisely discover all available WebView components and bridges in an app. Third, BridgeScope reconstructs the semantic information of all JavaScript Bridges and identifies the *sensitive bridges* that contain data flows to sensitive API invocations (such as *getLastLoction()*). Finally, BridgeScope generates test exploit code using the analysis results (such as the UI event sequences to trigger WebView components and data flow inside sensitive bridges).

To achieve high precision and scalability, BridgeScope applies fine-grained type, taint, and value analysis, which is implemented based using a novel *"shadowbox"* data structure. We refer to our analysis technique as "shadowbox analysis". Compared with state-of-the-art static approaches such as data flow tracking [4,33], shadowbox analysis is path- and value-sensitive, while preserving precision and scalability. We evaluated our *shadowbox* analysis technique using a generic benchmark (DroidBench[5]), and found that it achieved 94% precision.

Finally, we evaluated BridgeScope with 13,000 of the most popular free Android apps, gathered from Google Play across 26 categories. BridgeScope found a total of 913 potentially vulnerable apps that may enable various types of attacks such as stealing sensitive information, gaining privileged access by bypassing security checks (such as Same Origin Policy[6] in the web context), and other serious attacks that may result in monetary loss to device users. Furthermore, our evaluation on real-world malware apps also demonstrated that BridgeScope could identify malicious functionalities hidden in sensitive JavaScript Bridges, even when the associated malicious servers were unavailable.

In summary, we highlight our key contributions:

- We conduct a systematic study on how WebView and JavaScript Bridge are used by both benign apps and malware with diverse WebView implementations.
- We design a precise and scalable static detection system to automatically detect vulnerabilities caused by JavaScript Bridge.
- We evaluate our detection system BridgeScope with real-world popular apps and find 913 potentially vulnerable apps that could be exploited by attackers. On average, our system can vet an app within 7 s with a low false positive rate.

[5] https://github.com/secure-software-engineering/DroidBench.

[6] https://en.wikipedia.org/wiki/Same-origin_policy.

# 2 Problem Statement

## 2.1 Background: WebView and JavaScript Bridge

To understand the fundamental components of WebView, irrespective of any specific implementation, we devise a model, shown in Fig. 1, based on Android's default WebView which we find to be representative of most key properties that are important for our JavaScript Bridge analysis.

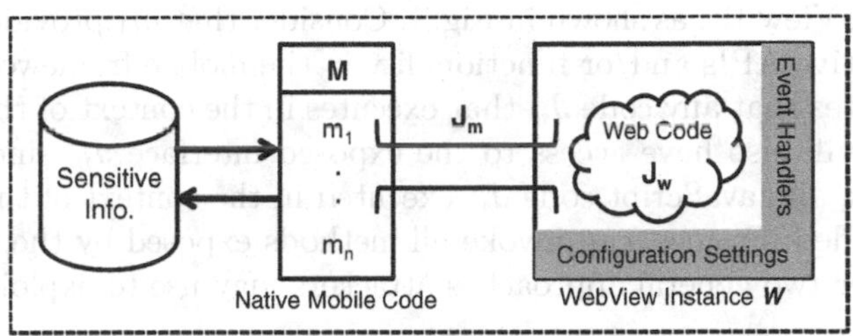


**Fig. 1.** Major modules in Android default WebView. In the example, Bridge $J_m$ enables interaction between web code $J_w$ and native code $M$.

**JavaScript Bridge.** The bridge $J_m$, shown in Fig. 1, allows interactions between the embedded web content $J_w$ and the mobile native code implemented in $M$ (the Bridge Object). Through its access to $M$, the web code in $J_w$ inherits access to the local resources and sensitive information in the mobile framework.

To enable bridges in WebView, all bridges must be registered by the API *addJavascriptInterface(BridgeObject, BridgeName)* in advance, where *BridgeObject* is a native object (i.e., an instance of a Java class such as $M$ in Fig. 1) that is being imported into the WebView instance $W$, and *BridgeName* is the object's reference name that can be used to directly access *BridgeObject* in the web context through $J_w$.

**Annotation.** In Android 4.2+, an annotation mechanism is introduced to restrict bridge access. In *BridgeObject*, only the methods that are explicitly annotated by '@JavaScriptInterface' can be invoked by JavaScript code.

**Configuration Settings.** Developers can configure a WebView component through its setting property. For instance, developers can enable/disable JavaScript in WebView. JavaScript is generally disabled by default requiring explicit activation by developers.

**Event Handler.** This mechanism allows developers to handle different events after WebView runs, which can be further utilized to provide additional security checks. For instance, the two event handlers *shouldOverrideUrlLoading*() and *shouldInterceptRequest*(), which are designed to handle URL and resources loading events, can be further used to restrict new web content loaded in WebView.

**Same Origin Policy (SOP).** In WebView, SOP is enabled to enforce access control on local data in the web layer between mutually distrusting parties. However, SOP is not extended to resources in the native layer, such as users' contact list.

### 2.2 Security Issues Caused by JavaScript Bridge and Their Impacts

To illustrate the general problem with JavaScript Bridges, consider an Android app that exposes several methods $\{m_1...m_n\} \in M$ through a bridge $J_m$ in an embedded WebView $W$, as shown in Fig. 1. Consider that $m_1$ provides privileged access to sensitive APIs and/or functionality in the mobile framework. The web platform dictates that any code $J_w$ that executes in the context of the embedded WebView $W$ will also have access to the exposed interface $J_m$ since $J_m \in J_w$. In other words, all JavaScript code $J_w$ executed in the context of the WebView, even in embedded iFrames, can invoke all methods exposed by the app in $M$.

We consider two general approaches attackers may use to exploit JavaScript Bridge's:

- *Direct Access To Sensitive APIs:* Attackers who can inject code into $W$ can then directly invoke sensitive functionality exposed through $J_m$. Attackers can also combine the use of multiple methods in $M$ for more stealthy attacks that may use one method to read data, and another method to write data to a remote server. This is a variant of the classic confused deputy access control problem [16]. In this scenario, the WebView $W$, as the deputy, will diligently allow access to both exposed methods $m_1$ and $m_2$, allowing an attacker to first invoke the request for sensitive information through $m_1$, and then append the returned data to another request to the communication-enabled exposed interface $m_2$. Additionally, even if $M$ does not include a method such as $m_2$, if the app has INTERNET permissions, then data from $m_1$ can still be leaked by $J_w$ through a JavaScript HTTP method.
- *Cross-Origin DOM Manipulation:* A more interesting attack scenario emerges when $m_n$ exposes an API that allows manipulation of the DOM in $W$, such as using $loadURL()$ or $loadDataWithBaseURL()$. As a result, an embedded iFrame in $W$ can inject cross origin JavaScript code to effectively circumvent the same origin policy (SOP) and execute cross-site-scripting-like attacks in $W$'s web origin. This is a violation of the same origin policy assumption, and can result in client-side XSS attacks using JavaScript Bridges. The root cause here is that the origin information is lost when JavaScript causes content to be loaded via a Bridge Object.

### 2.3 Sensitive APIs

We consider three type of *'sensitive'* system APIs, which we categorize as *source* (i.e., reading data from Android), *sink* (i.e., sending data out of mobile devices), and *danger* (i.e., dangerous operations) APIs. Specifically, we define "source

API" and "sink API" using a comprehensive categorization developed in a previous work [25]. Additionally, we treat any API that can access local hardware (such as camera), and cause charges on the user's device (e.g. SMS, phone calls), as a "danger API".

### 2.4 Threat Model

We focus on hybrid apps that enable JavaScript and *JavaScript Bridge*. We assume that the code written in C/C++ and implicit data flow inside apps have minimal influence for our analysis. Generally, we consider attack scenarios in the context of benign and malicious apps:

**Benign Apps.** In this scenario, we assume that HTML/Javascript code loaded in WebView of benign apps is untrusted. We also assume that web attackers cannot directly access the native context, but can inject malicious HTML/-JavaScript code to WebView through code injection attacks. We consider two ways for attackers to launch such attacks. Attackers can either compromise third-party websites, or inject/hijack network traffic (e.g., MITM attack) [3], such as the HTTP communication within WebView or third party Java libraries (e.g., ad libs [26]).

A much stronger assumption is that attackers may also hijack HTTPS traffic. Although this type of attack is difficult, it is still feasible, particularly considering how poorly/insecurely HTTPS is implemented/used in mobile apps [11,13].

**Malicious Apps.** We assume that an attacker writes a malicious app using WebView and JavaScript Bridge, and submits it to app marketplaces, such as Android official market 'Google Play'. To evade security vetting systems in app marketplaces, such as Google Bouncer[7], the app is designed in such a way that (1) WebView loads a remote web page, whose content is controlled by the attacker; (2) the malware's sensitive behaviors are conducted in JavaScript Bridge, while its command & control (CC) logic is implemented by JavaScript code in WebView; (3) initially, the CC code is not injected into the loaded web page, and it only becomes available at a specific time, such as after the app bypasses the security checks and is published.

## 3 Shadowbox Analysis

In this section, we present details about our shadowbox analysis technique. First, we highlight the advantages of our approach, compared with other state-of-the-art approaches. Then, we present definitions and concepts related to shadowbox. We also discuss more details about type, taint and value analysis respectively. Finally, we show how to apply shadowbox analysis to solve different challenges, such as the problem caused by common data structures.

---

[7] http://googlemobile.blogspot.com/2012/02/android-and-security.html.

### 3.1 Challenges

Type, taint, and value/string analysis are frequently used program analysis techniques [4,7,15,33]. However, the state-of-the-art approaches fall short of (1) precisely handling common data structures, such as list, hashmap, Android Bundle[8], Parcel[9], etc.; (2) maintaining path- and value-sensitivity while also remaining precise and scalable. These shortcomings may cause false negatives and false positives in analysis results.

**Path- And Value-Sensitivity.** To achieve high precision, it is critical to maintain path- and value-sensitivity. However, state-of-the-art work (such as Flowdroid [4] and Amandroid [33]) do not thoroughly maintain these properties. For instance, Listing 1.1 shows a snippet of a test case (from DroidBench) designed to test false positives of alias analysis. In this test case, sensitive information saved in '*deviceId*' is transferred to a field of an instance of the class '*A*' (Line 14), and then a sink API is called (Line 15), which merely sends out a constant string rather than the sensitive information. However, existing approaches, such as Flowdroid [4] and Amandroid [33], erroneously find a path from source to sink in this scenario due to path-insensitivity.

```
1  class A{ public String b ="Y";}
2  class B{ public A attr;}
3  ...
4  A b, q, y; B a, p, x;
5  a = new B(); p = new B();
6  b = new A();   q = new A();
7  if (Math.random() < 0.5) {x = a; y = b;}
8  else {x = p; y = q;}
9  x.attr = y;
10 q.b = deviceId; // source
11 sms.sendTextMessage("+49 1234", null, a.attr.b, null, null);//sink
```

**Listing 1.1.** A snippet of a test case for alias analysis in DroidBench

**Common Data Structures.** When a common data structure (e.g., list, hash map) is temporarily used to store tainted data (e.g., sensitive information), it may raise challenges to precisely track the sensitive data flow inside these data structures, since the position of taint data is difficult to determine. Most existing work (e.g., [4]) simply overtaints the entire data structure, which inevitably introduced false positives. Consider, for example, an array where only a single entry should be tainted (code shown in Listing 1.2). When line 4 is executed, only array[1] should be tainted. If, instead, the entire array is tainted, false positives are inevitably caused.

```
1 ArrayList<String> array = new ArrayList<String>();
2 String s = source();
3 array.add(s);                // array: [souce]
4 array.add(0, "element0");    // array: ["element0", source()]
```

**Listing 1.2.** An Example abstracted from real apps

BridgeScope solves this problem by performing fine-grained type, taint and value analysis using a '*shadowbox*' data structure as discussed in the following sections.

[8] https://developer.android.com/reference/android/os/Bundle.html.

[9] https://developer.android.com/reference/android/os/Parcel.html.

### 3.2 Concepts Related to Shadowbox

We define a *shadowbox* as the representation of an object (e.g. WebView). Generally, only tainted 'primitive variables' (e.g., integers), whose data type is primitive, and all 'non-primitive variables' (e.g., string and array) are boxed. The relevant concepts are defined as follows: (note that $v$ and $s$ represent a variable and a shadowbox, respectively)

- ***A variable v's representation*** $\langle scope_v, name_v \rangle$: Generally, $scope_v$ is the full name of a function (for local variables), an object (for regular fields), or a class name (for static fields), while $name_v$ is $v$'s name, which is usually a register name.
  Furthermore, to support inter-component communication (ICC) [33], the global but temporary representation `<global, intent>` is created to represent an intent message. To record a function $f$'s return value, the representation `<f, return>` is used.
- ***Points-to relationship:*** If a variable $v$ points to an object $o$, whose shadowbox is $s$, $v$ and $o$ have points-to relationship, which is represented by $v \longrightarrow s$.
- ***Alias relationship:*** If two variables $v_1$ and $v_2$, and their shadowboxes $s_1$ and $s_2$ stasify the following statement: $v_1 \longrightarrow s_1 \wedge v_2 \longrightarrow s_2 \wedge ID^{10}(s_1) = ID(s_2)$, $v_1$ and $v_2$ are alias. Such relationship is represented by $v_1 = v_2$.[10]
- ***Shadowbox dependency graph (SDG):*** A collection of points-to relationships: $\{(v, s)^* \mid v \longrightarrow s\}$. For convenience, we use $SDG(v)$, $SDG_v$, or $SDG(\langle scope_v, name_v \rangle)$ to represent the shadowbox pointed by $v$.
- ***Fields information in shadowbox (FDG):*** This is a variant of SDG: $\{(v, s)^* \mid v \longrightarrow s \wedge v \subset \text{'non-static fields ins'}\}$. Since $FDG$ is always bound with a shadowbox $s$, we use $FDG_s$ to indicate such relationship.

### 3.3 Type and Taint Analysis

Driven by the shadowbox concept, we define the analysis rules that implement type and taint analysis (Table 1). The analysis rules work directly on Dalvik opcode[11]. We use lower case letters to represent variables, with the exception of $e$ and $f$, which represent fields and functions, respectively. We use upper case letters for classes or data types. In the rules, operations on array are solved with the help of value analysis, as shown in Sect. 3.5.

### 3.4 Value and String Analysis

Given a target variable $v$ and its instruction $i$, $v$'s value is calculated by performing backward programming analysis along the analyzed path to update its "expression tree". The expression tree is subtly different with the regular binary expression tree [1]. The expression tree's leaf nodes correspond to system APIs (e.g., *getDeviceId*()), constants, JavaScript Bridge function input, and variables

[10] ID stands for the shadowbox's memory location in our static analysis.

[11] https://source.android.com/devices/tech/dalvik/dalvik-bytecode.html.

**Table 1.** Analysis rules

| | |
|---|---|
| $v_1 = v_2$ op $v_3$ | $\Rightarrow SDG(v_1)_{taint} = SDG(v_2)_{taint} \mid SDG(v_3)_{taint}$ |
| $v =$ new C | $\Rightarrow s =$ a new shadowbox; $s_{data\_type} = C$; $v \rightarrow s$ |
| $v_1 = v_2$ | $\Rightarrow v_1 \rightarrow SDG(v_2)$ |
| $v \in C$ | $\Rightarrow SDG(v)_{data\_type} = SDG(v)_{data\_type} \wedge C$ |
| function $f(...)\{...; return\ r;\}$ | $\Rightarrow \langle f, return\rangle \rightarrow SDG(r)$<br>$for\ v \in SDG_{vertexes},\ delete\ v\ if\ v.scope == f$ |
| $r = f(p_0, p_1, ...)$<br>function $f(p'_0, p'_1, ...)$ $\{...\}$ | $\Rightarrow \langle f, return\rangle \rightarrow null$<br>$\langle f, p'_0\rangle \rightarrow SDG(p_0)$; $\langle f, p'_1\rangle \rightarrow SDG(p_1); ...;$<br>$r \rightarrow SDG(\langle f, return\rangle)$ |
| $v = o.e$ | $\Rightarrow SDGv \rightarrow FDG_{SDG(o)}(e)$ |
| $v = C.e$ | $\Rightarrow SDG(v) \rightarrow \langle C, e\rangle$ |
| $o.e = v$ | $\Rightarrow FDG_{SDG(o)}(e) \rightarrow SDGv$ |
| $C.e = v$ | $\Rightarrow \langle C, e\rangle \rightarrow SDG(v)$ |
| $a[i] = v$ | $\Rightarrow$ Section 3.5 |
| $v = a[i]$ | $\Rightarrow$ Section 3.5 |

whose values is to be calculated (i.e., *variable leaf*), and the internal nodes correspond to functions (e.g., *string.replace*()) and operators. Initially, the root node of the expression tree is $v$. Starting from $i$, all variable leaves in the expression tree are kept being updated. If it is found that a variable $v_1$ is dependent on another variable $v_2$ or an expression $e_1$, $v_1$'s leaf node is replaced by $v_2$ or $e_1$. The analysis is continued till there are no variable leaves. To handle string operations, the associated functions are modelled. For example, the function *StringBuilder.append*() itself is treated as an internal node, and its function parameters are added as its children nodes.

Then, the target variable' value can be retrieved by resolving the expression tree. For this purpose, the expression tree is first converted to a regular expression using in-order traversal. During the conversion, functions in internal nodes are converted to proper operators. For example, *StringBuilder.append*() is replaced by +, and linked with the function's parameters (i.e., the children nodes). Then, we apply a lightweight solver to compute the expression's value, which is built on top of the Python function '*eval*()'.

### 3.5 Application of Shadowbox Analysis

**Path-Sensitivity.** We use the code shown in Listing 1.1 as the illustrative example. Before utilizing shadowbox analysis on the test case, SDG is first created by initializing shadowboxes of '*this*' and the corresponding function's parameters with their associated data types. Then, the analysis is applied on each instruction based on the rules defined in Sect. 3.3. When a conditional statement $c$ (Line 8) is encountered, the depth-first strategy is used and each path is analyzed sequentially. To keep the independence of each path, SDG is cloned and saved so that when a path is done, SDG is quickly restored for another path. Finally, when the sink API '*sendTextMessage*()' is encountered, the third parameter's shadowbox is read from SDG and checked to determine whether the parameter contains sensitive information.

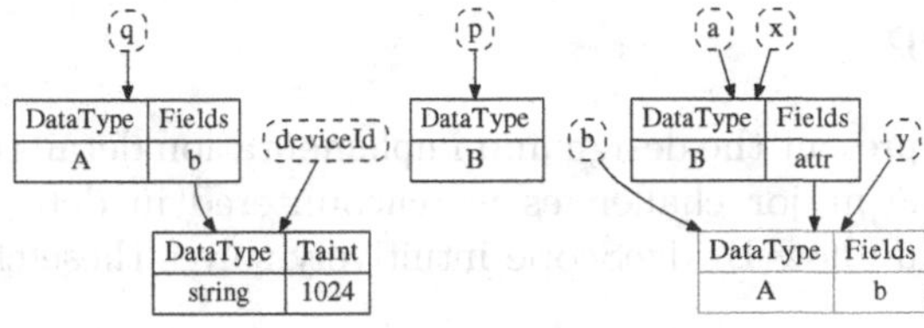


**Fig. 2.** SDG's partial content when sending text message, where cycles with dashed line are variable representations, and boxes with solid line represent corresponding shadowboxes. (Color figure online)

SDG's content (when the branch statement is true) is partially shown in Fig. 2.[12] By checking the shadowbox referenced by '*a.attr.b*' (the box with red line), we can learn that the third parameter is not tainted.

**HashMap and Linear Data Structures.** The propagation problem caused by common data structures is due to their lack of regular field information, which makes it difficult to locate target variables. To mitigate this problem, we model common data structures using 'shadowbox', and augment common data structures by adding explicit fields to them that enable us to apply our analysis rules and handle them similar to regular data structures.

We use keys in a hashmap as the explicit fields, since keys are always unique. We leverage value analysis to retrieve the keys' values, which are then treated as fields. Thus the instructions '`value = H.get(key)`' and '`H.get(key) = value`' can be converted to assignment statements '`value =` $FDG_H(key)$' and '$FDG_H(key)$ `= value`', where $H$ is an instance of hashmap.

We select the element position in linear data structures (such as list, array, Android Parcel, etc.) as the explicit fields. Thus the instructions '`value = array[index]`' and '`array[index] = value`' can be converted to assignment statements '`value =` $FDG_{array}(index)$' and '$FDG_{array}(index)$ `= value`'.

Most cases can be handled using the above intuition by computing *index*'s value in advance (Sect. 3.4), and converting it to a regular field. However, since an operation's *index* value is changeable, such as injecting a new element in the middle of a list, or merging two lists, we maintain the data structures' internal state (which is represented by $FDG$) during updates. For example, consider if an element $e$ is inserted into a list $L$ at the position $i$ through the API '$L.add(i, e)$'. $FDG_L$ can be updated to

$$\begin{aligned} FDG'_L = &\{(v, FDG_L(v)) \mid v \in FDG_L.fields \wedge v < i\} \\ &\cup \{(i, e) \mid i \rightarrow e\} \\ &\cup \{(v+1, FDG_L(v)) \mid v \in FDG_L.fields \wedge v >= i\}. \end{aligned}$$

Similarly, operations in Android Bundle and Parcel are also supported.

[12] Since most variable scopes are the same, scope information in variable representations is hidden to make SDG more concise.

## 4 BridgeScope

In this section, we present the design and implementation details of BridgeScope, and we explore the major challenges we encountered in detecting JavaScript Bridge problems and how BridgeScope intuitively solves these challenges.

### 4.1 Challenges and Solutions

**Semantic gap between web and native code.** This adds complexity to the analysis, especially when the suspicious command and control web code is not available, which is true for most cases.

To solve the problem, we assume that the code $O$ loaded in WebView is ***omnipotent***, which means $O$ has the capability to do anything through the JavaScript Bridge. Under this assumption, it is only necessary to focus on the analysis of JavaScript Bridge, which lowers the complexity and scope of our analysis.

However, actual code $R$ loaded in WebView has the following relationship with $O$: $R \subset O$, which means our initial assumption introduces false positives to our analysis, as it may be not feasible for attackers to launch code injection attacks in some cases. For instance, if a benign app's communications with remote servers are always properly protected, then even when there is a sensitive bridge found in the app, it is still hard to exploit.

To reduce false positives, we consider the complexity for attackers to launch attacks (i.e., *attack complexity*). We discuss more details in Sect. 5.

**Semantic gap between different WebView implementations.** As discussed in Sect. 2.1, there are multiple WebView implementations in the Android platform. The major challenge is to eliminate the semantic gap between different implementations to enable a generic analysis. For example, the default Android WebView uses `addJavascriptInterface(BridgeObject,BridgeName)` to enable a JavaScript Bridge, while rhino-based WebView uses `putProperty(scope, BridgeName, BridgeObject)`. Similarly, the default WebView in Android 4.2 and above requires the annotation '@JavascriptInterface', while the default WebView in older Android versions and Rhino does not use any annotation feature.

Rather than specifically hard-coding and addressing each different implementation and their syntax differences, we observe that all implementations have key common elements that follow the model shown in Sect. 2.1. Armed with that observation, we address this challenge by translating different implementations to an intermediate representation. This gives us an abstraction that lowers the semantic gap and eliminates the diversity to allow analysis that is agnostic of the specific implementation.

**Difficulty in identifying all JavaScript Bridges.** A quick but naive solution to identify Android's default WebView in 4.2 and above, as well as Crosswalk and Chromeview, is to directly search for annotations. However, this approach may introduce false negatives because it is not generic, different WebView implementations do not use the same annotation syntax, and annotated functions may only be known at runtime. While our generic WebView model supports the annotation mechanism, it is still not possible to apply a simple search approach. Specifically, due to the well-known program analysis *points-to* problem [30], *BridgeObject* cannot be easily identified, meaning that functions which are annotated are only identifiable at runtime. Additionally, it is error-prone due to annotation inheritance.

To address this challenge, we leverage a shadowbox dependency graph (see Sect. 3), which we use to first identify all possible WebView implementations, and further identify JavaScript Bridges for each WebView according to the semantics of WebView.

During analysis, a key consideration is to maintain the status of variables, especially WebView, so that critical information can be quickly extracted, such as the pair $\langle BridgeObject, BridgeName\rangle$. Then, all JavaScript Bridges can be extracted using the 'shadowbox' data structure and its dependency graph (see Sect. 3).

**Unknown semantics of functions in JavaScript Bridge.** Generally, the native end of the JavaScript Bridge is a black box, since its source code is not always readily available. It is challenging to reconstruct the semantics of each function in a bridge (i.e., bridge function), but it is a critical step in undersanding the functionality to decide which bridge is sensitive. To solve the problem, we use fine-grained data flow analysis on all functions of JavaScript Bridges by tracking their parameters and system sensitive information.

**Unknown input format of JavaScript Bridge.** Even when a sensitive bridge is found, it is still challenging to validate it since appropriately formatted input data is required. We mitigate the problem by applying several heuristics information gathered from our analysis results, such as the data flow information, key API semantic, etc.

### 4.2 System Overview

As shown in Fig. 3, our static analysis approach BridgeScope consists of four main components: WebView abstraction, WebView and bridge discovery, bridge analysis, and log analysis. Given an app, the WebView abstraction module firstly disassembles it to the Dalvik bytecode[13] and then abstracts all WebView implementations in the app by translating the different implementations of WebView to an 'intermediate representation'.

Next, starting from entry points of activities [4,21], type and value/string analysis based on shadowbox is performed to extract control flow graph (CFG), where type analysis is critical to resolve virtual function calls and solve points-to problem, and value/string analysis is useful to resolve Java reflection. Compared with existing approaches to generate CFG, our approach is fine-grained and complete.

[13] https://source.android.com/devices/tech/dalvik/dalvik-bytecode.html.

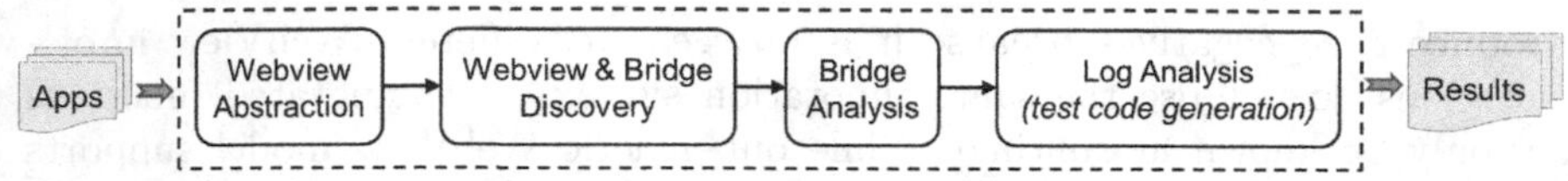


**Fig. 3.** Overview of BridgeScope

In addition, during the process, value/string analysis is also run specifically for two situations: (1) when JavaScript is enabled or disabled in WebView, the key parameter's value is computed; (2) When the pair '⟨*BridgeObject*, *BridgeName*⟩' is configured, *BridgeName*'s value is also computed.

Then, all methods in *BridgeObject* are further analyzed by means of data flow analysis to identify sensitive bridges. Finally, the log analysis module collects all analysis results from other modules and further generates heuristic information for the test attack code generation purpose.

### 4.3 WebView Abstraction

This module fills the semantic gap between different WebViews, which is done by translating different implementations of WebView into a generic 'intermediate representation'. We devise an 'intermediate representation' scheme, including common APIs (Table 2), and a generalized annotation mechanism.

**Table 2.** Generic WebView common APIs

| API | Description |
|---|---|
| *add_bridge(BridgeObject, BridgeName)* | Add JavaScript Bridge to WebView |
| *enable_js(boolean)* | Enable/disable JavaScript |
| *set_event_handler(event handler)* | Register event handler |
| *load(URL / local file / JavaScript code)* | Run WebView |

To support the annotation mechanism, which identifies Bridge Objects, we define the common annotation '*@JavaScriptBridge*' and apply it to all WebView instances, overwriting any specific annotation implementation such as in Android WebView in 4.2+ and Crosswalk.

We generalize WebView using shadowbox, whose structure is shown in Table 3. Generally, WebView contains three types of fields: (1) JsFlag, which indicates whether JavaScript is enabled; (2) Event Handler, which is used to react to different events (e.g., URL redirection, errors in web pages); (3) and JavaScript Bridge, which is a handle to a Bridge Object between the native and web context.

**Table 3.** The generic model representation of WebView (a) and JavaScript Bridge (b). Note that we use the special symbol '¡' to indicate that when the associated field is initialized or changed, it should be computed by value/string analysis immediately.

(a)

| DataType | Fields | | | |
|---|---|---|---|---|
| WebView | JsFlag (¡) | EventHandler | *Bridge#0* | *Bridge#1..* |

(b)

| DataType | Fields | |
|---|---|---|
| Bridge | BridgeObject | BridgeName(¡) |

## 4.4 WebView and Bridge Discovery

The goal of this module is to discover all WebView components and bridges. We apply type and value/string analysis based on shadowbox on the generalized WebView code (Sect. 4.3). This allows us to generate a complete control flow graph (CFG), and enables discovery of most WebViews and JavaScript Bridges within an app.

The analysis starts from entry points of Android Activities, since a WebView is almost always launched within an Activity. Even if a WebView is standalone or independent (such as Xbot [24]), we can still identify it after obtaining the CFG of the target app.

During analysis, data types of key variables, such as *BridgeObject*, are also for the further analysis (Sect. 4.5). Additionally, values of key variables, such as *JsFlag* and *BridgeName* (Sect. 4.3), are computed on demand with the help of value and string analysis. *JsFlag* can be used to filter out WebViews whose JavaScript is disabled (i.e., *JsFlag* is false), while *BridgeName* is helpful in attack code generation.

## 4.5 Bridge Analysis

The goal of the module is to identify sensitive bridges from all bridges in *BridgeObject*. To achieve the goal, it is critical to reconstruct the semantics and learn the functionality of all exposed functions in *BridgeObject* (i.e., bridge function), which are annotated with '@JavaScriptBridge' (Sect. 4.3). In BridgeScope, we apply taint analysis (Sect. 3) based on shadowbox on each function by tracking data flow of function parameters ($TP$) and system sensitive information ($TS$). To distinguish these two types of information, we define different taint value ranges: $[TP_{min}, TP_{max}]$, and $[TS_{min}, TS_{max}]$. Initially, parameters of a bridge function are tainted from left to right sequentially. Specifically, the $n$th parameter is assigned with the taint value $TP_{min} * 2^n$. During analysis, if a sensitive native API (Sect. 2.3) is invoked, we take a snapshot of their parameters' states (e.g., the associated shadowboxes), which will be analyzed further.

Finally, a bridge function's semantic information is reconstructed based on its data flow analysis result. A bridge function will be flagged as **sensitive** if: (1) its return is tainted by the value $t$ while $t \in [TS_{min}, TS_{max}]$, (2) or a sink API $s()$ is called while $s()$'s parameters are tainted, (3) or a danger API is invoked. Based on the above three scenarios, we categorize all bridge functions into ***SourceBridge***, ***SinkBridge***, and ***DangerBridge***, correlating to the API categorization as defined in Sect. 2.3.

As a result, an app can be flagged as **potentially vulnerable**, if a sensitive bridge function $f$ is found by BridgeScope. We use the following reasoning: (1) if $f \in SourceBridge$, it means that sensitive information can be obtained in the web context. Then, an attacker can send out sensitive information through network related APIs in the web context (like *XMLHttpRequest*()) or a sink JavaScript Bridge if it exists; (2) if $f \in SinkBridge$, security checks in event handlers in WebView, such as *shouldOverrideUrlLoading*(), can be evaded; (3) if $f \in DangerBridge$, a danger API can be accessed through $f$.

### 4.6 Log Analysis and Exploit Code Generation

BridgeScope collects a rich set of heuristics information for the app under analysis as it executes each module (Table 4). This information is useful to further analyze flagged sensitive bridges and to generate test attack code. Furthermore, inspired by SMV-Hunter [29], we retrieve required UI events for triggering target WebViews by analyzing the result of the 'WebView and bridge discovery' module.

**Table 4.** Collected Information

| Purpose | Collected information | Which module |
|---|---|---|
| Triggering WebView | UI Events | WebView & Bridge Discovery |
| Generating test code | *Domains* associated with WebView | |
| | ⟨*BridgeObject*, *BridgeName*⟩ | |
| | Semantics of bridge functions | Bridge Analysis |
| | SourceBridge,SinkBridge,DangerBridge | |

Algorithm 1 outlines our approach that leverages the above collected information to generate test code to verify discovered vulnerabilities. In the algorithm, a function *create_input*() is assumed to generate appropriate inputs for each bridge function. We implement it as a smart fuzzer using the following heuristics:

- Data Types: Based on data type information of parameters of bridge functions, which is gathered from type analysis, we can generate random but valid inputs [29].
- Bridge Function Name: The bridge function name itself also provides an important clue. For example, if a BridgeScope's name is *downloadImage*() and the input is of type String, then input is likely a URI of a picture file. In our fuzzer, we handle several keywords, such as "url", "email", "picture", "camera", "audio", "video", "SMS", "call" to provide typical input values.

**Algorithm 1.** Test Code Generation

```
function GENERATE_TEST_CODE
    for f in SourceBridge do
        input ← create_input(f);
        fname ← replace_bridgeobject_with_bridgename(P, f);
        add_test_code(X, "var r = fname(input)")  ▷ append the JavaScript code to the result X
        for d in Domains do                        ▷ bypass security check in event handler
            add_test_code(X, "XMLHttpRequest(http://d/r)")
        end for
        for f' in SinkBridge do
            input' ← create_input(f', "r");
            fname' ← replace_bridgeobject_with_bridgename(P, f');
            add_test_code(X, "fname'(input')")
        end for
    end for
    for f in SinkBridge ∪ DangerBridge do
        input ← create_input(f);
        fname ← replace_bridgeobject_with_bridgename(P, f);
        add_test_code(X, "fname(input)")
    end for
    return X
end function
```

- Semantics of bridge functions and key native APIs: We can also build input by utilizing the semantic information. For instance, assume there is a path in CFG from a bridge function to a sensitive API: $f(p_0 : string, p_1 : string) \rightsquigarrow sendTextMessage(v_0, null, v_2, null, null)$, where $v_0$ and $v_2$'s taint values are $TP_{min} * 2$ and $TP_{min} * 4$, respectively. The data flow in the bridge function includes $p_0 \rightsquigarrow v_0$ and $p_1 \rightsquigarrow v_2$. Since in $sendTextMessage()$, $v_0$ is the destination address, and $v_2$ is the message content to be sent, $p_0$ and $p_1$ are likely a phone number and message content. Therefore, the following input can be used to test the sensitive bridge function: `f("0123456789", "test")`.

## 5 Evaluation of BridgeScope

In this section, we present our evaluation of BridgeScope. First, we measure the performance of the programming analysis techniques by leveraging the generic benchmark DroidBench. Then, we evaluate BridgeScope's efficacy, precision, and overhead using 13,000 popular apps, and present our findings. Finally, we present some interesting case studies to illustrate the JavaScript Bridge vulnerability.

### 5.1 Performance of Shadowbox Analysis

We evaluate the precision of shadowbox analysis using the generic benchmark DroidBench 2.0. Our test results (Table 5) show BridgeScope's overall precision is 94%, compared to 80% and 91% for Flowdroid [4] and Amandroid [33], respectively, and BridgeScope's recall and F-score are also better than the others. Our use of shadowbox analysis benefits from its path- and value-sensitivity, and it is fine-grained, especially in handling common data structures.

**Table 5.** Testing Result on DroidBench. × represents suspicious data flows not detected, and ○ represents benign data flows flagged as suspicious. The number in {} represents the number of errors.

| DroidBench | BridgeScope | Flowdroid | Amandroid |
|---|---|---|---|
| Aliasing | | ○ | ○ |
| Android specific | ×× | ×× | ××× |
| Arrays and lists | | ○○○○ | ○○○○× |
| Callbacks | ×× | ○○× | ○○○○×××× |
| Emulator detection | ×× | ×× | ×× |
| Field/Object Sensitivity | | | |
| General java | ○○×× | ○{4}×××× | ○×× |
| Implicit flows | – | – | – |
| Interapp communication | | ○○○ | |
| ICC | ×××× | ○{16}×××× | ○××××× |
| Lifecycle | ○× | ○×× | ×××× |
| Reflection | | ××× | |
| Threading | × | × | ×{5} |
| Totally Found Paths $f$ | 100 | 127 | 101 |
| Precision $p = f/(f + \bigcirc)$ | 94% | 80% | 90% |
| Recall $r = \bigcirc/(\bigcirc/ + \times)$ | 83% | 82% | 75% |
| F-score $2 * p * r/(p + r)$ | 0.89 | 0.81 | 0.82 |

## 5.2 Performance of BridgeScope

**Dataset.** We use 13,000 apps that were collected from the Google Play app market. We crawled these apps from 26 categories, and extracted the top 500 most popular free apps for each category.

**Scalability.** We implemented BridgeScope in 8,157 lines of Python code on the top of the disassembly tool Apktool[14]. We deployed our tool on a university server, which is allocated with 20 CPU cores and 100 GB of memory. Due to Python's poor support for multiple threads, we run single process and single thread for the analysis (i.e., starting 20 processes for 20 apps each time). Finally, with the boost of the JIT (Just-in-Time) based Python interpreter (such as pypy[15]), the average analysis time of each process is 141 s. Thus, the average analysis time for each app is around 7 s. This suggests that BridgeScope is indeed capable of scaling to the level of real-worlds app markets to provide vulnerability detection services.

**Precision.** Among 13,000 apps, we find that 11,913 apps have at least one WebView component and 8,146 apps declare at least one JavaScript Bridge interface.

[14] https://ibotpeaches.github.io/Apktool/.

[15] https://pypy.org/.

In total, 913 apps were flagged as potentially vulnerable apps by BridgeScope, while a total of 1,530 sensitive bridge functions were found, including 56 bridge functions which could suffer from SOP Violation Attacks (Sect. 2.2).

**Measuring false positives and negatives.** A false positive occurs when an app is flagged as potentially vulnerable by BridgeScope, but has no vulnerability. A false negative occurs when an app is flagged as non-vulnerable by BridgeScope, but includes a JavaScript Bridge vulnerability.

Since it is hard to directly collect ground truth for the dataset, manual verification may be necessary, which is a difficult and tedious job for such a large dataset. To reduce the workload, we first design a dynamic verification module to automatically validate the potentially vulnerable apps (thus we do not need to manually validate all data) when analyzing false positives. Additionally, we manually analyzed a small set of 20 randomly chosen apps from those not marked as potentially vulnerable, which we used as the basis of measuring the false negative rate.

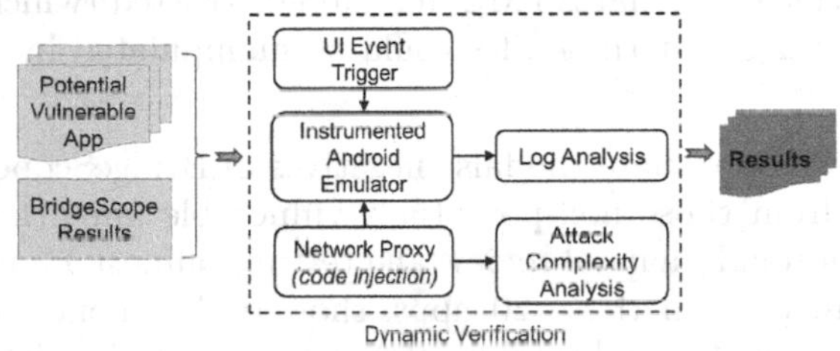


**Fig. 4.** Overview of the dynamic verification module

As shown in Fig. 4, our dynamic verification module is built around an *instrumented Android Emulator*, where all executed functions of apps under test are outputted, sensitive information is modified to special values, and native sink APIs parameters (e.g., WebView.load) are also outputted. In the module, *UI Event Trigger* [29] is used to input UI required event sequentially to trigger target WebViews, while *Network Proxy* is used to launch MITM attacks to inject attack code, which is generated using the example algorithm mentioned earlier (Algorithm 1).

In our evaluation we also hijack all network traffic, including HTTPS, so that we can further analyze the complexity faced by attackers who launch code injection attacks (i.e., *Attack Complexity Analysis*). We mainly consider three scenarios: (1) *HTTP*: the remote server is connected over HTTP; (2) *first-party HTTPS*: the remote server belonging to developers is connected over HTTPS; (3) *third-party HTTPS*: others. In Attack Complexity Analysis, we use the URL loaded by the WebView as input, and initiate a crawler to check all accessible URLs, similar to the approach in [14].

Finally, we check whether a potential vulnerability is successfully exploited by analyzing logs from the Android Emulator and proxy (i.e., *Log Analysis*).

If a bridge function $f$ satisfies: (1) $f \in SourceBridge$, it can be verified by checking executed functions, sink APIs parameters and proxys traffic. (2) $f \in SinkBridge \cup DangerBridge$, it can be verified by checking executed functions.

**False Positives.** By means of the dynamic verification module, we found that 617 potentially vulnerable apps flagged by BridgeScope are successfully exploited (i.e., they are surely not false positives). This reduces our manual verification job to only 296 non-verified potentially vulnerable apps. We then randomly selected 20 apps and manually analyzed them. We found most of them still contain vulnerable bridges that could be exploited. The reason they are missed by the dynamic verification module is because the dynamic module uses heuristics but cannot guarantee the completeness. For example, it may not always generate proper input formats of the JavaScript Bridges, such as the JSON string. There are 4 apps that use WebView to load local HTML files instead of connecting to Internet. While these 4 apps could be considered as false positives of BridgeScope (because our assumed network adversary may not be able to inject attack code in this case), we argue that they could still be vulnerable/exploited in an extended threat model in which external HTML files are not trusted (which could be also reasonable considering that these files could be manipulated by malicious apps in the phone).

**False Negatives.** To evaluate the false negatives of BridgeScope, we randomly selected 20 apps from those non-potentially-vulnerable apps that had at least one WebView. Thorough manual review and testing (almost 1 h per app) of how the WebViews are used in those 20 apps, showed that none were potentially vulnerable, suggesting that indeed our false negative rate is relatively low.

### 5.3 Overall Findings

**Diverse WebView implementations.** Based on our static analysis result, we found that WebView implementations are indeed diverse. Table 6 shows the distribution of different WebView implementations in our dataset.

**Table 6.** Diverse WebView implementations

| Android Default WebView | Mozilla Rhino Based WebView | Chromeview | XWalkView | Total |
|---|---|---|---|---|
| 11,823 | 526 | 20 | 0 | 11,913 |

**Evadable Security Checks in WebView event handlers.** As shown in Sect. 2, event handlers perform security checks on the URL to be connected. However, in our evaluation we found that the customized event handler did not properly protect sensitive information leakage. Once sensitive information is successfully obtained in the web context, it can always be directly sent out through a JavaScript API or by dynamically creating DOM elements [9].

**Attacking capability.** To further understand the attack capability on those potentially vulnerable apps, we analyze the different sinks and sensitive APIs of those confirmed potentially vulnerable apps and summarize the attack capabilities shown in Table 7. The most common attack enabled is to steal private information from content providers. This is due to the fact that a large number of potentially vulnerable apps use sensitive JavaScript Bridges to load authentication tokens from content providers. We also observe that attackers can launch diverse attacks including some critical attacks such as sending text messages, sending emails, and playing videos.

**Table 7.** Attacking capability distribution

| Attack capability | App number | Attack capability | App number |
|---|---|---|---|
| Leaking Content Provider Content | 241 | Sending text message by intent | 57 |
| Leaking the Device ID | 42 | Sending email by intent | 51 |
| Leaking phone numbers | 14 | Playing video by intent | 61 |
| Directly sending text message | 2 | Create calendar by intent | 171 |
| Downloading/Saving Picture | 344 | SOP Violation Attack | 41 |

**Table 8.** Difficulty to exploit vulnerabilities

| Network channel | HTTP | Third-Party HTTPS | HTTPS |
|---|---|---|---|
| Difficulty | Easy | Medium | Hard |
| Number | 224 | 103 | 290 |

**Attack complexity.** To reduce the false positive caused by our analysis assumption (Sect. 4.1) and further understand the relative difficulty of launching attacks on vulnerable apps, we define three attack complexity levels:

- *Hard:* The content in a vulnerable WebView is loaded over first-party HTTPS. In this case, those vulnerable JavaScript Bridges could be intentional bridges to the trusted JavaScript in the first-party content. However, it could still be attacked by hijacking HTTPS traffic [3], especially considering that HTTPS can be very poorly/insecurely implemented or used in mobile apps [11,13].
- *Medium:* The vulnerable WebView loads third-party content over HTTPS. It faces similar risks as above [3,11,13]. In addition, attackers could compromise third-party content (such as through a Content Delivery Network [20]) to inject the malicious JavaScript.
- *Easy:* The vulnerable WebView loads web content through HTTP. In this case, attackers can easily inject the malicious JavaScript into HTTP traffic.

Based on the above definitions, Table 8 shows the results of attacking complexity analysis of our automatically verified vulnerable apps. We can see that the majority of vulnerable apps are hard to attack, but we also note that most apps that fall into this category contain JavaScript Bridges that explicitly allow trusted JavaScript to access sensitive information from users. In other words, as long as the transport protocol is compromised, attacker capabilities are enhanced. Recent disclosures of the fragility of HTTPS [5,6] makes this scenario more trivial than not.

We also observe that there exists a large number of vulnerable apps using the HTTP protocol, which can be obviously easily attacked through code injection since communication is in clear text.

### 5.4 Case Studies

We present two interesting case studies of vulnerable apps here. In the interest of responsible disclosure, we avoid naming the specific apps at this time while we notify developers and coordinate possible fixes.

**Case 1: Advertisement library vulnerability.** In this case, the vulnerable app loads an advertisement library, which is a common practice in app development. However, this ad library contains a vulnerable WebView, which is used to communicate with the advertiser's website to retrieve advertising content over the HTTP protocol. BridgeScope detects only one vulnerable JavaScript Bridge imported into this vulnerable WebView. However, 56 methods are available in this vulnerable JavaScript Bridge. Among them, 19 are critical methods, which can be invoked by attackers to steal sensitive information (such as device ID, WIFI status, network operator name, and user's internal data) and download or delete files and folders in the device.

We found 12 apps in our dataset that used this vulnerable advertisement library, making all of them equally vulnerable.

**Case 2: Vulnerable browser apps.** Developers often extend WebView to quickly create and specify their own customized browser apps. Many specialized 'browsers' on the app market use this model. We crawled 100 popular browser apps from Google Play in January 2016. 74 of them are merely extensions of the standard WebView. BridgeScope successfully detected 6 vulnerable browser apps that can be exploited to leak sensitive information such as device ID (5 apps), phone number (1 app), serial number (1 app).

We also found one popular browsers app, downloaded by more than 100,000 users, which suffers from SOP Violation Attacks. The app is designed to provide an ad-free user experience by filtering out ads using a blacklist. A bridge function, named '$applyAdsRules(String\ url)$', checks whether the url is related to an advertisement website. If the url is 'safe', it will be sent to the app's main Activity to render it using the key API $WebView.loadUrl(url)$. This fits the pattern of the SOP violation attack, giving an attacker the ability to load content that he knows not to be blacklisted by the app's filter function to launch client-side XSS attacks.

Different from other apps, these browser apps have much larger attack surfaces since the website (e.g., third-party) to be accessed and the protocol used in communications (e.g., HTTP or HTTPS) are specified by users, making them relatively easy to attack by simply redirecting a user to an attacker-controlled website.

### 5.5 Results on Real-World Malware

In addition to finding potential vulnerabilities in benign apps, we also test our tool on real-world malware that uses JavaScript Bridge techniques. By searching reports from Honeynet [2] and Palo Alto Networks [24], we collected 23 malicious apps that were reported to employ JavaScript Bridge techniques.

By running BridgeScope on these malicious apps, we found a total of 68 sensitive bridges. Although the malicious servers were already down, BridgeScope still successfully identified malicious behaviors hidden in JavaScript Bridges, including leaking of sensitive information, sending text messages, and prompting fake notifications, which are the same as the report descriptions about these malware by Honeynet [2] and Palo Alto Networks [24].

## 6 Discussion

**Limitation in Static Analysis.** Similar to other existing static analysis tools [4,33], our work does not handle implicit data flow, or low level libraries written in C/C++, which may lead to false negatives. However, C/C++ library could be mitigated by modeling their functions, such as *system.arraycopy*(). We leave implicit data flow tracking as our future work.
**More comments on HTTPS.** In this paper, some of detected vulnerable apps require hijacking HTTPS in order to exploit them. We consider that while HTTPS may pose a higher level of complexity and difficulty for exploiting JavaScript Bridge vulnerabilities, it is still a realistic threat vector because HTTPS is widely implemented insecurely/poorly in mobile apps [11,13] and several recent high profile works also showed the inherent issues of HTTPS [5,6,20]. Therefore, once attackers can successfully hijack HTTPS, they can exploit our reported vulnerabilities to launch diverse critical attacks (shown in Table 7).

## 7 Related Work

**WebView Security.** Luo et al. [22] exposed attack vectors in WebView, and demonstrated the JavaScript Bridge vulnerability. Chin et al. [8] analyzed WebView vulnerabilities that result in excess authorization and file-based cross-zone scripting attacks. Mutchler et al. [23] did a generic large scale study on security issues (such as unsafe navigation and unsafe content retrieval) in Android apps equipped with WebView. Wu et al. [34] discussed file leakage problems caused by file:// and content:// schemes in WebView. Georgiev et al. [14] did a study on a popular third-party hybrid middleware frameworks. Hassanshahi et al. [17] studied the security issues caused by intent hyperlinks.

The JavaScript Bridge vulnerability is rooted in the conflict between security models of the native and web context [14], and the lack of privilege isolation [19]. The approach *NoFrak* proposed by [14] partially solves the conflict by extending the web's same original policy (SOP) to the local resources. Other works such as MobileIFC [28] also propose a similar concept of extending SOP to mediate access control between the mobile and web context within a hybrid app. Jin et al. [19] proposed a defense solution for JavaScript Bridge vulnerabilities in hybrid apps, with focus on privilege separation based on iFrame instances within the WebView. In [31], the authors proposed Draco, a uniform and fine-grained access control framework for web code running in Android default WebView.

**Privacy Detection And Protection.** Taint analysis is an effective approach for detecting privacy leakage. On Android, systems such as TaintDroid [10] and FlowDroid [4] are among some of the most well-known taint-based systems. Existing Android analysis tools [4,7,12,15,33] may be useful for detection of vulnerabilities. However, existing work either performed coarse-grained analysis, or imposed high performance overhead [7,18]. Furthermore, existing work could not handle the semantics of JavaScript Bridge and diverse WebView implementations.

## 8 Conclusion

The integration of mobile and web through the use of WebView requires compromises to be made in the security of both platforms. Subsequently, we find that the current design and practices in the implementation of WebView causes a class of generic vulnerabilities that can be exploited by attackers to cause serious problems on mobile devices. We implement an analysis framework, BridgeScope, which can automatically discover vulnerabilities in a hybrid mobile app and generate test attack code that is then automatically verified as a feasible exploit. Our system is implemented in Android, and we provide evaluation that shows our system is a feasible approach to automatically and precisely discover vulnerabilities at large scale.

**Acknowledgments.** This material is based upon work supported in part by the the National Science Foundation (NSF) under Grant no. 0954096 and 1314823. Any opinions, findings, and conclusions or recommendations expressed in this material are those of the authors and do not necessarily reflect the views of NSF.

## References

1. Binary Expression Tree. https://en.wikipedia.org/wiki/Binary_expression_tree
2. Is android malware served in theatres more sophisticated? http://www.honeynet.org/node/1081
3. Akhawe, D., Barth, A., Lam, P.E., Mitchell, J., Song, D.: Towards a formal foundation of web security. In: Computer Security Foundations Symposium (CSF) (2010)
4. Arzt, S., Rasthofer, S., Fritz, C., Bodden, E., Bartel, A., Klein, J., Le Traon, Y., Octeau, D., McDaniel, P.: Flowdroid: precise context, flow, field, object-sensitive and lifecycle-aware taint analysis for android apps. In: PLDI (2014)

5. Aviram, N., Schinzel, S., Somorovsky, J., Heninger, N., Dankel, M., Steube, J., Valenta, L., Adrian, D., Halderman, J.A., Dukhovni, V., Käsper, E., Cohney, S., Engels, S., Paar, C., Shavitt, Y.: Drown: breaking TLS using SSLv2. In: USENIX Security (2016)
6. Beurdouche, B., Bhargavan, K., Delignat-Lavaud, A., Fournet, C., Kohlweiss, M., Pironti, A., Strub, P.-Y., Zinzindohoue, J.K.: A messy state of the union: taming the composite state machines of TLS. In: IEEE Symposium on Security and Privacy (2015)
7. Calzavara, S., Grishchenko, I., Maffei, M.: Horndroid: practical and sound static analysis of android applications by SMT solving. In: IEEE European Symposium on Security and Privacy, EuroS&P (2016)
8. Chin, E., Wagner, D.: Bifocals: analyzing WebView vulnerabilities in android applications. In: Kim, Y., Lee, H., Perrig, A. (eds.) WISA 2013. LNCS, vol. 8267, pp. 138–159. Springer, Cham (2014). doi:10.1007/978-3-319-05149-9_9
9. Demetriou, S., Merrill, W., Yang, W., Zhang, A., Gunter, C.A.: Free for all!. assessing user data exposure to advertising libraries on android. In: NDSS (2016)
10. Enck, W., Gilbert, P., Chun, B.-G., Cox, L.P., Jung, J., McDaniel, P., Sheth, A.N.: Taintdroid: an information-flow tracking system for realtime privacy monitoring on smartphones. In: OSDI (2010)
11. Fahl, S., Harbach, M., Muders, T., Baumgärtner, L., Freisleben, B., Smith, M.: Why eve and mallory love android: an analysis of android ssl (in)security. In: ACM CCS (2012)
12. Fuchs, A.P., Chaudhuri, A., Foster, J.S.: Scandroid: Automated security certification of android applications. Manuscript, Univ. of Maryland (2009)
13. Georgiev, M., Iyengar, S., Jana, S., Anubhai, R., Boneh, D., Shmatikov, V.: The most dangerous code in the world: Validating ssl certificates in non-browser software. In: ACM CCS (2012)
14. Georgiev, M., Jana, S., Shmatikov, V.: Breaking and fixing origin-based access control in hybrid web/mobile application frameworks. In: NDSS, vol. 2014 (2014)
15. Gordon, M.I., Kim, D., Perkins, J., Gilham, L., Nguyen, N., Rinard, M.: Information-flow analysis of android applications in droidsafe. In: NDSS (2015)
16. Hardy, N.: The confused deputy: (or why capabilities might have been invented). ACM SIGOPS Operating Syst. Rev. **22**(4), 36–38 (1988)
17. Hassanshahi, B., Jia, Y., Yap, R.H.C., Saxena, P., Liang, Z.: Web-to-application injection attacks on android: characterization and detection. In: Pernul, G., Ryan, P.Y.A., Weippl, E. (eds.) ESORICS 2015. LNCS, vol. 9327, pp. 577–598. Springer, Cham (2015). doi:10.1007/978-3-319-24177-7_29
18. Huang, W., Dong, Y., Milanova, A., Dolby, J.: Scalable and precise taint analysis for android. In: ISSTA, pp. 106–117 (2015)
19. Jin, X., Wang, L., Luo, T., Du, W.: Fine-grained access control for HTML5-based mobile applications in android. In: Desmedt, Y. (ed.) ISC 2013. LNCS, vol. 7807, pp. 309–318. Springer, Cham (2015). doi:10.1007/978-3-319-27659-5_22
20. Liang, J., Jiang, J., Duan, H., Li, K., Wan, T., Wu, J.: When https meets CDN: a case of authentication in delegated service. In: IEEE Symposium on Security and Privacy (2014)
21. Lu, L., Li, Z., Wu, Z., Lee, W., Jiang, G.: Chex: statically vetting android apps for component hijacking vulnerabilities. In: ACM CCS (2012)
22. Luo, T., Hao, H., Du, W., Wang, Y., Yin, H.: Attacks on webview in the android system. In: ASCAC (2011)

23. Mutchler, P., Doupe, A., Mitchell, J., Kruegel, C., Vigna, G., Doup, A., Mitchell, J., Kruegel, C., Vigna, G.: A large-scale study of mobile web app. security. In: MoST (2015)
24. P.A. Networks. New Android Trojan Xbot Phishes Credit Cards and Bank Accounts, Encrypts Devices for Ransom. http://researchcenter.paloaltonetworks.com/2016/02/new-android-trojan-xbot-phishes-credit-cards-and-bank-accounts-encrypts-devices-for-ransom/
25. Rasthofer, S., Arzt, S., Bodden, E.: A machine-learning approach for classifying and categorizing android sources and sinks. In: NDSS, pp. 23–26 (2014)
26. Rastogi, V., Shao, R., Chen, Y., Pan, X., Zou, S., Riley, R.: Are these ads safe: detecting hidden attacks through the mobile app-web interfaces. In: NDSS (2016)
27. Sedol, S., Johari, R.: Survey of cross-site scripting attack in android apps. Int. J. Inform. Comput. Technol. **4**(11), 1079–1084 (2014)
28. Singh, K.: Practical context-aware permission control for hybrid mobile applications. In: Stolfo, S.J., Stavrou, A., Wright, C.V. (eds.) RAID 2013. LNCS, vol. 8145, pp. 307–327. Springer, Heidelberg (2013). doi:10.1007/978-3-642-41284-4_16
29. Sounthiraraj, D., Sahs, J., Greenwood, G., Lin, Z., Khan, L.: SMV-HUNTER: large scale, automated detection of SSL/TLS man-in-the-middle vulnerabilities in android apps. In: NDSS (2014)
30. Steensgaard, B.: Points-to analysis in almost linear time. In: POPL, New York, NY, USA, pp. 32–41 (1996)
31. Tuncay, G.S., Demetriou, S., Gunter, C.A.: Draco: a system for uniform and fine-grained access control for web code on android. In: ACM CCS (2016)
32. Wang, R., Xing, L., Wang, X., Chen, S.: Unauthorized origin crossing on mobile platforms: threats and mitigation. In: ACM CCS (2013)
33. Wei, F., Roy, S., Ou, X., et al.: Amandroid: a precise and general inter-component data flow analysis framework for security vetting of android apps. In: ACM CCS (2014)
34. Wu, D., Chang, R.K.C.: Indirect File Leaks in Mobile Applications. MoST (2015)

# Filtering for Malice Through the Data Ocean: Large-Scale PHA Install Detection at the Communication Service Provider Level

Kai Chen[1,2(✉)], Tongxin Li[3], Bin Ma[1,2], Peng Wang[4], XiaoFeng Wang[4], and Peiyuan Zong[1,2]

[1] SKLOIS, Institute of Information Engineering, Chinese Academy of Sciences, Beijing, China
{chenkai,mabin,zongpeiyuan}@iie.ac.cn

[2] School of Cyber Security, University of Chinese Academy of Sciences, Beijing, China

[3] Peking University, Beijing, China
litongxin@pku.edu.cn

[4] Indiana University, Bloomington, USA
{pw7,xw7}@indiana.edu

**Abstract.** As a key stakeholder in mobile communications, the *communication service provider* (*CSP*, including carriers and ISPs) plays a critical role in safeguarding mobile users against potentially-harmful apps (PHA), complementing the security protection at app stores. However a CSP-level scan faces an enormous challenge: hundreds of millions of apps are installed everyday; retaining their download traffic to construct their packages entails a huge burden on the CSP side, forces them to change their infrastructure and can have serious privacy and legal ramifications. To control the cost and avoid trouble, today's CSPs acquire apps from download URLs for a malware analysis. Even this step is extremely expensive and hard to meet the demand of online protection: for example, a CSP we are working with runs hundreds of machines to check the daily downloads it observes. To rise up to this challenge, we present in this paper an innovative "app baleen" (called *Abaleen*) framework for an *on-line* security vetting of an extremely large number of app downloads, through a high-performance, concurrent inspection of app content from the sources of the downloads. At the center of the framework is the idea of retrieving only a small amount of the content from the remote sources to identify suspicious app downloads and warn the end users, hopefully before the installation is complete. Running on 90 million download URLs recorded by our CSP partner, our screening framework achieves an unparalleled performance, with a nearly 85× speed-up compared to the existing solution. This level of performance enables an online vetting for PHAs at the CSP scale: among all unique URLs used in our study, more than 95% were processed before

**Electronic supplementary material** The online version of this chapter (doi:10.1007/978-3-319-66332-6_8) contains supplementary material, which is available to authorized users.


M. Dacier et al. (Eds.): RAID 2017, LNCS 10453, pp. 167–191, 2017.
DOI: 10.1007/978-3-319-66332-6_8

the completion of unfettered downloads. With the CSP-level dataset, we revealed not only the surprising pervasiveness of PHAs, but also the real impact of them (over 2 million installs in merely 3 days).

**Keywords:** Large scale · Communication service provide · Potentially-harmful apps

## 1 Introduction

With computing moving toward mobile platforms, also come new waves of mobile malware, which commits all sorts of malicious activities, ranging from fraud, code plagiarism to data theft and illegal surveillance. Such applications, re-branded as *potentially harmful apps* (PHA) by Google [20] to avoid the ambiguity of the term "malware", pose serious threats to the mobile ecosystem and therefore become the main focus of security defense by all major stake holders in mobile communications. On the front line are mobile app stores, such as Google Play and Amazon App Store, which implement malware checks to vet apps and protect their customers. Such protection, however, is far from perfect, particularly when it comes to detecting fraudulent or plagiarized apps, as evidenced by the recent discovery of fraud apps on app stores, including Google Play [5]. Further, there are hundreds of third-party stores around the world, whose app vetting could become sluggish, not to mention thousands of apps being downloaded directly from websites, not going through any security check. For such apps, the only party capable of observing their downloads and operations, and therefore at the position to provide additional protection for the end user is mobile carriers and ISPs, which we call *communication service provider* or *CSP* in our research.

**Challenges in the CSP-scale protection**. Today's CSPs are offering different kinds of value-added security services (e.g., AT&T Managed Security Services [2]) to their customers, which can potentially complement the protection already in place at app stores: particularly, for catching fraudulent and plagiarized apps (many of them are malware [15,28]) missed by typical app-store vetting, and for scanning those downloaded from non-app-store sources. However, in the absence of right technologies, such services entail significant burdens on the providers. A CSP has to process massive amount of data on the daily base: as an example, a world-leading CSP informed us that they observe over 30 million downloads of Android apps every day from a single region. Inspecting all such downloads for PHAs cannot be done through deep packet inspection, since app files today are compressed (in the ZIP format for Android APKs) and therefore their content cannot be directly observed from individual packets.

Alternatively, the CSP could temporarily retain all the packets in a download to reconstruct the app's package before scanning its content. This approach, however, is extremely expensive in terms of storage and computing, and unrealistic for a major CSP which is totally different form an individual organization that could easily reconfigure its firewalls to redirect or split app traffic for malware detection. Further, retaining packets for app scanning does not support online protection (that is, detecting suspicious apps before they are fully downloaded to customers' devices), unless the download process is suspended pending for the outcomes of a security check, which today's CSP simply will not do. Another hurdle for the packet retention approach is the legal and privacy concern. As an example, in the United Kingdom, the High Court of Justice issued a judicial order declaring that sections of the EU Data Retention Directive (which itself only allows retention of packet headers, not content [4]) prescribing indiscriminate data retention are incompatible with EU law and would be inapplicable from 31 March 2016 onwards [10].

To work around the legal barrier and control the cost, the CSP today chooses to download apps again from the URLs collected from the traffic it monitors and scan them off-line. The problem is that even this simple approach still brings in substantial overheads and can hardly provide any online protection to their mobile customers. As a prominent example, the CSP we are collaborating with told us that a major IT company helping them scan apps utilizes 500 servers to keep up with the pace of ever-growing app download traffic (30 million URLs per day now). Clearly, a more efficient and more sustainable alternative is in urgent need here.

**Our approach**. We believe that a practical solution is expected to fully respect today CSP's infrastructure, capability and legal constraints, and also serve to *complement* existing security protection put in place by other stake holders, app stores in particular. To this end, we present in this paper a new, highly efficient *online* app-download analysis framework, called *Abaleen* (app-baleen, as inspired by baleen whale's high-performance filtering system). Abaleen is designed to work under today's CSP infrastructure, and inspect massive amount of app-installing URLs within a short period of time, which allows the CSP to offer online protection, alerting to their subscribers even before an app's installation on the client when possible. For each ongoing app download, Abaleen concurrently utilizes the observed download URL to analyze the app data stored at the source the link points to. At the center of this new framework are the techniques that only *partially download* a very small amount of data (a few KB on average from a full package of 20 MB) from each stored APK for security checks (fraud and clone detection and other PHA scans), for the purpose of achieving extremely high performance (Sect. 3.2). More specifically, Abaleen framework supports security analysts to select different portions of an online app content for filtering and detecting various kinds of PHA, which further allows them to design customized filters and high-performance scanners (called *scanlet*). Examples include using an app's package name, checksum and signatures to determine, almost instantly, whether the app was seen before, regardless of different download URLs. For the app that was not, multiple scanlets will work on the APK, still using nothing more than a small set of downloaded data.

This partial-download and lightweight inspection framework turns out to be highly effective. Running our prototype on top of 90 million URLs provided by our CSP partner (from March 2nd to 4th in 2016, with 99% of the links reusable), Abaleen demonstrates that security checks over partial content work as effectively as much more heavyweight full downloads: almost all those detected by mainstream malware scanners were also captured by only inspecting 1 to 30% of their content. Further, our fraud and clone scanlets identified additional 10% PHAs never reported before (which have been manually confirmed and reported to the CSP), at a high precision (100% for fraud detection and 93% for clone detection). Most importantly, compared with the baseline solution (in which all the apps pointed by unique URLs are fully downloaded for duplicate removal and malware scan, as the CSP currently does), our approach improved the performance by almost 85 times, using merely 3 virtual-machine (VM) instances (8 cores, 2.5 GHz CPU, 16 GB memory) to analyze all the app installs the CSP receives per day. This performance enables the CSP to provide their customers real-time protection, sending out alerts even before an app has been installed on a mobile device. Indeed, our experiment shows that 95% of these download URLs were successfully analyzed before their APKs were fully downloaded.

**Findings.** Looking into the results of our analysis, we gained new insights into the illicit activities inside the Chinese mobile ecosystem, where Google Play cannot be accessed and the users tend to download apps from highly diverse sources. Particularly, our study shows that PHAs have been extensively propagated across the ecosystem. In just 3 days, already 2,263,643 downloads of 19,101 PHAs were observed. Among them are the PHAs that masquerade as the official apps of banks, online shopping sites, social networks and other organizations. Particularly, even two months after those apps were downloaded, still a fraud app impersonating JD.com, the largest Chinese e-commerce site, are missed by all 56 scanners on VirusTotal. As another example, the fake app for Bank of Communications, the 12th largest one in the world, is flagged by only a single scanner. Also interesting is the discovery of 17 different fake versions of WeChat, the largest Chinese social network app with 700 million users: those apps commit a wide spectrum of illicit activities, from credential stealing to aggressive advertising. Again, most alarming here is that so far, many of them are only flagged by Tencent, the developer of WeChat, among all 56 scanners hosted by VirusTotal. Actually, after two months, all these apps are still accessible from various web sources, indicating that the whole Chinese ecosystem (including mobile users) is less mature in terms of awareness of security risks. Further, we found that apps from major Chinese stores like 360 and Baidu are all delivered through various content-distribution networks (CDNs), and in many cases, even when a PHA was removed from the stores, it could still be downloaded from its CDN cache. This could potentially enable cyber criminals to continue to spread their PHAs even after the apps have been taken down by the app stores.

**Contributions.** The contributions of the paper are outlined as follows:

- *Highly scalable framework for online PHA detection.* The main contribution of this paper is an innovative framework that uses partial downloads to support online PHA detection at an extremely large scale. We demonstrate that by strategically picking up a small amount of app data from its online repository, security checks can be done as effectively as those performed on the fully-downloaded apps, and in a much faster way (85 × speed-up without undermining the quality of the PHA scan), which enables real-time online detection for end users.

- *New techniques to tune PHA detection to work with partial downloads*. Particularly, our new fraud and clone detection approaches leverage the icon, name, and UI similarity between a PHA and its impersonation target to efficiently identify suspicious apps, which requires only a small amount of data from an APK online and can therefore be easily integrated into the partial-download mechanism of the framework. We further show that only a small fraction of APK content is sufficient for modern Anti-Virus scanners to capture almost all PHAs.
- *New discoveries and insights*. Using Abaleen, we had the unique opportunity to analyze tens of millions of app download URLs, a scale never achieved in any prior study. Our study brought to light new findings about the Chinese mobile ecosystem, including the pervasiveness of security threats there (fraud, clone in particular) and the number of downloads by users. Such discoveries will contribute to better understanding of cyber criminals' strategies and techniques, and more effective protection of mobile users.

## 2 Background

**Android and PHA**. According to Netmarketshare [8], Android remains to be the most popular mobile operating system, with a 61.9% market share. With its biggest market share, Android is also the main target of PHA authors. In order to reach a large audience and gain their trust, a significant portion of PHAs today are designed to impersonate the apps associated with big organizations or other legitimate apps. Particularly, a fraudulent app can include a target organization's logo and name, and mimic its official app's UI layouts. At least some of these apps can get through today's app-store vetting. For example, it is reported that fake bank apps continue to pop up on Google play, victimizing the customers of the French bank, Industrial Bank of Korea (IBK), Israeli BankMirage and others, even for the party that does not have official app [5]. Also lacking in the vetting process is the detection of cloned apps, which are built by repackaging legitimate apps (e.g., AngryBird) with new functionalities, for the purpose of free-riding the latter's popularity to distribute the former.

**CSP-level protection**. Under the realistic threats of large-scale attacks, especially those involving extensive fraudulent charges on their subscribers, all major mobile carriers and ISPs today have security infrastructures in place to mitigate the security risks present in their networks. Also, they all provide additional security services to their customers, detecting signs of breaches from the customers' traffic and helping their incident investigations etc. Prominent examples include AT&T Managed Security Service [2] and Verizon Manged Security [9]. These services and infrastructures are mainly aimed at network-level protection, inspecting individual packets or collective features of traffic to identify botnets, SMS Spam, Phishing websites, etc.

The emergence of PHAs in mobile networks poses a new challenge to CSPs, since detecting these apps goes way beyond network-level defense: PHAs cannot be easily blocked by blacklisting their hosting domains and IPs, as many of them may belong to legitimate app stores; inspecting app-download packets or retaining packets for scanning is unrealistic on CSP level, as shown in Sect. 1. Up to our knowledge, today no effective techniques are there for timely scanning massive amount of APK download traffic going through the CSP and providing mobile users timely alerts especially before PHAs are installed on their devices, which is urgently needed by CSPs for extra profits (said by our CSP partner).

**Adversary model.** We consider an adversary who attempts to distribute PHAs through app stores and other online sources (e.g., forums and other public sites). He is capable of infiltrating some stores, using fraudulent, plagiarized (cloned) apps or other PHAs those stores are not well equipped to detect. On the other hand, *Abaleen was built for the purpose of detecting the suspicious apps hosted on the websites not within the adversary's control.* Those sites, including app stores and other application download portals, are the main channel for PHA propagation, since they attract most Android users and the PHAs there can easily reach a large audience. In the meantime, we do have protection in place to mitigate the threat from malicious sites, which might *cloak*, an *active attack tactic* that causes the content downloaded from the same URL differ based upon the requestor's IP and other information. Our techniques raise the bar for such attacks, making them more difficult to succeed, though we still cannot eliminate the threat (Sects. 3.2 and 5). Further assumed in our study is that the CSP intends to complement, rather than replace the existing defense at app stores, which has been confirmed by our industry partner. Finally, in our research, we focus on the apps installed through the unprotected HTTP protocol, whose traffic content, download URLs in particular, can be seen by the CSP. This is because almost all major app stores, except Google Play, are found to utilize HTTP for app installation. Prominent examples include Slideme, GetJar and all major Chinese markets. Particularly, in China where Google Play is inaccessible, almost all app download URLs are in plaintext and can be reused for collecting the same apps being downloaded (Sect. 4.1).

## 3 Design and Implementation

As mentioned earlier, a CSP-level online PHA analysis is expected to be highly efficient and extremely scalable, and also effective in complementing the security controls enforced by other stake holders in the mobile communications. The latter is important because the CSP is *not* meant to replace other parties, app markets in particular, in terms of end-user protection. Instead, it is supposed to provide another layer of defense against the PHAs missed by those parties.

### 3.1 Overview

Figure 1 illustrates the architecture of Abaleen, including a set of filters and lightweight scanlets. The filters perform a sequence of quick checks on massive amount

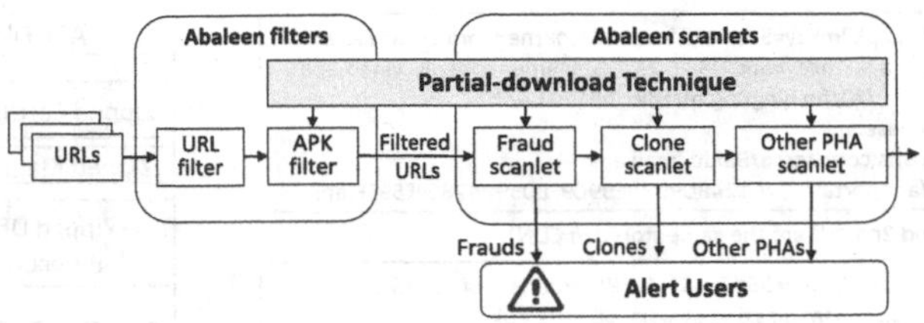


**Fig. 1.** Overview of our approach.

of app-download traces (i.e., the URLs) to remove those considered to be legitimate or seen before. Such filtering steps start with analyzing the download URLs, screening out duplicates (which is nontrivial, see Sect. 3.2) and those on a white list and immediately flagging those on a black list (an example is shown in Fig. 2). The follow-up filters run the partial-download technique to acquire the package name and signature from the APK pointed by each of the remaining links, identifying those issued by trusted parties or analyzed before (Sect. 3.2). In Fig. 2, the filter drops `Baidu_map.apk`, which is signed by Baidu (a party on the white list), and a FM radio app whose checksum and signature matches another app that Abaleen analyzed before. The traces significantly trimmed down in this way are then handed over to the scanlets, which further download partial app content (icon, names, XML files and others) to detect fraudulent, cloned and other suspicious apps (Sect. 3.3). In the example, the icon of the app from `139.196.26.149` is found to be similar to that of the Chase bank and its name also contains the word 'Chase', which causes an alert to the user (e.g., through SMS).

## 3.2 Abaleen Filters

A CSP typically observes a huge volume of app-download traffic, that is, a download URL including a `.apk` file or an HTTP response with its `Content-Type` set to "`application/vnd.android.package-archive`". As an example, our CSP partner reports at least 30 million downloads of Android apps every day from a region with a population of 20 million. Such URLs can be obtain as soon as their downloads start. Obviously, most of them belong to popular apps or are developed by reputable organizations. To quickly filter out these unlikely-harmful apps, a straightforward solution is to remove from the traffic the URLs all pointing to the same web locations and download the apps there only once, together with those signed by trusted parties. However, this turns out to be nontrivial, due to the variations in the URL parameters and the extensive use of the content distribution networks (CDNs).

**URL filtering**. Although many of download URLs pointing to the same web sources are identical and can therefore be easily removed, others look quite different. In some cases, the differences are caused by the parameters on a URL. To identify the parameters unrelated to the APK file, we tried to download the same app using various mobile devices in different places. To this end, we found some

**Fig. 2.** An example of our approach

**Fig. 3.** APK file (zip format)

parameters are apparently used to transport the information about the device installing the app and its owner, such as location, IMEI, IMSI, and even the content related to the owner's preferences (e.g., "mkey" and "f" in Fig. 2). The Abaleen filter removes all the parameters unrelated to the APK file to compare across the URLs their domains, paths and the APK names, keeping only one link for those showing up more than once. To prevent the adversary from taking advantage of the filter to deliver different code, we only remove the duplicates for the domains belonging to either known app stores (Amazon, Baidu, Tencent, etc.) or their CDNs.

Further complicating the filtering is the pervasiveness of CDNs, which enable the mobile user to acquire apps from the hosts close to her location but introduce a huge variation even in the domains of download URLs. Identification of CDNs is known to be hard and cannot be easily automated. What we did is to probe a set of largest app stores (e.g., 360, Baidu, Tencent) from different locations to find out the domains or IP addresses of the CDNs they use. Even though the CDN list collected in this way is by no means complete, it already helps reduce the number of download transactions: trimming down the 30 million download URLs from our CSP partner to around 1 million.

**Partial download**. To further cut down the volume of the download transactions to be scanned, we need to go beyond the URL-level screening, looking into the APK content to find the same apps stored at different places and the trusted apps hosted by less secure stores. Apparently this can only be done by downloading the whole app before its content can be inspected, as many IT companies do today (which was communicated to us by our CSP partner). The overheads introduced in this way, however, are tremendous: given that the average size of today's Android app is around 20 MB, scanning over merely 1 million apps requires transporting 20 TB data across the Internet and analyzing all of them, not to mention that a CSP has to go through at least tens of millions of app installs every day. Also the delays incurred by acquiring and evaluating apps' full content make it hard to timely respond to the security risk observed, alerting the user before a PHA is installed on her device.

A key observation in our research is that to find out whether an app is malicious, legitimate or seen before, oftentimes, only *part* of its content needs to be examined: for example, just looking at the certificate for the app's signature, we can filter out those signed by reputable organizations; by inspecting its checksum, we can remove the ones analyzed before and capture known PHAs. Note that such information cannot be falsified by the adversary as long as he does not control the hosting website (as considered in our adversary model), since they will be verified before the apps can be installed on the recipient devices. Actually, this "partial analysis" approach is fully supported by a modern data download technique implemented by almost every website today, which allows a download to start from any offset within an APK. Actually, this feature is supported by the HTTP 1.1 protocol [27] (page 52), which includes a header field called "Range". This field allows a request to specify the byte offset in the target file and the length of the content to be retrieved. Abaleen leverages this feature to pick up a small amount of information from the remote package for an efficient PHA analysis.

The challenge here is how to locate the necessary contents when an app is only remotely available. We notice that an APK file is in the ZIP format (Fig. 3), which includes the compressed versions of the app's contents (e.g., images, DEX bytecode) and a directory list that serves as the table of the contents (TOC), with the offset for each document within the ZIP file. The offset and length of the directory list in the ZIP file are specified in the EOCD (i.e., End of Central Directory Record) structure at the end of the ZIP file [11]. The length of EOCD is variable, which includes 22-byte data plus a variable-length comment. In our evaluation, the length of the whole EOCD never exceeds 200 bytes, which makes the TOC easy to retrieve for locating other documents inside the package. Specially, Abaleen first sends a request to the target APK file and retrieves its total length by reading the Content-Length field in the HTTP response header. Then, Abaleen sends another request to only retrieve the last 200 bytes by setting up the header field "Range" (the offset is set to the length of the file minus 200; the length is set to 200 bytes). From the retrieved data (i.e., EOCD), Abaleen knows the offset of TOC and its length. After retrieving TOC in a similar way, Abaleen can request the file entries that are needed for further analysis. Note that the downloaded data are actually not a ZIP file which cannot be directly decompressed. Our approach utilizes a dummy ZIP file with an app's directory list and all other downloaded elements placed at the right offsets of the file before running a standard tool (unzip) to extract them. In particular, the dummy ZIP file has the same size as the original APK, which uses the same dictionary and compressed files. Also the dictionaries in both files (the dummy file and the original APK) are located at the same position in their respective APKs. In this way, only a few KB is collected for an app.

**Fast app screening**. We note that, although the same app hosted on different stores cannot be identified from their install URLs, they all bear the same "META-INF/MAN-IFEST.MF" (containing the SHA-1 checksums of each individual file in the APK for signing the app) whose MD5 can serve as the checksum of an app. What Abaleen does is retrieving this file and searching for the checksum in the dataset of known APKs: a match found there causes the APK to be dropped; otherwise, its checksum is saved to the database together the results of the scan. Also used in this step is an app's "signature", that is, the public key on its X.509 certificate. Abaleen includes a white list of trusted app developers (e.g., Google, etc.). The apps signed by them are considered to be safe and will not be further inspected.

As mentioned in our adversary model (Sect. 2), the design of Abaleen is meant to detect the suspicious apps hosted on legitimate app stores and websites, which is the main channel for spreading PHAs today, given the popularity of the sites and their lack of adequate app-vetting protection. However, there are untrusted sites that may try to evade our techniques: such a site can deliver different content according to the user-agent of the visitor's browser (*user-agent cloaking*), the referer field in her download request (*referrer cloaking*), her IP address (*IP cloaking*) and whether she visits the site before (called *repeated cloaking*) [3]. Although this *active* attack is not within our adversary model, Abaleen does have necessary means to mitigate the threat.

Specifically, once deployed by the CSP, our approach can conduct partial downloads using the original request's user agent and referer, and different IP addresses. Given the large number of IP addresses under the CSP's control, it becomes almost impossible for the adversary to fingerprint the Abaleen filter's address. This approach also beats the repeated cloaking, since the adversary cannot find out whether our APK filter has visited his site before from its IP and therefore becomes more likely to treat it as a first-time visitor and deliver malicious payloads. In a more sophisticated cloak, specific to our design, the adversary might try to detect the partial-download behavior. However, requests for retrieving part of resources hosted by a website are common today. Also note that for an untrusted site, we only can contact it once to get its APK's `MANIFEST.MF`, which ensures that the site can no longer send us different content, even when it detects our intention later. This is because the file includes the app's signature, with the SHA-1 checksum for every single file in the APK. Therefore, even though we cannot guarantee to eliminate the cloaking attack, our techniques do raise the bar to the attack (see Sect. 5).

In terms of performance, our study shows that the Abaleen filters work effectively on the real-world data: in our experiment, the URL and APK filters removed 29,893,194 URLs from 30 million downloads (99.64%), within 12.51 h with 3 Virtual Machines, significantly reducing the workload for the follow-up scan step.

### 3.3 Abaleen Scanlets

After the bulk of the app-install transactions have been filtered out, Abaleen starts running various scanlets on the remaining download URLs to identify suspicious apps, which will cause an early warning to be issued to the subscribed user. Here we describe the extensible design of a general scanlet and three example scanlets integrated into our implementation.

**General design of scanlets.** As mentioned earlier, the scanlets are meant to be highly efficient, scalable and complementary to the protection at the app-store level. They are hosted by the extensible Abaleen framework under which both scanlets and PHA analyzers can be easily added and removed. Based on this design, Abaleen framework should supports security analysts both to easily port existing PHA detectors to the framework and to customize their own scanlets. Specifically, Abaleen framework allows security analysts to specify the elements in an APK file which should be partially downloaded, and also an algorithm to handle the downloaded components.

**Detecting frauds.** Fraudulent apps are a special category of PHAs that impersonate those released by big organizations (e.g., banks, payment card companies, and online retailers etc.) to reach a large audience, steal their sensitive information and perform other illicit or unwanted activities (e.g., advertising). Such PHAs often slip under the radar of today's app stores, whose vetting mechanisms are less effective against such a threat [18]. The key observation we have about these PHAs is that they have to plagiarize their target organizations' icons and names to deceive the users. As a result, they are actually exposed by this resemblance in the appearance but the difference in signing parties. Based upon such an observation, we built a scanlet that quickly scraps names and icons from APKs online to search a database with the symbols of large organizations and prominent apps. Those found matching there but carrying inconsistent signatures are reported to be potentially harmful. Note that such detection can be effectively done by only downloading an app's manifest (including its name and path for the icon) and icon image (the signature has already been retrieved by the APK filter), and therefore works highly efficiently, capable of alerting the end user even before her app download completes. Also, note that the programming trick like dynamic loading of icons does not work here because this will cause an icon change once the app is clicked by the user, which is highly unusual and suspicious.

However, this simple approach turns out to be more complicated than it appears to be: organizations can have multiple logos and PHA authors can change their targets' app names (e.g., from "Chase Mobile" to "Online Chase") and icons (e.g., adjusting their colors) but still make them deceptive to mobile users. As an example, Fig. 4 presents the icons of some suspicious apps, which are compared with the original Chase bank app that they might impersonate. These apps are identified through both a text analysis of their names and an image evaluation on their icons to control false positives. Both analyses are important, since an app carrying an icon similar to that of a different app could still be

**Fig. 4.** Icons of suspicious apps and the original Chase bank app.

legitimate: e.g., an app called "Financial assistant" includes a bank icon that looks like the image of ICBC (i.e., a famous bank in China). Following we describe the techniques that address these issues.

Our idea to defeat the name change trick is to identify a *key-term* ('Chase') perceived to represent an organization, which is then used to detect the app whose name involving that term. To do this in a largely automatic way, we collect a list of organizations (e.g., the top banks in different countries) and their official apps (by searching leading app stores), extract their names and try to find out whether a smaller unit within each name, such as a word or a phrase, can also describe the organization. For example, "JPMorgan Chase bank" can be represented by a single word "Chase". For this purpose, we leverage search engines: our approach extracts individual words and phrases within a name (e.g., "JPMorgan", "Chase", "bank", "JPMorgan Chase", "Chase bank") and searches them online; if the top (most relevant) result returned by the search points to the organization's website (which is found by searching for the organization's full name), we believe that the term is semantically tied to the organization, which we call *semantic terms*. Among all semantic terms, those that do not include any other semantic terms are picked out as the organization's key-terms. In the above example, "Chase" is a key-term while "Chase bank" is not. For the app with a Chinese name, we first perform word segmentation (using Jieba [6]) to identify the words from Chinese characters before extracting its key-terms from the words. Also for some organizations, their acronyms can also be their key-terms. For example, "BOA" is commonly perceived as "Bank of America", particularly when the app with that name also has a similar icon. These acronyms are found by searching online for the combination of initial letters of the words within an organization's full name or each of its non-single-word semantic term. Again, those finding us the organization's site are considered to be its key-terms.

In our research, we ran this approach on a list of 194 prominent organizations and 258 apps (including banks, payment services, insurance companies, online retailers, top games and social network apps) to automatically extract their key-terms and semantic terms. These terms were further used to harvest each organization's logos, by searching for them online (e.g., under Google Images, searching for "Chase Bank logo"). Top 50 images returned, after removing duplicates, were saved into our database and labeled by their corresponding key-terms[1].

[1] Those terms and images were manually inspected to ensure their correctness.

Altogether, our approach harvested 11,640 images for 194 organizations. The database is then used by the fraud detector for scanning the APK content partially downloaded from its website: the scanlet first looks for the presence of key-terms within an APK's name after removing from the name all non-letter characters (i.e., those not inside the English or Chinese letter set); when a match is found, it further checks the APK's icon and raises an alarm if the icon is found similar to any of the logos labeled by the key-terms.

The comparison between an icon and a logo can be done through an image similarity analysis. The algorithm we use is called *Perceptual Hashing* [24], which has been widely applied to find copyright infringement online. In a nutshell, the technique summarizes a set of perceivable features from an image and compares whether two images are close in terms of these features [23]. The state-of-the-art implementation can handle rotation, skew, contrast adjustment and other changes made by the PHA authors.

**Detecting clones.** For the CSP-level protection, a scanlet detecting clones is expected to be highly efficient, working only on a small portion of the APK. To this end, we leveraged an observation that the cloned apps tend to preserve the user interfaces (UIs) of the original apps, presumably in an attempt to impersonate the original apps to reach a large audience. As a result, UI-related components, particularly an app's UI layout files (in XML format), are largely intact in the cloned version [28]. Given the fact that such XML files are tiny, our scanlet can just retrieve them from an online APK, serving as a pre-filter to find out whether they strongly resemble those of known apps. Then Abaleen partially downloads the DEX code for clone detection. In this way, only very few bytes need to be downloaded.

Specifically, the visual structure of an app, including the features of its UI components (e.g., button, text field), is typically defined in its XML files. These components are represented through *View* elements (e.g., a single button) and further organized into *ViewGroup* (a special View containing other Views or ViewGroups). In Fig. 5, we show examples for Views (e.g., Button) and ViewGroups (e.g., LinearLayout). Such a hierarchical structure can be described by an *interface-graph* (*IGraph*): nodes represent Views and ViewGroups, which are connected by the edges that describe the inclusion of one element (e.g., a View) within the other (e.g., a ViewGroup). Such IGraphes are identical between the cloned and the original apps, when the repackaged version does not change the UIs, as found in today's PHAs. Note that changing UIs brings in risks to the PHA authors, making the apps less similar to the one they intend to impersonate and easier to notice by the user [15]. We ignore views with attribute "`visibility:none`" which makes UI components invisible to users. Also, though UIs can be dynamically generated, to make this happen, efforts need to be made to analyze and encode the UIs of the original apps, which raises the bar for the clone attack.

To enable a highly efficient similarity comparison across hundreds of thousands of apps, we developed a novel technique that identifies a set of structural and content features from each IGraph and maps these features to a

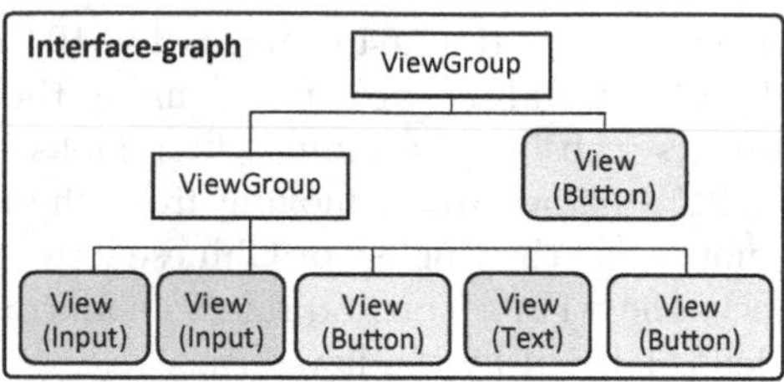


**Fig. 5.** An example of IGraph.

low-dimensional representative such as a number for evaluating the closeness of two graphs. Specifically, for each node in the graph, we describe it with a vector $v = \langle s, n, b, w \rangle$, where $s$ is a sequence number assigned to the node in the order determined by a deep-first traversal on the graph (i.e., the first one encountered in the traversal given 1, the next one given 2, and so on[2]), $n$ is the number of the UI elements on the node, $b$ is the number of the node's children, and $w$ is an index assigned to the UI type of the current node (e.g., button, image, etc.). We maps each node to a 4-dimensional space with each of these features being a coordinate, and then computes the geometric center of the whole graph as its representative: $v_{all} = (\sum_{e(p,q) \in IGgraph}(w_p \boldsymbol{v}_p + w_q \boldsymbol{v}_q))/(\sum_{e(p,q) \in IGraph}(w_p + w_q))$, where $v$ is called *vhash*, $e$ is the edge from node $p$ to $q$. Unlike the cryptographic hash, which cannot tolerate even a minor difference, the vhash is linear to the change on an IGraph: two XMLs' vhashes come close when their IGraphs are similar, and two different XMLs will have their vhashes distance apart. This allows us to sort the vhash values of known apps and run a binary search to help our scanlet quickly locate the apps carrying similar UIs (as described by their IGraphs).

In our research, our scanlet uses the vhash technique to compare the XMLs of an APK (only less than 1% of the file) against those of 500,000 apps we collected (which include prominent gaming apps, tools, etc.) before code comparison. Whenever the APK is found to share at least 80% of XMLs with a known app, it is considered to be a likely clone. To control false positives, we further used a white list to remove the XMLs belonging to SDKs and code templates (e.g., Umeng SDK, Android Support Libraries). Our study shows that this simple approach is capable of processing an APK within 2 s on average, has a high precision (0.008% false positives among all alarms) and importantly captured 1,563 PHAs never known before in our experiment (Sect. 4.2).

**Screening other PHAs.** We describe a lightweight scanlet to demonstrate how to combine existing scanners with Abaleen framework. As mentioned earlier, Abaleen is meant to be a highly scalable CSP-level framework that complements, rather than replaces, the protection already in place at mobile app stores. For this purpose, we design the scanlet built for screening app downloads from less reliable sources (particularly legitimate yet less protected stores and websites

[2] For each node, its child nodes with most children are visited first.

through which PHAs can easily reach a large audience) using existing scan results from leading stores and AV scanners (e.g., AVG, Qihoo-360).

Specifically, the scanlet simply lets go of all the apps passing the vetting of renowned sources documented by a white list. For other apps, the scanlet leverages the scan results of the identical app in the leading app markets. To this end, we need to search in the stores for the package name and checksum of each app from an unreliable source, which is actually complicated: this is because except Google Play, most other stores do not make such a search interface open to the public. To address this issue, we leveraged the observation that a URL scheme market://details?id=<package_name> proposed by Google [7] is actually supported by almost all the market apps (e.g., those for Amazon, Slideme, Baidu, 360, Tencent). Once the scheme is triggered by any Android app, a market app is invoked to download an APK using its package name from the corresponding online store. In our research, we reverse-engineered the protocols used by the market apps to query their stores and recovered the package-searching APIs for leading Chinese markets, as illustrated in Table 1. Using such APIs, our scanlets can directly retrieve from these stores the checksums of the apps with given package names (through partial download). Once the checksums match those of the apps downloaded from other legitimate but less protected sources, such apps are also quickly filtered out, without going through further evaluations.

**Table 1.** Protocols for searching package name in markets.

| Market | Protocol |
|---|---|
| Baidu | http://m.baidu.com/appsrv?...&action=detail&pkname=com.baidu.appsearch&pname=<package_name>& ... |
| Tencent | http://android.myapp.com/myapp/detail.htm?apkName=<package_name> |
| Qihoo | http://openbox.mobilem.360.cn/iservice/getAppDetail?...&pname=<package_name>& |

For the apps outside this fast lane, our scanlet downloads the code of the app (DEX and native code), typically only 20–30% of the package, which is most incriminating part of a PHA, including the program logics for malicious activities. Note that even though the PHA authors could hide attack code within resource files (e.g., images), the operations for loading and executing the code are still inside the DEX or native components of the app, and therefore can be detected from these components. Most importantly, our study shows that the code components, together with other ZIP and APK files within a package and its MD5, are all most AV scanners use to detect PHAs (see Sect. 4.2). Based upon this observation, our scanlet only downloads these code components from online APKs and sends them for a PHA scan by existing AV scanners.

## 4 Evaluation and Measurement

To understand the efficacy of Abaleen, we evaluated our prototype over 90 million APK download URLs provided by our CSP partner, which represent all app install transactions the CSP observed from a Chinese region with a 20 million population during three consecutive days. Since most apps were inside China, we deployed Abaleen in 3 VM instances hosted on the Aliyun cloud [1], a major Chinese cloud service provided by Alibaba. All instances have 8 cores, 16 GB memory. Two run Ubuntu Linux 14.04 with a 40 GB disk and one runs Windows with a 500 GB disk. The bandwidth it has for app download is about 4 MB per second on average.

### 4.1 Efficiency and Scalability

**Setting**. As mentioned earlier (Sect. 3), Abaleen takes two stages to inspect massive amount of download data: it first filters out the apps analyzed before and then runs fraud, clone and PHA scanlets on the remaining APKs. At each stage, a different amount of content needs to be partially downloaded: manifests, checksums and signatures first and then icons, XMLs and for a subset of apps, DEX, binary and HTMLs. Also additional time is spent on concurrently running fraud, clone and other PHA detection. In our research, we measured the time used in the whole process, and further compared the results with that of the straightforward alternative: downloading all apps after removing duplicate URLs for a PHA scan, as our CSP partner is currently doing.

**Table 2.** Number of URLs in each stage.

| | | Day 1 | Day 2 | Day 3 |
|---|---|---|---|---|
| Original | | 30 million | 30 million | 30 millon |
| Reusable | | 29.70 million | 29.68 million | 29.74 millon |
| Full download (Remove duplicates) | | 1,846,250 | 1,572,956 | 1,681,563 |
| Abaleen | after URL filter | 918,916 | 755,242 | 833,832 |
| | after APK filter | 106,806 | 40,054 | 47,549 |
| | fraud/clone detection | 106,806 | 40,054 | 47,549 |
| | PHA screening | 53,134 | 22,524 | 20,655 |

Table 2 shows the number of URLs and unique apps included in our dataset for each of the three days. Each day the CSP saw roughly 30 million download URLs, with 99% of them reusable (which can be used to download the same content multiple times). After removing duplicated URLs, about 1.8 million were left. By analyzing these URLs, our filters further trimmed down the install transactions the scanlets need to inspect. For the first day, a little more than 100,000 out of the 1.8 million remained after duplicate or legitimate apps were dropped. All these 100,000 were scanned by both fraud and clone scanlets, but only a little more than half of them, about 50,000, were outside three largest Chinese app stores that have proper app vetting in place (Baidu, Tencent, 360) and therefore needed to be partially downloaded (20 to 30%) for an additional PHA scan. Although still around 100,000 unique installs were seen on Day 2 and Day 3, respectively, the number of new apps (never seen in the prior days) went down, to 40,054 for the second day and 47,549 for the third day. To compare the number of bytes downloaded at each stage, we randomly selected 5000 apps and measured the sizes of their individual files. The results show that on average, only 0.24%, 2.17%, and 27.22% of the app need to be downloaded for APK filter, clone/fraud detection, and PHA screening, respectively.

To benchmark the performance of our system against the full-download approach, we randomly sampled 5000 apps from the whole dataset to measure the operation time of Abaleen at different stages against that for full downloads in the same VMs. 100 threads were run to concurrently collect the content from the APKs online.

**Results**. The results of this experimental study are presented in Table 3. On average, filtering an app took 0.098 s, retrieving its icon, manifest and XMLs needed 0.352 s and collecting its DEX, binary and others used 2.201 s. With these parameters, the whole dataset can be comfortably handled by the 3 VM instances. As an example, all the apps for Day 1 can be processed within 0.94 days. In contrast, downloading full APKs took 7.290 s on average using the same VM instances. Altogether, going through all 1.8 million apps with the partial download was about 55 times faster than the full-download solution on the first day. Further, it is important to note that the workload Abaleen faces decreases every day due to the overlapping between the apps downloaded cross days. On the third day, only 47,549 new apps needed to scan. At that point, the speed-up factor became roughly 85 times.

By comparing the time for app screening through Abaleen and that for fully downloading an APK, we found that Abaleen was much faster. Among all unique URLs in our study, more than 95% were processed before their apps were fully downloaded, showing that Abaleen is capable of supporting online PHA detection.

### 4.2 Effectiveness

**Fraud and clone detection**. Altogether, our fraud scanlet reported 289 suspicious APKs and the clone scanlet flagged 1,563. 17 of them passed VirusTotal and 845 were not detected by the leading anti-virus (AV) scanners we ran in our study, including AVG and Qihoo 360. From all those reported, we manually went through 150 random samples and found no false positive. To evaluate the false negative rate is difficult due to the lack of the ground truth for real fraud apps within the 90 million APK download URLs. What we did was to compare our detection results with a report of fraud apps given by our CSP partner. The comparison shows that all the fraud apps in the report were caught by our approach.

**Table 3.** The time (in seconds) for handling each app by Abaleen.

| | URL filter | APK filter | Fraud/clone | Other PHA | Full download |
|---|---|---|---|---|---|
| time (s) | 0.00001 | 0.098 | 0.352 | 2.201 | 7.290 |

To measure the false positive rate of clone, we randomly sampled 100 detected clones (after pre-filtering and partially downloading the code for comparison) and installed them on a device for a comparison with the original apps (those used for detecting the clones). We manually inspected those detected clones and found 1 false positive. This gives us a false detection rate (false positives vs. all detected) of 1% and a false positive rate (false positives vs. all apps analyzed) of 0.008% (= $1563 \times 1\%/(106806 + 40054 + 47549)$). The problem was caused by the shared libraries missed on our white list (built from the libraries within 2000 known legitimate apps).

**PHA screening.** For the PHA screening, what we wanted to understand is whether the scan on the partial content of APKs works as effectively as on the whole APKs. To do this, we randomly sampled 2,400 apps and submitted both their partial APKs (in a dummy ZIP file including DEX code, native code, other ZIP and APK files within the original APK package and its MD5) and complete ones to VirusTotal, a platform with 56 AV engines, and use the detection results of complete APKs as ground truth. 1,137 complete apps were flagged, while 1,101 (96.8% from 1,137) partial apps were also flagged, indicating that the partial content is effective for the PHA scan (only 3.2% apps undetected). We further ran AVG and Qihoo AV detector locally on all 96,313 apps (which are needed for PHA screening for all the three days, see Table 2) and found that 97.3% of PHAs detected from the complete APKs were also flagged by the scanners on their partial APKs. Our analysis on the remaining 2.7% apps shows that they were missed due to the MD5 of their partial APKs, which were calculated by the scanners to compare with their malware signatures. The MD5 signatures are known to be fragile, and many scanners (e.g., AVG) are not reliant upon them. Also, many app stores/websites provide MD5 for their apps, which can be utilized for PHA detection. Altogether, we conclude that the partial app content can bring in around 3% false negatives.

### 4.3 Measurement

From the 90 million real-world app-download URLs analyzed by Abaleen, we gained a rare opportunity to look into the PHA threat in the Chinese Android ecosystem from the CSP's perspective. Our study reveals the surprising pervasiveness of such apps in the traffic (19,101 in total): particularly, during merely three days, we observed 1,852 cloned and fraud apps impersonating a wide spectrum of legitimate apps, including bank and payment service and the largest Chinese social network. Many of them are never reported before and still missed by mainstream AV scanners even after two months. Also found in the study are the techniques the PHAs employ to evade detection, e.g., using legitimate apps' certificate. Further, even leading app stores apparently are less prepared for detecting fraud and clone PHAs, which can stay there for a long time. Even after being removed from the markets, PHAs could still be hosted by CDNs, which could continue to be used to victimize the mobile users. Also note that although the measurement study was performed in China, other countries (e.g., Russia, India, etc.) may have similar problems. These countries have many third-party markets in addition to Google Play. Even in the north America, third-party markets are still popular (e.g., Amazon, SlideME, etc.).

### 4.3.1 Landscape

**Magnitude of the PHA threat.** Altogether, Abaleen reported 19,101 PHAs from the 90 million download URLs collected by our CSP partner in three days, including 289 fraudulent apps, 1,563 app clones and 17,249 other PHAs, which were downloaded for 2,263,643 times in these days. Among them, 17 fraud apps were not flagged by any AV scanners *even two months after their download URLs were gathered.* Other fraud apps include those impersonating Bank of Communications, China Guangfa Bank, Wechat, JD (a leading Chinese e-commerce company) and China Mobile Online Office. Further, some PHA authors apparently are highly productive, creating 167 PHAs and spreading them to 17 different locations (app stores, download portals, etc.).

**Insights.** The most important insight from the study is that the whole Chinese ecosystem apparently are less mature in terms of security protection. Even though major app stores indeed made effort to enhance their app vetting, still a large number of fraud and clone PHAs fall through the cracks. Third-party stores are even more plagued by different kinds of PHAs, and a large number of mobile users download PHAs from various sources on the daily base. Even extremely dangerous Phishing apps, those impersonating banks, popular social network apps, etc., can be found from just a few days' traffic.

### 4.3.2 Understanding PHAs

**Fraud.** As mentioned earlier, within our traffic, totally 289 fraudulent apps were downloaded for 16,983 times. Most of them (83.7%) came from app markets or other legitimate download portals. Most of such apps do not copy the target's names, and instead, embed key-terms in their names to deceive the users. Looking into the UIs of such apps, we discovered that most of them include the views similar to those of the official apps, e.g., the screen for entering bank accounts and passwords, while the rest actually are quite different, only sharing icons and names with the official apps. The latter are mostly pushing advertisements and Phishing messages to the users, in the name of the organizations they impersonate.

We also found 17 zero day PHA. A prominent example is the phony app for JD.com, a leading Chinese e-commerce company. The app has been signed by the default AOSP (Android Open Source Project) certificate, and is capable of collecting the user inputs, including her login credential, and can also request installation of other PHAs, which once started cannot be stopped. The app appears to be a repackage of the official app but has been heavily obfuscated. It is remarkable that given the high profile of the victim, the fraud app has still not been detected by any AV scanner *after two months* (since Mar. 2nd, 2016, the first time it showed up in our trace).

**Clone**. We were surprised to find that 1,563 app clones were downloaded for 134,859 times in just three days. Some of them were developed to deceive the users for collecting their personal data, just like fraud apps. Others, however, possibly attempt to steal the original apps' advertisement revenues. 45.9% of those cloned apps were from majority appstore (Baidu, Tencent, Qihoo 360), while 54.1% from other download portals. Interestingly, we also discovered that 339 apps are actually the clones of a pornography app, which itself was flagged as malware by our CSP partner. This indicates that either these apps all came from the same author with different certificates or PHA authors even plagiarized the code of their peers. Another interesting observation is that some apps from different authors have an identical sequence of permissions added to their manifest, which may indicate that they were all repackaged using the same tool.

**Other PHAs**. As mentioned earlier, our Abaleen prototype runs AVG and Qihoo 360 as local scanners (for the purpose of avoiding upload of tens of thousands of apps to VirusTotal, see Sect. 4.2) for analyzing the partial content of the APKs that has not been checked by leading app stores. Altogether this step identified 17,249 PHAs from the three-days' traces, and 1,571 of them were signed by the default AOSP certificates. In addition to the classic harmful activities like Adware, SMS Trojan and Rootkit, there are 3 PHAs found to be able to infect both PCs and Android devices through HTMLs. Specifically, such an app injects a malicious script to HTML files, and when the script is running, all other HTMLs are further infected. These apps carry different signatures, which could imply that the same attack trick has been adopted by multiple PHA authors.

Some PHAs were found to utilize some simple techniques to evade detection. One of them is using random string to replace author information on an app's certificate, possibly to avoid the detection based upon the checksum of certificates. Also, we discovered that 514 PHAs include more than one certificate, many of these certificates are actually extracted from legitimate apps, which apparently are used to disguise a PHA as the legitimate one.

### 4.3.3 Propagation and Defense

**PHA hosting**. We found that many PHAs were downloaded from app stores (though less known ones), forums, app download portals and other legitimate sites, and only 3,483 from unknown places. Particularly, 46.3% fraud or clone apps were present on the leading Chinese app stores, Baidu, Tencent and Qihoo at the time the traces were collected, though 106 of them were removed when we analyzed them. Also, 22.6% of these apps were uploaded to multiple app markets. These findings indicate that indeed app stores and legitimate websites are the main channel for PHA propagation.

On the other hand, some PHAs did come from suspicious domains. From the 90 million download traces, we found a few likely malicious domains from which PHAs were delivered. Interestingly, the adversary apparently played a domain rotation trick to drive download traffic through related domains to a smaller set of IPs. For examples, we found that download requests for 7xk7r4.com1.z0.glb.clouddn.com and 7xnt11.com1.z0.glb.clouddn.com all pointing to the same IP address. Further, some suspicious domains impersonate legitimate ones, such as http://www.baidu.com.860ys.com and http://www.soso.com.860ys.com, where baidu.com and soso.com are all popular Chinese domains. Another observation is that the standard redirection trick for protecting malware hosting sites (such as those for drive-by downloads) is also used to hide PHA sites: we found that a download request for "http://www.huobaotv.net/194/e6%88%90%e4%ba%ba%e6%92%ad%e6%94%be%e5%99%a8_j2QFmY.apk" led to three redirections before the APK could be accessed.

**Defense in place.** In the presence of the serious PHA threat, the responses from the leading app stores, however, do not seem to be adequate. Specifically, in our research, we measured the time it takes for the app stores to clean their houses, as presented in Table 4. As we can see from the table, even after two months, most PHA URLs for those stores are still alive.

**Table 4.** Ratio of removed PHAs after two months.

| App store | Baidu | Qihoo-360 | Tencent |
|---|---|---|---|
| Ratio of removed PHAs | 24.8% | 3.8% | 18.0% |

Further complicating the situation is the extensive use of CDNs, as mentioned earlier (Sect. 3.2). Even after a PHA is dropped from an app store, its copy can still be cached by the store's CDN for a while, which can still be downloaded to victimize the user. In our research, we found that though some fraud or clone PHAs in the Tencent app store were no longer there, they could still be downloaded from Tencent's own CDN. To understand how long these code can still be around, we measured the duration between when they were removed from the store and the time they were no longer accessible from the CDN. We found that even 22 days after the apps' removal from the market, 19.3% of apps could still be downloaded from the CDN.

## 5 Discussion

**Website cloaking.** The design of Abaleen is meant to defend against the threat from the PHAs hosted by legitimate websites. These sites are supposed to deliver what a client asks for and not play the trick to change the app or its components according to the client's identity. In other words, the adversary in our assumptions is *passive*, who can deposit his PHA to a public site but does not have control on the download process. This model is realistic, since most apps today are installed from app stores, well-known application portals and other reasonable sources, even inside China, where Google Play is not accessible. In the meantime, risks do exist in which the adversary cheats mobile users into downloading PHAs from a malicious site (e.g., through social engineering). Although the threat is outside our adversary model, Abaleen is *not* defenseless in front of such attacks. As mentioned earlier (Sect. 3.2), a CSP has a plenty of resources (IP addresses in particular) to defeat the IP, referer and user-agent based cloaking used by today's malicious sites.

On the other hand, the adversary could adapt to our new technique, trying to detect the partial-download requests and deliver fake content. This attempt, however, is more complicated than it appears to be, due to the fact that a download starting from somewhere inside an APK is common nowadays for improving the reliability and performance of data transfer. Most importantly, our analysis shows that 47.9% of all 70,000 apps have their checksum files (MANIFEST.MF, the one used for signing apps) at the beginning of their packages while 45.6% include the files at the end of the APKs. Also, the start and the end of such a file can be easily identified, even when they are compressed. Therefore, Abaleen can run a multi-threaded download manager that breaks an APK into blocks and pretends to concurrently download all the blocks: whether the checksum file is at the head of the APK can be immediately found in this way (by checking whether the beginning a few bytes are "META-INF/"); if not, the manager can be set to first complete the download of the last 5% of the APK, which almost certainly includes the checksum file. Once the file is retrieved, the website can no longer cloak, since the file contains the SHA-1 for each document inside the package and signed by the app developer. This allows us to begin the partial download immediately after that. Note that multi-threaded download is widely used by ordinary Android users. Differentiating the behavior of Abaleen from the normal request, therefore, is challenging if not impossible, which certainly raises the bar for the attack.

**Evasion**. Further the PHA author might attempt to evade the security checks of our scanlets, for example, through using fake APK headers. However, fake APK headers will cause the APK install to fail on user's device. Attackers may also obfuscate app icons, names and XMLs files. As discussed in Sect. 3.2, such an attack cannot succeed without a significant effort, since the scanlets are all designed to tolerate certain levels of changes: e.g., we utilized the key-term search in the app name, perceptual hashing for image similarity comparison in the presence of color change and distortion, and vhash for fingerprinting the XMLs, which works even when the files have been moderately altered. On the other hand, further research is needed to better understand what the best evasion strategy the adversary may have in this situation. Also, our PHA scanlet filters out all the apps in the leading stores. This does not mean that these stores are PHA free. Instead, the CSP just does not want to replace the roles of the stores in user protection, which become prominent in recent years (e.g., Google's enhancement of Bouncer). Still the security implications here need further investigation.

**HTTPS.** Abaleen cannot handle encrypted download traffic. As mentioned earlier, most app markets and download portals today are using HTTP. Actually, once these app download sources decide to encrypt their traffic, the CSP is no longer at the position of detecting propagation of malicious content, simply because it can no longer see the traffic content. On the other hand, the app stores that utilize HTTPS, like Google Play, are those with proper security protection, while the stores and download portals choosing less protected communication mechanisms (HTTP here) tend to be less aggressive in vetting the apps they host and therefore are supposed to be the focus of our CSP level PHA analysis (assuming that these stores and portals are legitimate, see our adversary model). In our evaluation, 2,263,643 downloads of 19,101 PHAs were observed, within the 3-day traffic (including 90 million HTTP downloads) captured from a single city.

## 6 Related Work

**CSP-level threat identification.** Although PHA detection has been intensively studied [13,15,16,25,29], rarely has the problem been investigated from the CSP perspective. A prominent exception is the study on the malicious traffic observed by cellular carriers [22], which utilizes DNS requests from apps to understand the activities of mobile malware in the US. Interestingly, the study indicates that mobile app markets are relative safe and few attack instances were observed from the traffic. While this might be true back years ago in the US, the situation is certainly very different now in China, as we found in our study. Also remotely related to our work is the research on botnet detection, also at the CSP level (e.g., BotHunter [21]), which detects bots from their communication traffic. Our study, however, focuses on a large-scale screening of the apps being downloaded and installed, and therefore needs to address the challenge of analyzing mass amount of app content.

**Fraud and clone app detection.** Prior research on fraudulent apps often relies on the features extracted from the apps and various machine learning algorithms [12,19] to detect them. Unlike these approaches, the Abaleen scanlet is designed specifically for finding those impersonating legitimate apps, and can therefore utilize the similarity of their icons and names and difference in their signing parties to capture suspicious apps. Also note that as a screening framework, Abaleen is only supposed to identify those suspicious code, rather than using the thin information acquired by partial downloads to detect malware, though our scanlet indeed achieves a high accuracy in fraud detection.

Clone detection can be done through code analysis [14,17,31] or using other app data. Examples in the first category include those utilizing hashes [31], program dependence graphs [17], control flow graphs [14] for code similarity comparison. The latter includes the recent effort to use UIs for clone app detection: specifically, ViewDroid [30] and MassVet [15] statically construct an app's view graphs to compare them with the UIs of other apps. However, those approaches are still too heavyweight to be used for a CSP-level analysis. Droidmarking [26] detects cloned apps with the help of stakeholders, which is not suitable for CSP-level detection. Closely related to our work is DroidEagle [28], which also utilizes an app's XMLs to detect its clones. However, the approach is rather straightforward, relying on hash checksums over XMLs to compare UI layouts across apps. This treatment, however, is rather fragile, and can be easily evaded by the PHA authors by a minor adjustment of the files. By comparison, our clone scanlet runs vhash to summarize an XML file, which can tolerate moderate changes to the XML structures.

## 7 Conclusion

In this paper, we present the Abaleen framework to support CSP-level online screening of Android apps. The framework is built on an innovative partial-download technique, which enables retrieval of a small portion of APK content for PHA analysis. Running Abaleen on 90 million app-download URLs, we found that it achieved a nearly 85 times speed-up compared with the existing technique, which enables an online detection of PHAs, alerting users before download completion. Further by analyzing the apps detected, our study sheds new light on the PHA plague in the Chinese Android ecosystem.

**Acknowledgements.** We thank our shepherd Roberto Perdisci and anonymous reviewers for their valuable comments. We also thank VirusTotal for the help in validating suspicious apps in our study. Kai Chen was supported in part by NSFC U1536106, National Key Research and Development Program of China (Grant No. 2016QY04W0805), Youth Innovation Promotion Association CAS, and strategic priority research program of CAS (XDA06010701). The IU authors are supported in part by NSF CNS-1223477, 1223495, 1527141 and 1618493, and ARO W911NF1610127.

## References

1. Aliyun cloud. https://www.aliyun.com/
2. At&t managed security services. http://www.corp.att.com/gov/solution/network_services/mss.html
3. Cloaking. https://en.wikipedia.org/wiki/Cloaking
4. Data retention directive. https://en.wikipedia.org/wiki/Data_Retention_Directive
5. Fraudster phishing users with malicious mobile apps. https://info.phishlabs.com/blog/fraudster-phishing-users-with-malicious-mobile-apps
6. Jieba - chinese text segmentation. https://github.com/fxsjy/jieba
7. Linking to your products. https://developer.android.com/distribute/tools/promote/linking.html
8. Mobile/tablet operating system market share. https://www.netmarketshare.com/operating-system-market-share.aspx
9. Verizon managed security services. http://www.verizonenterprise.com/products/security/monitoring-analytics/managed-security-services.xml
10. Data retention across the eu (2016). http://fra.europa.eu/en/theme/information-society-privacy-and-data-protection/data-retention
11. Zip (file format) (2017). https://en.wikipedia.org/wiki/Zip_(file_format)

12. Abbasi, A., Albrecht, C., Vance, A., Hansen, J.: Metafraud: a meta-learning framework for detecting financial fraud. Mis Q. **36**(4), 1293–1327 (2012)
13. Arp, D., Spreitzenbarth, M., Hubner, M., Gascon, H., Rieck, K.D.: Effective and explainable detection of android malware in your pocket. In: NDSS (2014)
14. Chen, K., Liu, P., Zhang, Y.: Achieving accuracy and scalability simultaneously in detecting application clones on android markets. In: ICSE (2014)
15. Chen, K., Wang, P., Lee, Y., Wang, X., Zhang, N., Huang, H., Zou, W., Liu, P.: Finding unknown malice in 10 seconds: mass vetting for new threats at the google-play scale. In: USENIX Security, vol. 15 (2015)
16. Chen, K., Wang, X., Chen, Y., Wang, P., Lee, Y., Wang, X., Ma, B., Wang, A., Zhang, Y., Zou, W.: Following devil's footprints: cross-platform analysis of potentially harmful libraries on android and IOS. In: IEEE Symposium on Security and Privacy (SP), pp. 357–376. IEEE (2016)
17. Crussell, J., Gibler, C., Chen, H.: Attack of the clones: detecting cloned applications on android markets. In: Foresti, S., Yung, M., Martinelli, F. (eds.) ESORICS 2012. LNCS, vol. 7459, pp. 37–54. Springer, Heidelberg (2012). doi:10.1007/978-3-642-33167-1_3
18. Felt, A.P., Finifter, M., Chin, E., Hanna, S., Wagner, D.: A survey of mobile malware in the wild. In: Proceedings of the 1st ACM Workshop on Security and Privacy in Smartphones and Mobile Devices, pp. 3–14. ACM (2011)
19. Foozy, C.F.M., Ahmad, R., Abdollah, M.F.: Phishing detection taxonomy for mobile device. Int. J. Comput. Sci. **10**, 338–344 (2013)
20. Google. Google report: Android security 2014 year in review (2014). https://static.googleusercontent.com/media/source.android.com/en/security/reports/Google_Android_Security_2014_Report_Final.pdf
21. Gu, G., Porras, P.A., Yegneswaran, V., Fong, M.W., Lee, W.: Bothunter: detecting malware infection through ids-driven dialog correlation. In: Security (2007)
22. Lever, C., Antonakakis, M., Reaves, B., Traynor, P., Lee, W.: The core of the matter: analyzing malicious traffic in cellular carriers. In: NDSS (2013)
23. Monga, V., Evans, B.L.: Perceptual image hashing via feature points: performance evaluation and tradeoffs. IEEE Trans. Image Process. **15**, 11 (2006)
24. Niu, X.-M., Jiao, Y.-H.: An overview of perceptual hashing. Acta Electronica Sinica **36**(7), 1405–1411 (2008)
25. Rastogi, V., Chen, Y., Enck, W.: Appsplayground: automatic security analysis of smartphone applications. In: CODASPY, pp. 209–220 (2013)
26. Ren, C., Chen, K., Liu, P.: Droidmarking: resilient software watermarking for impeding android application repackaging. In: Proceedings of the 29th ACM/IEEE International Conference on Automated Software Engineering, pp. 635–646. ACM (2014)
27. RFC. Hypertext transfer protocol - http/1.1 (1999). http://www.ietf.org/rfc/rfc2616.txt
28. Sun, M., Li, M., Lui, J. Droideagle: seamless detection of visually similar android apps. In: Proceedings of the 8th ACM Conference on Security & Privacy in Wireless and Mobile Networks, p. 9. ACM (2015)
29. Yan, L.K., Yin, H.: Droidscope: seamlessly reconstructing the OS and dalvik semantic views for dynamic android malware analysis. In: USENIX Security (2012)
30. Zhang, F., Huang, H., Zhu, S., Wu, D., Liu, P.: Viewdroid: towards obfuscation-resilient mobile application repackaging detection. In: WiSec (2014)
31. Zhou, W., Zhou, Y., Jiang, X., Ning, P.: Detecting repackaged smartphone applications in third-party android marketplaces. In: CODASPY (2012)

# Android Malware Clustering Through Malicious Payload Mining

Yuping Li[1(✉)], Jiyong Jang[2], Xin Hu[3], and Xinming Ou[1]

[1] University of South Florida, Tampa, USA
yupingli@mail.usf.edu, xou@usf.edu
[2] IBM Research, Yorktown Heights, USA
jjang@us.ibm.com
[3] Pinterest, San Francisco, USA
huxinsmail@gmail.com

**Abstract.** Clustering has been well studied for desktop malware analysis as an effective triage method. Conventional similarity-based clustering techniques, however, cannot be immediately applied to Android malware analysis due to the excessive use of third-party libraries in Android application development and the widespread use of repackaging in malware development. We design and implement an Android malware clustering system through iterative mining of malicious payload and checking whether malware samples share the same version of malicious payload. Our system utilizes a hierarchical clustering technique and an efficient bit-vector format to represent Android apps. Experimental results demonstrate that our clustering approach achieves precision of 0.90 and recall of 0.75 for Android Genome malware dataset, and average precision of 0.98 and recall of 0.96 with respect to manually verified ground-truth.

## 1 Introduction

Triaging is an important step in malware analysis given the large number of samples received daily by security companies. Clustering, or grouping malware based on behavioral profiles is a widely-studied technique that allows analysts to focus their efforts on new types of malware. Multiple static [14,30], dynamic [2,22], and hybrid [12] analysis based clustering techniques have been proposed in the desktop malware domain.

With the rapid growth of Android smart devices, malicious Android apps have become a persistent problem. Security companies receive a list of (potential zero-day) malware on a daily basis [28]. Those apps that present certain suspicious behaviors but are not detected by any existing anti-virus scanners need to be further analyzed manually. Conducting clustering on those incoming

**Electronic supplementary material** The online version of this chapter (doi:10.1007/978-3-319-66332-6_9) contains supplementary material, which is available to authorized users.


M. Dacier et al. (Eds.): RAID 2017, LNCS 10453, pp. 192–214, 2017.
DOI: 10.1007/978-3-319-66332-6_9

malware apps can allow the analysts to triage their tasks by (a) quickly identifying malware that shares similar behaviors with known existing malware so they may not allocate much resources on it; and (b) selecting a few representative apps from each new malware cluster to prioritize their analysis.

We often observe that existing approaches to group Android malware based on their behaviors have provided limited capabilities. For example, existing Android malware detection products may report a family name for a detected sample; however, samples from one family can have multiple different versions of malicious code segments presenting significantly different behaviors. Therefore, the malware family information provided by AV products can be incomplete to describe crucial malicious code segments of Android malware.

Existing overall similarity analysis based clustering system cannot be immediately applied for Android malware clustering because the malicious code segments often constitute only a small fraction of an Android malware sample. In desktop malware clustering, the static or dynamic features are first extracted from target samples. Then a clustering algorithm (*e.g.*, hierarchical agglomerative clustering) is applied to group the samples such that samples within the same resulting group share high level of overall similarity. However, we note that overall similarity analysis performs poorly in Android malware clustering because of two common practices in Android malware development.

The first practice is repackaging. Malware writers may embed the malicious code inside an otherwise legitimate app, in which case the real malicious code segment is likely to be small compared to the original benign app. Our analysis shows that the ratio of the core malicious code segments to the entire app for a collection of 19,725 malware samples is between 0.1% and 58.2%. Given the small percentage of malicious code segments, the conventional clustering approach that is based on overall code similarity will not work well. For example, two malicious samples from different families can be repackaged based on the same original benign app, thus presenting high level of overall similarity. Likewise, Android malware variants with the same malicious code of one family can be repackaged into different original benign apps, thus presenting low level of overall similarity.

Another practice is utilizing shared library code. Android apps often include a variety of third-party libraries to implement extra functionalities in a cost-effective way. If the library code size is too large compared to the rest of the app, samples from different malware families may be clustered together simply because they share the same libraries. We measured the library code proportion of the 19,725 malware samples. For 13,233 of the samples that used at least one legitimate library, we found that the average library code ratio is 53.1% in terms of number of byte code instructions. This means a large portion of an Android app belongs to libraries. One approach to prevent those libraries from "diluting" the malicious code segments is to use a whitelist [4–6, 8, 10] to exclude all library code. However, previous work leverages only the names of libraries while building a whitelist as opposed to the content of libraries. We observed that malware authors injected their malicious code under popular library names, such as `com.google.ssearch`, `com.android.appupdate`, `android.ad.appoffer`, and `com.umeng.adutils`. Consequently, naïve whitelisting approaches inadvertently remove certain malicious payloads together with the legitimate library code from analysis. We found that about 30% of our analyzed Android malware families disguise their malicious payload under popular library names.

Due to the above two reasons, directly applying overall similarity analysis on Android apps will not be effective for Android malware analysis. A major challenge is to precisely identify the malicious code segments of Android malware. For simplicity, we refer to the core malicious code segments of Android malware as *malicious payload*. A payload can be an added/modified part of a repackaged malware app, or the entire code of "standalone" malware app excluding legitimate library code.

In this paper we propose an Android malware clustering approach through iterative mining of malicious payloads. Our main contributions include:

1. We design and implement an Android malware clustering solution through checking if apps share the same version of the malicious payloads. By reconstructing the original malicious payloads, our approach offers an effective Android malware app clustering solution along with fundamental insights into malware grouping.
2. We design a novel method to precisely remove legitimate library code from Android apps, and still preserve the malicious payloads even if they are injected under popular library names.
3. We conduct extensive experiments to evaluate the consistency and robustness of our clustering solution. Our experimental results demonstrate that our clustering approach achieves precision of 0.90 and recall of 0.75 for Android Genome malware dataset, and average precision of 0.984 and recall of 0.959 regarding manually verified ground-truth.

## 2 Overview of Android Malware Clustering System

Rather than directly conducting overall similarity analysis between Android malware samples, we first design a solution to precisely remove legitimate library code from Android apps. We consider the shared code segments (excluding legitimate library code) between the analyzed Android apps as candidate payload, and find all of the input Android apps through pairwise intersection analysis. For a group of $n$ apps, each input app will contribute to $n-1$ versions of candidate payloads.

After extracting all candidate payloads, we conduct traditional clustering analysis on all candidate payloads to group similar ones together. Base on several key insights that are learned from analyzing candidate payload clustering results, we design an effective approach to iteratively mine the payload clusters that are most likely to be malicious, and make sure that each input app will only contribute one version of malicious payload. Finally, we use the identified malicious payload clusters and payload-to-app association information to group the input Android malware apps. We describe this process in more details below.

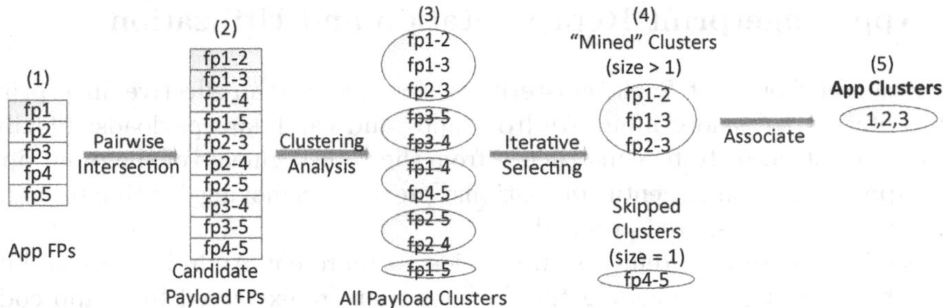


**Fig. 1.** Overview of the clustering system with five Android malware samples.

Figure 1 illustrates the overview of the clustering analysis system with five malware samples.

1. **Library code removal:** We convert malware samples into fingerprint representation, and design an effective approach to precisely remove legitimate library code from each app fingerprint. We denote the library-removed app fingerprints as fp1, fp2, fp3, fp4, and fp5 accordingly.
2. **Candidate payloads extraction:** We conduct a pairwise intersection analysis to extract all shared code segments (*e.g.*, candidate payloads) between input apps. Relying on the app fingerprint representation, we create candidate payload fingerprints, and record the payload-to-app association information. For example, fp1-2 indicates that this candidate payload is extracted from malware sample 1 and 2.
3. **Candidate payloads clustering:** We then perform hierarchical clustering on all candidate payloads with a predefined clustering similarity threshold $\theta$, *e.g.*, the candidate payload fingerprints fp1-2, fp1-3, and fp2-3 are grouped together as the largest payload cluster based on the overall payload similarity.
4. **Malicious payload mining:** After removing legitimate libraries, similar malicious payloads extracted from samples in the same malware family will become more *popular*[1] due to the "legitimate" reason of code reuse. Therefore, we design an iterative approach to mine the popular payload clusters from the clustering results, which are more likely malicious payload. For instance, candidate payload cluster containing fp1-2, fp1-3, and fp2-3 is selected as the most popular cluster. To ensure that each input app only contributes one version of final malicious payload, we simultaneously update the remaining payload clusters. *e.g.*, fingerprints fp1-4, fp1-5, fp2-4, fp2-5, fp3-4, and fp3-5 are then skipped because malware sample 1, 2 and 3 have already been "used".
5. **Malicious samples grouping:** We group the original Android samples based on payload mining results and payload-to-app association information such that the samples within each app cluster contains the same version of the malicious payload. For example, malware samples 1, 2, and 3 are grouped together based on the selected candidate payload cluster containing fp1-2, fp1-3, and fp2-3.

[1] Further intuition explanation and popularity criteria are included in Sect. 4.

# 3 App Fingerprint Representation and Utilization

As we can see from Sect. 2, the clustering system requires an effective fingerprint representation to denote input Android apps and candidate payloads. Ideally, the fingerprint needs to be constructed from the code segments of the input app and support two fundamental operations: precisely removing legitimate code, correctly extracting shared app code.

Based on these requirements, we decide to represent Android apps as bit-vector fingerprints, by encoding the features that are extracted from app code through feature hashing [13,14,26]. The value of each bit in the generated fingerprint is either 0 or 1, indicating whether the corresponding app has a specific feature or not.

This bit-vector format enables us to precisely remove legitimate library code (Sect. 3.2), extract shared code segments (Sect. 3.3), and reconstruct the original malicious payload (Sect. 3.4) by utilizing the bit manipulation capability.

## 3.1 Fingerprint Generation and Fingerprint Comparison

In this work, we use $n$-gram sequence of Dalvik bytecode to denote an Android app feature, and use a *bit-vector* fingerprint to represent the extracted features. The overall fingerprint generation process is shown in Fig. 2.

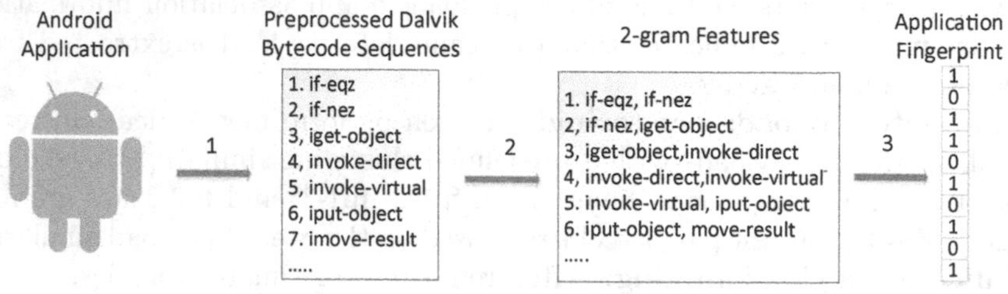


**Fig. 2.** Overall fingerprint generation procedure

For each Android app, we first use Dexdump [7] to disassemble `classes.dex` into Dalvik bytecode, then preprocess the Dalvik bytecode sequences to only include the major distinctive information and extract the $n$-gram features from the prepreocessed bytecode sequences. We follow similar approach to extract the distinctive information (*e.g.*, bytecode opcode) for feature construction as Juxtapp [11]. Since feature space is vital to support the key operations designed in this work, we decide to increase the feature space by including more generic but meaningful information from each bytecode instruction. The major distinctive information is separated into 4 categories and summarized in Table 1. Besides the feature differences shown in Table 1, we extract the $n$-gram features at the function level, while Juxtapp extracts $n$-gram features at the basic block level. For simplicity, we only show the Dalvik bytecode opcode sequences as the distinctive instruction information in Fig. 2.

**Table 1.** Major feature categories and main differences comparing with Juxtapp

| Feature category | Examples | Our approach | Juxtapp |
|---|---|---|---|
| Dalvik bytecode opcode sequences | sget, goto, return | ✓ | ✓ |
| Java VM type signatures | Z(*Boolean*), B(*byte*) | ✓ | |
| String value of `const-string` instructions | – | ✓ | |
| Type signatures for "invoked" functions | f(I,[B)Z | ✓ | |

After extracting all the $n$-gram features, we then encode all the features in a bit-vector format fingerprint through **feature hashing** technique using `djb2` hash function. During feature hashing process, we use a tuple $A(i, j)$ to represent a feature position, in which $i$ is the function offset indicating from which function the particular $n$-gram feature is extracted, and $j$ is the bytecode offset indicating the position of the $n$-gram feature within the corresponding function. Then the feature-to-bit information is stored in a map, in which the key is the bit index within the fingerprint indicating where the feature is stored, and the value is the list of feature tuples that are mapped to the bit location. With increased feature space, we hope to reduce majority of the random feature collisions, and allow each bit index to represent the same $n$-gram feature content.

Similar to the complete Android apps, individual legitimate libraries and the candidate malicious payloads are also represented in the same size of bit-vector fingerprints. The concrete $n$-gram size and the fingerprint size used for clustering are determined through analyzing the collision rate of random features, which is discussed in Sect. 6.2.

To measure the similarity between two fingerprints, we use the Jaccard index, or the Jaccard similarity, which is defined as the size of intersection divided by the size of union of two sets. Since each fingerprint is a bit-vector, we leverage cache-efficient bit-wise AND ($\wedge$) and bit-wise OR ($\vee$) operations to compute the intersection and the union. Then, the similarity of two fingerprints $\mathsf{fp_a}$ and $\mathsf{fp_b}$ is defined as follows:

$$Similarity(\mathsf{fp_a}, \mathsf{fp_b}) = \frac{S(\mathsf{fp_a} \wedge \mathsf{fp_b})}{S(\mathsf{fp_a} \vee \mathsf{fp_b})}, \qquad (1)$$

where $S(\cdot)$ denotes the number of 1-bits in the input.

Our fixed-sized bit-vector fingerprint representation also allows us to easily measure containment ratio in a similar fashion:

$$Containment(\mathsf{fp_a}, \mathsf{fp_b}) = \frac{S(\mathsf{fp_a} \wedge \mathsf{fp_b})}{S(\mathsf{fp_a})}, \qquad (2)$$

which measures how much of the content of $\mathsf{fp_a}$ is contained in $\mathsf{fp_b}$.

### 3.2 Fingerprint Based Library Code Removal

To precisely remove legitimate library code without excluding a possibly injected malicious payload, we exclude legitimate library code from an app by removing the *library-mapped* bits from the app bit-vector fingerprint. For each legitimate library, we collect its official jar file and disassemble it into Dalvik bytecode sequences; then apply the same feature hashing technique to map the $n$-gram features of the library code into a bit-vector fingerprint $\mathsf{fp_{lib}}$. We then flip all the bits in the library fingerprint to get $\overline{\mathsf{fp_{lib}}}$. Since the same features contained in an Android app and the library are mapped to the same bit positions in their fingerprint representation, we can exclude library-mapped bits from an app fingerprint by bit-wise ANDing $\overline{\mathsf{fp_{lib}}}$ and $\mathsf{fp_{app}}$. Figure 3 demonstrates the overall procedure to safely remove legitimate `twitter4j` library code from a malware sample.

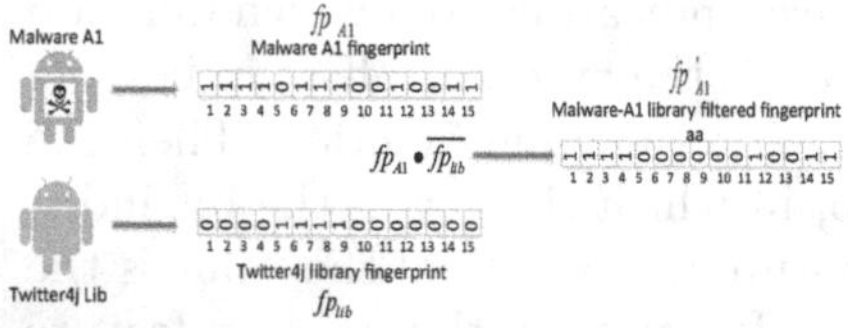


**Fig. 3.** Example procedure to safely remove legitimate "twitter4j" library code

**Fig. 4.** Extracting a candidate payload from two malware applications

We first conduct statistical analysis for the disassembled apps to identify the embedded legitimate libraries, and record the years when the target samples were created. We then obtain[2] the officially released library jar files to create the corresponding library fingerprints, and remove the library code from the analyzed apps. The library code removal process is applied only when an app contains code snippets that are defined under corresponding library namespaces.

In our implementation, each library is represented with an individual fingerprint. We encode multiple versions of the same library together in a single library fingerprint. This aggregated library representation may cause potential feature collision between the app code and the irrelevant versions of the library code. However, we empirically demonstrate in Sect. 6.3 that the library code removal process is precise because different versions of the same library typically share high level of code similarity due to code reuse, and the size of the single library is often smaller than the entire app.

### 3.3 Fingerprint Based Candidate Payload Extraction

The next operation is to extract malicious payloads from malware samples. We consider the shared code segments (after excluding legitimate libraries) between

[2] We randomly select one version of library in each year in case there are multiple versions of libraries released within the same year.

each malware sample pair to be a candidate malicious payload. For a group of malware samples, we obtain the intersection of every fingerprint pair of library-excluded samples, and consider the shared 1-bits between the sample fingerprints as a candidate payload fingerprint.

Figure 4 describes the intersection analysis procedure to extract a candidate malicious payload at a high level. For two malware samples we first build their fingerprints and exclude the legitimate library bits from the fingerprints. Then we pinpoint their shared 1-bits (*e.g.*, bits index 2, 3, and 4) as potentially malicious[3] bits and construct a candidate payload fingerprint.

During the candidate payload extraction process, we keep track of the association information between the candidate payload (*e.g.*, `A1-2`) and the corresponding samples (*e.g.*, `A1` and `A2`). We subsequently use the payload-to-app association information and the malicious payload mining results to group malware samples.

### 3.4 Fingerprint Based Malicious Payload Reconstruction

Using the bit-vector fingerprint representation, we can also define the cluster fingerprint for a version of the candidate payload cluster as the intersection of all the candidate payload fingerprints in the cluster. The 1-bits contained in the resulting cluster fingerprint can be viewed as the shared malicious bits for all input apps that share the same version of malicious payload.

Using the identified malicious bits from app fingerprints, we can then reconstruct the corresponding malicious payload code by checking the feature-to-bit mapping information that was recorded during feature hashing, which can be viewed as the reverse procedure of fingerprint generation. Given the identified malicious bits, we locate the feature tuples that are mapped to those identified malicious bits. We use each retrieved feature tuple to locate the $n$ lines of code where the $n$-gram feature is extracted, then reconstruct complete malicious code sequences by properly stitching the identified $n$ lines of code segments together.

In practice, feature collision is possible but becomes negligible with appropriate $n$-gram size and fingerprint size, thus we will rarely recover the irrelevant code. To certain extent, payload code reconstruction compensates feature hashing collisions (*e.g.*, resulting in missing $n$-grams) as far as the missing $n$-gram is within the overlapped original code sequences of recovered features. The reconstructed malicious payload code can be further inspected to verify its maliciousness.

## 4 Malicious Payload Mining

**Key insights:** (a) In practice, when feature hashing is configured to have a low collision rate, malware app fingerprints will not contain a large number of shared 1-bits unless they do share certain common features (*e.g.*, payload code

[3] malicious payload mapped.

snippets). (b) Likewise, if a target dataset contains malware samples that do share the same version of the malicious payload, then the candidate payload fingerprints extracted from those samples will contain similar shared 1-bits and be automatically clustered into the same group. (c) After removing legitimate library code from an app, similar malicious payloads have higher chances to form a *larger cluster* than the ones related to less popular libraries or coincidentally shared code segments. (d) Compared to coincidentally shared code segments, similar malicious payloads will have a *larger shared code base* because of "legitimate" reason of code reuse in the same malware family, and the fingerprints for the malicious payloads will have a larger amount of shared 1-bits.

Based on the above key insights, we design the following strategies to iteratively select representative candidate payload clusters based on payload *popularity*, which is determined based on the three criteria: the entry size of a payload cluster $l$, the number of distinct apps associated with a payload cluster $m$, and 1-bits count of a payload cluster fingerprint $k$.

- We count the number of candidate payload fingerprint entries in each cluster, and maximize the possibility of extracting core malicious payloads by selecting the clusters with the largest number of payload fingerprint entries. Payload cluster size $l$ is a direct indicator for the popularity of the shared code segments between malware samples, and such popular shared code is a good candidate for one version of malicious payloads since we have already filtered out popular legitimate library code.
- We measure the distinct apps $m$ that contribute to generating candidate payload fingerprints of each cluster, and select the clusters with the largest number of distinct apps if they have the same number of payload entries. Payload clusters that contain a large number of unique payload entries are often associated with a large number of distinct apps, and we use this app association information to break the tie in case the number of cluster entries are the same since distinct apps can be considered as another sign of comparative popularity.
- We obtain the intersection bits $k$ of payload fingerprint entries in each cluster as the cluster fingerprint. If two clusters are associated with the same number of distinct apps, we then select the one with the larger number of 1-bits in its cluster fingerprint. In this way, we can extract the payload with a larger code size, and it helps to increase the likelihood of getting malicious payloads together with shared libraries, and we subsequently exclude possibly remaining libraries later.
- During cluster selection, we keep track of which apps have been used to generate candidate payload fingerprints in the previously selected clusters, and consider already-selected apps as "inactive". We update the remaining payload clusters by removing candidate fingerprint entries that are associated with "inactive" apps. Skipping such fingerprints allows us to extract one version of the malicious payload from each app. This helps to merge all the shared core malicious code together, and only extract the widely shared malicious code between all apps, which also helps to reduce the probability of extracting non-malicious payload code.

- We omit a payload cluster if the corresponding cluster fingerprint contains less than the minimum $k$ number of 1-bits, meaning that the extracted code segments are too small. It forces the algorithm to break the current large payload cluster into smaller clusters with a larger code size, and prevent different malware families from being clustered together. We set the minimum number of 1-bits $k$ to 70 since the majority of the analyzed Android malware app fingerprints had more than 70 1-bits.
- We exclude a candidate payload cluster if it becomes empty after the update in the last step, or if the number of payload fingerprint entries is too small (*e.g.*, $l = 1$). This is because Clusters with only a single candidate payload entry provide little additional popularity information, and are more likely to contain less popular libraries or other coincidentally shared code snippets. We consider malware samples associated with such payload clusters as unclustered, and the unclustered app is evaluated as a singleton.

The shared payloads between Android samples can be library code segments, malicious payloads, copy-and-pasted code segments, or other coincidentally shared code segments. The above payload mining strategy enables us to select the most likely malicious candidate payload groups. Legitimate non-library reused code may be collected together with malicious payload only if it is shared across a significant number of apps. Otherwise, the less popular legitimate non-library code will be evidently excluded during the (popularity-based) payload mining procedure. If the same benign app is indeed used by many malware apps, we can further exclude original benign app code (*i.e.*, the legitimate non-library reused code) in a similar way to remove library code using a benign app fingerprint.

## 5 Optimize Overall Clustering Efficiency

According to the previously discussed malicious payload mining procedure, we will generate $\frac{n\times(n-1)}{2}$ versions of candidate payload fingerprints given $n$ malware samples, but the hierarchical clustering algorithm also has a quadratic complexity with respect to the number of analyzing targets. Due to the overall quartic complexity of the algorithm, directly using it to analyze large number of samples becomes a time-consuming task. Therefore, we further develop two methods to improve the scalability of the clustering analysis procedure, and hereafter refer them as Opt-1, and Opt-2.

### 5.1 Opt-1: Optimize Each Pairwise Computation

The first method to speed up the overall clustering process is to optimize each pairwise computation. Broder proposed minHash [3] to quickly estimate the Jaccard similarity of two sets without explicitly computing the intersection and the union of two sets. By considering our bit-vector fingerprint as a set, we apply minHash to further transform a large fingerprint into a smaller size signature, and calculate the similarity of minHash signatures to estimate the Jaccard similarity of the original fingerprints.

To apply minHash, we define a minHash function output of our bit-vector fingerprint $h(\mathsf{fp})$ to be the first non-zero bit index on a randomly permutated bits order of the fingerprint. We then apply the same minHash function to two fingerprint $\mathsf{fp_a}$ and $\mathsf{fp_b}$. This will generate the same minHash value when the first non-zero bit indexes for two fingerprints $\mathsf{fp_a}$ and $\mathsf{fp_b}$ are the same. Since the probability that the firstly encountered bit is a non-zero bit for $\mathsf{fp_a}$ and $\mathsf{fp_b}$ is conceptually the same as Jaccard similarity $Similarity(\mathsf{fp_a}, \mathsf{fp_b})$ [18], we use such probability $Pr[h(\mathsf{fp_a}) = h(\mathsf{fp_b})$ to estimate the original Jaccard similarity.

The probability estimation becomes more accurate if more independent minHash functions are used together. Formally, we define a minHash signature $sig(\mathsf{fp})$ to be a set of $k$ minHash function values extracted from $k$ round of random permutations over the fingerprint, and represent it as follows: $sig(\mathsf{fp}) = [h_1(\mathsf{fp}), h_2(\mathsf{fp}), ..., h_k(\mathsf{fp})]$. We denote the similarity of two minHash signatures as the ratio of equal elements between $sig(\mathsf{fp_a})$ and $sig(\mathsf{fp_b})$.

Instead of maintaining $k$ random permutations over the bit-vector, we follow a common practice for using minHash technique and use $k$ different hash functions to simulate $k$ random permutations, where each hash function maps a bit index to a value. In order to create $k$ hash functions, we first generate $k$ random numbers, then use FNV [9] hash algorithm to produce a basic hash output for each bit index, and finally apply XOR operation between each random number and the hash output to get the $k$ hash outputs. For each hash function, we select the smallest hash value (to simulate the first non-zero bit index) over all of the bit indexes of the fingerprint as the final hash output.

Note that the FNV hash value and the $k$ random numbers are all 32 bits unsigned integers, and they can be used to safely simulate random permutation over 512MB bit-vector fingerprint. In practice, the $k$ value usually needs to be larger than 100 to generate good enough results [18]. We set $k$ to be 256 in our experiments, and thus convert each bit-vector fingerprint into a 1 KB minHash signature.

In order to evaluate the potential impact of Opt-1 on accuracy, we conduct two experiments on the smallest 50 malware families[4]: one experiment (Exp-1) with no optimization, and another experiment (Exp-2) using Opt-1. We used the clustering output from Exp-1 as a reference, and measured the precision and recall of the clustering output from Exp-2. The precision and recall indicate how similar the two experiments results are, and are used to check the impact on accuracy brought by Opt-1.

Our experiments showed that on average Exp-2 took less than 83% time to complete compared to Exp-1 for the analyzed families, and the average precision and recall of the clustering output were 0.993 and 0.986. Opt-1 significantly reduce the overall memory consumption with minHash signature representation and improve the pairwise computation efficiency with almost zero accuracy penalty.

---

[4] We select those families since their family sizes are under 100 and all the experiments for those families can be finished within 1 h.

### 5.2 Opt-2: Employ approximate clustering

The previous optimization is still not sufficient for using the algorithm to analyze large scale malware samples. For instance, when analyzing with 2,000 samples, the algorithm will create 1,999,000 candidate payloads, and it results in approximately $2.0 \times 10^{12}$ pairwise comparison. Even 1% of the total comparison still takes lots of computation resources. To resolve the scalability issue for a large dataset input, we further adopt prototype-based clustering technique [16,22] to achieve approximate clustering.

Specifically, we randomly divide the target samples into small size (*e.g.*, 150) groups. For each group, we apply hierarchical clustering analysis on the shared payload within the group, and create a prototype fingerprint for each payload cluster by applying intersection analysis (to obtain all the shared 1-bit) among the payload fingerprints in each cluster. We then conduct hierarchical clustering analysis on all the collected prototype fingerprints. In this way, we represent a group of similar payload fingerprints with a single prototype fingerprint, and the algorithm proceeds with approximate clustering analysis using the prototype fingerprints instead of the original payload fingerprints.

We design two experiments to evaluate the impact of Opt-2 on accuracy: one experiment (Exp-3) using Opt-1 only, and another experiment (Exp-4) using Opt-1 and Opt-2. Due to the quartic complexity of the original algorithm, the overall analysis (using Opt-1 only) will get dramatically slower for analyzing larger number of malware samples. For instance, we found it takes about one day to analyze 1000 samples and more than five days to analyze 2000 samples for Exp-3. In order to conduct the evaluation within reasonable amount of time, we randomly select 70% of labeled samples from the largest 4 malware families and conduct the two experiments for each family. We used the clustering output generated by Exp-3 as reference, and measured the precision and recall of the clustering output generated by Exp-4 to evaluate the accuracy impact brought by Opt-2.

Our experiments showed that on average Exp-4 can speed up more than 95% compared to Exp-3, and the average precision and recall for the analyzed 4 families were 0.955 and 0.932. This optimization makes it feasible to apply our algorithm to analyze a bigger scale of malware families while providing a desirable trade-off option between speed and accuracy.

## 6 Experiments

In this section, we describe the data preparation procedure, and report malware clustering results and key findings of our experiments.

### 6.1 Data Preparation

We obtained a large collection of potentially malicious Android apps (ranging from late 2010 to early 2016) from various sources, include Google Play,

VirusShare [23] and third party security companies. In order to prepare ground-truth family labeling for the datasets, we queried the collected apps against VirusTotal [29] around April 2016, and used the scanning results to filter out potentially ambiguous apps.

To assign family labels to the collected malware samples, we applied the following steps: (1) tokenized VirusTotal scanning results and normalized the contained keywords, and then counted the total number of occurrences of each keyword. (2) removed all the generic keywords such as `Virus`, `Trojan`, and `Malicious`. (3) detected keyword aliases by calculating the edit distances between keywords. For example, `Nickyspy`, `Nickspy`, `Nicky`, and `Nickibot` were all consolidated into `Nickispy`. (4) assigned the dominant keyword as the family label for the sample. A keyword was considered as dominant if it satisfied two conditions: (a) the count of the keyword was larger than a predefined threshold $t$ (*e.g.*, $t = 10$), and (b) the count of the most popular keyword was at least twice larger than the counts of any other keywords.

**Table 2.** Clearly labeled malware families

| Name | Size | Name | Size | Name | Size | Name | Size | Name | Size |
|---|---|---|---|---|---|---|---|---|---|
| Dowgin | 3280 | Minimob | 145 | Erop | 48 | Vidro | 23 | Koomer | 15 |
| Fakeinst | 3138 | Gumen | 145 | Andup | 48 | Winge | 19 | Vmvol | 13 |
| Adwo | 2702 | Basebridge | 144 | Boxer | 44 | Penetho | 19 | Opfake | 13 |
| Plankton | 1725 | Gingermaster | 122 | Ksapp | 39 | Mobiletx | 19 | Uuserv | 12 |
| Wapsx | 1657 | Appquanta | 93 | Yzhc | 37 | Moavt | 19 | Svpeng | 12 |
| Mecor | 1604 | Geinimi | 86 | Mtk | 35 | Tekwon | 18 | Steek | 12 |
| Kuguo | 1167 | Mobidash | 83 | Adflex | 32 | Jsmshider | 18 | Spybubble | 12 |
| Youmi | 790 | Kyview | 80 | Fakeplayer | 31 | Cova | 17 | Nickispy | 12 |
| Droidkungfu | 561 | Pjapps | 75 | Adrd | 30 | Badao | 17 | Fakeangry | 12 |
| Mseg | 245 | Bankun | 70 | Zitmo | 29 | Spambot | 16 | Utchi | 11 |
| Boqx | 214 | Nandrobox | 65 | Viser | 26 | Fjcon | 16 | Lien | 11 |
| Airpush | 183 | Clicker | 58 | Fakedoc | 26 | Faketimer | 16 | Ramnit | 9 |
| Smskey | 166 | Golddream | 54 | Stealer | 25 | Bgserv | 16 | | |
| Kmin | 158 | Androrat | 49 | Updtkiller | 24 | Mmarketpay | 15 | | |

Although our malware labeling process may look similar to AVclass [27], we developed the approach independently without the knowledge of the AVclass; and both work was finished around the same time. The unlabeled samples were not included in the malware dataset for clustering analysis. In summary, we collected 19,725 labeled malware samples from 68 different families, and the detailed breakup of the malware samples is shown in Table 2.

Besides the above labeled malware dataset, we also collected Android Genome malware samples [34] to obtain an optimal clustering threshold, and randomly selected a list of 10,000 benign samples from AndroZoo [1] to evaluate the accuracy of the library removal procedure. In particular, we selected benign apps that were created around the same time (before Jan 1st, 2016) as most of the labeled malware samples, and their latest (Mar 2017) VirusTotal re-scanning results showed no malicious labels.

### 6.2 Feature Collision Analysis

The accuracy of the proposed clustering system and the correctness of the reconstructed malicious payloads relies on the assumption that unique features will be mapped to unique bit locations within the bit-vector fingerprint. Feature collision is directly impacted by two parameters: an $n$-gram size, and a bit-vector fingerprint size. To evaluate a feature collision rate, we varied the $n$-gram size (2 and 4) and the bit-vector fingerprint size, and then measured how many unique features were mapped to the same single bit position, i.e., feature collision. Figure 5 illustrates feature collision with regard to different $n$-gram sizes and fingerprint sizes.

The graph shows that feature collision occurs more frequently when the fingerprint size is small. The total number of unique features depends on the $n$-gram size. For the labeled malware, it was about 4.1 million for 2-gram features, and 14.4 million for 4-gram features. And for the benign dataset, it was about 15.2 million for 2-gram features, and 45.3 million for 4-gram features. According to the *pigeonhole principle*, when putting `N` unique features into `M` buckets, with $N > M$, at least one bucket would contain more than one unique features. This means that we need to set the bit-vector fingerprint size larger than the total number of unique features to reduce feature collision. Therefore, we set the default $n$-gram size to be 2 and default fingerprint size to be 1024 KB which provides 8,388,608 unique bit positions. With the above configuration, the unique feature per bit value was reduced to 0.49 to process the labeled malware dataset. Notice that the complete feature space is unlimited for our system due to the inclusion of arbitrary string values, however the true unique features contained in a certain dataset will be limited.

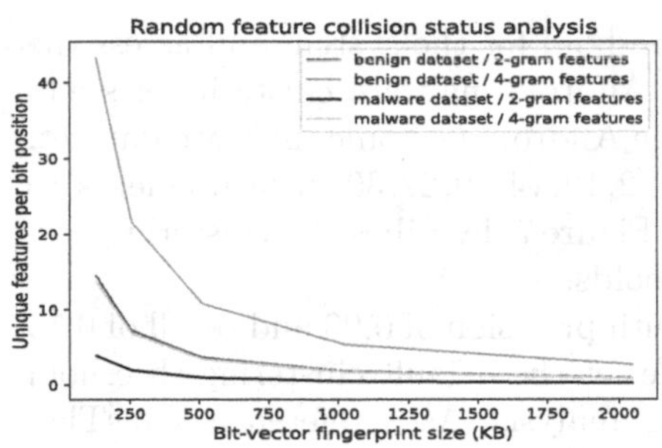

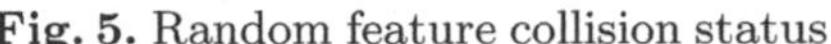

Fig. 5. Random feature collision status

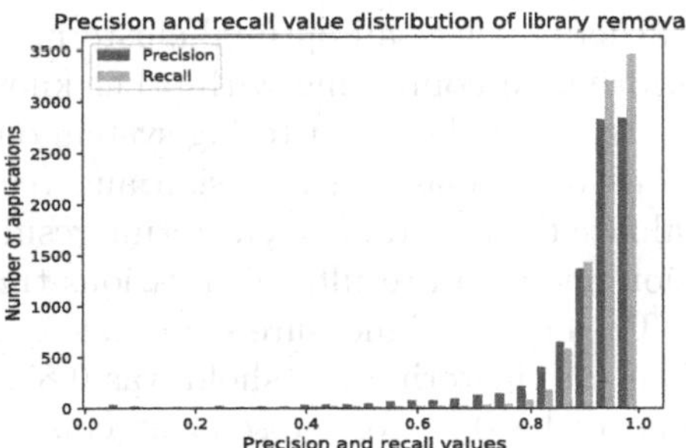


Fig. 6. Benign apps lib removal accuracy

### 6.3 Library Removal Accuracy

Besides the random feature collision discussed in the previous section, it is also possible that feature collision may happen between the app code and the irrelevant versions of the library code. To evaluate the library removal accuracy, we assumed the libraries used in benign samples were not purposefully manipulated, and measured the precision (*e.g.*, how much of the removed code is true library code) and recall (*e.g.*, how much of the true library code is removed) of library code removal results for the prepared benign samples. Particularly, we considered the code that were defined under the official library names in the benign samples as ground truth library code, and created the *true library code* fingerprint $\mathsf{fp}_{\mathsf{true}}$ by mapping all the features from the true library code to a bit-vector fingerprint. After removing the library code from each app, we identified the bit positions that were presented in the original app fingerprint and were removed subsequently; and used the identified bit positions to generate *removed library code* fingerprint $\mathsf{fp}_{\mathsf{removed}}$. Using the containment ratio calculation function as discussed in Sect. 3.1, library removal precision $\mathsf{P}_{\mathsf{lib}}$ is defined as $\frac{S(\mathsf{fp}_{\mathsf{true}} \wedge \mathsf{fp}_{\mathsf{removed}})}{S(\mathsf{fp}_{\mathsf{removed}})}$, and library removal recall $\mathsf{R}_{\mathsf{lib}}$ is defined as $\frac{S(\mathsf{fp}_{\mathsf{true}} \wedge \mathsf{fp}_{\mathsf{removed}})}{S(\mathsf{fp}_{\mathsf{true}})}$, where $S(\cdot)$ denotes the number of 1-bits in the bit-vector.

Figure 6 depicts the library removal precision and recall for the benign apps. We observed that 9,215 benign apps contained at least one legitimate library, and the median values for precision and recall were 0.94, 0.95, respectively. We manually inspected certain corner cases with poor precision or recall. The poor precision cases were due to incomplete true library code extraction, *e.g.*, an older version of Admob library contained obfuscated version of code which were not under `com.google` domain, thus not counted as true library code. The poor recall cases were due to excessive true library code inclusion, *e.g.*, all the code of the `Androidify` app was defined under `com.google` domain which made the distinction of library code obscure.

### 6.4 Malware Clustering Results

In order to select an optimal clustering threshold for the system and assess the performance comparing with other known Android malware clustering system, we first applied our clustering system on the Android Genome malware dataset. We used the classical precision and recall [2,12,14,19,22,30] measurements to evaluate the accuracy of clustering results. Figure 7 describes the clustering precision and recall results with various thresholds.

The highest F-measure score was 0.82 with precision of 0.90 and recall of 0.75 when the clustering threshold was 0.85. We set the default clustering threshold value to be 0.85 for subsequent clustering analysis. As a reference, ClusTheDroid [17] achieved precision of 0.74 and recall of 0.73 while clustering 939 of Android Genome malware samples.

Note that the clustering outputs produced by our system is per sub-version instead of per family, therefore it is more challenging to properly obtain fine-grained ground truth labels to evaluate the accuracy. In fact, this was the main

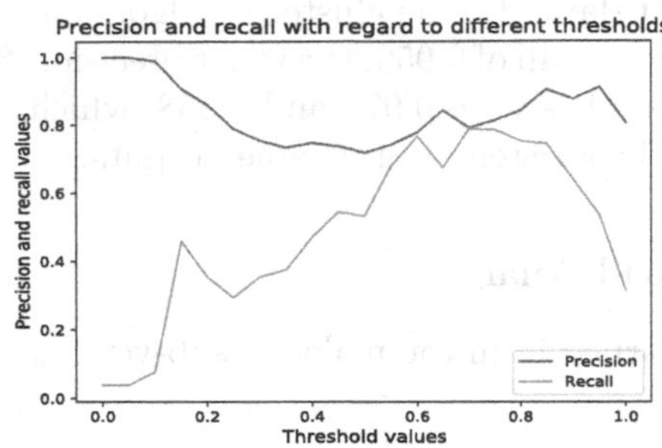


**Fig. 7.** Clustering results of Android Genome malware dataset

| Datasets | Samples | Clusters | Precision | Recall |
|---|---|---|---|---|
| D1 | 1064 | 33 | 0.977 | 0.972 |
| D2 | 1462 | 27 | 0.987 | 0.964 |
| D3 | 1708 | 29 | 0.985 | 0.978 |
| D4 | 1039 | 31 | 0.971 | 0.960 |
| D5 | 2277 | 29 | 0.988 | 0.989 |
| D6 | 1066 | 30 | 0.971 | 0.919 |
| D7 | 1256 | 29 | 0.985 | 0.981 |
| D8 | 1680 | 29 | 0.985 | 0.980 |
| D9 | 2074 | 31 | 0.996 | 0.858 |
| D10 | 1612 | 31 | 0.992 | 0.989 |

**Fig. 8.** Clustering results of different sub-version datasets

reason for a bit low recall of our system with respect to coarse-grained ground truth labels, *e.g.*, one Android malware family samples might contain multiple versions of malicious payloads. While reviewing the clustering results, we noticed that 13 families of the Genome dataset contained more than one versions of malicious payloads. For example, `Basebridge` contained 7 versions of malicious payloads with threshold of 0.85.

Therefore, we separated the labeled malware samples into sub-versions using the clustering system, and further designed several experiments to evaluate the clustering results with manually verified sub-version ground-truth. We manually verified the correctness of the sub-version cluster results. For the generated sub-version clusters, we first checked if the extracted payload was the indeed malicious. Since each version of the extracted payloads usually had similar class names and Dalvik code sequences, the maliciousness of the extracted payload can be spotted by checking the extracted class names (*e.g.*, similar pseudo-random pattern). In case the class names were not enough to determine its maliciousness, we then went through the reconstructed code segments and checked if there were any suspicious activities or behaviors, such as stealthily sending out premium SMS. After verifying the maliciousness of the extracted payload, we then randomly selected 3 samples from each sub-version group, and checked if the selected apps contained the same version malicious payload. Out of 19,725 malware samples that were labeled with 68 families, we obtained a total of 260 verified sub-version clusters, and each cluster corresponded to one version of the malicious payloads.

We considered the VirusTotal family labels together with the manually verified sub-version information as ground truth, and prepared 10 experiment datasets. For each dataset, we randomly selected 30 sub-versions from the entire ground truth dataset (*e.g.*, 260 sub-versions), then mixed the selected samples together as one input dataset. The resulting datasets had different overall sizes as each individual sub-version had different numbers of samples. The detailed dataset sizes and sample clustering results for the 10 datasets are presented in Fig. 8. On average, the sample clustering algorithm separated the input malware samples into 29.9 clusters, which was extremely close to the reference set (*i.e.*, 30 sub-versions). For the 10 experiment datasets, the clustering algorithm achieved average precision of 0.984 and average recall of 0.959, the worst precision and recall for clustering multiple malware families were 0.971 and 0.858, which suggests that the clustering system generated consistent and reliable outputs.

### 6.5 Key Findings for Malicious Payload Analysis

In this section, we report the key findings learned from the malware sub-version verification process.

**Significant library code ratio:** From the labeled malware datasets, we found that the average library code ratio was larger than 50% for the malware samples that contained at least one legitimate library. This highlights that existing Android malware similarity analysis work becomes ineffective without properly handling library code.

**Limited versions of malicious payloads:** During our experiments, we acquired 260 versions of malicious payloads from 68 labeled malware families while conducting clustering of each family. Among the 68 malware families, 27 families had only one version of malicious payload, and 5 families had more than 10 different versions of malicious payloads. For example, `Dowgin` was the largest malware family and had 23 versions of malicious payloads extracted.

**Malicious payload under popular namespaces:** We conducted manual analysis on the extracted malicious payloads, and noted that 29% of Android malware families injected their malicious payloads under popular namespaces, such as `com.google` and `com.android`, or legitimate advertisement library namespaces like `com.umeng`. Table 3 in Appendix includes the detailed malicious payload findings for the identified families. Since `com.google` and `com.android` are the main class names used by Android Open Source Project and Google Mobile Services, such malicious payloads can easily get overlooked.

## 7 Limitation

Our Android malware clustering approach is based on the assumption that malware authors often reuse the same malicious payload to create new malicious samples, and the obfuscated code sequences of malicious payload would largely remain the same if they are generated by the same obfuscation tool. This is consistent with our findings as listed in Sect. 6.5. Theoretically, advanced obfuscation techniques (e.g., class encryption or dynamic loading) can eventually break the assumption by generating a new version of a malicious payload for every new malware instance, or completely removing the original malicious payload from `classes.dex`. The attack and defense against malware obfuscation is a long-term arms race, and has already been observed in the traditional desktop malware analysis domain. For example, as observed in desktop malware research [15,20,24], independent systems might be desirable to specifically handle the de-obfuscation process. We consider it as a separate pre-processing step for malware analysis, and leave a comprehensive solution for advanced obfuscation as an orthogonal problem. In addition, using dynamic analysis with a sandbox can help further analyze malware. However, dynamic analysis also suffers from its own limitations, such as sandbox evasion and code coverage.

We believe that the Android malware analysis community can benefit from our work in several aspects. (a) It offers an alternative malicious payload extraction approach in which we can extract a more complete version of malicious payloads even if the malicious payloads are injected under popular library names or under existing functions. (b) It provides a viable solution for conducting Android malware clustering analysis by checking if malware samples contain the same version of malicious payloads. (c) Majority of Android malware samples are not obfuscated or obfuscated by simple obfuscation tools, even for the samples we collected recently. For example, within the extracted 260 versions of malicious payloads, we observed 181 of them had plain code, and only 79 of them used naming obfuscation, which was a simple basic obfuscation technique being used in practice. (d) As long as there are shared malicious code segments regardless of obfuscation among the samples from the same malware family, our algorithm extracts the shared patterns and uses them for deciding malware clustering output.

## 8 Related Work

### 8.1 Android Malware Clustering and App Similarity Analysis

Due to the challenges that are discussed in Sect. 1, existing Android malware clustering approaches have not been widely adopted yet. ClusTheDroid [17] was a system for clustering Android malware using 38 features extracted from profiles of reconstructed dynamic behaviors. Samra [25] extracted features from Android app manifest files, and could only cluster applications into two categories using K-means algorithm. Without properly excluding the features or behaviors that belong to the original benign apps or legitimate libraries, traditional clustering approaches would not be able to produce promising results.

Similarity analysis is essential for clustering, but existing Android application similarity analysis techniques were mainly designed to detect repackaged apps [11,31,33], and such overall similarity analysis based techniques cannot be directly applied for Android malware clustering for reasons described in Sect. 1. SMART [21] proposed a semantic model for Android malware analysis, but was mainly built for malware detection and classification. Both Juxtapp [11] and our system use $n$-gram bytecode features and feature hashing [13,14,26] as basic building blocks. However, Juxtapp excluded library code for further analysis if the core application component does not directly invoke it, which still couldn't differentiate a legitimate library and a bogus library with the same legitimate name. Furthermore, directly using Juxtapp to cluster Android malware will suffer the same limitations like other traditional clustering methods as it is based on overall similarity.

### 8.2 Android Malicious Payload Analysis

Malicious payload identification and extraction is essential for Android malware analysis. Zhou and Jiang [34] manually analyzed malicious payloads of Android malware and summarized the findings in the Android Malware Genome project. DroidAnalytics [32] presented a multi-level signature based analytics system to examine and associate repackaged Android malware. MassVet [5] analyzed graph similarity at the function level and extracted the shared non-legitimate functions as malicious payloads through commonality and differential analysis, and it applied a whitelist to exclude legitimate library code from analysis.

MassVet [5] is close to our work in that both extract malicious payloads from Android malware. However, similar to existing Android malware analysis work [4–6, 8, 10], MassVet simply used library name based whitelists to exclude popular library code, which can result in the failure of malicious payload extraction, and lead to false negatives in malware detection if malicious payloads are injected under popular library namespaces. In addition, due to the function level payload granularity of MassVet, it can not be easily designed to achieve payload-sharing based Android malware clustering, since the same function could be shared by different malware families, and the malware samples from the same family usually share multiple functions at the same time. Last but not least, MassVet won't be able to extract malicious payload injected under existing functions, while the instruction level payload granularity designed by our approach enables us to precisely identify one version of malicious payload from each Android malware, which includes all of the malicious components even if they are injected in existing functions or across different functions.

## 9 Conclusion

In this paper, we proposed a practical solution to conduct Android malware clustering. As an internal component, the fingerprint based library removal technique was used to distinguish a legitimate library and a bogus library that may share the same library name. Unlike traditional clustering techniques which examine the overall similarity, we achieved Android malware clustering by checking whether the analyzed Android malware samples shared the same version of malicious payload code. Compared with existing malicious payload extraction system, our approach extracts malicious payloads even if they were injected under popular library namespaces or under existing benign functions, and it provides a more complete picture of the whole malicious payload. Our comprehensive experimental results demonstrate that our clustering approach generates consistent and reliable outputs with high precision and recall.

**Acknowledgment.** This work was partially supported by the U.S. National Science Foundation under Grant No. 1314925, 1622402 and 1717862. Any opinions, findings and conclusions or recommendations expressed in this material are those of the authors and do not necessarily reflect the views of the National Science Foundation.

## References


1. Allix, K., Bissyandé, T.F., Klein, J., Le Traon, Y.: Androzoo: collecting millions of android apps for the research community. In: Proceedings of the 13th International Conference on Mining Software Repositories, pp. 468–471. ACM (2016)
2. Bayer, U., Comparetti, P.M., Hlauschek, C., Kruegel, C., Kirda, E.: Scalable, behavior-based malware clustering. NDSS **9**, 8–11 (2009)
3. Broder, A.Z.: On the resemblance and containment of documents. In: Compression and Complexity of Sequences 1997, Proceedings, pp. 21–29. IEEE (1997)
4. Chen, K., Liu, P., Zhang, Y.: Achieving accuracy and scalability simultaneously in detecting application clones on android markets. In: Proceedings of the 36th International Conference on Software Engineering, pp. 175–186. ACM (2014)
5. Chen, K., Wang, P., Lee, Y., Wang, X., Zhang, N., Huang, H., Zou, W., Liu, P.: Finding unknown malice in 10 seconds: mass vetting for new threats at the Google-play scale. In: USENIX Security Symposium, vol. 15 (2015)
6. Crussell, J., Gibler, C., Chen, H.: Attack of the clones: detecting cloned applications on android markets. In: Foresti, S., Yung, M., Martinelli, F. (eds.) ESORICS 2012. LNCS, vol. 7459, pp. 37–54. Springer, Heidelberg (2012). doi:10.1007/978-3-642-33167-1_3
7. Dexdump (2015). http://developer.android.com/tools/help/index.html
8. Egele, M., Brumley, D., Fratantonio, Y., Kruegel, C.: An empirical study of cryptographic misuse in android applications. In: Proceedings of the 2013 ACM SIGSAC Conference on Computer & Communications Security, pp. 73–84. ACM (2013)
9. Fowler, G., Noll, L.C., Vo, K.P.: Fnv hash (2015). http://www.isthe.com/chongo/tech/comp/fnv/
10. Grace, M., Zhou, Y., Zhang, Q., Zou, S., Jiang, X.: Riskranker: scalable and accurate zero-day android malware detection. In: Proceedings of the 10th International Conference on Mobile Systems, Applications, and Services, pp. 281–294. ACM (2012)
11. Hanna, S., Huang, L., Wu, E., Li, S., Chen, C., Song, D.: Juxtapp: a scalable system for detecting code reuse among android applications. In: Flegel, U., Markatos, E., Robertson, W. (eds.) DIMVA 2012. LNCS, vol. 7591, pp. 62–81. Springer, Heidelberg (2013). doi:10.1007/978-3-642-37300-8_4
12. Hu, X., Shin, K.G.: DUET: integration of dynamic and static analyses for malware clustering with cluster ensembles. In: Annual Computer Security Applications Conference (2013)
13. Hu, X., Shin, K.G., Bhatkar, S., Griffin, K.: Mutantx-s: scalable malware clustering based on static features. In: USENIX Annual Technical Conference, pp. 187–198 (2013)
14. Jang, J., Brumley, D., Venkataraman, S.: Bitshred: feature hashing malware for scalable triage and semantic analysis. In: Proceedings of the 18th ACM Conference on Computer and Communications Security, pp. 309–320. ACM (2011)
15. Kang, M.G., Poosankam, P., Yin, H.: Renovo: a hidden code extractor for packed executables. In: Proceedings of the 2007 ACM Workshop on Recurring Malcode, pp. 46–53. ACM (2007)
16. Kim, J., Krishnapuram, R., Davé, R.: Application of the least trimmed squares technique to prototype-based clustering. Pattern Recognit. Lett. **17**(6), 633–641 (1996)

17. Korczynski, D.: ClusTheDroid: clustering android malware. Master's thesis, Royal Holloway University of London (2015)
18. Leskovec, J., Rajaraman, A., Ullman, J.D.: Mining of Massive Datasets. Cambridge University Press, Cambridge (2014)
19. Li, Y., Sundaramurthy, S.C., Bardas, A.G., Ou, X., Caragea, D., Hu, X., Jang, J.: Experimental study of fuzzy hashing in malware clustering analysis. In: Proceedings of the 8th USENIX Conference on Cyber Security Experimentation and Test, p. 8. USENIX Association (2015)
20. Martignoni, L., Christodorescu, M., Jha, S.: Omniunpack: fast, generic, and safe unpacking of malware. In: Twenty-Third Annual Computer Security Applications Conference (ACSAC 2007), pp. 431–441. IEEE (2007)
21. Meng, G., Xue, Y., Xu, Z., Liu, Y., Zhang, J., Narayanan, A.: Semantic modelling of android malware for effective malware comprehension, detection, and classification. In: Proceedings of the 25th International Symposium on Software Testing and Analysis, pp. 306–317. ACM (2016)
22. Rieck, K., Trinius, P., Willems, C., Holz, T.: Automatic analysis of malware behavior using machine learning. J. Comput. Secur. **19**(4), 639–668 (2011)
23. Roberts, J.: VirusShare.com (2015). http://virusshare.com/
24. Royal, P., Halpin, M., Dagon, D., Edmonds, R., Lee, W.: Polyunpack: automating the hidden-code extraction of unpack-executing malware. In: Proceedings of the 22nd Annual Computer Security Applications Conference, pp. 289–300. IEEE Computer Society (2006)
25. Samra, A.A.A., Yim, K., Ghanem, O.A.: Analysis of clustering technique in android malware detection. In: 2013 Seventh International Conference on Innovative Mobile and Internet Services in Ubiquitous Computing (IMIS), pp. 729–733. IEEE (2013)
26. Santos, I., Nieves, J., Bringas, P.G.: Semi-supervised learning for unknown malware detection. In: Abraham, A., Corchado, M., González, S.R., De Paz Santana, J.F. (eds.) International Symposium on Distributed Computing and Artificial Intelligence. Advances in Intelligent and Soft Computing, vol. 91, pp. 415–422. Springer, Heidelberg (2011)
27. Sebastián, M., Rivera, R., Kotzias, P., Caballero, J.: AVCLASS: a tool for massive malware labeling. In: Monrose, F., Dacier, M., Blanc, G., Garcia-Alfaro, J. (eds.) RAID 2016. LNCS, vol. 9854, pp. 230–253. Springer, Cham (2016). doi:10.1007/978-3-319-45719-2_11
28. Snell, B.: Mobile threat report, what's on the horizon for 2016 (2016). http://www.mcafee.com/us/resources/reports/rp-mobile-threat-report-2016.pdf
29. Virustotal (2017). https://www.virustotal.com
30. Ye, Y., Li, T., Chen, Y., Jiang, Q.: Automatic malware categorization using cluster ensemble. In: ACM SIGKDD International Conference on Knowledge Discovery and Data mining (2010)
31. Zhang, F., Huang, H., Zhu, S., Wu, D., Liu, P.: Viewdroid: towards obfuscation-resilient mobile application repackaging detection. In: Proceedings of the 2014 ACM Conference on Security and Privacy in Wireless & Mobile Networks, pp. 25–36. ACM (2014)

32. Zheng, M., Sun, M., Lui, J.: DroidAnalytics: a signature based analytic system to collect, extract, analyze and associate Android malware. In: 2013 12th IEEE International Conference on Trust, Security and Privacy in Computing and Communications (TrustCom), pp. 163–171. IEEE (2013)
33. Zhou, W., Zhou, Y., Jiang, X., Ning, P.: Detecting repackaged smartphone applications in third-party Android marketplaces. In: Proceedings of the Second ACM Conference on Data and Application Security and Privacy, pp. 317–326. ACM (2012)
34. Zhou, Y., Jiang, X.: Dissecting android malware: characterization and evolution. In: 2012 IEEE Symposium on Security and Privacy (SP), pp. 95–109. IEEE (2012)

# A Detailed malicious payload mining results

**Table 3.** Malicious payload under popular libraries

| Family | Popular class names used |
|---|---|
| Nickispy | com.google.android.info.SmsInfo |
| | com.google.android.service.UploadService |
| Uuserv | com.uuservice.status.SysCaller.callSilentInstall |
| | com.uuservice.status.SilenceTool.MyThread.run |
| Fjcon | com.android.XWLauncher.CustomShirtcutActivity |
| | com.android.XWLauncher.InstallShortcutReceiver |
| Yzhc | com.android.Base.Tools.replace_name |
| | com.android.JawbreakerSuper.Deamon |
| Gumen | com.umeng.adutils.AdsConnect |
| | com.umeng.adutils.SplashActivity |
| Basebridge | com.android.sf.dna.Collection |
| | com.android.battery.a.pa |
| Spambot | com.android.providers.message.SMSObserver |
| | com.android.providers.message.Utils.sendSms |
| Moavt | com.android.MJSrceen.Activity.BigImageActivity |
| | com.android.service.MouaService.InitSms |
| Zitmo | com.android.security.SecurityService.onStart |
| | com.android.smon.SecurityReceiver.sendSMS |
| Mseg | com.google.vending.CmdReceiver |
| | android.ad.appoffer.Copy_2_of_DownloadManager |
| Droidkungfu | com.google.ssearch.SearchService |
| | com.google.update.UpdateService |
| Dowgin | com.android.qiushui.app.dmc |
| | com.android.game.xiaoqiang.jokes.Data9 |
| Fakeinst | com.googleapi.cover.Actor |
| | com.android.shine.MainActivity.proglayss_Click |
| Ksapp | com.google.ads.analytics.Googleplay |
| | com.google.ads.analytics.ZipDecryptInputStream |
| Bankun | com.google.game.store.bean.MyConfig.getMsg |
| | com.google.dubest.eight.isAvilible |
| Pjapps | com.android.MainService.SMSReceiver |
| | com.android.main.TANCActivity |
| Adwo | com.android.mmreader1030 |
| | com.google.ads.AdRequest.isTestDevice |
| Svpeng | com.adobe.flashplayer_.FV.doInBackground |
| | com.adobe.flashplayer_.FA.startService |
| Opfake | com.android.appupdate.UpdateService |
| | com.android.system.SurpriseService |
| Badao | com.google.android.gmses.MyApp |
| | com.android.secphone.FileUtil.clearTxt |

# Systems Security

# Stealth Loader: Trace-Free Program Loading for API Obfuscation

Yuhei Kawakoya[1(✉)], Eitaro Shioji[1], Yuto Otsuki[1], Makoto Iwamura[1], and Takeshi Yada[1,2]

[1] NTT Secure Platform Laboratories, Tokyo, Japan
{kawakoya.yuhei,shioji.eitaro,otsuki.yuto,iwamura.makoto}@lab.ntt.co.jp
[2] NTT Advanced Technology Corporation, Kawasaki, Kanagawa, Japan
takeshi.yada@ntt-at.co.jp

**Abstract.** Understanding how application programming interfaces (APIs) are used in a program plays an important role in malware analysis. This, however, has resulted in an endless battle between malware authors and malware analysts around the development of API [de]obfuscation techniques over the last few decades. Our goal in this paper is to show a limit of existing API de-obfuscations. To do that, we first analyze existing API [de]obfuscation techniques and clarify an attack vector commonly existed in API de-obfuscation techniques, and then we present *Stealth Loader*, which is a program loader using our API obfuscation technique to bypass all existing API de-obfuscations. The core idea of this technique is to load a dynamic link library (DLL) and resolve its dependency without leaving any traces on memory to be detected. We demonstrate the effectiveness of Stealth Loader by analyzing a set of Windows executables and malware protected with Stealth Loader using major dynamic and static analysis tools and techniques. The result shows that among other obfuscation techniques, only Stealth Loader is able to successfully bypass all analysis tools and techniques.

**Keywords:** API obfuscation · Windows · Program loader · Malware analysis

## 1 Introduction

Malware analysis is essential for fighting against cyber crime. Analysts take advantage of various analysis methods to reveal the behaviors of malware effectively. Windows userland APIs are important information sources for understanding the behaviors and intentions of malware since a sequence of APIs expresses significant part of the functionalities of malware. That is, the API is a fundamental factor for malware analysis.

---

**Electronic supplementary material** The online version of this chapter (doi:10.1007/978-3-319-66332-6_10) contains supplementary material, which is available to authorized users.


M. Dacier et al. (Eds.): RAID 2017, LNCS 10453, pp. 217–237, 2017.
DOI: 10.1007/978-3-319-66332-6_10

Malware authors understand this situation, so they try to hide APIs used in their malware by managing various obfuscation tricks [13,19,20,23]. One example is API redirection, which is an obfuscation technique that aims to confuse the control flows from call instructions to APIs by inserting junk code in the middle of the flows. Another example is DLL unlinking, which aims to make control flows from call instructions unreachable to the code of any recognized APIs. This is done by hiding loaded DLLs containing API code, which possibly becomes the destination of the control flows.

To fight against these API obfuscations, many API de-obfuscation approaches have been proposed in the past few decades [11,18,23]. For example, one approach aggressively collects traces of loaded DLLs from multiple sources, e.g., the Process Environment Block (PEB), Virtual Address Descriptor (VAD), or callback events, and creates a complete list of loaded DLLs. Another approach deeply performs a control flow analysis until it finds any API code reachable from call instructions in the original code by taking advantage of various static analysis techniques.

An essential step in these API de-obfuscations is API name resolution, i.e., relating a virtual memory address to an API name. To do that, API de-obfuscations have to identify the positions of loaded DLLs that contain API code. As far as we have investigated, to identify the positions of loaded DLLs, most existing API de-obfuscations are likely to depend on data structures that the underline operating system (OS) manages. For example, in the case of Windows, many analysis tools are designed to acquire the addresses of loaded DLLs from PEB or VAD. We consider that, behind this design, they expect that the Windows OS precisely manages loaded DLLs and keeps track of them by storing the information related to them in specific data structures. We also consider that this expectation possibly becomes an attack vector for malware authors to evade existing API de-obfuscations.

Our goal in this paper is to show a limitation of existing API de-obfuscations by actually attacking this expectation. To do that, we propose a new Windows API obfuscation technique and implement it in our prototype, *Stealth Loader*. The design principle of Stealth Loader is that it loads a DLL without leaving any traces in Windows-managed data structures. To achieve this, we have two approaches. The first is that we redesign each phase of program loading to become trace-free. The second is that we add two new features to a program loader; one is for removing some fields of the Portable Executable (PE) header of a loaded DLL from memory, and the other is for removing behavioral characteristics of Stealth Loader itself.

One effect of Stealth Loader is that a *stealth-loaded* DLL[1] is not recognized as a loaded DLL by analysis tools and even by the Windows OS because there is no evidence in Windows-managed data structures to recognize it. Due to this effect, calls of the functions exported from stealth-loaded Windows system DLLs, such as kernel32.dll and ntdll.dll, are not recognized as API calls because the DLLs are not recognized as loaded, i.e., analysis tools fail API name resolution.

[1] A DLL loaded by Stealth Loader.

The main challenge of this paper is to design a trace-free program loader without destroying the runtime environment for running programs. A program loader is one of the core functions of an OS. Therefore, simply changing the behavior of a program loader is likely to affect the runtime environment, and that change sometimes leads to a program crash. In addition, changes excessively specific to a certain runtime environment lose generality as a program loader. We need to redesign each step of the program loading procedure carefully while considering the effects on runtime environments that our changes may cause.

To demonstrate the effectiveness of Stealth Loader against existing API de-obfuscations, we embedded Stealth Loader into several Windows executables and analyzed them with major malware analysis tools. The result showed that all of these tools failed to analyze the invoked or imported APIs of stealth-loaded DLLs.

In addition, to show that the current implementation of Stealth Loader is practical enough for hiding malware's fundamental behaviors, we protected five real pieces of malware with Stealth Loader and then analyzed them by using a popular dynamic analysis sandbox, Cuckoo Sandbox [15]. The result of this experiment showed that pieces of malware whose malicious activities were obviously identified before applying Stealth Loader successfully hid most of their malicious activities after Stealth Loader was applied. Consequently, they could make Cuckoo Sandbox produce false negatives.

The contributions of this paper are as follows.

- We analyze existing API [de]obfuscation techniques and reveal a common expectation of API de-obfuscations which possibly becomes an attack vector for malware authors to bypass analyses and detections.
- We introduce *Stealth Loader*, a program loader using our Windows API obfuscation technique that exploits this attack vector.
- We demonstrate the effectiveness of Stealth Loader by analyzing Windows executables and real malware protected with Stealth Loader. The results show that Stealth Loader successfully evaded seven primary analysis tools.
- We discuss possible countermeasures against Stealth Loader. We present that Stealth Loader can evade API de-obfuscation techniques proposed in academic studies as well.

## 2 Problem Analysis

In this section, we explain existing API obfuscation and de-obfuscation techniques that are used in both major malware analysis tools and academic studies. Then, we clarify a common expectation shared in API de-obfuscations.

### 2.1 API Obfuscation

API obfuscation is a technique for hiding imported or invoked APIs from static or dynamic analysis tools, respectively. Malware authors often take advantage of this technique to protect their malware from being detected or analyzed. We

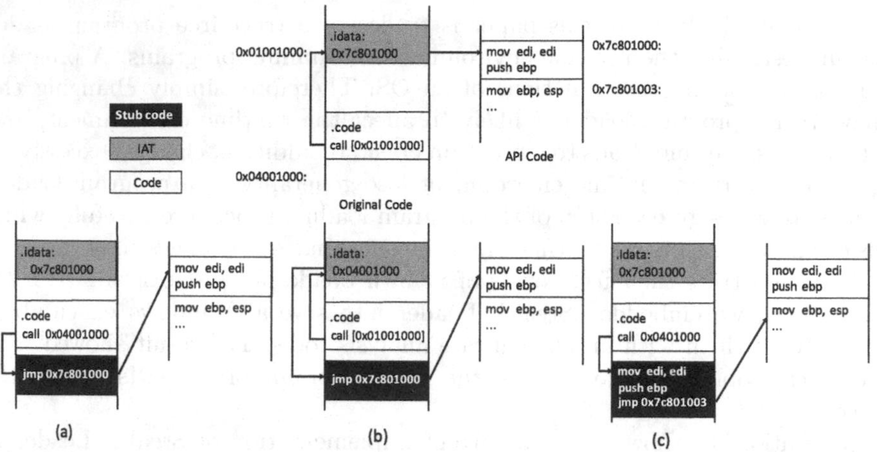


**Fig. 1.** Three patterns of API redirection. The upper one is the case of a normal Windows executable before applying API redirection. (a) is a case in which the reference of the call instruction is modified. (b) is a case in which the entry of IAT is modified. (c) is a case in which API redirection is conducted with stolen code.

first mention the basics of the PE format. Then, we explain IAT obfuscation and DLL unlinking as a technique against static analysis. Last, we explain API redirection as one technique against both static and dynamic analyses.

A PE executable usually has an import address table (IAT) and import name table (INT) to manage external APIs if it depends on them. IAT is a table that contains function pointers to APIs whose code is located in external DLLs. INT is also a table that contains the names of external APIs corresponding to IAT entries. Since these tables are referenced from the header of a PE executable, malware analysts can acquire the list of APIs that a piece of malware depends on from its PE header when they analyze a PE-format piece of malware.

To interfere with static analysis, malware often deletes INT and disconnects the reference to the tables from its PE header. This is called *IAT obfuscation*. Even if a piece of malware does not have any references to the tables from its PE header, since it keeps the list of APIs inside and restores it at runtime, it can sustain the feasibility of the original functionality.

DLL unlinking [11] is another technique for interfering with static analysis by obfuscating loaded DLLs. It makes control flows from call instructions unreachable to any APIs by hiding loaded DLLs that could possibly become the destination of the flows. Since a control flow of an external function call does not reach any memory area where a Windows system DLL is mapped, analysis tools fail to recognize this flow as an API call reference. This technique achieves this by removing the registered meta-information of the DLL from the lists of PEB, which is a data structure of Windows for managing loaded DLLs and their status in a process. Since some Windows APIs, e.g., EnumProcessModules, depend on PEB to extract loaded DLL lists, unlinked DLLs can avoid being listed by these APIs.

API redirection [23] is a technique for attacking both static and dynamic analyses by obfuscating API references. As Fig. 1-(a) shows, it modifies call instructions in the original code. Otherwise, as Fig. 1-(b) shows, it modifies IAT entries. With these modifications, it forces control flows to APIs in order to detour a stub, which executes junk instructions and finally jumps to APIs. By inserting a stub between an IAT entry or call instruction and API code, malware breaks the direct connection between the caller and callee of an API. Since many analysis tools expect API call instructions to directly refer to API code or at least via IAT, this technique can confuse their API resolution.

Additionally, advanced API redirection, shown in Fig. 1-(c), is involved with stolen code [23]. At the same time, when API redirection is applied, it copies some instructions at the entry of an API, i.e., `mov edi, edi` and `push ebp`, to right before the jmp instruction in the allocated buffer for a stub. An execution performed after running these instructions in the buffer is transferred to the instruction after the copied ones in API code, i.e., `mov ebp, esp`. By doing this, malware can avoid analyses that monitor the executions of an API at the entry instruction of an API, i.e., `mov edi, edi`.

## 2.2 API De-obfuscation

Malware analysts take advantage of API de-obfuscation techniques to clarify imported APIs or invoked APIs for static or dynamic analysis, respectively.

Regarding IAT obfuscation, it is necessary to reconstruct an obfuscated IAT and deleted INT. To reconstruct them, most existing IAT reconstruction tools, such as impscan (a plugin of The Volatility Framework [11]) and Scylla [14], follow four steps: acquiring a memory dump, finding IAT, resolving API, and repairing the PE header.

1. Run a target program until it resolves imported APIs and fills in IAT with the resolved addresses. Then, acquire a memory dump of it.
2. Find the original IAT by analyzing code sections of a target program, e.g., collecting memory addresses often referred by indirect call instructions, such as `call [0x01001000]`.
3. Resolve API names from each entry of the found IAT by identifying the loaded addresses of each DLL. Then, make a list of imported APIs.
4. Restore INT with the resolved API names and then update the pointers in the PE header to point to the found IAT and restored INT.

To defeat DLL unlinking, even if a loaded DLL is not listed on PEB, we can find the existence of an unlinked DLL by parsing VADs if we use ldrmodules, which is a plugin of The Volatility Framework [11]. In addition, Rekall [17] identifies loaded DLLs in memory dumps on the basis of the debug section included in the PE header of each loaded DLL. In a PE header, a globally unique identifier (GUID) can be contained, and Rekall sends a query to a Microsoft symbol server to find the DLL related to the GUID.

Some dynamic analysis tools, such as Cuckoo Sandbox [15], make the correspondence between addresses and API names by monitoring APIs or events. For example, by monitoring LoadLibrary, we can get both the loaded address of a DLL and its file name at the same time since the address is returned from this API and the file name is passed to this API.

To fight against API redirection, Sharif et al. [18] proposed an approach of statically analyzing control flows from call instructions until the flows reach any API code. Even if there is a stub between them, their approach can get over it by continuously analyzing flows to the end of a stub.

To overcome stolen code, shown in Fig. 1-(c), Kawakoya et al. [9] proposed a way of tracking the movement of API code with taint analysis. Their approach sets taint tags on API code and tracks them by propagating the tags to identify the position of copied instructions.

### 2.3 Analysis

A common intention of existing API obfuscations is to attack API name resolution, i.e., the intention is to make it difficult to relate a virtual memory address to an API name. If analysis tools fail to make the relationship between an executed virtual memory address with an API name, they fail to recognize an execution transfer from a virtual address to API code as an API call.

On the other hand, strategies existing API de-obfuscations take to fight against API obfuscations are either to complement lacking or hidden DLL information by finding the information from multiple data sources or to perform deeper code analysis until they reach a certain point where DLL information is found. In both cases, they rely on the meta-information of DLL, which is stored in some of the data structures the OS manages. In other words, they expect that the OS precisely manages loaded DLLs, keeps track of their loading and unloading, and stores their meta-information in certain data structures.

## 3 Design

We propose a new API obfuscation technique with *Stealth Loader*, which is a program loader that does not leave any traces of loaded DLLs in Windows-managed data structures. In this section, we present an overview of Stealth Loader and then introduce the design of it.

### 3.1 Overview

Figure 2 shows the components of Stealth Loader and how it works.

Stealth Loader is composed of exPEB, sLdrLoadDll, sLdrGetProcAddress, and Bootstrap. exPEB is the data structure to manage the meta-information of stealth-loaded DLLs. sLdrLoadDll and sLdrGetProcAddress are exported functions and the main components of Stealth Loader. sLdrLoadDll is used for loading a specified DLL in the way we explain in this Section, while sLdrGetProcAddress is used for retrieving the address of an exported function or variable from a specified stealth-loaded DLL. Bootstrap is a code snippet for resolving

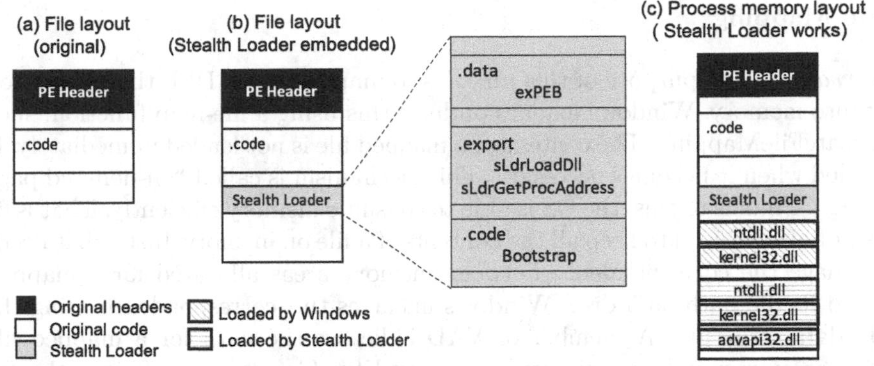


**Fig. 2.** How Stealth Loader works and its components. (a) is the file layout of an executable before Stealth Loader is embedded. (b) is the one after Stealth Loader is embedded and the components of Stealth Loader are also described. (c) is the process memory layout after Bootstrap has resolved the dependencies of an executable and stealth-loaded DLLs.

the API dependencies of an executable and stealth-loaded DLLs by using the two exported functions.

We first embed Stealth Loader into an executable which we want to protect. After an executable begins to run, Bootstrap code is executed. It identifies necessary DLLs for an executable and then loads them using sLdrLoadDll. At that time, it does not rely on Windows-loaded DLLs[2] to resolve the dependency of stealth-loaded DLLs. After loading all necessary DLLs and resolving APIs, the execution is transferred to the code of an executable from Bootstrap.

Our intention behind Stealth Loader is to attack API name resolution as other API obfuscations do. We achieve this by hiding the existences of loaded DLLs. This is the same intention as DLL unlinking, but our approach is more robust against API de-obfuscations. We tackle this from two different directions. The first is that we redesign the procedure of program loading to be trace-free. The second is that we add two new features to a program loader; one is for removing traces left on memory after completing DLL loading, and the other is for removing characteristic behaviors of Stealth Loader itself.

### 3.2 Program Loader Redesign

We first break the procedure of a program loader into three phases: code mapping, dependency resolution, and initialization & registration. Then, we observe what traces may be left at each phase for loading a DLL. On the basis of observation, we redesign each phase. In addition, we consider that the side effects caused by the redesigns are reasonable as an execution environment.

[2] DLLs loaded by Windows.

### Code Mapping

*Observation.* The purpose of this phase is to map a system DLL that resides on disk into memory. Windows loader conducts this using a file-map function, such as CreateFileMapping. The content of a mapped file is not loaded immediately. It is loaded when it becomes necessary. This mechanism is called "on-demand page loading." Thanks to this, the OS is able to consume memory efficiently. That is, it does not always need to keep all the contents of a file on memory. Instead, it needs to manage the correspondence between memory areas allocated for a mapped file and its file path on a disk. Windows manages this correspondence using the VAD data structure. A member of VAD indicates the path for a mapped file when the corresponding memory area is used for file mapping. This path of a mapped file in VAD becomes a trace for analysis tools to detect the existence of a loaded system DLL on memory. ldrmodules acquires the list of loaded DLLs on memory by parsing VADs and extracting the file paths of mapped files.

*Design.* Instead of using file-map functions, we map a system DLL using file and memory operational functions such as CreateFile, ReadFile, and VirtualAlloc to avoid leaving path information in VAD. The area allocated by VirtualAlloc is not file-mapped memory. Therefore, the VAD for the area does not indicate any relationship to a file. The concrete flow in this phase is as follows.

1. Open a DLL file with CreateFile and calculate the necessary size for locating it onto memory.
2. Allocate continuous virtual memory with VirtualAlloc for the DLL on the basis of size.
3. Read the content of an opened DLL file with ReadFile and store the headers and each section of it to proper locations in the allocated memory.

*Side Effect.* Avoiding file-map functions for locating a DLL on memory imposes on us two side effects. The first is that we have to allocate a certain amount of memory immediately for loading all sections of a DLL when we load the DLL. That means that we cannot use on-demand page loading. The second is that we cannot share a part of the code or data of a stealth-loaded DLL with other processes because memory buffers allocated with VirtualAlloc are not shareable, while ones where files are mapped are sharable. Regarding the first, recent computers have enough physical memory, so it would not be a big problem even if we could not consume memory efficiently. With regard to the second, we did not find any system DLL using shared memory with other processes in our experiments. Because of these reasons, we consider these effects to not be that significant.

### Dependency Resolution

*Observation.* The purpose of this phase is to resolve the dependency of a loading DLL. Most DLLs somehow depend on APIs exported from other DLLs. Therefore, a program loader has to resolve the dependency of a loading DLL to make

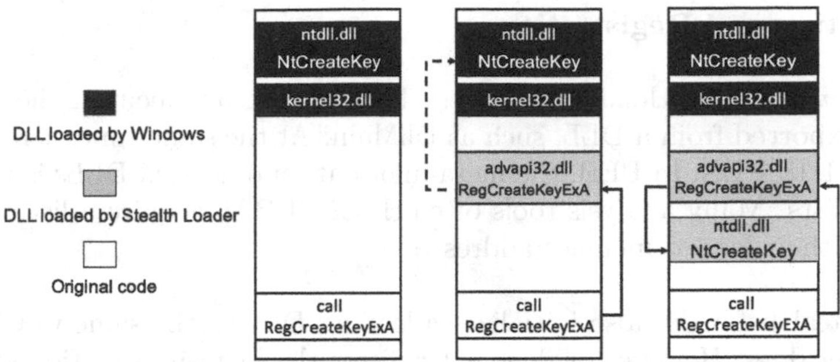


**Fig. 3.** Example of resolving dependency by Stealth Loader. (a) is the layout before Stealth Loader starts, (b) shows that the stealth-loaded advapi32.dll does not create a dependency on the Windows-loaded ntdll.dll, and (c) shows that the stealth-loaded advapi32.dll creates a dependency on the stealth-loaded ntdll.dll.

the DLL ready to be executed. When the Windows loader finds a dependency, and if a dependent DLL is already loaded into memory, it is common to use already loaded DLLs to resolve the dependency, as shown in Fig. 3-(b).

However, this dependency becomes a trace for analysis tools, i.e., behavioral traces. For example, if a stealth-loaded advapi32.dll has a dependency on a Windows-loaded ntdll.dll, the APIs of ntdll.dll indirectly called from advapi32.dll are possibly monitored by analysis tools. In other words, we can hide a call of RegCreateKeyExA, while we cannot hide one of NtCreateKey. Analysis tools can get similar behavior information from NtCreateKey as that from RegCreateKeyEx since RegCreateKeyEx internally calls NtCreateKey while passing almost the same arguments.

*Design.* To avoid this, Stealth Loader loads dependent DLLs by itself to resolve the dependency of a loading DLL. In the case of Fig. 3, it loads ntdll.dll by itself to resolve the dependency of advapi32.dll. As a result, after advapi32.dll has been loaded and its dependency has been resolved, the memory layout is like that shown in Fig. 3-(c). On the basis of this layout, when an original code calls RegCreateKeyExA, RegCreateKeyExA internally calls the NtCreateKey of stealth-loaded ntdll.dll. Therefore, this call is invisible to analysis tools even if a Windows-loaded kernel32.dll and ntdll.dll are monitored by them.

*Side Effect.* The side effect caused by this design is reduced memory space efficiency. That is, Stealth Loader consumes approximately twice as much memory for DLLs as the Windows loader since it newly loads a dependent DLL even if the DLL is already located on memory. We consider this side effect to not be that significant because recent computers have enough memory as we previously mentioned.

**Initialization and Registration**

*Observation.* Windows loader initializes a loading DLL by executing the initialize function exported from a DLL, such as DllMain. At the same time, it registers a loaded DLL to PEB. In PEB, the meta-information of loaded DLLs is managed by linked lists. Many analysis tools often check PEB to acquire a list of loaded DLLs and their loaded memory addresses.

*Design.* Stealth Loader also initializes a loading DLL in the same way as Windows loader does. However, it does not register the meta-information of loaded DLL to PEB to avoid being detected by analysis tools through PEB.

*Side Effect.* The side effect of this design is that stealth-loaded DLLs cannot receive events such as process-creation or process-termination. This is because these events are delivered to DLLs listed in PEB. We consider this effect to not be very significant because most system DLLs do not depend on these events at all as far as we have investigated. Most of them are implemented to handle only create-process and -thread events, which are executed mainly when the DLL is first loaded.

## 3.3 Stealthiness Enhancement

Apart from finding traces in Windows-managed data structures, there are other ways to identify the existence of a loaded DLL. In this subsection, we present the possibility of detecting loaded DLLs from characteristic strings in PE header of a certain DLL or behaviors of Stealth Loader itself. Then, we introduce our approaches to hiding the string patterns and behaviors.

**PE Header Removal.** Stealth Loader deletes some fields of the PE header on memory after it has loaded a DLL and resolved its dependency. This is because some of the fields may become a hint for analysis tools to inferring a DLL loaded on memory. For example, GUID is possibly included in the debug section of the PE header of a system DLL. Another example is that the tables of exported and imported API names of a system DLL, which are pointed from the PE header, also provide useful information for analysis tools. Like these examples, the PE header contains a lot of information for identifying a DLL.

In Stealth Loader, we delete the debug section, import name table, and export name table. Basically, the debug section is not used by the original code in a process under normal behavior; it is only used for debugging purposes. The import name table is necessary to resolve dependencies only when a DLL is being loaded. After it is completed, this table is not referenced from the code and data. Therefore, we can simply delete them after a DLL has been loaded.

Unlike the above two, we cannot simply delete the export name table since it is accessed after a DLL has been loaded in order to retrieve the address of an exported API of the loaded DLL at runtime. This is called "dynamic API resolution". Therefore, we prepared an interface, sLdrGetProcAddress, to resolve APIs exported from stealth-loaded DLLs. Also, we prepared a data structure, exPEB, in Stealth Loader to manage the exported API names and corresponding addresses of each stealth-loaded DLL. Thanks to them, we can delete the export name table as well without losing the dynamic API resolution capability of Stealth Loader.

**Reflective Loading.** *Reflective Loading* is used for hiding the API calls invoked from Stealth Loader itself. While the calls invoked from original code are successfully hidden by Stealth Loader, API calls invoked from Stealth Loader are still visible to analysis tools because Stealth Loader basically uses APIs exported from Windows-loaded DLLs. These exposed API calls give a chance for analysis tools to detect the existence of Stealth Loader because some of the behaviors of Stealth Loader are not often seen in normal programs. For example, `CreateFile(''kernel32.dll'')` is very characteristic since programs normally load a DLL with `LoadLibrary(''kernel32.dll'')` and do not open a Windows system DLL as a file with CreateFile. The position of Stealth Loader may allow analysis tools to perform a special analysis on Stealth Loader to extract loaded DLLs information from it.

To avoid this, we use Reflective Loading. The core idea of Reflective Loading is to copy all sections of an already loaded DLL to allocated buffers during the code mapping phase instead of opening a file and reading data from it. This idea is inspired by Reflective DLL injection, introduced in Fewer's paper [4], as a way of stealthily injecting a DLL into another process. We leveraged this to load a DLL as a part of Stealth Loader without opening the file of each DLL.

If a target DLL is not loaded at that time, we use the APIs of the stealth-loaded kernel32.dll to open a file, allocate memory, and conduct the other steps. kernel32.dll and ntdll.dll are always loaded because these DLLs are loaded by Windows as a part of process initialization. Thus, we can completely hide all API calls invoked by Stealth Loader from analysis tools monitoring API calls.

## 4 Implementation

We implement Stealth Loader on Windows 7 Service Pack 1. In this section, we explain dynamic API resolution of Stealth Loader and stealth-loadable APIs.

### 4.1 Dynamic API Resolution

Stealth Loader supports dynamic API resolution with sLdrLoadDll and sLdrGetProcAddress. When Stealth Loader loads a DLL depending on the LdrLoadDll or LdrGetProcedureAddress of ntdll.dll, e.g., kernel32.dll, it replaces the entries of IAT to the two functions in the loading DLL with pointers to sLdrLoadDll or sLdrGetProcAddress. Under this situation, when the original code attempts to dynamically load a DLL, for example, using LoadLibrary, which internally calls LdrLoadDll, the API call to LoadLibrary redirects to sLdrLoadDll and then Stealth Loader loads a specified DLL.

### 4.2 Stealth-Loadable APIs

In Stealth Loader, we support 12 DLLs: ntdll.dll, kernel32.dll, kernelbase.dll, gdi32.dll, user32.dll, shell32.dll, shlwapi.dll, ws2_32.dll, wininet.dll, winsock.dll, crypt32.dll, and msvcrt.dll. This means that we support in total 7,764 APIs exported from these 12 DLLs. The number of unsupported APIs is 1,633. The reasons we cannot support them are described in Appendix A. Since these reasons are very detailed and specific to the Windows 7 environment, we put them into this appendix. We can support more DLLs with no or at least little cost. However, we consider the current number of supported APIs to be enough for the purpose of this paper because we have already covered 99% (1018/1026) of the APIs on which IDAScope, a popular static malware analysis tool [16], focuses as important APIs. In addition, we also covered 75% (273/364) of the APIs on which Cuckoo Sandbox, a popular sandbox whose target APIs are selected by malware analysts [15], sets hooks for dynamic analysis. Regarding the remaining 25% of APIs, they separately reside in several DLLs in a small group.

## 5 Experiment

To show the feasibility of Stealth Loader, we conducted two types of experiments: one for comparing its resistance capability against existing analysis tools to other API obfuscations, and another for confirming its effectiveness with real malware.

### 5.1 Resistance

To show the resistance capability of Stealth Loader against existing API deobfuscation tools, we prepared test executables and analyzed them with seven major static and dynamic analysis tools that are primarily used in the practical malware analysis field. These tools are public available and cover various techniques we mentioned in Subsect. 2.2. Regarding the other techniques which are not covered by these tools, we qualitatively discuss the resistance capability of Stealth Loader against them in Subsect. 7.3 because they are not public available.

The test executables were prepared by applying Stealth Loader for nine Windows executables, calc.exe, winmine.exe, notepad.exe, cmd.exe, regedt32.exe, tasklist.exe, taskmgr.exe, xcopy.exe, and ftp.exe. After applying Stealth Loader for them, we verified if the executables were runnable without any disruptions and as functional as they had been before applying Stealth Loader by interacting with running test executables, such as clicking buttons, inputting keystrokes, writing and reading files, and connecting to the internet.

For comparison, we prepared tools using different API obfuscation techniques, that is, IAT obfuscation, API redirection which is explained in Fig. 1-(c), and DLL unlinking. Using the tools, we applied these techniques to the same nine Windows executables. We analyzed them with the same analysis tools and compared the results.

**Static Analysis.** In this experiment, we analyzed each test executable with four major static analysis tools, IDA [7], Scylla [14], impscan (The Volatility Framework [11]), and ldrmodules (The Volatility Framework [11]). IDA is a de-facto standard dis-assembler for reverse engineering. Scylla is a tool that reconstructs the destroyed IAT of an obfuscated executable. impscan and ldrmodules are plugins of The Volatility Framework for reconstructing IATs and making a list of all loaded modules on memory, respectively.

**Table 1.** Static and dynamic analysis resistance results

| API obfuscations | Static analysis | | | | Dynamic analysis | | |
|---|---|---|---|---|---|---|---|
| | IDA | Scylla | impscan | ldrmodules | Cuckoo | traceapi | mapitracer |
| Stealth Loader | ✓ | ✓ | ✓ | ✓ | ✓ | ✓ | ✓ |
| IAT Obfuscation | ✓ | | | N/A[a] | | | |
| API Redirection | ✓ | [b] | ✓ | N/A[a] | ✓ | ✓ | ✓ |
| DLL Unlinking | | ✓ | ✓ | | | | |

✓ indicates that obfuscation technique successfully evaded tool. Stealth Loader evaded all the tools.
[a] IAT Obfuscation and API Redirection are a technique for API obfuscation while ldrmodules is a tool for extracting loaded DLLs.
[b] When we manually gave the correct original entry point of a test executable to Scylla, it could identify imported APIs correctly. When we did not, it failed.

We explain how each analysis tool, except for IDA, resolves API. Scylla acquires the base addresses of loaded DLLs from the EnumProcessModules API, which internally references PEB and resolves API addresses with GetProcAddress. In addition, it heuristically overcomes API redirection. impscan also acquires the base addresses from PEB and resolves API addresses from the export address table (EAT) of each loaded DLL. ldrmodules acquires the base addresses from VAD.

*Procedure.* We first statically analyzed each test executable using each analysis tool, and then identified imported APIs. In the case of ldrmodules, we identified loaded DLLs. Then, we manually compared the identified imported APIs or loaded DLLs with ones we had acquired from the same executables before applying Stealth Loader.

*Result.* The left part of Table 1 shows the result of this experiment. Stealth Loader successfully defeated all static analysis tools, while the others were analyzed by some of them. This is because there were no hints for the analysis tools to acquiring the base addresses of loaded DLLs. IAT Obfuscation failed to defeat Scylla and impscan because these two tools are originally designed for reconstructing IAT by themselves in the way we explained in Subsect. 2.2. API redirection failed to evade Scylla because Scylla is designed for heuristically overcoming API redirection. DLL unlinking failed to evade ldrmodules because ldrmodules identified loaded DLLs through VADs, not PEB.

**Dynamic Analysis.** In this experiment, we analyzed each test executable with three dynamic analysis tools, Cuckoo Sandbox [15], traceapi [8], and mini_apitracer [21]. All of them are designed to monitor API calls. Cuckoo Sandbox is an open-source, dynamic malware analysis sandbox. traceapi is a sample tool of Detours, which is a library released from Microsoft Research for hooking API calls. mini_apitracer, shown as mapitracer in Table 1, is a plugin of DECAF [6], which is a binary analysis framework built on QEMU [2].

Each analysis tool relates API names and memory addresses as follows. Cuckoo acquires the base address of loaded DLLs from callback functions registered with the LdrRegisterDllNotification API and resolves API addresses with GetProcAddress. traceapi acquires the base address of loaded DLLs with LoadLibrary and resolves API addresses with GetProcAddress. mini_apitracer acquires the base addresses of loaded DLLs from PEB and resolves API addresses by parsing the EAT of each DLL.

*Procedure.* We first ran each test executable on each dynamic analysis environment and monitored the API calls. Then, we compared the monitored API calls with the ones we had collected from the same executable before applying Stealth Loader.

*Result.* The right part of Table 1 shows the results of this experiment. Stealth Loader successfully evaded all dynamic analysis tools, while the others were captured by some of them. IAT obfuscation totally failed because the dynamic analysis tools did not depend on IAT at all to identify the locations of APIs. API redirection successfully defeated all of them. This is because even though the dynamic analysis tools set hooks on the first instruction of each API for API monitoring, API redirection avoided executing them. As we explained in Subsect. 2.1, when an API is called API redirection transfers an execution to the code at a few instructions after the entry of the API. DLL unlinking also failed because the analysis tools calculated the locations of each API from the addresses of loaded DLLs and set hooks on each API before DLL unlinking had hidden DLLs.

### 5.2 Real Malware Experiment

The purpose of this experiment is to demonstrate that the current Stealth Loader implementation is practical enough for hiding the major characteristic behaviors of malware even though it has unsupported APIs.

*Procedure.* First, we collected 117 pieces of malware from VirusTotal [22] that were detected by several anti-virus products. At that time, we picked up four ones (DownloadAdmin, Win32.ZBot, Eorezo, and CheatEngine) from them because they were not obfuscated at all. We also picked one piece of malware (ICLoader) from 113 obfuscated ones as a representative case of obfuscated ones. Next, we applied Stealth Loader to the five pieces of malware. Then, using Cuckoo Sandbox, we analyzed both the malware before and after Stealth Loader was

**Table 2.** Real malware experiment results

| | without Stealth Loader | | | | with Stealth Loader | | | |
|---|---|---|---|---|---|---|---|---|
| Malware Name | Score | Signatures | Events | # of Calls | Score | Signatures | Events | # of Calls |
| DownloadAdmin | 3.6 | 11 | 16 | 9,581 | 1.8 | 5 | 12 | 224 |
| Win32.ZBot | 5.0 | 11 | 46 | 1,350 | 1.4 | 4 | 10 | 183 |
| Eorezo | 5.6 | 15 | 192 | 20,661 | 0.8 | 3 | 10 | 64 |
| CheatEngine | 4.8 | 12 | 209 | 126,086 | 1.6 | 5 | 10 | 120 |
| ICLoader | 4.0 | 11 | 33 | 3,321 | 4.0 | 11 | 38 | 1,661 |

Score is calculated from hit signatures, which are scored depending on severity of each behavior; score of less than 1.0 is benign, 1.0 - 2.0 is warning, 2.0 - 5.0 is malicious, and higher than 5.0 means danger. Signatures means number of hit signatures. Events indicates number of captured events. # of Calls is number of API calls captured by Cuckoo Sandbox.

applied. Last, we compared the results of the analyses in terms of the malicious score, the number of detected events, hit signatures, and monitored API calls. The malicious scores were calculated from observed behaviors matched with pre-defined malicious behavioral signatures [15].

To achieve the purpose of this experiment, we believe that the variety of malware's behaviors is more important than the number of malware. We also consider that the behaviors of the 4 pieces of malware (DownloadAdmin, Win32.ZBot, Eorezo, and CheatEngine) can cover the majority of behaviors, such as modifying a specific registry key or injecting code into another process, exhibited in all of the pieces of malware we collected for this experiment. This is because the signatures hit by analyzing the 4 ones contributed to detecting 637 out of 792 events which were generated by analyzing the 117 pieces of malware.

To ensure that Stealth-Loader-applied malware actually ran and conducted malicious activities, we configured Cuckoo Sandbox to write a memory dump file after each analysis had been done, and we then manually analyzed it with The Volatility Framework to confirm the traces which had been seen before applying Stealth Loader, such as created files or modified registries, were actually found.

*Result.* Table 2 shows the results of this experiment. Regarding DownloadAdmin, Win32.ZBot, Eorezo, and CheatEngine, Stealth Loader successfully hid the malicious behaviors and then the scores dropped to warning or benign from malicious or danger levels.

Regarding ICLoader, the score was the same before and after applying Stealth Loader because the same behaviors were observed. The reason is that this piece of malware acquires the base address of kernel32.dll by itself without depending on Windows APIs. That is, it directly accesses PEB, parses a list in PEB to find an entry of kernel32.dll, and then acquires the base address of kernel32.dll from the entry. From this base address, the malware acquires the addresses of LoadLibrary and GetProcAddress of the Windows-loaded kernel32.dll and then resolves the dependencies of the other APIs by using these two APIs. Since this malware does not use LoadLibrary or the equivalent APIs of the stealth-loaded kernel32.dll for dynamic API resolution, Stealth Loader did not have a chance to obfuscate the calls of dynamically resolved APIs invoked from this malware. We consider this to not be a limitation because our expected use case of Stealth Loader is to directly obfuscate compiler-generated executables, not already-obfuscated executables. This behavior, i.e., acquiring the base address of kernel32.dll through PEB, is a typical behavior of obfuscated executables.

## 6 Related Work

In this section, we briefly repeat the API obfuscation techniques which we mentioned in Sect. 2 for comparison with Stealth Loader and then explain other types of API obfuscations related to our research.

IAT obfuscation has the different target from Stealth Loader. It disturbs API name resolution by deleting INT and IAT and disconnecting to them from PE header, while Stealth Loader focuses on Windows-managed data structures, such as PEB or VAD. DLL unlinking obfuscates loaded DLLs. Its purpose is the same as Stealth Loader. However, DLL unlinking focuses on only PEB, not VAD, while Stealth Loader does on both. API redirection obfuscates the control flow from API call instructions to recognized API code whereas Stealth Loader attacks API name resolution. That is, Stealth Loader tries to make API code unrecognizable.

One piece of research close to us is Abrath et al.'s work [1]. They proposed a technique of linking Windows system DLLs statically with an executable and deleting imported API information from it to prevent API calls from being monitored. The effect of linking Windows system DLLs with an executable could be similar to the effect we obtained. However, static linked DLLs may lose the portability of a PE executable since system DLLs tend to depend on specific Windows versions and the size of a linked executable becomes larger.

Aside from the obfuscation techniques that we explained in Sect. 2.1, another type of obfuscation approach, called "API sequence obfuscation", has been proposed. Shadow Attack [13] is an API sequence obfuscation that works by partitioning one piece of malware into multiple processes. These multiple processes execute a part of the original behaviors of the malware. Illusion Attack [19] is another API sequence obfuscation that passes requested system call numbers and arguments via ioctl to an underlining kernel driver. From a monitoring tool viewpoint, it looks like a sequence of ioctl. These attacks mainly focus on scrambling executed API calls to avoid detection, while our approach focuses on hiding each API call to escape from both detection and analysis.

## 7 Discussion

In this section, we first discuss platform dependency of Stealth Loader. Then, we discuss other de-obfuscations and possible countermeasures against Stealth Loader.

### 7.1 Platform Dependency

As we mentioned in Sect. 4, the current Stealth Loader is implemented to run on Windows 7 environment. However, we believe that the design explained in Sect. 3 is also applicable to other Windows platforms including Windows 8 and 10. Of course, since Windows 8 and 10 have different implementations from Windows 7, we need an effort to make Stealth Loader runnable on these platforms without any issues. More concretely, we have to resolve some corner cases like we mentioned in Appendix A. In other word, the other part of this paper is applicable to other Windows platforms.

Regarding applying Stealth Loader to Linux, we consider that the designs of Stealth Loader are applicable to Linux platforms. Since Linux OS and libraries are less dependent each other than Windows ones, the implementation of Stealth Loader for Linux may become simpler than the one of Windows. We consider that Stealth Loader on Linux could make library calls invisible to library-call-monitoring tools, such as ltrace.

### 7.2 Other De-obfuscations

Eureka [18] relates the base address of a loaded DLL with a DLL file by monitoring NtMapViewOfSection API calls and extracting the specified file name and the return address. Since Stealth Loader does not use file-map functions at all, this API is not called when Stealth Loader loads a DLL. As a result, Eureka fails API name resolution, even though it overcomes stolen code or API redirection with performing deep program analyses.

API Chaser, proposed in [9] relates code with API name before starting an analysis by setting taint tags containing API name on the code. Then it keeps track of its relationship by propagating the tags during its analysis. Since it makes the relationship before Stealth Loader works, it may not be affected by Stealth Loader. However, it is widely known that tag propagation is disconnected at implicit flow code [3]. So, attackers are able to evade it by simply processing code with implicit flow without changing the value of it.

### 7.3 Countermeasures

**Monitor at Kernel Layer.** One countermeasure against Stealth Loader is monitoring at kernel layer. Stealth Loader has to depend on Windows system service calls, while it is independent of userland API code. Even though much useful information has already been lost when the executions of some APIs, e.g., network-related APIs, reach the kernel layer, a series of service system calls possibly provides a part of the whole picture regarding the behaviors of the executable protected with Stealth Loader.

**Specialized Analysis Environment.** Another one is to install hooks on system DLLs in an analysis environment before starting an analysis by modifying a file of each DLL on disk. This kind of modifications is likely to be detected and warned by Windows. However, since modified DLLs are loaded by not only benign processes but also processes protected with Stealth Loader, analysis tools probably identify the executions of APIs by the installed hooks when they are executed.

Instrumentation tools, such as Intel PIN [12], could possibly become a solution against Stealth Loader because they can possibly identify the locations of stealth-loaded DLLs by tracking the all memory reads and writes related to the DLLs. However, a major drawback of these tools is that they are easily detectable by malware. So, if malware analysts use these tools for analyzing Stealth-Loader-applied malware in practice, they need a further consideration for hiding these tools from malware.

**Detecting DLLs from Memory Patterns.** Scanning memory and finding specific patterns for a DLL may be effective. By preparing the patterns of each DLL in advance and scanning memory with these patterns, it could be possible to identify the modules loaded on memory. Also, comparing binaries using a different tool such as BinDiff [24] is also effective. By comparing the control flow of a Windows system DLL with that on memory, we could identify the existence of specific DLLs. However, since there are several binary- or assembly-level obfuscation techniques, such as [10], we need different counter-approaches to solve this type of problem.

**Inferring DLLs from Visible Traces.** Since current Stealth Loader avoids supporting some APIs as we explained in Appendix A, this fact may give static analysis tools a hint to infer a DLL. For example, if analysis tools identify the position of the IAT of a stealth-loaded DLL using the way we explained in Subsect. 2.1, they can probably specify the DLL from only visible imported APIs in the IAT. To solve this, we could take advantage of API redirection explained in Fig. 1-(c) in Subsect. 2.1. This type of API redirection modifies indirect API call instructions in original code with direct instructions which make the execution jump to a stub for each API. So, since there are no indirect API call instructions in original code, analysis tools are likely to fail to identify the IAT.

**Detecting Stealth Loader Itself.** Detecting Stealth Loader itself possibly becomes another direction to fight against Stealth Loader. One way is detecting specific byte patterns of Stealth Loader. While Stealth Loader hides its behaviors as we explained in Subsect. 3.3, the code or data of it may be likely to have specific patterns available to be detected. However, as we discussed above, several techniques, such as [10], have already proposed to avoid byte-pattern-based detection. If we apply one of them to Stealth Loader, we can avoid being detected.

**Restricting Untrusted Code.** One more direction is to prevent Stealth Loader from working at each phase. Policy enforcement, which is mentioned in safe loading [5], may be partially effective for that purpose. If there is a policy to restrict opening a system DLL for reading, Stealth Loader cannot map the code of a DLL on memory if it is not loaded by Windows yet. On the other hand, if the DLLs are already loaded by Windows, Reflective loading allows us to load them with Stealth Loader.

In addition, safe loading has a restriction to giving executable permissions. No other instances except for the trusted components of safe loading does not give executable permission to a certain memory area. Safe loader supports only Linux platform, however, if it would support Windows, safe loading may be able to prevent Stealth Loader from providing the executable permission to the code read from a DLL file.

## 8 Conclusion

We analyzed existing API [de]obfuscation techniques and clarified that API name resolution becomes an attack vector for malware authors to evade malware analyses and detections depending on API de-obfuscations. We also presented Stealth Loader and its implementation as a proof-of-concept to exploit the attack vector. Then, we demonstrated that Stealth Loader actually evaded all major analysis tools. In addition, we qualitatively showed that Stealth Loader can evade API de-obfuscations proposed in academic studies.

We do not consider that Stealth Loader is perfect. But we also consider that defeating Stealth Loader is not easy because none of the existing countermeasures discussed in Subsect. 7.3 can be come a direct solution against Stealth Loader. We consider that most existing malware analysis tools depend on more or less some of the API de-obfuscation techniques mentioned in this paper, implying that Stealth Loader can pose a serious real-world threat in the future.

## A The Reasons for Unsupported API

In this Appendix, we explain the reasons why we cannot support several APIs with Stealth Loader on Windows 7 platform.

### A.1 ntdll Initialization

ntdll.dll does not export the initialize function, i.e., DllMain does not exist in ntdll.dll, and LdrInitializeThunk, which is the entry point of ntdll.dll for a newly created thread, is also not exported. This inability of initialization leads to many uninitialized global variables, causing a program crash. As a workaround to this, we classified the APIs of ntdll.dll as to whether they are dependent on global variables or not by using static analysis. Then, we defined the APIs dependent on global variables as unsupported. As a result, the number of supported APIs for ntdll.dll is 776, while that of unsupported APIs is 1,992.

### A.2 Callback

APIs triggering callback are difficult to apply Stealth Loader to because these APIs do not work properly unless we register callback handlers in PEB. So, we exclude some of the APIs of user32.dll and gdi32.dll, which become a trigger callback from our supported APIs. To distinguish whether APIs are related to callbacks or not, we developed an IDA script to make a call flow graph and analyzed win32k.sys, user32.dll, and gdi32.dll using the script. Then, we identified 203 APIs out of 839 exported from user32.dll and 202 out of 728 exported from gdi32.dll.

### A.3 Local Heap Memory

Supporting APIs to operate local heap objects is difficult because these objects are possibly shared between DLLs. The reason is as follows. When a local heap object is assigned, this object is managed under the stealth-loaded kernelbase.dll. However, when the object is used, the object is checked under the Windows-loaded kernelbase.dll. This inconsistency leads to failure in the execution of some APIs related to the local heap object operation. To avoid this situation, we exclude the APIs for operating local heap objects from our supported API. As a result of static analysis, we found that local heap objects are managed in BaseHeapHandleTable, located in the data section of kernelbase.dll. Therefore, we do not support 6 APIs depending on this table in current Stealth Loader.

## References

1. Abrath, B., Coppens, B., Volckaert, S., De Sutter, B.: Obfuscating windows dlls. In: 2015 IEEE/ACM 1st International Workshop on Software Protection (SPRO), pp. 24–30. IEEE (2015)
2. Bellard, F.: Qemu, a fast and portable dynamic translator. In: USENIX Annual Technical Conference, FREENIX Track, USENIX, pp. 41–46 (2005)
3. Cavallaro, L., Saxena, P., Sekar, R.: On the limits of information flow techniques for malware analysis and containment. In: Zamboni, D. (ed.) DIMVA 2008. LNCS, vol. 5137, pp. 143–163. Springer, Heidelberg (2008). doi:10.1007/978-3-540-70542-0_8
4. Fewer, S.: Reflective dll injection. http://www.harmonysecurity.com/files/HS-P005_ReflectiveDllInjection.pdf
5. Gross, T.R., Hartmann, T., Payer, M.: Safe loading - a foundation for secure execution of untrusted programs. In: IEEE Symposium on Security and Privacy (2012), pp. 18–32 (2012)
6. Henderson, A., Prakash, A., Yan, L.K., Hu, X., Wang, X., Zhou, R., Yin, H.: Make it work, make it right, make it fast: building a platform-neutral whole-system dynamic binary analysis platform. In: Proceedings of the 2014 International Symposium on Software Testing and Analysis, ISSTA 2014, pp. 248–258. ACM, New York (2014)
7. Hex-Rays. https://www.hex-rays.com/
8. Hunt, G., Brubacher, D.: Detours: binary interception of win32 functions. In: Third USENIX Windows NT Symposium, USENIX, p. 8, July 1999

9. Kawakoya, Y., Iwamura, M., Shioji, E., Hariu, T.: API chaser: anti-analysis resistant malware analyzer. In: Stolfo, S.J., Stavrou, A., Wright, C.V. (eds.) RAID 2013. LNCS, vol. 8145, pp. 123–143. Springer, Heidelberg (2013). doi:10.1007/978-3-642-41284-4_7
10. Kruegel, C., Kirda, E., Moser, A.: Limits of static analysis for malware detection. In: Proceedings of the 23rd Annual Computer Security Applications Conference (ACSAC) 2007, December 2007
11. Ligh, M.H., Case, A., Levy, J., Walters, A.: The Art of Memory Forensics: Detecting Malware and Threats in Windows, Linux, and Mac Memory, 1st edn. Wiley Publishing, USA (2014)
12. Luk, C.-K., Cohn, R., Muth, R., Patil, H., Klauser, A., Lowney, G., Wallace, S., Reddi, V.J., Hazelwood, K.: Pin: building customized program analysis tools with dynamic instrumentation. In: Proceedings of the 2005 ACM SIGPLAN Conference on Programming Language Design and Implementation, PLDI 2005, pp. 190–200. ACM, New York (2005)
13. Ma, W., Duan, P., Liu, S., Gu, G., Liu, J.-C.: Shadow attacks: automatically evading system-call-behavior based malware detection. J. Comput. Virol. **8**(1), 1–13 (2012)
14. NtQuery. https://github.com/NtQuery/Scylla
15. Oktavianto, D., Muhardianto, I.: Cuckoo Malware Analysis. Packt Publishing, Birmingham (2013)
16. Plohmann, D., Hanel, A.: simplifire.idascope. In: Hacklu (2012)
17. Rekall. http://www.rekall-forensic.com/
18. Sharif, M., Yegneswaran, V., Saidi, H., Porras, P., Lee, W.: Eureka: a framework for enabling static malware analysis. In: Jajodia, S., Lopez, J. (eds.) ESORICS 2008. LNCS, vol. 5283, pp. 481–500. Springer, Heidelberg (2008). doi:10.1007/978-3-540-88313-5_31
19. Srivastava, A., Lanzi, A., Giffin, J., Balzarotti, D.: Operating system interface obfuscation and the revealing of hidden operations. In: Holz, T., Bos, H. (eds.) DIMVA 2011. LNCS, vol. 6739, pp. 214–233. Springer, Heidelberg (2011). doi:10.1007/978-3-642-22424-9_13
20. Suenaga, M.: A museum of API obfuscation on Win32. In: Symantec Security Response (2009)
21. Sycurelab. https://github.com/sycurelab/DECAF
22. VirusTotal. https://www.virustotal.com/
23. Yason, M.V.: The art of unpacking. In: Black Hat USA Briefings (2007)
24. Zynamics. https://www.zynamics.com/bindiff.html

# LAZARUS: Practical Side-Channel Resilient Kernel-Space Randomization

David Gens[1(✉)], Orlando Arias[2], Dean Sullivan[2], Christopher Liebchen[1], Yier Jin[2], and Ahmad-Reza Sadeghi[1]

[1] CYSEC/Technische Universität Darmstadt, Darmstadt, Germany
{david.gens,christopher.liebchen,ahmad.sadeghi}@trust.tu-darmstadt.de
[2] University of Central Florida, Orlando, FL, USA
{oarias,dean.sullivan}@knights.ucf.edu, yier.jin@eecs.ucf.edu

**Abstract.** Kernel exploits are commonly used for privilege escalation to take full control over a system, e.g., by means of code-reuse attacks. For this reason modern kernels are hardened with kernel Address Space Layout Randomization (KASLR), which randomizes the start address of the kernel code section at boot time. Hence, the attacker first has to bypass the randomization, to conduct the attack using an adjusted payload in a second step. Recently, researchers demonstrated that attackers can exploit unprivileged instructions to collect timing information through side channels in the paging subsystem of the processor. This can be exploited to reveal the randomization secret, even in the absence of any information-disclosure vulnerabilities in the software.

In this paper we present *LAZARUS* , a novel technique to harden KASLR against paging-based side-channel attacks. In particular, our scheme allows for fine-grained protection of the virtual memory mappings that implement the randomization. We demonstrate the effectiveness of our approach by hardening a recent Linux kernel with LAZARUS, mitigating all of the previously presented side-channel attacks on KASLR. Our extensive evaluation shows that LAZARUS incurs only 0.943% overhead for standard benchmarks, and therefore, is highly practical.

**Keywords:** KASLR · Code-reuse attacks · Randomization · Side channels

## 1 Introduction

For more than three decades memory-corruption vulnerabilities have challenged computer security. This class of vulnerabilities enables the attacker to overwrite memory in a way that was not intended by the developer, resulting in a malicious control or data flow. In the recent past, kernel vulnerabilities became more prevalent in exploits due to advances in hardening user-mode applications.

**Electronic supplementary material** The online version of this chapter (doi:10.1007/978-3-319-66332-6_11) contains supplementary material, which is available to authorized users.


M. Dacier et al. (Eds.): RAID 2017, LNCS 10453, pp. 238–258, 2017.
DOI: 10.1007/978-3-319-66332-6_11

For example, browsers and other popular targets are isolated by executing them in a sandboxed environment. Consequently, the attacker needs to execute a privilege-escalation attack in addition to the initial exploit to take full control over the system [4,17–19]. Operating system kernels are a natural target for attackers because the kernel is comprised of a large and complex code base, and exposes a rich set of functionality, even to low privileged processes. Molinyawe et al. [20] summarized the techniques used in the Pwn2Own exploiting contest, and concluded that a kernel exploit is required for most privilege-escalation attacks.

In the past, kernels were hardened using different mitigation techniques to minimize the risk of memory-corruption vulnerabilities. For instance, enforcing the address space to be writable or executable (W$\oplus$X), but never both, prevents the attacker from injecting new code. Additionally, enabling new CPU features like Supervisor Mode Access Prevention (SMAP) and Supervisor Mode Execution Protection (SMEP) prevents certain classes of user-mode-aided attacks. To mitigate code-reuse attacks, modern kernels are further fortified with kernel Address Space Layout Randomization (KASLR) [2]. KASLR randomizes the base address of the code section of the kernel at boot time, which forces attackers to customize their exploit for each targeted kernel. Specifically, the attack needs to disclose the randomization secret first, before launching a code-reuse attack.

In general, there are two ways to bypass randomization: (1) brute-force attacks, and (2) information-disclosure attacks. While KASLR aims to make brute-force attacks infeasible, attackers can still leverage information-disclosure attacks, e.g., to leak the randomization secret. The attacker can achieve this by exploiting a memory-corruption vulnerability, or through side channels. Recent research demonstrated that side-channel attacks are more powerful, since they do not require any kernel vulnerabilities [6,8,10,13,23]. These attacks exploit properties of the underlying micro architecture to infer the randomization secret of KASLR. In particular, modern processors share resources such as caches between user mode and kernel mode, and hence, leak timing information between privileged and unprivileged execution. The general idea of these attacks is to probe different kernel addresses and measure the execution time of the probe. Since the timing signature for valid and invalid kernel addresses is different, the attacker can compute the randomization secret by comparing the extracted signal against a reference signal.

The majority of side-channel attacks against KASLR is based on *paging* [8, 10,13,23]. Here, the attacker exploits the timing difference between an aborted memory access to an unmapped kernel address and an aborted memory access to a mapped kernel address. As we eloberate in the related work Sect. 7 the focus of the existing work is on attacks, and only include theoretical discussions on possible defenses. For instance, Gruss et al. [8] briefly discuss an idea similar to our implemented defense by suggesting to completely un-map the kernel address space when executing the user mode as it is done in iOS on ARM [16]. However, as stated by the authors [8] they did not implement or evaluate the security of their approach but only provided a simulation of this technique to provide a rough estimation of the expected run-time overhead which is around 5% for system call intensive applications.

*Goal and Contributions.* The goal of this paper is to prevent kernel-space randomization approaches from leaking side-channel information through the paging subsystem of the processor. To this end, we propose *LAZARUS* , as a novel real-world defense against paging-based side-channel attacks on KASLR. Our software-only defense is based on the observation that all of the presented attacks have a common source of leakage: information about randomized kernel addresses is stored in the paging caches of the processor while execution continues in user mode. More specifically, the processor keeps paging entries for recently used addresses in the cache, regardless of their associated privilege level. This results in a timing side channel, because accesses for cached entries are faster than cache misses. Our defense separates paging entries according to their privilege level in caches, and provides a mechanism for the kernel to achieve this efficiently in software. LAZARUS only separates those parts of the address space which might reveal the randomization secret while leaving entries for non-randomized memory shared. Our benchmarks show that this significantly reduces the performance overhead. We provide a prototype implementation of our side-channel defense, and conduct an extensive evaluation of the security and performance of our prototype for a recent kernel under the popular Debian Linux and Arch Linux distributions.

To summarize, our contributions are as follows:

- **Novel side-channel defense.** We present the design of *LAZARUS* , a software-only protection scheme to thwart side-channel attacks against KASLR based on paging.
- **Protoype Implementation.** We provide a fully working and practical prototype implementation of our defense for a recent Linux kernel version 4.8.
- **Extensive Evaluation.** We extensively evaluate our prototype against all previously presented side-channel attacks and demonstrate that the randomization secret can no longer be disclosed. We re-implemented all previously proposed attacks on KASLR for the Linux kernel. We additionally present an extensive performance evaluation and demonstrate high practicality with an average overhead of only 0.943% for common benchmarks.

## 2 Background

In this section, we first explain the details of modern processor architectures necessary to understand the remainder of this paper. We then explain the different attacks on KASLR presented by related work.

### 2.1 Virtual Memory

Virtual memory is a key building block to separate privileged system memory from unprivileged user memory, and to isolate processes from each other. Virtual

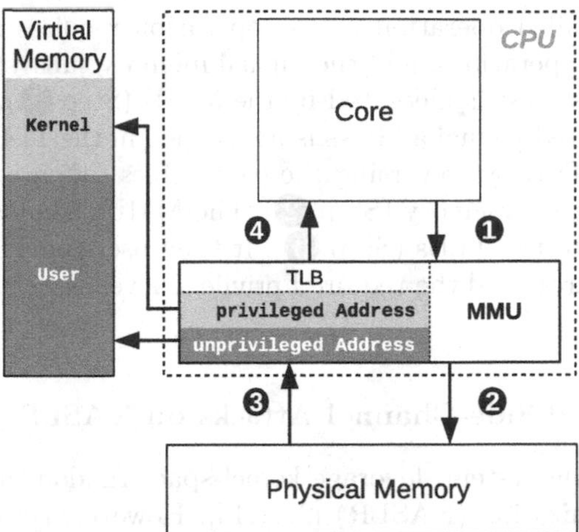


**Fig. 1.** When virtual memory is active, all memory accesses of the processor are mediated by the MMU ❶: it loads the associated page-table entry ❷ into the TLB from memory, checks the required privilege level ❸, and translates the virtual memory address into the corresponding physical memory address if and only if the current privilege level of the processor matches the required privilege level ❹.

memory is implemented by enforcing an indirection between the address space of the processor and the physical memory, i.e., every memory access initiated by the processor is mediated by a piece of hardware called the Memory Management Unit (MMU). The MMU translates the virtual address to a physical address, and enforces access control based on permissions defined for the requested address. The translation information as well as the access permissions are stored in a hierarchical data structure, which is maintained by the kernel, called the page table. The kernel isolates processes from each other by maintaining separate page tables for each process, and hence, different permissions. In contrast to processes, the kernel is not isolated using a separate page table but by setting the supervisor bit in page-table entries that translate kernel memory. In fact, each process page table contains entries that map the kernel (typically in the top part of the virtual address space). This increases the performance of context switches between the kernel and user applications because replacing the active page table forces the MMU to evict entries from its internal cache, called Translation Lookaside Buffer (TLB). The TLB caches the most recent or prominent page table entries, which is a sensible strategy since software usually exhibits (spatial or temporal) *locality*. Hence, all subsequent virtual-memory accesses, which are translated using a cached page-table entry, will be handled much faster.

Figure 1 shows the major components of virtual memory and their interaction. In the following we describe the MMU and the TLB in detail and explain their role in paging-based side-channel attacks.

The Central Processing Unit (CPU) contains one or more execution units (cores), which decode, schedule, and eventually execute individual machine instructions, also called operations. If an operation requires a memory access, e.g., load and store operations, and the virtual memory subsystem of the processor is enabled, this access is mediated by the MMU (Step ❶). If the page-table entry for the requested virtual address is not cached in the TLB, the MMU loads the entry into the TLB by traversing the page tables (often called a *page walk*) which reside in physical memory (Step ❷). The MMU then loads the respective page-table entry into the TLBs (Step ❸). It then uses the TLB entries to look up the physical address and the required privilege level associated with a virtual address (Step ❹).

## 2.2 Paging-Based Side-Channel Attacks on KASLR

All modern operating systems leverage kernel-space randomization by means of kernel code randomization (KASLR) [2,11,14]. However, kernel-space randomization has been shown to be vulnerable to a variety of side-channel attacks. These attacks leverage micro-architectural implementation details of the underlying hardware. More specifically, modern processors share virtual memory resources between privileged and unprivileged execution modes through caches, which was shown to be exploitable by an user space adversary.

In the following we briefly describe recent paging-based side-channel attacks that aim to disclose the KASLR randomization secret. All these attacks exploit the fact that the TLB is shared between user applications and the kernel (cf., Fig. 1). As a consequence, the TLB will contain page-table entries of the kernel after switching the execution from kernel to a user mode application. Henceforth, the attacker uses special instructions (depending on the concrete side-channel attack implementation) to access kernel addresses. Since the attacker executes the attack with user privileges, the access will be aborted. However, the time difference between access attempt and abort depends on whether the guessed address is cached in the TLB or not. Further, the attacker can also measure the difference in timing between existing (requiring a page walk) and non-existing mappings (immediate abort). The resulting timing differences can be exploited by the attacker as a side channel to disclose the randomization secret as shown recently [8,10,13,23].

*Page Fault Handler (PFH).* Hund, et al. [10] published the first side-channel attack to defeat KASLR. They trigger a page fault in the kernel from a user process by accessing an address in kernel space. Although this unprivileged access is correctly denied by the page fault handler, the TLBs are queried during processing of the memory request. They show that the timing difference between exceptions for unmapped and mapped pages can be exploited to disclose the random offset.

*Prefetch Instruction.* Furthermore, even individual instructions may leak timing information and can be exploited [8]. More specifically, the execution of the `prefetch` instruction of recent Intel processors exhibits a timing difference, which depends directly on the state of the TLBs. As in the case of the other side-channel attacks, this is used to access privileged addresses by the attacker. Since this access originates from an unprivileged instruction it will fail, and according to the documentation the processor will not raise an exception. Hence, its execution time differs for cached kernel addresses. This yields another side channel that leaks the randomization secret.

*Intel's TSX.* Transactional memory extensions introduced by Intel encapsulate a series of memory accesses to provide enhanced safety guarantees, such as rollbacks. While potentially interesting for the implementation of concurrent software without the need for lock-based synchronization, erroneous accesses within a transaction are not reported to the operating system. More specifically, if the MMU detects an access violation, the exception is masked and the transaction is rolled back silently. However, an adversary can measure the timing difference between two failing transactions to identify privileged addresses, which are cached in the TLBs. This enables the attacker to significantly improve over the original page fault timing side-channel attack [13,23]. The reason is that the page fault handler of the OS is never invoked, significantly reducing the noise in the timing signal.

# 3 LAZARUS

In this section, we give an overview of the idea and architecture of LAZARUS, elaborate on the main challenges, and explain in detail how we tackle these challenges.

## 3.1 Adversary Model and Assumptions

We derive our adversary model from the related offensive work [6,8,10,13,23].

- **Writable ⊕ Executable Memory**. The kernel enforces Writable ⊕ Executable Memory (W⊕X) which prevents code-injection attacks in the kernel space. Further, the kernel utilizes modern CPU features like SMAP and SMEP [12] to prevent user-mode aided code-injection and code-reuse attacks.
- **Kernel Address Space Layout Randomization (KASLR)**. The base address of the kernel is randomized at boot time [2,14].
- **Absence of Software-Based Information-Disclosure Vulnerability**. The kernel does not contain any vulnerabilities that can be exploited to disclose the randomization secret.
- **Malicious Kernel Extension**. The attacker cannot load malicious kernel extensions to gain control over the kernel, i.e., only trusted (or signed) extensions can be loaded.
- **Memory-corruption Vulnerability**. This is a standard assumption for many real-world kernel exploits. The kernel, or a kernel extension contains a memory-corruption vulnerability. The attacker has full control over a user-mode process from which it can exploit this vulnerability. The vulnerability

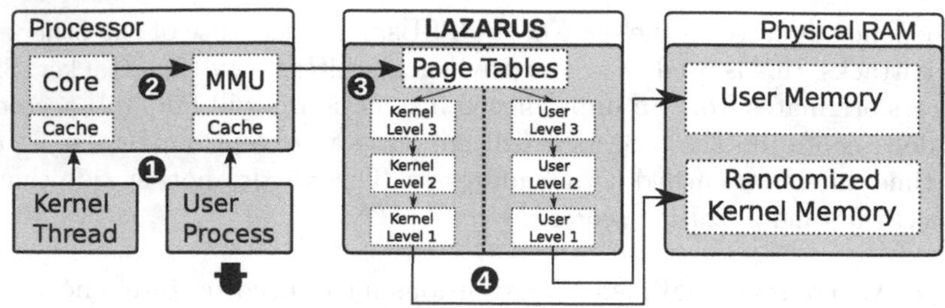


**Fig. 2.** The idea behind our side channel protection: An unprivileged user process (❶) can exploit the timing side channel for kernel addresses through shared cache access in the MMU paging caches (❷). Our defense mitigates this by enforcing (❸) a separation between different privilege levels for randomized addresses (❹).

enables the attacker to overwrite a code pointer of the kernel to hijack the control-flow of the kernel. However, the attacker cannot use this vulnerability to disclose any addresses.

While modern kernels suffer from software-based information-disclosure vulnerabilities, information-disclosure attacks based on side channels pose a more severe threat because they can be exploited to disclose information in the absence of software vulnerabilities. We address the problem of side channels, and treat software-based information-disclosure vulnerabilities as an orthogonal problem.

### 3.2 Overview

Usually, kernel and user mode share the same virtual address space. While legitimate accesses to kernel addresses require higher privilege, these addresses still occupy some parts of the virtual memory space that is visible to user processes. The idea behind our side-channel defense is to strictly and efficiently separate randomized kernel memory from virtual memory in user space.

Our idea is depicted in Fig. 2. Kernel execution and user space execution usually share a common set of architectural resources, such as the execution unit (Core), and the MMU. The attacker leverages these shared resources in the following way: in step ❶, the attacker sets up the user process and memory setting that will leak the randomization secret. The user process then initiates a virtual memory access to a kernel address.

Next, the processor invokes the MMU to check the required privilege level in step ❷. Since a user space process does not possess the required privileges to access kernel memory, any such access will ultimately be denied. However, to deny access the MMU has to look up the required privileges in the page tables. These are structured hierarchically with multiple levels, and separate caches on every level. Hence, even denied accesses constitute a timing side-channel that directly depends on the last cached level.

We address ❸ the root of this side channel: we separate the page tables for kernel and user space. This effectively prevents side-channel information from kernel addresses to be leaked to user space, because the MMU uses a different page table hierarchy. Thus, while the processor is in user mode, the MMU will not be able to refer to any information about kernel virtual addresses, as shown in step 4.

### 3.3 Challenges for Fine-Grained Address Space Isolation

To enable LAZARUS to separate and isolate both execution domains a number of challenges have to be tackled: first, we must provide a mechanism for switching between kernel and user execution at any point in time without compromising the randomized kernel memory (**C1**). More specifically, while kernel and user space no longer share the randomized parts of privileged virtual memory, the system still has to be able to execute code pages in both execution modes. For this reason, we have to enable switching between kernel and user space. This is challenging, because such a transition can happen either through explicit invocation, such as a system call or an exception, or through hardware events, such as interrupts. As we will show our defense handles both cases securely and efficiently.

Second, we have to prevent the switching mechanism from leaking any side-channel information (**C2**). Unmapping kernel pages is also challenging with respect to side-channel information, i.e., unmapped memory pages still exhibit a timing difference compared to mapped pages. Hence, LAZARUS has to prevent information leakage through probing of unmapped pages.

Third, our approach has to minimize the overhead for running applications to offer a practical defense mechanism (**C3**). Implementing strict separation of address spaces efficiently is involved, since we only separate those parts of the address space that are privileged and randomized. We have to modify only those parts of the page table hierarchy which define translations for randomized addresses.

In the following we explain how our defense meets these challenges.

*C1: Kernel-User Transitioning.* Processor resources are time-shared between processes and the operating system. Thus, the kernel eventually takes control over these resources, either through explicit invocation, or based on a signaling event. Examples for explicit kernel invocations are *system calls* and *exceptions*. These are synchronous events, meaning that the user process generating the event is suspended and waiting for the kernel code handling the event to finish.

On the one hand, after transitioning from user to kernel mode, the event handler code is no longer mapped in virtual memory because it is located in the kernel. Hence, we have to provide a mechanism to restore this mapping when entering kernel execution from user space.

On the other hand, when the system call or exception handler finishes and returns execution to the user space process, we have to erase those mappings again. Otherwise, paging entries might be shared between privilege levels. Since all system calls enter the kernel through a well-defined hardware interface, we can activate and deactivate the corresponding entries by modifying this central entry point.

Transitions between kernel and user space execution can also happen through *interrupts*. A simple example for this type of event is the timer interrupt, which is programmed by the kernel to trigger periodically in fixed intervals. In contrast to system calls or exceptions, interrupts are asynchronously occurring events, which may suspend current kernel or user space execution at any point in time.

Hence, interrupt routines have to store the current process context before handling a pending interrupt. However, interrupts can also occur while the processor executes kernel code. Therefore, we have to distinguish between interrupts during user or kernel execution to only restore and erase the kernel entries upon transitions to and from user space respectively. For this we facilitate the stored state of the interrupted execution context that is saved by the interrupt handler to distinguish privileged from un-privileged contexts.

This enables LAZARUS to still utilize the paging caches for interrupts occuring during kernel execution.

*C2: Protecting the Switching Mechanism.* The code performing the address space switching has to be mapped during user execution. Otherwise, implementing a switching mechanism in the kernel would not be possible, because the processor could never access the corresponding code pages. For this reason, it is necessary to prevent these mapped code pages from leaking any side-channel information. There are two possibilities for achieving this.

First, we can map the switching code with a different offset than the rest of the kernel code section. In this case an adversary would be able to disclose the offset of the switching code, while the actual randomization secret would remain protected.

Second, we can eliminate the timing channel by inserting dummy mappings into the unmapped region. This causes the surrounding addresses to exhibit an identical timing signature compared to the switching code.

Since an adversary would still be able to utilize the switching code to conduct a code-reuse attack in the first case, LAZARUS inserts dummy mappings into the user space page table hierarchy.

*C3: Minimizing Performance Penalties.* Once paging is enabled on a processor, all memory accesses are mediated through the virtual memory subsystem. This means that a page walk is required for every memory access. Since traversing the page table results in high performance penalties, the MMU caches the most prominent address translations in the Translation Lookaside Buffers (TLBs).

LAZARUS removes kernel addresses from the page table hierarchy upon user space execution. Hence, the respective TLB entries need to be invalidated. As a result, subsequent accesses to kernel memory will be slower, once kernel execution is resumed.

To minimize these perfomance penalties, we have to reduce the amount of invalidated TLB entries to a minimum but still enforce a clear separation between kernel and user space addresses. In particular, we only remove those virtual mappings, which fall into the location of a randomized kernel area, such as the kernel code segment.

# 4 Prototype Implementation

We implemented LAZARUS as a prototype for the Linux kernel, version 4.8 for the 64 bit variant of the x86 architecture. However, the techniques we used are generic and can be applied to all architectures employing multi-level page tables. Our patch consists of around 300 changes to seven files, where most of the code results from initialization. Hence, LAZARUS should be easily portable to other architectures. Next, we will explain our implementation details. It consists of the initialization setup, switching mechanism, and how we minimize performance impact.

## 4.1 Initialization

We first setup a second set of page tables, which can be used when execution switches to user space. These page tables must not include the randomized portions of the address space that belong to the kernel. However, switching between privileged and unprivileged execution requires some code in the kernel to be mapped upon transitions from user space. We explicitly create dedicated entry points mapped in the user page tables, which point to the required switching routines.

*Fixed Mappings.* Additionally, there are kernel addresses, which are mapped to fixed locations in the top address space ranges. These *fixmap* entries essentially represent an address-based interface: even if the physical address is determined at boot time, their virtual address is fixed at compile time. Some of these addresses are mapped readable to user space, and we have to explicitly add these entries as well.

We setup this second set of page tables only once at boot time, before the first user process is started. Every process then switches to this set of page tables during user execution.

*Dummy Mappings.* As explained in Sect. 3, one way of protecting the code pages of the switching mechanism is to insert dummy mappings into the user space page table hierarchy. In particular, we create mappings for randomly picked virtual kernel addresses to span the entire code section. We distribute these mappings in 2M intervals to cover all third-level page table entries, which are used to map the code section. Hence, the entire address range which potentially contains the randomized kernel code section will be mapped during user space execution using our randomly created dummy entries.

## 4.2 System Calls

There is a single entry point in the Linux kernel for system calls, which is called the system call handler. We add an assembly routine to execute immediately after execution enters the system call handler. It switches from the predefined user page tables to the kernel page tables and continues to dispatch the requested system call. We added a second assembly routine shortly before the return of the system call handler to remove the kernel page tables from the page table hierarchy of the process and insert our predefined user page tables.

However, contrary to its single entry, there are multiple exit points for the system call handler. For instance, there is a dedicated error path, and fast and slow paths for regular execution. We instrument all of these exit points to ensure that the kernel page tables are not used during user execution.

### 4.3 Interrupts

Just like the system call handler, we need to modify the interrupt handler to restore the kernel page tables. However, unlike system calls, interrupts can occur when the processor is in privileged execution mode as well. Thus, to handle interrupts, we need to distinguish both cases. Basically we could look up the current privilege level easily by querying a register. However, this approach provides information about the current execution context, whereas to distinguish the two cases we require the privilege level of the interrupted context.

Fortunately, the processor saves some hardware context information, such as the instruction pointer, stack pointer, and the code segment register before invoking the interrupt handler routine. This means that we can utilize the stored privilege level associated with the previous code segment selector to test the privilege level of the interrupted execution context. We then only restore the kernel page tables if it was a user context.

We still have to handle one exceptional case however: the non-maskable interrupt (NMI). Because NMIs are never maskable, they are handled by a dedicated interrupt handler. Hence, we modify this dedicated NMI handler in the kernel to include our mechanism as well.

### 4.4 Fine-Grained Page Table Switching

As a software-only defense technique, one of the main goals of LAZARUS is to offer practical performance. While separating the entire page table hierarchy between kernel and user mode is tempting, this approach is impractical.

In particular, switching the entire page table hierarchy invalidates all of the cached TLB entries. This means, that the caches are reset every time and can never be utilized after a context switch. For this reason, we only replace those parts of the page table hierarchy, which define virtual memory mappings for randomized addresses. In the case of KASLR, this corresponds to the code section of the kernel. More specifically, the kernel code section is managed by the last of the 512 level 4 entries.

Thus, we replace only this entry during a context switch between privileged and unprivileged execution. As a result, the caches can still be shared between different privilege levels for non-randomized addresses. As we will discuss in Sect. 5, this does not impact our security guarantees in any way.

# 5 Evaluation

In this section we evaluate our prototypical implementation for the Linux kernel. First, we show that LAZARUS successfully prevents all of the previously published side-channel attacks. Second, we demonstrate that our defense only incurs negligible performance impact for standard computational workloads.

## 5.1 Security

Our main goal is to prevent the leakage of the randomization secret in the kernel to an unprivileged process through paging-based side-channel attacks. For this, we separate the page tables for privileged parts of the address space from the unprivileged parts. We ensure that this separation is enforced for randomized addresses to achieve practical performance.

Because all paging-based exploits rely on the timing difference between cached and uncached entries for privileged virtual addresses, we first conduct a series of timing experiments to measure the remaining side channel in the presence of LAZARUS.

In a second step, we execute all previously presented side-channel attacks on a system hardened with LAZARUS to verify the effectiveness of our approach.

**Effect of LAZARUS on the Timing Side-Channel.** To estimate the remaining timing side-channel information we measure the timing difference for privileged virtual addresses. We access each page in the kernel code section at least once and measure the timing using the `rdtscp` instruction. By probing the privileged address space in this way, we collect a timing series of execution cycles for each kernel code page. The results are shown in Fig. 3.[1]

The timing side channel is clearly visible for the vanilla KASLR implementation: the start of the actual code section mapping is located around the first visible jump from 160 cycles up to 180 cycles. Given a reference timing for a corresponding kernel image, the attacker can easily calculate the random offset by subtracting the address of the peak from the address in the reference timing.

In contrast to this, the timing of LAZARUS shows a straight line, with a maximum cycle distance of two cycles. In particular, there is no correlation between any addresses and peaks in the timing signal of the hardened kernel. This indicates that our defense approach indeed closes the paging-induced timing channel successfully. We note, that the average number of cycles depicted for LAZARUS are also in line with the timings for cached page table entries reported by related work [8,13]. To further evaluate the security of our approach, we additionally test it against all previous side-channel attacks.

---

[1] For brevity, we display the addresses on the x-axis as offsets to the start of the code section (i.e., `0xffffffff80000000`). We further corrected the addresses by their random offset, so that both data series can be shown on top of each other.

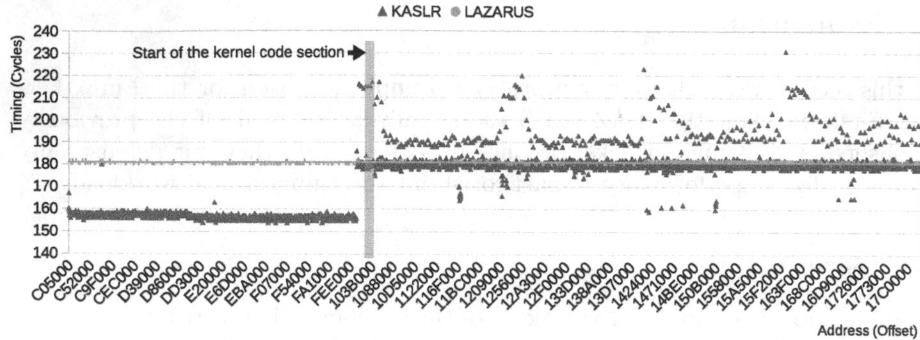


**Fig. 3.** Timing side-channel measurements.

**Real-World Side-Channel Attacks.** We implemented and ran all of the previous side-channel attacks against a system hardened with LAZARUS, to experimentally assess the effectiveness of our approach against real-world attacks.

*Page-fault handler.* The first real-world side-channel attack against KASLR was published by Hund et al. [10]. They noted that the execution time of the page fault handler in the OS kernel depends on the state of the paging caches. More specifically, they access kernel addresses from user space which results in a page fault. While this would usually terminate the process causing the access violation, the POSIX standard allows for processes to handle such events via *signals*. By installing a signal handler for the segmentation violation (`SIGSEGV`), the user process can recover from the fault and measure the timing difference from the initial memory access to the delivery of the signal back to user space. In this way, the entire virtual kernel code section can be scanned and each address associated with its corresponding timing measurement, allowing a user space process to reconstruct the start address of the kernel code section. We implemented and successfully tested the attack against a vanilla Linux kernel with KASLR. In particular, we found that page fault handler exhibits a timing difference of around 30 cycles for mapped and unmapped pages, with an average time of around 2200 cycles. While this represents a rather small difference compared to the other attacks, this is due to the high amount of noise that is caused by the execution path of the page fault handler code in the kernel.[2] When we applied LAZARUS to the kernel the attack no longer succeeded.

*Prefetch.* Recently, the `prefetch` instruction featured on many Intel x86 processors was shown to enable side-channel attacks against KASLR [8]. It is intended to provide a benign way of instrumenting the caches: the programmer (or the compiler) can use the instruction to provide a hint to the processor to cache a given virtual address.

[2] This was also noted in the original exploit [10].

Although there is no guarantee that this hint will influence the caches in any way, the instruction can be used with arbitrary addresses in principle. This means that a user mode program can prefetch a kernel virtual address, and execution of the instruction will fail siltently, i.e., the page fault handler in the kernel will not be executed, and no exception will be raised.

However, the MMU still has to perform a privilege check on the provided virtual address, hence the execution time of the `prefetch` instruction depends directly on the state of the TLBs.

We implemented the prefetch attack against KASLR for Linux, and succesfully executed it against a vanilla system to disclose the random offset. Executing the attack against a system hardened with LAZARUS we found the attack to be unsuccessful.

*TSX.* Rafal Wojtczuk originally proposed an attack to bypass KASLR using the Transactional Synchronization Extension (TSX) present in Intel x86 CPUs [23], and the attack gained popularity in the academic community through a paper by Jang et al. [13]. TSX provides a hardware mechanism that aims to simplify the implementation of multi-threaded applications through lock elision. Initially released in Haswell processors, TSX-enabled processors are capable of dynamically determining to serialize threads through lock-protected critical sections if necessary. The processor may abort a TSX transaction if an *atomic* view from the software's perspective is not guaranteed, e.g., due to conflicting accesses between two logical processors on one core.

TSX will suppress any faults that must be exposed to software if they occur within a transactional region. Memory accesses that cause a page walk may abort a transaction, and according to the specification *will not be made architecturally visible through the behavior of structures such as TLBs* [12]. The timing characteristics of the abort, however, can be exploited to reveal the current state of the TLBs. By causing a page walk inside a transactional block, timing information on the aborted transaction discloses the position of kernel pages that are mapped into a process: first, the attacker initiates a memory access to kernel pages inside a transactional block, which causes (1) a page walk, and (2) a segmentation fault. Since TSX masks the segmentation fault in hardware, the kernel is never made aware of the event and the CPU executes the abort handler provided by the attacker-controlled application that initiated the malicious transaction. Second, the attacker records timing information about the abort-handler execution. A transaction abort takes about 175 cycles if the probed page is mapped, whereas it aborts in about 200 cycles or more if unmapped [23]. By probing all possible locations for the start of the kernel code section, this side channel exposes the KASLR offset to the unprivileged attacker in user space.

Probing pages in this way under LAZARUS reveals no information, since we unmap all kernel code pages from the process, rendering the timing side channel useless as any probes to kernel addresses show as unmapped. Only the switching code and the surrounding dummy entries are mapped. However, these show identical timing information, and hence, are indistinguishable for an adversary.

### 5.2 Performance

We evaluated LAZARUS on a machine with an Intel Core i7-6820HQ CPU clocked at 2.70 GHz and 16 GB of memory. The machine runs a current release of Arch Linux with kernel version 4.8.14. For our testing, we enabled KASLR in the Linux kernel that Arch Linux ships. We also compiled a secondary kernel with the same configuration and LAZARUS applied.

We first examine the performance overhead with respect to the industry standard SPEC2006 benchmark [9]. We ran both the integer and floating point benchmarks in our test platform under the stock kernel with KASLR enabled. We collected these results and performed the test again under the LAZARUS kernel. Our results are shown in Fig. 4.

The observed performance overhead can be attributed to measurement inaccuracies. Our computed worst case overhead is of 0.943%. We should note that SPEC2006 is meant to test computational workloads and performs little in terms of context switching.

To better gauge the effects of LAZARUS on the system, we ran the system benchmarks provided by LMBench3 [22]. LMBench3 improves on the context switching benchmarks by eliminating some of the issues present in previous versions of the benchmark, albeit it still suffers issues with multiprocessor machines. For this reason, we disabled SMP during our testing. Our results are presented in Fig. 5.

We can see how a system call intensive application is affected the most under LAZARUS. This is to be expected, as the page tables belonging to the kernel must be remapped upon entering kernel execution. In general, we show a 47% performance overhead when running these benchmarks. We would like to remind the reader, however, that these benchmarks are meant to stress test the performance of the operating system when handling interrupts and do not reflect normal system operation.

In order to get a more realistic estimate of LAZARUS, we ran the Phoronix Test Suite [15], which is widely used to compare the performance of operating systems. The Phoronix benchmarking suite features a large number of tests which cover different aspects of a system, and are grouped according to the targeted subsystem of the machine. Specifically, we ran the system and disk benchmarks to test application performance. Our results are shown in Fig. 6. We show an average performance overhead of 2.1% on this benchmark, which is in line with our results provided by the SPEC and LMBench benchmarks. The worst performers were benchmarks that are bound to read operations. We speculate that this is due to the amount of context switches that happen while the read operation is taking place, as a buffer in kernel memory needs to be copied into a buffer from user space or remapped there.

Lastly, we ran the `pgbench` benchmark on a test PostgreSQL database and measured a performance overhead of 2.386%.

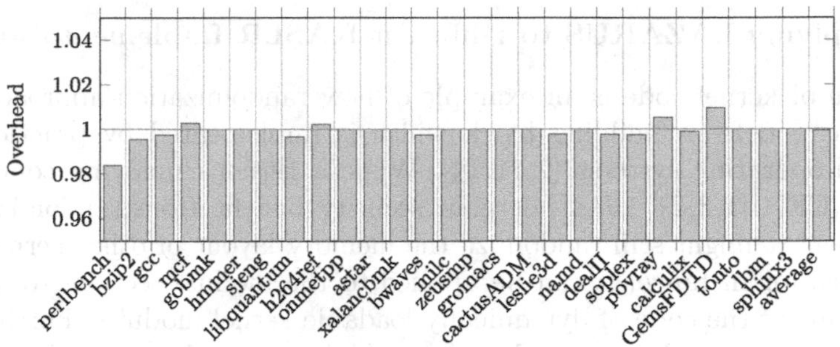


**Fig. 4.** SPEC2006 benchmark results

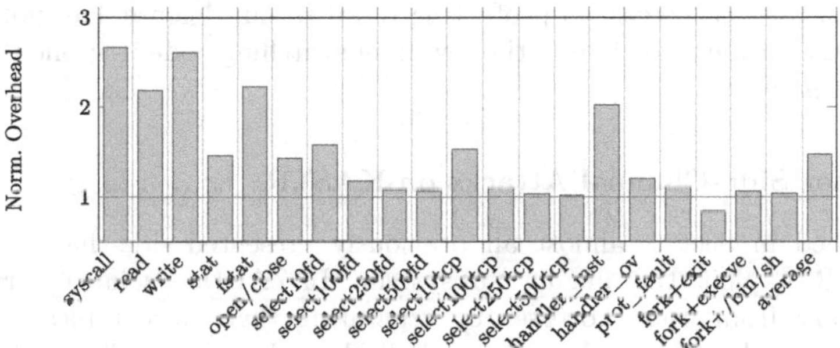


**Fig. 5.** LMBench3 benchmark results

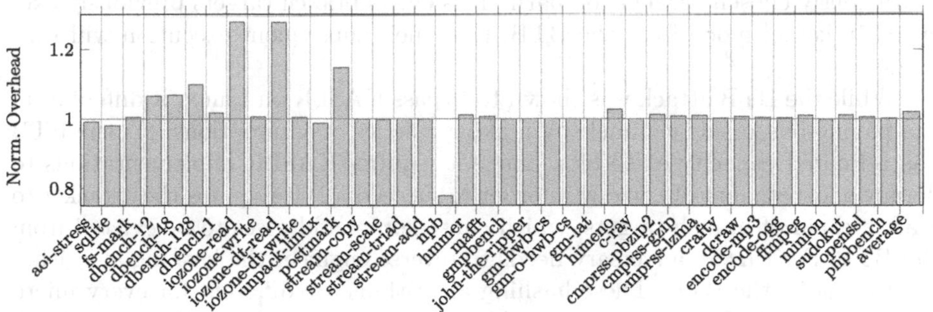


**Fig. 6.** Phoronix benchmark suite

# 6 Discussion

## 6.1 Applying LAZARUS to Different KASLR Implementations

Relocation of kernel code is an example of how randomization approaches can be used as a defense building block which is implemented by practically all real-world operating systems [2,11,14]. While a kernel employing control-flow integrity (CFI) [1,3,21] does not gain security benefit from randomizing the code section, it might still randomize the memory layout of other kernel memory regions: for instance, it can be applied to the module section, to hide the start address of the code of dynamically loadable kernel modules. Further, randomization was recently proposed as a means to protect the page tables against malicious modification through data-only attacks [5].

Since all of the publicly available attacks focus on disclosing the random offset of the kernel code section, we implemented our proof of concept for KASLR as well. Nonetheless, we note that LAZARUS is not limited to hardening kernel code randomization, but can be applied to other randomization implementations as well. In contrast to the case of protecting KASLR, our defense does not require any special treatment for hiding the low-level switching code if applied to other memory regions.

## 6.2 Other Side-Channel Attacks on KASLR

As explained in Sect. 2, almost all previously presented side-channel attacks on KASLR exploit the paging subsystem. LAZARUS isolates kernel virtual memory from user processes by separating their page tables. However, Evtyushkin et al. [6] recently presented the branch target buffer (BTB) side-channel attack, which does not exploit the paging subsystem for virtual kernel addresses.

In particular, they demonstrated how to exploit collisions between branch targets for user and kernel addresses. The attack works by constructing a malicious chain of branch targets in user space, to fill up the BTB, and then executing a previously chosen kernel code path. This evicts branch targets previously executed in kernel mode from the BTB, thus their subsequent execution will take longer.

While the BTB attack was shown to bypass KASLR on Linux, it differs from the paging-based side channels by making a series of assumptions: (1) the BTB has a limited capacity of 10 bits, hence it requires KASLR implementations to deploy a low amount of entropy in order to succeed. (2) it requires the attacker to craft a chain of branch targets, which cause kernel addresses to be evicted from the BTB. For this an adversary needs to reverse engineer the hashing algorithm used to index the BTB. These hashing algorithms are different for every micro architecture, which limits the potential set of targets. (3) the result of the attack can be ambiguous, because any change in the execution path directly effects the BTB contents.

There are multiple ways of mitigating the BTB side-channel attack against KASLR. A straightforward approach is to increase the amount of entropy for KASLR, as noted by Evtyushkin et al. [6]. A more general approach would be to introduce a separation between privileged an unprivileged addresses in the BTB. This could be achieved by offering a dedicated flush operation, however this requires changes to the hardware. Alternatively, this flush operation can emulated in software, if the hashing algorithm used for indexing the BTB has been reverse engineered. We implemented this approach against the BTB attack by calling a function which performs a series of jump instructions along with our page tables switching routine and were unable to recover the correct randomization offset through the BTB attack in our tests.

# 7 Related Work

In this section we discuss software and hardware mitigations against side-channel attacks that were proposed, and compare them to our approach.

## 7.1 Hardware Mitigations

*Privilege Level Isolation in the Caches.* Eliminating the paging side channel is also possible by modifying the underlying hardware cache implementation. This was first noted by Hund et al. [10]. However, modern architectures organize caches to be optimized for performance. Additionally, changes to the hardware are very costly, and it takes many years to widely deploy these new systems. Hence, it is unlikely that such a change will be implemented, and even if it is, existing production systems will remain vulnerable for a long time. Our software-only mitigation can be deployed instantly by patching the kernel.

*Disabling Detailed Timing for Unprivileged Users.* All previously presented paging side-channel attacks rely on detailed timing functionality, which is provided to unprivileged users by default. For this reason, Hund et al. [10] suggested to disable the `rdtsc` instruction for user mode processes. While this can be done from software, it effectively changes the ABI of the machine. Since modern platforms offer support for a large body of legacy software, implementing such a change would introduce problems for many real-world user applications. As we demonstrate in our extensive evaluation, LAZARUS is transparent to user-level programs and does not disrupt the usual workflow of legacy software.

## 7.2 Software Mitigations

*Separating Address Spaces.* Unmapping the kernel page tables during user-land execution is a natural way of separating their respective address spaces, as suggested in [8,13]. However, Jang et al. [13] considered the approach impractical, due to the expected performance degradation. Gruss et al. [8] estimated the performance impact of reloading the entire page table hierarchy up to 5%, by reloading the top level of the page table hierarchy (via the CR3 register) during a context switch, but did not provide any implementation or detailed evaluation of their estimated approach. Reloading the top level of the page tables results in a higher performance overhead, because it requires the processor to flush all of the cached entries. Address space separation has been implemented by Apple for their iOS platform [16]. Because the ARM platform supports multiple sets of page table hierarchies, the implementation is straightforward on mobile devices. For the first time we provide an improved and highly practical method of implementing address space separation on the x86 platform.

*Increasing KASLR Entropy.* Some of the presented side-channel attacks benefit from the fact that the KASLR implementation in the Linux kernel suffers from a relatively low entropy [6,10]. Thus, increasing the amount of entropy represent a way of mitigating those attacks in practice. While this approach was suggested by Hund et al. [10] and Evtyushkin et al. [6], it does not eliminate the side channel. Additionally, the mitigating effect is limited to attacks which exploit low entropy randomization. In contrast, LAZARUS mitigates all previously presented paging side-channel attacks.

*Modifying the Page Fault Handler.* Hund et al. [10] exploited the timing difference through invoking the page fault handler. They suggested to enforce its execution time to an equal timing for all kernel addresses through software. However, this approach is ineffective against attacks which do not invoke the kernel [8,13]. Our mitigation reorganizes the cache layout in software to successfully stop the attacks, that exploit hardware features to leak side channel information, even for attacks that do not rely on the execution time of any software.

*KAISER.* Concurrently to our work Gruss et al. implemented strong address-space separation [7]. Their performance numbers are in line with our own measurements, confirming that separating the address spaces of kernel and userland constitutes a practical defense against paging-based side-channel attacks. In contrast to LAZARUS, their approach does not make use of dummy mappings to hide the switching code, but separates it from the rest of the kernel code section (as outlined in 3.3.C2).

## 8 Conclusion

Randomization has become a vital part of the security architecture of modern operating systems. Side-channel attacks threaten to bypass randomization-based defenses deployed in the kernel by disclosing the randomization secret from unprivileged user processes. Since these attacks exploit micro-architectural implementation details of the underlying hardware, closing this side channel through a software-only mitigation efficiently is challenging. However, all of these attacks rely on the fact that kernel and user virtual memory reside in a shared address space. With LAZARUS, we present a defense to mitigate previously presented side-channel attacks purely in software. Our approach shows that side-channel information exposed through shared hardware resources can be hidden by separating the page table entries for randomized privileged addresses from entries for unprivileged addresses in software. LAZARUS is a necessary and highly practical extension to harden kernel-space randomization against side-channel attacks.

**Acknowledgment.** This work was supported in part by the German Science Foundation (project S2, CRC 1119 CROSSING), the European Union's Seventh Framework Programme (609611, PRACTICE), and the German Federal Ministry of Education and Research within CRISP.

Dean Sullivan, Orlando Arias, and Yier Jin are partially supported by the Department of Energy through the Early Career Award (DE-SC0016180). Mr. Orlando Arias is also supported by the National Science Foundation Graduate Research Fellowship Program under Grant No. 1144246.

## References

1. Abadi, M., Budiu, M., Erlingsson, Ú., Ligatti, J.: Control-flow integrity principles, implementations, and applications. ACM Transactions on Information System Security 13 (2009)
2. Cook, K.: Kernel address space layout randomization (2013). http://selinuxproject.org/~jmorris/lss2013_slides/cook_kaslr.pdf
3. Criswell, J., Dautenhahn, N., Adve, V.: Kcofi: complete control-flow integrity for commodity operating system kernels. In: 35th IEEE Symposium on Security and Privacy. S&P (2014)
4. CVEDetails: CVE-2016-4557 (2016). http://www.cvedetails.com/cve/cve-2016-4557
5. Davi, L., Gens, D., Liebchen, C., Ahmad-Reza, S.: PT-Rand: practical mitigation of data-only attacks against page tables. In: 24th Annual Network and Distributed System Security Symposium. NDSS (2017)
6. Evtyushkin, D., Ponomarev, D., Abu-Ghazaleh, N.: Jump over aslr: attacking branch predictors to bypass aslr. In: IEEE/ACM International Symposium on Microarchitecture (MICRO) (2016)
7. Gruss, D., Lipp, M., Schwarz, M., Fellner, R., Maurice, C., Mangard, S.: Kaslr is dead: long live kaslr. In: International Symposium on Engineering Secure Software and Systems. ESSoS (2017)
8. Gruss, D., Maurice, C., Fogh, A., Lipp, M., Mangard, S.: Prefetch side-channel attacks: bypassing smap and kernel aslr. In: Proceedings of the 2016 ACM SIGSAC Conference on Computer and Communications Security, pp. 368–379. ACM (2016)
9. Henning, J.L.: Spec cpu2006 benchmark descriptions. SIGARCH Comput. Archit. News **34**(4), 1–17 (2006). http://doi.acm.org/10.1145/1186736.1186737
10. Hund, R., Willems, C., Holz, T.: Practical timing side channel attacks against kernel space ASLR. In: 34th IEEE Symposium on Security and Privacy. S&P (2013)
11. Inc., A.: Os x mountain lion core technologies overview (2012). http://movies.apple.com/media/us/osx/2012/docs/OSX_MountainLion_Core_Technologies_Overview.pdf

12. Intel: Intel 64 and IA-32 architectures software developer's manual (2017). http://www-ssl.intel.com/content/www/us/en/processors/architectures-software-developer-manuals.html
13. Jang, Y., Lee, S., Kim, T.: Breaking kernel address space layout randomization with intel TSX. In: Proceedings of the 2016 ACM SIGSAC Conference on Computer and Communications Security, pp. 380–392. ACM (2016)
14. Johnson, K., Miller, M.: Exploit mitigation improvements in windows 8 (2012). https://media.blackhat.com/bh-us-12/Briefings/M_Miller/BH_US_12_Miller_Exploit_Mitigation_Slides.pdf
15. Larabel, M., Tippett, M.: Phoronix test suite (2011). http://www.phoronix-test-suite.com
16. Mandt, T.: Attacking the ios kernel: a look at "evasi0n"(2013). http://www.nislab.no/content/download/38610/481190/file/NISlecture201303.pdf
17. MITRE: CVE-2015-1328 (2015). https://cve.mitre.org/cgi-bin/cvename.cgi?name=CVE-2015-1328
18. MITRE: CVE-2016-0728 (2016). https://cve.mitre.org/cgi-bin/cvename.cgi?name=cve-2016-0728
19. MITRE: CVE-2016-5195 (2016). https://cve.mitre.org/cgi-bin/cvename.cgi?name=CVE-2016-5195
20. Molinyawe, M., Hariri, A.A., Spelman, J.: $hell on earth: from browser to system compromise. In: Blackhat USA. BH US (2016)
21. PaX Team: RAP: RIP ROP (2015)
22. Staelin, C.: lmbench: an extensible micro-benchmark suite. Softw. Pract. Experience **35**(11), 1079 (2005)
23. Wojtczuk, R.: Tsx improves timing attacks against kaslr (2014). https://labs.bromium.com/2014/10/27/tsx-improves-timing-attacks-against-kaslr/

# CFI CaRE: Hardware-Supported Call and Return Enforcement for Commercial Microcontrollers

Thomas Nyman[1,2(✉)], Jan-Erik Ekberg[2], Lucas Davi[3], and N. Asokan[1]

[1] Aalto University, Espoo, Finland
thomas.nyman@aalto.fi, n.asokan@acm.org
[2] Trustonic, Helsinki, Finland
{thomas.nyman,jee}@trustonic.com
[3] University of Duisburg-Essen, Duisburg, Germany
lucas.davi@wiwinf.uni-due.de

**Abstract.** With the increasing scale of deployment of Internet of Things (IoT), concerns about IoT security have become more urgent. In particular, memory corruption attacks play a predominant role as they allow remote compromise of IoT devices. Control-flow integrity (CFI) is a promising and generic defense technique against these attacks. However, given the nature of IoT deployments, existing protection mechanisms for traditional computing environments (including CFI) need to be adapted to the IoT setting. In this paper, we describe the challenges of enabling CFI on microcontroller (MCU) based IoT devices. We then present CaRE, the first *interrupt-aware* CFI scheme for low-end MCUs. CaRE uses a novel way of protecting the CFI metadata by leveraging TrustZone-M security extensions introduced in the ARMv8-M architecture. Its binary instrumentation approach *preserves the memory layout* of the target MCU software, allowing pre-built bare-metal binary code to be protected by CaRE. We describe our implementation on a Cortex-M Prototyping System and demonstrate that CaRE is secure while imposing acceptable performance and memory impact.

## 1 Introduction

*Cyber-Physical Systems* (CPS) are becoming pervasive across many application areas ranging from industrial applications (manufacturing), transport, and smart cities to consumer products. *Internet of Things* (IoT) refers to systems incorporating such devices with (typically always-on) communication capability. Estimates put the number of deployed IoT devices at 28 billion by 2021 [19]. Although programmable CPS devices are not new, connectivity makes them targets for network originating attacks. Gartner highlights device identity (management), code/data integrity and secure communication as the most important security services for IoT [23].

**Electronic supplementary material** The online version of this chapter (doi:10.1007/978-3-319-66332-6_12) contains supplementary material, which is available to authorized users.


M. Dacier et al. (Eds.): RAID 2017, LNCS 10453, pp. 259–284, 2017.
DOI: 10.1007/978-3-319-66332-6_12

The system software in IoT devices is often written in memory-unsafe languages like C [26]. The arms race [46] in runtime exploitation of general purpose computers and network equipment has shown us that memory errors, such as buffer overflows and use-after-free errors, constitute a dominant attack vector for stealing sensitive data or gaining control of a remote system. Over the years, a number of platform security techniques to resist such attacks have been developed and deployed on PCs, servers and mobile devices. These include protections against code injection and code-reuse attacks, such as *Control-Flow Integrity* [2] (CFI) and *Address Space Layout Randomization* [13,34] (ASLR) which aim to ensure the *run-time integrity* of a device.

CFI (Sect. 3.1) is a well-explored technique for resisting the code-reuse attacks such as *Return-Oriented Programming* (ROP) [44] that allow attackers in control of data memory to subvert the control flow of a program. CFI commonly takes the form of inlined enforcement, where CFI checks are inserted at points in the program code where control flow changes occur. For legacy applications CFI checks must be introduced by instrumenting the pre-built binary. Such binary instrumentation necessarily modifies the memory layout of the code, requiring memory addresses referenced by the program to be adjusted accordingly [27]. This is typically done through load-time dynamic binary rewriting software [15,37].

A prominent class of state-of-the-art CFI schemes is based on the notion of a *shadow stack* [14]: a mechanism that prevents overwriting subroutine return addresses on the call stack by comparing each return address to a protected copy kept in the shadow stack before performing the return. This effectively mitigates return-oriented programming attacks that stitch together instruction sequences ending in return instructions [44]. However, it presumes the existence of mechanisms to ensure that the shadow stack cannot be manipulated by the attacker.

As we argue in detail in Sect. 3.3, the type of IoT scenarios we consider have a number of characteristics that make traditional CFI mechanisms difficult to apply. First, IoT devices are typically architected as interrupt-driven reactive systems, often implemented as bare-metal software involving no loading or relocation. To the best of our knowledge, no existing CFI scheme is interrupt-aware. Second, IoT devices are often based on computing cores that are low-cost, low-power single-purpose programmable microcontrollers (MCUs). Countermeasures for general purpose computing devices, such as ASLR, often rely on hardware features (e.g., virtual memory) that are unavailable in simple MCUs. Prior CFI schemes for embedded systems, such as HAFIX [16], and the recently announced Intel Control-flow Enforcement Technology (CET) [30], require changes to the hardware and toolchain, access to source code and do not support interrupts.

On the positive side, hardware-based isolation mechanisms for MCUs have appeared not only in the research literature [12,18,31], but also as commercial offerings such as the recently announced TrustZone-M security extensions for the next generation of ARM microcontrollers (Sect. 2.2) providing a lightweight trust anchor for resource-constrained IoT devices [4]. However, since software (and updates) for IoT devices may come from a different source than the original equipment manufacturer (OEM), it is unrealistic to expect the software vendors to take responsibility for the instrumentation necessary for hardware-assisted CFI protection – OEMs in turn will be incentivized to distribute the same software to *all* devices, with and without hardware security extensions.

*Goal and Contributions.* We introduce the first hardware software co-design based security architecture that (i) enables practical enforcement of control-flow policies, (ii) addresses the unique challenges of low-end IoT devices with respect to CFI deployment, (iii) requires no changes to the underlying hardware, and (iv) operates directly on binary code thereby avoiding the need for source code. Specifically, we target control-flow integrity policies that defend against runtime attacks, such as ROP, that belong to the most prominent software attacks on all modern computing architectures, e.g., Desktop PCs [44], mobile devices [32], and embedded systems [21].

To this end we present the design and implementation of a novel architecture, CaRE (Call and Return Enforcement), accompanied with a toolchain for achieving robust run-time code integrity for IoT devices. We claim the following contributions:

- The first **interrupt-aware** CFI scheme for low-end MCUs (Sect. 4) supporting
  - **hardware-based shadow stack protection** by leveraging recently introduced TrustZone-M security extensions (Sect. 4.2).
  - a new binary instrumentation technique that is memory **layout-preserving** and can be realized **on-device** (Sect. 4.3).
- An implementation of CaRE on ARM Versatile Express Cortex-M Prototyping System (Sect. 4.4).
- A comprehensive evaluation (Sect. 5) showing that CaRE ensures CFI (Sect. 5.1), has a lower performance overhead (Sect. 5.2) compared to software-based shadow stack schemes while imposing comparable impact on program binary size (Sect. 5.3).

## 2 Background

### 2.1 ARM Architecture

ARM microprocessors are RISC-based computer designs that are widely used in computing systems which benefit from reduced cost, heat, and power consumption compared to processors found in personal computers. The ARM Cortex-M series of processors, geared towards low-cost embedded microcontrollers (MCUs), consists of core designs optimized for different purposes, such as small silicon footprint (M0), high energy efficiency (M0+), configurability (M3) or high performance (M4, M7). Cortex-M processors only support the 16-bit Thumb and mixed 16 and 32-bit Thumb-2 instruction sets. 32-bit Thumb-2 instructions are encoded as two 16-bit half-words. *ARMv8-M* [4] is the next generation instruction set architecture for M-class processors. The Cortex-M23[1] and Cortex-M33[2] are the first cores to support the ARMv8-M architecture. Both are compatible with other processors in the Cortex-M family, allowing (legacy) software re-use on these devices.

All 32-bit ARM processors feature 16 general-purpose registers, denoted `r0-r15`. Registers `r13-r15` have special names and usage models. These registers, including the program counter (`pc`) can be accessed directly. Cortex-M processors implement two stacks, the *Main* stack and *Process* stack. The stack pointer (`sp`) is *banked* between processor modes, i.e., multiple copies of a register exists in distinct register banks. Not all registers can be seen at once; the register bank in use is determined by the current processor mode. Register banking allows for rapid context switches when dealing with processor exceptions and privileged operations. Application software on Cortex-M processor executes in *Thread* mode where the current stack is determined by the *stack-pointer select* (`spsel`) register. When the processor executes an exception it enters the *Handler* mode. In Handler mode the processors always uses the Main stack. When executing in Handler mode, the *Interrupt Program Status Register* (`ipsr`) holds the exception number of the exception being handled. The `ipsr` may only be read using a `mrs` instruction used to access ARM system register, and is only updated by the processor itself on exception entry and exit (see *Exception behaviour* in Sect. 4.4).

*ARM calling standard.* As with all processors, ARM provides a *calling standard* that compiler manufacturers should use to resolve subroutine calls and returns in an interchangeable manner. In programs conforming to the ARM Architecture Procedure Call Standard (AAPCS) [3] subroutine calls may be performed either through a **B**ranch with **L**ink (`bl`) or **B**ranch with **L**ink and e**X**change (`blx`) instruction. These instructions load the address of the subroutine to the `pc` and the return address to the *link register* (`lr`). ARM processors do not provide a dedicated return instruction. Instead, a subroutine return is performed by writing the return address to the program counter `pc`. Hence, any instruction that can write to the `pc` can be leveraged as an effective return instruction. Two common effective return instructions are `bx lr` and `pop {..., pc}`. The `bx lr` instruction performs a branch to the return address stored in the link register `lr`. The `pop {..., pc}` in a subroutine epilogue loads the return address from the stack to the `pc`. The former is typically used in *leaf routines*, which do not execute procedure calls to other routines. The latter is typically preceded by a `push {..., lr}` instruction in the subroutine prologue, which in a *non-leaf routine* stores the return address in `lr` (possibly along with other registers that need to be saved) on the stack in preparation for calls to other routines.

---
[1] https://www.arm.com/products/processors/cortex-m/cortex-m23-processor.php.
[2] https://www.arm.com/products/processors/cortex-m/cortex-m33-processor.php.

## 2.2 TrustZone-M

*TrustZone-M* [4,48] (TZ-M) is a new hardware security technology present in the ARMv8-M architecture. In terms of functionality, it replicates the properties of processor supported isolation and priority execution provided by TrustZone-enabled Cortex-A application processors (TZ-A), but their respective architectural realizations differ significantly. Both TZ architectures expose a set of *secure state* non-privileged and privileged processor contexts beside their traditional *non-secure state* counterparts[3]. In both TZ variants the memory management is extended to enable splitting the device's physical memory into secure and non-secure regions.

In TZ-M, the only general purpose registers banked between the non-secure and secure states are the sp registers used to address the Main and Process stacks. The remaining general purpose registers are shared (not banked) between the non-secure and secure states. In practice this means that the secure state software is responsible for sanitizing any sensitive information held in any general purpose registers during a transition from secure to non-secure state.

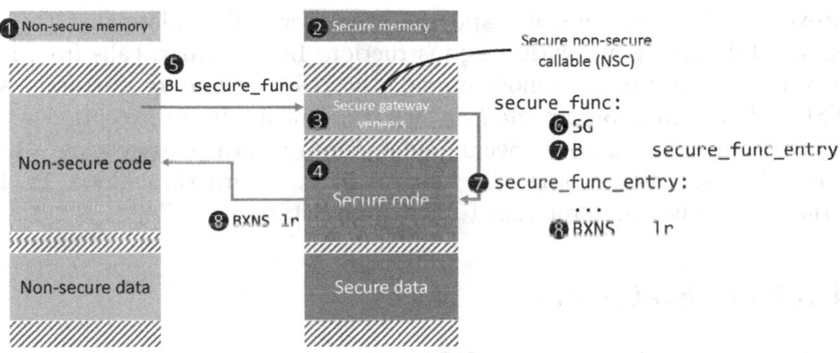


**Fig. 1.** ARMv8-M secure state call [48]

In TZ-A the entry to the secure state occurs via a dedicated hardware exception and the context switch is performed by the exception handler known as the Secure Monitor. In TZ-M the division between the secure and non-secure states is instead based on a memory map set up during device initialization which assigns specific regions of memory as either secure or non-secure. The transitions between secure and non-secure state occur *automatically* as the flow of execution is transferred from program code in non-secure memory to secure memory (and vice versa). Where in TZ-A the entry into the secure state typically has to manage VM and MMU configuration at the expense of thousands of processor cycles, TZ-M is geared towards embedded processors with no virtual memory support (at most a MPU). In TZ-M a switch of security state only takes a few processor cycles including a pipeline flush [48].

[3] Also referred to as the *secure world* and *normal world*.

The hardware support for the division of memory into secure and non-secure regions in ARMv8-M is a Secure Attribution Unit (SAU) inside the processor. The SAU is configurable while the processor executes in secure state. External interrupts may be routed to either non-secure state exception handlers, or secure state exception handlers based on the SAU configuration. Figure 1 denotes a typical memory layout for a TZ-M equipped device. Each memory region known to the SAU may be declared as either *Non-Secure* (❶), *Secure* (❷) or *Secure Non-Secure Callable* (NSC ❸). While Secure memory contains the secure program image and data, the NSC memory contains *secure gateway veneers*[4], i.e., branch instructions (❼) which point to the actual subroutine code in Secure memory (❹). The purpose of the NSC is to prevent non-secure program code to branch into invalid entry points in secure program code (such as into the middle of a function, as is often done in atleast ROP). To this end, the ARMv8-M instruction set also introduces a *Secure Gateway* (`sg`) instruction, which is included in the beginning of each veneer (❻) and acts as a call gate to the secure program code. From the non-secure program code a call to a secure subroutine is performed using a regular `bl` instruction (❺), targeting the corresponding veneer in the NSC. Calls targeting a memory address in the NSC will automatically cause a context switch to secure state, and the processor will validate that the call targets a valid entry point with a `sg` instruction. In particular, calls from non-secure state calling secure memory outside the NSC, or non-`sg` instructions in the NSC will fail in a *Secure Fault*, a new type of hardware exception which always traps into secure state. Secure subroutines return by executing a `bxns lr` instruction (❽), which otherwise behaves like a return through `bx lr`, but additionally switches the processor to non-secure state.

## 3 Problem Statement

### 3.1 Code-Reuse Attacks on ARM

Code-reuse attacks are a class of software exploits that allow attackers to execute arbitrary code on a compromised device, even in the presence of hardware countermeasures against code injection, such as W⊕X [28]. In a *return-to-libc* attack [45], the subroutine return address on the call stack is replaced by the address of an entry point to a subroutine in the executable memory of a process. The technique has been generalized into *Return-Oriented Programming* [44] (ROP) for the x86 architecture, which has since become the exploitation technique of choice for modern memory-safety vulnerability attacks. Subsequently ROP has been extended to various other CPU architectures [6,9,21], including ARM microprocessors [32].

Many code-reuse attacks on x86 platforms use unintended instruction sequences found by performing a branch into the middle of otherwise benign instructions. Such unintended sequences cannot be formed in the 32-bit ARM,

[4] http://www.keil.com/support/man/docs/armclang_link/armclang_link_pge1444644885613.htm.

or in the 16-bit Thumb instruction sets where branch target alignment is enforced on instruction load, and hence may only target the intended instruction stream. However, the presence of both 32-bit and 16-bit instructions in Thumb-2 code introduces ambiguity when decoding program code from memory. When decoding Thumb-2 instructions, ARM processors still enforce 2-byte alignment on instruction fetches, but the variable-length encoding allows the second half-word in a 32-bit Thumb-2 instruction to be interpreted as the first half-word of an unintended instruction. Such unintended instructions have been successfully utilized in prior work [35,36] to exploit ARM code.

It has been shown that, on both x86 and ARM, it is also possible to perform ROP attacks *without the use of return instructions* [8] in what has become to be known as *Jump-Oriented Programming* (JOP). On ARM platforms, JOP can be instantiated using indirect subroutine calls.

### 3.2 Control-Flow Integrity

A well known approach to address code-reuse attacks is enforcing the *Control-Flow Integrity* (CFI) of the code. The execution of any program can be abstractly represented as a *Control-Flow Graph* (CFG), where nodes represent blocks of sequential instructions (without intervening branches), and edges represent control-flow changes between such nodes (branch instructions). CFI enforcement strives to ensure that the execution of the programs conforms to a legitimate path in the program's CFG. CFI builds on the assumption that program code in memory is not writable (i.e., that memory pages can be marked W$\oplus$X) as a countermeasure against code injection attacks. Code immutability allows CFI checks to be omitted for nodes in the CFG that end in direct branch instructions [2,20], i.e., branches with a statically determined target offset. As a result, CFI is typically applied to nodes in the CFG that end in an indirect branch. Indirect branches are typically emitted for switch-case statements, subroutine returns, and indirect calls (subroutine calls to dynamic libraries, calls through function pointers, e.g. callbacks, as well as C++ virtual functions).

While the construction of the CFG can occur through static inspection of the program binary, the actual enforcement of CFI must occur at runtime. In inlined CFI enforcement the checks that validate control-flow changes are interspersed with the original program code at subroutine call sites, as well as in the subroutine prologue and epilogue. The insertion of these checks can be achieved through compiler extensions [10], or by binary machine-code rewriting. Binary instrumentation that adds additional instructions to a pre-built program binary by necessity modifies the memory layout of the code, and hence will require memory addresses referenced by the program to be adjusted accordingly.

Traditional ROP targets return instructions that read the return address off the program stack. A well known technique to enforce that subroutine returns target the original call site is the notion of a *shadow call stack* [14]. The shadow call stack is used to hold a copy of the return address. On subroutine return the return address on the shadow call stack is compared to the return address on the program stack. If they match, the return proceeds as usual. A mismatch in return addresses on the other hand indicates a failure of CFI and triggers an error which terminates the program prematurely. Recent results show that, in fact, shadow stacks are essential for the security of CFI [7].

### 3.3 CFI Challenges for Microcontrollers

We identify the following challenges in realizing CFI protection on IoT devices:

- **Interrupt awareness**: Since the software to be protected is a single, interrupt-driven bare-metal program, the CFI scheme needs to handle both interruptible code, as well as execution in interrupt contexts. To the best of our knowledge, no existing CFI scheme meets this requirement.
- **Hardware-based shadow stack protection**: Protection of shadow stack must leverage lightweight hardware-based trust anchors like TrustZone-M. The code size and performance overhead of purely software-based CFI is prohibitive on resource constrained devices and techniques for general purpose computing devices often rely on hardware (such as x86 segmentation support [2]) that is unavailable in simple MCUs.
- **Layout-preserving instrumentation**: Since software for MCUs is commonly deployed as monolithic firmware images with strict size requirements, CFI instrumentation must preserve memory layout of the image so as to avoid extensive rewriting and to minimize the increase in code size.
- **On-device instrumentation**: To avoid having to rely on the developer (or some other external entity) to perform the required instrumentation, the CFI scheme must be amenable to on-device instrumentation.

### 3.4 Adversarial Model

We consider a powerful adversary with arbitrary read-access to code memory and arbitrary read-write access to data memory of the non-secure state program. This model accounts for buffer overflows or other memory-related vulnerabilities (e.g. an externally controlled format string[5]) that, in practice, would allow adversaries to gain such capabilities. The adversary cannot modify code memory, a property that is achievable even on MCU class systems through widespread countermeasure against code injection (e.g. MPU-based W$\oplus$X). Nevertheless, arbitrary read-access necessitates a solution that is able to withstand information disclosure (the strongest attack scenario in Dang et al.s [14] evaluation of prior work on CFI). Our threat model is therefore similar to previous work on CFI, but we also consider an even stronger adversary who can exploit interrupt handling to undermine CFI protection.

This model applies even when an attacker is in active control of a module or thread within the same address space as the non-secure state program, such as gaining control of an unprotected co-processor on the *System-On-Chip* (SoC).

[5] CWE-134: Use of Externally-Controlled Format String https://cwe.mitre.org/data/definitions/134.html.

However, the adversary lacks the ability to read or modify memory allocated to the secure state software.

In this work, we do not consider *non-control data* attacks [46] such as *Data-Oriented Programming* [29]. This class of attacks can achieve privilege escalation, leak security sensitive data or even Turing-complete computation by corrupting memory variables that are not directly used in control-flow transfer instructions. This limitation also applies to prior work on CFI.

# 4 CFI CaRE

We now present CaRE (Call and Return Enforcement), our solution for ensuring control-flow integrity. CaRE specifically targets constrained IoT devices, which are expected to stay active in the field for a prolonged time and operate unattended with network (Internet) connectivity, possibly via IoT gateways. This kind of deployment necessitates the incorporation of software update mechanisms to fix vulnerabilities, update configuration settings and add new functionality.

We limit our scope to small, more or less bare-metal IoT devices. The system software is deployed as monolithic, statically linked firmware images. The secure and non-secure state program images are distinct from each other [1], with the secure state software stack structured as a library. The configuration of the SAU and the secure state program image is performed before the non-secure code is started. The entry to the secure state library happens through a well-defined interface describing the call gates available to non-secure software. Functions in the secure state are synchronous and run to completion unless interrupted by an exception. The system is interrupt-driven, reacting to external triggers. While it is possible that the non-secure state software is scheduled by a simple Real-Time Operating System (RTOS), the secure state software does not have separate scheduling or isolation between distinct software components for the simple reason that the device is single-purpose rather than a platform for running many programs from many stakeholders in parallel. Even when an RTOS is present, it is seldom necessary for non-secure state code to support dynamic loading of additional code sequences.

## 4.1 Requirements

Given the above target deployment scenario, we formulate the following requirements that CaRE should meet:

**Requirement 1.** *It must reliably prevent attacks from redirecting the flow of execution of the non-secure state program.*

**Requirement 2.** *It must be able to protect system software written in standard C and assembler conformant to the AAPCS.*

**Requirement 3.** *It must have minimal impact on the code footprint of the non-secure state program.*

**Requirement 4.** *Its performance overhead must be competitive compared to the overhead of software-based CFI schemes.*

We make the following assumptions about the target device:

**Assumption 1.** *A trust anchor, such as TZ-M, which enables isolated code execution and secure storage of data at runtime is available.*

**Assumption 2.** *All (secure and non-secure) code is subject to a* secure boot *sequence that prevents tampering of program and update images at rest. This bootstrap sequence itself is not vulnerable to code-reuse attacks, and routines in the bootstrap code are not invoked again after the device startup completes.*

**Assumption 3.** *All code is non-writable. It must not be possible for an attacker to modify the program code in memory at runtime.*

**Assumption 4.** *All data is non-executable. It must not be possible for an attacker to execute data as it were code. Otherwise, an attacker will be able to mount code injection attacks against the device.*

Assumption 1 is true for commercial off-the-shelf ARMv8-M MCUs. There also exist several research architectures, such as SMART [18], SANCUS [40], and Intel's TrustLite [31] that provide equivalent features. Assumption 2 is true for currently announced ARMv8-M SoCs[6]. Assumptions 3 and 4 are in line with previous work on CFI and can be easily achieved on embedded devices that are equipped with MPUs. These assumptions can be problematic in the presence of self-modifying code, runtime code generation, and unanticipated dynamic loading of code. Fortunately, most embedded system software in MCUs is typically statically linked and written in languages that compile directly to native code. Even when an RTOS is present, it is seldom necessary for non-secure state code to support dynamic loading of additional code sequences.

### 4.2 Architecture

Our design incorporates protection of a shadow call stack on low-end ARM embedded devices featuring TZ-M. The shadow call stack resides in secure memory, and is only accessible when the processor executes in the secure state. We also propose a *layout-preserving* binary instrumentation approach for Thumb code, with small impact to code footprint, and an opportunity for *on-device instrumentation* as part of code installation. The main aspect of this property is that the binary program image is rewritten without affecting its memory layout. Figure 2 shows an overview of the CaRE architecture.

The premise for CaRE is instrumentation of non-secure state code in a manner which removes all function calls and indirect branches and replaces them with dispatch instructions that trap control flow to a piece of monitor code, the *Branch*

[6] https://www.embedded-world.de/en/ausstellerprodukte/embwld17/product-9863796/numicro-m2351-series-microcontroller.

*Monitor* (❶), which runs in non-secure state. As a result, each subroutine call and return is now routed through the Branch Monitor. The Branch Monitor maintains the shadow stack by invoking secure functions (❷) only callable from the Branch Monitor, before transferring control to the original branch target. Other indirect branches, such as ones used to branch into switch case jump tables can be restricted by the Branch Monitor to a suitable range and to target direct branches in jump table entries. Thus, the Branch Monitor provides *complete mediation* of instrumented non-secure state code.

Apart from the Branch Monitor, the program image also contains bootstrap routines (labeled $b_n$) that are used to initialize the runtime environment (❸). Such routines may initially need to operate without a stack and other memory structures in place, and as such are typically hand written in assembler. Due to these constraints, the bootstrap routines are likely to deviate from usual AAPCS conventions. In particular, all calls are not guaranteed to result in a subsequent matching return as fragments of bootstrap routines may simply be chained together until eventually transferring control to the named C entry point marking the beginning of main program code. On the other hand, the initialization code is typically not entered again after control has been transfered to the main function until the device is reset.

Hence, from the perspective of maintaining control-flow integrity, both the Branch Monitor and bootstrap code exist outside benign execution paths encountered in the program during normal operation. Henceforth, we will refer to the code reachable from the main function as the *main program*. The CFG nodes labeled $f_n$ in Fig. 2 represent the instrumented main program (❹). The main program and bootstrap code do not share any routines (Assumption 2), even though routines belonging to one or the other may be interleaved in program memory. The main program code constitutes a *strongly connected component* within the *call graph*[7]. This observation leads us to consider the main program code as a complete ensemble in terms of instrumentation target. It can include an RTOS and/or interrupt handlers. Interrupts handlers labeled $h_n$ (❺), with the exception of the supervisor call handler that hosts the Branch Monitor, are considered to be part of the main program. Conceptually, interrupts may be reached from any node in the program's CFG.

By eliminating non-mediated calls and returns in the non-secure state main program, thus forcing each indirect branch through the Branch Monitor, we can unequivocally eliminate control-flow attacks that utilize such branches.

### 4.3 Instrumentation

The instrumentation must intercept all subroutine calls and returns. Furthermore, it should have minimal impact on code footprint. Prior shadow stack schemes either instrument the subroutine prologue and epilogue [10,14], or the call site [14], pushing the return address to the shadow stack upon a subroutine

[7] A call graph is a control-flow graph which represents the calling relationships between subroutines in a program.

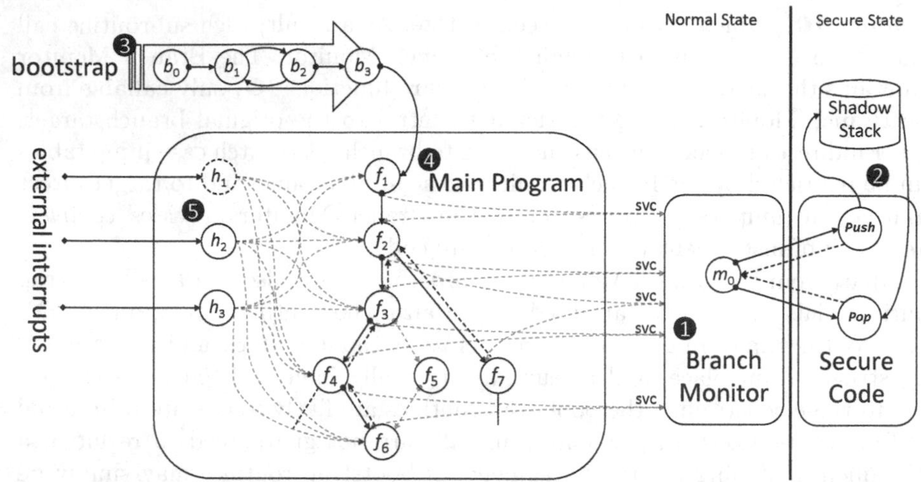


**Fig. 2.** CaRE overview

call, and validating the return address on top of the shadow stack upon return. We propose an alternative approach which is layout-preserving.

In uninstrumented code, the target address of direct subroutine calls (i.e., `bl` instructions with immediate operands) are encoded as `pc`-relative offsets (i.e., signed integer values). In other words, the destination address depends on the location of the branch instruction in memory. During instrumentation, we calculate the absolute destination address, and store it in a data structure, called the *branch table* which at runtime resides in read-only non-secure memory. Each destination address in this branch table is indexed by the memory address of the original branch instruction. The original branch instruction is overwritten with a *dispatch instruction*, which, when executed, traps into the Branch Monitor. At runtime, whenever an instruction rewritten in this fashion traps into the Branch Monitor, the Branch Monitor will lookup the destination address from the branch table, and redirect control flow to the original destination address.

In a similar manner, indirect branches corresponding to calls and effective returns are replaced with dispatch instructions. The destination address of the branches are only known at runtime, determined by a register value (`lr` in the case of effective returns), or by a return address stored on the program call stack, and hence do not influence the construction of the branch table during instrumentation.

To address JOP attacks, our CFI enforcement must also be able to determine legal call targets for indirect calls. In the case of indirect subroutine calls, the call target must be a valid entry point to the destination subroutine, i.e., the call must target the beginning of the subroutine prologue. The entry addresses are extracted from the symbol information emitted by the compiler for debug purposes. Further restriction of call targets is possible by means of static or dynamic analysis (see Sect. 6). Since CaRE only requires the addresses of entry points, not the full debug information, the entry points are included in the software image in a *call target table* on the device in a similar manner to the branch table. When an indirect call occurs, the Branch Monitor will match the branch target against this record of valid subroutine entry points.

In our implementation, we use the supervisor call `svc` instruction as the dispatch instruction, and place the Branch Monitor in the supervisor call exception handler. The `svc` instruction has a number of desirable properties which make it suitable as a dispatch. Firstly, it allows for an 8-bit comment field, which is ignored by hardware, but can be interpreted in software, typically to determine the service requested. We exploit this comment field to identify the type of the original instruction, overwritten during the instrumentation (e.g. `bl`, `blx`, `pop {..., pc}` etc.). Secondly, the supervisor call handler executes at the highest exception priority, allowing us to pre-empt execution to the Branch Monitor when instrumenting exception handlers. Lastly, because the `svc` in Thumb instruction is a 16-bit instruction, it can be used for instrumenting both 32-bit and 16-bit instructions. When replacing 32-bit instructions, e.g., a Thumb-2 `bl` instruction with an immediate operand, we use the sequence `0xb000`, which corresponds to the opcode for `add sp, #0` (effectively a NOP) as padding to fill the remaining 16 bits of the original `bl`.

### 4.4 Implementation

We implemented a proof-of-concept prototype of CaRE on the ARM Versatile Express Cortex-M Prototyping System MPS2+ configured as a Cortex-M23 CPU.

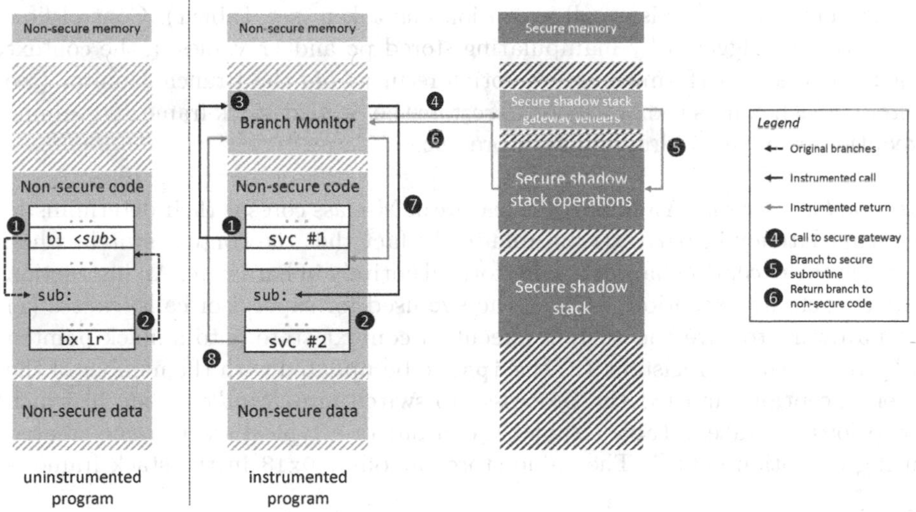


**Fig. 3.** CaRE instrumented control flow

We implemented a binary rewriter to perform the instrumentation on non-secure state binaries. It utilizes the Capstone disassembly engine[8] to identify control-flow instructions for rewriting.

Figure 3 illustrates the altered control-flow changes. When a dispatch instruction is encountered in the program (❶), instead of taking a control-flow transfer directly to the original target (❷), program execution is temporarily halted by a trap into the Branch Monitor (❸). The Branch Monitor will update the shadow stack maintained in secure memory by invoking secure shadow stack operations entry points in the gateway veneer (❹), which allow access to the secure state subroutines handling the actual update (❺). Upon completion, control is returned to the non-secure Branch Monitor code (❻), which finally redirects control flow to the intended destination (❼). The same sequence applies both for calls, and returns (❽).

*Branch Monitor.* The Branch Monitor is responsible for dispatching and validating control-flow transfers that occur during program execution. When invoked, it will first determine the reason for the trap based on the `svc` comment and trigger the corresponding branch handler routine within the Branch Monitor. The routine updates the shadow stack accordingly (pushes return address on subroutine calls, pops and validates return address on subroutine returns) and redirects the control flow to the intended target. For branches corresponding to direct subroutine calls a branch table lookup is needed since the target of a call is not anymore evident from the dispatch instruction. For indirect calls, the Branch Monitor verifies that each call targets a valid subroutine entry within the main program by looking up the target from the call target table.

As the Branch Monitor executes in the supervisor call handler, the main stack contains a context state stack frame corresponding to the processor state at the point the supervisor call exception was taken (see Table 1). Control-flow redirection is triggered by manipulating stored `pc` and `lr` values in the context stack frame and performing an exception return from the Branch Monitor (see below), which causes the processor to restore the context stack frame and resume execution from the address in the stored `pc`.

*Interrupt awareness.* An important feature of M-class cores is their deterministic interrupt latency in part attributable to the fact that the context-switch, while entering the exception handler, is performed entirely in hardware. An instruction that triggers an exception, such as the `svc` used for supervisor calls, causes (1) the hardware to save the current execution context state onto a stack pointed to by one of the `sp` registers, (2) the `ipsr` to be updated with the number of the taken exception, and (3) the processor to switch into *Handler mode* in which exceptions are taken. Table 1 shows the layout of a typical stack frame created during exception entry[9]. The value stored at offset `0x18` in the stack frame is

[8] http://www.capstone-engine.org/.

[9] In Cortex-M processors that implement the floating point extensions, the context stack frame may also contain the values of floating point registers.

**Table 1.** Context state stack frame layout [4]

| Offset | Stack contents | |
|---|---|---|
| 0x1C | xpsr | |
| 0x18 | pc | |
| 0x14 | lr | |
| 0x10 | r12 | |
| 0x0C | r3 | |
| 0x08 | r2 | |
| 0x04 | r1 | |
| 0x00 | r0 | ← sp |

the pc value at the point the exception was taken, and represents the return value from which program execution shall continue after the exception handler exits. To facilitate fast restoration of the saved context state, M-class processors support a special return sequence which restores the saved values on the stack into their corresponding registers. This sequence is known as an *exception return* and occurs when the processor is in Handler mode, and a special *Exception Return Value* (ERV) is loaded into the pc either via a pop instruction, or a bx with any register. ERVs are of the form 0xF*XXXXXXX*, and encode in their lower-order bits information about the current processor state and state before the current exception was taken. ERVs are not interpreted as memory addresses, but are intercepted by the processor as they are written to the pc. When this occurs, the processor will validate that there is an exception currently being handled, and that its number matches the exception number in the ipsr. If the exception numbers match, the processor performs an exception return to the processor mode specified by the ERV, restoring the previous register state from the current stack, including the stored pc. This causes the processor to continue execution from the point in the program at which the exception was originally taken. When multiple exceptions are pending, lower priority exceptions may be *tail-chained* which causes the processor to directly begin executing the next pending exception, without restoring the context state frame between exceptions.

Due to the fact that the context state stack frame contains a stored pc value that is restored on exception return, an exception handler with a vulnerability that allows an attacker to control the content of the context state frame on the stack constitutes a valid attack vector. This attack differs from a traditional ROP attack in that the attacker does not need to control the immediate lr value (which may reside only in the lr register), as during the execution of the exception handler lr contains merely the current ERV value. Instead, by manipulating the pc value in the context state stack frame, an attacker can cause an effective return from the exception handler to an arbitrary address. To avoid this, CaRE needs to be interrupt aware, and accurately record the correct return address for the exception handler onto the shadow stack. However, exceptions (when enabled) may be triggered by events external to the main program execution, effectively pre-empting the main program at an arbitrary position in the code, even during the execution of another exception handler (assuming an exception of higher priority arriving concurrently).

To tackle this challenge, we introduce *exception trampolines*. When an exception is received, the trampoline determines the return address, stores it on the shadow stack, and then proceeds to execute the original exception handler. The exception trampolines can be instrumented in place by rewriting the non-secure state exception vector and replacing the address of each exception with the address of a corresponding exception trampoline, that ends in a fixed branch to the original exception handler. That address is the original exception vector entry.

Since CaRE may interrupt the execution of another exception handler, we need to support a nested exception return, i.e. when the `pc` is being supplied with two consecutive return values in immediate succession. However, `pc` values in the `0xF0000000 - 0xFFFFFFFF` range are only recognized as ERVs when they are loaded to the `pc` either via a `pop` instruction, or a `bx` with any register (see Sect. 2.1). In particular, when an ERV is loaded to the `pc` as part of an exception return, it is instead interpreted as a memory address in an inaccessible range thus causing a hard fault in the processor. To overcome this, we also deploy *return trampolines*, small fragments of instruction sequences that contain the different effective return instructions originally present in the program image prior to binary rewriting. When the Branch Monitor returns from the supervisor call exception handler, it does so via the trampoline corresponding to the original return instruction.

# 5 Evaluation

## 5.1 Security Considerations

A key consideration for the effectiveness of CaRE is the ability of the Branch Monitor to perform complete mediation of indirect control-flow events in untrusted non-secure state program code. After all, any branch instruction for which an adversary can control the destination may potentially be used to disrupt the normal operation of the program. In practice, it is not possible to completely eliminate all instructions that may act as indirect branches from the non-secure state program image. In particular, the bootstrap code, the Branch Monitor itself and the return trampolines must remain uninstrumented. We argue that despite the Branch Monitor and bootstrap code being uninstrumented, CaRE is secure in terms of fulfilling Requirement 1. We demonstrate this with the following reasoning.

*Claim.* In order to maintain the control-flow integrity of the non-secure state program it is *sufficient* for the Branch Monitor to mediate calls that occur within the strongly connected component of the main program's call graph.

We base our reasoning on the following observations:

**Observation 1.** *The secure state software stack, and the Branch Monitor are trusted and cannot be disabled or modified.*

This follows from Assumptions 2 and 3. A secure boot mechanism protects the program code at rest and read-only memory protects it from modification at runtime.

**Observation 2.** *The main program has been instrumented in a manner which replaces* all *subroutine calls and indirect branch instructions with Branch Monitor calls.*

This follows simply from the operation of our instrumentation.
Based on these observations we formulate the following invariants:

**Invariant 1.** *Each subroutine within the main program has a fixed entry address that is the entry point for all control-transfer instructions (that are not returns) that branch to the subroutine.*

**Invariant 2.** *All control-transfer instructions in the main program that act as effective returns target a previously executed call site within the main program.*

Invariant 1 is true for all subroutines that are entered by control-transfer instructions where the destination address is an immediate operand that is encoded into the machine code instruction itself. This remains true after instrumentation as per Observations 1 and 2, as the destinations addresses are replicated read-only in the branch table, and the control-flow transfer for instrumented calls is mediated by the Branch Monitor. The entry address to an interrupt handler is the address recorded in the interrupt vector, and thus fixed, as interrupt handlers are not called directly from main program code.

As long as Invariant 1 holds control-flow transfers to an offset from the beginning of a subroutine are not possible. This includes branches that target 32-bit Thumb-2 instructions at a 16-bit offset[10], thus attempting to make use of the ambiguity in the Thumb-2 instruction set encoding.

Invariant 2 follows during benign execution from the structure of the program's call graph and Assumption 2. It remains true after instrumentation, notably *even* in the case the return addresses are compromised, because Observations 1, 2 and Invariant 1 imply that the Branch Monitor has complete mediation of control-flow transfers within the main program. Thus, the Branch Monitor has the ability to enforce that no return may target an address from which a matching call site has not been observed.

Based on this, and given that no instrumented subroutine call will ever occur from the bootstrap code nor from the Branch Monitor into the main program we may formulate the following corollaries:

**Corollary 1.** *No return within the main program may target the Branch Monitor.*

[10] Half-word alignment for branch instruction target addresses is enforced by the hardware itself.

**Corollary 2.** *No return within the main program may target the initialization code.*

Hence, as long as the Branch Monitor can correctly mediate all immediate branches corresponding to subroutine calls and all indirect branch instructions within the main program, the call/return matching performed by the Branch Monitor enforces that no control-flow transfers to outside the main program occur as a result of mediated calls.

We evaluated the effectiveness of our Branch Monitor implementation by attempting to corrupt control-flow data on the stack through a buffer overflow introduced into our sample binaries. We also performed simulations where we corrupted the target addresses kept in memory or registers for different branch types (both calls and returns) in a debugger. In each case, we observed the Branch Monitor detecting and preventing the compromised control flow.

### 5.2 Performance Considerations

The overhead CaRE adds to program execution is dependent on the number of subroutine calls and returns in the program. We evaluated the impact of CaRE on performance using microbenchmarks with varying proportions of subroutine calls (and returns) in relation to other instructions. Our microbenchmarks consisted of an event-based One-Time Password (OTP) generation algorithm that uses the Corrected Block Tiny Encryption Algorithm (XXTEA) block cipher algorithm, and a Hash-based Message Authentication Code (HMAC) implementation using the SHA256 cryptographic hash function. The size of the branch table was kept constant for each experiment. Our microbenchmarks contain only direct subroutine calls and all indirect branches corresponded to effective returns.

**Table 2.** Microbenchmark results. "*Monitor traps*" shows the number of Branch Monitor invocations during the execution of the microbenchmark routine. "*Ratio*" shows the ratio of instrumented control-flow transfer instructions in relation to other machine code instructions in the main program image.

| Program | Monitor traps | Ratio | Uninstrumented | Instrumented | Overhead |
|---|---|---|---|---|---|
| `otp` | 4 | $\frac{1}{956}$ | 0.53 ms | 0.59 ms | 0.07 ms |
| `hmac` | 80 | $\frac{1}{588.4}$ | 0.02 ms | 0.09 ms | 0.07 ms |

We also instrumented the *Dhrystone* 2.1 benchmark program [47] in order to estimate the performance impact on larger pieces of software. Dhrystone is a synthetic systems programming benchmark used for processor and compiler performance measurement. It is designed to reflect actual programming practice in systems programming by modeling the distribution of different types of high-level language statements, operators, operand types and locality sourced from contemporary systems programming statistics. In particular, it attempts

**Table 3.** Dhrystone results. The "*One run through Drystone*" column shows the average runtime through the Dhrystone benchmark for the "*Uninstrumented*" and "*Instrumented*" program versions respectively.

| Monitor traps | Ratio | One run through Drystone | | |
|---|---|---|---|---|
| | | Uninstrumented | Instrumented | Overhead |
| 34 | $\frac{1}{26.4}$ | 0.15 ms | 0.76 ms | 0.61 ms |

to reflect good programming practice by ensuring that the number of subroutine calls is not too low. Today Dhrystone has largely been supplanted by more complex benchmarks such as SPEC CPU bencmarks[11] and CoreMark[12]. The SPEC CPU benchmarks in particular have been used in prior CFI literature [2,14]. However, the SPEC suite is not practical to port to MCUs cores. The support library accompanying the Dhrystone benchmark contains both direct and indirect subroutine calls, and indirect returns. Other types of indirect branches were not observed in the main program portion of the samples.

All measurements were performed on an ARM Versatile Express Cortex-M Prototyping System MPS2+ FPGA configured as a Cortex-M23 processor executing at 25 MHz. Table 2 shows the results of the microbenchmarks and Table 3 shows the result for the Dhrystone benchmarks. According to the measurements the overhead of CaRE ranges between 13%–513%. The results compare favorably to existing software protection based shadow stack schemes with reported overheads ranging between 101%–4400% [10,20] (see Sect. 7).

### 5.3 Memory Considerations

While layout preserving instrumentation does not add instructions to the program image, the Branch Monitor and the constructed branch and call target tables and need to be placed in device memory. The Branch Monitor only needs to include the logic to handle branch variants present for a particular program image. For our microbenchmark program image the Branch Monitor implementation adds a fixed 700 bytes (5.1%) to the program image size. The branch table for the microbenchmarks program binary consists of 75 8-byte records, adding 600 bytes (4.3%) to the program image. Overall the memory consumption of our microbenchmark program increased by 9.4%. For our Dhrystone program image the Branch Monitor adds 1143 bytes (5.5%) and the branch and call target tables 1528 bytes (7.3%) and 376 bytes (1.7%). Overall the memory consumption of the Dhrystone program increased by 14.5%). The numbers for the Dhrystone program include full instrumentation of the support library.

[11] https://www.spec.org/benchmarks.html.

[12] http://www.eembc.org/coremark/about.php.

## 6 Extensions

*Function-Reuse Attacks.* The call target validation as presented in Sect. 4 does not fully address the issue of complete function reuse attacks within the main program code. An attacker might perform a pointer substitution where a pointer to one subroutine is exchanged for another subroutine. As both constitute valid call targets, the control-flow transfer would be allowed. Our instrumentation tools allow a human analyst to reduce the set of subroutines that may be subsitituted for each other by limiting the entries to the call target table known to be targeted by indirect subroutine calls, e.g. subrutines used as callback functions. However, as the call target may be computed by the program only at runtime, it is impractical to programatically fully explore all possible execution paths of a program during static analysis and pre-compute a complete CFG. This remains an open problem for any CFI scheme.

*Threading.* In our current implementation, the normal state software is limited to using the Main stack. In order to enable CFI for the rudimentary threading supported by Cortex-M processors, the Branch Monitor must be extended to maintain a separate shadow stack for return addresses on the Process call stack. The changes to the Branch Monitor are straightforward as it can consult the `spsel` register to determine which shadow stack to update.

*On-device instrumentation.* The layout-preserving instrumentation approach described in Sect. 4.3 has properties that make it suitable for performing binary rewriting on-device. Firstly, since it does not affect addresses resolved at link-time, it can be completed in a single pass over the binary image. Secondly, the logic consists of a simple search and replace of branch instruction patterns and branch table construction. While our current implementation relies on an separate tool for rewriting, it is straighforward to implement the needed instrumentation as part of the installation process on-device.

*Binary patching.* Another approach to performing the instrumentation required for CFI is *Binary patching* [5]. In binary patching, instrumented instructions are replaced with dispatch instructions to trampolines that are placed in unused memory. Compared to *binary rewriting* [27], binary patching does not require adjusting of *all* `pc`-relative offsets and thus has less impact to the program memory layout. However, as explained in Sect. 2, Thumb-2 code has properties that makes binary patching more challenging compared to the instrumentation approach described in Sect. 4.3; dispatch instructions used for ARM binary patching are typically 32-bit Thumb-2 `pc`-relative branches in order to encode a sufficient offset to reach the trampolines. If the instrumented instruction is 16 bits in size, the 32-bit dispatch instruction cannot be inserted without affecting the memory layout of the binary. Instead of adjusting all subsequent instructions, both the 16-bit target instruction, and another (16-bit or 32-bit) instruction is moved to the trampoline to make room for the dispatch instruction. If the moved instruction contains a `pc`-relative operation, it needs to be adjusted accordingly since the new location of the instruction will correspond to a different pc value. Even for a small instruction sets such as Thumb, the required logic to perform such adjustments is not in general practical to be implemented as part of the software update mechanism on a resource constrained device. Additionally, as trampolines may contain instructions moved from the instrumentation point, each instrumentation point requires a corresponding trampoline. However, for use cases where on-device instrumentation may not be a concern, a TZ-M protected shadow stack could be utilized with binary patching. This approach would have the advantage of not requiring Branch Monitor logic in the supervisor call handler.

## 7 Related Work

Code-reuse attack countermeasures have been a focal topic of research for the past decade. The most widely used mitigation technique against this class of attack is *Address Space Layout Randomization* (ASLR) [13,34]). ASLR relies on shuffling the executable (and the stack and heap) base address around in virtual memory, thus requiring an attacker to successfully guess the location of the target code (or data). This makes ASLR impractical for constrained devices that lack MMUs and where memory is a scarce resource.

Dang et al. [14] conduct a comprehensive evaluation of shadow stacks schemes in the face of different adversarial models. Dang et al.'s parallel shadow stack [14] and many traditional shadow stacks [24,25,38] are based on *unprotected shadow stacks*, e.g., their integrity can be compromised if the shadow stack location is known as they are located in the same address space as the vulnerable application. Shadow stacks protected by canary values [20,42] can withstand attacks that are limited to sequantial writes, but not arbitrary writes to specific memory addresses. Dang et al. identify only two schemes that operate under an equivalent adversary model as CaRE, in particular with regard to the ability to withstand disclosure of the shadow stacks location; Chiueh and Hsus Read-Only RAD [10] and Abadi et al.'s CFI scheme [2]. Read-Only RAD incurs a substantial overhead in the order of 1900%–4400% according to benchmarks by the authors. Abadi et al.'s protected shadow stack achieves a modest overhead between 5%–55% (21% on average). However, it makes use of x86 memory segments, a hardware feature not available on low-end MCUs. In contrast, CaRE provides equivalent security guarantees without requiring hardware features unique to high-end general purpose processors and compared to previous work on software-only protected shadow stacks, CaRE performs better.

In addition, we consider an even stronger adversary who can exploit interrupt handling to undermine CFI protection; this has been largely ignored in previous CFI works. Prior work, most notably ROPDefender [17] and PICFI [39] support *software exception handling*, particularly C++ exceptions. To the best of our knowledge, CaRE is the first scheme to protect *hardware interrupts* initiated by the CPU, a necessity for CFI in bare-metal programs. We make no claim regarding software exceptions, as our system model assumes C programs.

The prevalence of ROP and JOP exploitation techniques in runtime attacks on modern PC platforms has also prompted processor manufacturers to provide hardware support for CFI enforcement. In June 2016, Intel announced its *Control-flow Enforcement Technology* [30] that adds support for shadow call stacks and indirect call validation to the x86/x84 instruction set architecture. Similarly the ARMv8.3-A architecture provides *Pointer Authentication* (PAC) [43] instructions for ARM application processors that can be leveraged in the implementation of memory corruption countermeasures such as stack protection and CFI. Countermeasures suitable for resource-constrained embedded devices, however, have received far less attention to date. Kumar et al. [33] propose a software-hardware co-design for the AVR family of microcontrollers that places control-flow data to a separate *safe-stack* in protected memory. Francillon et al. [22] propose a similar hardware architecture in which the safe-stack is accessible only to return and call instructions. AVRAND by Pastrana et al. [41] constitutes a software-based defense against code reuse attacks for AVR devices. HAFIX [16] is a hardware-based CFI solution for the Intel Siskiyou Peak and SPARC embedded system architectures. SOFIA [11] is a hardware-based security architecture for the LEON3 soft microprocessor that provides software integrity protection and CFI through instruction set randomization.

## 8 Conclusion

Security is paramount for the safe and reliable operation of connected IoT devices. It is only a matter of time before the attacks against the IoT device evolve from very simple attacks such as targeting default passwords to advanced exploitation techniques such as code-reuse attacks. The introduction of lightweight trust anchors (such as TrustZone-M) to constrained IoT devices will enable the deployment of more advanced security mechanisms on these devices. We show why and how a well understood CFI technique needs to be adapted to low-end IoT devices in order to improve their resilience against advanced attacks. Leveraging hardware assisted security is an important enabler in CaRE, but it also meets other requirements important for practical deployment on small devices, such as interrupt-awareness, layout-preserving instrumentation and the possibility for on-device instrumentation. For small, interrupt-driven devices, the ability to ensure CFI in both interruptible code, as well for the code executing in interrupt contexts is essential.

**Acknowledgments.** This work was supported by the German Science Foundation (project S2, CRC 1119 CROSSING), Tekes—the Finnish Funding Agency for Innovation (CloSer project), and the Intel Collaborative Research Institute for Secure Computing (ICRI-SC).

## References

1. ARM compiler version 6.4 software development guide. http://infocenter.arm.com/help/topic/com.arm.doc.dui0773e (2015)

2. Abadi, M., Budiu, M., Erlingsson, U., Ligatti, J.: Control-flow integrity principles, implementations, and applications. ACM Trans. Inf. Syst. Secur. **13**(1), 4:1–4:40 (2009). http://doi.acm.org/10.1145/1609956.1609960
3. ARM Ltd.: Procedure Call Standard for the ARM Architecture (2009). http://infocenter.arm.com/help/topic/com.arm.doc.ihi0042d
4. ARM Ltd.: ARMv8-M Architecture Reference Manual.(2016). http://infocenter.arm.com/help/topic/com.arm.doc.ddi0553a.b
5. Brown, N.: Control-flow Integrity for Real-time Embedded Systems. Master's thesis, Worcester Polytechnic Institute, Worcester, MA, USA (2017)
6. Buchanan, E., Roemer, R., Shacham, H., Savage, S.: When good instructions go bad: generalizing return-oriented programming to risc. In: Proceedings of the 15th ACM Conference on Computer and Communications Security. CCS 2008, pp. 27–38. ACM, New York (2008). http://doi.acm.org/10.1145/1455770.1455776
7. Carlini, N., Barresi, A., Payer, M., Wagner, D., Gross, T.R.: Control-flow bending: on the effectiveness of control-flow integrity. In: Proceedings of the 24th USENIX Conference on Security Symposium. SEC 2015, pp. 161–176. USENIX Association, Berkeley (2015). http://dl.acm.org/citation.cfm?id=2831143.2831154
8. Checkoway, S., Davi, L., Dmitrienko, A., Sadeghi, A.R., Shacham, H., Winandy, M.: Return-oriented programming without returns. In: Proceedings of the 17th ACM Conference on Computer and Communications Security. CCS 2010, pp. 559–572. ACM, New York (2010). http://doi.acm.org/10.1145/1866307.1866370
9. Checkoway, S., Feldman, A.J., Kantor, B., Halderman, J.A., Felten, E.W., Shacham, H.: Can dres provide long-lasting security? the case of return-oriented programming and the AVC advantage. In: Proceedings of the 2009 Conference on Electronic Voting Technology/Workshop on Trustworthy Elections. EVT/WOTE 2009, p. 6. USENIX Association, Berkeley (2009). http://dl.acm.org/citation.cfm?id=1855491.1855497
10. Chiueh, T.C., Hsu, F.H.: Rad: a compile-time solution to buffer overflow attacks. In: 21st International Conference on Distributed Computing Systems, pp. 409–417, April 2001
11. de Clercq, R., Keulenaer, R.D., Coppens, B., Yang, B., Maene, P., d. Bosschere, K., Preneel, B., De Sutter, B., Verbauwhede, I.: Sofia: software and control flow integrity architecture. In: 2016 Design, Automation Test in Europe Conference Exhibition (DATE), pp. 1172–1177, March 2016
12. de Clercq, R., Piessens, F., Schellekens, D., Verbauwhede, I.: Secure interrupts on low-end microcontrollers. In: 2014 IEEE 25th International Conference on Application-Specific Systems, Architectures and Processors, pp. 147–152, June 2014
13. Cohen, F.B.: Operating system protection through program evolution. Comput. Secur. **12**(6), 565–584 (1993). http://dx.doi.org/10.1016/0167-4048(93)90054-9
14. Dang, T.H., Maniatis, P., Wagner, D.: The performance cost of shadow stacks and stack canaries. In: Proceedings of the 10th ACM Symposium on Information, Computer and Communications Security. ASIA CCS 2015, pp. 555–566. ACM, New York (2015). http://doi.acm.org/10.1145/2714576.2714635
15. Davi, L., Dmitrienko, A., Egele, M., Fischer, T., Holz, T., Hund, R., Nürnberger, S., Sadeghi, A.R.: MoCFI: a framework to mitigate control-flow attacks on smartphones. In: 19th Annual Network and Distributed System Security Symposium. NDSS 2012, February 5–8, San Diego, USA (2012). http://www.internetsociety.org/mocfi-framework-mitigate-control-flow-attacks-smartphones

16. Davi, L., Hanreich, M., Paul, D., Sadeghi, A.R., Koeberl, P., Sullivan, D., Arias, O., Jin, Y.: Hafix: hardware-assisted flow integrity extension. In: Proceedings of the 52Nd Annual Design Automation Conference. DAC 2015, pp. 74:1–74:6. ACM, New York (2015). http://doi.acm.org/10.1145/2744769.2744847
17. Davi, L., Sadeghi, A.R., Winandy, M.: Ropdefender: a detection tool to defend against return-oriented programming attacks. In: Proceedings of the 6th ACM Symposium on Information, Computer and Communications Security. ASIACCS 2011, pp. 40–51. ACM, New York (2011). http://doi.acm.org/10.1145/1966913.1966920
18. Eldefrawy, K., Francillon, A., Perito, D., Tsudik, G.: SMART: secure and minimal architecture for (Establishing a Dynamic) root of trust. In: 19th Annual Network and Distributed System Security Symposium. NDSS 2012, February 5–8, San Diego, USA, February 2012. http://www.eurecom.fr/publication/3536
19. Ericssson: Ericsson Mobility Report (2015). http://www.ericsson.com/res/docs/2015/mobility-report/ericsson-mobility-report-nov-2015.pdf
20. Erlingsson, U., Abadi, M., Vrable, M., Budiu, M., Necula, G.C.: Xfi: software guards for system address spaces. In: Proceedings of the 7th Symposium on Operating Systems Design and Implementation. OSDI 2006, pp. 75–88. USENIX Association, Berkeley (2006). http://dl.acm.org/citation.cfm?id=1298455.1298463
21. Francillon, A., Castelluccia, C.: Code injection attacks on harvard-architecture devices. In: Proceedings of the 15th ACM Conference on Computer and Communications Security. CCS 2008, pp. 15–26. ACM, New York (2008). http://doi.acm.org/10.1145/1455770.1455775
22. Francillon, A., Perito, D., Castelluccia, C.: Defending embedded systems against control flow attacks. In: Proceedings of the First ACM Workshop on Secure Execution of Untrusted Code. SecuCode 2009, pp. 19–26. ACM, New York (2009). http://doi.acm.org/10.1145/1655077.1655083
23. Gartner: Gartner Says Managing Identities and Access Will Be Critical to the Success of the Internet of Things (2015). http://www.gartner.com/newsroom/id/2985717
24. Giffin, J.T., Jha, S., Miller, B.P.: Detecting manipulated remote call streams. In: Proceedings of the 11th USENIX Security Symposium, pp. 61–79. USENIX Association, Berkeley (2002). http://dl.acm.org/citation.cfm?id=647253.720282
25. Giffin, J.T., Jha, S., Miller, B.P.: Efficient context-sensitive intrusion detection. In: Proceedings of the Network and Distributed System Security Symposium. NDSS 2004 (2004)
26. Eclipse IoT Working Group, IEEE IoT, AGILE IoT and IoT Council: IoT Developer Survey 2017 (2017). https://ianskerrett.wordpress.com/2017/04/19/iot-developer-trends-2017-edition/
27. Habibi, J., Panicker, A., Gupta, A., Bertino, E.: DisARM: mitigating buffer overflow attacks on embedded devices. In: Qiu, M., Xu, S., Yung, M., Zhang, H. (eds.) NSS 2015. LNCS, vol. 9408. Springer, Cham (2015). doi:10.1007/978-3-319-25645-0_8
28. Hewlett-Packard: Data Execution Prevention (2006). http://h10032.www1.hp.com/ctg/Manual/c00387685.pdf
29. Hu, H., Shinde, S., Adrian, S., Chua, Z.L., Saxena, P., Liang, Z.: Data-oriented programming: on the expressiveness of non-control data attacks. In: IEEE Symposium on Security and Privacy, SP 2016, San Jose, CA, USA, May 22–26, 2016, pp. 969–986 (2016). http://doi.ieeecomputersociety.org/10.1109/SP.2016.62

30. Intel: Control-flow Enforcement Technology Preview (2016). https://software.intel.com/sites/default/files/managed/4d/2a/control-flow-enforcement-technology-preview.pdf
31. Koeberl, P., Schulz, S., Sadeghi, A.R., Varadharajan, V.: TrustLite: a security architecture for tiny embedded devices. In: Proceedings of the Ninth European Conference on Computer Systems. EuroSys 2014, pp. 10:1–10:14. ACM, New York (2014). http://doi.acm.org/10.1145/2592798.2592824
32. Kornau, T.: Return Oriented Programming for the ARM Architecture. Master's thesis, Ruhr-University Bochum (2009). http://static.googleusercontent.com/media/www.zynamics.com/en//downloads/kornau-tim-diplomarbeit-rop.pdf
33. Kumar, R., Singhania, A., Castner, A., Kohler, E., Srivastava, M.: A system for coarse grained memory protection in tiny embedded processors. In: Proceedings of the 44th Annual Design Automation Conference. DAC 2007, pp. 218–223. ACM, New York (2007). http://doi.acm.org/10.1145/1278480.1278534
34. Larsen, P., Homescu, A., Brunthaler, S., Franz, M.: Sok: automated software diversity. In: Proceedings of the 2014 IEEE Symposium on Security and Privacy, SP 2014, pp. 276–291. IEEE Computer Society, Washington, DC (2014). http://dx.doi.org/10.1109/SP.2014.25
35. Le, L.: ARM Exploitation ROPMap. BlackHat USA (2011)
36. Lian, W., Shacham, H., Savage, S.: Too LeJIT to quit: extending JIT spraying to ARM. In: Kirda, E. (ed.) Proceedings of NDSS 2015. Internet Society, February 2015
37. Microsoft: Enhanced Mitigation Experience Toolkit (2016). https://www.microsoft.com/emet
38. Nebenzahl, D., Sagiv, M., Wool, A.: Install-time vaccination of windows executables to defend against stack smashing attacks. IEEE Trans. Dependable Secur. Comput. **3**(1), 78–90 (2006). http://dx.doi.org/10.1109/TDSC.2006.14
39. Niu, B., Tan, G.: Per-input control-flow integrity. In: Proceedings of the 22nd ACM SIGSAC Conference on Computer and Communications Security. CCS 2015, pp. 914–926. ACM, New York (2015). http://doi.acm.org/10.1145/2810103.2813644
40. Noorman, J., Agten, P., Daniels, W., Strackx, R., Van Herrewege, A., Huygens, C., Preneel, B., Verbauwhede, I., Piessens, F.: Sancus: low-cost trustworthy extensible networked devices with a zero-software trusted computing base. In: Proceedings of the 22nd USENIX Conference on Security. SEC 2013, pp. 479–494. USENIX Association, Berkeley (2013). http://dl.acm.org/citation.cfm?id=2534766.2534808
41. Pastrana, S., Tapiador, J., Suarez-Tangil, G., Peris-López, P.: AVRAND: a software-based defense against code reuse attacks for AVR embedded devices. In: Caballero, J., Zurutuza, U., Rodríguez, R.J. (eds.) DIMVA 2016. LNCS, vol. 9721, pp. 58–77. Springer, Cham (2016). doi:10.1007/978-3-319-40667-1_4
42. Prasad, M., Chiueh, T.: A binary rewriting defense against stack based overflow attacks. In: Proceedings of the USENIX Annual Technical Conference, pp. 211–224 (2003)
43. Qualcomm Technologies Inc: Pointer Authentication on ARMv8.3. (2017). https://www.qualcomm.com/media/documents/files/whitepaper-pointer-authentication-on-armv8-3.pdf
44. Shacham, H.: The geometry of innocent flesh on the bone: return-into-libc without function calls (on the x86). In: Proceedings of the 14th ACM Conference on Computer and Communications Security. CCS 2007, pp. 552–561. ACM, New York (2007). http://doi.acm.org/10.1145/1315245.1315313
45. Designer, S.: lpr LIBC RETURN exploit (1997). http://insecure.org/sploits/linux.libc.return.lpr.sploit.html

46. Szekeres, L., Payer, M., Wei, T., Song, D.: Sok: eternal war in memory. In: Proceedings of the 2013 IEEE Symposium on Security and Privacy. SP 2013, pp. 48–62. IEEE Computer Society, Washington, DC (2013). http://dx.doi.org/10.1109/SP.2013.13
47. Weicker, R.P.: Dhrystone: a synthetic systems programming benchmark. Commun. ACM **27**(10), 1013–1030 (1984). http://doi.acm.org/10.1145/358274.358283
48. Yiu, J.: ARMv8-M architecture technical overview (2015). https://community.arm.com/docs/DOC-10896

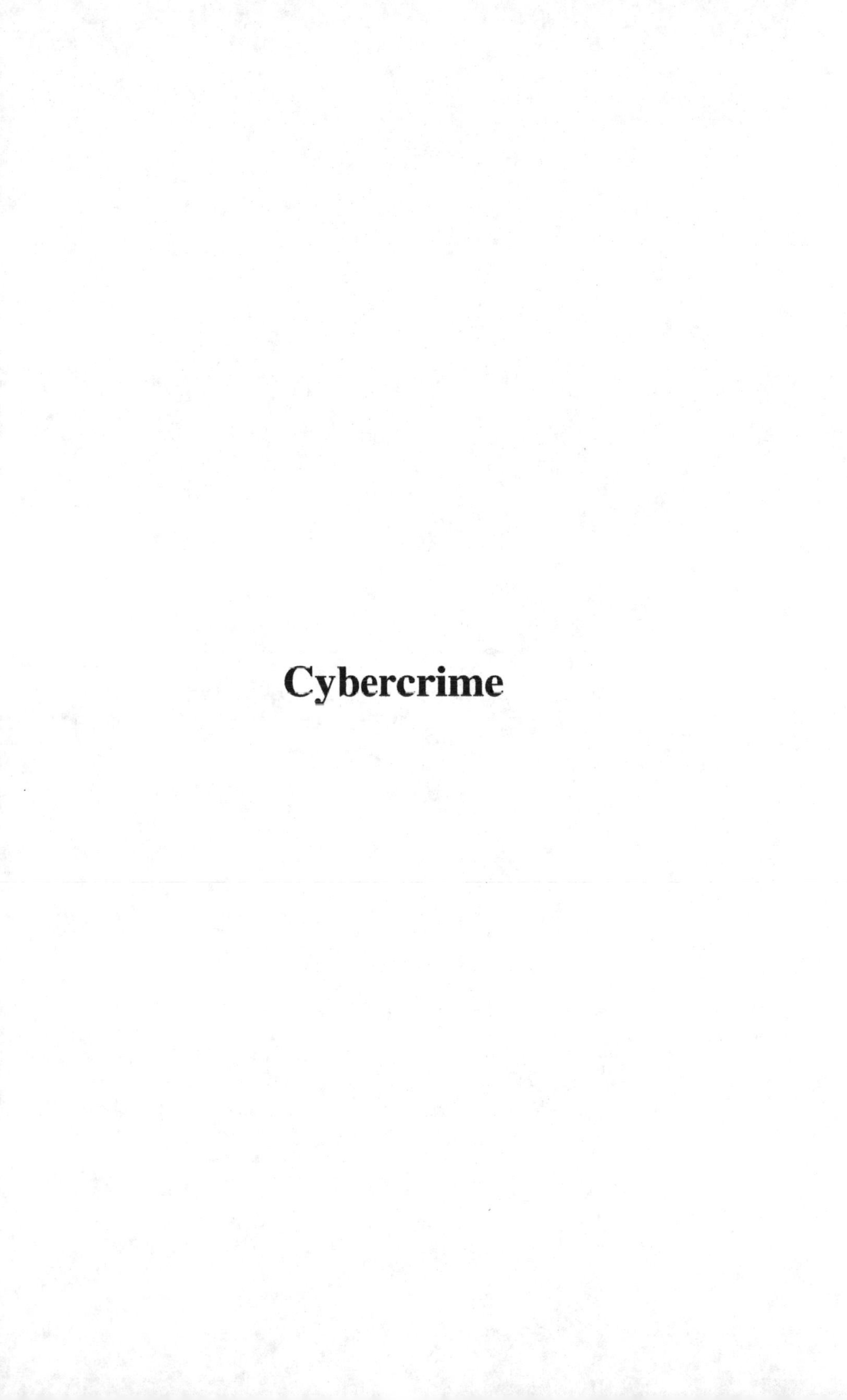

# Cybercrime

# Mining on Someone Else's Dime: Mitigating Covert Mining Operations in Clouds and Enterprises

Rashid Tahir[1(✉)], Muhammad Huzaifa[1], Anupam Das[2], Mohammad Ahmad[1], Carl Gunter[1], Fareed Zaffar[3], Matthew Caesar[1], and Nikita Borisov[1]

[1] University of Illinois Urbana-Champaign, Urbana, USA
{tahir2,huzaifa2,mahmad11,cgunter,caesar,nikita}@illinois.edu
[2] Carnegie Mellon University, Pittsburgh, USA
anupamd@cs.cmu.edu
[3] Lahore University of Management Sciences, Lahore, Pakistan
fareed.zaffar@lums.edu.pk

**Abstract.** Covert cryptocurrency mining operations are causing notable losses to both cloud providers and enterprises. Increased power consumption resulting from constant CPU and GPU usage from mining, inflated cooling and electricity costs, and wastage of resources that could otherwise benefit legitimate users are some of the factors that contribute to these incurred losses. Affected organizations currently have no way of detecting these covert, and at times illegal miners and often discover the abuse when attackers have already fled and the damage is done.

In this paper, we present *MineGuard*, a tool that can detect mining behavior in *real-time* across pools of mining VMs or processes, and prevent abuse despite an active adversary trying to bypass the defenses. Our system employs hardware-assisted profiling to create discernible signatures for various mining algorithms and can accurately detect these, with negligible overhead (<0.01%), for both CPU and GPU-based miners. We empirically demonstrate the uniqueness of mining behavior and show the effectiveness of our mitigation approach($\approx$99.7% detection rate). Furthermore, we characterize the noise introduced by virtualization and incorporate it into our detection mechanism making it highly robust. The design of MineGuard is both practical and usable and requires no modification to the core infrastructure of commercial clouds or enterprises.

**Keywords:** Cryptocurrency · Cloud abuse · Hardware Performance Counters

---

**Electronic supplementary material** The online version of this chapter (doi:10.1007/978-3-319-66332-6_13) contains supplementary material, which is available to authorized users.


M. Dacier et al. (Eds.): RAID 2017, LNCS 10453, pp. 287–310, 2017.
DOI: 10.1007/978-3-319-66332-6_13

## 1 Introduction

For most popular cryptocurrencies, such as Bitcoin and Litecoin, it is not profitable to mine using one's own resources unless the mining is carried out using specialized hardware [17]. However, the exercise can be of value if carried out on "stolen" resources, such as pools of hijacked VM instances or resources acquired under false pretexts (e.g., for research). This has incentivized both hackers [8,11,18] and unethical employees, such as professors [15], academic researchers and students mining on university-owned resources [10,26]. Even IT admins [7] have been found doing covert cryptomining. One researcher, for instance, misused NSF-funded supercomputers to mine for Bitcoins costing the university upwards of $150,000 [44]. On two other noteworthy occasions, NAS device botnets secretly mined for DogeCoin and Monero amounting to $600,000 and $82,000 respectively, before the covert operations were eventually discovered and shut down [14,29]. There are several other instances of employees and hackers secretly mining for coins in both the corporate [5] and government sectors [4].

This covert abuse of "borrowed" resources is not limited to enterprises and has also been observed in commercial clouds and datacenters [11]. The sheer amount of resources needed for a covert cryptomining operation are readily available in a cloud setting. Furthermore, since mined coins can easily be transferred to the attacker using a simple anonymized wallet address, it makes the "get away" scheme straightforward [1]. As a result, numerous instances of this targeted cloud abuse have already been uncovered, whereby attackers successfully *broke* into clouds and deployed cryptominers at a massive scale by spawning numerous VM instances dedicated exclusively to mining [9,11,18]. The advent of GPU clouds, such as those operated by Amazon and Microsoft, have further incentivized attackers to transfer their operations onto clouds and leverage the power of parallel computing, as GPUs often have higher hash rates and perform better for certain mining algorithms.

In this paper we present MineGuard, a simple hypervisor tool based on hardware-assisted behavioral monitoring, which accurately detects the signature of a miner. Specifically, our system uses Hardware Performance Counters (HPCs), a set of special-purpose registers built into modern processors, to accurately track low-level mining operations or events within the CPU and GPU with minimal overhead. This gives MineGuard the ability to accurately detect, in real-time, if a VM is trying to mine for cryptocurrency, without incurring any substantial slowdown (<0.01%). MineGuard is built on the observation that for attackers to mine for any cryptocurrency, they will have to repeatedly run the core Proof-of-Work (PoW) algorithm that the currency is based on (such as Scrypt [32] for Litecoin) millions of times at the very least. Such repeated runs would substantially influence the count of certain HPCs in a particular way, which we can detect using a runtime checker. We empirically demonstrate very high detection rates (≈99.7%), low false positives (<0.25%) and false negatives (<0.30%). Furthermore, our system does not modify any hypervisor code and leverages commonly available tools such as *perf* [19], thus making it easy to deploy and use in cloud and enterprise environments. We believe that attackers cannot deceive MineGuard as (1) it attempts to catch the inherent mining behavior essential for mining and (2) it is more privileged than a VM and hence difficult to bypass. We make the following contributions:

**Behavioral Analysis of Cryptomining:** We perform a first-of-its-kind comprehensive study to explore the behavior of cryptocurrency mining focusing on micro-architectural execution patterns. Specifically, (1) we show that CPU/GPU signatures of mining and non-mining applications differ substantially; (2) different implementations of the same coin exhibit similar signatures due to the same underlying PoW algorithm, meaning that mining should be detectable by profiling an algorithm instead of the executing binaries (to overcome polymorphic malware) and (3) surprisingly, profiles of various coins exhibit overlapping signatures, despite having different PoW algorithms.

**HPC Monitoring in Virtual Environments:** While prior work has demonstrated the use of HPCs for malware detection, their utility and feasibility in a *virtualized* context has largely been ignored. We characterize the noise that is introduced into each HPC value individually due to virtualization, and show the best-fit distribution for this noise in each case. Our findings indicate that certain counters have a very pronounced noise-distribution, which can be used to error-correct the signatures. In contrast, some HPCs show negligible effects of noise. To incorporate this noise into our behavior profiles we develop a step-by-step signature creation process that captures an evolving profile of mining malware in increasingly noisier environments making our detection robust under different virtualized environments.

**Userspace Detection Tool:** We build a user space tool, MineGuard, that can run on top of any hypervisor or host OS and perform real-time detection. MineGuard has a negligible overhead, a small size footprint, is hard to evade, and cannot be compromised by malicious VMs. We believe MineGuard can be extended for other resource-intensive malware with minor modifications and serves as a valuable addition to the cloud security toolbox.

**Paper Organization:** We discuss the cost of covert cryptomining in Sect. 2 and how HPCs can be used to detect such miners in Sect. 3; followed by our system design in Sect. 4, methodology in Sect. 5 and evaluation in Sect. 6. Limitations are presented in Sect. 7 and related work in Sect. 8. Finally, we conclude in Sect. 9.

## 2 Understanding the Cost of Covert Cryptomining

Apart from using compromised accounts and hijacked VM instances for mining, hackers can also exploit the freemium business model of clouds. They can amass the complimentary resources allocated to individual accounts and build a large valuable pool [48,51], e.g., building an unlimited "slack space" on top of small free storage shares in Dropbox [43]. This issue has recently gained more traction amongst cloud providers with Google expressly forbidding any mining-related activity in its free tier resources [27]. Furthermore, providers also offer free resources under other specialized programs, such as to app developers and students. These resources can also be abused in the aforementioned manner. As evidence to these freeloading issues, researchers recently constructed a mining botnet on Amazon entirely out of free resources [11]. The mining botnet was capable of generating cryptocurrency worth thousands of dollars and went completely undetected, despite its large footprint and conspicuous behavior.

These covert and cleverly concealed mining operations are a serious financial concern for admins. First, they waste valuable resources. Second, to maximize the hash rates hackers push CPUs/GPUs to full compute capacity for extended periods of time. This increases power consumption and generates heat, both of which impact operating costs [6]. Hence, it is imperative that mining deployments be thwarted before different losses stack up.

Users can't prevent this abuse as attackers can easily get root access and bypass security mechanisms or simply spawn their own VMs using stolen accounts. Similarly, providers and admins also struggle to mitigate these mining rigs [18], as they cannot distinguish mining from other types of workloads from outside the VM. Traditional VM instrospection techniques, such as analyzing memory dumps [41] or virtual disk monitoring [45], could be used but they have a large overhead and do not scale well. Also, if vendors start "peeking" into customers' VMs (e.g., by analyzing memory dumps), they run the risk of compromising the confidentiality and privacy of sensitive user data and computations.

Hence, a tool like MineGuard that proactively detects mining-related abuse (on free and stolen/compromised instances) and does not directly look at user data or code, is needed as a part of the provider's security toolbox.

## 3 Using Hardware Performance Counters

Past work has shown the effectiveness of hardware-based monitoring for malware detection [34,35,53–55] using architectural and microarchitectural execution patterns. The approach is predominantly characterized by an extremely low performance overhead making it ideal for real-time monitoring on latency sensitive systems. We build upon these past works and present the design of a system based on Hardware Performance Counters (HPCs) for detecting mining behavior on clouds/enterprises. HPCs, outlined in Table 2 later on, are a set of special purpose registers internal to the processor that record and represent the runtime behavior and characteristics of the programs being executed. Common examples include counts of page faults, executed instructions, cache misses etc. Though developed to aid application developers in fine-tuning their code, HPCs can also be used for behavior profiling without directly looking at code and data. Other than the fact that HPCs are extremely fast, their choice as the main detection metric is based on the following insights.

First, miners need to run the core PoW algorithm of a coin repeatedly, millions of times. If an algorithm A alters a few specific HPCs, say counters X, Y and Z, as part of the main hashing operations, then the values for these three counters should dwarf counts of all other (relatively under utilized) HPCs given that algorithm A has to run millions of times. This implies that a very strong signature can be constructed based on the relevant counters of a particular algorithm, such as Scrypt [32] or CryptoNight [2]. If an adversary tries to stay under the radar by mining conservatively, then the hash rates will take a hit and profits will decline correspondingly making the exercise less lucrative. Also, since the processor will remain relatively under utilized, power and cooling costs will stay at manageable levels, making mining less of a nuisance for cloud vendors.

Second, any computation can only ever add to the values of HPCs and has no way of reducing counter values, as opposed to software-based defenses, which the attacker can subvert and alter. Hence, if an adversary mines for a coin, they will have no way of reducing counter values to avoid detection, and will be flagged with high likelihood. An adversary however, can try and neutralize the signature by increasing the values of other HPCs not associated with the PoW algorithm. But to do so successfully, the adversary has to overcome two *hard* challenges. First and foremost, they have to figure out a computation that **only** affects HPCs other than the ones related to the mining algorithm. In other words, there can be no overlap in the counters altered by the miner and the computation in question. Otherwise, the signature of the miner will only be bolstered further. Second, and more importantly, they have to run the secondary computation millions of times so that counter values are approximately equalized. However, the extra load on the system would greatly diminish the hash rate of the miner, reducing their profits.

Finally, HPCs are low-level registers and can be directly accessed by the hypervisor, requiring no modifications to the guest OS or applications. Furthermore, an adversary that manages to compromise a VM, even with root access, will not be able to falsify the values of the HPCs as the hardware does not allow this.

## 4 Design and Signature

The design of MineGuard was influenced by the following observations: First, unlike generic malware that can exploit users in novel ways, miners have to stick to the core PoW algorithm on which a cryptocurrency is based. This means that if a signature is built specifically for the algorithm, various implementations, even polymorphic and metamorphic ones, would be detectable. Second, detection has to be performed in a manner oblivious to the VM so that a malicious party cannot identify if they are being profiled or not, lest they start behaving differently. In addition, if a malicious entity does start behaving differently to cover up its tracks, it should incur a massive penalty, thereby defeating the whole purpose of the attack. Third, the detection mechanism has to be more privileged than the mining entity for obvious reasons. Finally, given the massive scale of clouds, the mechanism needs to be highly scalable with low performance overhead.

Given these stringent requirements, a hardware-assisted mechanism that can be executed on the host OS or the hypervisor emerged as the only logical candidate. As shown in Fig. 1A, MineGuard comprises of three components: A Profiler, a Detection Agent, and a Mitigation Agent. These three components run on each server in the cloud on top of the host or the hypervisor.

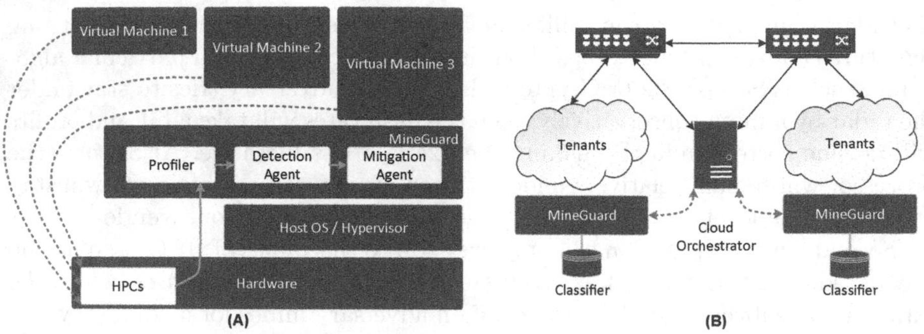


**Fig. 1.** **(A)** Inner components of a MineGuard instance. **(B)** Overview of MineGuard. Sequentially: MineGuard checks for current HPC values against the classifier. If a match occurs, it discovers all other VMs of the tenant and shuts down/suspends these VMs if they are also found mining.

The Profiler instruments each VM in real-time by polling the HPCs with a 2 s interval. The interval length is an adjustable metric, as MineGuard can use any user-defined sampling frequency to increase the accuracy even further. However, since mining is a long-term activity usually carried out for several hours at the very least (as opposed to short-term malware) we can easily afford to utilize large sampling intervals. This has the benefit of minimizing MineGuard's resource usage and does not effect the quality of the signature giving highly accurate detection rates as shown in Sect. 6. Furthermore, long intervals before repolling for HPCs, minimizes the overhead experienced by legitimate users as their VMs are profiled less often.

The Detection Agent runs the current HPC values against a classifier trained to detect mining behavior. If the classifier outputs a positive match, the Detection Agent flags the VM. Once a VM is flagged, the Mitigation Agent suspends it temporarily and determines the location of all VMs belonging to that tenant by contacting the cloud orchestrator as shown in Fig. 1B. All of the tenant's VM are then put to further screening by the Detection Agents on their corresponding servers. If more matches occur in this phase, the Mitigation Agents shut down those suspicious VMs as well.

**Signature Creation:** To incorporate the noise introduced by virtualization, we use a three-phased approach to creating accurate and precise mining signatures for both CPUs and GPUs. For our purposes, a signature is a time series of performance counter values of an application over a specified interval of time. To generate such time series, in the first phase, we run miners for various coins in a native environment and profile only the mining processes using *perf* [19] with a sampling rate of 2 s (empirically chosen for ease and accuracy). This gave us noise-free *process-level* HPC-based signatures for numerous coins. For GPUs we used *nvprof* [3]. The signature that we obtain during this phase is cleaned so that the bootstrapping code of the miner is not considered and only the signature for the core PoW algorithm is captured. We call this signature the OS-level signature. In the second phase, we run miners inside VMs to cater to *noise* that is induced by executing in a virtualized environment. No additional processes are run on the VMs other than the default OS ones and our cryptominers, giving us pure *VM-level* signatures. This phase corresponds to a scenario in which an attacker uses dedicated VM instances for mining coins. Finally, in the last phase, we perform mining inside VMs that are already running other jobs and processes. This allows us to capture signatures in the presence of maximum noise. We repeat our experiments for various popular and common cloud workloads running in parallel with a cryptocurrency miner. Signatures generated during this phase are called *VM-Interference* signatures. The aforementioned scheme, explicitly captures the effects of virtualization-induced noise and workload-induced noise both of which are a must for efficient detection of mining activity.

**Signature Database:** MineGuard's signature database, which we use to train the classifier, is very small in size for numerous reasons. First, unlike generic malware, miners have to stick to a core PoW algorithm. Whether the miner is polymorphic, metamorphic or heavily obfuscated, the core algorithm, which we profile in our system, remains the same. Since there are a finite number of coins, and consequently a limited number of proof-of-work algorithms, added to the fact that there is no such thing as a zero-day coin, our resulting signatures are few in number (<100). This makes our signature database small. And, since each signature in the database is distinct and prominent compared to other common cloud workloads, as shown in Sect. 6, the classifier is able to build its inner models successfully.

## 5 Methodology

Before we jump into the results, we explain our prototype implementation and test environment, and present details of the cryptocurrencies, miners and benchmarks we used for testing and evaluation.

**MineGuard Implementation:** We implemented MineGuard in userspace using a combination of C++, Python and Bash. We used C++ for the signature creation and detection modules, and Bash and Python scripts for profiling VMs and collecting and organizing data. We used an open source random forest library [25] for the bagged decision tree implementation, and *perf/perf-KVM* [19] and *nvprof* [3] for CPU and GPU profiling, respectively. Upon deployment, a driver script samples any given process (application/miner/VM) for 2 s (equivalent to one test vector), formats the test vector and passes it to the predict module to classify the process. Excluding the random forest library, the entire MineGuard infrastructure only requires 282 lines of code. We have also made the source code and training/test data publicly available at the following URL: https://bitbucket.org/mhuzai/mineguard/overview.

**Testbed:** All experiments were performed on a machine with an Intel Core-i7 2600 K processor (Sandy Bridge), an NVIDIA GTX 960 GPU (Maxwell) and

**Table 1.** Cryptocoins we used along with their PoW algorithms and CPU/GPU miners.

| Cryptocurrency | Proof-of-work algorithm | CPU miner | GPU miner |
|---|---|---|---|
| Bitcoin | SHA256 | cpuminer-multi-windows, bfgminer-5.1.0, cgminer-2.11.4 | – |
| Bytecoin | CryptoNight | cpuminer-multi-windows | ccMiner-cryptonight-0.17 |
| Dash | X11 | cpuminer-multi-windows | ccMiner-1.6.6-tpruvot |
| Litecoin | Scrypt | cpuminer-multi-windows | cudaminer-2014-02-28 |
| Quarkcoin | BLAKE, Blue Midnight Wish, GrØstl, JH, SHA-3 and Skein | cpuminer-multi-windows | ccMiner-1.6.6-tpruvot |
| Vertcoin | Lyra2RE | cpuminer-multi-windows | ccMiner-1.6.6-tpruvot |
| Ethereum | Ethash (Modified Dagger-Hashimoto) | ethminer-1.3.0 | ethminer-1.3.0 |
| Zcash | Equihash | nheqminer-0.5c | nheqminer-0.5c |

8 GB of DDR3 RAM. We ran Linux 3.16.0-44 for both desktop (native) and server (virtualized) environments. For collecting CPU-based training data, each application was profiled for 20 s, with one sample being collected every 2 s, for a total of 10 samples per application and miner. This provided ample data for high accuracy classification with negligible overhead (discussed in Sect. 6). For GPU-based training data, samples were only collected once at the end of a 120 s execution window - unlike *perf*, *nvprof* does not allow live periodic sampling of running applications.

**Cryptocurrencies and Miners:** Other than Bitcoin, the seven additional cryptocurrencies listed in Table 1 are still actively mined using CPUs and GPUs, and hence together comprise a realistic group for mining in the cloud. Furthermore, the currencies were chosen to evaluate a variety of mining algorithms and provide maximum coverage across the entire algorithm-space for mining-related PoW algorithms. The coins were also chosen to represent a large fraction of the market cap for mine-able coins (excluding Ripple, which cannot be mined, or coins with similar PoW algorithms, like Monero which is based on the same algorithm as Bytecoin). To mine these coins, we used cryptominers that were open-source and readily available online. Table 1 lists the cryptominers and mining algorithms for each of the cryptocurrencies used. Each miner was run using as

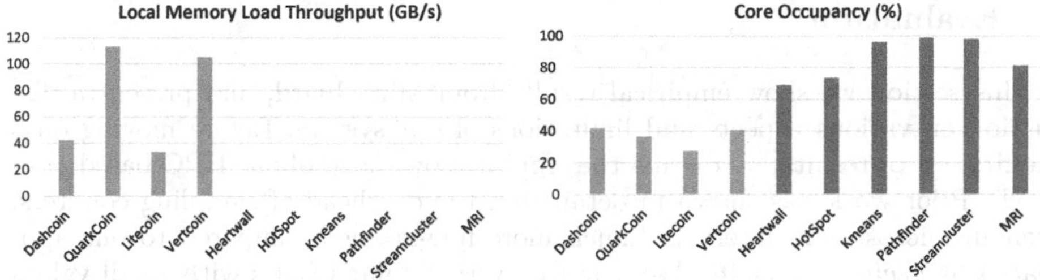


**Fig. 2.** Difference in behavior of GPU miners and GPU applications. Miners are shown in red; applications are shown in blue. (Color figure online)

many cores as available on the test system (8 cores for both the non-virtualized and virtualized environment) and public mining pools were used to mine coins. Using public pools ensured that our signature also incorporated the I/O aspects of miners, in addition to the dominant compute aspects. Finally, each miner was profiled in three different operating environments; **OS** (running standalone in a host OS), **VM** (running standalone in a guest OS) and **VM+Int** (running simultaneously with interfering applications in a guest OS).

**Benchmarks and Cloud Workloads:** To obtain signatures for non-mining applications, we chose various workloads from representative benchmark suites like CloudSuite (v3.0) [37], SPEC 2006 [20], Rodinia [33] and Parboil [49]. The benchmarks were chosen to cover a wide variety of domains, such as Hadoop workloads, scientific computing, AI simulations, data mining, graph analytics, web searching etc.; and a wide variety of workload characteristics such as compute and memory intensity, branch and cache behavior, and latency vs. throughput sensitivity. Furthermore, our mix of benchmarks consisted of both single-threaded and multi-threaded applications. We tested a total of 39 applications which we feel are representative of a real-world cloud setting.

**Classification Algorithm and Evaluation Metrics:** For evaluating our multi-class classification problem, we resorted to standard metrics like—*precision*, *recall*, and *F-score* [47] which is the harmonic mean between precision and recall. Since we do not know the underlying distribution of the different features for miners, we tried out different non-parametric classifiers like k-Nearest Neighbor (k-NN), Multiclass Decision Tree and Random Forest. We found that in general, ensemble-based approaches like Random Forest outperformed the other classifiers. During training, features from all applications (i.e., both miners and non-miners) were used to train the classifier. We used a random forest with 50 decision trees. In the test phase, the classifier predicted the most probable class for an unseen feature vector.[1]

[1] Unless otherwise stated, all experiments perform binary classification.

## 6 Evaluation

In this section we show empirical results from MineGuard, and present a discussion on various aspects and limitations of our system. Before moving onto the first set of results, we discuss the empirical overhead of our HPC-based approach. Prior work has shown in detail that the overhead of sampling counters, even in microsecond intervals (much more fine-grained compared to our approach), is *negligible* [35,46]. We observed very similar results with small values (<0.01%) for various polling intervals, hence, we do not present results for the overhead incurred due to space limitations and instead focus on other details surrounding MineGuard. Additionally, we found that the average time required to match a new sample against the classifier was 8 ms, bulk of which was spent in file I/O such as formatting the profiling data and reading the signature from disk. However, unnecessary I/O can be eliminated by keeping the signature in main memory. Finally, actual classification only took *32* μ*s*, showcasing the low overhead nature of our design.

**Uniqueness of GPU Mining Signatures:** As explained above, MineGuard uses HPC-based signatures to detect miners in real time. We justify our choice of HPCs by demonstrating the uniqueness of mining behavior on GPU instances compared to other common and popular GPU-based workloads. Figure 2 presents this comparison between mining software and some popular and common GPU workloads taken from the Rodinia [33] and Parboil [49] GPU-benchmark suites. The figure shows the behavior of two different profiling metrics, out of a total of 28 GPU metrics, across four miners and six applications. We ran these experiments for several other benchmarks from the aforementioned benchmark suites and found consistent results. However, those results have been omitted for brevity. Some observations from our GPU results are discussed below.

Miners have significantly less core occupancy (number of actual threads out of maximum possible threads) than non-mining applications. This is due to the fact that, in general, it is a good practice to run as many threads as optimally possible on a GPU core, and therefore non-mining applications tend to have high core occupancy. Miners, on the other hand, also optimize for memory per warp (the basic unit of execution in NVIDIA GPUs), and aim to avoid creating bottlenecks in the memory system. Consequently, they usually exhibit low core occupancies.

Another noticeable difference between miners and non-mining applications is their usage of local memory. Local memory in NVIDIA GPUs is used for register spilling and per-thread local data. However, despite its name, local memory physically resides in the main memory of the GPU and as such it is not as fast as scratchpads or texture caches. As a result, GPU application programmers tune their code to minimize local memory usage as much as possible. As can be seen in Fig. 2, the six different non-mining applications have in fact no local memory usage (an exception is MRI, which does use local memory but does so minimally). Miners, in stark contrast, exhibit high usage of local memory. This is a consequence of the fact that mining algorithms require a significant number of registers and this in turn results in a significant number of register spills (note: the high register usage of these algorithms also contributes to the low core occupancy).

As evident, there is a marked difference between the performance counter profiles of GPU miners and typical GPU applications. It is precisely these differences that our classification algorithm relies upon to detect miners with high accuracy.

**Uniqueness of CPU Mining Signatures:** As with GPU-based miners, we collected HPC-based signatures for CPU-based miners as well. These signatures were then compared to common CPU-based workloads from CloudSuite and the SPEC2006 benchmark suite to distinguish CPU miners from non-mining applications. The unique and distinct characteristics of CPU-based miners, similar to their GPU counterparts, can be seen in Fig. 3. The figure shows subgraphs for two different HPCs, out of a total of 26 CPU HPCs shown later in Table 2. Both subgraphs show a live-trace of a HPC's value during the execution of a CPU-based miner mining Litecoin and four non-mining applications; namely data caching (memcached server), AI (game of Go), H264 (hardware video encoding) and NAMD (molecular dynamics). The results from other benchmarks have been omitted for clarity.

In both graphs, the mining signature stands out. Since miners repeatedly run a small set of computations over and over again for millions of times, their resource usage is consistent throughout their execution. In other words, miners generally do not exhibit irregular *phases* as most common applications do. Rather, miners possess regular and structured phases. This consistency in signature is represented by a step function like recurring pattern in both graphs (red line).

On the other hand, non-mining applications and workloads have phases that are noticeably different. While the phases are, like miners, repeated in regular intervals, the behavior of each phase is much more irregular and possesses a high degree of variance (a finding consistent with prior research [35]). These patterns are particularly visible for H264 (black line). For example, the L1 Store curve of H264 is rhythmic but irregular, and, in fact, we found that troughs in load count

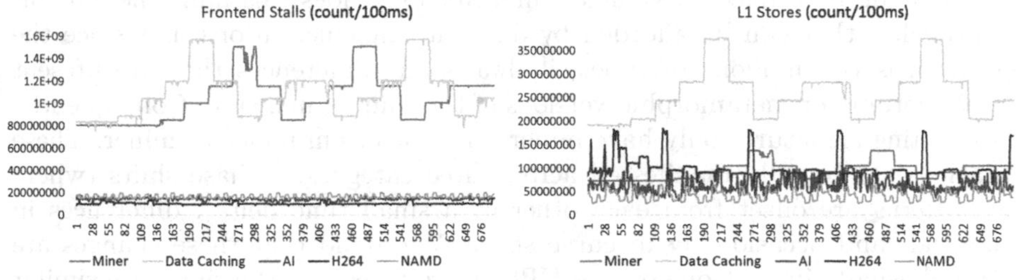


**Fig. 3.** Difference in behavior of a Litecoin CPU miner and four representative CPU applications. The x axis shows time in units of 100 ms (miner in red). (Color figure online)

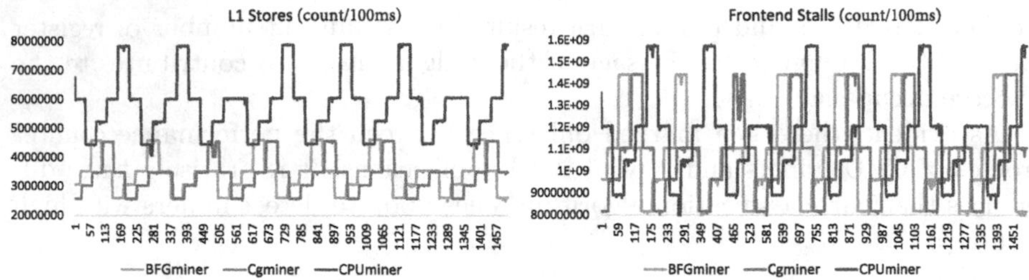


**Fig. 4.** Similarity in behavior of three different Bitcoin mining softwares. The x axis shows time in units of 100 ms.

correspond to peaks in store count. Similarly, another interesting observation is that for the Litecoin miner, the curves for the HPCs closely follow each other - an increase in one is accompanied by an increase in the other, which is generally not the case in the other workloads. Finally, even though data caching exhibits a slight similarity to Litecoin for these two HPCs, it is quite different for all metrics taken together. We take away the following insight from these results: CPU-miners exhibit a unique HPC-based signature and this signature can be effectively leveraged to detect virtual machines that are performing cryptocurrency mining.

**Signature Homogeneity Within a Coin:** Hackers usually employ various techniques and mechanisms to bypass detection mechanisms. They use polymorphic, metamorphic and obfuscated malware to fool anti-virus software and runtime checkers by completely overhauling their codebase. To show MineGuard's resilience against these techniques, we demonstrate how three completely different miner implementations that are mining the same coin still exhibit the same HPC-based signature.

Figure 4 shows two graphs, one per HPC, for three different miners all mining for Bitcoin. The implementations of these miners are quite different from one another, however, the graphs all show similar HPC patterns, thereby backing our claim that the mining signature is consistent across different implementations. The reason behind this, as mentioned previously, is that at their core, all miners have to abide by a fixed PoW algorithm. Not only does this limit the amount of variability that can be afforded by different implementations, but since the algorithm is run millions of times, it dwarfs any differences that are present in polymorphic or metamorphic versions of the mining malware. Consequently, the resulting signatures only have minor variations from miner to miner. These variations are broadly manifested across three categories. Phase shifts (where the patterns are offset from each other by a small time delta), differences in magnitude and occasionally in curve shape. We found that these changes are rare and usually impact one or two HPCs largely keeping the signature similar across implementations. MineGuard exploits this uniformity during its detection phase allowing it to catch altered versions of a mining malware.

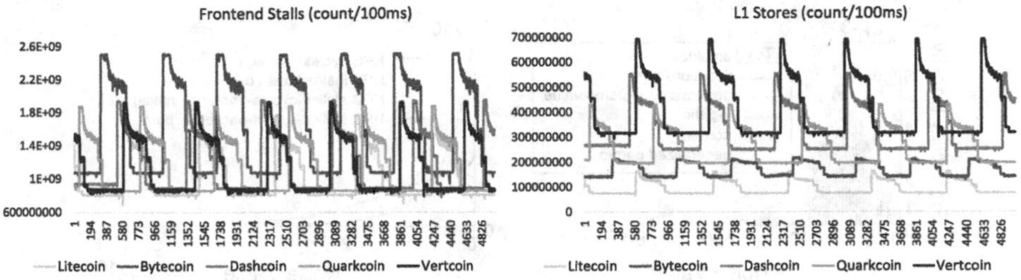


**Fig. 5.** Similarity in behavior of various cryptocurrencies (algorithms). The x axis shows time in units of 100 ms.

**Signature Homogeneity Across Coins:** We also claim that different cryptocurrencies have similar signatures due to the nature of cryptomining. As evidence, we present the signatures of five different cryptocurrencies in Fig. 5. The figure shows a subset of the signatures of cryptominers mining Litecoin, Bytecoin, Dashcoin, Quarkcoin and Vertcoin. It is immediately obvious that all five signatures follow the same pattern - periods of constant computation (the flat part of the curves, corresponding to hashing) punctuated by phases of exponentially decaying irregular code that executes when new blocks are found, the mining difficulty is changed, I/O is performed, etc. The only differences are in the magnitudes of the various HPC values, which can be attributed to different PoW algorithms having higher or lower operation counts. However, when looking at the combined signature of all HPCs, the similarities dwarf the differences, as shown in Fig. 5.

**Effects and Characterization of Noise:** So far, we have discussed the signatures of miners and various other applications that were obtained in a non-virtualized environment (OS). Although these signatures aptly present the similarities and differences between various miners and non-mining applications, they do not account for VM noise that would naturally be added when the aforementioned software are executed in a virtualized environment (guest OS) and profiled from the hypervisor. Since monitoring virtual machines is the primary role of MineGuard, we characterize this noise and study its effects on mining signatures.

By performing per feature noise profiling (on both OS and VM environments using all miner and cloud workloads) for all 26 HPCs (see Table 2), we found that roughly one-fourth of the counters show variation in values due to noise e.g., cycles, instructions, stalled-cycles-fronted, context switches etc. Figure 6A shows the process via which we arrived at the best fit, which was determined using the Akaike Information Criterion (AIC) [28]. The empirical data points (blue bars) represent the noise added as we moved from native to in-VM execution. The colored curves represent various distributions superimposed on top. As evident, a vivid pattern can be extracted based on the distribution and later used for error correction. Similarly, Fig. 6B shows the probability density functions for a few HPC counters. The best fit distributions in the depicted cases were *Nakagami* (cycles, stalled-cycles-frontend) and *Burr* (instructions, stalled-cycles-backend)

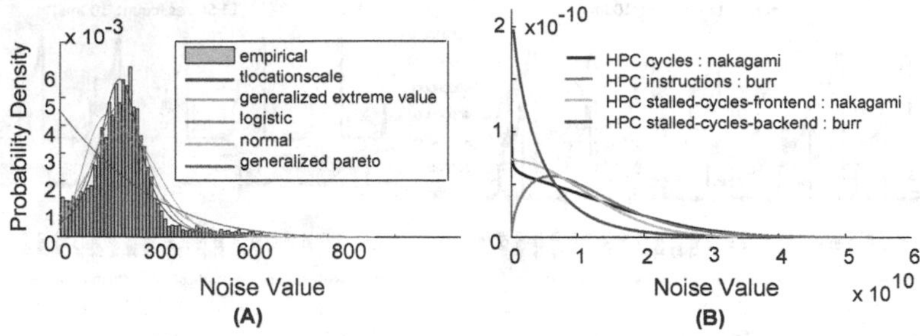


**Fig. 6.** **(A)** The fitting process via which we arrive at the final best fit distribution ($t$Location-Scale) for the context switch counter (ID 10). **(B)** Noise distribution for number of instructions counter (ID 2). The best fit distribution in this case is Burr.

distributions. Other HPCs, such as context switches, followed the $t$Location-Scale distribution. We found that three-fourths of the counters have negligible change to their values or patterns when we move from OS to VM. This fact justifies our choice of HPCs for MineGuard given that virtualization has limited impact on HPCs. Furthermore, if necessary, the discovered distributions can be factored into the signatures to develop error-corrected profiles for even more robust and accurate signatures.

To visually demonstrate how this noise distorts signatures, we present graphs for native vs in-VM execution of miners in Fig. 7A. The graph depicts the values of the L1 Loads counter. The curves have become more jagged and noisy as the system processes of the guest OS influence counter values, but their involvement results in a *minimal degradation* of the signature. For example, the peaks and troughs can still be clearly seen. Similarly, the slopes are unchanged and the noisy plateaus are still flat, preserving the consistent behavior of miners. All this follows from the fact that most HPCs do not suffer from virtualization-induced noise as shown above and maintain unique patterns and characteristics associated with mining.

**MineGuard Under an Active Adversary:** In an attempt to throw off MineGuard, a clever attacker could selectively create noise in the HPCs by running computations in parallel that influence counters not involved in mining. This would artificially inflate the values and modify patterns of certain HPCs that are irrelevant to the mining signature and appear as a benign workload to the classifier. To check the effectiveness of this scheme we performed an experiment with Litecoin where we modified the miner's code to run a computation in parallel that predominantly affects the set of mining-orthogonal counters (HPCs not showing significance use during mining). We measured how increasing the number of threads for the extra computation negatively impacts the total hash rate along with the corresponding reduction in MineGuard's detection accuracy. Figure 7B captures this relationship for 100 different runs of the aforementioned experiment. As expected, increasing the number of threads for the camouflaging computation severely degrades the hash rate (base hash rate is approximately

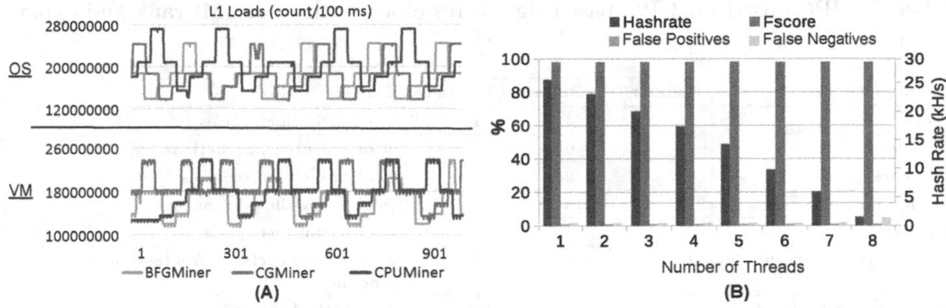


**Fig. 7.** **(A)** Effect of virtualization-induced noise on L1 Loads for various miners all mining for Bitcoin. The x axis shows time in increments of 100 ms. **(B)** Degradation of mining hash rate as the number of masking threads is increased. The hash rate falls consistently while the detection rate remains constant throughout, with only a slight increase in false negatives as 8 threads are used.

30 kH/s). However, it has very little impact on the detection rate meaning that the exercise would not be of benefit to the attacker. Granted, the experiment covers only a small subset of the overall computation space available to the attacker, we still feel that the impact suffered by the hash rate will be much more severe compared to the hit taken by the classifier in nearly all cases.

**Feature (Counter) Selection:** We now present a formal approach to feature (counter) selection to determine the importance of each counter, both by itself and in relation to other counters. When looking at each counter individually, we use mutual information to determine its importance. The mutual information (MI) of two random variables is a measure of the mutual dependence between the two variables. More specifically, it quantifies the "amount of information" (in units such as bits or entropy) one random variable contributes to generating a unique signature for the miner. When looking at multiple features together, their importance as a whole is represented by joint mutual information (JMI), a measure of the features' combined entropy. JMI can then be used to rank features from most important to least important. In turn, the ranking can be used to choose the minimum number of features that provide the best classification accuracy.

Table 2 lists the 26 different counters that were available on our system. To obtain MI and JMI for each counter, we used FEAST, an open source toolbox for feature selection algorithms [31]. The entropy (MI) of all 26 counters, both in an OS setting and in a VM setting, is shown in Fig. 8. It can be seen that features can be broadly divided into three categories. First, certain features like feature ID 1 (clock cycles), 5 (bus cycles) and 8 (task clock) hold a significant amount of information in both OS and VM environments. Second, features like feature ID 9 (page faults) and 10 (context switches) contribute negligibly to the classification process in both environments. Finally, the remaining features provide varying amounts of information depending upon the environment. While

**Table 2.** HPCs used for CPU-based signatures along with their JMI rank and explanation.

| Name of counter | Counter ID | OS rank | VM rank | Explanation |
|---|---|---|---|---|
| cycles | 1 | 4 | 4 | # of CPU clock cycles |
| instructions | 2 | 6 | 6 | # of executed instructions |
| branches | 3 | 2 | 19 | # of branch instructions |
| branch-misses | 4 | 16 | 15 | # of mispredicted branches |
| bus-cycles | 5 | 8 | 1 | # of useful bus cycles |
| stalled-cycles-frontend | 6 | 1 | 5 | # of stalled cycles in frontend of pipeline |
| stalled-cycles-backend | 7 | 11 | 16 | # of stalled cycles in backend of pipeline |
| task-clock | 8 | 3 | 3 | CPU time in milliseconds |
| page-faults | 9 | 26 | 26 | # of page faults |
| context-switches | 10 | 24 | 24 | # of context switches |
| cpu-migrations | 11 | 25 | 25 | # of migrations of profiled app |
| L1-dcache-loads | 12 | 13 | 14 | # of loads at L1 data cache |
| L1-dcache-load-misses | 13 | 21 | 13 | # of load misses at L1 data cache |
| L1-dcache-stores | 14 | 7 | 7 | # of stores at L1 data cache |
| L1-dcache-store-misses | 15 | 14 | 8 | # of store misses at L1 data cache |
| L1-dcache-prefetch-misses | 16 | 18 | 17 | # of misses at L1 cache that did not benefit from prefetching |
| L1-icache-load-misses | 17 | 15 | 10 | # of instruction fetches missed in the L1 instruction cache |
| LLC-loads | 18 | 12 | 11 | # of loads at the Last Level Cache |
| LLC-stores | 19 | 20 | 2 | # of loads that missed in the data TLB |
| LLC-prefetches | 20 | 9 | 20 | # of stores that queried the data TLB |
| dTLB-loads | 21 | 5 | 12 | # of stores at the Last Level Cache |
| dTLB-load-misses | 22 | 17 | 21 | # of prefetches at the Last Level Cache |
| dTLB-stores | 23 | 10 | 9 | # of loads that queried the data TLB |
| dTLB-store-misses | 24 | 23 | 22 | # of stores that missed in the data TLB |
| iTLB-loads | 25 | 19 | 23 | # of instruction fetches that queried the instruction TLB |
| iTLB-load-misses | 26 | 22 | 18 | # of instruction fetches that missed in the instruction TLB |

the general trends are the same in both environments, the differences between the two graphs present the importance of performing feature selection for each environment.

We present feature ranking results for both OS and VM environments based on JMI in Table 2. Feature rankings mimic the patterns observed in MI - certain features like 2 (instructions) do not change rank while others like 3 (branches) change rank significantly. Another interesting observation is that system level events like page faults and context switches have a low rank while purely hardware-based events like loads and stores are ranked highly in both scenarios.

**Classification Accuracy:** We now present results for MineGuard's miner detection performance in both closed and open world setting. A **closed world setting** is a scenario in which every cryptocurrency that MineGuard can be

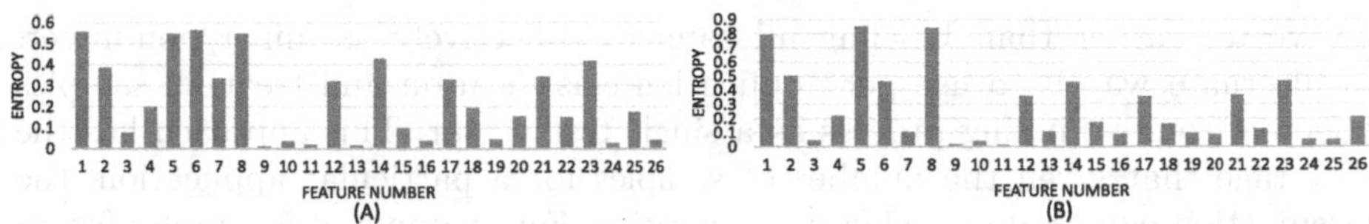


**Fig. 8.** The mutual information (entropy) contained within each hardware performance counter for **(A)** an OS environment, **(B)** a VM environment.

requested to detect is a part of the signature database. The test sample may vary from the signatures stored in the database but as we have previously shown, miners have unique and consistent signatures, increasing the likelihood if the test sample is from a miner, it will be matched to a miner in the signature database.

**Table 3.** Classification results for three different operating environments in a closed world setting. Each result's 95% confidence interval is written in brackets.

| Closed world scenario | F-score (CI) | False positives (CI) | False negatives (CI) |
|---|---|---|---|
| OS-Level | 99.69% (0.13%) | 0.22% (0.11%) | 0.29% (0.25%) |
| VM-Level | 99.69% (0.17%) | 0.27% (0.14%) | 0.26% (0.18%) |
| VM-Interference | 99.15% (0.11%) | 2.12% (0.29%) | 0.04% (0.03%) |
| Open world scenario | F-score (CI) | False positives (CI) | False negatives (CI) |
| OS-Level | 94.91% (1.02%) | 4.50% (1.13%) | 2.58% (1.64%) |
| VM-Level | 93.58% (1.33%) | 5.63% (1.61%) | 4.52% (2.41%) |
| VM-Interference | 95.82% (0.86%) | 6.77% (1.45%) | 2.53% (1.54%) |

Table 3 shows our results for this scenario where all values are reported after 100 runs. Since MineGuard has been trained on every cryptocurrency in the test set, it achieves an exceptionally high miner detection accuracy. It achieves ≈99.5% accuracy with a false positive rate (FPR) of 0.22% and false negative rate (FNR) of 0.29% when classifying miners running solely in either the OS and VM setting. *This equates to near-perfect miner detection and implies that if a known cryptocurrency is being mined in an OS or a VM, MineGuard will detect it almost every time.* When classifying miners running with other applications, the average *F-score* drops to 99.15% and FPR increases to 2.12%, while FNR remains at ≈0%. Even in an **open world setting**, where all test signatures are unseen (i.e., miners in the test set are unknown to the classifiers), MineGuard still achieves accuracy ≈95% for all three cases. Though the results are slightly worse than a closed world setting, they are still satisfactory overall. Furthermore, as we explain in Sect. 7, unseen signatures are rare as zero-day coins are an unlikely scenario.

The results shown in Table 3, have been computed on a per sample basis. This means that the classifier treats each 2 s sample of HPC values as an independent test vector rather than labeling all samples collectively as miner/non-miner. An alternate way is to use per application classification and treat all samples collected from a running process as a single test vector. This approach has the advantage that given the number of samples for a particular application, the classification can be done using various ratios. For example, if 5 samples for an application are available, if one is categorized as miner the entire application is labeled as a miner. Similarly, we can use a scheme where all samples need to be classified as a miner or use a simple majority rule (3 out of 5 classified as miner then app is miner). In each case, the corresponding F-score, FPR and FNR would be different. In Table 4, we present open world results for a simple majority scheme (though other settings can also be used such as classification based on 33% match or 75% match etc.) using per application testing.

**Table 4.** Classification results for three different operating environments in a open world setting when all samples are treated collectively (per application processing).

| Open world scenario | F-score (CI) | False positives (CI) | False negatives (CI) |
|---|---|---|---|
| OS-Level | 93.85% (2.68%) | 0.0% (0.0%) | 9.70% (3.77%) |
| VM-Level | 91.67% (3.16%) | 0.0% (0.0%) | 16.33% (5.83%) |
| VM-Interference | 96.32% (1.75%) | 0.0% (0.0%) | 7.99% (4.10%) |

The results show that the F-score is still high. The corresponding FPRs for our simple majority scheme are zero in all cases, which eliminates the primary concern in our setting as legitimate tenants would rarely be flagged or shut down. The reason for the 0% FPR is that previously, we were classifying each 2 s HPC sample individually. In such a scenario there is a possibility that a particular sample belonging to a non-miner exhibits HPC values matching those of a miner (perhaps due to a hashing intensive phase in the execution). However, since now we're looking at all samples of a single application collectively, the chances of all samples being hashing intensive (or even a majority of them) for a non-miner app are rare and hence the 0% FPR. The corresponding FNRs are a bit high, however this is less of a concern for the following reasons. First, since mining is commonly a long-term activity the attacker will eventually get flagged in a subsequent scan even if he evades the classifier once or twice. Second, if the attacker uses multiple VMs to form a personal mining pool, then with high likelihood one of their VMs will get flagged (even if other VMs successfully evade the classifier), which would trigger MineGuard to immediately scan all other VMs that are part of the same deployment again and if more VMs are caught, the cloud provider can do a more comprehensive check of the entire deployment using VMI or other more invasive tools.

Taken collectively, these results indicate that MineGuard is extremely adept at identifying miners running in any operating environment. Even in the worse case of detecting miners running in noisy environments, it achieves very high accuracy.

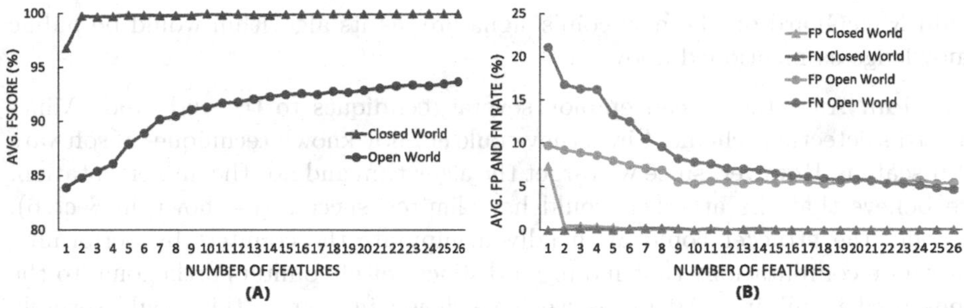


**Fig. 9.** Accuracy of miner classification in a VM environment, in terms of **(A)** average *F-score*, **(B)** average false positive rate and average false negative rate, as the number of features is increased.

**Effect of Signature Size on Accuracy:** Figure 9 captures the relationship between the size of the signature (number of top counters used) and the accuracy of detection in a VM environment for both open and closed world settings. As shown in Fig. 9A, for the closed world scenario (triangles) even when only 2 counters are used, we achieve an average *F-score* above 99.5%, an average false positive rate (FPR) below 0.5% and an average false negative rate (FNR) of approximately 0, shown in Fig. 9B. This implies that MineGuard can actually work with very small signature footprints speeding up all processes from profiling to matching. Similarly, in the open world case (circles) with only 3 counters the average F-score is around 85% and jumps to 90% if we consider the top 7 counters. Increasing the size further brings marginal increases that ultimately take the detection rate close to 95% for all 26 counters. An opposite downward trend is observed in the average values of FP and FN for the open world case as shown in Fig. 9B, with the rates declining all the way to roughly 5% when the entire vector of HPCs is used. These numbers might appear a bit high, but as we argue in Sect. 7 the open world case is highly unlikely as unseen mining algorithms are an extremely rare possibility.

## 7 Discussion

We discuss a few aspects of our work in this section and explore potential limitations.

**Custom or Zero-Day Cryptocurrency:** Is MineGuard vulnerable to zero-day or custom coins? We believe it is not. By definition, zero-day or custom coins do not exist because for a coin to have any dollar value, it first needs to have a known PoW algorithm, needs to be recognized by the cryptocommunity as mathematically sound and has to be adopted at a moderate-to-large scale for the core network to exist. Therefore, the first time a new piece of malware for some new coin makes an appearance in the wild, it would already be well-known in the cryptocurrency community, giving cloud vendors enough time to train MineGuard on the new coin's signature, as its algorithm would be public knowledge as mentioned above.

**Evasion:** An attacker can employ several techniques to try and evade MineGuard's detection scheme. First, they could employ known techniques of software obfuscation. However, since we target the algorithm and not the implementation, we believe that the attacker would have limited success (as shown in Sect. 6). Second, the attacker could artificially manipulate the counters by performing alternate computations that modify a distinct set of counters orthogonal to the ones used in mining. Again, as we have shown in Sect. 6, this would severely penalize the hash rate of the attacker while having very limited impact on his chances of evading MineGuard. Thirdly, the attacker could attempt to stay under the radar and mine at an extremely low hash rate. Theoretically, this is a limitation since the attacker can evade MineGuard by sticking to low hash rates. However, we argue that the whole exercise becomes non-profitable for the attacker and nullifies the whole point of mining on clouds. Furthermore, low hash rates eliminate the original problem of resource abuse making it less of a nuisance. Finally, the attacker could try to determine when the VM is being profiled by MineGuard and stop mining temporarily. However, there are numerous issues with this evasion scheme. First, since there is no measurable profiling overhead, it is hard for an adversary to tell if their VM is being profiled. Second, instead of monitoring the VMs in a round-robin fashion, the hypervisor can monitor the VMs randomly, making it impossible to predict when a VM would be profiled.

**Coin Diversity:** We could not perform analysis on all cryptocurrencies available in the market and chose to work with a popular subset (choosing coins with distinct algorithms and ignoring those which were forks of popular coins) as shown in Table 1. Additionally, with the above restriction in mind we selected coins that collectively comprise the largest share of market cap. Also, we justify our choice by highlighting that most cryptocurrency exchanges, like Kraken [23], only deal with the top 25–30 cryptocurrencies, as other altcoins have exceptionally low dollar value and profit margins from transactions are very low [22]. Moreover, documented cases of cryptocurrency Trojans have been mostly limited to the top 10–15 coins [12,13,16,21,24]. Hence, attackers avoid wasting precious hashes on less valuable coins, which is why we chose our subset of popularly used coins. Nevertheless, we list this as a limitation, since the possibility, however minute, of an excluded coin's signature matching a cloud app still remains.

## 8 Related Work

Cloud abuse has become a hot topic of research. Recent efforts [40,52] have been geared towards developing a sound understanding of the problems and vulnerabilities inherent to clouds. Others have demonstrated novel ways of exploiting these vulnerabilities by building practical systems that are of value to attackers, such as file sharing applications [51], unlimited storage banks [43] and email-based storage overlays [48]. To mitigate these concerns, researchers have proposed various Virtual Machine Introspection (VMI) approaches [36,42,45]. However, some of these are voluntary and require user participation [30], which of course the attacker wants no part of, and others have a large overhead [41]. Furthermore, these VMI-based approaches are designed to observe the memory, disk and processor state of customers' VMs, which is a serious privacy concern given the sensitive nature of customer data.

A different yet related line of work attempts to describe the infrastructure and mechanism of mining botnets. Huang et al. [39] present a thorough investigation of mining ecosystems in the wild. They claim that mining is less profitable than other malicious activities, such as spamming or booter-renting (DDoS for hire), and should be used as a secondary monetizing scheme. However, we believe that it is unfair to compare mining profits with other monetizing activities as the price of coins varies substantially over time and as of this writing, the value of one Bitcoin is a $1000 (and rising) as opposed to $100 in 2013, which demonstrates that mining can generate an order of magnitude more revenue now. Furthermore, as mining uses an orthogonal set of resources (CPU/GPU and memory) compared to DDoS attacks (network), we postulate that botnet-herders should maximize their profits by running various resource-disjoint monetizing activities in parallel making a strong case for covert cryptomining. Indeed, Sophos Security presented evidence that mining botnets could potentially generate around $100,000 per day of profits for herders [8].

Finally, there has been much research on detecting generic malware using architectural and microarchitectural execution patterns, such as HPCs, with differing results. Demme et al. [35] built a system for detection of generic malware and demonstrate the feasibility of the design based on ARM (Android) and Intel (Linux) platforms. Other researchers [38,50,55] have also used low-level hardware features to promising success, furthering the work of Demme et al. In addition to generic malware, HPCs have also been successfully used to detect kernel-level rootkits [53], side-channel attacks [34], firmware modifications [54] etc. However, none of these previous works try to accommodate the noise introduced by virtualization, as we do in this work.

## 9 Conclusion

We present MineGuard, a userspace tool that prevents abuse of resources at the hands of hackers interested in mining cryptocurrencies on others' resources. Whether the mining operation is local (restricted to one VM) or being conducted in a pool of participating VMs, MineGuard can successfully detect and shutdown the illegitimate mining "ring". We empirically demonstrate that our design imposes negligible overhead to legitimate tenants and can detect mining in real-time with high precision. If multiple VMs are involved in mining, MineGuard can collaborate with other MineGuard instances to expose the entire footprint of the mining deployment. For detection, MineGuard uses signatures based on Hardware Performance Counters for both CPU and GPU-based miners. The fact that MineGuard runs on top of the hypervisor or the host OS prevents miners running inside the VMs from subverting it despite root access on the guest. We also account for the noise generated as a result of virtualization to provide error correction for our detection mechanisms. In the future, we plan to extend MineGuard to accurately detect other types of malwares in highly multiplexed and virtualized environments.

## References


1. Bitcoin Anonymizer TOR Wallet. https://torwallet.com/
2. CryptoNight. https://en.bitcoin.it/wiki/CryptoNight
3. CUDA Toolkit Documentation. https://tinyurl.com/z7bx3b3
4. Government employee caught mining using work supercomputer. https://tinyurl.com/mrpqffd
5. ABC employee caught mining for Bitcoins on company servers (2011). https://tinyurl.com/lxcujtx
6. Data Center Power and Cooling. CISCO White Paper (2011)
7. How to Get Rich on Bitcoin, By a System Administrator Who's Secretly Growing Them On His School's Computers (2011). https://tinyurl.com/lwx8rup
8. The ZeroAccess Botnet - Mining and Fraud for Massive Financial Gain (2012). https://tinyurl.com/ldgcfao
9. Online Thief Steals Amazon Account to Mine Litecoins in the Cloud (2013). https://tinyurl.com/mzpbype
10. Harvard Research Computing Resources Misused for Dogecoin Mining Operation (2014). https://tinyurl.com/n8pzvt6
11. How Hackers Hid a Money-Mining Botnet in the Clouds of Amazon and Others (2014). https://tinyurl.com/mowzx73
12. List of Major Bitcoin Heists, Thefts, Hacks, Scams, and Losses (2014). https://bitcointalk.org/index.php?topic=576337
13. Mobile Malware Mines Dogecoins and Litecoins for Bitcoin Payout (2014). https://tinyurl.com/q828blg
14. NAS device botnet mined $600,000 in Dogecoin over two months (2014). https://tinyurl.com/myglgoa
15. US Government Bans Professor for Mining Bitcoin with A Supercomputer (2014). https://tinyurl.com/k3ww4rp
16. Adobe Flash Player Exploit Could Be Used to Install BitCoinMiner Trojan (2015). https://tinyurl.com/lhxzloa
17. Cloud Mining Put to the Test- Is It Worth Your Money? (2015). https://tinyurl.com/zquylbo
18. Developer Hit with $6,500 AWS Bill from Visual Studio Bug (2015). https://tinyurl.com/zm3pzjq
19. Perf Tool Wiki (2015). https://tinyurl.com/2enxbko
20. Standard Performance Evaluation Corporation (2015). https://www.spec.org/benchmarks.html
21. Trojan, C.: A Grave Threat to BitCoin Wallets (2016). https://tinyurl.com/k73wdaq
22. Crypto-Currency Market Capitalizations (2016). https://coinmarketcap.com/
23. Kraken Bitcoin Exchange (2016). https://www.kraken.com/
24. Linux. Lady. 1 Trojan Infects Redis Servers and Mines for Cryptocurrency (2016). urlhttps://tinyurl.com/ka9ae4c

25. Randomized Decision Trees: A Fast C++ Implementation of Random Forests (2016). https://github.com/bjoern-andres/random-forest
26. Student uses university computers to mine Dogecoin (2016). https://tinyurl.com/lubeqct
27. Supplemental Terms and Conditions For Google Cloud Platform Free Trial (2017). https://tinyurl.com/ke5vs49
28. Akaike, H.: A new look at the statistical model identification. IEEE TAC 19 (1974)
29. Marosi, A.: Cryptomining malware on NAS servers (2016)
30. Baek, H.W., Srivastava, A., van der Merwe, J.E.: Cloudvmi: virtual machine introspection as a cloud service. In: 2014 IEEE International Conference on Cloud Engineering (2014)
31. Brown, G., Pocock, A.C., Zhao, M., Luján, M.: Conditional likelihood maximisation: a unifying framework for information theoretic feature selection. In: JMLR (2012)
32. Percival, C., Josefsson, S.: The Scrypt Password-Based Key Derivation Function. IETF (2012)
33. Che, S., et al.: Rodinia: A benchmark suite for heterogeneous computing. In: Proceedings of the 2009 IEEE International Symposium on Workload Characterization (2009)
34. Chiappetta, M., Savas, E., Yilmaz, C.: Real time detection of cache-based side-channel attacks using hardware performance counters. IACR Cryptol. ePrint Archive **2015**, 1034 (2015)
35. Demme, J., Maycock, M., Schmitz, J., Tang, A., Waksman, A., Sethumadhavan, S., Stolfo, S.J.: On the feasibility of online malware detection with performance counters. In: The 40th Annual ISCA (2013)
36. Dinaburg, A., Royal, P., Sharif, M.I., Lee, W.: Ether: malware analysis via hardware virtualization extensions. In: ACM CCS (2008)
37. Ferdman, M., Adileh, A., Koçberber, Y.O., Volos, S., Alisafaee, M., Jevdjic, D., Kaynak, C., Popescu, A.D., Ailamaki, A., Falsafi, B.: Clearing the clouds: a study of emerging scale-out workloads on modern hardware. In: ASPLOS (2012)
38. Garcia-Serrano, A.: Anomaly detection for malware identification using hardware performance counters. CoRR (2015)
39. Huang, D.Y., Dharmdasani, H., Meiklejohn, S., Dave, V., Grier, C., McCoy, D., Savage, S., Weaver, N., Snoeren, A.C., Levchenko, K.: Botcoin: monetizing stolen cycles. In: NDSS (2014)
40. Idziorek, J., Tannian, M.: Exploiting cloud utility models for profit and ruin. In: IEEE CLOUD (2011)
41. Jiang, X., Wang, X., Xu, D.: Stealthy malware detection and monitoring through VMM-based "out-of-the-box" semantic view reconstruction. ACM Trans. Inf. Syst. Secur. **13**(2), 12:1–12:28 (2010)
42. Lengyel, T.K., Neumann, J., Maresca, S., Payne, B.D., Kiayias, A.: Virtual machine introspection in a hybrid honeypot architecture. In: CSET (2012)
43. Mulazzani, M., Schrittwieser, S., Leithner, M., Huber, M., Weippl, E.R.: Dark clouds on the horizon: using cloud storage as attack vector and online slack space. In: 20th USENIX Security Symposium (2011)
44. National Science Foundation Office of Inspector General: SEMIANNUAL REPORT TO CONGRESS (2014)
45. Payne, B.D., Lee, W.: Secure and flexible monitoring of virtual machines. In: ACSAC (2007)
46. Sembrant, A.: Low Overhead Online Phase Predictor and Classifier. Master's thesis, UPPSALA UNIVERSITET (2011)

47. Sokolova, M., Lapalme, G.: A systematic analysis of performance measures for classification tasks. Inf. Process. Manage. **45**, 427–437 (2009)
48. Srinivasan, J., Wei, W., Ma, X., Yu, T.: EMFS: email-based personal cloud storage. In: NAS (2011)
49. Stratton, J.A., et al.: Parboil: A revised benchmark suite for scientific and commercial throughput computing. In: IMPACT Technical report (2012)
50. Tang, A., Sethumadhavan, S., Stolfo, S.J.: Unsupervised anomaly-based malware detection using hardware features. In: Stavrou, A., Bos, H., Portokalidis, G. (eds.) RAID 2014. LNCS, vol. 8688, pp. 109–129. Springer, Cham (2014). doi:10.1007/978-3-319-11379-1_6
51. Tinedo, R.G., Artigas, M.S., López, P.G.: Cloud-as-a-gift: effectively exploiting personal cloud free accounts via REST apis. In: IEEE CLOUD (2013)
52. Vaquero, L.M., Rodero-Merino, L., Morán, D.: Locking the sky: a survey on IaaS cloud security. Computing **91**(1), 93–118 (2011)
53. Wang, X., Karri, R.: Numchecker: detecting kernel control-flow modifying rootkits by using hardware performance counters. In: The 50th Annual DAC (2013)
54. Wang, X., Konstantinou, C., Maniatakos, M., Karri, R.: Confirm: Detecting firmware modifications in embedded systems using hardware performance counters. In: ICCAD (2015)
55. Yuan, L., Xing, W., Chen, H., Zang, B.: Security breaches as PMU deviation: detecting and identifying security attacks using performance counters. In: APSys (2011)

# BEADS: Automated Attack Discovery in OpenFlow-Based SDN Systems

Samuel Jero[1(✉)], Xiangyu Bu[1], Cristina Nita-Rotaru[2], Hamed Okhravi[3], Richard Skowyra[3], and Sonia Fahmy[1]

[1] Purdue University, West Lafayette, IN, USA
{sjero,bu1,fahmy}@purdue.edu
[2] Northeastern University, Boston, MA, USA
c.nitarotaru@neu.edu
[3] MIT Lincoln Laboratory, Lexington, MA, USA
{hamed.okhravi,richard.skowyra}@ll.mit.edu

**Abstract.** We create BEADS, a framework to automatically generate test scenarios and find attacks in SDN systems. The scenarios capture attacks caused by malicious switches that do not obey the OpenFlow protocol and malicious hosts that do not obey the ARP protocol. We generated and tested almost 19,000 scenarios that consist of sending malformed messages or not properly delivering them, and found 831 unique bugs across four well-known SDN controllers: Ryu, POX, Floodlight, and ONOS. We classify these bugs into 28 categories based on their impact; 10 of these categories are new, not previously reported. We demonstrate how an attacker can leverage several of these bugs by manually creating 4 representative attacks that impact high-level network goals such as availability and network topology.

## 1 Introduction

Software-defined networking (SDN) is an attractive alternative to traditional networking, offering benefits for large enterprise and data-center networks. In SDNs, the control and management of the network (*i.e.*, the control plane) is separated from the delivery of data to the destinations (*i.e.*, the data plane). Such a separation offers enhanced manageability, flexibility, and programmability to the network administrators, enabling them to perform better resource allocation, centralized monitoring, and dynamic network reconfiguration.

DISTRIBUTION STATEMENT A. Approved for public release: distribution unlimited. This material is based upon work supported by the Department of Defense under Air Force Contract No. FA8721-05-C-0002 and/or FA8702-15-D-0001. Any opinions, findings, conclusions or recommendations expressed in this material are those of the author(s) and do not necessarily reflect the views of the Department of Defense.

**Electronic supplementary material** The online version of this chapter (doi:10.1007/978-3-319-66332-6_14) contains supplementary material, which is available to authorized users.


M. Dacier et al. (Eds.): RAID 2017, LNCS 10453, pp. 311–333, 2017.
DOI: 10.1007/978-3-319-66332-6_14

SDN's benefits, however, come at a cost to security. The programmability and malleability of the network presents new attack surfaces. In addition to the network-based attacks applicable to traditional networks, new attack vectors are available to an attacker to maliciously impact the network functionality by manipulating, poisoning, or abusing the malleable network logic. For example, we show that ARP spoofing attacks have broader impact in SDNs because of the centralized control. In particular, many controllers maintain a centralized ARP cache and implement Proxy ARP to resolve ARP queries, making the impact of poisoning this cache much broader than in traditional networks.

Recent efforts at the intersection of SDN and security have focused on developing new languages for SDN programming, some of which offer formally verifiable guarantees [9,15,30,43], such as flow rule consistency [16,18,40]. Some work has focused on possible attacks from the data plane to control plane and vice versa [44]. Protocol-level attacks and corresponding defenses have also been studied [7,10,16,42]. Finally, the dynamism and agility offered by SDNs has been leveraged to build new defenses [11,13,25]. Several of these approaches have identified specific attacks in the context of SDNs [7,10,16,38,42,44]. These efforts highlight the need for systematic approaches to find attacks in SDNs.

In order to systematize OpenFlow testing, the Open Networking Foundation created conformance test documents for OpenFlow 1.0.1 [32] and 1.3.4 [34]. Following these documents, the SDN community started two projects, OFTest [8] and FLORENCE [29]. Both of them focus only on OpenFlow switches and consist of manually written tests. OFTest supports 478 manually written tests for OpenFlow 1.0–1.4, while FLORENCE supports 18 manually written tests for OpenFlow 1.3. Examples of tests performed are: `AllPortStats`, which "Verif[ies] [that] all port stats are properly retrieved" for OFTest and `Port Range test` to "Verify that the switch rejects the use of ports that are greater than OFPP_MAX and are not part of the reserved ports" for FLORENCE.

Both OFTest and FLORENCE focus on testing how well a switch conforms to the OpenFlow specification. However, OpenFlow is a configuration protocol; it specifies *how* a controller instructs a switch to do something, but not *what* the controller should tell the switch to do. As a result, many bugs and attacks on SDNs arise from incorrect assumptions in the controller software about the switches. Frameworks like OFTest and FLORENCE that exclude the controller from the testing process are unable to find such issues.

Further, conformance testing is not sufficient to detect attacks. In fact, the Open Flow Foundation conformance testing documents explicitly state: *"This document does not include requirements or test procedures to validate security, interoperability or performance."* Previous work on automated attack finding on communication protocols has been confined to distributed systems [23] and transport protocols [12] which are less complex than SDN systems.

In this work, we develop BEADS, a framework to automatically and systematically test SDN systems for attacks resulting from malicious switches and malicious hosts. Our framework automatically generates and tests thousands of scenarios involving malicious switches that do not obey the OpenFlow protocol and malicious hosts that do not obey the ARP protocol. BEADS combines known techniques such as Byzantine fault injection, semantically-aware testcase generation, and black box testing to test whole SDN systems comprising OpenFlow switches, controllers, and hosts. As such it differs from existing SDN testing tools in the following aspects: (1) it supports malicious (Byzantine) participants – hosts and switches; (2) it does not require access to the code of the switch or controller; (3) it targets attacks at a deeper layer than simple parsing (that can be tested using simple random fuzzers); (4) it achieves higher coverage by using message grammar and *semantically-aware* test case generation; (5) it can test controller algorithms like routing, topology detection, and flow rule management by also including the controller in its test cases; (6) it makes better use of resources by performing targeted and preferential search. BEADS is publicly available at https://github.com/samueljero/BEADS.

Using BEADS, we identify bugs that trigger error messages, network topology or reachability changes, or increased load. We then show that these bugs can be exploited with damaging impacts on SDN networks. Our results show the importance of malicious testing for SDNs as well as the practicality of blackbox testing for such systems. Our contributions are:

- We create BEADS, a framework to automatically find malicious switch- and host-level attacks. BEADS combines network emulation with software switches and real SDN controllers running in a virtualized environment. It takes a blackbox approach to the SDN switches and controller and does not require access to the source code of either. Attack scenarios are automatically generated based on message grammar and the protocol semantics associated with special fields (such as port). BEADS uses four criteria to detect bugs: error messages, network topology changes, reachability changes, and controller or switch load.
- We use BEADS to automatically test almost 19,000 scenarios, and find 831 unique bugs across four well-known SDN controllers: Ryu [45], POX [27], ONOS [5], and Floodlight [39]. We classify these bugs into 28 categories based on their impact; 10 of these categories have not been previously reported. Outcomes include preventing the installation of flow rules network-wide, periodic switch disconnections, inducing packet loss in the data plane, denial of service against the controller, and removing network links.
- We construct and implement 4 representative attack scenarios using several bugs we identified to break high-level network goals such as availability, reachability, and network connectivity. The scenarios are (1) TLS Man-in-the-Middle, (2) Web Server Impersonation, (3) Breaking Network Quarantine, and (4) Deniable Denial of Service. We demonstrate the feasibility of these attack scenarios on real SDN controllers.
- We have notified the SDN vendors of bugs we found. Ryu has issued a patch (CD2,CD3 in Table 2) while ONOS has confirmed that the latest version is no longer impacted (EP1 in Table 2).

**Roadmap.** Section 2 specifies the threat models. Section 3 describes the design of BEADS. Section 4 discusses the bugs we found and presents our attack demonstrations. Section 5 discusses some limitations of BEADS while Sect. 6 summarizes related work and Sect. 7 concludes the paper.

## 2 Threat Model

We consider a threat model where the attacker can control compromised SDN switches or end-hosts connected to the SDN. We consider malicious switches because prior work has shown that many SDN switches can be easily compromised due to running operating systems with poor security defaults, out of date software, and minimal updates [35,36] and, once compromised, they can influence the entire control plane. Note that if communication is not conducted over secure channels, a man-in-the-middle attacker can control otherwise uncompromised switches and hosts. We do not consider malicious controllers.

*Malicious Switches.* Attackers who have compromised an OpenFlow switch can confuse SDN controllers via malicious OpenFlow messages. This ability is unique to SDNs and can confuse the controller about the network topology and the locations of target hosts [7,10]. Additionally, a malicious OpenFlow switch can mount a DoS attack against the controller by sending OpenFlow messages, spoofed or legitimate, at a very high rate. Some controllers enforce per-switch OpenFlow rate limits in an attempt to mitigate this type of attack [7]. Recent work has shown that OpenFlow switches are extremely vulnerable to attackers, running old, unsecured software versions with default/hidden administrator accounts, out of date software, and minimal updates [35,36].

Our analysis focuses on how malicious switches can disrupt or degrade *other* parts of the network (*e.g.,* QoS on other switches or making the controller redirect distant traffic through a compromised switch) via the control-plane. Thus, we do not consider pure data-plane attacks (*e.g.,* dropping packets). We model malicious switches as having the following basic capabilities with respect to OpenFlow messages between the switch and controller:

**Drop (percentage).** This action drops a particular type of OpenFlow message with a given probability specified as a parameter, for example `barrier_request drop 20`. This emulates a malicious switch that does not send these messages or ignores them after receiving them.

**Duplicate (times).** This action duplicates a particular type of OpenFlow message a certain number of times given as a parameter. For example `barrier_reply duplicate 5` means the malicious switch duplicates this messages 5 times.

**Delay (msec).** This action delays a particular type of OpenFlow message by a given number of milliseconds, emulating a malicious switch that delays processing a request or taking some action; for example, `of_hello delay 1000`.

**Change (field, value).** This action modifies a particular field of a particular type of OpenFlow message with a particular value. Modifications supported include setting a particular value as well as adding or subtracting a constant. We select the modification values to be likely to trigger problems based on the field type. This typically includes values like 0, minimum field value, and maximum field value. This basic strategy corresponds to a malicious switch that performs a different action or returns different information than that requested by the controller. Examples of this action include `flow_add change priority 42` or `flow_removed change reason 12`.

*Malicious Local Hosts.* Attackers who have compromised a host that is directly connected to an SDN, like a server or a user workstation, can launch attacks to confuse the SDN controller about the network topology and the location of target hosts, in order to hijack a target host or traffic of interest [7,10]. These are primarily attacks that target the Address Resolution Protocol (ARP) [37] since ARP is one of the few protocols that hosts can use to manipulate the SDN control plane. Prior work has also pointed out that hosts can inject or tunnel LLDP packets [7,10]. However, we need not separately consider such hosts because they appear to the network as malicious switches, which we already consider.

For ARP, SDN has brought back known vulnerabilities because, while traditional networks have deployed defenses against ARP spoofing, these defenses have not been adapted for SDNs. Unlike traditional network switches that maintain their own local ARP tables, operate on L2/L3 networks, and can be checked to prevent ARP poisoning attacks, SDN switches consist of a programmable flow table and leave the SDN controllers to check for ARP corruption. Such controllers do not currently implement ARP spoofing defenses. Moreover, some controllers (including POX and ONOS) maintain a centralized ARP cache and implement Proxy ARP to resolve ARP queries. This creates a single, centralized ARP cache for the entire network. Poisoning this cache has broader network-wide impact rather than limited subnetwork-wide impact as in traditional networks.

We model malicious or compromised local hosts as follows:

**ARP-location-injection (victim-MAC, victim-IP).** The malicious host injects ARP packets with the spoofed Ethernet source address of the victim to make the controller believe that the victim is at the same port as the attacker. Example: `ARP-location-injection 00:00:00:00:00:04 10.0.0.4`.

**ARP-map-injection (attacker-MAC, victim-IP).** The malicious host injects ARP packets that indicate a mapping between the victim's IP and the attacker's MAC. This disrupts the IP-to-MAC mapping, and leads the controller to believe that the attacker has the victim's IP address. An example of this attack would be `ARP-map-injection 00:00:00:00:00:01 10.0.0.4`.

## 3 BEADS Design and Implementation

We first describe the design principles behind BEADS and then provide more details about each component.

### 3.1 Design Goals

There are several guiding principles behind BEADS: automation of attack generation and attack search, realism by testing real-world implementations of complete SDN systems generalizable to many different implementations independent of language and operating system, reproducibility of the results, high coverage of test scenarios, efficient use of resources, and last but not least, focus on *security* (rather than conformance) by supporting malicious switches and hosts.

Our main goal is to test real-world implementations of complete SDN systems. This requires including switches, controllers, and hosts in our tests to be able to capture their interplay. Similarly, our tests would ideally include the physical hardware and operating systems running the various system nodes, the production network connecting the physical hardware, and the actual application binaries running on the operating systems. However, using physical hardware to test all possible configurations and operating systems is not scalable and prohibitively expensive. We address this challenge by choosing a virtualized environment that supports different operating systems and languages, and network emulation using Mininet [21] that enables strong control over the network, while still being close enough to a real-world installation.

Another design goal is to run actual implementations of the system of interest without discriminating based on programming language, compiler, toolkit, or target operating system, and without imposing restrictions solely for visibility into algorithmic behavior. Ideally, we should use the same implementation that will be deployed. We achieve this goal by using a *proxy* to create the behavior of the malicious switch. Malicious host behavior is injected directly into the real data-plane, similarly enabling the use of unmodified switches and controllers.

Finally, a major goal for our test case generation is to create meaningful, semantically-aware test cases that can go beyond testing parsers. One simple method to generate an attack strategy is to use random fuzzing where the entire packet or some of its fields are replaced with random strings. While random fuzzing has been used successfully to test API inputs, it would have a low success rate for OpenFlow messages. OpenFlow messages are complex data structures involving many layers of nested objects as well as other syntactic and semantic dependencies. Although any packet can be represented as a bit string, the majority of bit strings are not valid OpenFlow messages. Hence, the majority of test cases generated by random fuzzing only test the OpenFlow message parser while the attacks we are interested in lie at a much deeper layer, in the algorithms creating and processing those messages. Basic knowledge of the packet format or fields helps generate valid, meaningful messages by satisfying the syntactic requirement. However, an ideal testing tool should also consider the semantic meaning of different packet fields. For example, it should treat a field representing a switch port number differently from a field representing an IP address, and treat the switch port number differently from the length of an embedded structure. This approach enables testing on semantically meaningful, yet problematic values for a field—for example IP addresses actually in the network—and provides a means for tuning the testing to focus on particular types or locations of attacks. Similarly, our test generation creates tests with malicious hosts and switches at multiple locations in our test topology to ensure that our results are general and not tied to a specific topology.

## 3.2 Design Details

Our automated attack discovery platform, BEADS, is depicted in Fig. 1. We separate the attack strategy generation functionality controlled by a *Coordinator* from the testing of a strategy in an SDN system controlled by an *Execution Manager* (*Manager* for short). Several managers can run in parallel under the reign of one coordinator. The coordinator has three roles: generate attack strategies, assign those strategies to different managers for testing, and receive feedback about the execution of those strategies and their results. The attack strategies are generated based on the format of the messages and on the network topology in order to choose what entity (host or switch) will behave maliciously. The coordinator generates strategies for both malicious host and malicious switch behavior and decides how to interleave them. The coordinator uses feedback from the execution and testing of prior strategies for future strategy generation.

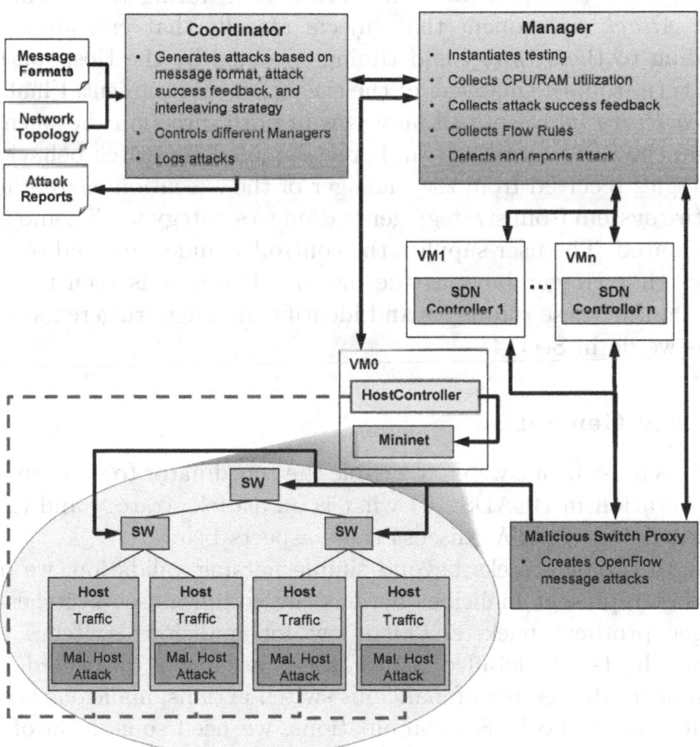


**Fig. 1.** BEADS framework design

The (execution) manager controls the execution environment for a set of attack strategy tests. This environment consists of an SDN, with a given topology, a specified placement and type of attackers (hosts and/or switches), as well as a list of attack strategies and a mechanism for interleaving host and switch strategies. BEADS combines network emulation using software switches and emulated hosts with real SDN controllers running in a virtualized environment. We select Mininet for emulation because it offers the flexibility to test different network topologies and traffic patterns while providing attack isolation and increased reproducibility. Mininet exhibits high fidelity through the use of real network stacks, software switches, and real traffic. We leverage virtualization to run a wide range of SDN controllers independent of required operating systems, libraries, or system configurations. BEADS does not require access to the source code of the OpenFlow implementation in the switch or controller.

The manager uses Mininet to create an emulated data-plane network consisting of SDN switches and emulated hosts capable of both generating normal network traffic and injecting host-based attacks. This network is controlled using OpenFlow by one or several controllers running on a separate virtual machine, as depicted in Fig. 1. A *Host Controller* running on the same virtual machine as Mininet controls the hosts connected to the testing network. Each host has a *Traffic* component that generates the traffic used during testing, and a *Malicious Host Attack* component that injects attacks that emulate a malicious host according to the strategy and timing specified by the HostController and received in turn from the manager of the execution environment. Finally, a *Malicious Switch Proxy* intercepts all messages in both directions between the SDN switches and the SDN controllers and creates malicious switch behavior according to strategies received from the manager of the execution environment.

The entire system from strategy generation to strategy testing and bug detection is automated. The user supplies the controller under test and receives a list of strategies that trigger bugs as the output. The user is then responsible to manually examine these strategies and identify the bugs triggered and any fixes required, as we do in Sect. 4.

### 3.3 Strategy Generation

Two questions must be answered to enable the coordinator to perform automatic strategy generation in BEADS: (1) what is an attack strategy and (2) when to inject an attack strategy. We discuss these aspects below.

In order to target attacks beyond simple parsing validation, we use attack strategies that represent malicious actions (by compromised switches or hosts) which target protocol packets: OpenFlow for malicious switches and ARP for malicious hosts. A detailed list of these actions is presented in Sect. 2. BEADS supports the testing of malicious switch actions, malicious host actions, and combinations of both. For combinations, we need some form of coordination between malicious host and malicious switch actions, as they are launched from independent components, not necessarily connected. We currently provide a basic level of coordination between these strategies based on time relative to the start of each test; *i.e.*, we specify the time at which different malicious switch and malicious host actions occur relative to the start of the test.

The injection points differ for malicious hosts and malicious switches. In the case of malicious switches, the attack is executed by a malicious proxy which has the ability to modify or affect the delivery of OpenFlow messages as discussed in Sect. 2. At the start of each test we define a set of one or more malicious switches. For these switches, we then use send-based attack injection; *i.e.*, when the proxy receives an OpenFlow message to/from these switches, it takes any actions relevant to that message type, and forwards the message to its destination. To curtail state space explosion, we only consider strategies where the same action is applied to every message of a given type. These strategies manipulate the delivery or fields of OpenFlow messages based on their message type and individual message fields. For instance, a strategy may be to duplicate `features_reply` messages 10 times or to modify the `in_port` field of a `packet_out` message to 7. Our malicious proxy supports all manipulations discussed in Sect. 2, including dropping, duplicating, and delaying messages based on message type, as well as modifying message field values based on message type.

Our testing applies this procedure to a list of strategies that we automatically generate based on the OpenFlow message formats and semantics associated with their fields. This list of strategies includes our message delivery attacks for each message type and manipulations of each field in each message type. The field values we use in our field manipulations are based on the field type, and are chosen to be likely to cause unexpected behavior. This includes setting values to zero, and the minimum and maximum values that the field can handle. For fields representing switch ports, we also consider all real switch ports as well as OpenFlow virtual ports like `CONTROLLER`. When selecting strategies to test, we only consider strategies for message types that we observe actually occurring in communication between the switch and controller. Because controllers usually do not use all the messages detailed in the OpenFlow specification, this dramatically reduces the number of strategies we need to test.

For malicious hosts, we consider the injection of ARP packets as discussed in Sect. 2. We again define a list of malicious hosts at the start of each test. We use time-based attack injection with these malicious hosts, where we launch attacks for a few seconds at different times during each test. The exact time of attack, duration, and frequency of packet injection are configurable.

This automatic strategy generation enables us to quickly and easily generate tens of thousands of strategies in a manner that considers both message structure and protocol semantics. In contrast, DELTA [24] uses blind fuzzing, supplemented with a few manual tests. It is able to generate an unbounded number of strategies, but considers neither message structure nor protocol semantics. OFTest and FLORENCE make no attempt at strategy generation and rely on a manually developed set of tests. As a result, FLORENCE only tests 18 different scenarios and OFTest only covers a few hundred. BEADS is able to generate several orders of magnitude more tests in a fraction of the time. While number of test cases does not perfectly correspond with amount of search space covered, this does strongly suggest that BEADS can cover a much larger portion of the search space, especially in combination with the new attacks that we find.

### 3.4 Impact Assessment

Once we have executed a strategy, we automatically determine the impact based on a variety of system and network characteristics. Our framework collects several outputs and, at the end of each test, checks them for conditions indicating a deviation from normal behavior and a possible vulnerability. If such conditions are detected, we automatically schedule a re-test of the strategy to make sure that the failure is repeatable. If it is, we declare this strategy to be a vulnerability.

We use four methods to determine if a tested strategy leads to unexpected behavior: (1) OpenFlow error messages, (2) network configuration changes, (3) network reachability failures, and (4) controller or switch resource usage.

Since BEADS aims to identify actions that are the most damaging to the network, we gradually filter actions based on their impact. First, we consider the error messages, then the static network state, then the network connectivity, and finally the controller and switch resource usage. Below we provide more details about each of these and the rationale for considering them.

**OpenFlow Error Messages.** One mechanism we use to observe protocol deviation is monitoring the OpenFlow connections for error messages. Error messages are sent when an OpenFlow device (switch or controller) fails to parse an OpenFlow message or the message indicates an invalid or unsupported option. These messages indicate an anomalous condition in the OpenFlow connection, and that some desired change to the network was not performed.

**Network State.** One of the most powerful indicators of undesirable changes in the network are changes in the network state, including changes to routing, access control lists (ACLs), and priorities of flows in the network. We define *network state* as the state of the flow rules at each switch. The manager collects the flow rules from all switches at the end of each test, canonicalizes them, and compares them to reference flow rules from a benign run.

Unfortunately, the network state is not completely deterministic. Part of our canonicalization process filters out known non-deterministic elements (timestamps, etc.). Additionally, we use multiple benign test runs to detect other non-deterministic elements and filter them out. Note that without detailed knowledge of the application algorithms the SDN controller has implemented we cannot decide whether a given non-deterministic rule is correct.

**Reachability.** Another protocol deviation indicator we use is pair-wise connectivity tests. In particular, our test system uses pair-wise ICMP pings and `iperf` to verify that all hosts are reachable from all other hosts. This is extremely effective in detecting spoofing attacks and attacks on connectivity. It also detects many manipulations of flow rules that our network state detection mechanism cannot detect due to non-determinism.

**Controller or Switch Resource Usage.** The final protocol deviation indicator we use is monitoring the RAM and CPU time used by the SDN controller and switches. Excessive usage, compared to a benign baseline, indicates an opportunity for denial of service, where the ability of the switches or controller to process messages and packets in a timely fashion is impaired.

### 3.5 Implementation

We use KVM for virtualization and Mininet for the emulated network. The hosts were written in Python and use `iperf` and `ping` for traffic generation, and the scapy library[1] for malicious host attack injection. The hosts communicate with a *HostController* Python script to execute malicious host attacks, generate traffic in the network, and conduct reachability tests on the network.

We insert our malicious proxy into the path between the Open vSwitch[2] software switches started by Mininet and our SDN controllers by simply having the proxy listen for TCP connections on a specified port and address, and supplying this port and address to Mininet as the address of the controller. When a switch connects, the proxy opens a second TCP connection to the controller and passes messages back and forth, modifying the message as required by the strategy. The proxy is implemented in C++ and leverages the C version of the Loxigen[3] library to parse and modify OpenFlow messages.

## 4 Experimental Results

We present the results obtained by applying BEADS to four SDN controllers: ONOS, POX, Ryu, and Floodlight. We then demonstrate the impact of these bugs with 4 real attacks.

### 4.1 Methodology

We applied BEADS to ONOS 1.2.1, POX version eel[4], Ryu 3.27, and Floodlight 1.2. For ONOS we used its default forwarding, which uses topology detection and shortest path routing along with proxy ARP, and a flow rule idle time of 30 s; for POX, we used the `proto.arp_responder`, `openflow.discovery`, `openflow.spanning_tree`, and `forwarding.l2_multi` modules to enable topology detection and shortest path routing along with proxy ARP; for Ryu, we used the `simple_switch` module, which emulates a network of learning switches; for Floodlight, we used its default forwarding, which uses topology detection and shortest path routing, and a flow rule idle time of 90 s.

The emulated network was created using Mininet 2.2.1 and Open vSwitch 2.0.2. While BEADS supports OpenFlow versions 1.0–1.5, our testing was done

[1] http://www.secdev.org/projects/scapy/.
[2] http://openvswitch.org/.
[3] https://github.com/floodlight/loxigen.
[4] Commit `4ebb69446515d9d9a0d5a002243cdca3c411520b` from 9/24/2015.

with OpenFlow 1.0 because it was the default negotiated by Open vSwitch and none of the SDN controllers we tested make use of the additional features introduced in later versions of OpenFlow. We configured Mininet with a simple two-tier tree topology of three switches and four hosts. The malicious switches and hosts vary depending on the test being run.

Our testing was done on a hyper-threaded 20 core Intel Xeon 2.4 GHz system with 125 GB of RAM. Each test takes about 60 s. We parallelize the tests by running between 2 and 6 managers simultaneously. Testing required around 200 h of total computation per tested SDN controller.

Table 1 presents a summary of tested scenarios and bugs found. We tested 6,996 strategies for ONOS, 4,286 for POX, 3,228 for Ryu, and 4,330 for Floodlight. Not all the controllers take advantage of the complete functionality of OpenFlow, and as we test only the messages that are actually used by the tested system, the number of testing scenarios for each controller depended on the implemented and used OpenFlow functionality. As a result, we tested significantly more strategies for ONOS because ONOS automatically polls every switch for statistics about flow rules and ports periodically using the OpenFlow `flow_stats_*` and `port_stats_*` messages. The other controllers do not poll for statistics and so have no need to use these message types, effectively utilizing a much smaller portion of the OpenFlow protocol. Similarly Ryu's learning switch behavior requires no topology detection which reduces the number of messages it uses. We found a total of 831 unique bugs, with 178 common to all four controllers and a further 134 common to two or three controllers. Table 1 also shows the detection criteria (Sect. 3.4) for each bug.

**Table 1.** Summary of tested scenarios and bugs.

| SDN controller | Total tested | Bugs found | Error msg. | Net. state | Reachability | Res. usage |
|---|---|---|---|---|---|---|
| ONOS | 6, 996 | 578 | 104 | 372 | 102 | 0 |
| POX | 4, 286 | 487 | 121 | 335 | 29 | 2 |
| Ryu | 3, 228 | 251 | 48 | 168 | 32 | 3 |
| Floodlight | 4, 330 | 577 | 95 | 478 | 4 | 0 |
| Total | 18, 840 | 1, 893 | 368 | 1, 353 | 167 | 5 |

### 4.2 Detailed Results

We analyze all 831 unique bugs, based on their outcome, and present a summary in Table 2.

**OpenFlow Operation Stall (OS)–No Known Mitigations.** Several bugs have the common outcome of preventing or delaying OpenFlow operations that may affect multiple switches. By ignoring or dropping `barrier_request` and `barrier_reply` messages or changing their transaction IDs, a malicious switch can stall the installation of flow rules forming a path through that switch as we

**Table 2.** Discovered bugs, each line corresponds to several bugs grouped by message and action. Note that some bugs may occur multiple times, in different categories for different controllers. FL = Floodlight.

| Outcome | Name | Strategy | Num | Controllers | New |
|---|---|---|---|---|---|
| OpenFlow operation stall | OS1 | Drop barrier messages | 4 | POX | No |
| | OS2 | Change xid in barrier messages | 12 | POX | No |
| | OS3 | Drop flow_add | 3 | ALL | No |
| Periodic switch disconnect | SD1 | Change version,type,length fields of handshake messages | 197 | ALL | No |
| | SD2 | Duplicate handshake messages | 20 | ONOS | Yes |
| | SD3 | Change version,type,length of barrier_request/barrier_reply | 36 | ONOS/POX/FL | No |
| | SD4 | Change version,type,length in flow_add/flow_delete/flow_removed | 48 | ALL | No |
| | SD5 | Change version,type,length in packet_in/packet_out | 46 | ALL | No |
| | SD6 | Change version,type,length in port_mod/echo_reply/echo_request | 42 | POX/RYU/FL | No |
| | SD7 | Change version,type,length in of_*_stats_reply/of_*_stats_request | 68 | ONOS | No |
| | SD8 | Change role in of_nicira_controller_role_* | 12 | ONOS/FL | No |
| | SD9 | Add CONTROLLER port to features_reply/port_status | 15 | ONOS/POX/FL | Yes |
| Data-plane loss | DP1 | Delay/drop packet_in/packet_out | 17 | ALL | No |
| | DP2 | Mod buffer_id in pkt_in/flow_add | 8 | ALL | No |
| Flow rule modification | FM | Change flow rule match, actions, etc. in flow_add | 162 | ALL | No |
| Port config modification | PC | Change port_mod to change port configuration | 39 | POX | No |
| Packet location hijacking | LH1 | Change port where packet was received in packet_in | 14 | ALL | No |
| | LH2 | Change port for packet_out | 14 | ALL | No |
| Empty packet_ins | EP1 | Change inner packet length to 0 in packet_in | 1 | ONOS | Yes |
| | EP2 | Set packet_in length=0 | 2 | POX/RYU/FL | No |
| Controller DoS | CD1 | Delay flow_add | 2 | POX | No |
| | CD2 | Change length to 0 on any message | 8 | RYU | Yes |
| | CD3 | Change inner packet length to 0 in packet_in | 2 | RYU | Yes |
| Link detection failure | LD | Change port lists in features_reply/port_status | 33 | ONOS/POX/FL | Yes |
| Broken ARP broadcast | BB | Change port lists in features_reply/port_status | 20 | ONOS/FL | Yes |
| Unexpected flowrule removal | FR1 | Change flow_stats_reply such that flow rule entry does not match | 8 | ONOS | Yes |
| | FR2 | Change flow_stats_reply such that packet_count is constant | 4 | ONOS | Yes |
| Unexpected broadcast | UB | Change port_in field of the packet_out message | 6 | POX/RYU | Yes |

discovered in POX. A similar operation stall occurs when dropping or ignoring `flow_add` messages; the flow will eventually be inserted, but it will take extra messages and controller processing. These bugs are due to the design of OpenFlow and there are no known mitigations.

**Periodic Switch Disconnect (SD)–Some Mitigations.** We found many bugs that cause the malicious switch to periodically disconnect. This causes topology churn and prevents the installation of flow rules or the delivery of `packet_in`/`packet_out` messages. It takes about 3 s for the network to fully recover from one of these events, although the TCP level disconnection is only about half a second.

While most of these bugs are unavoidable and due to the reception of invalid OpenFlow messages, we did identify two subcategories of these bugs that can be easily fixed. The first of these, consists of duplication of ONOS handshake messages. The state machine ONOS uses to control its handshake with a switch is not tolerant to message duplication. As a result, duplicating these messages results in a connection reset. This could be avoided by designing the handshake state machine to tolerate duplication.

The second subcategory of these bugs operates by modifying the `features_reply` message sent during the initial handshake to ONOS or POX to include a port with number 0xFFFD. This triggers a disconnection by the malicious switch the next time an ARP flood occurs, which might be hours later. The disconnection occurs because this port number (in OpenFlow 1.0) indicates the controller and results in an invalid `packet_in` being sent to the controller. These bugs can be mitigated by modifying the controller to sanity check the list of ports received from the switch.

**Data-Plane Loss (DP)–No Known Mitigations.** While we do not explicitly consider data-plane level attacks, we found several bugs which can trigger data-plane packet loss. All the controllers we tested are vulnerable to dropping occasional data-plane packets as a result of malicious switches discarding `packet_in` or `packet_out` messages. A different method to induce data loss is to target the buffering of packets at malicious OpenFlow switches by corrupting the buffers indicated in `packet_in` or `packet_out` messages. This causes the buffered packet to eventually be dropped. These bugs can have particularly large impacts on small flows like ARP and DNS where installing flow rules makes little sense. We are not aware of any known mitigations against these bugs.

**Flow Rule Modification (FM)–No Known Mitigations.** Another class of bugs disrupts flow rules from the controller by modifying `flow_add` messages. This enables the attacker to affect the timeout, priority, and match fields and masks of flow rules in malicious switches as well as the actions performed on a match. Our testing found a number of modifications that cause network-wide denial of service, but specific changes to small sets of flows are also possible. We are not aware of any known mitigations against these bugs.

**Port Config Modification (PC)–No Known Mitigations.** Similar to the flow rule modification, a compromised switch can mislead a controller as to the configuration of its ports by modifying `port_mod` messages. This configuration primarily consists of the port's enabled or disabled state and whether it has broadcast enabled. Our testing found a number of specific modifications that cause broad, network-wide denial of service, but these bugs could also be used for specific modifications targeting specific topology changes in networks. We are not aware of any known mitigations against these bugs.

**Packet Location Hijacking (LH)–No Known Mitigations.** Several bugs allow a malicious switch to change the apparent source port of a packet sent to the controller and the apparent destination port of packets send by the controller. This hijacking of packet locations has dramatic and wide spread effects across the network, including topology detection, MAC learning, and reactive forwarding. Note that the topology poisoning attacks identified in prior efforts [7,10] apply these bugs to LLDP traffic on particular ports to carefully forge specific links without breaking the entire network. While attacks forging LLDP packets can be mitigated using cryptographic techniques, the more general bugs are more difficult to address, and we are not aware of any known mitigations.

**Empty `packet_in`'s (EP)–Some Mitigations.** We identified a bug in the ONOS controller where sending a `packet_in` message with a zero-length payload packet triggers a NULL pointer exception in the processing thread. ONOS's design separates the processing of messages from different switches into different threads. As a result, this exception causes this switch's to terminate, disconnecting the malicious switch, but allows the controller to continue running. We reported this bug to the ONOS project, which confirmed it and verified that it was no longer present in their most recent release.

However, a second bug exists which effectively prevents all topology detection and useful reactive forwarding through a compromised switch on any controller. The bug is exploited by configuring the compromised switch to send `packet_in` messages with a payload length of at most zero bytes. This means that no packet headers will be sent to the controller, which can then do nothing useful with the message, preventing topology detection, MAC learning, and reactive forwarding. Preventing these bugs would require an update to the OpenFlow specification to disallow very small payload lengths.

**Controller DoS (CD)–Some Mitigations.** We identified several possible bugs that can overload and DoS the controller. One unavoidable way to do this is simply to delay the installation of flow rules in malicious switches, causing a flood of `packet_in` messages. This bug has been identified by several other studies, including [7,42,44]. Note that ONOS and Floodlight partially mitigate this bug by tracking flow rules to prevent repeated insertion attempts. The only complete mitigation is to proactively insert all needed flow rules and never send packets to the controller.

We also identified two new bugs that crash the Ryu controller. The first of these causes an infinite loop when receiving an OpenFlow message with a zero-length header while the second terminates the controller with an uncaught exception when a packet_in message with a zero length payload is received. We reported these bugs to the Ryu project, which has patched both.

**Link Detection Failure (LD)–Some Mitigations.** This bug works against implementations of the LLDP protocol to prevent a correct global topology from being constructed by a vulnerable controller. It exists in ONOS, Floodlight, and POX; Ryu is not vulnerable only because it does not attempt to construct a global view of the topology, but simply emulates a set of learning switches. Link detection is typically implemented by having the controller send LLDP packets out of each port on each switch that it knows about and observing where the packet_in messages containing those packets arrive. From the packet_in message, the controller knows what port the packet was received on, allowing it to identify a unidirectional link between the port where this packet was sent and the port where it was received.

This bug tampers with the list of ports sent by a malicious switch in the features_reply and port_status messages that the controller uses to enumerate available switch ports. If ports are omitted in these messages, no LLDP packets will be sent on them, which means no links can form from those ports. Without knowledge of these links, the controller is limited in its ability to route packets and may be unable to reach certain destinations.

These bugs can be substantially mitigated by monitoring received packet_in messages and looking for previously unknown ports. If such ports are observed, the controller can begin to send LLDP packets on those ports and emit an alert about a malicious or buggy switch sending inconsistent information.

**Broken ARP Broadcast (BB)–Some Mitigations.** This bug is conceptually similar to the link detection failure bug except that it applies to the network edge ports of a malicious switch that are directly connected to hosts instead of to other switches. It enables an attacker to render target hosts unreachable in a network running ONOS or Floodlight. Both controllers identify edge ports as those that have not received LLDP packets and are thus not connected to other switches and only broadcast ARP requests on these ports. However, by relying solely on the port lists from features_reply and port_status messages, certain ports may be omitted from those messages and hidden from the controller, preventing ARP broadcasts on those ports. This is despite other traffic from those ports. This causes hosts behind these omitted ports of malicious switches to be effectively unreachable. This lasts until each target host sends an ARP request of its own, at which point the controller receives the ARP request and learns the location of the target host. Much like link detection failure bugs, monitoring received packet_in messages can substantially mitigate these bugs.

**Unexpected Flow Rule Removal (FR)–Complete Mitigations.** These bugs confuse the ONOS controller into removing flows that it installed on a malicious switch, complicating debugging and directing suspicion away from the malicious switch. This bug occurs because ONOS manages the flow rules in switches with a very heavy hand. In particular, it will remove any flow rule in the switch that it did not insert and will track the usage of flow rules and request removal of flows rules that have been idle for some amount of time. As a result, by modifying the flow rule information returned to ONOS in the `flow_stats_reply` message, a malicious switch can make a flow rule appear idle or appear sufficiently different that ONOS does not recognize it and orders its removal. These bugs can be mitigated by relying on the ability of OpenFlow switches to automatically remove flow rules based on idle timeouts [31,33] and ensuring that all expected rules are accounted for before beginning removal.

**Unexpected Broadcast Behavior (UB)–Partial Mitigations.** OpenFlow `packet_out` messages include a special broadcast option that asks a switch to broadcast the included packet out of all ports with broadcast enabled that are not the port on which this packet was received. However, this mechanism is vulnerable to subtle changes in behavior that cause unexpected packet forwarding and cripples learning-switch type routing. This bug occurs when the `packet_out` message is modified by a malicious switch to change the `in_port`, which results in the packet being broadcast by the malicious switch out of the port on which it was received. This has impact on learning switch routing because broadcasting packets in this manner causes switches to learn incorrect locations for hosts resulting in connectivity losses. These bugs can be detected by linking packets sent at one switch with those received by other switches.

### 4.3 Attack Demonstrations

We demonstrate that one can weaponize the bugs in Table 2 into powerful attacks with potentially disastrous consequences. We manually develop exploits for a few of the bugs we discover and present these weaponized examples below. All attacks were manually implemented and tested using BEADS. The network topology was a simple tree with three switches and four hosts.

**TLS Man-in-the-Middle.** The security of TLS against man-in-the-middle attacks relies on a correctly implemented certificate-based PKI and active user involvement. Unfortunately, attackers can leverage maliciously obtained certificates [22] or tools like SSLStrip [26] to observe (and potentially modify) confidential information exchanged between client and server.

We implemented this scenario using the Ryu controller, which provides learning switch routing. We assume that the attacker has access to a compromised switch on path as well as a host that is not currently on the path between client and server. We use the FM bug to alter the flow table of the attacker-controlled switch to insert his host, potentially performing an SSL man-in-the-middle attack, into the path between the target client and server. Additional rules must be inserted using the FM vulnerability to ensure that each switch only sees packets with addresses that conform to the network topology.

**Web Server Impersonation.** In this scenario, an attacker wishes to impersonate an internal web server. We use the ONOS controller (we believe POX is vulnerable to a similar attack) and a malicious host at an arbitrary location in the network. We used the ARP-location-injection bug to confuse the controller into believing that the target webserver is now located on the same port as the attacker. All future connections from new or idle hosts are then sent to the attacker. Since ONOS uses a global Proxy ARP cache, the attacker can be anywhere on the network. This effect lasts until the target server starts a new connection with a host that causes a `packet_in` to the controller. This will reset the target server's location and end the attack.

If the switch to which the target server is connected is compromised, the attacker can increase the duration of this attack by also using the DP1 vulnerability to drop all `packet_in` messages from the target to the controller. This prevents the target server from ever re-asserting its old location and causes the attack to last indefinitely.

**Break Network Quarantine.** This scenario considers an attacker who has found useful information (*e.g.*, PII, credit card data, intellectual property, *etc.*) but induced a network quarantine in the process, and must transfer that data to an external server despite the imposed isolation.

In our demonstration of this attack, the Ryu controller is implementing a firewall and attempting to quarantine a target host from the rest of the network by dropping all packets from its port. The attacker is assumed to control an arbitrary switch in the network and is trying to send traffic from the target host to elsewhere in the network to exfiltrate discovered data. We use the CD2 bug for this attack, which causes the controller to enter an infinite loop and become unresponsive. Eventually, the switches in the network detect the failed connection and enter standalone mode, at which point they fall back to conventional Layer-2 Ethernet learning switches. This purges the flow table and enables all-to-all connectivity, allowing the attacker to exfiltrate the data. We were able to successfully demonstrate this attack against Ryu.

**Deniable Denial of Service.** In this scenario an adversary wishes to degrade network performance while remaining undetected for as long as possible. Whole-network effects such as controller crashes are thus undesirable, as are any actions that are easily traceable to attacker-controlled entities.

We implemented this attack scenario using ONOS. To stealthily disrupt network service, we use an infinite sequence of SD9 bugs. This bug uses a malformed `features_reply` message to cause disconnection of the malicious switch on the next ARP flood, which may be a long time after the message was sent. Blame for the disconnection will be placed on the controller because of the invalid `packet_out` message that triggers the disconnection, thereby directing suspicion away from the malicious switch. Using this attack, each ARP flood caused the malicious switch to disconnect from the controller, resulting in about 3 s of impaired service. ARP floods occurred 4 times in our tests, but an attacker could use normal ARP requests for non-existent hosts to increase that by a factor of 10. We successfully tested this attack against ONOS.

## 5 Discussion and Limitations

BEADS does not find fully weaponized attacks ready to launch against a target. Instead, it identifies strategies that cause significant impact on the network stemming from one or more bugs much like stack-overflow vulnerabilities, there is still manual effort needed to write an exploit that uses the bug in a targeted way. This includes fixing the malicious host or switch locations, as the bugs themselves exist irrespective of network location.

Many of the bugs found by BEADS allow a malicious switch to impact other switches or hosts indirectly. While a malicious switch always has the ability to impact such devices directly, there are two reasons it might want to use indirect methods instead. First, it makes it difficult to identify the malicious party by making the controller appear responsible for the undesirable behavior. Second, if a switch does not protect its connection with the controller using TLS, these bugs allow a Man-In-The-Middle attacker to maliciously control the switch using OpenFlow alone. Prior work has established that a significant number of SDN switches are not using TLS to protect their communication with the controller, making this a promising attack avenue [35,36].

Because BEADS is designed to detect bugs in the SDN control plane, we do not include metrics like latency, throughput, and packet drop rate in our detection. These are important data plane metrics, but provide little to no information about the control plane, and thus for our testing.

Our malicious proxy is stateless, and thus cannot coordinate modifications of particular requests or responses. Instead, it applies actions based on the type of each message. This maps well to OpenFlow's use of separate types for most requests, responses, and commands and reduces the attack generation search space. Adding additional state to this proxy could enable the discovery of more complex attacks, but at the cost of an exponential increase in the search space.

## 6 Related Work

**Network testing and debugging.** The work that is closest to ours is DELTA [24]. DELTA also evaluates the whole SDN system, including both controller and switches. However, it focuses on the SDN controller's northbound interface and uses only blind fuzzing without regard for message structure or probable vulnerabilities on the OpenFlow southbound interface. BEADS focuses on the southbound interface and uses message format and semantic information to provide much better test coverage, especially against controller algorithms like routing and topology detection. As a result, BEADS finds all the malicious switch attacks that DELTA finds and several that DELTA does not.

Other closely related efforts are OFTest [8] and FLORENCE [29]. Both of these tools test OpenFlow switches using manually written tests focusing on conformance to the OpenFlow specification. Since these tools do not consider the controller, they are unable to find bugs and attacks in the controller software based on incorrect assumptions about the switches.

Another work related to ours is NICE [6], which uses model checking and symbolic execution to test SDN controller applications using network invariants. NICE differs from our work in that it focuses on non-malicious SDN testing, while we focus on malicious attacks. NICE was only shown to scale to simple first-generation SDN controllers (*e.g.,* NOX). The second generation of SDN controllers we test, like ONOS and Ryu, include orders of magnitude more code, which would substantially complicate the symbolic execution. In particular, topology generation requires the controller to send messages to the switches on a timer which is not supported in NICE. BEADS successfully tests ONOS and other large, second-generation SDN controllers. Finally, while NICE models switches and hosts, our approach uses real (software) switches and real applications. OFTEN [20] (an extension of NICE) adds real switches, but it cannot test for performance attacks. Further, neither NICE nor OFTEN consider sending the switches malformed messages and both are dependent on difficult-to-design network state invariants for bug detection.

STS [41] is another work looking at network debugging. This work develops a method to minimize network execution traces containing bugs for OpenFlow networks. To test their trace minimizing technique, they develop a network event fuzzer that randomly injects events like link failures or packets into a network and use it to find seven new bugs in five SDN controllers. Unlike the STS fuzzer, our work focuses on manipulating the OpenFlow messages themselves and identifies which of these messages are likely to lead to attacks.

**Attacks and defenses in SDN.** Work that studies SDN attacks includes exploration of protocol attacks [10], saturation attacks [42,44], and controller-switch communication attacks [4]. Several defense and verification techniques have been proposed to ensure that flow rules do not violate invariants [1,2,16–18]. These verification approaches focus on logic errors in rules, as opposed to malicious manipulation of the SDN. The work by Mekky *et al.* [28] allows efficient inspection and filtering of higher network layers in SDNs. Kotani and Okabe [19] filter `packet_in` messages according to predefined rules to protect the controller. LineSwitch [3] mitigates control plane saturation DoS attacks by applying probabilistic black-listing. Recently, Spiffy [14] was proposed to detect link-flooding DDoS attacks in SDNs by applying rate changes to saturated links. None of these approaches considers the problem of automatic attack identification.

## 7 Conclusion

We have developed a framework, BEADS, to automatically find attacks in SDN systems. BEADS considers attacks caused by malicious hosts or switches by using semantically-aware test case generation and considering the whole SDN system (switches, controllers, and hosts). We used BEADS to automatically test almost 19,000 scenarios on four controllers and found 831 unique bugs. We classified these into 28 categories based on their impact; 10 of which are new. We demonstrated through 4 attacks how an attacker can use these bugs to impact high-level network goals such as availability, network topology, and reachability.

**Acknowledgements.** We thank William Streilein and James Landry for their support of this work as well as our shepherd, Guofei Gu, and anonymous reviewers for their helpful comments on this paper. This material is based in part upon work supported by the National Science Foundation under Grant Numbers CNS-1654137 and CNS-1319924. This work is sponsored by the Department of Defense under Air Force Contract #FA8721-05-C-0002. Opinions, interpretations, conclusions and recommendations are those of the author and are not necessarily endorsed by the United States Government.

## References

1. Al-Shaer, E., Al-Haj, S.: FlowChecker: Configuration analysis and verification of federated OpenFlow infrastructures. In: Proceedings of ACM SafeConfig, pp. 37–44 (2010)
2. Al-Shaer, E., Marrero, W., El-Atawy, A., Elbadawi, K.: Network configuration in a box: towards end-to-end verification of network reachability and security. In: Proceedings of ICNP, pp. 123–132 (2009)
3. Ambrosin, M., Conti, M., De Gaspari, F., Poovendran, R.: LineSwitch: efficiently managing switch flow in software-defined networking while effectively tackling DoS attacks. In: Proceedings of ASIA CCS, pp. 639–644 (2015)
4. Benton, K., Camp, L.J., Small, C.: OpenFlow vulnerability assessment. In: Proceedings of HotSDN, pp. 151–152 (2013)
5. Berde, P., Gerola, M., Hart, J., Higuchi, Y., Kobayashi, M., Koide, T., Lantz, B., O'Connor, B., Radoslavov, P., Snow, W., et al.: ONOS: towards an open, distributed SDN OS. In: Proceedings of HotSDN, pp. 1–6 (2014)
6. Canini, M., Venzano, D., Peresini, P., Kostic, D., Rexford, J.: A NICE way to test OpenFlow applications. In: Proceedings of NSDI (2012)
7. Dhawan, M., Poddar, R., Mahajan, K., Mann, V.: SPHINX: detecting security attacks in software-defined networks. In: Proceedings of NDSS (2015)
8. Floodlight Project: Github - floodlight/oftest: Openflow switch test framework (2016). https://github.com/floodlight/oftest
9. Foster, N., Harrison, R., Freedman, M.J., Monsanto, C., Rexford, J., Story, A., Walker, D.: Frenetic: a network programming language. ACM SIGPLAN Not. **46**, 279–291 (2011)
10. Hong, S., Xu, L., Wang, H., Gu, G.: Poisoning network visibility in software-defined networks: new attacks and countermeasures. In: Proceedings of NDSS, pp. 8–11 (2015)
11. Jafarian, J.H., Al-Shaer, E., Duan, Q.: OpenFlow random host mutation: transparent moving target defense using software defined networking. In: Proceedings of HotSDN, pp. 127–132 (2012)
12. Jero, S., Lee, H., Nita-Rotaru, C.: Leveraging state information for automated attack discovery in transport protocol implementations. In: 45th IEEE/IFIPDSN, pp. 1–12. IEEE Computer Society (2015)
13. Kampanakis, P., Perros, H., Beyene, T.: SDN-based solutions for moving target defense network protection. In: Proceedings of WoWMoM (2014)
14. Kang, M.S., Gligor, V.D., Sekar, V.: SPIFFY: inducing cost-detectability tradeoffs for persistent link-flooding attacks. In: Proceedings of NDSS (2016)
15. Katta, N.P., Rexford, J., Walker, D.: Logic programming for software-defined networks. In: Workshop on Cross-Model Design and Validation (XLDI), vol. 412 (2012)

16. Kazemian, P., Chang, M., Zeng, H., Varghese, G., McKeown, N., Whyte, S.: Real time network policy checking using header space analysis. In: Proceedings of NSDI, pp. 99–111 (2013)
17. Kazemian, P., Varghese, G., McKeown, N.: Header space analysis: static checking for networks. In: Proceedings of NSDI, pp. 113–126 (2012)
18. Khurshid, A., Zhou, W., Caesar, M., Godfrey, P.B.: Veriflow: verifying network-wide invariants in real time. In: Proceedings of NSDI (2013)
19. Kotani, D., Okabe, Y.: A packet-in message filtering mechanism for protection of control plane in OpenFlow networks. In: Proceedings of ANCS, pp. 29–40 (2014)
20. Kuzniar, M., Canini, M., Kostic, D.: OFTEN testing OpenFlow networks. In: European Workshop on Software Defined Networking (EWSDN), pp. 54–60 (2012)
21. Lantz, B., Heller, B., McKeown, N.: A network in a laptop: rapid prototyping for software-defined networks. In: Proceedings of HotNets (2010)
22. Leavitt, N.: Internet security under attack: the undermining of digital certificates. Computer **44**(12), 17–20 (2011)
23. Lee, H., Seibert, J., Hoque, E., Killian, C., Nita-Rotaru, C.: Turret: a platform for finding attacks in unmodified implementations of intrusion tolerant systems. In: IEEE ICDCS (2014)
24. Lee, S., Yoon, C., Lee, C., Shin, S., Yegneswaran, V., Porras, P.: DELTA: a security assessment framework for software-defined networks. In: Network and Distributed System Security Symposium. Internet Society (2017)
25. Lim, S., Ha, J.I., Kim, H., Kim, Y., Yang, S.: A SDN-oriented DDoS blocking scheme for botnet-based attacks. In: Proceedings of ICUFN, pp. 63–68 (2014)
26. Marlinspike, M.: New tricks for defeating SSL in practice. BlackHat DC, February 2009
27. McCauley, M.: About POX (2013). http://www.noxrepo.org/pox/about-pox/
28. Mekky, H., Hao, F., Mukherjee, S., Zhang, Z.L., Lakshman, T.: Application-aware data plane processing in SDN. In: Proceedings of HotSDN, pp. 13–18 (2014)
29. Natarajan, S.: Github - snrism/florence-dev: Sdn security test framework (2016). https://github.com/snrism/florence-dev
30. Nelson, T., Ferguson, A.D., Scheer, M.J., Krishnamurthi, S.: Tierless programming and reasoning for software-defined networks. In: Proceedings of NSDI, pp. 519–531 (2014)
31. Open Networking Foundation: OpenFlow switch specification (1.0) (2009)
32. Open Networking Foundation: Conformance test specification for OpenFlow switch specification 1.0.1 (2013). https://www.opennetworking.org/images/stories/downloads/sdn-resources/onf-specifications/openflow-test/conformance-test-spec-openflow-1.0.1.pdf
33. Open Networking Foundation: OpenFlow switch specification (1.5.0) (2014)
34. Open Networking Foundation: Conformance test specification for OpenFlow switch specification 1.3.4 - basic single table conformance test profile (2015). https://www.opennetworking.org/images/stories/downloads/working-groups/OpenFlow1.3.4TestSpecification-Basic.pdf
35. Pickett, G.: Abusing software defined networks. In: Defcon (2014)
36. Pickett, G.: Staying persistent in software defined networks. In: BlackHat (2015)
37. Plummer, D.: Ethernet address resolution protocol: Or converting network protocol addresses to 48.bit ethernet address for transmission on ethernet hardware. RFC 826 (1982)
38. Porras, P., Cheung, S., Fong, M., Skinner, K., Yegneswaran, V.: Securing the software-defined network control layer. In: Proceedings of NDSS (2015)

39. Project Floodlight: Floodlight OpenFlow Controller (2016)
40. Reitblatt, M., Foster, N., Rexford, J., Schlesinger, C., Walker, D.: Abstractions for network update. In: Proceedings of ACM SIGCOMM, pp. 323–334 (2012)
41. Scott, C., Wundsam, A., Raghavan, B., Panda, A., Or, A., Lai, J., Huang, E., Liu, Z., El-Hassany, A., Whitlock, S., Acharya, H., Zarifis, K., Shenker, S.: Troubleshooting blackbox SDN control software with minimal causal sequences. In: Proceedings of SIGCOMM, pp. 395–406. ACM (2014)
42. Shin, S., Gu, G.: Attacking software-defined networks: a first feasibility study. In: Proceedings of HotSDN, pp. 165–166 (2013)
43. Shin, S., Porras, P., Yegneswaran, V., Gu, G.: A framework for integrating security services into software-defined networks. In: Proceedings of Open Networking Summit (2013)
44. Shin, S., Yegneswaran, V., Porras, P., Gu, G.: Avant-guard: scalable and vigilant switch flow management in software-defined networks. In: Proceedings of CCS, pp. 413–424 (2013)
45. The Ryu Project: Ryu SDN framework using OpenFlow 1.3. Website (2014). https://osrg.github.io/ryu/

# Trapped by the UI: The Android Case

Efthimios Alepis and Constantinos Patsakis(✉)

Department of Informatics, University of Piraeus,
80, Karaoli & Dimitriou, 18534 Piraeus, Greece
kpatsak@gmail.com

**Abstract.** Mobile devices are highly dependent on the design of user interfaces, since their size and computational cost introduce considerable constraints. UI and UX are interdependent since UX measures the satisfaction of users interacting with digital products. Therefore, both UX and UI are considered as top priorities among major mobile OS platforms. In this work we highlight some pitfalls in the design of Android UI which can greatly expose users and break user trust in the UI by proving how deceiving it can be. To this end, we showcase a series of attacks that exploit side channel information and poor UI choices ranging from sniffing users' input; resurrecting tapjacking, to wiping users' data, in Android from KitKat to Nougat.

## 1 Introduction

Modern mobile devices have penetrated our everyday life at an unprecedented rate. An indicator of this trend is that despite the fact that commodity smartphones date back to less than a decade, globally there are more smartphone users than desktop users. In terms of capabilities, while they can be considered as a stripped down version of modern computers, their various embedded sensors provide them additionally allowing them to sense their location through *e.g.* the GPS, their position through the compass, or even the motion of a device through accelerometers. This knowledge allows smartphones to adjust the user interface and the provided information in real-time in a way that fits better for the user and the corresponding environment.

More than simply managing all this information in a computational efficient way, mobile devices are subject to size constraints as the attached monitor which acts as both an input and an output modality of interaction is rather small and a lot of functionality has to be squeezed into it in the most intuitive way so as not to confuse users when interacting with the device. As a result, mobile UIs contain a lot of components and information in a rather confined setting. Therefore, while the resulting UI seems rather simple, it is in fact fairly complex. Furthermore, since all mobile applications share the same small screen, they end up getting stacked one on top of the other which prevents users from determining

**Electronic supplementary material** The online version of this chapter (doi:10.1007/978-3-319-66332-6_15) contains supplementary material, which is available to authorized users.


M. Dacier et al. (Eds.): RAID 2017, LNCS 10453, pp. 334–354, 2017.
DOI: 10.1007/978-3-319-66332-6_15

to which application the foreground component belongs to. Nevertheless, users have absolute trust in the UI: they expect that what they are presented is exactly what it claims to be.

Smartphone UIs have received a lot of attention over the last years, with numerous researchers revealing vulnerabilities that lead to a significant number of OS patches and precautionary measures, with Android; due to its popularity, receiving most of them. In this paper, we present new attack vectors that we have discovered which not only bypass recent countermeasures integrated in Android, but more importantly, these attacks, in many cases, are for more malicious than the reported in current state of the art.

After reviewing the related scientific literature, we argue that one may categorise Android UI attacks into two main categories. The first category consists of attacks that utilize window dialogs that hold the `SYSTEM_ALERT_WINDOW` signature level permission, allowing them to be shown on top of all other apps; e.g. [41]. Android Toast messages are an exception in this category, since they require no permission, however have some significant limitations, as it is discussed in the next section. The second set of attacks consists of applications that manage to determine the foreground app and consequently present a fake application to steal sensitive user information; e.g. [18]. However, at the time of writing, these attacks have either low or zero impact since their underlying security issues have been already addressed. For the first category of attacks, the `SYSTEM_ALERT_WINDOW` permission requires special handling by the user, after the installation of an app to be granted. Additionally, after the introduction of API level 23, special intents (e.g. `ACTION_MANAGE_OVERLAY_PERMISSION` [11]) and checks (e.g. `canDrawOverlays()` [11]) have been introduced to harden the UI and disable third party apps from arbitrarily drawing over other apps. Regarding the second set of attacks, again several countermeasures have been applied during the last years. Moreover, Android ActivityManager's class method getRunningTasks(), has been deprecated in API level 21 and is no longer available to third party applications [2], while ActivityManager's class `getRunningAppProcesses()` returns a list of only the caller application's package name as of API level 22.

In our work we use quite different attack vectors to achieve these results, which, to the best of our knowledge and according to our reports to Google; see Table 1 for details, had not been studied yet. Our proposed attacks exploit some of the properties of the most generic Android OS mechanisms, such as Android activities and Intents. Hence, not only do we succeed in delivering a wide range of attacks to the Android OS through seemingly benign apps; they do not request any dangerous permission, but we also provide proofs that these vulnerabilities exist for far too many years, up to the latest versions. These attacks may range from stealing sensitive input and installing apps without users' knowledge, to wiping the user's phone, even in the latest versions of Android AOSP (SDK 25). In addition, we have successfully uploaded our proof of concept applications to Google Play, bypassing the security checks from the Bouncer; the system which analyses applications in Google Play for malicious functionality [27,31], further proving the significance of the threats.

While much effort has been made in Android towards countering UI redressing attacks, for instance since Marshmallow, the user is presented with a notification screen whenever an overlay is detected, the ground truth is that most of these defense mechanisms have been partially deployed, allowing an adversary to launch a wide set of attacks. Table 1a provides an overview of our contributions stating some of the Android's design goals and linking them with both our findings and the way that these findings can be used maliciously.

More precisely, in this work we demonstrate that many security standards of Android's UI can be easily bypassed with the use of inherent mechanisms that do not require any special permission from the user. To this end, our presented attacks either exploit the knowledge of what the foreground app is (SDK<24), or lure the user to use arbitrary UIs and result in a series of "unwanted" actions. Based on the methods that will be presented, an adversary can launch several serious attacks, ranging from sniffing sensitive and private data, to gaining administrative privileges that allow the adversary to reset the device, wipe user's data, or even cover the installation of new downloaded apps. A summary of the attacks presented in this work, their applicability to specific Android versions and the percentage of current devices affected by them, are illustrated in Table 1b. It should be noted that the reported results have not been tested to API levels below 19 as these devices not only represent a small market share, but they have been long deprecated.

## 2 Related Work

Android User Interfaces take place in three-dimensional space, where the two dimensions control the horizontal and vertical positioning of controls inside a mobile window respectively, while the other controls the "depth". The latter dimension refers to the different "layers" of UI graphic elements which are placed on a mobile screen and it is defined from the level of the screen towards the user's eyes. Hence, as far as activities are concerned, the "outermost" activity is practically the active one. However, there are also other types of graphic elements that may appear on a mobile screen, such as dialogs. Dialogs consist of controls that may appear on top of activities to interact with the users, usually providing some kind of information. For managing all the UI elements on the Z axis, there is a dedicated Android interface, namely *WindowManager* [12], used by the apps to bound to a particular display.

In terms of user interaction, Android's activities and dialog windows have significant differences between them. First and foremost, activities have a much more complex lifecycle which consists of special states and their corresponding events that are triggered during their lifecycle. On the contrary, dialogs are usually either informative or prompt users for making a decision, and therefore have much shorter and less complex lifecycle. Furthermore, all activities have to be declared inside the app manifest file, whereas there is no such requirement for

**Table 1.** Summary of our attacks and their applicability.

| Design goal | Findings | Issue | Malicious usage |
|---|---|---|---|
| Apps should not access users' private files without specific dangerous permissions (*e.g.* access to the contents of the device's Wallpaper storage) [6] | Apps, without any permission, have read access to the contents of the device's Wallpaper | 219663 224516 | Using the Wallpaper image we create a fake pin/pattern screen and sniff users' pins and patterns. |
| Apps should not be aware of users' current foreground app [2]. | All apps in Android versions prior to Nougat have access to /proc/ file system and can determine the foreground app without requesting any permission. | 233504 | Having actual knowledge of the foreground app we launched attacks involving the app's UI which resulted in sniffing user input data. |
| Only apps that hold the signature permission `SYSTEM_ALERT_WINDOW` should be allowed to draw over other apps and on a part of the screen [7]. | We achieved this goal by using simple Android's activities and without requiring any permission. This way, arbitrary number of sized activities can be stacked over other apps. | 233504 234399 | We draw over very special OS UI elements involving systems settings, managing to use system apps (phone calls, sms, etc) and third party apps to either complete a malicious action or sniff personal data. We also manage to install new apps. |
| Every app is able to retrieve a list of all of the device's installed applications [10]. | Works as intended. | | Having actual knowledge of the installed applications, an adversary can create fake UIs that mimic the real applications. To convince the user in launching the fake UI, the adversary can issue fake notifications or create fake shortcuts. |
| Even when a UI element is drawn over another app, in critical cases all the background interactions must be either disabled or notify the user. This mechanism has been activated for all dangerous runtime permissions since SDK 23. | While Android successfully detects overlays in dangerous permission settings, it fails to do detect them in signature permissions, such as `SYSTEM_ALERT_WINDOW`, `BIND_ADMIN`, etc, or even when using Package manager. | 233504 | We can escalate privileges of zero permission apps to gain signature permissions for them (*e.g.* admin rights, change device settings, system alerts) or to download and install new apps. |
| Each application should have its own notifications so that the user could know its source. | As of API level 23 the developer can provide arbitrary icons for the notification and either provide an arbitrary title (API<24) or strip the application's name (API>23). | 233790 | An adversary can push malicious notifications to the user, tricking him into launching forged activities that mimic the look and feel of installed legitimate apps. |
| Applications are able to create shortcuts to facilitate users in launching them. For security reasons, the icon and the corresponding label must be unique and uniquely identifiable by the user | As of API level 19, apps holding the INSTALL_SHORTCUT permission are allowed to create shortcuts to the home screen with arbitrary icons and labels. | 234044 | A malicious app creates a fake shortcut of a legitimate installed app to the user's home screen, tricking the user in interacting with a malicious app instead of the legitimate one and resulting in private data leakage. |

(a) Overview of main contributions and comparison with design goals in Android.

| Android Version | Nougat | Marshmallow | Lollipop | KitKat | Available in Google Play | Vulnerable devices(%) |
|---|---|---|---|---|---|---|
| **Tested API level** | 25 | 23 | 22 | 19 | | |
| **Sniff lock pin/pattern** | ✓ | ✓ | ✓ | ✓ | ✓ | 86.3 |
| **Sniff data from foreground apps** | | ✓ | ✓ | ✓ | ✓ | 85.6 |
| **Unauthorized actions through OS apps** | ✓ | ✓ | ✓ | ✓ | ✓ | 86.3 |
| **Gain escalated privileges** | ✓ | ✓ | ✓* | ✓* | ✓ | 86.3 |
| **Interfere UI of legitimate apps** | ✓ | ✓ | ✓ | ✓ | ✓ | 86.3 |
| **Fake apps mimicking legitimate apps** | ✓ | ✓ | ✓ | ✓ | ✓ | 86.3 |
| **Forged notifications** | ✓** | ✓ | | | ✓ | 30.3 |
| **Forged shortcuts** | ✓ | ✓ | ✓ | ✓ | ✓ | 30.3 |
| **Install applications** | ✓ | ✓ | ✓ | ✓ | ✓ | 86.3 |
| **Revised tapjacking** | ✓ | ✓ | ✓ | ✓ | ✓ | 86.3 |
| **Market share (%)** | 0.7 | 29.6 | 33.4 | 22.6 | | |

(b) Attacks and applicability. *: On API>22 more signature runtime permissions are available *e.g.* `SYSTEM_ALERT_WINDOW` and `WRITE_SETTINGS`. **: On API> 23 the title of the notification is fetced from the app title. Nonetheless, one could declare a name with many spaces or dashes to trick the user.

dialog windows. Following the same logic, an app's activity can also be launched from other apps using *intents*, a special Android mechanism to enable a kind of "communication" between applications through asynchronous messages. Consequently, there is a strong relationship between activities and intra- and inter-app navigation, which makes them one of the fundamental building blocks of apps on the Android platform.

At this point it is essential to clarify how Android UI elements interact with each other inside or outside the scope of an app. In principle, a dialog window cannot appear outside the scope of its calling app; *i.e.* appear on top of another app's activity, unless this app is granted the `SYSTEM_ALERT_WINDOW` permission. While there is an exception to this rule inside Android, concerning the "Toast" window, this type of windows have limited functionality and very short lifetime (maximum 3.5 s). Moreover, the `SYSTEM_ALERT_WINDOW` permission is a signature level permission; far more strict than dangerous permissions, and allows an application to create windows shown on top of all other apps by using the `TYPE_SYSTEM_ALERT` option. According to Google Developer resources [7]: "*Very few apps should use this permission; these windows are intended for system-level interaction with the user*". Apparently, while many applications may request this permission, this permission is actually neither automatically granted nor the user is notified about it during installation. Therefore, a permission management screen is presented to the user to grant it [7] and to allow the application to draw on top of the others. Table 2 provides an overview of the properties of all UI elements that are able to draw over other apps have.

On the contrary, a newly launched activity is by default, and without requiring any permission, able to appear on top of another app. This is the usual and obvious way of interaction inside Android OS where apps appear on top of others, usually as a result of users' actions, creating a kind of an application stack. Activities which are launching other activities or other apps' activities and sometimes even return results, are a commonplace in Android and are thus thoroughly supported through the Android Intent [5] mechanism. Notably, up to recently, each application would have been actually stacked on top of the others covering them entirely, as the size of each application would have been equal to the screen's size. This is not the case any more as several features, recently introduced in Android's UI, are providing more complex stacks such as messaging apps' "chatheads"; through `SYSTEM_ALERT_WINDOW` permission, and Multi-Window [8].

### 2.1 Attacks to the UI

In principle, one of the main goals of malware is to perform unauthorised actions on victims' devices and for achieving this an adversary may use various approaches. Nonetheless, if the adversary cannot find a vulnerability to penetrate into the user's device either remotely or by getting physical access to it, one alternative way would be to trick the user into performing the malicious action himself. To this end, the adversary may use social engineering methods to convince the user to *e.g.* install a malicious application or change specific OS

**Table 2.** Android UI elements over other apps.

| UI window type | Required permission | Manifest declaration | Focusable | Duration | Launch from service |
|---|---|---|---|---|---|
| Toast messages | | Not required | | 3.5 s | |
| Alert messages | SYSTEM_ALERT_WINDOW | Not required | ✓ | No limit | |
| System alerts | SYSTEM_ALERT_WINDOW | Not required | ✓ | No limit | ✓ |
| Keyguards* | | Required | ✓ | No limit | ✓ |
| Normal activity | | Required | ✓ | No limit | ✓ |
| Transparent activity | | Required | ✓ | No limit | ✓ |
| Small shaped activity | | Required | ✓ | No limit | ✓ |
| Notification | | Not required | | No limit | ✓ |

settings. Obviously, the application must not raise an alert to the user indicating its maliciousness, otherwise the user will not perform the task.

However, even if the user is tricked into installing a malicious app, this does not guarantee that the adversary will accomplish his/her goals. For instance, if the adversary has the goal of stealing a user's password, then the embedded security mechanisms of the operating system may prevent the adversary from this theft. To overcome this obstacle, many malicious applications try to trick users into providing the necessary input directly to them. An obvious method to achieve this is by disguising themselves as legitimate apps so as to trick users into providing the input to them. Another approach, which is very often used in mobile devices due to their UI, is to provide a transparent layer on top of the legitimate application and thus to steal the sensitive user input.

In literature, several attacks targeting Android relevant to our work are documented. Despite the fact that transparent elements in browsers were used as the first UI redressing attacks, we are not studying them hereafter since they target an entirely different environment. Besides, these attacks cannot recover the sensitive information nor can perform the actions that we target in our attacks. To the best of our knowledge, the first attempts to escape the browser environment can be attributed to Richardson [32] and Johnson [22]. Nevertheless, these attacks were quite limited as *e.g.* they used a simple toast. The actual successful UI redressing attack can be attributed to Niemietz and Schwenk [30] who ported them to Android. The authors managed to create an overlay which is "touch transitive" in that the clicks are also transferred to the application which is positioned below it. In that scenario for example, the user is tricked into clicking at specific points on the screen while his clicks are also parsed to the dialer application which sits below the app. In that way, the user performs an unauthorised call to a premium number without realising it.

The attack of Chen et al. [18] starts from a side channel attack to the underlying GUI system. While in principle the attack can be launched to any GUI, the authors focus on Android and more precisely try to infer the activity that is displayed from the foreground application based on shared memory. First, the authors monitor offline the memory counters (virtual and physical) of an application as they are recorded in `procfs`. That is, they monitor the memory consumption of each activity in an application by tracking the memory allocation of the corresponding `/proc/[pid]/statm` file. The hypothesis is that the transition from one activity to another has a specific memory footprint that can be used to create a unique signature in a target app. Based on this signature, the adversary can infer the foreground application and the corresponding activity. By monitoring network traffic through `/proc/net/tcp6` one can further improve the results. Based on this input, the adversary may determine whether, for instance, the victim is presented with the login screen of a sensitive app or he/she is being asked to enter payment details. Therefore, he can timely bring his malicious app in the foreground with a replicated UI and trick the user into disclosing the sensitive information.

Bianchi et al. in [16] categorise all Android UI attacks under the general umbrella of GUI confusion attacks. Despite the countermeasures that are discussed in this work, of special interest to our work is the reported leakage of foreground application by `profs`. In this case, the leakage is from the file `/proc/[pid]/cgroups` whose contents change from `/apps/bg_non_interactive` to `/apps` when an app is sent to the foreground. Recently, Fernandes et al. [21] showed that one could exploit the use of a defense mechanism such as the aforementioned one, by monitoring the binder IPC calls in `/sys/kernel/debug/binder`. This allows an adversary to know when the scan has finished and to timely present user with a fake activity to steal the sensitive data. To overcome this drawback, Fernandes et al. provide a more advanced mechanism which mitigates such attacks.

The attacks of Ying et al. [41] can be considered quite narrow and the assumptions that the authors make are rather strong. Firstly, the attack is mainly focused on custom ROMs where the ecosystem is very different compared to Android AOSP, as there is a lot of customisation and radically different implementations even for native libraries. Actually, the authors exploit one of these features, more precisely the `SYSTEM_ALERT_WINDOW` permission to draw on top of other windows. Notably, to grant this permission to an application the user has to perform a set of actions post installation [7]. Using Tacyt[1] to estimate the exposure from this attack vector, we identified 235,059 versions in Google Play and 28,533 version outside it which use this permission. The reason for this choice is that Tacyt downloads all the apps from Google Play and all their versions in daily basis, analyses them and provides an interface to mine part of this information. Due to the implementation of Tacyt, the responses are in per app version and not per app, nonetheless, they provide a very good snapshot of available Android apps. Notably, the latter numbers contradict the reported ones by Ying et al. [41]. For Android AOSP, their attack cannot be considered valid as none of the big corporations which are explicitly granted this permission by Google would try to exploit it as such actions would most probably put them out of business immediately. Alternatively, the user has to be tricked into performing a set of unusual and very dangerous actions.

---

[1] https://www.elevenpaths.com/technology/tacyt/index.html.

Currently, there are several reported possible countermeasures to UI redressing attacks [1,21,28,29,38]. Nonetheless, in terms of state of practice we consider as baseline the latest version of Android AOSP, which at the time of writing is 7.1.1. The reasons for this choice is that while several defense mechanisms are implemented for quite old Android versions *e.g.* Android 4.4 and they actually account for a low percentage of market share which has currently been left unsupported. Additionally, Google has issued several security features in the newer versions to tackle many of these attacks, and introduced new UI features, some of which are exploited by our attacks. Notwithstanding the above, the attacks that we demonstrate here can be launched to a plethora of Android versions, illustrating that the defense mechanisms are rather low. For a more thorough overview of this field, the interested reader may refer to [37].

## 3 The Attacks

The following paragraphs present the backbone of our attacks. After introducing our threat model, we provide the necessary technical details and research findings that enable the realisation of our attacks. Based on these findings, we detail how an adversary can take advantage of them to launch an attack.

### 3.1 Threat Model

Like most attacks on Android, we assume that the victim has been tricked into installing a malicious app [19,20,36]. To minimize the risk of alerting the user that the app might be malicious, we minimize the requirement for permissions, by requesting access only to the Internet. The latter is a weak assumption, since after the radical changes in Android 6, the new permission model considers this access as a normal permission. Practically, the user is not notified about it, yet the permission is automatically granted and cannot be revoked. Therefore, our threat model assumes that the device has not been compromised via a root exploit. In fact, as we are going to show, most of our attacks can be applied to the latest version of Android. Therefore, our malicious apps are assumed to be unprivileged and managed to trick Bouncer and be shared through Google Play.

To provide stealthiness to our app, instead of just using Internet to communicate the commands and results, we use Firebase. The idea behind this choice is that Firebase provides a nice hide out for the execution of our attack since the channel is considered secure and trustworthy, as it is powered by Google, and the traffic is also considered legitimate as many applications use it to store information. Additionally, it facilitates the development lifecycle as Android has many native API calls to exchange information with Firebase. In this regard, the use of Firebase can be considered similar to the use of Facebook, Twitter, etc. by social botnets [23] to hide their communication with the C&C server.

### 3.2 Drawing over Other Activities

Microphone and touchscreen inputs can be considered as the most sensitive information on a smartphone, as they constitute the primary inputs to the device. While for the former the main security mechanisms can be found in the transport layer, for the latter the mechanisms are embedded in the operating system. This is perhaps the reason why a significant number of corresponding attacks has already been reported. For instance, apart from the obvious keylogger applications, an attacker may try to recover information from leaks (potential or malicious) of the software keyboard [17], processor's cache [24], motion sensors [14, 39], distortions of the wireless signals from finger motions [42], hand motion [26], audio [25], video [33] or both [34] to infer user's input.

In our approach, we exploit Android's UI and side channel information to either steal or interfere with the user's input. In what follows we discuss how one can draw on top of other activities. Practically, this is split in two cases: one where a transparent overlay activity covers another one, and one where one or more non transparent activities partially cover other activities.

For the former case we use typical Android manifest theme declarations. More specifically we have used the `Theme.Translucent.NoTitleBar` parameter in the activities' theme declaration to make an activity transparent and extend it to full screen. In the cases where "on-screen" actions, such as clicks, or key input through the supplementary presence of a keyboard needs to be recorded, the transparent layout was supplied with corresponding `KeyListener` and `ClickListener` objects. Notably, drawing over the Android UI by utilizing a transparent activity was seamless, as a "layer" since any visible view on the transparent activity is seen as visible on the mobile screen (*e.g.* TextViews, Buttons, etc.). The latter case was more demanding as activities whose size is smaller than the screen are statistically quite "rare" in Android apps. Moreover, apart from this constraint, we required to leave user interaction pass through the outer space of the activity. To achieve these, we defined *Application Theme* styles that contained the following items as elements:

```
<item name="android:windowIsFloating">true</item>
<item name="android:windowIsTranslucent">true</item>
<item name="android:windowBackground">@android:color/transparent</item>
<item name="android:windowNoTitle">true</item>
```

Then, a crucial step was to override the activity's `onCreate()` method to define some additional parameters. Namely, a `WindowManager.LayoutParams` object was created whose `dimAmount` was set to 0 and it was flagged with the attributes `FLAG_LAYOUT_NO_LIMITS` and `FLAG_NOT_TOUCH_MODAL`. To position the sized floating activity on the screen, one can fine tune several parameters of the corresponding `LayoutParam` *e.g.* "Gravity" parameters, or actual position through (X,Y) on-screen coordinates. Finally, to make an activity "wrap" around its contents (*e.g.* ImageViews) its `layout_width` and `layout_height` parameters have to be defined to take the `wrap_content` value, instead of the default `match_parent` default value. Notably, the aforementioned properties, can be used to create arbitrary stacks of activities on top of others, allowing an adversary to create an interface as in Fig. 1a, where only part of the activity on the bottom can be seen, nonetheless, the interaction (click) is passed to it. The fact that arbitrary number of sized activities can overlay other apps can also be used to create a grid on top of the screen as illustrated in Fig. 1b. Both of these approaches, concerning a number of floating, sized activities are used in our research for a wide variety of attacks that range from permission escallation attacks, to revisiting tapjacking, as it is illustrated in the next section.

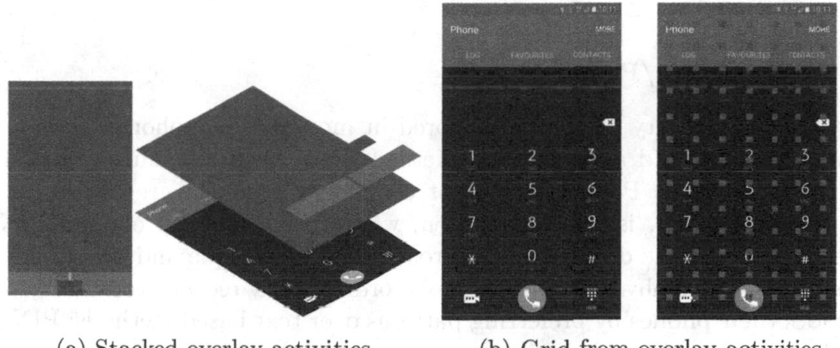


(a) Stacked overlay activities. (b) Grid from overlay activities.

**Fig. 1.** Exploiting floating Android activities.

### 3.3 Tricking Users to Open Apps

In API level 4 Google introduced notifications to Android. As the name suggests, this mechanism notifies users about application events. To create a notification there is no permission needed to be granted. From API level 11, one must denote the text of the notification; through `setContentText` which accepts a string variable, the title of the notification; through `setContentTitle` which also accepts a string variable, and the notification icons for the status bar and the notification view, using `setSmallIcon` and `setLargeIcon` respectively [9]. As of API level 23, both icons can be set dynamically using custom bitmaps. Prior to API level 23, only the `setLargeIcon` provided this feature, as `setSmallIcon` required an integer which denoted the resource ID in the application's package of the drawable to use. Practically, this means that a developer can now fetch all the content of a notification; strings and icons, from the Internet, without having any restriction from the declared app resources in the package. Notably, these attacks emerged since API level 23. While one could long press on the icon of a notification to see its properties, which would actually show the user the correct app, this cannot be considered a normal user interaction, as it beats the purpose of the notifications and cannot be expected to be performed regularly.

Shortcuts are an easy way to launch applications beyond going through the list of installed applications. To this end, they are created in the home screen of Android so that the user can quickly find the apps she uses most often. While the user can create shortcuts for her apps and arrange them in the home screen, applications can also do it when deemed necessary, as long as they have declared the normal permission `INSTALL_SHORTCUT` in their manifest. The underlying mechanism to create a shortcut is intents [4], so the developer has to declare three variables: a string which denotes the caption of the shortcut (`EXTRA_SHORTCUT_NAME`), a string which denotes the "action" of the intent to be launched (`setAction`), and its icon as a bitmap (`EXTRA_SHORTCUT_ICON`). Again, as in the previous case of notifications, all the parameters for the creation of app shortcuts can be set dynamically, using Internet resources.

### 3.4 Sniffing PIN/Pattern

Due to the sensitivity of the data stored in modern smartphones, a wide set of authentication and authorization methods have been introduced to prevent unauthorised access. Perhaps the most common mechanism, regardless of the underlying platform, is the lock screen, where users have to enter a PIN or pattern to unlock the device. The approach is rather simple and provides baseline security from physical intrusion. According to a recent study [35], most users lock their phones by preferring patterns over text based methods; PIN and passphrase.

While in some versions there might be some minor filename changers, by default, the pattern is stored as an unsalted SHA-1 hash in `/data/system/gesture.key` file, while the PIN or passphrase are stored in `/data/system/password.key` as a concatenation of the password's SHA-1 and MD5 hash values. Contrary to the patterns, the text-based passwords use a salt which is stored in the `/data/system/locksettings.db`. Clearly, due to the location where these files are stored, users and applications cannot access them neither for reading nor for writing them. Therefore, attacks to recover the unlocking code are focused either to cases where one has access to the storage and manipulates it to *e.g.* remove the protection mechanism or to sniff the password by side channel attacks [13,40,42].

While the user is not allowed to read nor modify the content of the two aforementioned files, an application is able to determine which is the locking modality that is used. To achieve it, the application must simply request the file size of the two files. Obviously, the file whose size is a positive number indicates which of the two modalities is used, as both files exist in the filesystem regardless of which modality the user prefers.

To replicate the lock screen's UI, one also needs to collect the user's wallpaper. Notably, in Android, all applications are allowed to access device's wallpaper by requesting the `getDrawable` property without the need for declaring any dangerous permission, as reported by the Authors, in Security Issue 219663. This choice can be considered rather dubious as users would most often use personal photos as their wallpaper. Clearly, apart from the use described in our attack, this feature also enables apps to profile users since the content of the wallpaper could reveal social connections, religious and political beliefs or even sexual preferences.

Combining the above information we are able to prepare the screen that is be presented to the user when he wants to unlock the phone, since the device's secure lock background image is almost always the blurred version of the user's wallpaper. The malicious application is seemingly harmless and can consist of several activities. Obviously, the fake lock screen functions as the real one, yet it records all touch events, which are stored and transmitted to the adversary to recover the unlocking code. The interface and steps of our attack for the case of pattern locked smartphone are illustrated in Figs. 2a and b.

To accomplish an attack that will result in sniffing a user's lock screen pin or pattern, our approach requires the implementation of a BroadcastReceiver class that will be capable of listening for screen-off events, (`ACTION_SCREEN_OFF`), while our app is running on the foreground. In other words, the actual initialization of our attack is triggered by the user, not when she tries to unlock her mobile phone by using the power button, but on the contrary when she locks her phone so that she will subsequently unlock it for the next use. As a result, our fake lock screen will be brought to the foreground after the screen-off event and will remain there invisible until the moment the user tries to unlock her smartphone. However, due to Android OS's restrictions for security reasons, this "special" kind of broadcast receiver cannot be registered in the app's manifest but only programmatically on runtime, nor can it be associated with a different activity than the one that registered the receiver. To overcome these restrictions our app registers the broadcast receiver programmatically through a "dummy" activity and most importantly the same activity is also used to create the fake lock screen. We accomplish this "transformation" of the dummy activity into the desired one by hiding all the views that were used in it and by replacing them with visible ones that where previously hidden, which comprise the "desired" fake lock screen activity. Of course, the device's specs are "welcomed" by attackers in order to "fine tune" the attack, such as screen size and screen fonts, and thus produce a "convincing" result. In order to force our fake lock screen precede the real lock screen when the victim presses the power button, some special flags are used, such as the `FLAG_SHOW_WHEN_LOCKED` parameter. Finally, while the user interacts with our fake lock screen we manage to create a simple path data structure where each (X,Y) coordinate regarding touch screen events and movements is recorded, `ACTION_DOWN`, `ACTION_UP` and `ACTION_MOVE`. Obviously, analysing this data structure can straightforwardly reveal a victim's lock screen pattern. Certainly, producing a fake lock screen that consists of UI controls to capture a 4 digit screen lock is simpler.

### 3.5 Inferring Foreground Application

For obvious security and privacy reasons, Android prevents applications from inferring which application is on the foreground. Nonetheless, it allows applications to know, without requesting any dangerous permission, which applications are installed in the device, as well as which ones are currently running; the latter only applies for all Android versions prior to Nougat. While these permissions and restrictions are performed in the SDK, one may dig into the OS layer to retrieve this information.

Android is practically a Linux system and as most of the Unix-like systems it follows the same approach for handling its filesystems. One well-known, yet special filesystem is `procfs` which is utilised to store the information of the processes that are executed by the operating system. While accessing the information in this filesystem is well protected, in terms of reading and altering the stored information this does not actually prevent side leakages. In principle, in Android these mechanisms are more strict as each application is a separate user, and as such, each application is prevented from accessing the "internals" of the other. Nonetheless, some metadata are publicly available to all applications.

Special concern should be paid to the `oom_adj_score` file. To understand the importance of this parameter we will discuss some Android specific features of process management. In principle, Android runs is mobile devices which have constrained resources, whereas many refinements have been introduced by Google in order to allow Android to perform resource allocation and release. Since the device has limited memory, Android performs the following steps to achieve stability. If there is memory free, Android uses Zygote to launch a new VM. However, if there is not any free memory, it has to close the last user application. In this regard, each application is given a `oom_adj_score`, stored under `/proc/[pid]/`. By monitoring the aforementioned files, and pruning all the system applications, one can easily determine which is the application which is less probable to be killed, which eventually, is the foreground app.

## 4 Use Cases and Implemented Attacks

To demonstrate our attacks and highlight their importance, we have prepared a set of different attack scenarios that reveal different exposures from the Android UI. Some representative interfaces of the attacks that we launched are illustrated in Fig. 2. In these screenshots we have deliberately created a sloppy interface for most of the attacks so that the reader can easily determine the overlayed activity as well as the exposed functionality. As discussed in the previous section, an adversary can easily present either transparent or sized activities on top of the benign ones to provide the necessary look and feel and trick the user into performing illegal actions and/or sniff input data.

While one could argue that the activities and their resources must be declared in the manifest, one can easily bypass this restriction by simply using webviews that cover the whole activity. In this regard, an adversary can load dynamically any interface he wants. Note that the adversary through his malicious app already knows which apps are installed in the victim's device, also illustrated in Fig. 2, so he can easily prepare the appropriate interface and load it dynamically when deemed necessary. Therefore, in what follows, we consider the creation and delivery of the forged interface as a trivial part of the attack that is made mostly through Firebase.

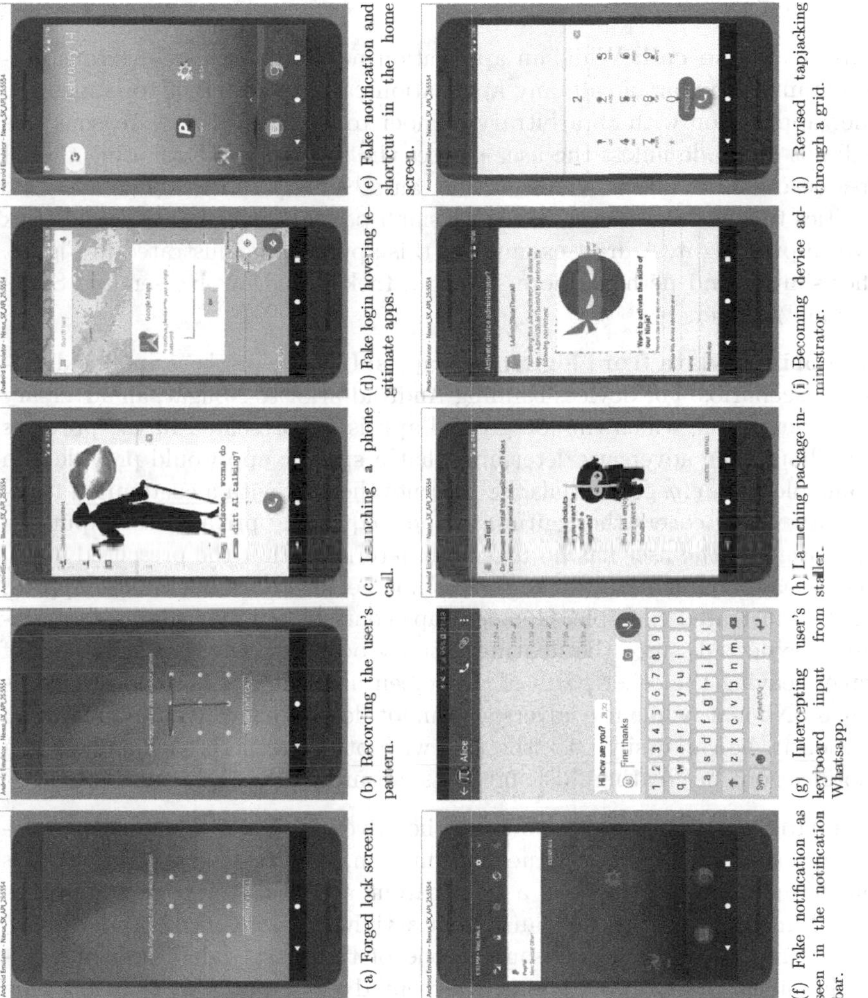

(a) Forged lock screen.

(b) Recording the user's pattern.

(c) Launching a phone call.

(d) Fake login hovering legitimate apps.

(e) Fake notification and shortcut in the home screen.

(f) Fake notification as seen in the notification bar.

(g) Intercepting user's keyboard input from Whatsapp.

(h) Launching package installer.

(i) Becoming device administrator.

(j) Revised tapjacking through a grid.

**Fig. 2.** Various UI redressing attacks.

The lifecycle of our attacks is the following. Initially, Malory, the adversary, uploads the malicious app in Google Play; as already reported our apps bypass Bouncer's filters, and the user is tricked into downloading the app and installing it since it requires no special permissions. Then, the app sends through Firebase all the necessary input from the victim's phone. Next, Malory delivers all her payload for the attacks through Firebase. Depending on the installed apps and Android version, the malicious app either timely launches a forged activity or overlays a benign app.

**Starting a phone call:** While an application needs to have a dangerous permission granted to start a call, any application can use an intent to launch the "Phone" application with an arbitrary number to call. For obvious reasons this call will not be made unless the user presses the call button. Exploiting the UI features described in the previous section, an adversary can easily create a set of activities to cover the screen, leaving a small part of the call button and trick the user in pressing it. A draft example of this approach is illustrated in Fig. 2c. Another similar and perhaps more stealth attack would involve sending SMSs to premium numbers.

**Sniffing private data from legitimate apps:** In this case there are two different attack scenarios. For devices running Android prior to Nougat, an adversary is able to determine which the foreground app is, as presented in the previous section. Should the adversary determine that a specific app would provide him with valuable data *e.g.* credentials, he presents the user with a customised floating activity which covers the legitimate app, requesting private user input. As shown in Fig. 2d, the user has no means to determine that the presented activity (shown as a common app dialog) does not belong to the legitimate app. In fact in the illustrated example, Google Maps continues to function in the background as expected, since the floating activity occupies only a specific part of the screen leaving the other parts of the screen unaffected. Considering devices running on Nougat, while the adversary cannot determine which the foreground application is, he can easily trick the user with other methods such as injecting fake notifications or creating fake shortcuts, all mimicking legitimate ones.

**Intercepting sensitive input:** Should the adversary know which is the foreground application via side channel information, as discussed in the previous section, he can present the user a transparent activity. A typical example is illustrated in Fig. 2g where the transparent activity accompanied by a keyboard allows the user to type her message to one of the most widely used messenger applications, Whatsapp. Having intercepted the input, the malicious app displays a message that something went wrong to smoothly return to normal execution.

**Fake notifications:** Based on the latter restriction in Nougat, about determining the foreground app, we tried a different approach: force the user to open a desired application. To achieve this, we exploited the fake notification mechanism, discussed in the previous section. Therefore, we created a malicious app that downloads dynamically both the notification icons and the notification message. Since the adversary knows which the installed apps are, he can easily create a forged notification for one of the victim's apps. In Figs. 2e and f we illustrate this in Nougat using PayPal as the target app. As shown in these screenshots, the user has no means to determine that the foreground activity does not belong to PayPal. As already discussed, the notification in Fig. 2f may not contain the app name, yet the user most probably will not notice it. Clearly, in Marshmallow, since the name restriction does not apply, the user cannot tell the actual difference, as the forged notification will be identical to the real one. Finally, it should be noted that notifications are used as shortcuts, so the user does not spend much time in trying to determine whether there is a name or not; in the case of Nougat, he will trust the icon.

**Fake shortcuts:** Another approach to trick the user into launching the forged activity of the malicious app is to create a fake shortcut on the mobile's home screen. While Android has its application menu locked so that applications cannot add more icons, the same does not apply for the home screen. There, any application using the normal permission `INSTALL_SHORTCUT` can create a shortcut with the icon and name of a legitimate and installed application, as described in the previous section. However, the shortcut actually launches the forged activity from the malicious app and not the legitimate one.

**Installing applications:** Further to performing actions within the scope of the installed applications, an adversary could also trick the user into performing actions within the scope of the operating system per se. For obvious reasons, one would expect that an application would not be allowed to cover activities over them, nonetheless, this is not the case. A profound example is the case of the install manager. Notably, an adversary could download an application from the Internet, by simply using an intent to the browser, or by other means such as utilizing Google Drive, using local files, etc. Practically, using the "Intent" way means that the app does not request Internet permission. Once the download of the APK is finished, the Package Manager is automatically invoked and the malicious app presents the user an activity as in Fig. 2h, to trick him and install another app. In the less sinister scenario, the adversary manages to raise his stats, while in the more sinister, the adversary tricks the user into installing an application which has more dangerous payload and the user would have never downloaded from Google Play.

**Becoming administrator:** In Android 2.2 [3], Google introduced a mechanism that allows users to grant device administration features to specific applications in order to facilitate enterprise applications and to provide them means to apply stricter policies and device management. To this end, an application which is granted this permission can among other features restart the device or wipe its data. To facilitate the installation procedure, Android provides a shortcut so that the application requesting this permission can present the user with this screen. While one would expect that this activity would not be accessible and no one would be able to interact with it once it loses focus, this restriction does not apply. As illustrated in Fig. 2i an adversary can cover the activity with the techniques described in the previous section to trick the user into granting some of the most dangerous permissions. Notwithstanding this deceit, the same security gap is present is other highly dangerous activities, *e.g.* installing custom certificates, granting access to user's notifications to name a few. Apparently, the user can be easily tricked into being blocked from his own device, wiping his own data or even giving full remote access to his data.

**Tapjacking revisited:** The basic concept of most tapjacking attacks in the literature is to create a transparent overlay which exploits a vulnerability in Android's UI to catch the event of user tapping the screen and then passing it to the underlying application. To the best of our knowledge all of these attacks are now obsolete as of Marshmallow. A different approach however is to exploit the grid concept with many sized transparent activities of Fig. 1b. The twist in this approach is that we do not try to pass the event to the underlying application, but we exploit the size of users' fingers, as well as the fact that a "sized" activity can even have a surface of a few pixels. Since the activities can also be transparent and can overlay any application, the malicious app can sense where the user's finger is and derive the user's input. Eventually, if the screen is covered by many small transparent activities, touch events will be sensed by the grid, while the interaction with the underlying application will also exist. Notably, in this scenario, the adversary does not need to know the foreground app, as the malicious app logs almost all user tapping so he can later infer sensitive application such as PINs, credentials, keyboard typing etc. To demonstrate the applicability of this attack we created a proof of concept, yet to facilitate the reader, the sized activities are marked red in Fig. 2j, but in the original, they are transparent.

## 5 Conclusions

User interfaces are tightly entwined with user experience, especially regarding user-smartphone interaction. However, the efforts in improving user interfaces may hinder OS security, as app lifecycles are more complex. All the reported attacks, accompanied with the corresponding proof of concept have been already communicated to Google. In some cases, the Android Security team has already responded and provided corresponding software patches, yet other issues are still under investigation.

Considering the notifications and the shortcuts related issues we believe that both users and developers cannot efficiently protect themselves, unless actions in the side of the operating system are taken. Such actions include enforcing the creation of notifications and shortcuts to pass strictly through resource bound parameters. This way, software systems that statically analyse apps installation packages would be able to detect malicious content, such as duplicated third party logos and potentially harmful string values. When Android OS is abused for either tricking users into making *e.g.* unwanted calls, or for escalating malicious apps privileges, we believe that all the involved in these actions activities must be reviewed to handle events when they lose focus and they are overlaid, so that users are notified accordingly. Notably, this mechanism has been partially deployed *e.g.* in Marshmallow's dangerous run-time permissions dialogs. Another alternative would be to disable all OS activity controls when other UI elements appear in front of them. The latter is done in Google Play app, where the presence of a front layer disables some "dangerous" choices, such as the pressing of the "install" app button. The diversity of the two approaches signifies that the problem is known to Google, yet not to its entity, as the patches were applied per case and not generically.

Unfortunately, the aforementioned countermeasures do not apply for the cases of third party apps, therefore the OS could consider adopting them only for the cases where OS activities are involved. That is because many applications provide "floats" in the front most UI screen layer and users find them very usefull, such as the "chatheads" dialogs that are quite common in chatting apps. Implementing the aforementioned solutions could either cause malfunctioning in a large number of applications or continuous annoying alerts, which would negatively affect UX. Subsequently, this raises the need for alternate countermeasures for the third party apps. Towards this direction, a plausible incitement would be to face these security problems differently and enable apps to protect themselves from malicious software. All Android activities are able to "detect" even the slightest changes in their interaction with the user UI, utilizing the Android activities' lifecycle states. That is, overriding the appropriate methods (*e.g.* `onPause` method for detecting dialogs, or `onStop` method when the activities are fully covered by other UI elements) and act accordingly, like disabling or hiding their "sensitive" UI elements, or even alerting their users.

It is also worth noticing that while intents are extremely helpful in providing intercommunication between Android applications, they can be considered a covert channel in terms of permissions, as they provide an out of the loop way of using data and device resources. This is rather important as in static code analysis, one cannot trace this through the corresponding manifest file or the low level API calls, as intents do not map to the framework's methods. This way, they bypass security checks, increasing the complexity to approaches such as Backes et al. [15] as it requires to determine interdependencies between apps.

Concluding, we may state that due to the lack of visible resources that would allow users to determine which the "actual" foremost app is, users have immediate and absolute trust to their OS that the presented apps are the ones they claim to be. It is the authors' strong belief that by providing some more rules and permissions in the Android's UI handling mechanisms in combination with improving security concerns in app development by developers themselves, would lead to the elimination of the majority of the Android UI related security issues raised in this work.

**Acknowledgments.** This work was supported by the European Commission under the Horizon 2020 Programme (H2020), as part of the *OPERANDO* project (Grant Agreement no. 653704) and is based upon work from COST Action *CRYPTACUS*, supported by COST (European Cooperation in Science and Technology). The authors would like to thank *ElevenPaths* for their valuable feedback and granting them access to Tacyt.

## References


1. AlJarrah, A., Shehab, M.: Maintaining user interface integrity on android. In: 2016 IEEE 40th Annual Computer Software and Applications Conference (COMPSAC), vol. 1, pp. 449–458. IEEE (2016)
2. Android Developer: ActivityManager – getRunningTasks. https://developer.android.com/reference/android/app/ActivityManager.html#getRunningTasks(int). Accessed 28 Mar 2017
3. Android Developer: Device administration. https://developer.android.com/guide/topics/admin/device-admin.html. Accessed 28 Mar 2017
4. Android Developer: Intent. https://developer.android.com/reference/android/content/Intent.html. Accessed 28 Mar 2017
5. Android Developer: Intents and intent filters. https://developer.android.com/guide/components/intents-filters.html. Accessed 28 Mar 2017
6. Android Developer: Manifest.permission – READ_EXTERNAL_STORAGE. https://developer.android.com/reference/android/Manifest.permission.html#READ_EXTERNAL_STORAGE. Accessed 28 Mar 2017
7. Android Developer: Manifest.permission – SYSTEM_ALERT_WINDOW. https://developer.android.com/reference/android/Manifest.permission.html#SYSTEM_ALERT_WINDOW. Accessed 28 Mar 2017
8. Android Developer: Multi-window support. https://developer.android.com/guide/topics/ui/multi-window.html. Accessed 28 Mar 2017
9. Android Developer: Notification.builder. https://developer.android.com/reference/android/app/Notification.Builder.html. Accessed 28 Mar 2017
10. Android Developer: PackageManager – getInstalledApplications. https://developer.android.com/reference/android/content/pm/PackageManager.html#getInstalledApplications. Accessed 28 Mar 2017
11. Android Developer: Settings. https://developer.android.com/reference/android/provider/Settings.html#ACTION_MANAGE_OVERLAY_PERMISSION. Accessed 28 Mar 2017
12. Android Developer: WindowManager. https://developer.android.com/reference/android/view/WindowManager.html. Accessed 28 Mar 2017
13. Aviv, A.J., Gibson, K., Mossop, E., Blaze, M., Smith, J.M.: Smudge attacks on smartphone touch screens. In: Proceedings of the 4th USENIX Conference on Offensive technologies, pp. 1–7. USENIX Association (2010)
14. Aviv, A.J., Sapp, B., Blaze, M., Smith, J.M.: Practicality of accelerometer side channels on smartphones. In: Proceedings of the 28th Annual Computer Security Applications Conference, pp. 41–50. ACM (2012)
15. Backes, M., Bugiel, S., Derr, E., McDaniel, P., Octeau, D., Weisgerber, S.: On demystifying the android application framework: re-visiting android permission specification analysis. In: 25th USENIX Security Symposium (USENIX Security 2016), pp. 1101–1118. USENIX Association, Austin (2016)
16. Bianchi, A., Corbetta, J., Invernizzi, L., Fratantonio, Y., Kruegel, C., Vigna, G.: What the app is that? Deception and countermeasures in the android user interface. In: Proceedings of the 2015 IEEE Symposium on Security and Privacy, pp. 931–948. IEEE Computer Society (2015)

17. Chen, J., Chen, H., Bauman, E., Lin, Z., Zang, B., Guan, H.: You shouldn't collect my secrets: thwarting sensitive keystroke leakage in mobile IME apps. In: 24th USENIX Security Symposium (USENIX Security 2015), pp. 657–690. USENIX Association, Washington, D.C. (2015)
18. Chen, Q.A., Qian, Z., Mao, Z.M.: Peeking into your app without actually seeing it: UI state inference and novel android attacks. In: 23rd USENIX Security Symposium (USENIX Security 2014), pp. 1037–1052. USENIX Association, San Diego (2014)
19. Faruki, P., Bharmal, A., Laxmi, V., Ganmoor, V., Gaur, M.S., Conti, M., Rajarajan, M.: Android security: a survey of issues, malware penetration, and defenses. IEEE Commun. Surv. Tutorials **17**(2), 998–1022 (2015)
20. Felt, A.P., Finifter, M., Chin, E., Hanna, S., Wagner, D.: A survey of mobile malware in the wild. In: Proceedings of the 1st ACM Workshop on Security and Privacy in Smartphones and Mobile Devices, pp. 3–14. ACM (2011)
21. Fernandes, E., Chen, Q.A., Paupore, J., Essl, G., Halderman, J.A., Mao, Z.M., Prakash, A.: Android UI deception revisited: attacks and defenses. In: Grossklags, J., Preneel, B. (eds.) FC 2016. LNCS, vol. 9603, pp. 41–59. Springer, Heidelberg (2017). doi:10.1007/978-3-662-54970-4_3
22. Johnson, K.: Revisiting android tapjacking (2011). https://nvisium.com/blog/2011/05/26/revisiting-android-tapjacking/
23. Kartaltepe, E.J., Morales, J.A., Xu, S., Sandhu, R.: Social network-based botnet command-and-control: emerging threats and countermeasures. In: Zhou, J., Yung, M. (eds.) ACNS 2010. LNCS, vol. 6123, pp. 511–528. Springer, Heidelberg (2010). doi:10.1007/978-3-642-13708-2_30
24. Lipp, M., Gruss, D., Spreitzer, R., Maurice, C., Mangard, S.: Armageddon: cache attacks on mobile devices. In: 25th USENIX Security Symposium (USENIX Security 2016), pp. 549–564. USENIX Association, Austin (2016)
25. Liu, J., Wang, Y., Kar, G., Chen, Y., Yang, J., Gruteser, M.: Snooping keystrokes with mm-level audio ranging on a single phone. In: Proceedings of the 21st Annual International Conference on Mobile Computing and Networking, pp. 142–154. ACM (2015)
26. Liu, X., Zhou, Z., Diao, W., Li, Z., Zhang, K.: When good becomes evil: keystroke inference with smartwatch. In: Proceedings of the 22nd ACM SIGSAC Conference on Computer and Communications Security, pp. 1273–1285. ACM (2015)
27. Lockheimer, H.: Android and security. http://googlemobile.blogspot.com/2012/02/android-and-security.html. Accessed 28 Mar 2017
28. Malisa, L., Kostiainen, K., Och, M., Capkun, S.: Mobile application impersonation detection using dynamic user interface extraction. In: Askoxylakis, I., Ioannidis, S., Katsikas, S., Meadows, C. (eds.) ESORICS 2016. LNCS, vol. 9878, pp. 217–237. Springer, Cham (2016). doi:10.1007/978-3-319-45744-4_11
29. Marforio, C., Masti, R.J., Soriente, C., Kostiainen, K., Capkun, S.: Hardened setup of personalized security indicators to counter phishing attacks in mobile banking. In: Proceedings of the 6th Workshop on Security and Privacy in Smartphones and Mobile Devices, pp. 83–92. ACM (2016)
30. Niemietz, M., Schwenk, J.: UI redressing attacks on android devices, blackHat Abu Dhabi (2012)
31. Oberheide, J., Miller, C.: Dissecting the android bouncer. In: SummerCon (2012)
32. Richardson, D.: Android tapjacking vulnerability (2010). https://blog.lookout.com/look-10-007-tapjacking/

33. Shukla, D., Kumar, R., Serwadda, A., Phoha, V.V.: Beware, your hands reveal your secrets! In: Proceedings of the 2014 ACM SIGSAC Conference on Computer and Communications Security, CCS 2014, pp. 904–917. ACM, New York (2014)
34. Simon, L., Anderson, R.: Pin skimmer: inferring pins through the camera and microphone. In: Proceedings of the Third ACM Workshop on Security and Privacy in Smartphones and Mobile Devices, pp. 67–78. ACM (2013)
35. Van Bruggen, D.: Studying the impact of security awareness efforts on user behavior. Ph.D. thesis, University of Notre Dame (2014)
36. Vidas, T., Votipka, D., Christin, N.: All your droid are belong to us: a survey of current android attacks. In: Proceedings of the 5th USENIX Conference on Offensive Technologies, p. 10. USENIX Association (2011)
37. Wu, L., Brandt, B., Du, X., Ji, B.: Analysis of clickjacking attacks and an effective defense scheme for android devices. In: IEEE Conference on Communications and Network Security. IEEE (2016)
38. Wu, L., Du, X., Wu, J.: Effective defense schemes for phishing attacks on mobile computing platforms. IEEE Trans. Veh. Technol. **65**(8), 6678–6691 (2016)
39. Xu, Z., Bai, K., Zhu, S.: Taplogger: inferring user inputs on smartphone touchscreens using on-board motion sensors. In: Proceedings of the Fifth ACM Conference on Security and Privacy in Wireless and Mobile Networks, pp. 113–124. ACM (2012)
40. Ye, G., Tang, Z., Fang, D., Chen, X., Kim, K.I., Taylor, B., Wang, Z.: Cracking android pattern lock in five attempts (2017)
41. Ying, L., Cheng, Y., Lu, Y., Gu, Y., Su, P., Feng, D.: Attacks and defence on android free floating windows. In: Proceedings of the 11th ACM on Asia Conference on Computer and Communications Security, pp. 759–770. ACM (2016)
42. Zhang, J., Zheng, X., Tang, Z., Xing, T., Chen, X., Fang, D., Li, R., Gong, X., Chen, F.: Privacy leakage in mobile sensing: your unlock passwords can be leaked through wireless hotspot functionality. Mobile Inf. Syst. **2016**, 8793025:1–8793025:14 (2016)

# Cloud Security

# SGX-LAPD: Thwarting Controlled Side Channel Attacks via Enclave Verifiable Page Faults

Yangchun Fu[1], Erick Bauman[2(✉)], Raul Quinonez[2], and Zhiqiang Lin[2]

[1] Google Inc., Mountain View, USA
yangchun.fu@utdallas.edu
[2] The University of Texas at Dallas, Richardson, USA
{erick.bauman,raul.quinonez,zhiqiang.lin}@utdallas.edu

**Abstract.** To make outsourcing computing more practical, Intel recently introduced SGX, a hardware extension that creates secure enclaves for the execution of client applications. With SGX, instruction execution and data access inside an enclave are invisible to the underlying OS, thereby achieving both confidentiality and integrity for outsourced computing. However, since SGX excludes the OS from its trusted computing base, now a malicious OS can attack SGX applications, particularly through controlled side channel attacks, which can extract application secrets through page fault patterns. This paper presents SGX-LAPD, a novel defense that uses compiler instrumentation and enclave verifiable page fault to thwart malicious OS from launching page fault attacks. We have implemented SGX-LAPD atop Linux kernel 4.2.0 and LLVM 3.6.2. Our experimental results show that it introduces reasonable overhead for SGX-nbench, a set of SGX benchmark programs that we developed.

**Keywords:** SGX · Trusted Execution · Controlled channel attack · Page fault

## 1 Introduction

Trusted computing, or Trusted Execution Environment (TEE), is a foundational technology to ensure confidentiality and integrity of modern computing. Over the past few decades, a considerable amount of research has been carried out to search for practical ways for trusted computing, e.g., by using a formally verified operating system (OS) [16], or using a virtual machine monitor (VMM), hypervisor [9,25], system management mode (SMM) [30], and even BIOS [28] to monitor the kernel and application integrity, or with hardware support [17]. Increasingly, hardware based technologies for TEE (e.g., TPM [20], TrustZone [23]) have rapidly matured. The most recent advancement in this direction is the Intel Software Guard eXtensions (SGX) [13,18].

**Electronic supplementary material** The online version of this chapter (doi:10.1007/978-3-319-66332-6_16) contains supplementary material, which is available to authorized users.


M. Dacier et al. (Eds.): RAID 2017, LNCS 10453, pp. 357–380, 2017.
DOI: 10.1007/978-3-319-66332-6_16

At a high level, SGX allows an application or part of an application to run inside a secure enclave, which is an isolated execution environment. SGX hardware, as a part of the CPU, prevents malicious software, including the OS, hypervisor, or even low-level firmware (e.g., SMM) from compromising its integrity and secrecy. SGX provides opportunities for securing many types of software such as system logs [15] and computer games [5]. The isolation enabled by SGX is particularly useful in cloud computing, where customers cannot control the infrastructure owned by cloud providers. Haven [6] pioneered the idea of enabling unmodified application binaries to run on SGX in a cloud by utilizing a library OS [22]. VC3 [24] demonstrated privacy-aware data analytics in the cloud. Ohrimenko et al. [19] presented a number of privacy preserving multi-party machine learning algorithms running in SGX machines for cloud users, while Chandra et al. [7] provide a more scalable solution on larger models using randomization.

Unfortunately, since SGX excludes the OS kernel from its trusted computing base, SGX enclave programs can certainly be attacked by the underlying OS. A powerful demonstration of this is controlled channel attacks, which can extract application secrets using the page fault patterns of an enclave's execution [31]. In particular, by controlling the page table mappings of an enclave program, a malicious OS can observe a number of patterns regarding an application's page access footprint, such as the number of page faults, the base virtual address of the faulting pages, the sequence of page faults, and even the timing of page faults. If an attacker also has the binary code of the enclave program, he or she can recover a lot of secrets (e.g., text documents, outlines of JPEG images) based exclusively on the page access patterns.

Given such a significant threat from page-fault side channel attacks, it is imperative to design new defenses. Thus in this paper we present SGX-LAPD, a system built atop both OS kernel and compilers to ensure that the LArge Pages are verifieD by the enclave (LAPD) and attacker triggered page faults are detectable by the enclave itself. The key insight is that page-fault side channel attacks are very effective when the OS uses 4 KB pages; if we can enlarge the page size, most programs will trigger few code page faults—and data page faults can also be significantly reduced (by three orders of magnitude if we use MB level pages). Thus, the challenge lies in how to make sure that the OS has cooperated and really provided large pages to the enclave programs.

Since the only trust for SGX programs is the underlying hardware and the enclave code itself, we have to rely on the enclave program itself to verify whether an OS indeed has provided large pages. As a page-fault attack often incurs significant delays during cross-page control flow transfers, an intuitive approach would be to detect the latency at each cross small-page control flow transfer point. However, there is no reliable way of retrieving the hardware timing information inside the enclave (e.g., `RDTSC` instruction is not supported in SGX v1 [14]), and meanwhile it can also be attacked by the OS. Note that `RDTSC` reads the Time-Stamp Counter from the TSC MSR which can be modified by `WRMSR` instruction [3].

Also, the API sgx_get_trusted_time provided by Intel SGX SDK is also only available in simulation mode.

Interestingly, we notice that each enclave contains a data structure, EXINFO, that tracks the page fault address if a page fault causes the enclave exit [14]. Therefore, we can detect whether an OS has indeed provided large pages by traversing this data structure when there is a page fault. However, when to incur a page fault is decided by the OS, and the enclave program has to deliberately trigger a page fault for such a verification. Therefore, if we can instrument the enclave program to automatically inject a page access and then verify whether a page fault was triggered by checking the EXINFO data structure, we can then detect whether the underlying OS has cooperated. SGX-LAPD is designed exactly based on this idea.

We have implemented SGX-LAPD atop a recent Linux kernel 4.2.0 and LLVM 3.6.2. Specifically, we implemented an OS kernel module to enable the OS to support large page tables, and we implemented a compiler pass in LLVM to recognize the cross small-page control flow transfer points and insert the self-verification code. We have evaluated our system using a number of benchmarks. In order to test SGX-LAPD on actual SGX hardware, we had to port a benchmark, since there are no existing SGX programs to test. We therefore manually created SGX-nbench, a modified version of nbench 2.2.3 running on real SGX hardware. Our experimental results show that SGX-LAPD introduces reasonable performance overhead for the tested benchmarks.

In short, we make the following contributions:

- We present SGX-LAPD, a system that uses large paging via kernel module and self-verifiable page faults through compiler instrumented code to defeat the controlled side channel attacks.
- We have also developed a new SGX benchmark suite SGX-nbench, for measuring the performance overhead of real SGX programs.
- We have evaluated SGX-LAPD with SGX-nbench and showed that it introduces reasonable overhead for detecting both non-present and non-executable page fault attacks.

## 2 Background and Related Work

In this section, we provide the background on the page fault side channel attacks using a running example in Sect. 2.1, and then discuss the possible defenses and related work in Sect. 2.2. Finally, we reveal how an enclave program handles exceptions in Sect. 2.3, which comprises the basic knowledge in order to understand our defense.

### 2.1 The Page-Fault Side Channel Attack

An SGX enclave program is executed in user mode (ring-3), and it has to ask the underlying OS to provide resources such as memory, CPU, and I/O. As such, this gives a hostile OS (ring-0) the opportunity to attack enclave programs from various vectors, such as manipulating system call execution (e.g., Iago [8] attacks) or controlling page fault access patterns to infer the secrets inside enclave programs [31].

The virtual memory pages of a process are managed by the underlying OS. Specifically, when launching a new process, the OS first creates the page tables and initializes the page table entries for virtual addresses specified in the application binary. When a process is executed, if the corresponding virtual page has not been mapped in the page table yet, a page fault exception will occur, and the CPU will report the faulting address as well as the type of page access (read or write) to the page fault handler, which will be responsible for mapping the missing pages. When a process terminates, the OS will delete the virtual to physical mappings and reclaims all the virtual pages.

Page faults for SGX processes are treated in the same way as regular processes, with the only difference that the page fault handler can observe just the base address of the faulting address. Therefore, by controlling the page table mappings, a hostile OS can observe all of the page access patterns of a victim SGX process. If the attacker also has the detailed virtual address mappings (e.g., when owning a copy of the SGX enclave binary), such a page fault attack is extremely powerful as demonstrated by Xu et al. [31].

**A Running Example.** To understand clearly the nature of the page fault side channel attack, we use example code from [31] as a running example to explain how SGX-LAPD works to defeat this attack. The source code of this example is shown in Fig. 1(a). At a high level, this enclave program takes user input `GENDER` and returns a welcome string based on whether the `GENDER` is `MALE` or `FEMALE`. To show this program is vulnerable to the page fault attack, we compile its source code using LLVM deliberately with the option "`align-all-function=12`" that aligns each function at a 4 KB boundary. The resulting disassembled code for this example is presented in Fig. 1(b), where five control flow transfer instructions inside `WelcomeMessage` are highlighted.

We can notice that a hostile OS can infer whether a user enters `MALE` or `FEMALE` to the program by observing the page fault profiles. Specifically, when all other pages except 0x404000 are marked unmapped: if a subsequent page fault accesses page 0x403000 (for control flow transfer "`callq WelcomeMessageForFemale`"), then an attacker can infer `GENDER` is `FEMALE`; otherwise an attacker can conclude `GENDER` is `MALE` when page 0x402000 is accessed.

### 2.2 Possible Defenses and Related Work

In the following, we examine various possible defenses. At a high level, we categorize them into hardware assisted and software based defenses.

**Hardware-Assisted Defenses.** As the hardware of a system is usually in the TCB, it can be helpful to utilize the hardware to enforce security.

```
const char* WelcomeMessageForMale()
{
    char* mesg = "Hello sir!";
    return mesg;
}
const char* WelcomeMessageForFemale()
{
    char* mesg = "Hello madam!";
    return mesg;
}
const char* WelcomeMessage(GENDER s)
{
    const char* mesg;
    if (s == MALE) { //MALE
        mesg = WelcomeMessageForMale();
    } else { //FEMALE
        mesg = WelcomeMessageForFemale();
    }
    return mesg;
}
```

(a) Source Code

```
402000 <WelcomeMessageForMale>:
402000: 55                   push   %rbp
402001: 48 89 e5             mov    %rsp,%rbp
...
          402012: c3                       retq
...
403000 <WelcomeMessageForFemale>:
403000: 55                   push   %rbp
403001: 48 89 e5             mov    %rsp,%rbp
...
403012: c3                   retq
...
404000 <WelcomeMessage>:
404000: 55                   push   %rbp
404001: 48 89 e5             mov    %rsp,%rbp
404004: 48 83 ec 10          sub    $0x10,%rsp
404008: 89 7d fc             mov    %edi,-0x4(%rbp)
40400b: 85 ff                test   %edi,%edi
40400d: 74 07                je     404016 <WelcomeMessage+0x16>
40400f: e8 ec ef ff ff       callq  403000 <WelcomeMessageForFemale>
404014: eb 05                jmp    40401b <WelcomeMessage+0x1b>
404016: e8 e5 df ff ff       callq  402000 <WelcomeMessageForMale>
40401b: 48 89 45 f0          mov    %rax,-0x10(%rbp)
40401f: 48 8b 45 f0          mov    -0x10(%rbp),%rax
404023: 48 83 c4 10          add    $0x10,%rsp
404027: 5d                   pop    %rbp
404028: c3                   retq
```

(b) Disassembled Code

**Fig. 1.** Our running example.

- **Enclave Managed Paging.** A very intuitive approach is to allow the enclave itself to manage the paging (i.e., self-paging [12]). Once the enclave has been granted this capability, it can disable paging out sensitive pages, or enforce large pages, etc.
- **Hardware Enforced Contractual Execution.** Recently, Shinde et al. [27] proposed having the hardware enforce a contract between the application and the OS. Such a contract states that the OS will leave a certain number of pages in memory; if a page fault that violates the contract does occur, the hardware reports the violation to the secure application.

While the hardware-assisted approaches sound appealing, they have to modify the hardware to add new mechanisms, such as securely delivering the page fault address to the application page fault handler without relying on the OS. In addition, hardware modifications require significant time before widespread adoption is possible.

**Software-Based Defenses.** Software defenses have significant advantages over hardware modifications, one of which is that they can work on existing platform. We focus more on software defenses due to this. Note that software approaches can have the freedom of rewriting the binary code or recompiling the program source to add new capabilities on the enclave program. A number of defenses can be designed:

- **ORAM.** ORAM [11,21] is a technique for hiding the memory contents and access patterns of a trusted component from an untrusted component. Initially it was a software obfuscation technique, but recently there has been increasing interest in applying ORAM to build practical cloud storage. Theoretically, ORAM can be applied to protect the page fault patterns, but ORAM has large space requirements and high overhead.
- **Normalization.** Another approach is to make sensitive portions of the code behave identically for all possible inputs. However, this is difficult because not only must all page accesses be identical, but also each execution branch should take the same time to execute. Meanwhile, as demonstrated by Shinde et al. [27] in their use of deterministic multiplexing to execute the sensitive code, such an approach runs the risk of imposing extremely high overhead (up to 4000X), as the execution of any path must also perform all the page faults that every other path might make.
- **Randomization and Noise Injection.** Alternatively, if the code is hard to normalize, then we can introduce randomization and noise to make attacks harder. For instance, we can apply the same principle as ASLR [29] by performing fine-grained randomization (e.g., [4,10]) of code and data locations to hide from an attacker what code or data is actually being accessed, or inject noise into normal program behavior to hide legitimate page accesses among random fake ones. However, the challenge lies in how to make the randomization or noise indistinguishable from the normal page fault patterns.
- **Detection.** If an application is able to detect a controlled page fault attack, then it has the ability to abort execution before an attacker can extract the secret. However, the challenge lies in extracting the unique signatures for this attack. Recently, T-SGX [26] leverages code instrumentation and Transactional Synchronization Extensions (TSX) mechanism to detect whether there is any exception occurs inside a transaction. Similar to T-SGX, we also take a detection approach and we both use compiler instrumentation to insert the detection logic. However, the difference is that T-SGX relies on TSX whereas SGX-LAPD does not depend on this hardware feature and instead it uses large pages.

### 2.3 Exception Handling Inside SGX

Since a page fault is an exception and SGX-LAPD needs to use some internal enclave data structures for the defense, we would like to examine in greater detail how SGX handles exceptions. The following study is based on the trace from a real SGX platform by executing our instrumented running example and confirmed with the description from the SGX programming reference [14].

By design, an exception will trigger an asynchronous enclave exit (AEX), and the CPU execution has to leave the enclave and come back through an ENTER or ERESUME instruction. In general, there are 10 exceptions [14] an SGX enclave can capture, and the type of the exception is stored in the EXITINFO.VECTOR field, which is at offset 0xA0 in the GPRSGX region, as illustrated in Fig. 2. Note that the 4 bytes of EXITINFO contain the information that reports the exit reasons (i.e., which exception) to the software inside the enclave, and the first byte is the VECTOR field. The GPRSGX region holds the processor general purpose registers as well as the AEX information. Among the 10 exceptions, we are interested in GP, general protection fault, which is caused by illegal access, e.g., accessing thread control structure (TCS) inside an enclave and PF, the page fault exception. Exceptions such as DV (divide by zero), BP (int 3 for debugging), and UD (undefined instruction, e.g., executing CPUID inside enclave) etc., are out of our interest, though they are all handled similarly as GP by the CPU.

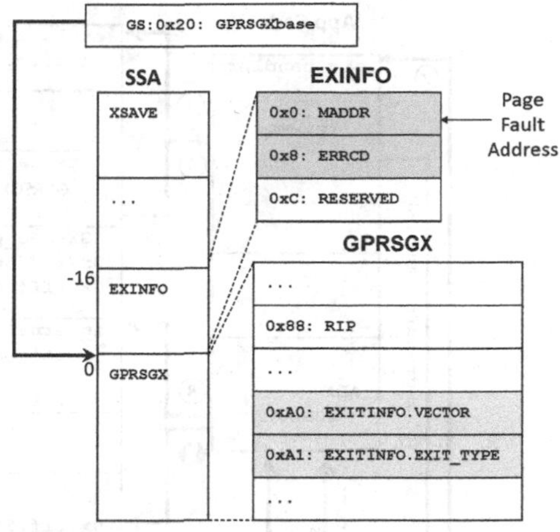


**Fig. 2.** The layout of involved enclave data structures.

**Page Fault Exceptions.** An exception is handled by system software first, and then by the application defined code. A page fault exception can be entirely handled by the system software (only requires 3 steps of execution), but other exceptions such as GP, DV, or UD require 8 steps, as illustrated in Fig. 3.

Specifically, when an exception occurs, SGX hardware will automatically store the fault instruction address in the GPRSGX.RIP field and the exception vector in the GPRS.EXITINFO.VECTOR field (Step ❶), and meanwhile inform the CPU of the instruction to be executed next, which is defined as the Asynchronous Exit Pointer (AEP, which is normally just an ERESUME instruction). This is because an exception needs to be handled by system software, and the enclave internal address should not be exposed to the system software; the CPU will just execute AEP after handling the exception, so the address is not exposed. Also note that there are only two instructions that can enter an enclave: EENTER and ERESUME. EENTER always starts the execution at the enclave_entry address whereas ERESUME will use the internally maintained GPRSGX.RIP as the starting address.

For a page fault exception, SGX hardware will also store the fault address in MADDR as well as the corresponding error code (ERRCD) in the EXINFO structure, whose layout is presented in Fig. 2. Note that EXINFO and EXITINFO are two different data structures, and EXINFO is only used for PF and GP exceptions, though both of them are stored in the State Save Area (SSA) page.

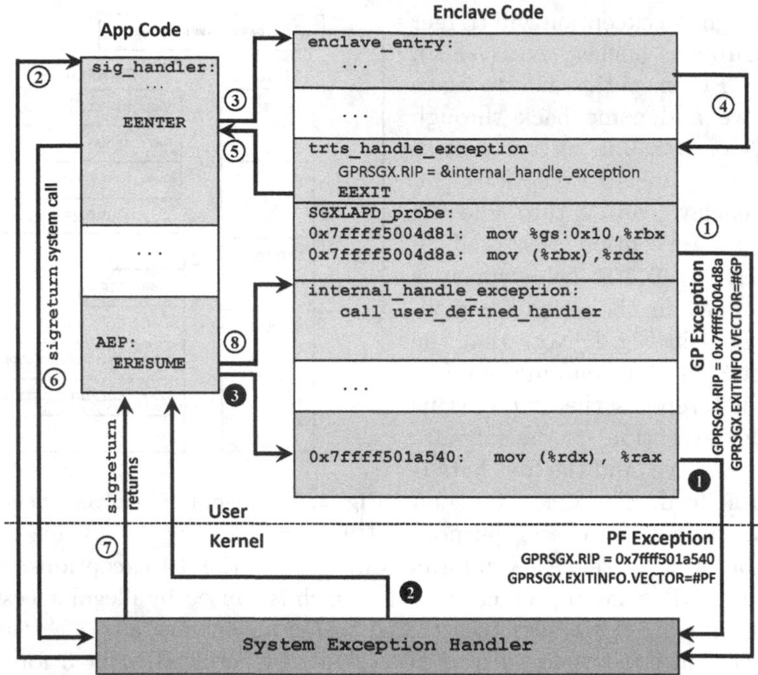


**Fig. 3.** Detailed CPU control flow transfers in SGX enclave exception handling.

After the system software maps the missing page (Step ❷) for the page fault exception, the CPU will continue the execution in user space to execute the ERESUME instruction, which restores registers and returns control to where the exception occurred. Again, the ERESUME instruction is stored at address called AEP, which is defined by the EENTER instruction. After executing ERESUME (Step ❸), the CPU will continue the execution at the fault address that is captured by GPRSGX.RIP. For other exceptions such as GP, the CPU has to execute 8 steps to eventually resolve that exception.

**Non-Page Fault Exceptions.** Some exceptions cannot be completely resolved by the system software. In this case, the event will be triggered again if the enclave is re-entered using ERESUME to the same fault instruction (e.g., a divide by 0 instruction). Therefore, SGX supports resuming execution at a different location (to skip the fault instruction for instance). However, the fault instruction address is internally stored in GPRSGX.RIP field by the hardware inside enclave, and we must rely on the enclave code to update GPRSGX.RIP to a different instruction location, and then ERESUME to this new location. To tell the enclave and update GPRSGX.RIP, we have to use the EENTER instruction and then EEXIT.

Take a GP exception as an example, as illustrated in Fig. 3: when enclave code accesses data in TCS (thread control structure, which is not supposed to be accessed by the enclave code), it triggers a GP exception (Step ①). The hardware stores the fault instruction address at `GPRSGX.RIP` and the exception number, namely #GP, in `EXITINFO.VECTOR`. Meanwhile, the hardware also passes the `AEP` address to the system software, which is the next instruction to be executed after handling the exception. The system exception handler processes this exception as SIGSEGV, which cannot be completely resolved without collaboration with the enclave code. Therefore, the control flow goes to the user space `sig_handler` (Step ②), which works together with the `trts_handle_exception` function inside the enclave to resolve the exception. More specifically, after learning more details about this exception, `sig_handler` executes `EENTER` at Step ③ and then the execution goes to the `enclave_entry` point.

Note that `enclave_entry` is defined in the enclave binary and initialized by `EINIT`, and `EENTER` will start to execute enclave code at `enclave_entry`, which normally contains a dispatch table. In our exception handling case, it will call trusted exception handling function `trts_handle_exception` (Step ④) to reset `GPRSGX. RIP` to the address of the `internal_handle_exception` function, and then it executes `EEXIT` at Step ⑤ to continue the execution of `signal_handler`, which further executes system call `sigreturn` (Step ⑥) to trap to the kernel. Then at Step ⑦, the `sigreturn` system call will return to `AEP`, which will execute `ERESUME` instruction (Step ⑧). Having set up the `GPRSGX.RIP` value with `internal_handle_ exception`, enclave code will execute this function, call the corresponding user defined handler if there is one, and continue the execution.

**To Capture Page Fault Exceptions** SGX hardware will not automatically report a page fault exception to `EXINFO` and `EXITINFO` unless the `EXINFO`-bit (namely `SECS. MISCSELECT[0]`) is set, and this bit can be controlled in SGX-v2, not in the current market available SGX v1. We have verified this observation in a real SGX-v2 machine with the help from the Intel SGX team. Note that `SECS` is the enclave control structure, which contains meta-data used by the hardware to protect the enclave and is created by the `ECREATE` instruction. Enclave developers can set the `SECS.MISCSELECT` field before invoking `ECREATE` to create the enclave. Once the `EXINFO`-bit is set, both GP and PF will be reported in the `EXINFO` structure. Therefore, an enclave can inject a GP exception to probe whether `EXINFO`-bit has been set, as we have demonstrated in the `SGXLAPD_probe` code in Fig. 3.

## 3 System Overview

### 3.1 Scope and Assumptions

The focus of this paper is on defending the controlled channel attacks, which can be more specifically termed as page fault attacks. There are two types of page fault attacks: code page fault and data page fault. As a first step, we focus on the code page fault attacks and leave the protection of data page fault attacks to future work. Also, we focus on the Linux platform.

We assume the SGX hardware and the enclave program itself are trusted. While we wish for the OS to provide large pages, the OS may not cooperate and may cheat the enclave programs. Therefore, we will verify whether an OS indeed provides large pages from the application itself. Regarding the SGX hardware, the market available one is Skylake, and we focus on the x86-64 architecture. Typically, under this architecture, the CPU supports 4K and 2M page sizes [2]. We use 2M large pages. Also, we assume an attacker has a binary code copy of our enclave code, the same threat model as in [31].

### 3.2 Challenges and Approaches

**Key Idea.** The goal of SGX-LAPD is to minimize page fault occurrence by using large pages (i.e., 2 MB). However, an OS may not provide large pages to the enclave program, and therefore the key idea of SGX-LAPD is to verify from the enclave itself whether an OS provides it 2 MB or 4 KB size pages. To perform the verification, fortunately we have another observation: if the OS is hostile and only provides 4 KB size pages, but if there is no controlled page fault attack, the execution will still be normal; but if there is such an attack, then a cross 4 KB page control flow transfer will trigger a page fault. If we have set the enclave to report page fault exceptions to `EXINFO`, we can detect this attack by checking the `MADDR` field in this data structure. Also, another reason to use 2 MB pages is to minimize the page fault occurrences for enclave code, since most programs have less than 2 MB code. If we do not use large pages, we cannot differentiate whether the page fault is malicious or benign when a real page fault occurs.

**Challenges.** However, there are still two major challenges we have to solve:

- **How to insert the verification code.** We certainly cannot manually insert the verification code into the enclave binary, as that would be error-prone and not scalable. Instead, we must resort to either binary code rewriting or compilers to automatically insert our code. Meanwhile, not all control flow transfers need the verification; we only need to check those that cross 4 KB page boundaries and we must identify them to insert our code.
- **How to perform the verification.** At each cross 4 KB page control flow transfer, we need to know how to traverse the `EXITINFO` and `EXINFO` structures inside the enclave in order to retrieve data such as the fault address. Meanwhile, we also have to decide whether the fault is legal or not since there could exist enclaves that have more than 2 MB code.

**Approaches.** To address the first challenge, we decide to modify a mainstream compiler, LLVM, to automatically insert the large page verification code, which will be executed at run-time inside an enclave to make sure the OS really cooperates. The reason why we selected a compiler approach is because SGX essentially comes with a set of new instructions, and it requires an ecosystem change for applications to really take advantage of its security features (unless one is directly running a legacy application inside the enclave using a library OS).

We use the insight we learned in Sect. 2.3 to address the second challenge. Specifically, we notice that inside the enclave, `%gs:0x20` always points to the `GPRSGX` region (as illustrated in Fig. 2), from which we can easily reach `EXINFO`, which is at `(%gs:0x20)-16`, and `EXITINFO`, which is at `(%gs:0x20)+ 0xA0`. To allow legal control flow transfers across 2M page boundaries, our instrumented code will also collect the source address of the control flow transfer in addition to the target fault address. If this transfer crosses to another 2 MB page, it will be considered legal. Next, we present our detailed verification algorithm using our running example.

### 3.3 The Verification Algorithm

The page fault exception attack can be triggered in two ways. The first and most straightforward way is to manipulate the page mapping (i.e., the P-bit in the page table) and make the target page unmapped. Then any code execution access will trigger a non-present (NP) page fault. This approach has been used by Xu et al. [31]. However, we also determined that there is a second way to perform the attack by making the page non-executable when CPU paging mode is PAE or IA-32e to trigger a non-executable (NX) page fault. Therefore, we provide two strategies to detect these faults.

```
0000000000404000 <WelcomeMessage>:
 404000:  55                      push   %rbp
 404001:  48 89 e5                mov    %rsp,%rbp
 404004:  48 83 ec 10             sub    $0x10,%rsp
 404008:  89 7d fc                mov    %edi,-0x4(%rbp)
 40400b:  85 ff                   test   %edi,%edi
 40400d:  eb 2f                   jmp    40403e <WelcomeMessage+0x3e>
          ...
 40403e:  74 69                   je     4040a9 <WelcomeMessage+0xa9>
 404040:  9c                      pushfq
 404041:  50                      push   %rax
 404042:  56                      push   %rsi
 404043:  52                      push   %rdx
 404044:  48 8d 35 b5 ef ff ff    lea    -0x104b(%rip),%rsi
 40404b:  65 48 8b 04 25 20 00    mov    %gs:0x20,%rax
 404052:  00 00
 404054:  c6 80 a0 00 00 00 00    movb   $0x0,0xa0(%rax)
 40405b:  8a 16                   mov    (%rsi),%dl
 40405d:  8a 90 a0 00 00 00       mov    0xa0(%rax),%dl
 404063:  80 fa 0e                cmp    $0xe,%dl
 404066:  75 05                   jne    40406d <WelcomeMessage+0x6d>
 404068:  e8 a3 c4 ff ff          callq  400510 <abort@plt>
 40406d:  5a                      pop    %rdx
 40406e:  5e                      pop    %rsi
 40406f:  58                      pop    %rax
 404070:  9d                      popfq
 404071:  e8 8a ef ff ff          callq  403000 <WelcomeMessageForFemale>
 404076:  eb 2f                   jmp    4040a7 <WelcomeMessage+0xa7>
          ...
 4040a7:  eb 36                   jmp    4040df <WelcomeMessage+0xdf>
 4040a9:  9c                      pushfq
          ...
 4040da:  e8 21 df ff ff          callq  402000 <WelcomeMessageForMale>
 4040df:  48 89 45 f0             mov    %rax,-0x10(%rbp)
 4040e3:  48 8b 45 f0             mov    -0x10(%rbp),%rax
 4040e7:  48 83 c4 10             add    $0x10,%rsp
 4040eb:  5d                      pop    %rbp
 4040ec:  9c                      pushfq
          ...
 40411b:  c3                      retq
```

**Fig. 4.** Final disassembled code for function `WelcomeMessage` after SGX-LAPD instrumentation for non-present page fault detection.

We note that in terms of detection capability, the NX page fault approach can detect all attacks including both non-present and non-executable faults. However, the NP page fault approach cannot detect non-executable page faults. Therefore, in practice we recommend the use of the NX approach. Only when the CPU is set in non PAE nor IA-32e mode will the NP approach be useful. We provide both approaches just for the completeness of the defense.

**(I). Detecting NP Page Faults.** Since we have instrumented our verification code in the enclave binary at each cross 4 KB-page control flow transfer point, we just need to invoke a target page read (basically inject an explicit page fault) and check whether indeed there is a page fault. If so, a page fault attack is confirmed by checking field `EXITINFO.VECTOR`. To show how SGX-LAPD really performs this, we illustrate the final disassembly of function `WelcomeMessage` in our running example in Fig. 4.

We can notice that for the four direct control flow transfers in `WelcomeMessage` (Fig. 1), we each instrumented 49 bytes of code right before them. The last control flow transfer instruction `retq` has 47 bytes of instrumented code. More specifically, for the first ("`je 404049`") and third ("`jmp 4040df`") control flow transfers, our instrumented code directly performs a within-page jump (i.e., "`jmp 40403e`" and "`jmp 4040a7`") because there is no need for the verification, whereas for the second ("`callq 403000`"), and forth ("`callq 402000`") direct function call, and fifth ("`retq`") function return, our instrumented code first injects a target page read, and then traverses `EXITINFO` in `SSA` to detect whether there is a real page fault.

The full disassembly of our page fault verification code for the second control flow transfer "`callq 403000`" is presented in Fig. 4 from `0x404040` to `0x404070`. In particular, our instrumented code will first save the flag register via `pushfq`, `rax`, `rsi`, and `rdx` in the stack, and then load the target address into `rsi`, i.e., "`lea -0x104b(%rip), %rsi`". After that, it loads the base address of `GPRSGX` into `%rax`, and assigns a zero to the field `EXITINFO.VECTOR` (to clear any prior exceptions recorded in the vector). Then *it performs a one-byte memory read access at the target address*, i.e., "`mov (%rsi), %dl`", to inject a page fault to test if there is any controlled side channel on the target page. After that, the enclave code checks the `EXITINFO.VECTOR` field. If it is set to be `0xe`, a page fault is detected (because there is a page fault for the three just executed instructions, and it must come from attack since enclave memory is not supposed to be swapped out) and we `abort` the execution; otherwise, we pop those saved registers and continue the execution.

**Detecting NX Page Faults.** Instead of using "`mov (%rsi), %dl`" to inject a read page fault, we need to really execute the target page in order to detect the NX page fault if there is any. The verification can be performed at either the destination page or the source page (if we inject a `callq *%rsi` and `retq` pair in the source and target).

If we perform the verification at the destination page, we need to track the source address (because we need to allow cross 2 MB transfers) because a target page can be invoked by many different sources. On the other hand, since at each control flow transfer point we already know the source address, we decide to take the second approach, namely inject a `callq *%rsi` in the source page, and a `retq` in the target page to quickly return. To this end, we need to inject a `retq` in the beginning of each determined basic block, and probe the page fault by quickly returning from the target. We omit the details for brevity here since most of the code is similar to those in Fig. 4.

## 4 Detailed Design

An overview of SGX-LAPD is illustrated in Fig. 5. There are three key components: an SGX-LAPD-compiler and SGX-LAPD-linker that work together to produce the enclave code that contains large page verification code at any cross-small page control flow transfer points, and an SGX-LAPD kernel module that runs in kernel space to provide the 2 MB pages for enclave code. In this section, we provide the detailed design for these three components.

### 4.1 SGX-LAPD-Compiler

The goal of SGX-LAPD-compiler is to automatically insert the 4 KB page fault detection code into each cross page control flow transfer (CFT) at various instructions such as `call/jmp/jcc/ret`. In particular, our compiler needs to track the source and target addresses for the CFTs, and also needs to keep the starting address of the inserted code such that we can later patch our instrumented code to NOP instructions (or other semantically equivalent ones) if the CFT is within a page. Note that only after the code is generated can this patching be performed (by our SGX-LAPD-linker) because we do not know the final concrete address before that.

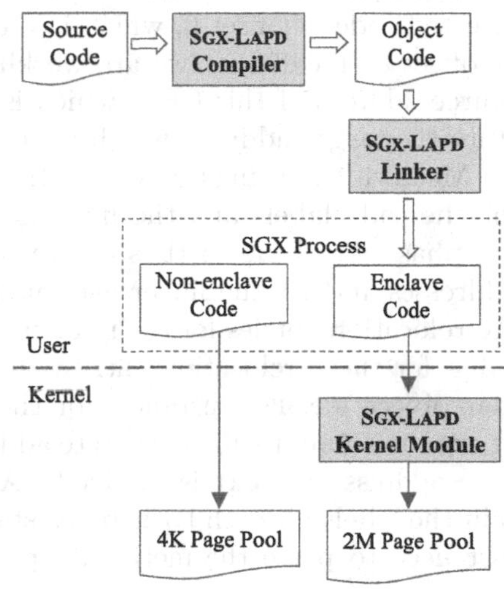


**Fig. 5.** SGX-LAPD overview.

**The Meta-data Used by Our Compiler.** We define a data structure that tracks (1) the starting address of the inserted code, (2) the source, and (3) the target address, for each encountered CFT (except `retq` since we do not know its target address statically). We store this information in a special data section we created and we call it

**Fig. 6.** Examples of SGX-LAPD instrumented code label and the corresponding meta-data.

.SgxLapdCodeLabel. An example of these code labels is presented in Fig. 6. In particular, for the first CFT "je 20c4", we store the starting address of the inserted code at offset 0, which is the symbolic code label .LINST2_0_12. Then at offset 8 (recall that we are working on a 64-bit architecture), we store the source address of this CFT, which is .LINST2_0_11. Finally, at offset 0x10, we store the target address, which is .LINST2_1_8.

Meanwhile, during the compilation phase, we only know the symbol addresses for the code labels and the final concrete address is resolved during the linking phase. We have to thus create relocation entries to store these code label addresses and let the linker eventually resolve them. To this end, we also create relocation entries for each .SgxLapdCodeLabel item. After compilation, the value for these relocation entries will be the logic address within that particular object file. For instance, for the first entry .LINST2_0_12, whose value is .text+0x0200d, its final concrete address will be resolved by the linker (once the base address of .text is resolved). Also, mainstream compilers typically maintain the labels for each basic block starting address and CFT target address. We just need to parse the meta-data provided by compilers and use them for our purposes.

**The Instrumentation Algorithm.** At a high level, to perform the instrumentation, our compiler will iterate through each compiled function right after the code generation phase. For each basic block within a function, we will look for the CFT instructions (i.e., call/jmp/ret and conditional jumps jcc). For each CFT instruction, we get its source address and destination address and store them in the corresponding .SgxLapdCodeLabel section. Note for retq, since we do not know its target address statically, no target address meta data is needed for this instruction.

Since there are different types of CFTs, we have to instrument slightly different verification code. Note that the size difference is due to the different instructions used to fetch the target address for different CFT. Specifically, to detect *NP page faults*, we insert 49 bytes of assembly code if it is a direct CFT, and this assembly code is formed from a macro template with symbols as macro parameters. For indirect CFT, we insert 50 bytes of assembly if it is an indirect CFT through memory (e.g., "call (%rax)"), otherwise 45 bytes if it uses register (e.g., "call %rax"), right before the CFT instructions. For return CFT, we insert 47 bytes of assembly. For *NX page fault* detection, we insert 56 bytes, 57 bytes, 52 bytes, and 53 bytes respectively each for direct CFT, indirect CFT through memory, indirect CFT through register, and return CFT. We also store the starting address of the inserted code into .SgxLapdCodeLabel for direct CFTs. Note that the inserted assembly code will use the destination address symbol for the direct CFTs, and these symbol addresses will be automatically resolved during the linking phase. For all indirect CFTs (e.g., "callq %rax" and retq), we will directly use the correspondingly *run-time* value to access the target page in the inserted assembly code. In other words, we do not need to generate any meta-data for indirect CFTs as their target addresses are computed at runtime, and they also do not need patching.

### 4.2 SGX-LAPD-Linker

**Symbol Address Resolution.** The compiler generates the object file for each input source file using a logic address starting at offset 0. The function or global variable references are all through symbols. Their concrete addresses are not known until linking time, when the linker combines the same section (e.g., `.text`, `.data`) from each object file. To assist the linker in calculating the address for each symbol, there is a relocation entry specifying the relative address to its section. SGX-LAPD leverages this mechanism, and generates symbols for each label that we want to know the final address of into the `.SgxLapdCodeLabel` section and the corresponding relocation record into the `.RELOCATION` section. Later, in the linking phase, the linker can resolve the concrete address for each label. For example, `.LINST2_0_12` is resolved as `0x40400d`, as shown in Fig. 6.

**Code Optimization.** Our SGX-LAPD-compiler has instrumented each CFT due to the fact that we do not know whether any of these transfers will cross a 4 KB page boundary in the final executable. Once the code is finally linked, we can scan the final executable to patch the overly instrumented code.

Thanks to our tracked meta-data, it becomes extremely simple to patch this code. Specifically, we know where to start the patching because our `.SgxNypdCodeLabel` section tracks the starting address of the instrumented code. We also know whether an instrumented CFT crosses a 4 KB page boundary or not because we also know the source and destination addresses of this transfer from `.SgxNypdCodeLabel`. Note that `retq` is not included in this optimization since its destination address is unknown statically.

While we could patch all the inserted bytes to `NOP` instructions, we can just insert an unconditional jump to directly skip the unnecessary code instead. We also know how many bytes our instrumented code occupies (e.g., 49 bytes for direct CFT for non-present page fault detection). As such, we can directly rewrite the first two bytes in the beginning of the instrumented code to an unconditional jump instruction (e.g., "`eb 2f`" to skip the remaining 47 bytes of the 49 bytes of inserted code), as shown in the example code for the first and third CFT instructions in Fig. 4.

### 4.3 SGX-LAPD-Kernel Module

The last component of SGX-LAPD is the kernel module that is responsible for providing 2 MB pages for enclave code. While we can rewrite the OS kernel to provide 2 MB pages for all processes, such a design would waste page resources for many other non-SGX processes. Therefore, we design a kernel module to exclusively manage the page tables for enclave code.

Meanwhile, to really use SGX, Intel provides a number of hardware level data structures such as the Enclave Page Cache Map (EPCM) to manage the enclave page cache (EPC), a secure storage used by the CPU to store the enclave pages [14]. An enclave must run from the EPC, which is protected from non-enclave memory accesses. The EPC is initialized by the BIOS during boot time, and later each enclave process can use privileged instructions such as `ENCLS`

[EADD] to add a page. In other words, we can directly instrument the corresponding SGX kernel code to manage the enclave process page tables.

In particular, the SGX kernel module is responsible for the management of enclave memory allocation and virtual-to-physical mapping. Each enclave page is allocated from a pool of EPC pages, and each EPC page has a size of 4 KB. The process of adding an EPC page into an enclave is by first mapping a 4 KB virtual page to a 4 KB EPC page, then copying the corresponding contents to that EPC page via the EADD instruction. While our SGX-LAPD-kernel module cannot directly add a 2 MB EPC, it groups 512 small pages into a 2 MB page. Note that those 512 smaller pages need to be contiguous in the physical address space, and the physical address of the first page is 2 MB aligned. The SGX kernel module manages all the EPC pages and knows the physical address for each EPC page. We can control which physical pages are mapped to EPC pages.

## 5 Implementation

We have implemented SGX-LAPD for X86-64 Linux. We did not implement anything from scratch; instead we implemented SGX-LAPD-compiler atop LLVM 3.6.2, SGX-LAPD-linker atop `ld-2.24`, and SGX-LAPD-kernel module atop the Intel SGX kernel driver. Below we share some implementation details of interest.

Specifically, we modified the LLVM compilation framework to add a new `Machine Function` pass into the LLVM backend. This new pass operates on LLVM's machine-dependent representation code. Note that our pass is running in the end of the compilation phase, so the code is ready to be emitted into assembly code. This also ensures that our inserted code is not optimized out by other passes. Inside this pass, we iterate each instruction within each basic block in order to identify all CFT instructions. For each CFT, the page fault detection code is inserted into the same basic block before the CFT instruction. We also add a new data section named `.SgxLapdCodeLabel` inside `MCObject FileInfo` class during the initialization phase. The `.SgxLapd CodeLabel` section is like the debug info section and can be removed by using the "`strip -R .SgxLapdCodeLabel`" command. Later in `AsmPrinter`, where the object file is created, we emit the meta data into the `.SgxLapdCodeLabel` section. In total, we added 1,500 LOC to the LLVM framework.

To perform the linking of our compiled code, we modified the linker script to make sure the binary will be loaded into a 2MB-aligned starting address. Our linker also needs to use the meta-data inside the final ELF to optimize our instrumented code. We implemented our own optimization pass and integrated with linker `ld`. Basically, we parse the ELF header to locate the `.SgxLapd CodeLabel` section. Then the meta-data is used to decide whether each control flow transfer crosses a 4 KB page boundary. Control flow transfers that happen inside the same page or cross a 2 MB page boundary are considered valid (no verification check) and thus we insert unconditional jump to skip the verification code for those CFTs. In total, we added 150 LOC into `ld`.

Finally, we modified the Linux SGX kernel driver (initially provided by Intel) to support 2 MB paging, which is only applied to the code pages of an enclave binary. Note that the data pages are still 4 KB. We first instrumented `enclave_create` in the SGX kernel driver to record the base loading address and size of an enclave binary. We also make sure the EPC pages allocated to the enclave binary are contiguous and starting at a 2 MB aligned physical address. Until an `EINIT` is executed, the enclave is not permitted to execute any enclave code, so before the execution of `EINIT`, all the enclave pages have been assigned and initialized. We can group each block of 512 small pages into a 2 MB page by modifying the page table for the enclave process. In total, we added 200 LOC into the SGX kernel driver.

## 6 Evaluation

In this section, we present our evaluation result. We first describe how we create the benchmark programs and set up the experiment in Sect. 6.1, and then describe detailed result in Sect. 6.2.

### 6.1 The Benchmark and Experiment Setup

We have tested SGX-LAPD using two set of benchmarks: one is a manually ported nbench 2.2.3, which we call SGX-nbench, that runs atop a real SGX platform, and the other is the SPEC2006 benchmark that was not ported to SGX. It is important to note that no SGX applications currently exist that we can directly test, but we want to test the results of real SGX performance imposed by our solution. We therefore manually ported nbench into our SGX-nbench, which can be used to measure the true performance for any real SGX solutions. Meanwhile, since porting program to SGX platform requires non-trivial effort, SPEC2006 is in not running atop SGX enclave. We used SPEC2006 to exclusively measure how heavy of code instrumentation is for real programs.

**SGX-nbench.** We ported nbench 2.2.3, which contains 10 tests, to SGX-nbench. Specifically, we ported each benchmark to run inside an enclave in order to measure actual enclave performance. The difficulty of this task is that porting an application to run in SGX is nontrivial; libraries will not be available unless they are statically linked, and all system calls must be made outside the enclave. In addition, enclaves cannot execute certain instructions. Therefore, much of the code must be restructured in order to run inside an enclave. Porting a benchmark of the size and complexity of SPEC is a formidable task, so we focused on porting the more reasonably-sized nbench to measure real enclave performance.

In order to minimize the modifications to nbench, we moved only the minimal code required to run the timed portion of each benchmark into an enclave, and we left the rest of the benchmark code on the host application side. Specifically, we created an enclave application that we linked with modified nbench code; all the timing code stays outside the enclave, and the modified nbench code performs enclave calls to run the initialization code and timed code. The enclave contains the benchmark initialization functions (each benchmark needs to allocate one or more buffers and initialize them with starting data before the benchmark) and iteration functions (each benchmark performs $n$ iterations until $n$ is large enough that the elapsed time is greater than $min$ seconds).

Our port added 5,279 LOC, modified 150 LOC, and removed 447 LOC from nbench 2.2.3. About half of the added LOC comprised enclave code or host application enclave initialization code, while the other added LOC were added to call the enclave functions for each of the benchmarks.

**SPEC2006.** We directly compiled SPEC2006 by using `clang` compiled from our modified LLVM framework. There are 31 benchmarks provided by SPEC2006, but only 21 are written in C/C++. We selected those 21 benchmarks to evaluate SGX-LAPD. In total, there are 12 integer benchmarks and 7 floating-point benchmarks. `998.specrand` and `999.specrand` are the common random number generator for integer suite and floating-point suite respectively.

**Experiment Setup.** All the benchmarks are compiled with Clang. Our tested platform is Ubuntu 14.04 with Linux Kernel 4.2.0, and our hardware is a 4-core Intel Core i5-6200U Skylake CPU running SGX-v1 at 2.3 GHz with 4G DDR3 RAM.

### 6.2 Results

We complied the benchmarks with three settings: without Instrumentation, with Non-Present page fault Detection (NPD) and with Non-eXecutable page fault Detection (NXD). The evaluation tries to measure the overhead added to the compiler and programs caused by the instrumentation.

SGX-LAPD **Compiler.** Table 1 presents the building details for the SPEC2006 and SGX-nbench. To show how much code we needed to insert for each program, we reported the number of CFTs for each benchmark. We report the number of direct CFTs in the 3rd column and the number of indirect CFTs in the 4th column. We also show the static binary size for each benchmark after compilation. The number of CFTs correlates with the size of the binary code; a larger code size will have more CFTs. Space overhead is due to the inserted code, so a program with more CFTs will have a higher space overhead. Table 1 shows that `400.perlbench` and `403.gcc` have the largest space overhead. Note that `445.gobmk` is as large as `403.gcc`, but only one-third is code. Hence, its space overhead is small. For SGX-nbench, we only report the size of code inside the enclave. On average, SGX-LAPD increases the static binary size by 213% with NPD and 244% with NXD.

In terms of compilation time, SGX-LAPD only introduces small overhead to the compiler. The building time for SPEC2006 is increased from 5672 s to 5745 s, with only additional 73 s more time. The building time for SGX-nbench is increased from 1.4 s to 1.6 s.

SGX-LAPD **Linker.** In the linking phase, SGX-LAPD will optimize out the unnecessary instrumentation code. To show the efficiency of our optimization, we reported the number of patches for each benchmark in Table 1. As mentioned in Sect. 4.1, each direct CFT is associated with one piece of meta-data to record

**Table 1.** The building results for SPEC2006 and SGX-nbench

| Benchmark | w/o Instrumentation | | | w/ NPD | | | w/ NXD | | |
|---|---|---|---|---|---|---|---|---|---|
| | Size (KB) | #Direct CFT | #InDirect CFT | #Patch | Size (KB) | Increase (%) | #Patch | Size (KB) | Increase (%) |
| 400.perlbench | 1086 | 50152 | 1881 | 33375 | 5266 | 384.9 | 34651 | 5818 | 435.7 |
| 401.bzip | 90 | 2029 | 120 | 1454 | 262 | 191.1 | 1572 | 286 | 217.8 |
| 403.gcc | 3218 | 143634 | 5190 | 95564 | 15170 | 371.4 | 101562 | 16738 | 420.1 |
| 429.mcf | 19 | 338 | 32 | 265 | 47 | 147.4 | 296 | 51 | 168.4 |
| 433.milc | 132 | 3665 | 234 | 1497 | 440 | 233.3 | 2341 | 484 | 266.7 |
| 444.namd | 327 | 6527 | 113 | 4653 | 863 | 163.9 | 5675 | 935 | 185.9 |
| 445.gobmk | 3382 | 26701 | 2369 | 15185 | 5642 | 66.8 | 15838 | 5962 | 76.3 |
| 447.dealII | 3240 | 101938 | 5722 | 70494 | 11596 | 257.9 | 80068 | 12856 | 296.8 |
| 450.soplex | 375 | 13867 | 1467 | 7719 | 1551 | 313.6 | 9742 | 1723 | 359.5 |
| 453.povray | 1027 | 32399 | 1747 | 16508 | 3739 | 264.1 | 21304 | 4107 | 299.9 |
| 456.hmmer | 303 | 11108 | 478 | 6117 | 1227 | 305 | 8048 | 1355 | 347.2 |
| 458.sjeng | 136 | 4541 | 189 | 2686 | 516 | 279.4 | 3118 | 564 | 314.7 |
| 462.libquantum | 47 | 1113 | 104 | 592 | 139 | 195.7 | 727 | 155 | 229.8 |
| 464.h264ref | 653 | 12533 | 875 | 8466 | 1721 | 163.6 | 9492 | 1869 | 186.2 |
| 470.lbm | 19 | 140 | 20 | 71 | 31 | 63.2 | 110 | 31 | 63.2 |
| 471.omnetpp | 655 | 25196 | 2503 | 6234 | 2819 | 330.4 | 11028 | 3175 | 384.7 |
| 473.astar | 43 | 1062 | 90 | 647 | 135 | 214 | 888 | 147 | 241.9 |
| 482.sphinx3 | 186 | 6186 | 299 | 3315 | 702 | 277.4 | 3926 | 774 | 316.1 |
| 483.xalancbmk | 4250 | 140253 | 9892 | 92143 | 16522 | 288.8 | 95686 | 18538 | 336.2 |
| 988.specrand | 7 | 19 | 10 | 19 | 11 | 57.1 | 19 | 13 | 85.7 |
| 999.specrand | 7 | 19 | 10 | 19 | 11 | 57.1 | 19 | 13 | 85.7 |
| SGX-nbench | 273 | 848 | 91 | 615 | 408 | 49.5 | 732 | 412 | 50.9 |
| Average | 885 | 26558 | 1520 | 16711 | 3128 | 212.5 | 18493 | 3455 | 244.1 |

the instrumented code information. SGX-LAPD Linker scans that information to find all the direct CFTs for which the verification code does not need to be run and patches them with an unconditional branch. The patch number for NXD approach is larger. Currently, SGX-LAPD does not instrument the library code. We cannot use `call-ret` pair to check page fault, and thus verification code of CFT to library call need to be skipped. Note that this should not be a limitation of SGX-LAPD since in real application, the enclave code is built in static linked binary [1]. SGX-LAPD can instrument all the enclave code.

**Runtime Performance.** SGX-LAPD slows down the program execution time, which is caused by the additional page fault detection code inserted before each cross-page CFT. We evaluated the slowdown in both SPEC2006 and our own SGX-nbench. For SPEC2006, we measured the execution time overhead for each benchmark by running the instrumented benchmarks on their reference data sets 10 times, with a maximum variance of 2%. In Fig. 7, we present the execution time overhead for each SPEC2006 benchmark, shown as a percent increase over the normalized baseline performance of the non-instrumented version of each benchmark. Similar to space overhead, the NXD approach has a larger execution

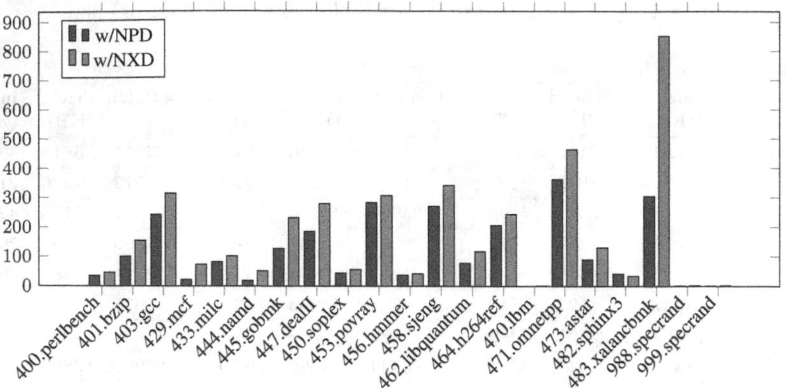


**Fig. 7.** Percent overhead for each of the SPEC2006 benchmarks.

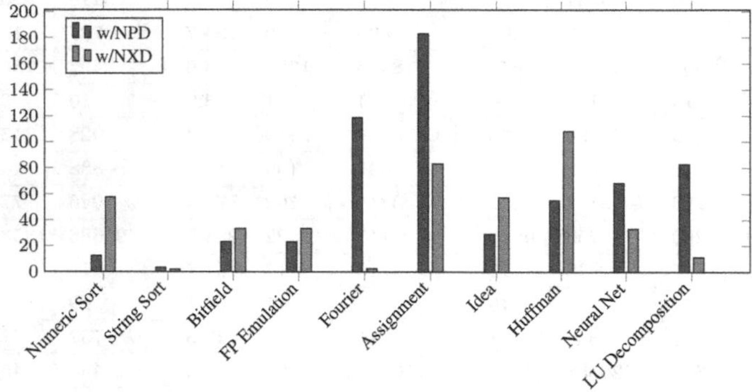


**Fig. 8.** Percent overhead for each of the SGX-nbench benchmarks.

time overhead than NPD. In general, benchmarks with a larger number of CFTs will have higher overhead. As shown in Table 1, most of the verification code in `483.xalancbmk` cannot be skipped, which is why it has the largest overhead. On average, NPD introduces 120% overhead on SPEC2006, while NXD introduces 183% overhead.

For SGX-nbench, we used the performance result reported by the benchmark itself. In particular, SGX-nbench runs its benchmarks multiple times, taking the mean and standard deviation until it reaches a confidence threshold such that the results are 95% statistically certain. In Fig. 8, we present the execution time overhead for each SGX-nbench benchmark, shown as a percent increase over the normalized baseline of the non-instrumented version. The average overhead of SGX-nbench is only 60% with NPD and 42% with NXD, smaller than SPEC2006. This is because SGX-LAPD only instruments the code inside the enclave. The host application code is not instrumented and has no overhead. This demonstrates the true performance of SGX-LAPD in real SGX programs.

## 7 Discussion

SGX-LAPD relies on the enclave code itself to detect page faults and verify whether an OS indeed provides large pages. All the code outside the enclave is not trusted, which means both the user level `sig_handler` and the kernel level system exception handler can be malicious. According to the detailed steps in exception handling described in Fig. 3, we can notice that an attacker can execute the eight step exception handling instead of the three step page fault handling to reset the `GPRSGX.RIP` to some other instructions. But this relies on collaboration from the enclave code, which is trusted. Therefore, we have to note that such an attack is impossible unless the enclave code itself is compromised.

Meanwhile, we note that there might exist a race condition for a malicious OS to reset the `EXITINFO.VECTOR` right after entering the enclave as illustrated in Fig. 4. More specifically, a malicious OS can first launch the page fault attack, causing `EXITINFO.VECTOR` to be set. When control returns to the enclave again but before our verification code, the malicious OS injects another interrupt (e.g., timer interrupt or other faults such as GP) and makes the enclave exit again (to reset `EXITINFO.VECTOR` and evade our detection). Fortunately, such an attack is challenging to launch. In particular, to launch this attack, attackers have to execute the enclave program using single step execution; otherwise it will be very challenging for them to control the timing. However, there is no way to execute enclave program using single step in the deployment mode (only debugging mode can), and attackers must rely on the extremely low probability to inject the interrupt or exception right after entering the enclave and before our checking code. But this time window is extremely short (just a few instructions).

In addition, there is a lot of room for further improvement of SGX-LAPD, particularly on where to instrument our detection code. For instance, our current design overly inserts a lot of intra-page control flow transfer page fault detection code in the enclave binary, though we have patched the binary to skip executing that code. While our current design can be acceptable for small enclave binaries, especially considering the fact that we already ask the SGX to provide 2 MB pages for the enclave code (such a design already wastes a large volume of space), we certainly would like to further eliminate this unnecessary code. We believe this would require iterative processing and instruction relocation. We leave this to one of our future works. On the other hand, if we were able to precisely identify the input-dependent CFTs, we would not have to insert excessive amounts of detection code. Therefore, the second avenue for future improvement is to identify the input-dependent CFTs. However, this is also a non-trivial task for a compiler since it would require a static input taint analysis. We leave this to another of our future works.

Finally, SGX-LAPD only stops code page fault attacks; attackers can still trigger data page faults. As mentioned in Sect. 3.1, we leave the defense for data page fault attacks to future work. We also would like to note that practical controlled channel attacks often require two kinds of page fault patterns, as demonstrated by Xu et al. [31]. The first is the code page pattern which indicates the start or end of a specific function. The second can be either a code page fault pattern or a data page fault pattern, but it critically depends on the first code page fault pattern to be effective. By removing only code page fault patterns, SGX-LAPD can still make data page fault attacks much harder.

## 8 Conclusion

We have presented SGX-LAPD, a system that leverages enclave verifiable large paging to defeat controlled page fault side channel attacks based on the insight that large pages can significantly reduce benign page fault occurrence. A key contribution of SGX-LAPD is a technique that explicitly verifies whether an OS has provided large pages by intentionally triggering a page fault at each cross small page control flow transfer instruction and validating with the internal SGX data structure updated by the hardware. We have implemented SGX-LAPD with a modified LLVM compiler and an SGX Linux kernel module. Our evaluation with a ported real SGX benchmark SGX-nbench shows that, while space and runtime overhead can be somewhat high, as a first step solution SGX-LAPD can still be acceptable especially considering the difficulties in fighting for the controlled side channel attacks. Finally, the source code of SGX-LAPD is available at https://github.com/utds3lab/sgx-lapd, and the source code of SGX-nbench is available at https://github.com/utds3lab/sgx-nbench.

**Acknowledgement.** We thank Mona Vij from Intel for the assistance of the test with SGX-v2. We are also grateful to the anonymous reviewers for their insightful comments. This research was partially supported by AFOSR under grant FA9550-14-1-0119, and NSF awards CNS-1453011, CNS-1564112, and CNS-1629951. Any opinions, findings, conclusions, or recommendations expressed are those of the authors and not necessarily of the AFOSR and NSF.

## References

1. Intel software guard extensions (Intel SGX) SDK. https://software.intel.com/en-us/sgx-sdk
2. The Linux kernel archives. https://www.kernel.org/doc/Documentation/vm/hugetlbpage.txt
3. Intel 64 and IA-32 architectures software developer's manual (2015). http://www.intel.com/content/dam/www/public/us/en/documents/manuals/64-ia-32-architectures-software-developer-manual-325462.pdf
4. Backes, M., Nürnberger, S.: Oxymoron: making fine-grained memory randomization practical by allowing code sharing. In: USENIX Security Symposium (2014)
5. Bauman, E., Lin, Z.: A case for protecting computer games with SGX. In: Proceedings of the 1st Workshop on System Software for Trusted Execution, p. 4. ACM (2016)
6. Baumann, A., Peinado, M., Hunt, G.: Shielding applications from an untrusted cloud with haven. In: Proceedings of the 11th Symposium on Operating Systems Design and Implementation (OSDI), Broomfield, pp. 267–283, October 2014

7. Chandra, S., Karande, V., Lin, Z., Khan, L., Kantarcioglu, M., Thuraisingham, B.: Securing data analytics on SGX with randomization. In: Proceedings of the 22nd European Symposium on Research in Computer Security, Oslo, September 2017
8. Checkoway, S., Shacham, H.: Iago attacks: why the system call API is a bad untrusted RPC interface. In: Proceedings of the 18th International Conference on Architectural Support for Programming Languages and Operating Systems (ASPLOS), Houston, pp. 253–264, March 2013
9. Chen, X., Garfinkel, T., Lewis, E.C., Subrahmanyam, P., Waldspurger, C.A., Boneh, D., Dwoskin, J., Ports, D.R.: Overshadow: a virtualization-based approach to retrofitting protection in commodity operating systems. In: Proceedings of the 13th International Conference on Architectural Support for Programming Languages and Operating Systems (ASPLOS XIII), Seattle, pp. 2–13. ACM (2008)
10. Giuffrida, C., Kuijsten, A., Tanenbaum, A.S.: Enhanced operating system security through efficient and fine-grained address space randomization. In: USENIX Security Symposium, pp. 475–490 (2012)
11. Goldreich, O.: Towards a theory of software protection and simulation by oblivious rams. In: Proceedings of the Nineteenth Annual ACM Symposium on Theory of Computing, pp. 182–194. ACM (1987)
12. Hand, S.M.: Self-paging in the Nemesis operating system. In: OSDI, vol. 99, pp. 73–86 (1999)
13. Hoekstra, M., Lal, R., Pappachan, P., Phegade, V., Del Cuvillo, J.: Using innovative instructions to create trustworthy software solutions. In: Proceedings of the 2nd International Workshop on Hardware and Architectural Support for Security and Privacy (HASP), Tel-Aviv, pp. 1–8 (2013)
14. Intel: Intel software guard extensions programming reference (rev2), 329298-002US, October 2014
15. Karande, V., Bauman, E., Lin, Z., Khan, L.: Securing system logs with SGX. In: Proceedings of the 12th ACM Symposium on Information, Computer and Communications Security, Abu Dhabi, April 2017
16. Klein, G., Elphinstone, K., Heiser, G., Andronick, J., Cock, D., Derrin, P., Elkaduwe, D., Engelhardt, K., Kolanski, R., Norrish, M., Sewell, T., Tuch, H., Winwood, S.: seL4: Formal verification of an OS kernel. In: Proceedings of the ACM SIGOPS 22nd Symposium on Operating Systems Principles (SOSP 2009), pp. 207–220 (2009)
17. McCune, J.M., Parno, B.J., Perrig, A., Reiter, M.K., Isozaki, H.: Flicker: an execution infrastructure for TCB minimization. In: Proceedings of the ACM EuroSys Conference, Glasgow, pp. 315–328, March 2008
18. McKeen, F., Alexandrovich, I., Berenzon, A., Rozas, C.V., Shafi, H., Shanbhogue, V., Savagaonkar, U.R.: Innovative instructions and software model for isolated execution. In: Proceedings of the 2nd International Workshop on Hardware and Architectural Support for Security and Privacy (HASP), Tel-Aviv, pp. 1–8 (2013)
19. Ohrimenko, O., Schuster, F., Fournet, C., Mehta, A., Nowozin, S., Vaswani, K., Costa, M.: Oblivious multi-party machine learning on trusted processors. In: 25th USENIX Security Symposium (USENIX Security 2016), Austin, pp. 619–636. USENIX Association, August 2016
20. Perez, R., Sailer, R., van Doorn, L., et al.: vTPM: virtualizing the trusted platform module. In: Proceedings of the 15th USENIX Security Symposium (Security), Vancouver, pp. 305–320, July 2006
21. Pinkas, B., Reinman, T.: Oblivious RAM revisited. In: Rabin, T. (ed.) CRYPTO 2010. LNCS, vol. 6223, pp. 502–519. Springer, Heidelberg (2010). doi:10.1007/978-3-642-14623-7_27

22. Porter, D.E., Boyd-Wickizer, S., Howell, J., Olinsky, R., Hunt, G.C.: Rethinking the library OS from the top down. In Proceedings of the 16th International Conference on Architectural Support for Programming Languages and Operating Systems (ASPLOS), Newport Beach, pp. 291–304, March 2011
23. Santos, N., Raj, H., Saroiu, S., Wolman, A.: Using ARM TrustZone to build a trusted language runtime for mobile applications. In: ACM SIGARCH Computer Architecture News, vol. 42, pp. 67–80. ACM (2014)
24. Schuster, F., Costa, M., Fournet, C., Gkantsidis, C., Peinado, M., Mainar-Ruiz, G., Russinovich, M.: VC3: Trustworthy data analytics in the cloud using SGX. In: Proceedings of the 2015 IEEE Symposium on Security and Privacy (2015)
25. Seshadri, A., Luk, M., Qu, N., Perrig, A.: SecVisor: a tiny hypervisor to provide lifetime kernel code integrity for commodity OSes. In: Proceedings of Twenty-First ACM SIGOPS Symposium on Operating Systems Principles (SOSP 2007), Stevenson, Washington, DC, pp. 335–350 (2007)
26. Shih, M.-W., Lee, S., Kim, T., Peinado, M.: T-SGX: eradicating controlled-channel attacks against enclave programs. In: Proceedings of the 2017 Annual Network and Distributed System Security Symposium (NDSS), San Diego (2017)
27. Shinde, S., Chua, Z.L., Narayanan, V., Saxena, P.: Preventing your faults from telling your secrets: defenses against pigeonhole attacks. arXiv preprint arXiv:1506.04832 (2015)
28. Sun, K., Wang, J., Zhang, F., Stavrou, A.: SecureSwitch: BIOS-assisted isolation and switch between trusted and untrusted commodity OSes. In: Proceedings of the 19th Annual Network and Distributed System Security Symposium (NDSS), San Diego, February 2012
29. PaX Team: Pax address space layout randomization (aslr). http://pax.grsecurity.net/docs/aslr.txt
30. Wang, J., Stavrou, A., Ghosh, A.: HyperCheck: a hardware-assisted integrity monitor. In: Jha, S., Sommer, R., Kreibich, C. (eds.) RAID 2010. LNCS, vol. 6307, pp. 158–177. Springer, Heidelberg (2010). doi:10.1007/978-3-642-15512-3_9
31. Xu, Y., Cui, W., Peinado, M.: Controlled-channel attacks: deterministic side channels for untrusted operating systems. In: Proceedings of the 2015 IEEE Symposium on Security and Privacy (2015)

# Secure In-Cache Execution

Yue Chen(✉), Mustakimur Khandaker, and Zhi Wang

Florida State University, Tallahassee, FL 32306, USA
{ychen,khandake,zwang}@cs.fsu.edu

**Abstract.** A cold boot attack is a powerful physical attack that can dump the memory of a computer system and extract sensitive data from it. Previous defenses focus on storing cryptographic keys off the memory in the limited storage "borrowed" from hardware chips. In this paper, we propose EncExec, a practical and effective defense against cold boot attacks. EncExec has two key techniques: spatial cache reservation and secure in-cache execution. The former overcomes the challenge that x86 processors lack a fine-grained cache control by reserving a small block of the CPU's level-3 cache exclusively for use by EncExec; the latter leverages the reserved cache to enable split views of the protected data: the data stored in the physical memory is always encrypted, and the plaintext view of the data is strictly confined to the reserved cache. Consequently, a cold boot attack can only obtain the encrypted form of the data. We have built a prototype of EncExec for the FreeBSD system. The evaluation demonstrates that EncExec is a practical and effective defense against cold boot attacks.

## 1 Introduction

A cold boot attack is a powerful physical attack that can extract sensitive data from the physical memory[1] of a computer system. It exploits the fact that, contrary to the common belief, memory chips may retain their contents for seconds after the power is lost and considerably longer at a low temperature [14,27]. An attacker can dump the memory of a victim computer by freezing and transplanting its memory units to a computer under his control or rebooting it to a malicious operating system (OS). Sensitive data can then be extracted from the dumped memory [14]. Lots of sensitive data sit in the memory for a long time [7]. For example, whole-disk encryption protects the document at rest in case the computer is lost or stolen. However, the disk encryption key (or its derived sub-keys) often sits in the memory in plaintext and thus vulnerable to the cold boot attack. Cold boot attacks have also been demonstrated against mobile devices, even though their memory units are soldered onto the motherboard [23,28], by

[1] For brevity, we refer to the physical memory as the memory and the CPU cache as the cache.

**Electronic supplementary material** The online version of this chapter (doi:10.1007/978-3-319-66332-6_17) contains supplementary material, which is available to authorized users.


M. Dacier et al. (Eds.): RAID 2017, LNCS 10453, pp. 381–402, 2017.
DOI: 10.1007/978-3-319-66332-6_17

freezing and rebooting them to the recovery mode. The attacker then uses a tool to extract sensitive data from the phone, including passwords, contacts, photos, and emails. Cold boot attacks have become a major security and privacy concern.

A few defenses have been proposed to address cold boot attacks on the x86 [12,21,22,26] and ARM [10] platforms. In principle, they re-purpose existing hardware features to keep cryptographic keys off the memory. For example, AESSE [21], TRESOR [22], LoopAmnesia [26], and ARMORED [10] store a single AES key in SSE registers, debug registers, performance counters, and NEON registers, respectively. By doing so, the key will never leave the CPU and consequently not be contained in the memory dump. However, the amount of storage provided by these "borrowed" registers is very limited. It is often too small for cryptographic algorithms that use longer keys (e.g., RSA). They also interfere with normal operations of these registers. From another perspective, Copker [12] temporarily disables caching and uses the cache-as-RAM technology [9] to implement RSA. However, Copker severely degrades the system performance when it is active because caching has to be completely disabled. On recent Intel processors with a shared Level-3 (L3) cache, Copker has to disable caching on *all* the cores. Moreover, these systems focus solely on securing cryptographic algorithms while completely ignoring other sensitive data in the process (one reason is that they do not have large enough secure storage for them). Sensitive data, such as user accounts and passwords, can be scattered in the process address space as the memory is allocated, copied, and freed [7]. This calls for a stronger protection against cold boot attacks that can protect not only cryptographic keys but also sensitive data.

In this paper, we propose EncExec, a system that can securely execute a whole program, or a part of it, in the cache. Data protected by EncExec have split views in the memory and the (reserved) cache: data stored in the memory are always encrypted; they are decrypted into the cache only when accessed. EncExec guarantees that the decrypted data will *never* be evicted to the memory. As such, the reserved cache is desynchronized from the memory. Even though the data are encrypted in the memory, the CPU can still access the unencrypted data from the cache because the cache precedes the memory. Consequently, the memory dump contains just the encrypted view of the protected data. Their unencrypted view only exists in the cache and will be lost when the power is reset or the system is rebooted. To enable split views of the protected data, EncExec relies on two key techniques, spatial cache reservation and secure in-cache execution. The former reserves a small block of the cache by carefully managing the system's physical memory allocation. A key challenge here is the lack of direct control of the cache in the x86 architecture – there are instructions to enable/disable the cache and to invalidate the whole cache or a cache line, but there is no fine-grained control over how data is cached and evicted by various levels of caches. Without precise control of cache replacement, the unencrypted data in the cache could be accidentally leaked to the memory. To address that, we observe that x86 processors use the n-way set-associative cache organization. EncExec thus can reserve a small block of the cache by reserving all the physical memory cached by it. Additionally, the CPU will not spontaneously evict a cache line unless there are cache conflicts. EncExec thus can prevent the unencrypted data from being evicted to the memory by avoiding conflicts for the reserved cache. EncExec's second technique utilizes the reserved cache to protect sensitive data by desynchronizing the cache and the memory.

EncExec can be used in two modes. In the first mode, a process is given a block of the secure memory for storing its critical data. The process can decide which data to protect. From the process' point of view, this block of memory can be used just like the regular memory. In the second mode, EncExec uses the reserved cache to protect the whole data of the process. Specifically, it uses the reserved cache as a window over the process' data, similar to demand paging. The data in the window are decrypted in the cache and remain in the cache until they are replaced by EncExec. The data out of the window only exist in the memory and stay encrypted. Note that window-based encrypted execution alone is not secure because the (unencrypted) window often contain critical data due to program locality. For example, a web server's private key most likely is in the window because it is constantly being used to encrypt and decrypt web traffic. Without strict cache control provided by EncExec's first technique, the unencrypted data can be evicted to the memory and obtained by an attacker. Between these two modes, the first one is more practical because a process has the best knowledge of its data and the reserved cache is still relatively small for large programs. The first mode can support more processes simultaneously. However, it does require some changes to the program.

We have built a prototype of EncExec for the FreeBSD 10.2 operating system. Our prototyping experience shows that EncExec can be easily integrated into the kernel and provide an effective defense against cold boot attacks. The performance overhead is very minor for the first mode, while the overhead for the second mode as expected depends mostly on the process' program locality.

## 2 System Design

### 2.1 Design Goals and Assumptions

EncExec aims at protecting a process' sensitive data against cold-boot attacks. Specifically, it reserves a small block of the (L3) cache and uses the reserved cache to securely execute the whole process or a part of it in the cache. We have the following design goals for EncExec:

- *Data secrecy*: the plaintext view of the protected data should only exist in the cache. It must be encrypted before being evicted to the memory. The key to encrypt the data must be protected from cold boot attacks as well.
- *Data quantity requirement*: most early defenses can only secure small cryptographic keys. A practical solution should support cryptographic algorithms such as RSA that use large keys.
- *Performance isolation*: the cache is critical to the overall system performance. EncExec reserves a small portion of the L3 cache for its use. It should not incur

large performance overhead for other processes whether EncExec is active or not; i.e., the performance impact of EncExec is isolated from concurrent processes.
- *Application transparency*: when operating in the whole-data protection mode, EncExec should be transparent to the protected process. An unmodified user program should be able to run under EncExec just like on a normal OS (but slower).

**Threat Model:** the attacker is assumed to have physical access to the victim's device. He can launch a cold-boot attack either by transplanting the (frozen) memory units to a computer under his control [14] or by rebooting it to a tiny malicious OS [23,28]. We assume that the attacker does not have malware, such as a kernel rootkit, installed on the victim's device, otherwise he could simply obtain the memory through the malware without resorting to cold-boot attacks. This threat model covers the common scenarios where cold-boot attacks may be attempted. For example, many business laptops lost in public places have encrypted hard disks and are protected by screen locks.

Since the attacker has physical control over the device, he could launch other physical attacks. For example, external expansion buses like FireWire may be exploited to directly access the physical memory via DMA. Some devices have enabled debug ports (e.g., the JTAG port on a mobile phone). The attacker can attach a debugger to these ports and fully control the system. More exotic attacks, such as monitoring or injecting data on the buses, often require sophisticated equipment and aplenty financial support. In this paper, we consider these attacks out of the scope and assume they are prevented by other defenses, such as using IOMMU to prevent DMA attacks and disabling debug ports.

A process may have close interaction with its external environment. Sensitive data could leak to the environment. For example, a word processor often stores parsed documents in temporary files. This problem has been addressed by a number of previous systems [24]. In this paper, we assume the data transferred out of the process maintain their secrecy by, say, encrypting the file system and network communications. Of course, the keys for encryption need to be protected (by EncExec).

### 2.2 Design Overview

Figure 1 shows the overall architecture of EncExec. The user space of a process consists of code and data sections. EncExec focuses on protecting the process' data against cold boot attacks but leaves the code as is. This is based on the assumption that the data more likely contain sensitive information that needs protection, while the code is often publicly available and does not carry private user information. Nevertheless, EncExec can also be applied to protect the code if needed. In Fig. 1, the protected data remain encrypted in the memory all the time, the decrypted data are stored in the part of the L3 cache reserved by EncExec. EncExec uses the L3 cache to minimize its performance impact because

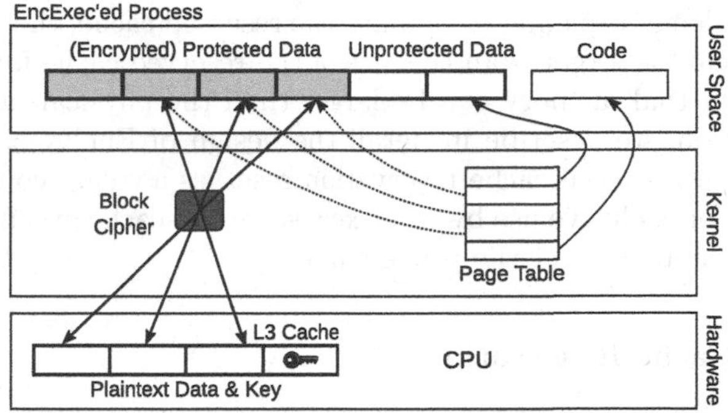


**Fig. 1.** Overall architecture of EncExec. Three pages of the protected data is in the window.

recent Intel processors have large, unified, inclusive L3 caches[2]. Moreover, the L3 cache is *physically indexed* and *physically tagged*. Physical addresses thus solely determine the allocation of this cache. To enable the split views of the data, EncExec uses the reserved cache as a (discontinuous) window over the protected data. The data in the window is decrypted and fully contained within the cache. Since the cache precedes the memory, the CPU directly accesses the decrypted data in the cache when it tries to access the data in the window. The data out of the window remains encrypted in the memory and unaccessible to the CPU. EncExec extends the kernel's virtual memory management (VMM) to strictly control the process' data access so that no plaintext data will be evicted to the memory due to cache conflicts. Specifically, only the protected data in the window (as well as the code and unprotected data) are mapped in the process' address space. If more protected data are used than the window size, EncExec selects a page in the window for replacement, similar to demand paging in the OS. Because a page table can only map memory in pages, the reserved cache must be page-aligned, and its size is a multiple of the page size. We use the hardware-accelerated AES (AES-NI [16]) in the counter mode for encryption. Both the key and the initial vector are randomly generated, and the key and sub-keys are securely stored in the reserved cache to protect them from cold boot attacks.

This architecture can support both modes of EncExec. In the first mode, EncExec provides the process with a block of secure memory. Any data stored in this memory is guaranteed to be protected from cold boot attacks. The process can decide when and how to use this memory. As such, the program needs to be (slightly) modified. For example, we can modify a cryptographic library so that its stack and session data are allocated from the secure memory. In the second mode, EncExec protects the complete data of a process. This mode is transparent to the protected process; no changes to the program are necessary.

[2] An unified cache stores both code and data. An inclusive L3 cache includes all the data cached by the L1 and L2 caches.

Because we use demand-paging to manage the reserved cache, the amount of the protected data can be larger than the size of the reserved cache for both modes, similar to how virtual memory can be larger than the physical memory. In the rest of this section, we describe in detail the design of EncExec. EncExec has two key techniques: spatial cache reservation reserves a small, continuous block of the L3 cache for exclusive use by EncExec, secure in-cache execution leverages the reserved cache to protect the process data.

### 2.3 Spatial Cache Reservation

EncExec's first technique reserves a small part of the L3 cache for its use. This is a challenging task on the x86 architecture because x86 transparently manages cache assignment and replacement. It does not provide explicit and fine-grained control of the cache. A process has no direct control over how its data are cached, and the CPU decides transparently which cached line[3] to be replaced when there is a cache conflict. To replace a cache line, the CPU first evicts the old contents back to the memory and then loads the new contents from the memory. EncExec needs to precisely control how the protected data are cached and how the cache is replaced to avoid conflicts in the reserved cache. Without this control, the CPU can evict some of the reserved cache to the memory, leaking the unencrypted data to the physical memory. To address that, EncExec enforces the following two rules:

- *Rule 1*, the protected data are only cached by the reserved cache, and no other memory is cached by the reserved cache. Consequently, neither the kernel itself nor other processes can cause the reserved cache to be evicted.
- *Rule 2*, the amount of the *accessible* (decrypted) protected data must be less than the size of the reserved cache. They thus always fit in the reserved cache. Consequently, the protected data themselves cannot cause the reserved cache to be evicted.

These two rules prevent conflicts in the reserved cache caused by other processes and by the protected data themselves, respectively. With these two rules, EncExec can guarantee that the decrypted data remain in the CPU cache, unobtainable by cold boot attacks.

EncExec enforces these two rules by leveraging the cache architecture and the replacement algorithm of x86 processors. Modern x86 processors often have a large shared L3 cache. Figure 2 shows the cache architecture of an Intel Core-i7 4790 processor. There are three levels of caches. Each CPU core has dedicated L1 and L2 caches, but all the four cores share a single large L3 cache. The L1 cache is split into an instruction cache (IL1) and a data cache (DL1), each 32 KB in size. The L2 and L3 caches are unified in that they cache both code and data. L1 and L2 caches are relatively small in size (64 KB and 256 KB, respectively), but the L3 cache is capacious at 8 MB. Even though the L1 and L2 caches are

[3] A cache line is the unit of data transfer between the cache and the memory. Recent x86 processors use a cache line of 64 bytes.

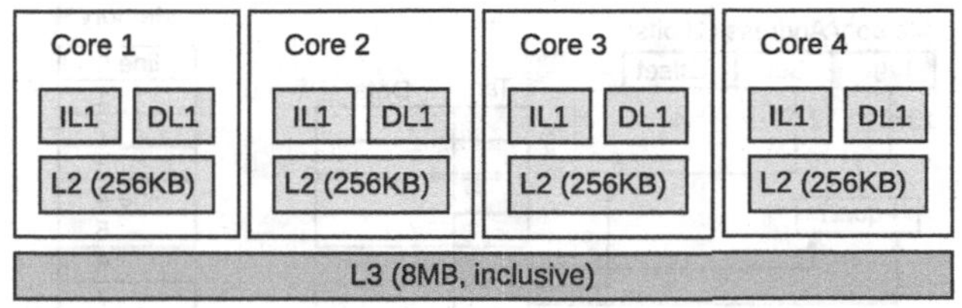


**Fig. 2.** Intel Core i7 cache architecture

small, they are more important to the overall system performance because they are faster and closer to CPU cores. It is thus impractical to reserve any part of the L1 or L2 cache, especially because EncExec has to reserve the cache in pages (4 KB at least). Another important feature of the L3 cache for EncExec is inclusivity. An inclusive L3 cache is guaranteed to contain all the data cached by the L1 and L2 caches. The CPU will not bypass the L3 cache when it accesses the memory. Without inclusivity, the CPU could evict the unencrypted data to the memory directly from the L1 or L2 cache and load the encrypted data directly from the memory to the L1 or L2 cache. The former leaks the unencrypted data to the memory, while the latter causes the program to malfunction. Recent Intel processors have large, unified, inclusive L3 caches. However, old processors like Pentium 4 have non-inclusive L2 caches (they do not have an on-chip L3 cache) and thus cannot be used by EncExec. In addition, we assume the cache is set to the write-back mode instead of the write-through mode. This is because in the write-through mode the CPU keeps the cache and the memory in sync by writing any updates to the cached to the memory as well. Most OSes use the write-back mode for the main memory due to its better performance.

EncExec takes control of all the physical memory cached by the reserved cache so that no other processes can use that memory and cause eviction of the reserved cache (rule 1). The actual memory EncExec has to control is decided by the CPU's cache organization. Specifically, the memory and the cache are divided into equal-sized cache lines (64 bytes). The memory in a line is cached or evicted as a whole. Intel processors use the popular $n$-way set-associative algorithm to manage the cache [15]. Figure 3 shows a simple 2-way set-associative cache with a cache line of 16 bytes to illustrate the concept. This cache is organized into 8 cache lines, and each two consecutive lines are grouped into a set. This cache thus has 8 cache lines in 4 sets. Meanwhile, the memory address (16 bits) is divided into three fields: the `offset` field (4 bits) specifies the offset into a cache line. This field is ignored by the cache since the memory is cached in lines; the `set` field (2 bits) is an index into the cache sets. A line of the memory can be cached by either line in the indexed set; the last field, `tag`, uniquely identifies the line of the physical memory stored in a cache line. During the cache fill, the CPU selects one line of the indexed set (evict it first if it is used) and loads the new memory line into it. The tag is stored along with the data in the cache line. During the cache lookup, the CPU compares the tag of the address to the two

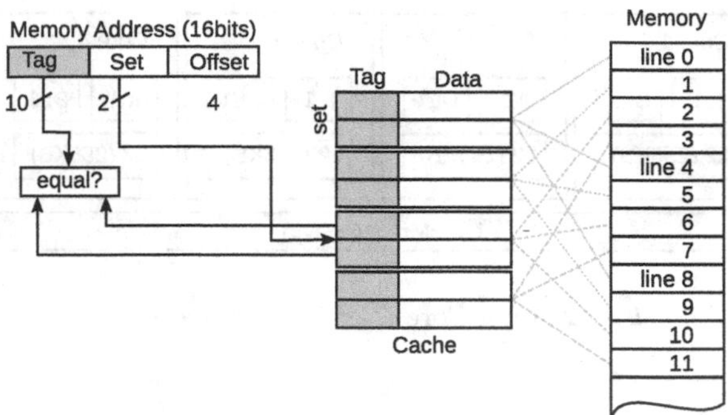


**Fig. 3.** 2-way set-associative cache, 8 cache lines in 4 sets. Each cache line is 16 bytes.

tags in the indexed set simultaneously. If there is a match, the address is cached (a cache hit); otherwise, a cache miss has happened. The CPU then fills one of the lines with the data. Note that all the addresses here are physical addresses as the L3 cache is physically indexed and physically tagged.

The L3 cache of Intel Core-i7 4790 is a 16-way set-associative cache with a cache line size of 64 bytes [15]. Therefore, the `offset` field has 6 bits to address each of the 64 bytes in a cache line. The width of the `set` field is decided by three factors: the cache size, the cache line size, and the associativity. This processor has an 8 MB L3 cache. The `set` field thus has 13 bits ($\frac{8M}{64\times16} = 8192 = 2^{13}$); i.e., there are 8,192 sets. The `tag` field consists of all the leftover bits. If the machine has 16 GB ($2^{34}$) of physical memory (note the L3 cache is physically tagged), the *tag* field thus has 15 bits ($34 - 6 - 13 = 15$).

EncExec relies on the page table to control the use of the reserved memory (Sect. 2.4). A page table can only map page-sized and page-aligned memory. Therefore, EncExec has to reserve at least a whole page of the L3 cache. Even though this processor supports several page sizes (4 KB, 2 MB, and 1 GB), we only reserve a smallest page of the cache (4 KB, or 64 lines) to minimize the performance overhead. However, we have to reserve 64 cache sets instead of 64 cache lines because this cache uses 16-way set-associative and all the cache lines in the same set have to be reserved together (as the CPU may cache our data in any line of a set). The actual amount of the reserved cache accordingly is 64 KB. These reserved cache sets must be continuous and the first set is page-aligned so that together they can cache a whole page of the physical memory. In our prototype, we reserve the cache sets from index 8,128 (`0x1FC0`) to index 8,191 (`0x1FFF`). Figure 4 shows the format of memory addresses that are cached by these selected sets. EncExec needs to take control of all physical pages conforming to this format (rule 1), which total $\frac{1}{128}$ of the physical memory. For example, it needs to reserve **128** MB physical memory on a machine with **16** GB of RAM. As mandated by rule 2, EncExec cannot use more data than the reserved cache size in order to avoid cache conflicts. Therefore, we can use 16 pages (64 KB) of the reserved 128 MB memory at a time. Note that the amount of the protected

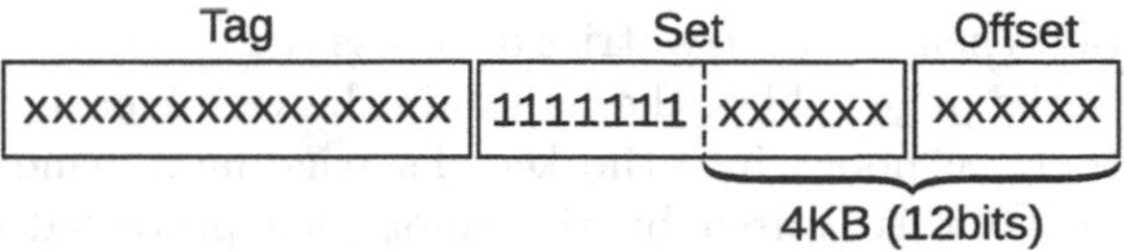


**Fig. 4.** Addresses that map to the reserved cache (bits marked with x can be either 0 or 1)

data can be larger than 16 pages because we use demand paging to manage the reserved cache. Moreover, an attacker that controls an unprotected process (e.g., using JavaScript in a browser) cannot evict EncExec's reserved cache because the reserved physical memory is not mapped in that process's virtual address space (remember that the L3 cache is physically indexed and physically tagged).

### 2.4 Secure In-Cache Execution

EncExec's second technique, secure in-cache execution, splits the views of the protected data between the memory and the reserved cache: the data remain encrypted in the memory, and their plaintext view only exists in the cache. In other words, we need to desynchronize the memory and the cache. There are three requirements for this to happen: *first*, the cache must be configured to use the write-back mode so that data modified in the cache will not be written through to the memory; *second*, the L3 cache is inclusive of the L1 and L2 caches so that the CPU always accesses the memory through the L3 cache; *third*, there are no conflicts in the reserved cache so that the CPU will not evict any reserved cache line. The first two requirements are guaranteed by the hardware and the existing kernels. The third requirement is fulfilled by EncExec's second technique.

EncExec's first technique takes control of all the physical pages that may be cached by the reserved cache. As long as we use no more protected data than the size of the reserved cache, they can fit in the reserved cache without conflicts, and any changes to these data, including decryption, stay within the cache. To continue the previous example, we select 16 pages out of the reserved 128 MB physical memory and use these pages for securing the protected data. We call these pages plaintext pages. In order to desynchronize the cache and the memory, we only need to copy the encrypted data to a plaintext page and decrypt them there. The decrypted data remain in the cache since there are no cache conflicts. However, we often need to protect more data than that can fit in plaintext pages. To address that, EncExec's second technique leverages demand paging to protect a large amount of data.

In demand paging, a part of the process can be temporarily swapped out to the backing store (e.g., a swap partition) and be brought into the memory on-demand later [25]. For EncExec, the original memory of the protected data serves as the swap for plaintext pages. The data are brought into and evicted from plaintext pages when necessary. The page table is used to control the process' access to the data. When the process tries to access the unmapped data (marked as non-present in the page table), the hardware delivers a page fault exception to the kernel. EncExec hooks into the kernel's page fault handler and checks whether the page fault is caused by the unmapped protected data. If so, it tries to allocate a plaintext page for the faulting page. If none of the plaintext pages are available, EncExec selects one for replacement. Specifically, it first encrypts the plaintext page and copies it back into its original page (note the original page is a non-reserved page). EncExec then decrypts the faulting page into this plaintext page and updates the page table if necessary. To initiate the protection, EncExec encrypts all the protected data, flushes their cache, and unmaps them from the process' address space. As such, EncExec can completely moderate access to the protected data. By integrating EncExec into the kernel's virtual memory management, we can leverage its sophisticated page replacement algorithm (e.g., the LRU algorithm) to select plaintext pages for replacement. Note that the second technique alone is not secure because plaintext pages often contain (most recently used) sensitive data due to program locality. Without the first technique, there is no guarantee that plaintext pages will not be evicted to the memory and become vulnerable to cold boot attacks. It is thus necessary for both techniques to work together.

EncExec needs to frequently encrypt and decrypt the protected data. The cryptographic algorithm thus plays an important role in the overall performance of the protected process. Recent CPUs have built-in hardware support to speed up popular cryptographic algorithms. For example, most Intel CPUs now feature hardware acceleration for AES, a popular block cipher, through the AES-NI extension [16]. EncExec uses hardware-accelerated ciphers when available. Our prototype uses AES-128 in the counter mode. Therefore, each block of the protected data can be encrypted/decrypted independently. To protect the (randomly generated) key from cold boot attacks, we dedicate one plaintext page to store the key, its derived sub-keys, and other important intermediate data. Initial vectors are stored for each page of the data. It is not necessary to protect the secrecy of initial vectors, but they should never be reused.

## 3 Implementation

We have implemented a prototype of EncExec based on the FreeBSD operating system (64-bit, version 10.2) [1]. FreeBSD's virtual memory management has an interesting design that enables multiple choices for implementing EncExec. Our prototype is based on the Intel Core-i7 4790 CPU with 16 GB of memory. Other CPUs with a similar cache architecture can be used by EncExec as well. For example, the Xeon E5-2650 processor has a 20 MB shared, inclusive L3 cache organized as 20-way set-associative. In the rest of this section, we describe our prototype in detail.

### 3.1 Spatial Cache Reservation

EncExec reserves a block of the L3 cache by owning all the physical pages cached by it, i.e., physical pages whose addresses are all 1's from bit 12 to bit 18 (Fig. 4). In other words, EncExec reserves one physical page every 128 pages[4]. EncExec can only use 16 of these pages as plaintext pages to protect data so that these pages can be completely contained in the reserved cache.

Modern operating systems have a sophisticated, multi-layer memory manage system to fulfill many needs of the kernel and the user space. For example, physical memory is often allocated in pages by the buddy memory allocator, and kernel objects are managed by the slab memory allocator to reduce fragmentation [1]. The slab allocator obtains its memory from the physical page allocator, forming a layered structure. Given this complexity, EncExec reserves its physical pages early in the booting process when the kernel is still running in the single processor mode. Memory allocated after enabling the multi-processor support is harder to reclaim – an allocated page may contain kernel objects accessed concurrently by several processors. Simply reclaiming it will lead to race conditions or inconsistent data.

When FreeBSD boots, the boot loader loads the kernel image into a continuous block of the physical memory, starts the kernel, and passes it the layout of the physical memory discovered by the BIOS (through `e820` memory mappings). The kernel image is large enough to contain several reserved physical pages that need to be reclaimed. The kernel uses several ad-hoc boot-time memory allocators to allocate memory for the booting process (e.g., `allocpages` in `sys/amd64/amd64/pmap.c`. We modify these allocators to skip the reserved pages. If a large block of memory (i.e., more than 127 pages) is allocated, we save the location and length of the allocated memory in order to fix it later. A typical example is the array of `vm_page` structures. There is one `vm_page` structure for each physical page. This structure thus could be really large.

By now, the kernel still runs on the simple boot page table. The kernel then replaces it with a new, more complete page table (`create_pagetables` in `sys/amd64/amd64/pmap.c`). x86-64 has a huge virtual address space. This allows the kernel to use it in ways that are not possible in 32-bit systems. For example, the kernel has a dedicated 4TB area that directly maps all the physical memory, including the reserved pages. This is called the direct map. Accordingly, the kernel can access any physical memory by adding the offset of this area to the physical address (`PHYS_TO_DMAP(pa)`). It is not necessary to unmap plaintext pages from the direct map because EncExec needs to directly access them (e.g., to decrypt a page). Another area in this new page table maps in the kernel. As mentioned earlier, the kernel is large enough to contain several reserved pages. If we find such a page when creating the page table, we allocate a non-reserved page, copy the contents from the original page, and map this page in the page

[4] This number is decided by the CPU's cache architecture. For example, EncExec reserves one physical page every 512 pages on the aforementioned Xeon E5-2650 CPU.

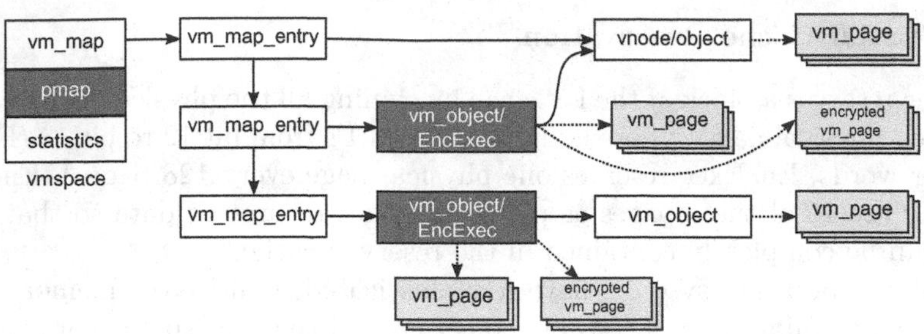


**Fig. 5.** Virtual memory structures for a process. Dark rectangles mark the possible placements for EncExec.

table[5]. This essentially replaces all the reserved pages in the kernel map with non-reserved pages. The kernel then switches to the new page table and continues the booting process. To make sure that no reserved pages exist in this new page table (except the DMAP area), we write a small kernel function to scan the new page table for reserved pages. No reserved page was found in the new page table.

Eventually, the kernel adds the left-over physical pages to the run-time page allocator (`vm_page_startup` in `sys/vm/vm_page.c`). We hook into this function and reserve pages as they are being added to the allocator. We also hook into the kernel's whole-cache flushing function (`wbinvd`). By doing so, we can encrypt the plaintext pages first to prevent the unencrypted data from being leaked to the memory. The CPU may temporarily power down a part of its caches in some power management states. In our implementation, we disable the CPU power management when EncExec is active and re-enable it otherwise.

### 3.2 Secure In-Cache Execution

With EncExec, the protected data remain encrypted in the memory; they are loaded and decrypted into the reserved cache on demand. This essentially adds another layer to the kernel's demand paging: the memory serves as the backing store for plaintext pages, while the swap partition services as the backing store for the memory. EncExec manipulates the page table to desynchronize the cache and the plaintext pages. FreeBSD's virtual memory management has a unique design that provides two alternative choices in the placement of EncExec.

Figure 5 shows the kernel data structures that manage the process address space in FreeBSD. The top level structure, `vmspace`, represents the whole address space. It is a container for other related structures. Two notable such structures are `vm_map` and `pmap`. FreeBSD separates the address space layout (`vm_map`) from the page table management (`pmap`). `vm_map` describes the process' virtual address space layout using a list of `vm_map_entry` structures. Each `vm_map_entry` specifies a continuous block of the process' address space, including its start and

[5] The kernel uses 2 MB large pages to map its data. We break them down into 4 KB pages first.

end addresses and its permissions (read/write/execute). Each `vm_map_entry` is backed by a chain of `vm_objects`. A `vm_object` describes the origin of the data for this entry and the backing store to swap in and out the data. There are three types of `vm_objects`. Named `vm_objects` represent files. Program sections like the code and data sections use named `vm_objects` because their initial contents are loaded from the program binary. Anonymous `vm_objects` represent sections that are zero-filled on the first use, such as uninitialized data sections and heap sections. Shadow `vm_objects` hold a private copy of the locally modified pages (represented by `vm_pages`). Every `vm_object` has an associated pager interface that decides how to swap in and swap out the object's associated data. For example, anonymous `vm_objects` use the swap pager to store data in the swap partition. The `pmap` structure consists of architecture-specific data and functions to manage the process' page table. Every CPU architecture defines its own pmap structure but implements the common `pmap` API. As such, other kernel modules do not need to be concerned with the details of page tables. `Pmap` can decide when and how to map a page. For example, it can unmap a page from the process' address space as long as the page is not pinned by the upper vm layers.

This design enables two feasible ways to implement EncExec in the FreeBSD kernel: it can either be implemented as a shadow object or in the `pmap` module. We chose the latter because it is simpler and more likely to be applicable to other OSes (e.g., Linux). Specifically, a `vm_map_entry` can be backed by a chain of `vm_objects`. Objects ahead in the chain precede over these later in the chain. When a page fault happens, the page fault handler searches for the faulting page along the chain of `vm_objects`. It returns the first located page without checking the rest of the chain. This chain of objects is essential to many features of FreeBSD's virtual memory design, such as copy-on-write where the kernel creates a shadow object of the original one for both the parent and the child and marks the original object read-only. If either process tries to modify a shared page, the kernel makes a copy of the page and gives it to the corresponding shadow object. This new copy overshadows the original shared page. EncExec can be similarly implemented as a shadow object by using plaintext pages to store the data and the original (non-reserved) memory as the backing store. However, this design introduces additional complexity to the kernel's already tangled virtual memory system [20]. For example, EncExec's shadow object should always be the first object in the chain, otherwise plaintext pages could be copied to `vm_objects` earlier in the chain and leaked to the memory. EncExec thus has to monitor any changes to the object chain. If a new object is inserted before EncExec's shadow object, EncExec must move its object to the head of the chain. Reordering objects is not supported by FreeBSD. Additionally, it is hard to apply this design to other kernels that do not have a similar structure (e.g., Linux).

The `pmap` module also has the needed support for EncExec: by design, `pmap` is allowed to unmap a page from the process' address space as long as the page is not pinned. The page fault handler will ask `pmap` to remap that page if it is later accessed. Moreover, `pmap` maintains a reverse mapping for each physical page, which keeps track of all the processes and virtual addresses a physical page is mapped. EncExec uses reverse mapping to completely disconnect a shared page from all the processes, otherwise some processes might incorrectly access the encrypted data. `Pmap` also tracks the page usage information for page replacement. EncExec can leverage this information to optimize its own page replacement.

EncExec first picks 15 reserved pages as the plaintext pages and unmaps all the protected data from the process' address space. If a page is shared by multiple processes, EncExec removes it from other processes as well. EncExec then returns to the user space to resume the process. When the process accesses its protected data, a page fault will be triggered. The page fault handler searches its data structures and asks `pmap` to map in the data (`pmap_map` in `pmap.c`). EncExec intercepts this request, allocates a plaintext page, decrypts the target page into it, and maps it into the process. At any time, no more than 15 plaintext pages can be used by the protected process. If more are needed, EncExec will pick a plaintext page in use for replacement. In addition, the FreeBSD kernel might proactively map-in (also called pre-fault) a page, expecting the process to access it in the near future. No page fault will be triggered when the process accesses this page later. In our prototype, we disable pre-faulting for the protected data sections to save the limited plaintext pages. The process may also perform file I/O with the protected memory. For correctness, we temporarily restore the affected pages and unmap them from the process' address space. When these pages are accessed by the user space again, page faults will be triggered. This signals the end of the file I/O operation. We then re-enable the protection for these pages.

## 4 Evaluation

In this section, we evaluate the security and performance of our EncExec prototype. All the experiments were conducted on a desktop with a 3.6 GHz Intel Core i7-4790 CPU and 16 GB of memory. The system runs 64-bit FreeBSD for x86-64, version 10.2. To test its performance, we run various benchmarks in the FreeBSD ports and the benchmarks of mbed TLS [2]. Mbed TLS, formerly known as PolarSSL, is a popular, portable, open-source TLS library developed by ARM.

### 4.1 Validation

We first validate that we can actually desynchronize the cache and plaintext pages. Theoretically, updates to the plaintext pages should be confined to the reserved cache because neither the kernel nor other processes can cause cache conflicts with EncExec, and we never use more plaintext pages than the size of the reserved cache. Consequently, the CPU should not evict the cached plaintext pages. However, x86 does not provide instructions to directly query the cache line status. To address that, we first validate that none of the reserved pages are used by the kernel or unprotected processes. Specifically, we write a simple kernel function that scans a page table for reserved pages. We apply this function to all the active page tables in the system. No reserved pages are found to be mapped in these page tables, except plaintext pages in the kernel's direct map area. As mentioned before, we use direct map to encrypt/decrypt plaintext pages. We also unmap plaintext pages from the direct map when EncExec is not in use. If the kernel accesses any of these pages, a page fault will be triggered and the kernel will crash itself. None of these happen during our experiment. Moreover, we conduct an experiment to validate de-synchronization of the cache and the plaintext pages. Specifically, we write all zeros to a plaintext page and then execute the `wbinvd` instruction, which writes back the modified cache lines and invalidates the internal caches. Now, the cache and the page have been synchronized and the memory of this page is guaranteed to contain all zeros. Next, we modify the plaintext page. Any changes should remain in the cache. To check that, we discard the modified cache lines by executing the `invd` instruction and read the plaintext page again. The plaintext page should contain all zeros. This is indeed the case. It shows that the plaintext page and the cache have been desynchronized.

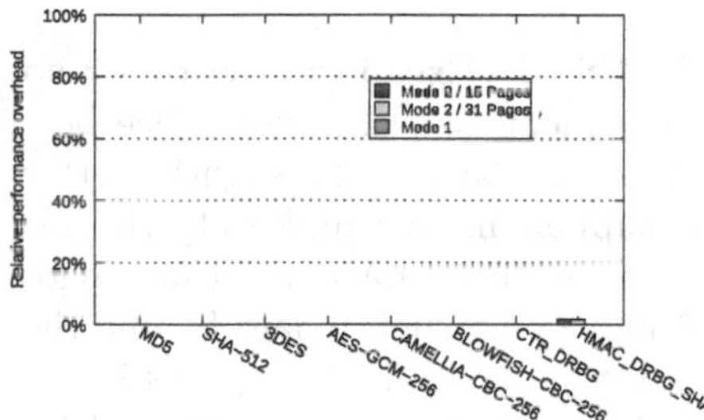


**Fig. 6.** Overhead of common cryptographic algorithms.

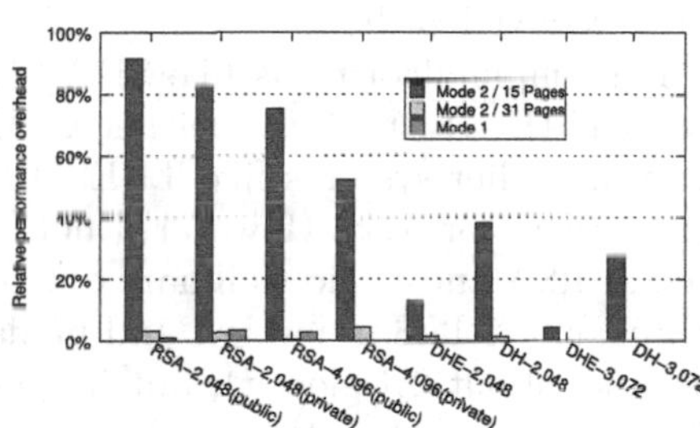


**Fig. 7.** Overhead of RSA and DH handshakes.

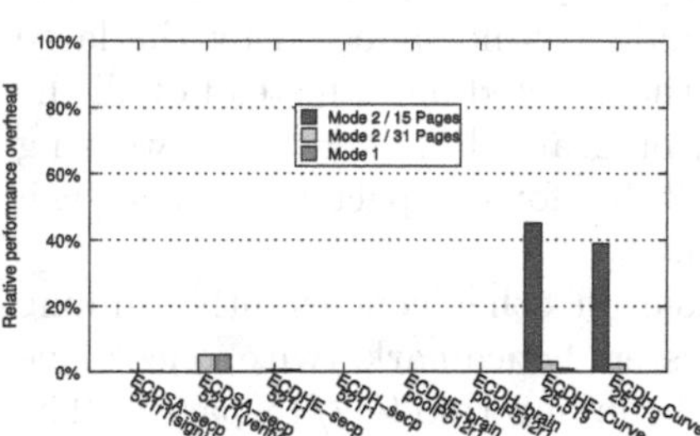


**Fig. 8.** Overhead of Elliptic Curve algorithms.

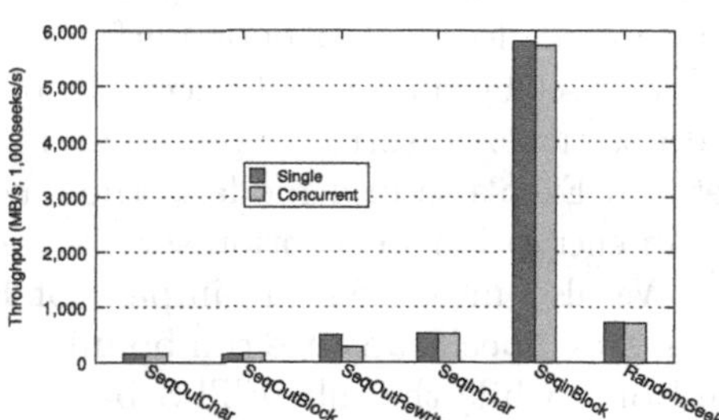


**Fig. 9.** Performance of Bonnie. The unit on Y-axis is MB/sec and thousand-seeks/sec (for RandomSeeks only).

### 4.2 Performance Evaluation

EncExec uses the hardware-accelerated AES (AES-NI) to encrypt and decrypt data. Our measurements show that it takes about 3 µs on average to encrypt/decrypt 4 KB data using 128-bit AES algorithm. Therefore, there is an extra 3 µs or so delay to load a data page and 6 µs if it's necessary to replace an existing page. This delay is the most significant source of EncExec's overhead, but it is hard to reduce this delay.

We use the official benchmarks from mbed TLS to measure the performance overhead of EncExec. These benchmarks consist of a wide range of cryptographic algorithms. The results are presented in Figs. 6, 7, and 8. The overhead is calculated relative to the baseline performance, i.e., the performance of mbed TLS on the original FreeBSD system. The "mode 1" bars give the overhead of mbed TLS protected by the first mode of EncExec. Specifically, we modified the source code of mbed TLS to allocate the session data and the stack from the secure memory. The "mode 2" bars give the overhead of mbed TLS protected by the second mode of EncExec, i.e., we protect all its data sections with EncExec. We experimented with both 15 and 31 plaintext pages. In the latter, we changed our prototype to double the reserved cache (32 pages, or 128 KB). This set of experiments represents the most practical use cases of EncExec, given the limited size of the reserved cache.

For simple algorithms like SHA-512 and AES, EncExec incurs virtually no overhead (Fig. 6) because neither CPU nor the memory is a performance bottleneck. Earlier systems like TRESOR [22] have similar or even slightly better performance for AES. However, EncExec can support more complex algorithms, such as RSA and Diffie-Hellman, due to its larger secure storage. For those algorithms, mbed TLS in mode 1 and mode 2/31 pages only slightly lags behind the baseline (about 2% slower), but its performance under mode 2/15 pages is significantly slower than the baseline. For example, it can only achieve about 8.4% of the baseline performance for RSA-2048 public key encryption and 16.7% for RSA-2048 private key encryption. This can be explained with the working set model [25]. Clearly, the working set of these benchmarks is larger than 15 pages but less than (or around) 31 pages. With only 15 plaintext pages, thrashing is guaranteed, leading to poor performance. Mode 1 is not affected by the large working set because it only needs to protect the selected data, instead of all the data sections. Nevertheless, many real-world programs have very large working set. EncExec's second mode is thus more suitable for compact programs, such as an encryption/decryption service program.

We also measured the impact of EncExec on other concurrently running processes. Specifically, we run bonnie, a file system benchmark, twice, once alone and once while the mbed TLS benchmark is running (mode 2/15 pages). The results are shown in Fig. 9. These two runs have almost identical performance for most of the six tests except the third one: the concurrent run is about 43% slower. This overhead likely is not caused by EncExec but instead the result of the kernel's scheduling algorithm: both benchmarks have very low initial CPU usage. It is likely that they will be scheduled to run on the same CPU core.

When bonnie is running its third test, the mbed TLS benchmark starts to run the RSA-related tests and uses more than 80% of the CPU. Temporarily, the mbed TLS benchmark preempts bonnie and degrades its performance. This is supported by the fact that bonnie uses 19.9% of the CPU time in the single run for this test, but it only receives 11.1% of the CPU time in the concurrent run. In the following tests, bonnie uses more than 100% of the CPU time and will be scheduled to a different CPU core than the mbed TLS benchmark. The performance of the mbed TLS benchmark remains mostly the same. To verify this hypothesis, we simultaneously run bonnie and the mbed TLS benchmark without EncExec. The similar results are observed a little bit earlier than the concurrent run with EncExec. This is because the mbed TLS benchmark runs faster this time. Overall, this result is not surprising: a process protected by EncExec and other processes cannot interfere with each other through the L3 cache, but they can still interact through the L1 and L2 caches if they are scheduled *to the same core*. Meanwhile, there is no interference through the cache if they are scheduled to different cores because each core has its own L1 and L2 caches. This strong performance isolation makes EncExec a more practical defense against cold boot attacks.

## 5 Discussion

In this section, we discuss some potential improvements to EncExec and related issues.

**Impact on L1 and L2 Caches:** EncExec controls all the physical pages cached by the reserved cache. This allows EncExec to precisely control the replacement of the reserved cache. These pages are also cached by the L1 and L2 cache. This naturally raises the question of whether EncExec reserves some of the L1 and L2 cache, as an side effect. L1 and L2 caches are critical to the overall system performance as they are smaller, faster, and closer to CPU cores. Reserving even a small part of them could severely harm the system performance. Fortunately, EncExec does not reserve any of the L1 and L2 cache. This is because each L1 and L2 cache line can cache more physical lines than a L3 cache line does. For example, Intel Core i7-4790 has 256 KB of L2 cache and 64 KB of L1 cache (instruction + data). Its L2 cache uses the 8-way set-associative algorithm. Accordingly, the set field for the L2 cache is 9 bits ($\frac{256K}{64\times8} = 512 = 2^9$), and the tag field is 19 bits. Therefore, each L2 cache line caches $2^{19}$ lines of the physical memory, most of which are not reserved by EncExec. Therefore, EncExec does not reserve any of the L1 or L2 cache lines. Nevertheless, it changes access patterns of the L1 and L2 caches. Some L1 and L2 cache lines may see more activities and some less.

**Thrashing Control:** EncExec can protect either the selected sensitive data or all the data. In the latter case, thrashing could happen if the process' working set is larger than the reserved cache. To relieve that, we could reserve more cache and use processors with a larger L3 cache. For example, the Xeon E5-2670 processor has a 20 MB shared L3 cache with 20-way set-associative. EncExec can use 40 plaintext pages (or 160 KB) if we reserve 8 KB of the cache space. Recent Intel CPUs partition the L3 cache among their cores. Specifically, each core has its own slice of the CPU's L3 cache which acts like a N-way set-associative cache. Physical RAM is assigned (equally) to these slices using an undisclosed hash algorithm [17–19,29]. This design allows more cache pages to be reserved by EncExec since cache slices operate mostly independently [29]. Even though these improvements allow EncExec to support a larger working set, the reserved cache is still not enough for complex programs. For these programs, the developers should use EncExec to protect only the sensitive data. Most cryptographic algorithms have a small working set that fits in EncExec's reserved cache.

**Large Page Sizes:** EncExec controls all the physical pages cached by the reserved cache. For example, our prototype reserves one physical page every 128 pages. This precludes the use of larger pages in the kernel. As previously mentioned, x86 processors support several page sizes, including 4 KB, 2 MB, and 1 GB. They often have separate TLB (translation look-aside buffer) entries for small pages and large pages. Using large pages can thus reduce the TLB pressure for small pages. The kernel uses 2 MB pages to map its own code and data. However, EncExec has to reserve 4 small pages from every 2 MB page. A kernel with EncExec therefore cannot use large pages. In our prototype, we break large kernel pages into small ones and reclaim the pages we need to reserve. There are two possible workarounds for the kernel to continue using large pages. First, we can compile the kernel so that no code or data will be allocated to the reserved page. The kernel still maps itself with large pages, but none of the reserved pages are actually accessed at runtime. This leaves a number of unused holes in the kernel's address space. As long as these pages are not touched by the kernel, they will not conflict with EncExec. Second, we can restore kernel large pages when EncExec is not in use. The user may not always need the protection of EncExec. For example, he may use EncExec when accessing his bank accounts but not when browsing random Internet sites. This solution will eliminate EncExec's idle performance overhead.

In addition, some I/O devices (e.g., graphic cards) may use large continuous blocks of physical address space for memory-mapped I/O (MMIO). MMIO accesses the device's (on-board) I/O memory instead of the RAM. Memory-mapped I/O will not interfere with EncExec because I/O spaces are often configured to be uncachable in order to correctly interact with I/O devices. Reading/writing I/O memory thus will not cause cache fill or eviction.

**Intel SGX:** Intel SGX is a powerful and complex extension to Intel CPUs. It creates a trusted execution environment, called enclave, for trusted apps. The enclave's code and data are encrypted in the memory and only decrypted in the CPU cache. SGX's TCB (trusted computing base) consists of only the CPU and the app itself. Therefore, the enclave is protected from cold boot attacks, bus snooping attacks, and malicious high-privileged code (e.g., the hypervisor). SGX has many other useful features, such as remote attestation that can ensure the initial integrity of the trusted app. Compared to SGX, EncExec works on the existing commodity Intel and other CPUs with a similar cache architecture, while SGX is only available in the new Intel CPUs. EncExec is also very lightweight: accessing the protected data in EncExec is instant and does not require time-consuming context switches. A context switch in SGX could be very expensive since it has to flush the TLB and perform various checks [5]. EncExec can also support unmodified programs. Moreover, the design of SGX is vulnerable to cache-based side-channel attacks [8]. By protecting data in the reserved cache, EncExec can provide some (limited) protection against cache side-channel attacks targeting that data, even though the side-channel defense is not the focus of this paper.

## 6 Related Work

**Cold Boot Attacks and Defenses:** the first category of related work consists of cold boot attacks and defenses. A cold boot attack exploits the fact that frozen DRAM keeps its contents for a relatively long period of time. It has been demonstrated against both desktop computers [14,27] and mobile phones [23,28]. A cold boot attack can be launched by either transplanting the frozen memory to a machine controlled by the attacker or booting a small kernel to dump the memory. Most existing defenses focus on re-purposing hardware storage to protect (small) cryptographic keys [10,21,22,26] or execute cryptographic algorithms [12] on the chip. For example, AESSE [21], TRESOR [22], LoopAmnesia [26], and ARMORED [10] protect an AES key in the SSE registers, debug registers, performance counters, and NEON registers, respectively. These "borrowed" registers naturally can only support compact cryptographic algorithms, but they do not have enough space for algorithms like RSA that have larger memory footprints. Compared to this line of work, EncExec can support all these algorithms.

Copker uses the cache-as-RAM technology [9] to run cryptographic algorithms in the cache. It can also support more complex algorithms such as RSA. However, Copker has very high context switch overheads – it has to force the calling CPU core, as well as any cores that share a cache with it, to enter the no-fill mode of caches. This poses a severe limit on the number of concurrent processes that can use Copker. For example, it can only support *one* process at a time on the Intel Core i7 CPU used in our prototype because the L3 cache is shared by all the cores. Most recent and near-future Intel CPUs all have a similar cache architecture. EncExec does not have these limitations. For example, it can support multiple concurrent processes and has a close to native performance if used properly. Mimosa uses hardware transactional memory to protect private (RSA) keys from memory disclosure [13]. EncExec also supports large RSA keys and can transparently protect the whole data sections. Both EncExec Mimosa require changes to the OS kernel although EncExec's changes are more invasive. On the other hand, Mimosa requires special hardware support (hardware transactional memory); thus it is not applicable to other architectures.

CaSE combines the cache-as-ram technology and ARM TrustZone to create a system that can protect the data from both cold-boot attacks and the compromised operating system [30]. The flexible cache control of the ARM platform allows CaSE to have lower performance overhead than Copker but similar to EncExec. EncExec instead works on the x86 architecture that lacks find-grained cache control. A recent system called RamCrypt [11] uses moving-window based encryption to protect the process data, similar to our second technique. As mentioned before, this technique alone is potentially susceptible to cold boot attacks because the recently-used unencrypted (sensitive) data can be evicted to the memory and become vulnerable to cold boot attacks.

**Other Related Work:** EncExec can protect the whole process data from cold boot attacks. Overshadow uses the hypervisor-assisted whole process encryption to protect an application from the untrusted OS kernel [6]. PrivateCore vCage is a virtual machine monitor that implements full-memory encryption for guest VMs by actively managing the whole L3 cache [3]. EncExec focuses on protecting applications. It reserves a small portion of the L3 cache and relies on demand paging to support larger protected data. XnR leverages demand paging to prevent an attacker from reading the randomized code [4]. RamCrypt similarly uses that technology to protect the process data from cold boot attacks [11]. HIveS manipulates the CPU's physical memory layout to hide malware in the I/O memory address space to avoid detection by memory forensic tools [31].

## 7 Summary

We have presented the design, implementation, and evaluation of EncExec, a practical and effective defense against cold boot attacks. EncExec has two key techniques: spatial cache reservation reserves a small block of the L3 cache, and secure in-cache execution uses demand paging to protect sensitive process data. Under the protection of EncExec, the sensitive data are always encrypted in the memory, and the plaintext data are confined to the reserved cache. Consequently, cold boot attacks can only obtain the encrypted data. The evaluation results demonstrate the effectiveness and practicality of EncExec.

**Acknowledgments.** We would like to thank the anonymous reviewers for their insightful comments that helped improve the presentation of this paper. This work was supported in part by the US National Science Foundation (NSF) under Grant 1453020. Any opinions, findings, and conclusions or recommendations expressed in this material are those of the authors and do not necessarily reflect the views of the NSF.

## References

1. FreeBSD. https://www.freebsd.org
2. SSL Library mbed TLS/PolarSSL. https://tls.mbed.org
3. Trustworthy Cloud Computing with vCage. https://privatecore.com/vcage/

4. Backes, M., Holz, T., Kollenda, B., Koppe, P., Nürnberger, S., Pewny, J.: You can run but you can't read: preventing disclosure exploits in executable code. In: Proceedings of the 2014 ACM SIGSAC Conference on Computer and Communications Security (CCS 2014) (2014)
5. Baumann, A., Peinado, M., Hunt, G.: Shielding applications from an untrusted cloud with haven. ACM Trans. Comput. Syst. **33**(3), 8 (2015)
6. Chen, X., Garfinkel, T., Lewis, E.C., Subrahmanyam, P., Waldspurger, C.A., Boneh, D., Dwoskin, J., Ports, D.R.: Overshadow: a virtualization-based approach to retrofitting protection in commodity operating systems. In: Proceedings of the 13th International Conference on Architectural Support for Programming Languages and Operating Systems (ASPLOS XIII) (2008)
7. Chow, J., Pfaff, B., Garfinkel, T., Christopher, K., Rosenblum, M.: Understanding data lifetime via whole system simulation. In: Proceedings of the 13th Conference on USENIX Security Symposium (SSYM 2004), vol. 13 (2004)
8. Costan, V., Devadas, S.: Intel SGX explained. https://eprint.iacr.org/2016/086.pdf
9. Nallusamy, E.: A framework for using processor cache as RAM (CAR). http://www.coreboot.org/images/6/6c/LBCar.pdf
10. Götzfried, J., Müller, T.: ARMORED: CPU-bound encryption for android-driven ARM devices. In: Proceedings of 8th International Conference on Availability, Reliability and Security, Regensburg (2013)
11. Götzfried, J., Müller, T., Drescher, G., Nürnberger, S., Backes, M.: RamCrypt: kernel-based address space encryption for user-mode processes. In: Proceedings of the 11th ACM Symposium on Information, Computer and Communications Security (ASIA CCS 2016). ACM (2016)
12. Guan, L., Lin, J., Jing, B.L.: Copker: computing with private keys without RAM. In: Proceedings of the 21th Network and Distributed System Security Symposium (NDSS 2014) (2014)
13. Guan, L., Lin, J., Luo, B., Jing, J., Wang, J.: Protecting private keys against memory disclosure attacks using hardware transactional memory. In: Proceedings of the 2015 IEEE Symposium on Security and Privacy (SP 2015), pp. 3–19. IEEE Computer Society, Washington, DC (2015)
14. Halderman, J.A., Schoen, S.D., Heninger, N., Clarkson, W., Paul, W., Calandrino, J.A., Feldman, A.J., Appelbaum, J., Felten, E.W., Remember, L.W.: Cold-boot attacks on encryption keys. In: Proceedings of the 17th USENIX Conference on Security, San Jose (2008)
15. Hennessy, J.L., Patterson, D.A.: Computer Architecture: A Quantitative Approach. Morgan Kaufmann, San Francisco (2012)
16. Intel: Intel 64 and IA-32 Architectures Software Developerś Manual, February 2014
17. Irazoqui, G., Eisenbarth, T., Sunar, B.: S \$ A: a shared cache attack that works across cores and defies VM sandboxing-and its application to AES. In: Proceedings of the 36th IEEE Symposium on Security and Privacy, pp. 591–604. IEEE (2015)
18. Liu, F., Yarom, Y., Ge, Q., Heiser, G., Lee, R.B.: Last-level cache side-channel attacks are practical. In: Proceedings of the 36th IEEE Symposium on Security and Privacy, pp. 605–622 (2015)
19. Maurice, C., Scouarnec, N., Neumann, C., Heen, O., Francillon, A.: Reverse engineering intel last-level cache complex addressing using performance counters. In: Bos, H., Monrose, F., Blanc, G. (eds.) RAID 2015. LNCS, vol. 9404, pp. 48–65. Springer, Cham (2015). doi:10.1007/978-3-319-26362-5_3

20. McKusick, M.K., Neville-Neil, G.V., Watson, R.N.: The Design and Implementation of the FreeBSD Operating System. Addison-Wesley Professional, London (2014)
21. Müller, T., Dewald, A., Freiling, F.C.: AESSE: a cold-boot resistant implementation of AES. In: Proceedings of the Third European Workshop on System Security, Paris (2010)
22. Müller, T., Freiling, F.C., Dewald, A.: TRESO: runs encryption securely outside RAM. In: Proceedings of the 20th USENIX Conference on Security, San Francisco (2011)
23. Müller, T., Spreitzenbarth, M.: FROST: forensic recovery of scrambled telephones. In: Proceedings of the 11th International Conference on Applied Cryptography and Network Security, Banff (2013)
24. Onarlioglu, K., Mulliner, C., Robertson, W., Kirda, E.: PrivExec: private execution as an operating system service. In: Proceedings of the 2013 IEEE Symposium on Security and Privacy (SP 2013). IEEE Computer Society, Washington, DC (2013)
25. Silberschatz, A., Galvin, P.B., Gagne, G.: Operating System Concepts. Wiley, Harlow (2012)
26. Simmons, P., Amnesia, S.T.: A software-based solution to the cold boot attack on disk encryption. In: Proceedings of the 27th Annual Computer Security Applications Conference, Orlando (2011)
27. Lest We Remember: Cold-boot attacks on encryption keys. https://citp.princeton.edu/research/memory/
28. FROST: Forensic Recovery Of Scrambled Telephones. http://www1.informatik.uni-erlangen.de/frost
29. Yarom, Y., Ge, Q., Liu, F., Lee, R.B., Heiser, G.: Mapping the Intel last-level cache. https://eprint.iacr.org/2015/905.pdf
30. Zhang, N., Sun, K., Lou, W., Hou, Y.T.: CaSE: cache-assisted secure execution on ARM processors. In: Proceedings of the 2016 IEEE Symposium on Security and Privacy (SP 2016) (2016)
31. Zhang, N., Sun, K., Lou, W., Hou, Y.T., Jajodia, S.: Now you see me: hide and seek in physical address space. In: Proceedings of the 10th ACM Symposium on Information, Computer and Communications Security, ASIA (CCS 2015). ACM (2015)

# Scotch: Combining Software Guard Extensions and System Management Mode to Monitor Cloud Resource Usage

Kevin Leach[1(✉)], Fengwei Zhang[2], and Westley Weimer[3]

[1] University of Virginia, Charlottesville, VA 22903, USA
kjl2y@virginia.edu
[2] Wayne State University, Detroit, MI 48202, USA
fengwei@wayne.edu
[3] University of Michigan, Ann Arbor, MI 48109, USA
weimerw@umich.edu

**Abstract.** The growing reliance on cloud-based services has led to increased focus on cloud security. Cloud providers must deal with concerns from customers about the overall security of their cloud infrastructures. In particular, an increasing number of cloud attacks target resource allocation in cloud environments. For example, vulnerabilities in a hypervisor scheduler can be exploited by attackers to effectively steal CPU time from other benign guests on the same hypervisor. In this paper, we present Scotch, a system for transparent and accurate resource consumption accounting in a hypervisor. By combining x86-based System Management Mode with Intel Software Guard Extensions, we can ensure the integrity of our accounting information, even when the hypervisor has been compromised by an escaped malicious guest. We show that we can account for resources at every task switch and I/O interrupt, giving us richly detailed resource consumption information for each guest running on the hypervisor. We show that using our system incurs small but manageable overhead—roughly 1 µs every task switch or I/O interrupt. We further discuss performance improvements that can be made for our proposed system by performing accounting at random intervals. Finally, we discuss the viability of this approach against multiple types of cloud-based resource attacks.

## 1 Introduction

The growing ubiquity of Software- and Infrastructure-as-a-Service has led to an increase in the cloud computing market. Spending on cloud computing infrastructure is projected to reach $38 billion in 2016 [14]. At the same time, the National Vulnerability Database shows that there are 226 security vulnerabilities in Xen, 99 vulnerabilities for VMWare ESX, and 98 vulnerabilities for KVM

**Electronic supplementary material** The online version of this chapter (doi:10.1007/978-3-319-66332-6_18) contains supplementary material, which is available to authorized users.


M. Dacier et al. (Eds.): RAID 2017, LNCS 10453, pp. 403–424, 2017.
DOI: 10.1007/978-3-319-66332-6_18

hypervisors [29]. As a result, there is additional concern over security breaches in cloud environments [20,26].

Such vulnerabilities have already led to exploits related to the improper allocation of cloud resources. For instance, resource-freeing attacks [35] allow a malicious VM guest to take one resource from a victim VM (e.g., more CPU time). Similarly, vulnerabilities in hypervisor schedulers have been documented [32,49]. Hypervisor vulnerabilities may permit a malicious customer to acquire cloud resources for free or at the expense of a victim. As a result, there is a need for cloud providers to guarantee levels of service and billing accountability to their customers using their infrastructure [24].

Cloud providers make use of virtualization platforms such as the Xen hypervisor [18]. Resource allocation is performed by the hypervisor according to the provider's configuration corresponding to the customer's service level. For example, a cloud provider might offer more CPU time to a customer that pays more money—this policy would be enforced by the hypervisor's scheduler. However, malicious customers that exploit vulnerabilities in the hypervisor may be able to evade this policy, obtaining more resources than would be dictated by their service levels.

In this paper, we present SCOTCH (Securely Communicating Objective, Transparent Cloud Health), a technique that leverages two x86 features to accurately account for resources consumed by virtual machines: System Management Mode (SMM) and Software Guard eXtensions (SGX). SMM permits transparent access to CPU registers and memory in the underlying operating system, hypervisor, and guests. SGX allows the creation of encrypted regions called enclaves that isolate critical execution from a potentially-compromised hypervisor or operating system. We can use SMM to track the resources consumed by each guest such that (1) potentially malicious guests are unaware, and (2) we can detect previously undetected resource accounting attacks. While SMM asynchronously measures resource usage, this information can be securely conveyed to an individual userspace enclave using SGX. This novel combination of SMM and SGX enables a new method of accurately measuring and securely communicating resource usage information in virtualized environments.

We evaluate a prototype of our technique based on the Xen hypervisor. We show that our technique takes roughly 1 μs to check resource usage during each context switch and interrupt. We also show how this fixed 1 μs cost can be amortized across multiple context switches and interrupts by randomly choosing intervals in which to check resource consumption. Next, we discuss the tradeoff between the quantity of a resource that can be stolen by a malicious guest compared to the overhead our technique incurs. Finally, we discuss the types of attacks for which SCOTCH is capable of providing accurate resource accounting information where other approaches cannot. We note that SCOTCH does not automatically decide whether malicious activity is occurring; a direct comparative study against such techniques remains future work.

We make the following contributions:

- A technique for accurately and transparently measuring system resources consumed by guest VMs running under a hypervisor,
- A prototype implementation employing the proposed technique for Xen, and
- An experimental evaluation of the prototype measuring accuracy and overhead of the proposed technique.

## 2 Background

In this section, we discuss three topics relevant to our proposed technique. First, we introduce System Management Mode, a special execution mode built into x86-based CPUs that permits transparent, isolated execution. Second, we discuss the Xen hypervisor and the types of vulnerabilities that could be leveraged by a malicious customer to gain or otherwise misuse cloud resources. Third, we introduce Intel Software Guard eXtensions (SGX), another set of instructions that enable our approach.

### 2.1 System Management Mode

System Management Mode (SMM) is a CPU mode available in all x86 architecture. It is similar to Real and Protected Modes. Originally designed for facilitating power control, recent work has leveraged SMM for system introspection [28,43], debugging [45], and other security tasks [44,46]. In brief, the CPU enters SMM upon a System Management Interrupt (SMI). While in SMM, the CPU executes the System Management Handler (SMI Handler), a special segment of code loaded from the Basic Input/Output System (BIOS) firmware into System Management RAM (SMRAM), an isolated region of system memory [6]. Upon completing executing the SMI Handler, the CPU resumes execution in Protected Mode.

We use SMM as a trusted execution environment for implementing our resource accounting functions. SMM has been available on all x86 platforms since the 386, so it is widely available for usage on commodity systems. In addition, the underlying operating system is essentially paused while the SMI handler executes. This isolated execution provides transparency to the operating system. We trust SMM for two main reasons: (1) SMRAM can be treated as secure storage because it is inaccessible by Protected and Real Modes, and (2) the SMI handler requires only a small trusted code base because it is stored in the BIOS and cannot be modified after booting when properly configured.

The SMI handler is stored as part of the BIOS. Typically, vendors ship SMI handler code specific to their platforms. Upon powering the system, the BIOS loads the SMI handler code into SMRAM before loading the operating system. After loading the SMI handler, the BIOS prevents further modifications to the SMI handler by locking down SMRAM. On Intel and AMD platforms, this is implemented using a write-once model-specific register (MSR); upon setting a specific bit, no other changes can be made to SMRAM (or the associated MSR). Thus, even if the hypervisor becomes completely compromised, the underlying SMI handler performing our resource accounting task will remain intact. The SMI handler is, by default, loaded into a 4 KB region of memory, called the ASEG segment. We can alternatively load the SMI handler into another segment of memory called TSEG to allocate more space, often as much as 8 MB.

Finally, as SMRAM is isolated in hardware (i.e., it cannot be mapped by the MMU unless the CPU is in SMM), a hypothetical DMA attack would not be able to corrupt resource accounting information stored in SMRAM.

### 2.2 Xen Credit Scheduler and Resource Accounting

Xen [18] is a widely-deployed open source hypervisor. Xen is responsible for multiplexing multiple independent guest virtual machines. In a cloud environment, customers are given access to guest VMs with different configurations according to how much they pay. For instance, a customer may pay more to the cloud provider for a VM configured with more memory, disk space, or nominal CPU time.

Xen uses the Xen Credit Scheduler [1] by default to manage CPU time. The Credit scheduler allocates virtual *credits* to each Virtual CPU (VCPU) that wants CPU time. Each VCPU can be given more or fewer credits depending on the service level paid for. That is, the scheduler can distribute more credits to one customer's VCPU over another's based on how much is billed for CPU time. Every context switch, the scheduler decides which VCPU to run next based in part on the number of credits that VCPU currently has. While there are other schedulers Xen can be run with (Cherkasova et al. [13] provide a comparison), the Credit scheduler is the most commonly deployed scheduler.

Critically, Xen runs a helper function (`burn_credits` in the `sched_credit.c` file) at a regular interval that deducts credits from the currently executing VCPU. In brief, this function approximates CPU usage over time by polling the currently-executing context. Previous research [24,32,49] discussed in Sect. 7 has already explored vulnerabilities related to this approximation. If a malicious guest knows about the interval at which `burn_credits` is executed, the guest can measure time precisely and yield the CPU before the credits are accounted for. In doing so, a malicious attacker can potentially use CPU time without being billed for it.

In addition, Xen maintains credit information (and other metadata) about each guest in memory. Guests that escape the VM [15] could potentially alter such data, yielding incorrect accounting (and later, billing) information. For example, by deducting credits more rapidly from a benign victim guest, the victim's apparent CPU consumption could be made to exceed its real consumption.

### 2.3 Software Guard eXtensions

Intel SGX is another new set of instructions that permits the creation of *enclaves* in userspace [23]. These enclaves are encrypted regions of memory (code and data) that cannot be accessed from outside of the enclave context. SGX allows computation to occur securely, even if the operating system or hypervisor is malicious.

SGX is intended to secure local computation; I/O instructions are illegal while inside an enclave. Instead, SGX-based applications must call out (via `OCALLs`) to switch to untrusted OS code to execute I/O on behalf of the enclave. SGX applications are therefore unable to monitor other activity happening on the system (e.g., through shared memory or device I/O) securely. In this paper, we use SMM to measure system-wide usage and then report this information to the end user via an SGX enclave application.

## 3 Threat Model

In this section, we discuss three types of attacks against which Scotch is capable of reliably accounting: (1) scheduler attacks, (2) resource interference attacks, and (3) VM escape attacks. These attacks increase in terms of expressive power and detriment against a hypervisor.

### 3.1 Scheduler Attacks

We consider an attacker capable of exploiting vulnerabilities in the hypervisor's scheduler to acquire system resources for the malicious VM at the expense of a victim VM. This approach allows the attacker to prevent the victim from accessing rightful resources and also allows the attacker to perform expensive computations for free.

Figure 1a shows the non-attack scenario, a potential schedule of two benign CPU-bound VMs competing for CPU time on one physical CPU. Both guests 1 and 2 are given equal time, and when the VMM assesses which VM to bill, each guest is billed for its fair share of CPU time. However, as shown in the attack scenario in Fig. 1b, a malicious guest could yield at precise times to avoid when the VMM attempts to assess which guest is running. As a result, a malicious VM could appear to never consume CPU time. Zhou et al. [49] showed that such an attack can consume the vast majority of CPU time under proper conditions.

### 3.2 Resource Interference Attacks

Resource interference attacks work by exploiting VM multi-tenancy. That is, all VM guests on a single hypervisor will have to share the underlying physical resources at some point (e.g., there is only one system bus). A clever attacker VM can execute precise, calculated workloads that could impact the performance of other victim VMs or simply improve its own performance. For example, Resource Freeing Attacks [35] work by forcing a victim VM to free up a resource for the attacker to use. For example, the victim might be running a webserver, in which case the attacker can flood requests to the victim, cause it to block on I/O, and free up CPU time for the attacker. In this paper, we consider an attacker capable of degrading victim guest performance in this manner.

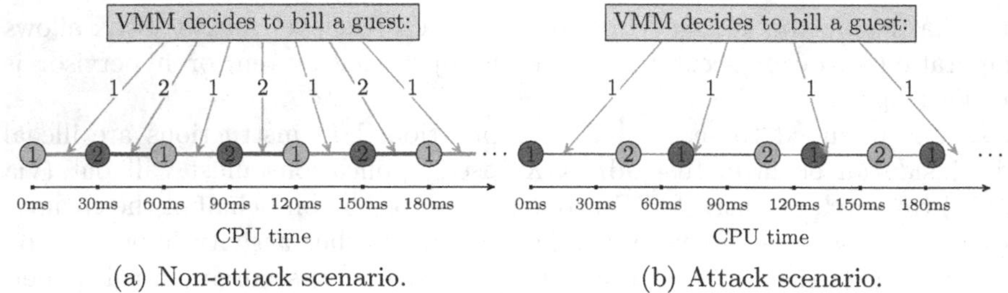


(a) Non-attack scenario. (b) Attack scenario.

**Fig. 1.** Resource accounting scenario. A potential schedule of two benign VMs (denoted 1 and 2) with ideal CPU-bound workloads. The orange arrows represent when a VMM would poll which guest is running as part of determining billing. The accounting information inferred is accurate over time. In (b), a malicious guest closely controls CPU usage so that the benign guest (1) appears to use all of the CPU time. (Color figure online)

### 3.3 VM Escape Attacks

Virtualization technologies, such as Xen, nominally isolate guest VMs from one another. Indeed, with full hardware virtualization, each guest believes it has control of an entire system. However, vulnerabilities inevitably find their way into hypervisors that allow malicious guests to escape out of the virtualization environment and execute arbitrary code within the hypervisor context [15,27]. Naturally, such attacks can have a devastating impact on cloud providers, potentially exposing private or valuable data to the attacker. In this paper, we consider an attacker capable of escaping the guest context, and taking over the VMM.[1]

In this paper, we do not assume VM escape attacks that completely disable the system. For instance, it is very possible that a VM escape attack could compromise the hypervisor and stop executing all guests, or an attacker could attempt to disable network communications in the SMI handler with the Remote System. These sorts of denial-of-service (DoS) attacks can often be detected with timeouts and are out of scope for this work. Instead, we consider escape attacks where the attacker is capable of corrupting data structures related to resource usage.

## 4 Architecture

The goal of the SCOTCH architecture is to provide accurate and transparent resource accounting for cloud computing systems. This is done via resource accounting code that measures resources consumed by each guest residing on a hypervisor during every task switch and interrupt. We take advantage of hardware support to provide incorruptible accounting code and data storage as well as tamper-proof event-based invocation.

[1] We assume the attacker can gain ring 0 (i.e., kernel) privilege after escaping the guest VM environment.

Figure 2 illustrates our system architecture. We have two or more systems in our approach. First, one or more Protected Systems run Virtual Machine Monitor (VMM) software capable of hosting multiple benign or malicious VM guests. Each Protected System reliably collects resource consumption information about each guest, periodically reporting this information to an SGX enclave. The SGX enclave stores all of the resource consumption information from the VMs on the Protected System for further processing or analysis in a way that cannot be read or tampered with by a malicious guest, operating system, or hypervisor. In our implemented prototype of Scotch, we consider one Protected Machine with one SGX enclave.

### 4.1 Resource Accounting Workflow

The Protected Machine described in Fig. 2 is responsible for collecting reliable and tamper-resistant resource consumption information about each VM guest whether it is malicious or benign. To accomplish this goal, we will discuss five steps (marked ①–⑤ in Fig. 2) taken by the Protected System to ensure the integrity of the resource accounting information.

In step ①, the VMM is engaged by a VM guest through preemption or a hypercall to service an I/O request. Using hardware support (q.v. Sect. 5), we capture all such events, and execute our custom resource accounting code (denoted step ②). Note that the VM guest could be malicious or benign—we make no distinction in our approach because we are simply computing accurate and tamper-resistant resource accounting so that benign customers are eventually notified of the resources actually consumed.

During a context switch, step ② invokes an SMI, causing our accounting code to run in the SMI handler. Using further hardware support, we can convert certain types of I/O and event interrupts into SMIs. For instance, when a VM's time quantum elapses, a timer raises an interrupt telling the VMM to switch guests. In Scotch, we change such interrupts to invoke SMIs instead. Invoking an SMI is critically important to the continued reliability of accounting information provided by our system.

In step ③, our accounting code records which VM guest will run next as well as the time elapsed since the last time our code executed (i.e., the last context switch event). This information is recorded in an isolated region of system memory, inaccessible from the hypervisor (or guest) context. For I/O events, we record information about what type of I/O is being done. For recording resource consumption besides CPU time, capturing these I/O events allows us to reason about whether a guest is consuming disk or network.

In step ④, our accounting code finishes executing and transfers control back to the guest. We do not pass control back to the hypervisor because a compromised hypervisor may change the result of a task switch event (cf. time-of-check-to-time-of-use attacks). For example, during a context switch, the hypervisor scheduler will select a new guest to run. If one were to perform resource accounting before the hypervisor finalizes the scheduling decision, a compromised hypervisor could spoof which guest will run next, perform accounting, and then

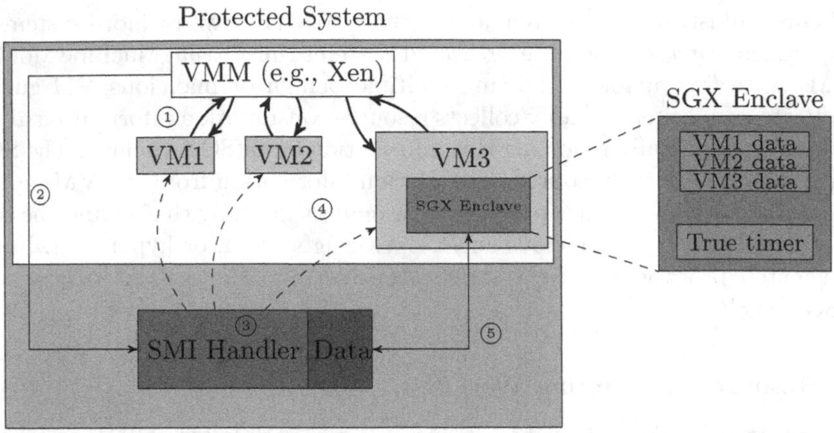

**Fig. 2.** High level overview of SCOTCH. The system contains one Protected System running VMM software containing a number of benign and malicious guests. One of the benign guests has an SGX enclave application running that receives accounting information from our tamper-resistant resource monitoring code. The annotations ①–⑤ correspond to the order of events in an indicative workflow. We assume benign guests are motivated to know their resource consumption.

run a different guest. Instead, in SCOTCH we invoke the resource accounting code right before control would have been transferred to the guest. After our accounting code completes, control flows directly to the correct guest.

Finally, step ⑤ represents a task that is completed occasionally. It is possible that a malicious guest that escapes to the hypervisor could corrupt data. In particular, if such an attacker is trying to hide the resources they consume, they might corrupt timers on the hypervisor that we use to measure the amount of time each guest spends consuming a resource. In such cases, we could use the SMI handler code (Step ②) to occasionally request time information from a trusted remote server (cf. Spectre [43]).

**Cost of Accounting.** Recall that our approach invokes SMIs to reliably execute our resource accounting code. The invocation of the SMI and the resource accounting code itself both incur overhead on the hypervisor. This, in turn, affects the performance of the guests on the system, even if no malicious guests are running. For example, assuming a CPU-bound workload in which all guests consume all of their allocated time quanta, adding our resource accounting code essentially increases the amount of time taken to complete a context switch. Thus, deploying SCOTCH means accepting an associated performance loss in order to gain high accuracy, tamper-resistant resource accounting information.

As we discuss in Sect. 6, we also consider an alternative scenario to mitigate performance impact by invoking our code at different intervals. Ideally, we would invoke our accounting code on every possible task switch and I/O interrupt event. However, we could instead elect to invoke our code every $x$ such events, where

$x$ is some random interval from 1 to some maximum interval. Essentially, every time an interrupt or task switch occurs, we flip a coin to decide whether to invoke our resource accounting code. This requires adding such decision code to the hypervisor, which could be noticed (or altered) by malicious, escaped guests. However, we propose this approach as a means to significantly improve performance on diverse workloads. This option allows a cloud provider to trade off resource accounting granularity and overhead.

## 5 Implementation

In this section, we discuss how we implement our approach on a real system. Recall there are five steps in our workflow from Fig. 2:

1. Capture interrupts and task switch events,
2. Redirect interrupts to invoke resource accounting code,
3. Compute resource usage impact of the current event,
4. Transfer CPU control to next guest, and
5. Relay accounting information into a trusted SGX enclave running within a VM guest.

Capturing these interrupts depends on features from Intel's Virtualization (VT-x) extension. In particular, we use VT-x's intercept capability, which allows us to control what happens as a result of a diverse array of events that can happen during execution, including task switching and interrupts. VT-x supports intercepting other events such as when a guest executes certain instructions, but we do not use this feature in SCOTCH. After intercepting task switches and I/O interrupts, we execute our resource accounting code.

We use System Management Mode (SMM) to implement our resource accounting code. We invoke a System Management Interrupt (SMI), which causes the CPU to save its state and transfer control to the SMI handler. The SMI handler is stored in the BIOS and loaded into the special SMRAM memory region upon booting the system. SMRAM is only addressable by SMM, and so any hypervisor or guest code running in Protected or Long Mode are not capable of reading or writing our SMI handler code. We overwrite the SMI handler with custom resource accounting code, which is then executed every time we assert an SMI.

SMIs can be asserted in several ways according to the platform's chipset. For our prototype, we use the AMD 800 series chipset. This platform supports invoking SMIs by writing to the legacy I/O port `0xb0` [5]. By executing `outb` instructions, we can invoke SMIs. Alternatively, we can also write to offset `0x9b` of the SMI control register of the advanced configuration and power interface (ACPI) MMIO configuration space.[2] Writes to this address causes an SMI to occur. Once an SMI is asserted, the CPU switches to SMM and begins executing the SMI handler at a fixed offset. Finally, we can also assert SMIs by configuring timing registers to deliver SMIs at configurable intervals.

[2] On our platform, the specific physical address was `0xfed8029b`.

We wrote a custom SMI handler that locates the VM guests residing on the system, identify which one was executing when the SMI occurred, and updates resource account information about that guest. On x86 machines, the control register CR3 contains a pointer to the physical location of the page directory associated with a process—in Xen, the CR3 value can uniquely identify guests. We maintain a map of CR3 register values to VM guest IDs. We can also compute the location of the Virtual Machine Control Structure (VMCS) of each guest, which contains information about virtualized timers (and other information related to VM guest context). In our prototype, we have two guest VMs executing on one physical core—this setup simplifies identifying which guest is currently executing.

Recall that our SMI handler is invoked for one of two reasons: task switching or interrupt servicing. During a task switch, the VMCS page contains a pointer to the next guest that will run after the task switch completes. In other words, we know which guest will run next but not the guest that just completed running. Nonetheless, we can record current timestamp $t_1$ using the `rdtsc` instruction. Then, when the next task switch occurs, we can get another timestamp $t_2$, and use the difference $t_2 - t_1$ to estimate the amount of CPU time consumed by the guest that was previously executing. For interrupts, we can determine which IRQ was involved using the VMCS, from which we can determine the device that caused the interrupt. For our current prototype, we track the number of interrupts and associated IRQs corresponding to each guest.

After our resource accounting SMI handler completes, it switches back to Protected Mode to resume normal execution. Executing an `RSM` instruction restores the previous state and configuration registers. Ultimately, in our prototype, this transfers control of the CPU to the next guest task to execute without any space for the VMM to execute any instructions. Thus, even if the hypervisor is compromised, it does not have an opportunity to change the results of a task switch or interrupt event after we have completed our accounting code. This approach allows a highly granular and accurate view of resource consumption of each guest.

Next, we relay our accounting information to the SGX enclave, which stores data for later analysis in an isolated space. We cannot use SGX-related instructions while in SMM [23]. Instead, we perform several steps to get the data into the SGX enclave. First, we create a normal userspace stub program in the virtual machine guest containing the SGX enclave. This stub program contains a page of memory for arbitrary data, and code to marshall that data into the SGX enclave (via `EENTER`). We use the SMI handler to check the integrity of the stub program to detect potential tampering. Next, we note the physical address of this starting page, and the SMI handler writes its accounting data into that location. We configure the SMI handler to transfer control to the stub code after exiting SMM (by changing save state). The stub code (executing in Protected Mode at ring 3) then places that data into the enclave. This approach allows us confidence that the accounting data is securely relayed to user space.

Finally, we implement a network card driver in the SMI handler to communicate with the Remote System for accurate, external timing information. A similar approach was used in Spectre [43] and MalT [45]. We use symmetric key encryption with a key stored in SMRAM transmitted by the Remote System as the BIOS is booting the Protected System. This ensures that the key is stored securely before the Protected System has an opportunity to load potentially-compromised hypervisor code.

## 6 Evaluation

In this section, we evaluate Scotch. We present experimental results and discussion. We seek to answer the following research questions:

**RQ1** Can we perform accurate resource accounting during scheduler attacks?
**RQ2** What is the overhead of our accounting approach on benign workloads?
**RQ3** Can we accurately account resources during resource interference attacks?
**RQ4** Can we perform accurate resource accounting during VM escape attacks?
**RQ5** How do our CPU-based techniques apply to other resources?

### 6.1 Experimental Setup

Our experiments were carried out on an Intel Core i7-7700HQ 2.8 GHz CPU with 32 GB of memory. We ran two identical Ubuntu 15.04 guests, each given 256 MB of memory and 1CPU core. We recorded the physical memory addresses of each guest's Virtual Machine Control Structure (VMCS) to ease experimentation. For ground truth data, we used Xen's built-in instrumentation, xentrace [3]. Xentrace behaves similarly to perf in that it can monitor for certain events and record resource usage. For some research questions, we developed our own attacks to mimic the behavior of possible attacks that would occur in the wild. Those implementations are detailed in the appropriate sections that follow.

### 6.2 RQ1: Scheduler Attack

Our first research question asks whether our system is capable of accurately recording CPU time consumption when a malicious guest uses a scheduler attack to steal CPU time. For this experiment, we have one malicious guest VM and one victim guest VM competing for the same amount of CPU time on a physical core. We wrote ten variants of the Xen credit scheduler, each of which gives the malicious VM an increasing amount of CPU time by influencing credit allocation in the scheduler. This is similar to the pseudo-attack implemented in [24], though we effect changes in the credits assigned to each guest over time to achieve changes in CPU time.

The ten scheduler variants are meant to represent varying degrees severity of a given attack—during each accounting period, each variant will randomly decide whether to deduct credits from the attacker VM, with variant $n$ being

$4n\%$ likely to skip credit deduction. That is, scheduler variant 10 is 40% likely to skip the deduction of credits on the attacker VM. This means that, over time, the attacker will have more credits and thus more time to get scheduled.

We ran several benchmark applications in both guests using each of the ten scheduler variants: pi, gzip, and PARSEC [11]. Computing pi represents a highly CPU-bound workload, while gzip on a large random file represents a more mixed CPU and I/O-bound workload. The PARSEC benchmark suite has been used previously in the area of cloud performance and economics [37,39]. Under benign circumstances, each guest should get 50% of the CPU time regardless of workload. When the attack variants are considered, an increasing amount of CPU time should be allocated to the attacker.

**Table 1.** Ratio of attacker VM CPU time to guest VM CPU time.

| | Scheduler attack severity level | | | | | | | | | | |
|---|---|---|---|---|---|---|---|---|---|---|---|
| | Benign | 1 | 2 | 3 | 4 | 5 | 6 | 7 | 8 | 9 | 10 |
| Scotch | 1.00 | 1.04 | 1.07 | 1.10 | 1.13 | 1.17 | 1.21 | 1.26 | 1.31 | 1.36 | 1.41 |
| Ground truth | 0.99 | 1.05 | 1.09 | 1.12 | 1.15 | 1.17 | 1.20 | 1.25 | 1.30 | 1.35 | 1.39 |

Table 1 shows the results of this experiment. We ran each benchmark program for five minutes measuring the CPU time allocated. We report the ratio between the attacker VM and victim VM CPU time for both Scotch and xentrace [3]. Furthermore, we average the results of all benchmarks. We note that, under benign circumstances, Scotch and xentrace both report a ratio of 1.0. However, as the attack becomes more severe, the attacker VM gets a higher ratio of CPU time, again validated against xentrace. This pattern is consistent across all workloads. Overall, Scotch performs accurate resource accounting even in the face of severe scheduler attacks.

### 6.3 RQ2: Overhead

We note that executing our isolated SMI handler resource accounting code takes additional time during each context switch and interrupt. Our SMI handler code takes $2248 \pm 69$ cycles to execute. On our 2.8 GHz platform, that corresponds to about 1 µs. However, acquiring granular resource accounting information means this 1 µs cost must be incurred every context switch and every interrupt. In contrast, a typical VM switch takes roughly 20,000 cycles, or roughly 7.1 µs. Adding our resource accounting code thus increases context switching time 14%. However, in purely CPU-bound workloads, Xen uses a 30 ms default quantum per guest. Thus, the context switching time is amortized into the 30 ms runtime per quantum. In other words, every 30 ms of useful work requires a total of 8.1 µs overhead in Scotch, compared to 7.1 µs overhead in default systems. Thus, we can estimate the additional system overhead incurred by Scotch on CPU-bound workloads with:

$$\frac{|8.1\,\mu\text{s} - 7.1\,\mu\text{s}|}{(30\,\text{ms} + 7.1\,\mu\text{s})} = 33 \times 10^{-6}\text{additional overhead}$$

That is, our system incurs an additional .0033% overhead by using our system. As I/O operations typically take much longer in comparison to CPU-bound computation, this overhead reasonably approximates the worst-case overhead incurred by SCOTCH.

However, for the complete picture, we must also consider more realistic mixed CPU- and I/O-bound workload. Using gzip, we compressed a large randomly-generated file for a total of 5 min. The file was twice the size of guest system memory preclude caching the entire file and force operations to go all the way to disk. We measured the amount of CPU time and the amount of time spent servicing disk requests using our approach. In five minutes, there were 8070 context switches in which 214.59 s of CPU time were consumed. Thus, we can estimate the amount of CPU time consumed after each context switch with:

$$\frac{214.59\,\text{s}}{8070\,\text{switches}} = 26.6\,\text{ms},$$

which is reasonable (for reference, recall the standard quantum in Xen is 30 ms): gzip would be spending some amount of time executing CPU-bound compression code. Using the formula above, we get an additional overhead of 0.0038%.

In contrast, there were 1371 interrupts going to disk, which took a total of 85.42 s. This corresponds to 62.3 ms per interrupt. Using a similar formula above, we can estimate the additional overhead incurred on disk-bound interrupt events. For interrupts, this additional overhead is 0.0016%. Both values represent a significant improvement over existing SMM-based work [24]. While part of this improvement is due to faster SMI-handler code, much of the overhead depends on the underlying capability of the CPU to switch into SMM. Previous work has found SMI handler code takes on the order of 10 μs [43, 45]. That said, even with a 100-fold increase in execution time of our SMI handler code, we still incur an overhead below 1%.

Note that we can further improve performance using an interval-based approach. Instead of invoking our code on every task switch or I/O interrupt, we can instead invoke our code after $x$ such events, where $x$ is a random number between 1 and some maximum interval. This random interval approach prevents transient resource attacks from going unnoticed because such attacks cannot learn a pattern for our resource accounting invocation. Thus, in the long run, such an approach maintains high accuracy with regard to resource accounting, but features a lower overhead. That said, spreading out the interval does create an opportunity for a sophisticated attacker to hide malicious activity; such an attacker could risk a certain amount of detection (determined by the measurement interval) by attempting to steal resources and counting on not be measured with our approach. Ultimately, the end user must decide the level of granularity of resource accounting information they need in comparison to the amount of overhead incurred by SCOTCH.

### 6.4 RQ3: Resource Interference Attacks

We also consider accounting in the face of resource interference attacks [35]. SCOTCH is capable of maintaining accurate resource accounting information even in the presence of such attacks. Because SCOTCH is invoked on every task switch and I/O interrupt, we maintain an accurate picture of resource consumption by construction. For example, as discussed in Sect. 3.2, a resource freeing attack may work by causing a victim to block on I/O and thus free up CPU time for the attacker—but they still involve standard task switching and I/O interrupts. Thus, in such an attack, SCOTCH will accurately report that one guest is blocked on I/O and that the other is using the CPU.

We note that resource interference attacks often rely on an attacker's knowledge of a victim's workload. We reiterate that SCOTCH does not detect or prevent such an attack per se (although an analyst may do so by inspecting the resource accounting information). Instead, SCOTCH provides a guarantee about the quality and accuracy of resource accounting information our system delivers, even in the face of such attacks. This represents an improvement over previous approaches [12,24], which neither detect nor prevent nor accurately account for resource usage in the presence of such attacks.

### 6.5 RQ4: VM Escape Attacks

Next, we discuss the viability of using SCOTCH even when the hypervisor has been compromised completely. Attacks such as Venom [15] or CloudBurst [27] allow a malicious VM guest to exploit vulnerabilities in the underlying hypervisor to escape the virtualized environment and execute arbitrary code in the hypervisor context. These are particularly dangerous attacks because they have the potential to compromise all of the other VM guests on the hypervisor. Additionally, such attacks are capable of changing resource allocation arbitrarily, potentially influencing ultimate billing for benign customers. In such cases, SCOTCH can provide accurate resource accounting information that can be used to provide accurate billing for all customers.

Recall that our resource accounting code is stored in isolated SMRAM. Even if an attacker is allowed ring 0 privilege in the underlying hypervisor, there is not a way for such an attacker to either (1) change previously-collected accounting information, or (2) change the accounting code itself. While ring 0 code could influence configuration registers and invoke spurious SMIs, a cursory analysis of the data transmitted to the Remote System would reveal such behavior. Additionally, such an attacker is not able to change SMM-related configuration registers because they are locked before the BIOS transfers control to the hypervisor.

However, malicious ring 0 code could alter kernel structures (Direct Kernel Object Manipulation [30]) or sensitive registers to influence accounting information before it is seen by the SMI handler. An attacker could, for instance, write the TSC register so that it appears a particular guest has consumed fewer cycles than it actually has, leading to an accounting discrepancy. In such cases, we could employ an instruction-level instrumentation approach similar to MALT [45] while kernel code executes to detect TSC writes or other malicious DKOM activity.

### 6.6 RQ5: Beyond CPU Time

RQ1 discusses experiments related to CPU time as a resource. However, SCOTCH is also capable of accurately recording VM guests' consumption of other system resources as well. First, by invoking our code on every I/O interrupt as well as every task switch, we have the opportunity to examine consumption of peripheral devices (e.g., network and disk). As discussed in Sect. 5, VT-x allows us to gather information about the cause of the interrupt via the VMCS. Second, we do not give the hypervisor an opportunity to execute any code after the interrupt occurs—instead, after our resource accounting code executes, we transfer control to the next guest VM that was supposed to run after the interrupt completed. In doing so, there is no opportunity for a compromised hypervisor to alter the results of an interrupt to make it appear as though a different resource had been consumed.

### 6.7 Threats to Validity

SCOTCH is a system meant to provide accurate resource accounting information in the cloud so that end customers have greater assurance that they are billed correctly according to the resources they really consume. While we have conducted experiments validating the high accuracy and low overhead of our approach, we discuss some assumptions we have made in conducting this evaluation.

First, we did not experiment using a test in the wild. For example, we implemented a resource-based attack by directly modifying the scheduler's behavior. We favored this approach because it admits controlled experimentation: it allowed us to vary how much of the CPU time was being stolen. We believe this represents different modalities of attackers with varying goals—some attackers may wish to operate more stealthily for longer periods of time, while others might operate more blatantly. We believe a controlled attack such as the one we have created is reasonably indicative of a variety of attacker behavior. Similarly, the benchmark workloads we evaluated on may not generalize. We attempted to mitigate this threat by including both microbenchmarks (CPU-bound and mixed) as well as the PARSEC [11] benchmarks which have been previously used in the area of cloud performance.

Second, invoking SMIs may cause perturbations in the behavior of certain caching mechanisms. For instance, the instruction cache might be cleared, and different chipsets and CPUs may perform other tasks while switching to SMM. Attacks abusing knowledge of this low-level detail have been documented [41,42]. In this paper, we assume that the hardware is trusted and that hardware-level bugs that admit such attacks are out of scope.

Third, while DMA attacks would be unable to affect the integrity of data stored in SMRAM or within the SGX enclave, there is a potential opportunity for an attacker to compromise data while it is being marshalled into the enclave from SMM. In SCOTCH, we configured the system to immediately transfer control to the enclave entry code after resuming from SMM. Depending on the platform's

RSM implementation, there may be a small window to corrupt that marshalled data.

Finally, modifying the SMI handler to enable SCOTCH requires some degree of trust in the hardware vendor's BIOS code. Several attacks against SMM and related firmware have been discovered [17,25]; such attacks could compromise the resilience of data collected by SCOTCH. We can mitigate such concerns by using open source firmware where available, such as Coreboot [16] as used in SPECTRE [43] and MALT [45]. This would allow evaluating the firmware before deployment while trusting a restricted set of closed-source vendor code.

### 6.8 Evaluation Conclusions

Unlike previous approaches, SCOTCH was able to perform accurate resource accounting in the face of scheduler attacks, producing results that were within 2% of the ground truth. SCOTCH increases the cost of each context switch by 14%, which corresponds to a .0033% overhead for CPU-bound workloads and a .0016% overhead on more mixed workloads. This can be mitigated by accounting at random intervals, trading off granularity for overhead. By construction, SCOTCH provides accurate accounting in the face of resource interference attacks, since such attacks still use standard task switching and I/O interrupts. SCOTCH also provides accurate accounting in the presence VM escape attacks, since even the hypervisor cannot tamper with SMRAM or SMI handler code. In addition to accurately measuring CPU time, techniques in SCOTCH can address resources such as disk and network I/O that are processed through interrupts. Overall, SCOTCH provides transparent and accurate resource accounting for virtual machine guests.

## 7 Related Work

In this section, we discuss four main areas of related work: (1) Resource accounting techniques that propose helping cloud providers guarantee a particular service level to their customers, (2) SMM-based system protection techniques, (3) SGX-based system protection techniques, and (4) other multi-tenancy virtualization studies.

### 7.1 Resource Accounting

Chen et al. [12] propose Alibi, a system for verifiable resource accounting. It places a reference monitor underneath the service provider's software platforms (i.e., nested virtualization). Jin et al. [24] propose another verifiable resource accounting mechanism for CPU and memory allocation even when the hypervisor is compromised. Similar to our system, their approach also uses SMM as a trusted execution environment to account the resource usage. However, our system differs from previous work in the following ways:

1. By invoking our resource accounting code every context switch and interrupt, we can derive a granular resource usage report for each guest. This allows a rapid identification of discrepancies in resource usage. By contrast, Jin et al. employ a polling technique that requires running the analysis for a long time before a conclusion can be made—if an attacker is trying to be stealthy by stealing fewer resources, our approach can be used to more quickly identify such behavior, possibly within a few context switches, depending on the workload.
2. In addition, the manner in which our resource accounting code is invoked guarantees that we do not miss transient events—other techniques that employ polling for resource auditing may miss malicious guests that learn their polling behavior. For instance, Wang et al. [38] provides a systematic analysis of evasion attacks (i.e., transient attacks) for polling-based SMM systems. In such attacks, the adversary can circumvent the defense mechanisms by studying their polling behavior. With Scotch, if a malicious guest wants CPU time, control must transfer to it at some point, at which point our SMI handler will be invoked.
   However, this guarantee comes at the price of performance. As noted in Sect. 6, our resource accounting code incurs an additional 1 µs per task switch and I/O event. We can tune this depending on the end-user's needs, instead invoking our code on random intervals to amortize the 1 µs cost. Ultimately, the 1 µs cost corresponds to a worst-case additional overhead of .0033%, which may be low enough for most applications.
3. Scotch requires no nested virtualization and retains a small Trusted Code Base (TCB) within SMM. In contrast, Alibi [12] incurs a higher overhead, roughly 6% CPU and 700% I/O, much of which is due to nested virtualization. Additionally, Alibi incorporates the KVM codebase, significantly increasing the TCB.
4. Finally, Scotch is capable of reporting accurate accounting information in the presence of a malicious guest capable of escaping the virtualization environment. An escaped guest might be able to change resource usage information recorded by the hypervisor (e.g., credits consumed in the Xen scheduler to hide oddities in consumed CPU time). However, as we store this information in SMRAM, we can derive an accurate report of resource usage without relying on data structures stored in the hypervisor.

In addition to works from academia, several industrial systems have been introduced for resource accounting [4,31,36]. For instance, Amazon AWS provides a tool called CloudWatch [4], which is a monitoring service for AWS cloud resources that provides system-wide visibility to resources consumed by cloud applications.

### 7.2 SMM-Based Approaches

To the best of our knowledge, only Jin et al. [24] have proposed an SMM-based cloud resource accounting technique. Their approach is called Hardware-Assisted

Resource Accounting (HRA). This technique is limited by its dependency on random polling. By sampling which VCPU (and therefore which VM guest) is currently executing, HRA relies on a large sample size to approximate a sort of Gantt chart of VM running time. Additionally, HRA relies on data structures in the hypervisor to coarsely approximate memory consumption. In contrast, by measuring resource consumption every context switch and interrupt, SCOTCH can rapidly determine accurate resource consumption information.

Additionally, there are several other SMM-based systems that are not directly used in securely reporting hypervisor resource consumption. These systems instead focus on detecting malicious activity [43], hiding keystrokes from the OS [44], and securing peripheral devices [46]. Furthermore, systems like HyperCheck [47] and HyperSentry [8] have been used to verify the integrity of a running hypervisor. Finally, MALT [45] proposed a transparent, remote debugging framework for use in analyzing stealthy malware or attacks capable of escaping a VM or rooting a system. Besides using SMM for defense, attackers use it for malicious purposes like implementing stealthy rootkits [19,33]. For example, the National Security Agency (NSA) uses SMM to build advanced rootkits such as DEITYBOUNCE for Dell and IRONCHEF for HP Proliant servers [2].

### 7.3 SGX-Based Approaches

Previous SGX-based systems such as Haven [10] ported system libraries and a library OS into an SGX enclave, which forms a large TCB. Arnautov et al. [7] proposed SCONE, a secure container mechanism for Docker that uses SGX to protect container processes from external attacks. Hunt et al. [21] developed Ryoan, a SGX- based distributed sandbox that enables users to keep their data secret in data-processing services. These two papers did not propose techniques to reduce the attack surface of computation inside enclaves or reduce the performance overhead imposed by SGX paging. Schuster et al. [34] developed VC3, an SGX-based trusted execution environment to execute MapReduce computation in clouds.

### 7.4 Other VM Multi-tenancy Studies

Zhang et al. [48] presented a class of memory denial-of-Service attacks in multi-tenant cloud servers, showing that a malicious VM may cause significant performance degradation of the victim VM by causing contention in storage-based and scheduling-based resources. Bates et al. [9] discussed using side-channel attacks to recover private information about co-resident VM guests. Similarly, Inci et al. [22] exploited side-channel information to acquire RSA keys from victim guests. SCOTCH does not address these sorts of attacks. We instead focus on scenarios in which attackers actively attempt to consume more resources for themselves at the expense of victim guests.

## 8 Future Work

In Sect. 3, we discussed three classes of attacks where SCOTCH can provide accurate resource accounting information. However, we also discuss *transplantation* attacks in which an escaped VM guest moves malicious code into a victim guest so that the victim computes and accesses resources on behalf of the malicious guest. SCOTCH and similar accounting systems are not currently capable helping detect such attacks or otherwise automatically deciding whether malicious activity occurs. Even with perfectly accurate resource consumption information, the victim VM in this case would appear as though it were consuming resources as normal, and so the victim would end up being billed for work initiated by the attacker. We believe that such attacks would require detecting either the escape itself (i.e., detecting the vulnerability or exploit causing the guest to escape the virtualized environment) or detecting disparities from the normal workload performed by the benign guest. In the future, we would like to incorporate such detection into SCOTCH.

Additionally, we see SCOTCH as seeding the development of a general approach to securing interrupts and peripheral I/O. Currently, SGX does not support any form of secure communication outside the scope of the enclave. Existing work such as SGXIO [40] has investigated trusted I/O paths with peripheral devices. SCOTCH can target a similar application—by interacting with peripheral devices in SMM, we have the opportunity to attest firmware on potentially malicious devices, whereas SGXIO requires trusting a hypervisor containing a driver. We intend to explore securing I/O using SCOTCH's combination of SMM and SGX.

## 9 Conclusion

The growing popularity of cloud-based virtualization services, coupled with the increasing number of security vulnerabilities in hypervisors, presents a compelling need for accurate and transparent virtual machine resource accounting. We introduce SCOTCH, an architecture that uses System Management Mode on x86-based systems to carry out resource accounting and store information in an isolated manner that cannot be tampered with by a compromised guest or hypervisor. By accounting for resources at every task switch and I/O interrupt, our system is accurate in the presence of certain classes of attacks, such as scheduler attacks and resource interference attacks, by construction. SCOTCH produced results that were within 2% of the ground truth, while incurring a .0016% overhead on indicative workloads. Because SMRAM is isolated, SCOTCH can even provide accurate information in the face of VM escape attacks. Overall, SCOTCH provides transparent and accurate resource accounting for virtual machine guests.

## References


1. Credit Scheduler. http://wiki.xensource.com/xenwiki/CreditScheduler
2. NSA's ANT Division Catalog of Exploits for Nearly Every Major Software/Hardware/Firmware. http://Leaksource.wordpress.com
3. Xentrace. http://linux.die.net/man/8/xentrace
4. Amazon AWS: Amazon CloudWatchamazon cloudwatch. https://aws.amazon.com/cloudwatch
5. AMD: AMD RS800 ASIC family BIOS developer's guide (2010)
6. AMD. AMD64 architecture programmer's manual, Volume 2: System Programming (2013)
7. Arnautov, S., Trach, B., Gregor, F., Knauth, T., Martin, A., Priebe, C., Lind, J., Muthukumaran, D., O'Keeffe, D., Stillwell, M.L., et al.: SCONE: secure Linux containers with Intel SGX. In: 12th USENIX Symposium Operating Systems Design and Implementation (2016)
8. Azab, A.M., Ning, P., Wang, Z., Jiang, X., Zhang, X., Skalsky, N.C.: HyperSentry: enabling stealthy in-context measurement of hypervisor integrity. In: Proceedings of the 17th ACM Conference on Computer and Communications Security (CCS 2010) (2010)
9. Bates, A., Mood, B., Pletcher, J., Pruse, H., Valafar, M., Butler, K.: Detecting co-residency with active traffic analysis techniques. In: Proceedings of the 2012 ACM Workshop on Cloud computing security workshop, pp. 1–12. ACM (2012)
10. Baumann, A., Peinado, M., Hunt, G.: Shielding applications from an untrusted cloud with haven. ACM Trans. Comput. Syst. (TOCS) **33**(3), 8 (2015)
11. Bienia, C., Kumar, S., Singh, J.P., Li, K.: The PARSEC benchmark suite: characterization and architectural implications. In: Proceedings of the 17th International Conference on Parallel Architectures and Compilation Techniques, pp. 72–81. ACM (2008)
12. Chen, C., Maniatis, P., Perrig, A., Vasudevan, A., Sekar, V.: Towards verifiable resource accounting for outsourced computation. In: Proceedings of the 9th ACM SIGPLAN/SIGOPS International Conference on Virtual Execution Environments (VEE 2013) (2014)
13. Cherkasova, L., Gupta, D., Vahdat, A.: Comparison of the three CPU schedulers in Xen. SIGMnfluencingformance Eval. Rev. **35**(2), 42–51 (2007)
14. Columbus, L.: Roundup of cloud computing forecasts and market estimates (2016). http://www.forbes.com/sites/louiscolumbus/2016/03/13/roundup-of-cloud-computing-forecasts-and-market-estimates-2016/
15. Common Vulnerability Database: VENOM: CVE-2015-3456, Xen 4.5 VM escape attack (2015)
16. Coreboot: Open-Source BIOS. http://www.coreboot.org/
17. Domas, C.: The memory sinkhole. BlackHat, USA (2015)
18. Dragovic, B., Fraser, K., Hand, S., Harris, T., Ho, A., Pratt, I., Warfield, A., Barham, P., Neugebauer, R.: Xen and the art of virtualization. In: Proceedings of the ACM Symposium on Operating Systems Principles (2003)
19. Embleton, S., Sparks, S., Zou, C.: SMM rootkits: a new breed of OS independent malware. In: Proceedings of the 4th International Conference on Security and Privacy in Communication Networks (SecureComm 2008) (2008)
20. Garcia, A.: Target settles for $39 million over data breach (2015). http://money.cnn.com/2015/12/02/news/companies/target-data-breach-settlement/

21. Hunt, T., Zhu, Z., Xu, Y., Peter, S., Witchel, E.: Ryoan: a distributed sandbox for untrusted computation on secret data. In: 12th USENIX Symposium on Operating Systems Design and Implementation (OSDI 2016), pp. 533–549. USENIX Association (2016)
22. Inci, M.S., Gulmezoglu, B., Irazoqui, G., Eisenbarth, T., Sunar, B.: Seriously, get off my cloud! Cross-VM RSA key recovery in a public cloud. Technical report, IACR Cryptology ePrint Archive (2015)
23. Intel: Intel software guard extensions programming reference (2014). https://software.intel.com/sites/default/files/managed/48/88/329298-002.pdf
24. Jin, S., Seol, J., Huh, J., Maeng, S.: Hardware-assisted Secure Resource Accounting under a Vulnerable Hypervisor. In: Proceedings of the 11th ACM SIGPLAN/SIGOPS International Conference on Virtual Execution Environments (VEE 2015) (2015)
25. Kallenberg, C., Kovah, X.: How many million bioses would you like to infect? (2015). http://legbacore.com/Research_files/HowManyMillionBIOSesWouldYouLikeToInfect_Whitepaper_v1.pdf
26. Kelion, L.: Apple toughens iCloud security after celebrity breach (2014). http://www.bbc.com/news/technology-29237469
27. Kortchinsky, K.: CLOUDBURST: a VMware guest to host escape story. In: Black Hat USA (2009)
28. Leach, K., Spensky, C., Weimer, W., Zhang, F.: Towards transparent introspection. In: 23rd IEEE International Conference on Software Analysis, Evolution and Reengineering (2016)
29. National Institute of Standards, NIST: National vulnerability database. http://nvd.nist.gov. Accessed 10 May 2016
30. Prakash, A., Venkataramani, E., Yin, H., Lin. Z.: Manipulating semantic values in kernel data structures: attack assessments and implications. In: 2013 43rd Annual IEEE/IFIP International Conference on Dependable Systems and Networks (DSN), pp. 1–12. IEEE (2013)
31. Ren, G., Tune, E., Moseley, T., Shi, Y., Rus, S., Hundt, R., Profiling, G.-W.: A continuous profiling infrastructure for data centers. IEEE Micro (2010)
32. Rong, H., Xian, M., Wang, H., Shi, J.: Time-stealer: a stealthy threat for virtualization scheduler and its countermeasures. In: Qing, S., Zhou, J., Liu, D. (eds.) ICICS 2013. LNCS, vol. 8233, pp. 100–112. Springer, Cham (2013). doi:10.1007/978-3-319-02726-5_8
33. Schiffman, J., Kaplan, D.: The SMM rootkit revisited: fun with USB. In: Proceedings of 9th International Conference on Availability, Reliability and Security (ARES 2014) (2014)
34. Schuster, F., Costa, M., Fournet, C., Gkantsidis, C., Peinado, M., Mainar-Ruiz, G., Russinovich, M.: Vc3: trustworthy data analytics in the cloud using SGX. In: 2015 IEEE Symposium on Security and Privacy (SP), pp. 38–54. IEEE (2015)
35. Varadarajan, V., Kooburat, T., Farley, B., Ristenpart, T., Swift, M.M.: Resource-freeing attacks: improve your cloud performance (at your neighbor's expense). In: Proceedings of the 2012 ACM conference on Computer and communications security, pp. 281–292. ACM (2012)
36. VMware Inc.: vCenter chargeback manager. https://www.vmware.com/products/vcenter-chargeback
37. Wang, H., Jing, Q., Chen, R., He, B., Qian, Z., Zhou, L.: Distributed systems meet economics: pricing in the cloud. HotCloud **10**, 1–6 (2010)

38. Wang, J., Sun, K., Stavrou, A.: A dependability analysis of hardware-assisted polling integrity checking systems. In: Proceedings of the 42nd Annual IEEE/IFIP International Conference on Dependable Systems and Networks (DSN 2012) (2012)
39. Wang, L., Zhan, J., Luo, C., Zhu, Y., Yang, Q., He, Y., Gao, W., Jia, Z., Shi, Y., Zhang, S., et al.: Bigdatabench: a big data benchmark suite from internet services. In: 2014 IEEE 20th International Symposium on High Performance Computer Architecture (HPCA), pp. 488–499. IEEE (2014)
40. Weiser, S., Werner, M.: SGXIO: generic trusted I/O path for Intel SGX. In: Proceedings of the Seventh ACM on Conference on Data and Application Security and Privacy (CODASPY 2017), pp. 261–268, New York. ACM (2017)
41. Wojtczuk, R., Rutkowska, J.: Attacking Intel trust execution technologies (2009). http://invisiblethingslab.com/resources/bh09dc/Attacking%20Intel%20TXT%20-%20slides.pdf
42. Wojtczuk, R., Rutkowska, J.: Attacking SMM memory via Intel CPU cache poisoning (2009)
43. Zhang, F., Leach, K., Sun, K., Stavrou, A.: SPECTRE: a dependable introspection framework via system management mode. In: Proceedings of the 43rd Annual IEEE/IFIP International Conference on Dependable Systems and Networks (DSN 2013) (2013)
44. Zhang, F., Leach, K., Wang, H., Stavrou, A.: Trustlogin: securing password-login on commodity operating systems. In: Proceedings of the 10th ACM Symposium on Information, Computer and Communications Security, pp. 333–344. ACM (2015)
45. Zhang, F., Leach, K., Wang, H., Stavrou, A., Sun, K.: Using hardware features for increased debugging transparency. In: Proceedings of the 36th IEEE Symposium on Security and Privacy (2015)
46. Zhang, F., Wang, H., Leach, K., Stavrou, A.: A framework to secure peripherals at runtime. In: Kutyłowski, M., Vaidya, J. (eds.) ESORICS 2014. LNCS, vol. 8712, pp. 219–238. Springer, Cham (2014). doi:10.1007/978-3-319-11203-9_13
47. Zhang, F., Wang, J., Sun, K., Stavrou, A.: HyperCheck: a hardware-assisted integrity monitor. In: IEEE Transactions on Dependable and Secure Computing (2013)
48. Zhang, T., Zhang, Y., Lee, R.B.: Memory dos attacks in multi-tenant clouds: Severity and mitigation. arXiv preprint arXiv:1603.03404 (2016)
49. Zhou, F., Goel, M., Desnoyers, P., Sundaram, R.: Scheduler vulnerabilities and coordinated attacks in cloud computing. J. Comput. Secur. **21**(4), 533–559 (2013)

# Network Security

# Linking Amplification DDoS Attacks to Booter Services

Johannes Krupp[1(✉)], Mohammad Karami[2], Christian Rossow[1], Damon McCoy[3], and Michael Backes[1,4]

[1] CISPA, Saarland University, Saarbrücken, Germany
johannes.krupp@cispa.saarland
[2] Google, Inc., Mountain View, CA, USA
mkarami@google.com
[3] New York University, New York, USA
[4] MPI-SWS, Saarbrücken, Germany

**Abstract.** We present techniques for attributing amplification DDoS attacks to the booter services that launched the attack. Our k-Nearest Neighbor ($k$-NN) classification algorithm is based on features that are characteristic for a DDoS service, such as the set of reflectors used by that service. This allows us to attribute DDoS attacks based on observations from honeypot amplifiers, augmented with training data from ground truth attack-to-services mappings we generated by subscribing to DDoS services and attacking ourselves in a controlled environment. Our evaluation shows that we can attribute DNS and NTP attacks observed by the honeypots with a precision of over 99% while still achieving recall of over 69% in the most challenging real-time attribution scenario. Furthermore, we develop a similarly precise technique that allows a victim to attribute an attack based on a slightly different set of features that can be extracted from a victim's network traces. Executing our $k$-NN classifier over all attacks observed by the honeypots shows that 25.53% (49,297) of the DNS attacks can be attributed to 7 booter services and 13.34% (38,520) of the NTP attacks can be attributed to 15 booter services. This demonstrates the potential benefits of DDoS attribution to identify harmful DDoS services and victims of these services.

## 1 Introduction

Distributed Denial-of-Service (DDoS) attacks have become commoditized by DDoS-for-hire services, commonly called *booters* or *stressers* [7,19]. A large number of booter services advertise their services openly as an economical platform for customers to launch DDoS attacks. At the same time DDoS attacks are increasing in number and in magnitude. This proliferation of DDoS attacks has caused many network and website operators to rank this type of attack as one of

**Electronic supplementary material** The online version of this chapter (doi:10.1007/978-3-319-66332-6_19) contains supplementary material, which is available to authorized users.


M. Dacier et al. (Eds.): RAID 2017, LNCS 10453, pp. 427–449, 2017.
DOI: 10.1007/978-3-319-66332-6_19

the largest threats facing them [13]. This barrage of DDoS attacks has increased the demand for Content Delivery Networks (CDNs) and Software Defined Networking defenses that can absorb and filter these attacks [5]. In turn, this has prompted attackers to react by devising increasingly efficient methods of bypassing or overwhelming defenses. The result is an escalating technological arms-race between DDoS attackers and defenders that at times has congested segments of the core Internet infrastructure as collateral damage [17].

Despite the proliferation of DDoS services and attacks, little progress has been made on attributing the services that are launching these attacks on behalf of their customers. Most ideas for attribution focus on IP traceback mechanisms [16,21–23,30] to trace the source of spoofed IP packets, which require ISPs to assist and so far have not been widely deployed. This has resulted in most of these attacks being unattributed unless the attackers unveil themselves. While it is important to create strong technological DDoS defenses, we argue that there is also benefit in investigating other methods that enable attribution of DDoS attacks to the services responsible for launching these attacks. For instance, some of these booter services—seven out of 23 services that we studied—claim they are benign services by advertising as "stress-testing" services intended to be used only by authorized administrators. For example, one of these services included this statement on their website, *"We provide a professional and legal ip stresser service which is based on a massive 20 dedicated server backend, ensuring that your server is tested to its limits."* Attribution can remove this veil of legitimacy and assist efforts to undermine these services by allowing victims and law enforcement to attribute which booter services were responsible for an attack. Attribution also enables measuring the scale of these services and prioritizing undermining the larger services that are causing more harm. In order to assist ongoing investigations, we are continually sharing information from our study on DDoS attacks and booter services with the European Police Office (Europol), the United States Federal Bureau of Investigation (FBI) and large ISPs or backbone providers.

In this work, we show that it is possible to build supervised learning techniques that allow honeypot amplifier operators and victims to accurately attribute attacks to the services that launched them. To begin, we identify three key features that honeypot operators can record to construct a supervised $k$-NN classifier that can attribute attacks. In order to validate our method, we subscribed to 23 booter services and generated a ground truth data set of attacks to booter service mappings[1]. Validation of our classifier using the ground truth self-attack data set shows that it is highly precise at attributing DNS and NTP attacks with a precision of over 99% at 69.35% recall in the worst case of real-time attribution. When retrospectively attributing attacks, the recall even increases to 86.25%. Executing our classifier over the set of all attacks observed by the honeypots shows that 25.53% (49,297) of the DNS attacks can be attributed to 7 booter services and 13.34% (38,520) of the NTP attacks can be attributed to 15 booter services.

[1] Our ethical framework for these measurements is based on previous studies that have used this methodology [7,20].

Finally, we show that a $k$-NN classifier can also be used *by victims* to attribute DDoS attacks to the service that launched the attack. Our findings demonstrate that many of the attacks we observed can be attributed to a small set of booter services that are operating relatively openly. Our ability to attribute large numbers of attacks to a small set of booter services and sharing of this information with Europol and the FBI to assist in active investigations demonstrates the usefulness of our attribution methods.

In summary, we frame our contributions as follows:

- We present a $k$-NN-based classifier that attributes amplification DDoS attacks observed by honeypots with a precision of over 99% while still achieving recall of over 69% in the most challenging real-time attribution scenario.
- We present a similarly precise technique that allows a DDoS victim to attribute attacks based on features extracted from a victim's network traces.
- We attribute 25.53% (49,297) of the DNS attacks to 7 booter services and 13.34% (38,520) of the NTP attacks to 15 booter services.

## 2 Background

### 2.1 Threat Model

Amplification DDoS constitutes a powerful attack in which an adversary aims to exhaust the bandwidth of a victim's host or network by inducing a large volume of traffic. Towards this, the attacker abuses multiple servers as so called *amplifiers*. These servers offer UDP based protocols prone to amplification, i.e., the server's response is significantly larger than the corresponding request sent to the server. At least 14 protocols suffer from this flaw [18], such as NTP and DNS, leading to a multitude of servers that can be exploited as amplifiers. Given the connection-less nature of UDP, an attacker can redirect the servers' responses to the victim by simply spoofing the source IP address in requests. Due to amplification ratios of a factor of 5 to 4500 [18], an attacker that sends requests at a rate of some Mbit/s can still cause attack traffic at Gbit/s-scale.

Furthermore, we are concerned with a special type of attacker: *booter services*. These offer platforms for DDoS-as-a-service, often under the disguise of "stress-testing", where customers can request various types of attacks for a small fee. The booter will then launch these attacks using its infrastructure. Our threat model thus contemplates four parties: *Customers*, who commission attacks; *booters*, who conduct the actual attacks; *amplifiers*, who are exploited to amplify traffic; and *victims*, who are the targets of such attacks.

The aim of this paper is to attribute attacks to booters, when observed from either the victim's or an amplifier's perspective. This is non-trivial, as from the victim's perspective the attack seems to stem from the amplifiers. Similarly, from an amplifier's perspective, the requests seem to be legitimate requests by the victim (due to the use of spoofed source IP addresses by the booter). While ultimately one would like to identify the customer, only the booter, amplifiers, and the victim are directly participating in an attack. Nonetheless, since the booter has a business relation to the customer, pinpointing the booter behind an attack constitutes an important step towards this goal.

### 2.2 Ethical Considerations

As part of our study we subscribed to 23 booters and conducted a controlled set of self DDoS attacks. Furthermore, we also leveraged honeypots for amplification attacks. We settled on this methodology for collecting a ground truth data set of mappings between observed attacks and the services that launched these attacks after finding that no data set available to us could be used to validate our DDoS attribution techniques. Before we began performing these self DDoS attacks we carefully attempted to minimize the harms and maximize the benefits associated with our methodology based on observations from previous studies that launch self-attacks in order to measure booter's attacks [7, 20].

We received an exemption from our Institutional Review Board (IRB), since our study did not include any personally identifiable information. In addition, we consulted with our institution's general counsel, who advised us not to engage with any DDoS service that advertised using botnets and to cease active engagement with any booter service that we realized was using botnets.

An analysis of TTL values observed by the honeypots indicated that it is unlikely any of the booter services we subscribed to used botnets. Based on the guidance of our institution's general counsel, our victim server was connected by a dedicated 1 Gbit/s network connection that was not shared with any other servers. We also obtained consent from our ISP and their upstream peering points before conducting any DDoS attack experiments. We also minimized the attack durations, notified our ISP before launching any attack and had a protocol in place to end an attack early if it caused a disruption at our ISP.

We purchased subscriptions from 23 booter services. When doing so, we selected the cheapest option, which ranged from \$6–\$20 and averaged \$12 per month, to minimize the amount of money given to these services. In total, we spent less than \$400 and no individual booter service received more than \$40 in payments as part of the measurements in this paper[2]. All payments were made using PayPal and we assumed that proper controls were put in place at PayPal to mitigate the risk of money flowing to extremist groups. As part of our design methodology, we minimized the amount of money paid and targeted a small set of booters to obtain a valuable ground truth data set.

Our method created some harm to amplifiers and their upstream peering points by consuming bandwidth resources. The largest amount of bandwidth consumed was 984.5 kbit/s for NTP amplifiers and the least was 16.7 kbit/s for DNS amplifiers, similar to those reported in a previous study [7].

Over the course of our experiments we did not receive any complaints from the operators of these amplifiers. We limited our attacks to 30 s. Based on

[2] To put this into perspective: Previous studies of these booters have shown that they have thousands of paid subscribers and generate revenues of over \$10,000 per month [7, 19].

analysis from a previous study that used a similar methodology [7], these short duration attacks enable us to observe about 80% of the amplifiers used by a given booter service and reduce the harm we cause to misconfigured amplifiers.

Similarly, the use of DDoS honeypots might also incur harm on the Internet. We used AmpPot, a honeypot proposed by Kraemer et al. [8]. To avoid contributing to DDoS attacks, AmpPot limits the rate of requests and deploys automatic IP blacklisting: The honeypots will stop responding for one hour to any IP address sending more than 10 requests per minute. This limits the maximum amount of data sent to a DDoS victim to a few kilobytes. For a more detailed ethical discussion on AmpPot we refer the reader to [8].

## 3 Amplification Attack Data Set

To investigate if and how amplification attacks can be attributed to their originating booter service, we established two data sets that help us to gain insights into the overall amplification attacks, but also to find concrete attack instances caused by individual booters. In Sect. 3.1, we describe how we leverage amplification honeypots to gain insights into global amplification attacks. In Sect. 3.2, we discuss how we use booters and launch controlled attacks against ourselves to learn about attack techniques of certain attackers.

### 3.1 Honeypot Attacks

Although the general threat of amplification attacks has been known for years, actual attack insights are only documented in anecdotal evidence, such as attacks against Spamhaus or OVH at hundreds of Gbit/s attack volume. To collect insights into the set of global amplification attacks, we leverage data collected by AmpPot [8], a honeypot proposed by Krämer et al. AmpPot emulates seven UDP-based protocols that have known amplification vectors and will thus eventually be abused as part of real-world DDoS amplification attacks (QOTD, CharGen, DNS, NTP, RIPv1, MSSQL, and SSDP). Krämer et al. observed that attackers will eventually find such honeypots via Internet scans, and start abusing them as potential reflectors shortly thereafter. AmpPot thus serves as an eye on global amplification attacks, and due to the nature of the attack traffic, can also observe who is being attacked and when.

In December 2014, eleven globally-distributed honeypots with single static IP addresses were deployed, and have been operated continuously since then. In November 2015, a twelfth honeypot was added, listening on 48 static IP addresses. This honeypot employs a special feature named *Selective Response*, where each source scanning for amplifiers will find a unique set of 24 IP addresses[3] [10].

We set our analysis period to two months from December 9, 2015 to February 10, 2016. In this period, the honeypots observed 570,738 amplification attacks

[3] The idea behind this is to imprint a unique fingerprint on each scanner. Letting each scanner find 24 IP addresses maximizes the total number of fingerprints.

(8,918 attacks per day on average). However, given that RIPv1, MSSQL, and QOTD combined account for less than 5% of these, we decided to exclude those protocols from our analyses.

### 3.2 Self-attacks

The honeypots give us valuable insights into global attacks, but do not give us indications where the attacks were coming from. Previous studies have identified so-called booter services ("booters") as being responsible for a large number of amplification attacks [6,7,20]. In an attempt to learn attack characteristics of these booters, we signed up at these services and then launched short-lived amplification attacks against a target in our control.

To start launching self-attacks and correlating them with the traffic seen at the honeypots, our first task was to identify booter services to cover in the study. Absent a centralized location for finding booters, we located services via search engines and advertisements on underground forums. We selected a total of 23 services offering amplification attacks based on NTP, DNS, CharGen and SSDP. When selecting these booters, we tried to include services that we speculated to be more stable and have more subscribers based on reviewing user feedback on underground forums. To minimize the amount of money we paid to these abusive services, we kept the number of covered booters relatively small.

Table 1 provides an overview of the booter services[4] that we cover and the amplification attack types they offer. NTP was the most popular attack protocol, followed by DNS. 16 of the 23 services clearly advertise malicious DDoS attacks. In contrast, seven services hide their malicious intention behind "stressing" services, a seemingly benign way to verify the resilience of a network against DDoS attacks. However, not a single service performs any kind of attack target validation. That is, service subscribers can specify any IP address (or domain) that should be attacked, regardless of whether the target is under the control of the client. This shows the clear malicious intention behind all 23 booter services.

**Table 1.** Covered booter services

| | AUR | BAN | B01 | B02 | B03 | CRI | DOW | EXI | EXO | KST | INB | NET | RAW | SER | STA | ST1 | ST2 | ST3 | ST4 | SYN | THU | VDO | WEB |
|---|---|---|---|---|---|---|---|---|---|---|---|---|---|---|---|---|---|---|---|---|---|---|---|
| CharGen | ✓ | ✓ | ✓ | ✓ | ✓ | | ✓ | | ✓ | ✓ | | ✓ | ✓ | ✓ | | | | | ✓ | ✓ | ✓ | | ✓ |
| DNS | ✓ | ✓ | | ✓ | ✓ | | ✓ | ✓ | | | ✓ | | ✓ | ✓ | ✓ | ✓ | ✓ | ✓ | | ✓ | ✓ | ✓ | ✓ |
| NTP | ✓ | ✓ | ✓ | ✓ | ✓ | ✓ | ✓ | ✓ | ✓ | ✓ | ✓ | ✓ | ✓ | ✓ | ✓ | ✓ | | ✓ | ✓ | ✓ | ✓ | ✓ | ✓ |
| SSDP | ✓ | ✓ | ✓ | ✓ | ✓ | | ✓ | | ✓ | ✓ | ✓ | ✓ | | | ✓ | ✓ | ✓ | | ✓ | | ✓ | ✓ | |

Booter services maintain front-end sites that allow their customers to purchase subscriptions and launch attacks using simple web forms. We created custom crawlers to automate the task of visiting the websites of covered booters and launching attacks directed at our own target. Using this automation,

[4] To avoid unintentionally advertising booter services covered in this study, we replace the name of booter services by the first three letters of their domain name. The last letter is replaced by a number in the case of name collisions.

daily attacks were launched for each covered booter and attack type. A total of 13 booter services were covered within the first week of starting the self-attacks on December 9, 2015 and by January 14, 2016 all 23 booters were covered.

**Labeling Self-attacks:** As we instructed all booters to attack the same target, we had to find a mechanism to separate between multiple consecutive self-attacks to assign (booter) labels to the attack traffic. To this end, we initially relied on the time that attacks were initiated. To account for clock skew, we left 10 min between consecutive attacks and used a grace period of ±3 min for matching. On January 14, we started to use a distinct victim IP per booter service as an improved matching criterion. Based on the same criterion, we then also mapped the self-attacks to attacks observed at the honeypots.

**Table 2.** Overview over self-attacks

| Protocol | Booters | Launched attacks | Observed | | |
|---|---|---|---|---|---|
| | | | At victim | At honeypots | >100 pkts. |
| CharGen | 16 | 608 | 417 | 35 | 33 |
| DNS | 19 | 676 | 452 | 173 | 100 |
| NTP | 22 | 823 | 577 | 421 | 373 |
| SSDP | 16 | 560 | 351 | 1 | 0 |
| Total | 23 | 2667 | 1797 | 630 | 506 |

Table 2 gives an overview over the self-attacks. We launched a total of 2667 CharGen, DNS, NTP and SSDP attacks using 23 booter services. Interestingly, only around 2/3 of the attacks we initiated were observed at the victim. This can be explained by our observation of maintenance issues that some booter websites have. Sometimes booter websites provide the user interface for selecting a particular attack type that is temporarily non-functional. To users it appears that the attack has been successfully launched, but no actual attack traffic is generated as a result of initiating such attacks.

The DDoS honeypots observed many NTP attacks (73.0%) and DNS attacks (38.3%), but only a small fraction of the CharGen attacks (8.4%) and only a single SSDP attack. Furthermore, while the honeypots observed some traffic belonging to 630 attacks, in only 506 cases did we record more than 100 requests. We inspected the reasons why the honeypots missed large portions of SSDP and CharGen attacks. To this end, we investigated the attack traffic towards our victim to learn the preferences of attacks in choosing reflectors. In both cases, we found that the vast majority of the reflectors that were abused by multiple booters send responses that are significantly larger than the ones configured in AmpPot. This indicates that the honeypots' SSDP and CharGen responses were too small to be attractive for attackers, and adversaries preferred other reflectors with better amplification. We leave further investigations on reflector selection strategies open for future work and focus on DNS and NTP in the following.

**Multi-branding Booters:** During the sign-up phase, we noticed that some booters were visually similar. Investigations have revealed that one miscreant follows a multi-branding strategy, i.e., sells the same service via different booter names that shared similar web front-ends. It became apparent that attacks from `RAW` and `WEB` shared characteristics, and also their sign-up page of the web interface was equivalent in appearance and HTML code. We further analyzed those two booters by launching application layer (layer 7) attacks against our victim server. Layer 7 attacks usually abuse public HTTP proxy servers to hide the identity of back-end servers involved. However, some proxies reveal the identity of the requesting clients in the `X-Forwarded-For` field of the HTTP header. Based on this observation, we were able to verify that these two booters used shared back-end infrastructure. We thus conclude that `RAW` and `WEB` are likely to be operated by the same individuals and will regard them as equivalent.

## 4 Characteristic Attack Features

We will now introduce characteristic attack patterns that we can use to train our classifier for attribution purposes. We first describe various characteristics that we have observed to repeat across subsets of attacks at the honeypots. We then describe how we leverage these observations as features to summarize attacks.

### 4.1 Attack Observations

While analyzing the attacks captured by the honeypots, we observed the following three properties that repeated across subsets of the attacks.

**Honeypot Sets:** Although eleven honeypots were active since the end of 2014, few attacks (1.63%) abused all of them simultaneously. In fact, more than 60% of all DNS- and NTP-based attacks abused five honeypots or less. This indicates that attackers either perform only partial scans of the Internet, or choose a subset of the discovered amplifiers in subsequent attacks.

Interestingly, we observed that honeypot sets seem to be *reused* across multiple attacks, i.e., even in attacks against different victims or on different days. To further investigate this observation, we analyzed amplifiers seen in self-attacks from a few example booter services over time, shown in Fig. 1. The entries on the heat maps show the ratio of abused amplifiers that were shared per booter and attack protocol on two consecutive days each. With the exception of DNS, there is a high level of overlap for attacks based on NTP, CharGen, and SSDP, suggesting that booters reuse their set of amplifiers for a protocol for some time. The low overlap for attacks based on DNS is likely caused by frequent rescans to account for the relatively high IP churn rate of DNS amplifiers [11].

In addition, we verified that two simultaneous attacks towards the same victim on different protocols showed little overlap in the sets of honeypots abused.

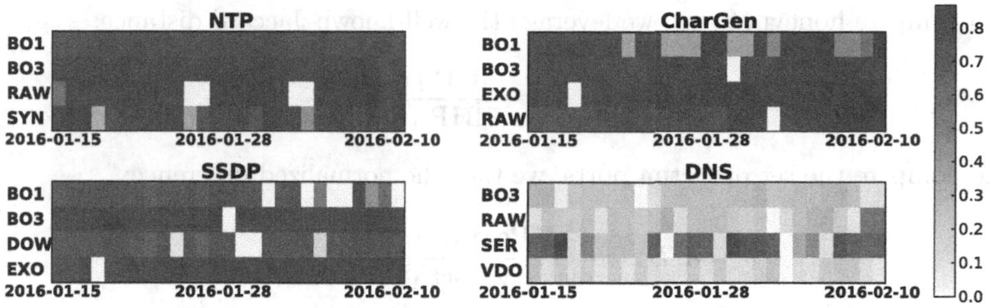


**Fig. 1.** Overlap of amplifier sets between consecutive dates.

This could indicate that the set of amplifiers might be specific to the protocol, which intuitively can be explained by the small overlap of systems that suffer from amplification vulnerabilities for multiple protocols.

**Victim Ports Entropy:** While one UDP port determines the amplification protocol (e.g., DNS, NTP, etc.), the other determines the *victim port* on which the victim will receive the reflected responses. Since an attacker has virtually no restrictions on setting the victim port, we expected to observe the two obvious choices: Choosing one victim port per attack, or choosing an individual victim port for every request. Surprisingly, in addition to that, we also observed attacks where requests shared a small number of victim ports. One explanation could be that attackers use multiple threads for attacking, and that they choose a different victim port *per thread*. In addition, we verified that a significant number of booter services actually ask their clients to choose the victim port, giving a reason why the number of source ports is frequently restricted to one.

**Time-to-Live Values:** The Time-to-Live (TTL) value in the IP packet indicates how many hops a packet has traversed from the attack source to the honeypot. As already observed by Krämer et al. [8], for one particular attack, a honeypot will usually only see one (or very few) TTL value(s). We can thus conclude that most attacks likely stem from a single source, which motivates further investigations in finding this particular source sending spoofed traffic. Additionally, the vast majority of requests have a TTL >230. This suggests that attackers use a fixed initial TTL of 255 in their generated packets, as otherwise we would see a wider distribution.

### 4.2 Distance Function

In order to leverage these observations in a classifier, we next introduce a distance function based on the above features. Given two attack instances A and B, such a function is used to determine how dissimilar the two instances are. For an attack A, we will denote the set of honeypots used by $\mathbf{HP}_A$, the set of victim ports observed by $\mathbf{VPort}_A$, and the set of TTLs received at honeypot $hp$ by $\mathbf{TTL}_{hp,A}$.

To compare honeypot sets, we leverage the well-known Jaccard distance:

$$d_{hp}(A,B) = 1 - \frac{|\mathbf{HP}_A \cap \mathbf{HP}_B|}{|\mathbf{HP}_A \cup \mathbf{IP}_B|}$$

To compare the set of victim ports, we take the normalized difference:

$$d_{vp}(A,B) = \frac{\big||\mathbf{VPort}_A| - |\mathbf{VPort}_B|\big|}{\max\left(|\mathbf{VPort}_A|, |\mathbf{VPort}_B|\right)}$$

Finally, to compare TTLs, we compute the overlap of their histograms[5]

$$d_{\text{hist}}(S,T) = 1 - \frac{\sum\limits_x \min(S(x),T(x))}{\sum\limits_x \max(S(x),T(x))}$$

and then average this overlap over all honeypots involved in *both* attacks:

$$d_{ttl}(A,B) = \frac{\sum\limits_{hp \in \mathbf{HP}_A \cap \mathbf{HP}_B} d_{\text{hist}}\left(\mathbf{TTL}_{hp,A}, \mathbf{TTL}_{hp,B}\right)}{|\mathbf{HP}_A \cap \mathbf{HP}_B|}$$

From these three sub-functions we compute a weighted average as the overall distance function. We set the weights to $w_{hp} = 5$, $w_{vp} = 1$, and $w_{ttl} = |\mathbf{HP}_A \cap \mathbf{HP}_B|/2$. Note that our methodology is independent from the weights and the analyst can choose any weights according to her needs. We assigned a smaller weight to the victim port feature, as it relies on inputs with little entropy given just three cases: a single victim port, a few victim ports, or many victim ports. For the TTL feature, we assign a higher weight if the two attacks have more honeypots in common, as we assume that coinciding TTLs for *multiple* honeypots have a much higher significance than those for only a single honeypot.

## 5 Honeypot Attack Attribution

We now leverage the aforementioned features to identify which booter has caused which attacks observed at a honeypot. The core idea is to use supervised machine learning techniques to attribute an attack observed at a honeypot to a particular booter service. We will first use our ground truth data set to show the performance and resilience of our classifier in various situations. Afterwards, we will apply the classifier to the entire data set of attacks collected by the honeypots.

[5] To account for fluctuation in TTLs due to route changes, we apply smoothing to the histograms using a binomial kernel of width 6, which corresponds to a standard deviation of $\sigma \approx 1.22$.

### 5.1 Description

Finding the true origin of an amplification attack is a non-trivial problem, because—from the reflector's perspective—all packets carry spoofed headers. Using our attack distance metric, we showed that attacks from the same booter service exhibit similar characteristics and this observation turns the problem of finding the origin of an attack into a classification problem. The collected self-attack data set can be used for training and validating a classifier. Since the number of attacks observed strongly varies between booters, we decided to use the *k-Nearest Neighbor* ($k$-NN) algorithm due to its resilience to such imbalances. In $k$-NN, to determine the label of an instance, the set of its $k$ nearest neighbors is computed. Next, every neighbor casts a vote for its own label, and finally the instance is given the label of the majority of its neighbors.

Additional care has to be taken, as our training data set is not exhaustive and may miss data for some booters. That is, not all attacks can be attributed to a booter that we know. Therefore, we use a cutoff threshold $t$ to introduce a label for an **unknown** classification result. When classifying an item $i$, we only consider the $k$ nearest neighbors that can be found in the neighborhood of radius $t$ centred around item $i$. If no item from the training data set lies within this neighborhood, the item $i$ is assigned the label **unknown**. To find a well-suited and conservative threshold, we analyzed our ground truth data set using our distance function and hierarchical clustering. From those clusters, we then computed the average distance between attacks within a cluster and took the 95th percentile over all. This results in $t = 0.338$ for DNS and $t = 0.236$ for NTP.

Furthermore, as shown in Sect. 4.1, booters rescan to find new lists of amplifiers on a regular basis. To reflect this during classification, we only consider elements from the training data set no more than 7 days apart, which approximately corresponds to the maximum rescan frequency we observed for booters.

When using $k$-NN, the choice of $k$ is highly critical for the performance of the classifier. One common approach is to learn the value of $k$ from the training data set using *n-fold cross-validation* (CV). In n-fold CV, the training data set is partitioned into $n$ equally sized sets. Then, the classifier is trained on $n - 1$ of these sets, and the final set is used for validation. This process is repeated $n$ times, until every set has been used as the validation set once. For finding $k$ we thus perform 10-fold CV for all $k \in \{1, 3, 5\}$ as part of the training phase of the classifier. We restrict $k$ to odd values to avoid ties in the voting phase. We only consider $k \leq 5$, because about $2/3$ of the clusters contain less than five attacks.

To assess the performance of our classifier, we first define the *false positive rate* (FPR), *precision* and *recall* metrics, as well as *macro-averaging*. Intuitively, the FPR for a label $l_i$ (in our case, a particular booter) is the fraction of elements that were incorrectly assigned the label $l_i$ while their true label was *not* $l_i$. In a similar vein, precision is the ratio with which the classifier was correct when assigning label $l_i$, while recall is the ratio with which the classifier is able to re-identify elements with true label $l_i$. Let $\mathsf{tp}_i$ be the number of items *correctly* classified to have label $l_i$ (*true positives*), let $\mathsf{tn}_i$ be the number of items *correctly* classified to *not* have label $l_i$ (*true negatives*), let $\mathsf{fp}_i$ be the number of items *incorrectly* classified to have label $l_i$ (*false positives*), and let $\mathsf{fn}_i$ be the number of items *incorrectly* classified to *not* have label $l_i$ (*false negatives*). Then the FPR is defined as $\mathsf{fpr}_i = \mathsf{fp}_i/(\mathsf{fp}_i + \mathsf{tn}_i)$, precision as $\mathsf{p}_i = \mathsf{tp}_i/(\mathsf{tp}_i + \mathsf{fp}_i)$, and recall as $\mathsf{r}_i = \mathsf{tp}_i/(\mathsf{tp}_i + \mathsf{fn}_i)$. To compute overall performance measures from these per-class metrics, we employ macro-averaging, i.e., first computing $\mathsf{fpr}$, $\mathsf{p}$, and $\mathsf{r}$ *per class* and averaging the respective results afterwards, as this will avoid bias due to imbalance in our ground truth data. Thus booters for which we were able to collect more datapoints do *not* influence the results more strongly. However, since we strongly prefer mislabeling an attack as `unknown` over incorrectly attributing it to a wrong booter, we only weigh the `unknown` label with $\frac{1}{8}$.

### 5.2 Validation

To validate our classifier, we defined three experiments on our labeled self-attack data set: First, we conducted 10-fold CV to assess how well our classifier can correctly attribute attacks (E1). Second, to estimate how well our classifier deals with attacks from booters *not* contained in the training data set, we used leave-one-out CV on the booter level (E2). This means that the attacks from all but one booter constitute the training set, and all attacks from the omitted booter are used for validation, checking if these attacks are correctly labeled as `unknown`. Third, we were also interested in the performance of classifying attacks in real-time (E3), i.e., training only on labeled observations *prior* to the attack.

**Table 3.** Honeypot-driven experimental results

(a) DNS

| | | BAN | EXI | RAW | SER | ST1 | ST2 | VDO |
|---|---|---|---|---|---|---|---|---|
| | samples (#) | 10 | 1 | 49 | 11 | 10 | 18 | 1 |
| E1 | correct (%) | 90 | 0 | 82 | 82 | 100 | 78 | 0 |
| | unknown (%) | 10 | 100 | 18 | 18 | 0 | 22 | 100 |
| | wrong (%) | | | | | | | |
| E2 | unknown (%) | 100 | 100 | 100 | 100 | 100 | 100 | 100 |
| | wrong (%) | | | | | | | |
| E3 | correct (%) | 70 | 0 | 67 | 73 | 70 | 67 | 0 |
| | unknown (%) | 30 | 100 | 33 | 27 | 30 | 33 | 100 |
| | wrong (%) | | | | | | | |

(b) NTP

| | | AUR | BAN | B01 | B02 | B03 | CRI | DOW | EXI | NET | RAW | SER | ST1 | ST3 | ST4 | SYN | THU | VDO |
|---|---|---|---|---|---|---|---|---|---|---|---|---|---|---|---|---|---|---|
| | samples | 28 | 15 | 40 | 1 | 12 | 27 | 21 | 4 | 1 | 78 | 16 | 19 | 18 | 24 | 5 | 1 | 63 |
| E1 | correct | 100 | 87 | 78 | 0 | 100 | 96 | 90 | 50 | 0 | 99 | 100 | 100 | 94 | 100 | 80 | 0 | 100 |
| | unknown | 0 | 13 | 23 | 100 | 0 | 4 | 10 | 50 | 0 | 1 | 0 | 0 | 6 | 0 | 20 | 100 | 0 |
| | wrong | | | | | | | | | CRI: 100 | | | | | | | | |
| E2 | unknown | 100 | 100 | 100 | 100 | 100 | 74 | 100 | 100 | 0 | 100 | 100 | 100 | 100 | 100 | 100 | 100 | 100 |
| | wrong | | | | | | NET: 26 | | | CRI: 100 | | | | | | | | |
| E3 | correct | 89 | 67 | 57 | 0 | 92 | 81 | 76 | 25 | 0 | 88 | 88 | 84 | 78 | 92 | 60 | 0 | 97 |
| | unknown | 11 | 33 | 43 | 100 | 8 | 19 | 24 | 75 | 0 | 12 | 13 | 16 | 22 | 8 | 40 | 100 | 3 |
| | wrong | | | | | | | | | CRI: 100 | | | | | | | | |

Table 3 shows the results for both DNS and NTP. For each experiment we give the percentage of attacks correctly attributed to its booter, the percentage of attacker the classifier labeled as **unknown**, as well as the percentage of attacks that were misclassified, along with their putative label. Additionally, the first row states the number of attacks contained in our data set[6]. Note that in the second experiment (E2) every column regards a classifier trained on the entire data set *except* the corresponding booter; hence the classifier is correct when assigning the **unknown** label in this case.

In the 10-fold CV (E1) our DNS classifier correctly attributed 78% or more of the attacks for each booter. Exceptions are the cases of `EXI` and `VDO`, for which our data set only contains a single attack, which naturally cannot be attributed correctly due to lack of training data. All the remaining attacks were labeled as **unknown**. In fact, the DNS classifier never attributed an attack to a wrong booter in all three experiments. This is especially remarkable in the leave-one-out scenario (E2), when the classifier was not trained on data for one of the booters. That is, even in this case our classifier did not lead to false accusations, showing the resilience of the classifier against attacks stemming from booters *not* contained in the training set. Of course, this resilience comes at the cost of higher false negative rates in the other experiments (E1 & E3), as we prefer the classifier to label an attack as **unknown** over attributing it to the wrong booter. This could possibly be alleviated by obtaining more training data per booter. The last experiment (E3) simulates the performance of the classifier in a real-time scenario, i.e., when classifying an attack only based on training data that was obtained *prior* to the attack. In contrast to this, the first experiment (E1) measured the performance when classifying attacks after the fact. Since booters regularly rescan for amplifiers and update their set of amplifiers accordingly, our classifier will achieve a performance worse than in the first experiment (E1). However, even in the real-time attribution setting, we could still attribute at least 67% of all attacks without any incorrect attributions. The loss compared to E1 can be explained by the fact that the first attack of a booter can never be correctly classified due to lack of prior training data.

In the case of NTP, we achieved an overall attribution rate of 78% or more in the 10-fold CV (E1) for most booters, with the exception of those which occur only once in the data set. Remarkably, the cases of `EXI` and `SYN` show that the classifier also performs reasonably well even for small amounts of training data. The NTP classifier generates misclassifications. However, this only stems from a few attacks by `NET` and `CRI`, which exhibit precisely the same characteristics. While we suspect that `NET` and `CRI` share the same infrastructure, we were not able to verify this assumption by leveraging layer 7 attacks (as done previously for `RAW` and `WEB`). The same two attacks are also the cause for the only misclassifications in the leave-one-out scenario (E2), as about a quarter of attacks from `CRI` were attributed to `NET`, when the classifier was not trained on data from `CRI`. In the real-time scenario (E3), the NTP classifier attributed over 76% of the attacks in most cases, even outperforming the DNS classifier. Since NTP

[6] This effectively provides the entire confusion matrix for each experiment.

experiences less amplifier churn, booters can use the same amplifier set for a longer period of time, i.e., an attack is more likely to use a set of amplifiers for which the classifier already observed a training sample. A notable exception here is B01, for which only 57% of the attacks could be attributed, despite the large number of attacks contained in the data set. This indicates that B01 performs rescans more frequently than other booters.

Averaging over booters for which the data set contains more than one attack, our classifier achieves a macro-averaged precision of 100.00% and recall of 86.25% in E1 for DNS, and 99.74% and respectively 91.01% for NTP. In the case of real-time attribution (E3), the precision stays similarly high (100.00% for DNS, 99.69% for NTP), while the recall drops to 69.35% and respectively 76.73%.

### 5.3 Attribution

After validating the classification mechanism, we now turn to applying it to our entire data set of attacks observed at the honeypots (excluding the self-attacks). Due to their low entropy, we excluded attacks that were only observed by a single honeypot. This left 266,324 NTP-based and 161,925 DNS-based attacks. For both we trained our classifier on all self-attacks collected from December 9 to February 10.

Our NTP classifier attributed 38,520 attacks (14.46%) to one of the booters it was previously trained on and our DNS classifier attributed almost a third of all attacks (49,297, 30.44%) to a booter. Note that not all attacks observed at the honeypots have to be caused by booters; they can also be caused by malevolent parties that do not offer their attack capabilities on an online platform. Furthermore, since we only trained our classifier on a limited set of booters, our classifier cannot possibly achieve a classification rate of 100%. Still, attributing a considerable amount of attacks to the booters of our training set indicates that the booters we considered are used very actively.

## 6 Victim-Driven Attack Attribution

Based on the success of the classifier that allows *honeypot operators* to attribute DDoS attacks, we now aim to build a similar classification method that will enable *victims* to attribute attacks based on features that can be extracted from victims' network traces. The core idea is to isolate a set of features that are directly observable by the victim and that can precisely attribute attacks to a particular booter service using a similar $k$-NN-classifier algorithm.

### 6.1 Description

Motivated by the fact that each booter abuses characteristic sets of amplifiers, we use the set of amplifiers as seen in the victim's attack traces as a feature for training our victim-driven classifier. However, the TTL value of the attack source used in the honeypot operator attribution technique is not directly observable by a victim, so we cannot use this feature in our victim based attribution method. The loss of the TTL value feature is mostly compensated for by the victim being able to see a larger set of amplifiers used by the booter service.

As we will show, this single feature is sufficient to build a classifier that can accurately attribute NTP, SSDP, and CharGen attacks from the victim's perspective. The one exception is that the set of open DNS resolvers used by individual booter services are less stable over time, likely due to churn. As a result, relying on the set of amplifiers as the sole feature for classifying DNS attacks will not provide the same classification performance as for the other three attack types. Therefore, we must identify additional entropy to improve the accuracy of our victim-based DNS attack classification technique. Based on our analysis of DNS attack traces captured at our victim server, we noticed that each booter service tends to send spoofed *ANY* requests for a very small number of mostly non-overlapping domain names. We thus complement the feature of amplifier sets with an additional feature over the set of domain names resolved in DNS attacks. That is, for DNS, the Jaccard index is computed both for the set of amplifiers and for the set of resolved domains, and the similarity score is the mean of the two computed Jaccard indices. For all other protocols (NTP, SSDP, and CharGen), we use the Jaccard index computed over the set of amplifiers.

In the victim-driven data set, all attacks are labeled with the booter service and we do not have any `unknown` attacks. However, we will evaluate the situation of unattributed attacks by performing the same E2 leave-one-out CV experiment as in Sect. 5.2. Given this, we select a cutoff threshold $t$ to introduce a label for an `unknown` classification result that is used in the same way as in Sect. 5.2. We choose a conservative threshold of $t = 0.55$ for CharGen, $t = 0.60$ for DNS, $t = 0.55$ for NTP, and $t = 0.45$ for SSDP. In order to select the threshold value, the score of correct classifications and incorrect classifications were manually checked and a reasonably conservative value was selected for each attack type. Only attack instances in the training set for which the similarity score is no less than $t$ were considered as potential neighbors. If no neighbor could be found for a test instance, it was classified as `unknown`.

### 6.2 Validation

To validate the results of our victim-driven classifier, we perform the same experiments as in Sect. 5.2. Table 4 shows the result of our victim-driven classifier experiments for DNS and NTP[7].

In E1, our DNS classifier achieved high attribution rates of 80% or more, except for `B02`, `EXI`, `EXO`, and `VDO`, where a large fraction was also marked as `unknown`. However, in five cases the classifier also mistook attacks from one booter as coming from another. The higher number of false positives for DNS is attributable to the less stable set of DNS amplifiers abused by booters. These results are worse than those for the honeypot-driven classifier, possibly due to the fact that unlike organic sets of amplifiers, the honeypots do not churn over

[7] Results for CharGen and SSDP can be found in Sect. A.1.

**Table 4.** Victim-driven experimental results

(a) DNS

| | | AUR | BAN | BO2 | BO3 | EXI | EXO | NET | RAW | SER | ST1 | ST2 | ST3 | STA | SYN | THU | VDO |
|---|---|---|---|---|---|---|---|---|---|---|---|---|---|---|---|---|---|
| | samples | 25 | 10 | 2 | 27 | 7 | 25 | 19 | 81 | 36 | 21 | 51 | 18 | 21 | 25 | 24 | 60 |
| E1 | correct | 96 | 80 | 0 | 89 | 29 | 60 | 95 | 96 | 100 | 95 | 98 | 83 | 100 | 100 | 100 | 43 |
| E1 | unknown | 4 | 20 | 100 | 4 | 71 | 36 | 0 | 4 | 0 | 5 | 2 | 11 | 0 | 0 | 0 | 52 |
| E1 | wrong | | | | VDO 7 | | NET 4 | EXO 5 | | | | | SYN 6 | | | | BO3 5 |
| E2 | unknown | 100 | 100 | 100 | 74 | 86 | 64 | 47 | 98 | 100 | 100 | 100 | 89 | 48 | 56 | 96 | 92 |
| E2 | wrong | | | | THU 4<br>VDO 22 | RAW 14 | NET 12<br>STA 24 | EXO 42<br>STA 11 | SYN 2 | | | | SYN 11 | EXO 43<br>NET 10 | VDO 8<br>ST3 36 | BO3 4 | BO3 5<br>SYN 3 |
| E3 | correct | 76 | 60 | 50 | 81 | 14 | 40 | 79 | 75 | 92 | 71 | 82 | 83 | 86 | 92 | 96 | 28 |
| E3 | unknown | 24 | 40 | 50 | 19 | 86 | 56 | 5 | 22 | 8 | 29 | 18 | 17 | 0 | 4 | 4 | 72 |
| E3 | wrong | | | | | | NET 4 | EXO 16 | SYN 1<br>EXI 1 | | | | | EXO 14 | ST3 4 | | |

(b) NTP

| | | AUR | BAN | BO1 | BO2 | BO3 | CRI | DOW | EXI | EXO | KST | NET | RAW | SER | ST1 | ST3 | ST4 | STA | SYN | THU | VDO |
|---|---|---|---|---|---|---|---|---|---|---|---|---|---|---|---|---|---|---|---|---|---|
| | samples | 23 | 15 | 40 | 3 | 28 | 27 | 27 | 7 | 61 | 20 | 29 | 82 | 15 | 21 | 19 | 27 | 22 | 28 | 22 | 61 |
| E1 | correct | 100 | 100 | 95 | 0 | 100 | 100 | 96 | 71 | 97 | 100 | 86 | 100 | 100 | 100 | 89 | 100 | 91 | 100 | 95 | 100 |
| E1 | unknown | 0 | 0 | 5 | 100 | 0 | 0 | 4 | 29 | 3 | 0 | 0 | 0 | 0 | 0 | 11 | 0 | 9 | 0 | 5 | 0 |
| E1 | wrong | | | | | | | | | | | EXO 10<br>CRI 3 | | | | | | | | | |
| E2 | unknown | 100 | 100 | 100 | 100 | 100 | 74 | 100 | 100 | 34 | 100 | 10 | 100 | 100 | 100 | 100 | 93 | 100 | 93 | 100 | 100 |
| E2 | wrong | | | | | | NET 26 | | | NET 66 | | EXO 86<br>CRI 3 | | | | | SYN 7 | | ST4 7 | | |
| E3 | correct | 87 | 73 | 90 | 0 | 96 | 89 | 81 | 43 | 90 | 80 | 69 | 98 | 87 | 86 | 74 | 93 | 77 | 86 | 86 | 97 |
| E3 | unknown | 13 | 27 | 10 | 100 | 4 | 11 | 19 | 57 | 10 | 20 | 17 | 2 | 13 | 14 | 26 | 7 | 23 | 14 | 14 | 3 |
| E3 | wrong | | | | | | | | | | | EXO 10<br>CRI 3 | | | | | | | | | |

time. Misclassifications are even more prevalent in our E2 experiment, where in some cases the classifier confused over half of the attacks. While the number of misclassifications could be reduced by lowering the cutoff threshold, this would also cause a higher rate of `unknown` results in the other two experiments. Finally, in E3 the classifier shows similar performance compared to E1, with a slight degradation. However, this is expected, since if a booter service has just rescanned we will have no training samples that match the current set of amplifiers.

For NTP the victim-driven classifier generally performs better than for DNS. In the 10-fold CV (E1), the classifier correctly attributed 71% or more of the attacks for every booter, in many cases even more than 85%. As before, `BO2` marks an exception due to the small number of attacks that were recorded for this booter. As already observed in the honeypot-based classifier, attacks from `NET` and `CRI` showed similar behavior. A third booter, `EXO`, that was only observed in the victim-based data set exhibits similar traits as well. While we were not able to verify that these booters are just different front ends of a multibranding booter, they account for almost all of the misattributions not only for NTP but also for CharGen. In E2 the classifier achieves a perfect result for most booters, with the exception of the previously mentioned group and two confusions between `ST4` and `SYN`. Again, the results of our real-time classification experiment (E3) are as expected, with attribution rates of over 69% in all cases, except for `EXI`, whose recall drops from 71% to only 43%, due to the small number of attacks observed from this booter.

Overall, the victim-driven classifier achieves a macro-averaged precision of 91.65% and recall of 79.03% for DNS, while for NTP it performs better with 94.58% and respectively 91.07%.

## 7 Discussion

We now discuss potential ways to evade our attribution implementation and describe general limitations of our approach that we have not discussed so far.

### 7.1 Evasion

While our attribution methods have proven to work well as of now, they may be susceptible to evasion attempts by miscreants. A *mimicry* attacker could try to be attributed as someone else by following our methodology, i.e., learning the attack profile of another booter and copying its behavior. For example, she could use the same set of reflectors as the other booter for her own attacks. However, this involves a significant increase in terms of effort in comparison to Internet-wide scans. In addition, our TTL-based features are much harder to copy, as they encode the location of the booter service and are subject to changes for other booter locations. While such mimicry attacks are possible [2], given the complexity and overhead, we do not believe that attackers trying to trigger a *false* attribution constitute an actual risk in practice. For similar arguments, attackers that share lists of reflectors with each other would partially poison our analysis, but again TTL-based attribution may be safe against this. Our use of the set of domain names resolved as a feature for our victim-driven DNS classifier can be evaded by booter services selecting a larger pool of domain names that result in large replies and cycling through this pool.

An *evasive* attacker could try to evade our classification mechanisms. Attackers have full control over the traffic they generate, and thus could add noise. For example, one could randomize the set of reflectors used in the attacks, or spoof the initial TTL value within a range of possible values. It is unclear if a classifier could still keep up with such evasion attempts, but it may be possible to add additional features to enrich the classification, such as other characteristics (e.g., IP packet IDs, DNS transaction IDs), as those have shown characteristic patterns even if they were randomized [8]. In addition, honeypots that selectively respond to scan requests may survive such randomization [10]. Even if attackers randomize the set of reflectors, any subset will still be a subset of a unique mapping to a scanner. Lastly, randomizing the traffic does also incur a performance overhead to attackers, as they cannot reuse pre-generated packets.

Finally, attackers could try to map out the honey amplifiers using probing messages [3] if the honeypot amplifier data was made public for the DDoS service to use as an oracle. To avoid this evasion technique, access to the honeypot amplifier data is restricted to vetted entities, such as researchers and LEAs.

### 7.2 Limitations

Our in-the-wild experiments faced some limitations, as discussed in the following:

**Honeypot Coverage:** Regardless of our attempts to maximize the coverage of the honeypots, they missed significant fractions of the self-attacks, especially for SSDP and CharGen. This can be addressed by framing larger emulated responses to make the honeypots more attractive to attackers. The coverage for two of the main protocols, DNS and NTP, was significant, though, covering about 57% of the self-attacks. We therefore argue that our results are representative at least for these two protocols. In addition, there is no limitation of our methodology that would restrict its applicability to the two well-tested protocols.

**Multi-source Attribution:** We assumed that attacks are caused by single sources (booters). If botnets launched amplification attacks, our features (e.g., TTL) would be unstable. To give an upper bound of attacks launched by botnets, we searched for attacks with several TTL values, as this—among other reasons—might be caused by distributed traffic sources. Less than 9.5% of attacks at the honeypots show more than 2 TTL values at a honeypot.

**Other Attacks:** Other types of DDoS attacks, such as SYN flooding or HTTP-based attacks, do not use reflectors and are thus not traceable with our proposed methods. Note that amplification attacks constitute the most common bandwidth exhaustion attack. This is also demonstrated by the fact that all booters advertise amplification attacks, while support for other attack types (e.g., HTTP-based attacks) is far less popular. To put things into perspective: we observed more than 8,900 amplification attacks per day.

## 8 Related Work

The general risk of amplification attacks was first illustrated in Paxon's seminal paper on reflection attacks [15] and then by Rossow's recent overview of amplification vulnerabilities in 14 UDP-based network protocols [18]. A wealth of further work analyzed amplification attacks, such as attempts to monitor and reduce the number of reflectors [1,4,11], analyses on detailed amplification vectors in specific protocols [4,12,24–26], studies on the impact of DDoS attacks [29], and proposals to detect and defend against amplification DDoS attacks [5,9,18,28].

Orthogonal to these studies, we investigated ways to perform *attribution* for amplification DDoS attacks. While concepts for closing the root cause of amplification attacks (IP spoofing) are well-known [14], little success has been made in *identifying* the spoofing sources. Our work thus constitutes an important element for law enforcement to identify and act upon information of booter services that are responsible for the majority of attacks. We follow a similar goal to IP traceback mechanisms [16,21–23,30], i.e., to find the source of "bad" (such as spoofed) traffic. While we also aim to reveal the source of the bad traffic, we focus on attack services rather than locating the networks that cause the traffic.

In addition, the working principles behind the methods are inherently different. Most IP traceback methods are deterministic and can be guaranteed to find the correct source of traffic. However, at the same time, they impose requirements that are often not met in practice, such as that providers have to mark IP packets or collaborate to find traffic paths. In contrast, our proposed mechanism advances the field in that we do not require such a collaborative effort. In fact, despite being known for decades, automated traceback mechanisms have not been deployed by many providers. To tackle this problem, our approach merely requires a set of honeypots that anybody can set up, enabling a single party to perform attribution. On the other hand, our approach is limited to mapping amplification attacks to booter services, whereas traceback mechanisms could trace back any type of DoS traffic—down to the network that caused it.

Closely related to our work is AmpPot, as proposed by Krämer et al. [8]. This honeypot technology has enabled us to monitor thousands of DDoS attacks per day. We combine such data with observations of attack traffic emitted by booters, introducing the new concept of attributing amplification attacks to booters.

Our work was motivated by various research papers that shed light onto booter services using forensic analyses. Karami and McCoy were the first to monitor such booter services, studying the adversarial DDoS-As-a-Service concept [6] and observing that booters are a source for amplification attacks. Similarly, Santanna et al. analyze leaked databases and payment methods of 15 booters [19]. Related to our idea to fingerprint booters, Santanna et al. performed self-attacks of 14 booter services and also observed that the set of reflectors chosen by booters may have overlap across attacks [20]. We build upon this observation, find further correlations for attacks of booter services, and propose to use theses for attack attribution. Karami et. al. [7] provide a detailed view on the subscribers and victims of three booters. They provide early attempts to map the infrastructures of booters, but do not perform any kind of attribution between attacks and booters or infrastructures.

Wang et al. [27] have studied the dynamics of attack sources of DDoS botnets, showing distinct patterns per botnet. While the authors provide first results that might enable them to predict future attack sources, they do not further investigate this matter. Our work is different in motivation and techniques in multiple respects. First, booters follow a completely different methodology than DDoS botnets, which rarely use IP spoofing. Second, we can leverage the observation that attackers scan for "attack sources" (amplifiers). Third, we perform attack attribution rather than prediction.

Recently, Krupp et al. [10] showed how to uncover the *scan infrastructures* behind amplification DDoS attacks, which in some cases could also be identified to be the attacking infrastructure. Although their work might seem similar to ours at first, there are key differences both in the goal and the methodology: While they use probabilistic reasoning to identify the scanners that provide the necessary reconnaissance for attacks, we use machine learning techniques to link attacks to the originating booters. Moreover, both approaches serve different demands: while their work aids in adding pressure on providers to cease illegal activities, our paper helps to generate forensic evidence that a particular booter has caused a specific attack, which can prove useful in prosecution.

## 9 Conclusion

Our work presented the first deep exploration of techniques for attributing amplification DDoS attacks to booter services. We present two precise attribution techniques based on carefully chosen features as part of a $k$-NN classifier. In order to evaluate the effectiveness of our techniques, we subscribed to a small set of booter services and launched self-attacks to collect a ground truth set of attack-to-booter-service mappings. We discuss the ethical framework used to collect this data set, which is similar to that of a previous study [7].

Our honeypot-driven technique attributes DNS and NTP attacks with a very high precision of over 99% while still achieving recall of over 69.35% in the most challenging real-time attribution scenario. Further analysis has revealed that 25.53% (49,297) of the observed DNS attacks can be attributed to just 7 booter services and 13.34% (38,520) of the NTP attacks can be attributed to 15 booter services. We have shared these findings with law enforcement agencies to help them prioritize legal actions against the wealth of booter services.

Our second technique extracts features out of a victim's network's traces and attributes attacks from the *victim's perspective*, which opens the possibility to offer a centralized DDoS attribution service. Using this technique, victims can learn the source of the attacks they face and could even compare two attacks to determine if they have been launched by the same actor (booter).

**Acknowledgements.** This work was supported in part by the German Federal Ministry of Education and Research (BMBF) through funding for the Center for IT-Security, Privacy and Accountability (CISPA) under grant 16KIS0656, by the European Union's Horizon 2020 research and innovation program under grant agreement No. 700176, by the US National Science Foundation under grant 1619620, and by a gift from Google. Any opinions, findings, and conclusions or recommendations expressed in this material are those of the authors and do not necessarily reflect the views of the sponsors.

## A Appendix

### A.1 Additional Experimental Results

Table 5 shows our experimental results for victim-driven attribution for CharGen (precision 92.86%, recall 89.24%) and SSDP (precision 92.15%, recall 81.41%).

**Table 5.** Victim-driven experimental results for CharGen and SSDP

(a) CharGen

| | | AUR | BAN | BO1 | BO2 | BO3 | DOW | EXO | KST | NET | RAW | SER | ST1 | ST4 | SYN |
|---|---|---|---|---|---|---|---|---|---|---|---|---|---|---|---|
| | samples | 26 | 3 | 41 | 2 | 27 | 27 | 60 | 21 | 18 | 78 | 42 | 20 | 26 | 26 |
| E1 | correct | 96 | 0 | 93 | 100 | 100 | 100 | 97 | 76 | 89 | 99 | 100 | 100 | 100 | 100 |
| | unknown | 4 | 100 | 7 | 0 | 0 | 0 | 3 | 24 | 11 | 1 | 0 | 0 | 0 | 0 |
| | wrong | | | | | | | | | | | | | | |
| E2 | unknown | 100 | 100 | 100 | 100 | 100 | 63 | 48 | 100 | 39 | 100 | 76 | 100 | 100 | 100 |
| | wrong | | | | | | SER 37 | NET 52 | | EXO 61 | | DOW 24 | | | |
| E3 | correct | 88 | 33 | 80 | 50 | 96 | 85 | 93 | 57 | 78 | 96 | 86 | 90 | 92 | 88 |
| | unknown | 12 | 67 | 20 | 50 | 4 | 11 | 7 | 43 | 22 | 4 | 14 | 10 | 8 | 12 |
| | wrong | | | | | | SER 4 | | | | | | | | |

(b) SSDP

| | | AUR | BAN | BO1 | BO2 | BO3 | DOW | EXO | KST | NET | ST1 | ST2 | STA | VDO |
|---|---|---|---|---|---|---|---|---|---|---|---|---|---|---|
| | samples | 20 | 17 | 40 | 2 | 27 | 28 | 60 | 21 | 28 | 17 | 17 | 25 | 49 |
| E1 | correct | 95 | 76 | 95 | 0 | 100 | 96 | 98 | 95 | 100 | 18 | 88 | 96 | 100 |
| | unknown | 0 | 24 | 5 | 100 | 0 | 4 | 2 | 5 | 0 | 82 | 12 | 4 | 0 |
| | wrong | VDO 5 | | | | | | | | | | | | |
| E2 | unknown | 95 | 100 | 100 | 100 | 100 | 100 | 100 | 100 | 100 | 100 | 100 | 100 | 90 |
| | wrong | VDO 5 | | | | | | | | | | | | AUR 10 |
| E3 | correct | 80 | 59 | 85 | 0 | 96 | 86 | 95 | 81 | 86 | 12 | 71 | 88 | 98 |
| | unknown | 20 | 41 | 15 | 100 | 4 | 14 | 5 | 19 | 14 | 88 | 29 | 12 | 0 |
| | wrong | | | | | | | | | | | | | AUR 2 |

## References


1. The Spoofer Project. http://spoofer.cmand.org
2. Backes, M., Holz, T., Rossow, C., Rytilahti, T., Simeonovski, M., Stock, B.: On the feasibility of TTL-based filtering for DRDoS mitigation. In: Proceedings of the 19th International Symposium on Research in Attacks, Intrusions and Defenses (2016)
3. Bethencourt, J., Franklin, J., Vernon, M.: Mapping internet sensors with probe response attacks. In: Proceedings of the 14th Conference on USENIX Security Symposium (2005)
4. Czyz, J., Kallitsis, M., Gharaibeh, M., Papadopoulos, C., Bailey, M., Karir, M.: Taming the 800 pound gorilla: the rise and decline of NTP DDoS attacks. In: Proceedings of the Internet Measurement Conference 2014. ACM (2014)
5. Gilad, Y., Goberman, M., Herzberg, A., Sudkovitch, M.: CDN-on-Demand: an affordable DDoS defense via untrusted clouds. In: Proceedings of NDSS 2016 (2016)
6. Karami, M., McCoy, D.: Understanding the emerging threat of DDoS-as-a-service. In: LEET (2013)
7. Karami, M., Park, Y., McCoy, D.: Stress testing the booters: understanding and undermining the business of DDoS services. In: World Wide Web Conference (WWW). ACM (2016)
8. Krämer, L., Krupp, J., Makita, D., Nishizoe, T., Koide, T., Yoshioka, K., Rossow, C.: AmpPot: monitoring and defending against amplification DDoS attacks. In: Bos, H., Monrose, F., Blanc, G. (eds.) RAID 2015. LNCS, vol. 9404, pp. 615–636. Springer, Cham (2015). doi:10.1007/978-3-319-26362-5_28

9. Kreibich, C., Warfield, A., Crowcroft, J., Hand, S., Pratt, I.: Using packet symmetry to curtail malicious traffic. In: Proceedings of the 4th Workshop on Hot Topics in Networks (Hotnets-VI) (2005)
10. Krupp, J., Backes, M., Rossow, C.: Identifying the scan and attack infrastructures behind amplification DDoS attacks. In: Proceedings of the 23rd ACM Conference on Computer and Communications Security (CCS) (2016)
11. Kührer, M., Hupperich, T., Rossow, C., Holz, T.: Exit from hell? reducing the impact of amplification DDoS attacks. In: Proceedings of the 23rd USENIX Security Symposium (2014)
12. Kührer, M., Hupperich, T., Rossow, C., Holz, T.: Hell of a handshake: abusing TCP for reflective amplification DDoS attacks. In: Proceedings of the 8th USENIX Workshop on Offensive Technologies (WOOT 2014) (2014)
13. A. Networks. Worldwide Infrastructure Security Report (2015). https://www.arbornetworks.com/images/documents/WISR2016_EN_Web.pdf
14. Ferguson, P., Senie, D.: BCP 38 on Network Ingress Filtering: Defeating Denial of Service Attacks which employ IP Source Address Spoofing (2000). http://tools.ietf.org/html/bcp.38
15. Paxson, V.: An analysis of using reflectors for distributed denial-of-service attacks. Comput. Commun. Rev. (2001)
16. Perrig, A., Song, D., Yaar, A.: StackPi: A New Defense Mechanism against IP Spoofing and DDoS Attacks. Technical report (2003)
17. Prince, M.: The DDoS That Almost Broke the Internet (2013). https://blog.cloudflare.com/the-ddos-that-almost-broke-the-internet/
18. Rossow, C.: Amplification hell: revisiting network protocols for DDoS abuse. In: Proceedings of NDSS 2014 (2014)
19. Santanna, J., Durban, R., Sperotto, A., Pras, A.: Inside booters: an analysis on operational databases. In: 14th IFIP/IEEE International Symposium on Integrated Network Management (IM) (2015)
20. Santanna, J.J., van Rijswijk-Deij, R., Hofstede, R., Sperotto, A., Wierbosch, M., Granville, L.Z., Pras, A.: Booters - an analysis of DDoS-As-a-Service attacks. In: 14th IFIP/IEEE International Symposium on Integrated Network Management (IM) (2015)
21. Savage, S., Wetherall, D., Karlin, A., Anderson, T.: Practical network support for IP traceback. In: ACM SIGCOMM Computer Communication Review, vol. 30. ACM (2000)
22. Snoeren, A.C., Partridge, C., Sanchez, L.A., Jones, C.E., Tchakountio, F., Kent, S.T., Strayer, W.T.: Hash-based IP traceback. In: ACM SIGCOMM Computer Communication Review, vol. 31. ACM (2001)
23. Song, D.X., Perrig, A.: Advanced and authenticated marking schemes for IP traceback. In: Proceedings of the 20th Annual Joint Conference of the IEEE Computer and Communications Societies. IEEE (2001)
24. Sun, X., Torres, R., Rao, S.: DDoS attacks by subverting membership management in P2P systems. In: Proceedings of the 3rd IEEE Workshop on Secure Network Protocols (NPSec) (2007)
25. Sun, X., Torres, R., Rao, S.: On the feasibility of exploiting P2P systems to launch DDoS attacks. J. Peer-to-Peer Networking Appl. **3** (2010)
26. van Rijswijk-Deij, R., Sperotto, A., Pras, A.: DNSSEC and its potential for DDoS attacks - a comprehensive measurement study. In: Proceedings of the Internet Measurement Conference 2014. ACM (2014)

27. Wang, A., Mohaisen, A., Chang, W., Chen, S.: Capturing DDoS attack dynamics behind the scenes. In: Almgren, M., Gulisano, V., Maggi, F. (eds.) DIMVA 2015. LNCS, vol. 9148, pp. 205–215. Springer, Cham (2015). doi:10.1007/978-3-319-20550-2_11
28. Wang, X., Reiter, M.K.: Mitigating bandwidth-exhaustion attacks using congestion puzzles. In: Proceedings of the 11th ACM Conference on Computer and Communications Security (CCS) (2004)
29. Welzel, A., Rossow, C., Bos, H.: On measuring the impact of DDoS botnets. In: Proceedings of the 7th European Workshop on Systems Security (EuroSec) (2014)
30. Yaar, A., Perrig, A., Song, D.: Pi: a path identification mechanism to defend against DDoS attacks. In: Proceedings of the IEEE Symposium on Security and Privacy (S&P) (2003)

# Practical and Accurate Runtime Application Protection Against DoS Attacks

Mohamed Elsabagh[1(✉)], Dan Fleck[1], Angelos Stavrou[1], Michael Kaplan[2], and Thomas Bowen[2]

[1] George Mason University, Fairfax, VA 22030, USA
{melsabag,dfleck,astavrou}@gmu.edu
[2] Vencore Labs, Red Bank, NJ 07701, USA
{mkaplan,tbowen}@vencorelabs.com

**Abstract.** Software Denial-of-Service (DoS) attacks use maliciously crafted inputs aiming to exhaust available resources of the target software. These application-level DoS attacks have become even more prevalent due to the increasing code complexity and modular nature of Internet services that are deployed in cloud environments, where resources are shared and not always guaranteed. To make matters worse, many code testing and verification techniques cannot cope with the code size and diversity present in most services used to deliver the majority of everyday Internet applications. In this paper, we propose *Cogo*, a practical system for early DoS detection and mitigation of software DoS attacks. Unlike prior solutions, *Cogo* builds behavioral models of network I/O events in linear time and employs Probabilistic Finite Automata (PFA) models to recognize future resource exhaustion states. Our tracing of events spans then entire code stack from userland to kernel. In many cases, we can block attacks far before impacting legitimate live sessions. We demonstrate the effectiveness and performance of *Cogo* using commercial-grade testbeds of two large and popular Internet services: Apache and the VoIP OpenSIPS servers. *Cogo* required less than 12 min of training time to achieve high accuracy: less than 0.0194% false positives rate, while detecting a wide range of resource exhaustion attacks less than seven seconds into the attacks. Finally, *Cogo* had only two to three percent per-session overhead.

**Keywords:** Software DoS · Early detection · Slow-rate attacks · Probabilistic Finite Automata

## 1 Introduction

Software availability is a major concern for the success of today's interconnected Internet services. As technologies become more advanced and complex, servicing

**Electronic supplementary material** The online version of this chapter (doi:10.1007/978-3-319-66332-6_20) contains supplementary material, which is available to authorized users.


M. Dacier et al. (Eds.): RAID 2017, LNCS 10453, pp. 450–471, 2017.
DOI: 10.1007/978-3-319-66332-6_20

an ever increasing number of users and devices, they become much harder to properly design and test against inputs and runtime conditions that may result in resource exhaustion and, eventually, denial-of-service (DoS). Recent surveys clearly indicate that business owners are concerned about DoS attacks over other security concerns [6,8]. A system is vulnerable to resource exhaustion attacks if it fails to properly regulate the resources that can be allocated to individual user sessions and the service overall. Resource DoS attacks can target system resources such as memory, computing (CPU), and I/O including file access and traditional network resources [21,23,37]. Contrary to the common belief, resource exhaustion attacks are increasing in numbers, becoming even more prevalent and risky when compared to network layer attacks [1,21].

Recent work by Elsabagh et al. [25] proposed Radmin, a system for detecting DoS attacks at the application layer. Radmin operated by learning (offline) and enforcing (online) resource consumption patterns of programs. Radmin showed promising results; however, it had a quadratic training time complexity in the training data size that makes it prohibitive to apply to large code bases. Moreover, Radmin was tested on stateless traffic and synthetic attacks rather than on live traffic and known attacks used in practice. Radmin also did not cover network state and I/O which are common targets for attacks. Another limitation was that Radmin was heavily dependent on "normal" patterns of pure resource utilization without modeling the rate at which individual resources were acquired and released. As we show in our experiments, lack of taking into consideration when individual resources were allocated can lead to prolonged evasion by Slow-rate [11] attacks, violating the early detection goal of Radmin.

In this paper, we propose *Cogo* as a novel Probabilistic Finite Automata (PFA) based system for runtime detection and mitigation of software resource exhaustion DoS attacks. *Cogo* fully addresses all the aforementioned limitations of Radmin, enabling early detection of real-world attacks in many cases before they are able to affect the service operation or quality. Our approach operates in two phases: offline and online. In the offline phase, *Cogo* monitors the entire resource consumption behavior of the target program — including its network I/O — and builds PFA models that characterize the program's resource behavior over time. *Cogo* monitors network I/O at the individual socket level and supports monitoring of containerized processes. To reduce modeling complexity, we introduce an efficient PFA learning algorithm that operates in linear time. During the online phase, *Cogo* actively monitors the program and detects deviations from the learned behaviors. It attributes anomalies to the specific threads and connections causing them, allowing for selectively limiting resource utilization of individual sessions that may violate the models.

We built a working prototype implementation of *Cogo* by extending the code base of Radmin [25] which offered several integrated user/kernel tracing capabilities and an extensible PFA detection engine. We extended Radmin by supporting new low-level network I/O monitoring, process migration, and monitoring containerized processes. Extending Radmin allowed us to benchmark our approach

in a unified way and provide comparative results.[1] We discuss two case studies using real-world attacks and commercial-grade testbeds against The Apache HTTP Server [2] and the VoIP OpenSIPS [9] server. In our experiments, *Cogo* achieved a significant improvement in training time over Radmin, requiring only few minutes instead of days to train and build the models. This is significant since in real-world systems training data are expectantly large in size. In addition to short training time, *Cogo* achieved a low false positive rate (FPR) (0.019% for Apache, 0.063% for OpenSIPS) using small models (76 MB for Apache, 55 MB for OpenSIPS). Moreover, *Cogo* swiftly detected the attacks in less than seven seconds into their execution, resulting in **zero** downtime in some cases. Its runtime overhead is negligible. it increased the latency by $0.2 \pm 0.3$ ms per request on average, resulting in two to three percent per-session overhead.
To summarize, this study makes the following contributions:

- Demonstrates *Cogo* as a system for early detection and mitigation of resource exhaustion DoS attacks against real-word complex Internet services. Our approach extends prior work on Radmin [25] by enabling network stack tracing from the application to the kernel, monitoring containerized processes, and attaching to running processes.
- Presents and discusses a linear time training algorithm that reduces the training and model building time complexity.
- Studies the effectiveness of *Cogo* using realistic testbeds with real-world attacks on Apache and the VoIP OpenSIPS server. The results demonstrate that *Cogo* is suitable for large-scale deployment as it is scalable, accurate, has low false positives, and can mitigate real-world attacks.

## 2 Assumptions and Threat Model

*Cogo* focuses on DoS attacks that occur at the application layer such as algorithmic, state, and protocol-specific attacks. Volumetric attacks targeting the network and transport layers, as well as other attack vectors such as code execution and memory exposure are outside the scope of this work. We assume that attackers have full knowledge of the internals of the attacked program and can craft benign-looking inputs that prevent the attacked program from serving legitimate clients (a DoS attack). To protect a program with *Cogo*, we assume the availability of benign training inputs that cover the typical desired behavior of the program. *Cogo* uses kernel tracing; our prototype currently supports only Linux and Unix-like operating systems since they power the majority of servers.[2] However, the approach itself does not place restrictions on the runtime environment and can be ported to other operating systems with little effort.[3]

[1] By building on Radmin, *Cogo* inherits other monitoring sensors from Radmin such as CPU and memory sensors.

[2] Market share of operating systems by category: https://en.wikipedia.org/wiki/Usage_share_of_operating_systems.

[3] For Microsoft Windows, kernel tracing can be implemented using the Event Tracing for Windows (ETW) kernel-mode API: https://msdn.microsoft.com/en-us/windows/hardware/drivers/devtest/adding-event-tracing-to-kernel-mode-drivers.

We only focus on detection; proper remediation strategies after attack detection should be implemented by the operator and are outside the scope of this work. Nevertheless, *Cogo* offers the option to migrate the offending process or session to another server, reduce its resource priority, or terminate it based on a configurable policy. Finally, we assume that attackers can be local or remote, but cannot overwrite system binaries or modify the kernel.

## 3 The *Cogo* System

*Cogo* operates in two phases: offline training phase and online detection phase. In the offline phase, *Cogo* monitors the behavior of the target program on benign inputs and collects a trace of network I/O measurements. The measurements are sequences of raw data that include the event type (socket open, close, send, receive), the consumption amount of the related resource (number of owned sockets, traffic rate per socket), and meta data such as the PID, the socket inode number, and timestamps.

The raw resource consumption amounts are encoded (quantized) over a countable finite alphabet $\Sigma$ (a finite set of symbols). $|\Sigma|$ is a tuning parameter, typically less than 16 for a maximum of 16 different consumption levels. Encoding is done by mapping (many-to-few) each raw resource consumption value to one symbol from $\Sigma$. This is necessary since the PFAs (state machines) only work with a finite set of values. Since encoding is a typical step in constructing finite automata from arbitrary values, and due to space constraints, we refer interested readers to [25,26] for more detail.[4]

*Cogo* constructs multiple PFAs from the measurements, one PFA per resource type. The PFAs capture both the spatial and temporal network I/O patterns in the measurements. In the online phase, *Cogo* executes the PFAs as shadow state machines along with the target program and raises an alarm if a deviation of the normal behavior is detected. *Cogo* detects anomalous behavior using the statistical properties of the PFAs — namely the transition probabilities on the PFA edges. In the following, we discuss how *Cogo* monitors network I/O and its PFA learning and detection algorithms.

### 3.1 Network Tracing

*Cogo* monitors the network activity of the target program by intercepting the traffic and socket events that happen in the context of target processes inside the kernel. Specifically, it monitors all socket creation and destruction events triggered by the target processes and tracks traffic sent or received on those sockets. *Cogo* computes the transmit (TX) and receive (RX) rates per second from the size and direction of the monitored traffic.

*Cogo* differentiates sockets from regular file descriptors inside the kernel as follows: First, it retrieves a target process task structure in kernel space using

[4] We use "measurements" to refer to encoded measurements in the rest of this paper.

the global process identifier (PID). (The task structure is the actual structure that represents the process inside the kernel.) It traverses the task structure and extracts the file descriptors table owned by the process. For each file descriptor, *Cogo* extracts the inode object associated with the file descriptor. (The inode object is a kernel structure that contains all needed information to manipulate and interact with a file descriptor. An inode represents each file in a file system, including regular files and directories, as well as special files such as sockets, devices, and pipes.) *Cogo* checks if the inode object contains an embedded (allocated member) socket object. If found, *Cogo* marks the corresponding file descriptor of the inode as a socket descriptor. *Cogo* tracks all identified sockets by their low-level unique inode numbers throughout their lifetime.

For each identified socket, *Cogo* extracts the socket Internet protocol family from the socket kernel structure. (The protocol family defines the collection of protocols operating above the Internet Protocol (IP) layer that utilize an IP address format. It can be one of two values: INET6 and INET for the IPv6 and IPv4 protocol families, respectively.) This is essential for determining how to interpret the socket network addresses. Given a socket protocol family, *Cogo* extracts the local and foreign addresses and port numbers, if available. Foreign port numbers may not be available if the socket is a listening or a datagram socket.

*Cogo* intercepts all transmit and receive socket events that occur in the context of the monitored process in kernel space, including regular I/O operations such as streamed and datagram I/O, asynchronous I/O (AIO) operations, and operations utilizing a socket iterator. *Cogo* collects the direction (TX or RX) and size of the traffic, and associates them with the corresponding socket inode number. The TX and RX rates are computed periodically per socket. The period length is configurable (defaults to 1 s). To minimize memory and runtime overhead, *Cogo* installs a kernel timer that ticks once per period length, requiring minimal memory per socket as only the last tick timestamp and total traffic size need be kept in memory. It also minimizes runtime overhead by avoiding unnecessary context switches to compute the rates. *Cogo* also monitors the socket status: connected or disconnected. When a socket disconnects or is freed by the kernel, *Cogo* purges any structures associated with that particular socket from its kernel memory.

### 3.2 Training and Learning

*Cogo* employs Probabilistic Finite Automata (PFA) based learning and detection. *Cogo* builds one PFA for each monitored resource: one PFA for socket creation and destruction, one PFA for TX rate, and one PFA for RX rate. *Cogo* uses the PFAs to compute the probability of observed measurements in the online phase. In the following, we present a training algorithm that runs in time linear in the measurements length, making *Cogo* attractive and realistic for real-world deployment.

**Constructing Bounded Generalized Suffix Trees.** To construct each resource PFA, first, *Cogo* builds a bounded Generalized Suffix Tree (GST) from the resource measurements. (A suffix tree is a tree containing all suffixes of a given string. A GST is a suffix tree for a *set* of strings.) Given a set of strings $S$ over an alphabet $\Sigma$ (a finite set of symbols), a GST over $S$ contains a path from the root to some leaf node for each suffix in $S$. Each edge in the GST is labeled with a non-empty substring in $S$; the labels of outgoing edges from the same node must begin with unique symbols. A GST can be constructed in linear time and space $O(n)$ where $n$ is the total number of symbols in $S$, using Ukkonen's algorithm [36]. A GST allows efficient implementations of several string query operations over sets of strings such as linear time substring searching and finding the longest common substring among all the strings in the set. *Cogo* limits the depth of the GST by processing the measurements into non-overlapping subsequences of maximum length $L$.[5] This bounds the depth of the GST to $L$ and the space requirements per GST to $O(|S|L)$.

After constructing the bounded GST, *Cogo* counts the number of occurrences of each substring in the tree. This corresponds to the number of leaf nodes in the subtree rooted at each node in the tree. These counts are computed in a single depth-first traversal of the GST. For each parent-child nodes in the tree, the ratio between the child's count to the parent's count gives the conditional probability of seeing the first symbol of the corresponding child substring after the parent's. More formally, the prediction probability of a symbol $s_j$ after a substring $s_i s_{i+1} \dots s_{j-1}$ can be computed as:

$$P(s_j | s_i s_{i+1} ... s_{j-1}) = \frac{count(s_i s_{i+1} ... s_{j-1} s_j)}{count(s_i s_{i+1} ... s_{j-1})}, \quad (1)$$

which *Cogo* computes on-the-fly during the depth-first traversal of the GST to count the substrings, and stores it in each child node in the tree.

**Inferring the PFAs.** *Cogo* infers a PFA from the GST. Each PFA is a 5-tuple $(\Sigma, Q, \pi, \tau, \gamma)$, where: $\Sigma$ is a finite set of symbols processed by the PFA; $Q$ is a finite set of states, and $q^\circ \in Q$ is the start state; $\tau\colon Q \times \Sigma \rightarrow Q$ is the state transition function; and, $\gamma\colon Q \times \Sigma \rightarrow [0,1]$ is the transition probability function.

To infer a PFA from the GST, *Cogo* starts by creating a forest of unconnected PFA nodes where each node has a unique ID and corresponds to exactly one node in the GST. It then traverses the GST in depth-first order: For each edge between each parent (source) and child (destination) nodes in the GST, *Cogo* checks the length of the edge label. If the label has exactly one symbol, *Cogo* adds a transition between the corresponding source and destination nodes in the PFA, sets the transition probability to the child node probability in the GST, and sets the transition symbol to the edge label. If the edge has a label of length

[5] We found that non-overlapping subsequences were sufficient for large-scale deployments. However, it may be desired to overlap subsequences to maximize fidelity of very small datasets.

greater than one, i.e., the label is a substring consisting of multiple symbols, *Cogo* adds nodes to the PFA corresponding to each inner symbol in the label; adds a PFA transition from the source state to the node corresponding to the first symbol in the label; and adds another transition from the last inner symbol in the label to the destination node. Formally put, given the edge $u \xrightarrow{s_i s_{i+1} \ldots s_j} v$ in the GST, *Cogo* adds the following path to the PFA: $u' \xrightarrow{s_i, count(u[s_i])/count(u)} \bullet \xrightarrow{s_{i+1}, 1.0} \ldots \xrightarrow{s_{j-1}, 1.0} \bullet \xrightarrow{s_j, 1.0} v'$ where $u'$ and $v'$ are the corresponding nodes in the PFA of $u$ and $v$. Recall that transitions in the PFA hold both a transition symbol and an emitted probability.

At this stage, this initial PFA contains paths that correspond to the substrings from the GST, and can be used for prediction so long as the *entire* substring is in the tree. However, if the next symbol following some substring is not in the tree, then a Markovian decision need be made since it may still be possible to predict the symbol using a shorter suffix. For this, the GST suffix links are used to find the next immediate suffix. In a GST, the node corresponding to the string $s_i \ldots s_j$ has a suffix link (a pointer) to the internal node corresponding to the string $s_{i+1} \ldots s_j$, i.e., its immediate suffix. This enables *jumping* to the next available context (history) in constant time. *Cogo* utilizes the suffix links to complete the PFA construction in the following manner: For each node $u$ (visited during the depth-first traversal) and for each symbol $\sigma \in \Sigma$ that does not mark any outgoing edge from $u$, *Cogo* follows the suffix links starting from $u$ until:

1. An internal node $v$ is reached where the first symbol of the substring represented by that node equals $\sigma$. In this case, *Cogo* adds a transition between the corresponding two nodes to $u$ and $v$ in the PFA. It sets the transition symbol to $\sigma$ and the transition probability to that stored in $v$ in the GST.
2. The root of the GST is reached and it has an edge with a label that begins with $\sigma$ to some child node $v$. Here, *Cogo* adds a transition between the corresponding $u$ and $v$ nodes in the PFA. It sets the transition symbol to $\sigma$ and the transition probability to that stored in $v$.
3. The root is reached but it has no outgoing edges for $\sigma$. In this case, a loop-back transition on $\sigma$ from $u$ to itself is added and the transition probability is set to $\rho_{min}$ (a small predefined value for the minimum transition probability).

Since the GST contains all suffixes, the resulting PFA would contain outgoing edges from the start state that never prefixed the training sequences. This can result in the PFA accepting anomalous behavior if an attack occurs at the very beginning of execution of a target process. *Cogo* eliminates those spurious transitions by keeping a set of the initials of the training sequences and pruning outgoing start state transitions from the PFA that do not correspond to those initials. This is done in constant time ($|\Sigma|$ comparisons). Using a single depth-first traversal, *Cogo* also removes any transitions that have a probability less than or equal to $\rho_{min}$ and replaces them with loop-back transitions with $\rho_{min}$ probability. During the same traversal, *Cogo* normalizes the probabilities across outgoing edges from each node.

**Minimizing the PFAs.** The PFA may contain redundancy such as unreachable states (because of eliminated transitions) or overlapping paths, resulting in unnecessary space overhead. To overcome this, *Cogo* minimizes the PFA using the following greedy approach. The goal is to reduce the size of the PFA as much as possible without incurring excessive training overhead, i.e., reduction time has to be linear in the size of the PFA. The minimization algorithm is based on the insight that paths farther away from the PFA root (the start state) are more likely to overlap sine they represent longer substrings.

*Cogo* iterates over the PFA in breadth-first order. Each time it visits a new state $u$, it searches for all previously visited states that are fully equivalent to the $u$. Two states are fully equivalent if they have the same outgoing transitions with the same transition symbols, probabilities, and destination states for each transition. *Cogo* groups all the equivalent states into a single state set. This process continues till all states in the PFA are visited, producing a set family of states. After that, all equivalent states set are removed and replaced with a single state in the PFA. The process is repeated on the resulting PFA till any of the following conditions occur: (*1*) Tthe PFA stops changing. (*2*) The minimization ratio, i.e., the size of the resulting PFA divided by the size of the old PFA, drops below some user defined threshold $\theta$ (defaults to 0.1). (*3*) The number of repetitions exceeds a user chosen threshold $\zeta$ (defaults to 100). The 2nd condition terminates the minimization stage once a diminishing returns point is reached. The 3rd condition gives the user the ability to control the hidden constant $c$ of the minimization complexity $O(cn)$. This completes the construction of the PFA. Figure 1 illustrates an example of a bounded GST and the PFA inferred by *Cogo* from the set $\{01001101, 01010100\}$ where $L = 4$, i.e., the effective set is $\{0100, 1101, 0101, 0100\}$. The figure also shows how to compute the probability of the sequence 010 using the PFA.

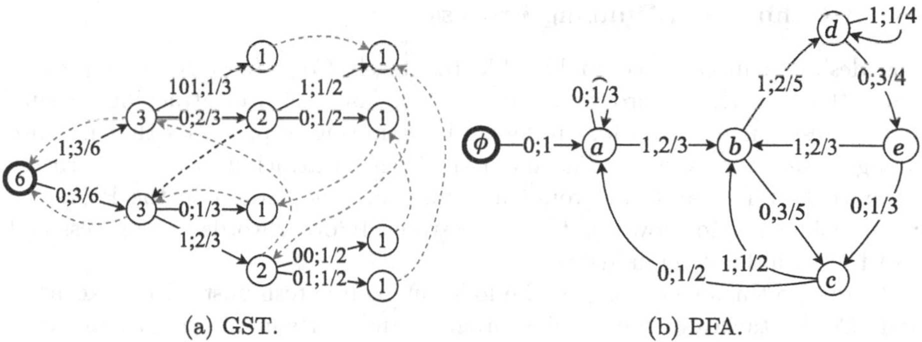


**Fig. 1.** Bounded GST and final PFA produced by *Cogo* from the strings {01001101, 01010100} with maximum depth $L = 4$. Each edge in the GST has a substring and a transition probability. Dotted edges are suffix links in the GST. Each edge in the PFA has one symbol and a transition probability. Low probability edges are not shown for simplicity. To compute $P(010)$, we walk $\phi \rightarrow a \rightarrow b \rightarrow c$, giving $1 * 2/3 * 3/5 = 2/5$.

### 3.3 Detection

In the online phase, *Cogo* executes the PFAs as shadow state machines to the monitored program. Each measurement symbol results in a transition in the corresponding PFA of that measured resource type. Computing the probability of a sequence of symbols using a PFA reduces to walking the path corresponding to the symbols in the PFA, one transition at a time. This enables constant time online detection with minimal state keeping overhead, since only the current state and the transition symbol determine the next state.

For a sequence of $n$ measurements, a PFA allows us to compute the prediction probability in $O(n)$ time and $O(1)$ space. Given a PFA $M$ and a string of measurements $s = s_1 \ldots s_l$, and assuming that $M$ is currently in state $q_j$, we walk $M$ (for each $s_i \in s$) where each transition *emits* the transition probability. The prediction probability of $s$ by $M$ is computed as the multiplication of all emitted probabilities along the walked path. *Cogo* decides that the sequence $s$ is anomalous if the sequence resulted in at least $t$ low probability transition in the PFA. Specifically, *Cogo* performs the following test:

$$\left|\{\gamma(q_j, s_i) \leq \rho_{min}, i \in 1 \ldots l\}\right| \begin{cases} \leq t \rightarrow accept \\ > t \rightarrow reject \end{cases} \tag{2}$$

where $\gamma(q_j, s_i)$ is the transition probability of symbol $s_i$ outgoing from state $q_j$, $q_{j+1} = \tau(q_j, s_i)$ gives the next PFA state, and $t$ is the tolerance level. Recall that *Cogo* builds the PFAs such that low probability transitions are loop-back transitions, therefore they do not result in a state change in the PFA. This allows *Cogo* to offer tolerance by *forgetting* up to $t$ low probability transitions. If a sequence results in more than $t$ low probability transitions, *Cogo* raises an alarm.

### 3.4 Attaching to a Running Process

It is desirable in practice to be able to attach *Cogo* to a running process rather than starting a program under *Cogo*. For instance, attaching to running processes is essential for on-demand monitoring of processes that migrate among a cluster of servers. The main challenge in attaching to a run process in our context is that *Cogo* would not know in which states in the PFAs the process might be, nor how it got to those states. In other words, the process and the PFAs would not be in sync.

To resolve this, we developed the following non-deterministic PFA executor: First, *Cogo* attaches to the running program and starts monitoring at any arbitrary point in its execution. As measurements arrive, for each PFA for the target program, *Cogo* executes the PFA in a non-deterministic fashion by finding all paths that correspond to the incoming measurements, producing a set of potential paths $\mathcal{P}$ that the monitored process might have executed along. As more measurements arrive, *Cogo* extends each path in $\mathcal{P}$ by one transition at a time and checks if the detector accepts or rejects the new paths. A rejected path is eliminated from $\mathcal{P}$. Eventually, either all paths in $\mathcal{P}$ are eliminated or only a single path remains. If all paths are eliminated, meaning the process has deviated, *Cogo* raises an alarm. If a single path remains, then the PFA and the process have been successfully synchronized and *Cogo* returns to normal operation.

### 3.5 Seeing Through Containers

It is typical that web applications are deployed in isolated instances, i.e., multiple instances of the web server would be running in isolation from each other on the same host. Each instance gets its own isolated view of the systems resources — including file system, CPU, RAM, and network interfaces. Common isolation techniques are either based on full virtualization (e.g., virtual machines) or operating-system-level virtualization using software containers (e.g., OpenVZ, LXC, and Docker). Full virtualization does not pose an issue for *Cogo* since *Cogo* can be deployed inside the web server VM itself. On the other hand, containers abstract out the OS kernel, making it impossible to deploy *Cogo* inside an isolated container since *Cogo* requires kernel access. Therefore, *Cogo* needs to be deployed on the host (outside the containers) yet monitor processes running inside isolated containers.

The main hurdle of seeing through containers is that PIDs inside a container are *local* to that container, i.e., they only identify the process inside that container PID namespace. Quoting from the Linux kernel manual, "a namespace wraps a global system resource in an abstraction that makes it appear to the processes within the namespace that they have their own isolated instance of the global resource."[6] The local PID serves no meaning outside the container where a process is running. Instead, the process is identified by a different *global* PID only known to the host running the container. Without knowledge of the global PID of a process, *Cogo* cannot attach and monitor that process in kernel space since the global PID is the PID seen by the kernel tracer in kernel space. Note that there are no containers or namespaces in kernel space.

We implemented a container-aware global PID resolver to be able to identify processes running in namespaces. First, *Cogo* starts the process in a *suspended* state *inside* the container and gets the process id in the container namespace (NSPID). (The NSPID from the loader process is the PID local to the container where the process is running.) This is possible by creating a custom loader process that outputs its NSPID and its namespace identifier (NSID), then sends a stop signal to *itself*. (The NSID is a unique namespace identifier.) When the loader process receives a continue signal, it loads the desired target program via a call to the `exec` system call. Given the NSPID and NSID, *Cogo* searches all namespaces on the host system for a matching child NSID that contains a matching NSPID. Once identified, *Cogo* extracts the global PID of the process from the identified child namespace. It then attaches to that process (the loader) using the global PID and sends it a continue signal. Upon receiving the continue signal

[6] The Linux kernel manpage for namespaces is available at: http://man7.org/linux/man-pages/man7/namespaces.7.html.

by the loader, it loads and executes the desired target using the `exec` system call, replacing the process image but retaining any PIDs. *Cogo* then continues normal operation.

## 4 Implementation

We implemented *Cogo* by extending the code base of Radmin [25]. Radmin offered several integrated kernel space and user space tracing capabilities and an extensible PFA engine, which allowed us to implement and benchmark *Cogo* in a unified way. Figure 2 illustrates the architecture of *Cogo* within Radmin. We extended Radmin's kernel tracer to support network I/O monitoring, and implemented *Cogo*'s learning and detection algorithms by extending Radmin's PFA engine which originally only supported a quadratic time PFA construction (q-PFA in the figure). We also extended the framework to support attaching to running processes and monitoring containerized processes.

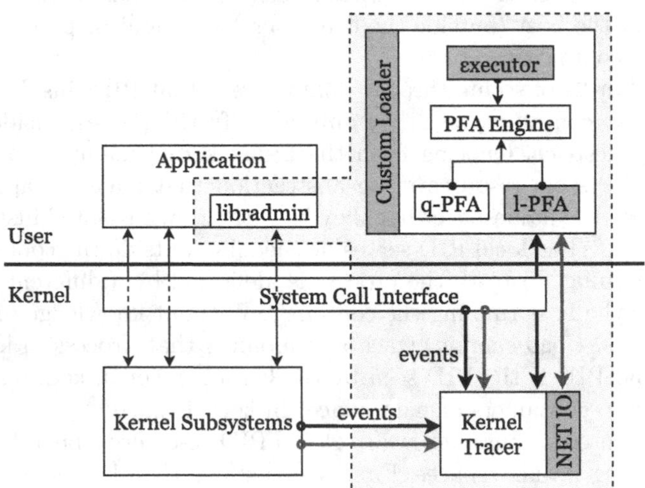


**Fig. 2.** *Cogo*'s architecture within Radmin. *Cogo* extends Radmin with a network I/O monitoring module, the linear PFA construction component, a non-deterministic PFA executor, and a custom loader to resolve namespace PIDs.

We extended Radmin's kernel tracer to support network I/O monitoring by attaching handlers to the relevant tracepoints [24] in the kernel. Kernel tracepoints are special points in the executable kernel memory that provide hooks to various events in the kernel. The hooks call functions (probes) that are provided at runtime by kernel modules. *Cogo* provided a handler for each tracepoint where it collected and reported the measurements to the rest of Radmin as needed. Each tracepoint executes in the context of the process that triggered the event. *Cogo* filters out process contexts using the global PIDs of the monitored processes.

**Table 1.** Kernel tracepoints hooked by *Cogo* for network I/O monitoring.

| Kernel tracepoint | Description |
|---|---|
| `socket.create` | A socket is allocated |
| `socket.close` | A socket is closed and released |
| `socket.sendmsg, socket.writev, socket.aoi_write, socket.write_iter` | Data is being sent on a socket |
| `socket.recvmsg, socket.readev, socket.aoi_read, socket.read_iter` | Data is received on a socket |

It supports monitoring a single process, all processes part of one program, or all processes in a process tree. Table 1 lists the relevant tracepoints that *Cogo* hooked to monitor network state.

## 5 Evaluation

We measured the detection accuracy, earliness, and overhead of *Cogo* on two large-scale server applications that are commonly targeted by application layer DoS attacks: Apache [2], the world's most used web server software; and OpenSIPS [9], the famous free VoIP server and proxy implementation of the session initiation protocol (SIP) [33]. The testbeds used Docker containers for isolation and CORE [15] for network emulation.

### 5.1 HTTP Attacks on Apache

Our Apache testbed is depicted in Fig. 3. It consisted of a server running Apache, one User Agent (UA) node for benign clients, and one Weaponized User Agent (W-UA) node for attackers. UA and W-UA consisted of Docker containers running HTTP clients. We generated benign traffic using an HTTP client model derived from Choi-Limb [22]. From the mean and standard deviation for various model parameters for the data set reported in [22], we used a nonlinear solver to calculate approximate distribution parameters for the distribution found to be a good fit in Choi-Limb. We represented each client using one instance of the HTTPerf [7] benchmark. For each client, we generated a workload session using a unique seed and the distilled distribution parameters. The session consisted of a series of requests with a variable think time between requests drawn from the client model. We generated the workload session in HTTPerf's workload session log format (wsesslog). Each client request contained as URL parameters a random request length padding and a requested response size drawn from the client model. The Apache server hosted a CGI-bin web application that simulated real deployments. For each client HTTP request, the server responded with content equal in byte length to the requested response size.

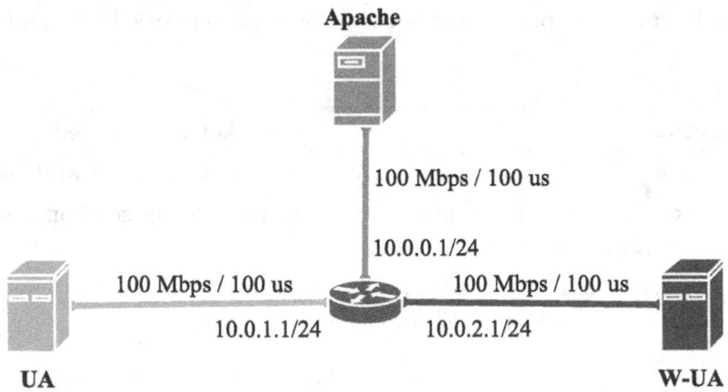


**Fig. 3.** HTTP DoS testbed used in our experiments, including the Apache server, a User Agent (UA) node where benign clients reside, and a Weaponized User Agent (W-UA) node where attacks originate from.

Attack traffic originated from the W-UA node. We used the HTTP application layer DoS benchmark SlowHTTPTest [4] which bundles several Slow-rate [11] attack variants. (Slow-rate attacks are low-bandwidth application layer DoS attacks that use legitimate albeit slow HTTP requests to take down web servers.) Two famous examples of Slow-rate attacks are Slowloris [12] and Slowread [5]. In Slowloris, attackers send the HTTP request headers as slowly as possible without hitting the connection timeout limit of the server. Its Slowread variant sends the headers at normal speeds but reads the response as slowly as possible. If enough of these slow requests are made in parallel, they can consume the entire server's application layer connections queue and the server becomes unable to serve legitimate users. Slow-rate attacks typically manifest in an abnormally large number of relatively idle or slow sockets.

We built *Cogo* model for Apache using 12 benign traffic runs, each of which consisted of one hour of benign traffic. We set the number of benign clients to 100. Note that each benign client is a whole workload session. For testing, we performed several experiments using blended benign and attack traffic by injecting attack requests at random points while serving a benign load. Testing is performed by running Apache under *Cogo* in detection mode, serving one hour worth of benign requests from 100 benign clients and 100 Slow-rate clients (attackers). The number of attackers represents the total concurrent SlowHTTPTest attack connections. We limited the attack duration to 15 min. We configured Apache to serve a maximum of 100 concurrent connections at any moment in time.

We performed each experiment with and without *Cogo*. We configured *Cogo* to kill the offending Apache worker process when an attack is detected.[7] Finally, we experimented with two types of attackers: non-aggressive attackers that seep

[7] More advanced remediation policies can be used, such as blocking offending source IPs, rate limiting, or protocol-specific recovery. We opted for process termination for simplicity as remediation is not the focus of *Cogo*.

in the server at a very slow rate, and aggressive attackers that bombard the server with as many concurrent connections as possible. For non-aggressive attackers, we set the SlowHTTPTest connection rate to one connection per second. For aggressive attackers, we set the connection rate to the server capacity, i.e., 100 connections per second.

**Detection Results.** Table 2 summarizes the results. It took *Cogo* only about 12 min to build a model for Apache from the benign measurements. This is about a 505× improvement over Radmin which took more than four days to construct a model from the same measurements. The savings in training time came at the expense of a slight increase in the model size (from 34 MB to 76 MB) which is acceptable and does not pose a bottleneck. The model is only loaded once at startup of *Cogo*; detection time is invariant of the model size as each measurement point results in exactly one transition in one of the PFAs.

*Cogo* achieved a very low false positive rate (FPR) at 0.0194% (about 91% better than Radmin). We believe the reason for this reduction in FPR is that *Cogo* retains longer low-probability paths in the PFA as the detection algorithm limits transition probabilities rather whole path probabilities as in Radmin. For the most part, false positives (FPs) were encountered during startup or shutdown of Apache which from experience has shown considerable variability.

**Table 2.** Summary of results for Apache. The number of requests was 473,558.

| Item | Radmin | *Cogo* | Improvement |
|---|---|---|---|
| Training time (sec.) | 379,661 | **752** | ▼ 505× |
| Model size (MB) | **34** | 76 | ▲ 0.45× |
| FPs, FPR | 1,116, 0.2357% | **92, 0.0194%** | ▼ 12× |
| Downtime (sec; non-aggressive) | 137 | **0** | ▼ ∞ |
| Downtime (sec; aggressive) | 58 | **7** | ▼ 8.3× |

Figures 4 and 5 depict the availability of Apache against non-aggressive and aggressive attacks. *Cogo* successfully prevented Apache from going down against non-aggressive attacks. As the attack connections were idling at the server side, *Cogo* detected anomalous transmit and receive rates and terminated the attacked Apache workers. This occurred within seven seconds from connection establishment. Against the same attacks, Apache under Radmin remained down for longer than two minutes. For aggressive attacks, Apache protected with Radmin was down for one minute, compared to only seven seconds under *Cogo*.

### 5.2 VoIP Attacks on OpenSIPS

Next, we considered detection of resource attacks on VoIP servers as telephony systems have increasingly become targets of DDoS attacks evidenced during the

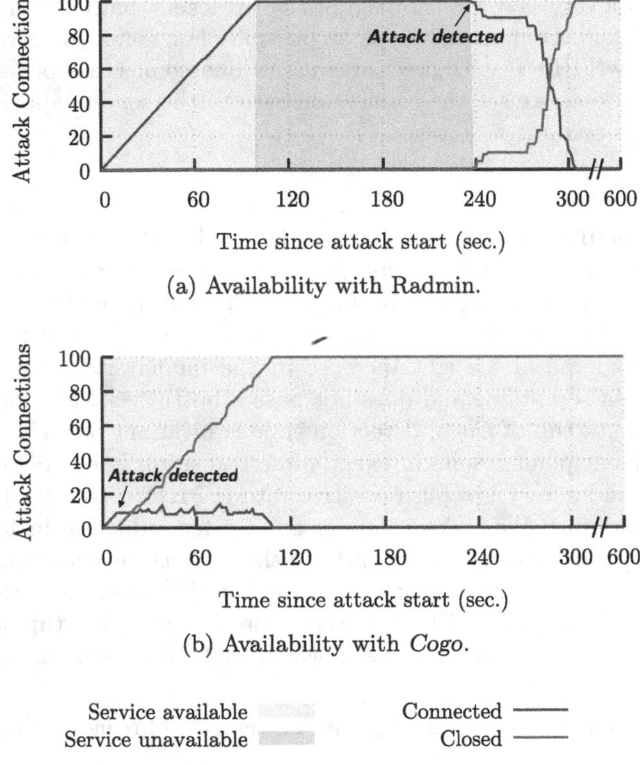


**Fig. 4.** Apache server availability against non-aggressive Slow-rate attacks. With Radmin, the server was down for more than two minutes. There was no downtime under *Cogo*.

2015 attack on the Ukrainian power grid [13]. To establish and manage calls, VoIP servers rely on Session Initiation Protocol (SIP) [33] which is known to be vulnerable to exhaustion and overload, even under benign conditions [29]. Overload can be caused by a variety of legitimate SIP behaviors such as response duplication, call forwarding, and call forking (conference calls) which result in large numbers of control packets that may congest servers. Similarly, excessive transactions cause system resource exhaustion in stateful servers when the number of requests exceeds the finite memory available to track each call state machine. An adversary who wishes to cause DoS can do so by initiating calls that exercise these legitimate but atypical resource intensive behaviors and thus degrade server performance — all while blending in with normal traffic (without malformed packets or specification violations) to circumvent defenses such as scrubbing or bandwidth limitation. In the following we evaluate *Cogo* against these protocol attacks on a representative SIP testbed based on OpenSIPS [9].

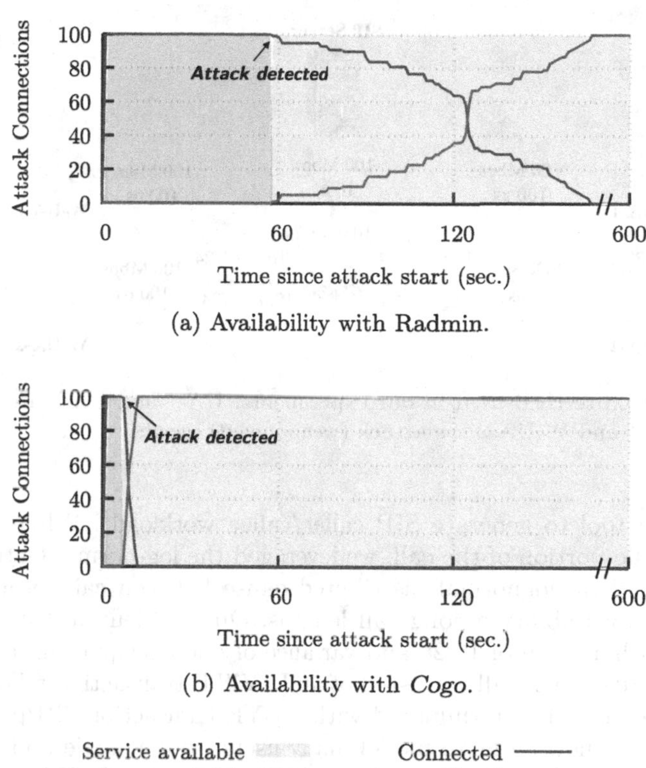


**Fig. 5.** Apache server availability against aggressive Slow-rate attacks. *Cogo* reduced the server down time by at least a factor of eight, down from 58 s to only seven seconds.

**Testbed and Procedure.** Our SIP DDoS testbed, shown in Figure 6, consisted of a SIP server and pairs of SIP user agents and weaponized agents that serviced simultaneous callers and attackers. The SIP server ran OpenSIPS 2.2 and was configured using the residential configuration generated by the OpenSIPS configuration tools. OpenSIPS used fixed-size shared and private memory across its child processes (32 MB and 16 MB respectively). To exacerbate memory exhaustion at the server, we adjusted the *wt_timer* of the OpenSIPS to 32 s (the recommended value in the RFC) which corresponds to the length of time a transaction is held in memory after it has completed. Though intended to help absorb delayed messages after the transaction completed, it also inadvertently reserves memory that could otherwise be made available to handle new calls. For the following experiments, we considered a small enterprise or large residential deployment, thus end-to-end delays from UA to server were minimal (ten ms) and link bandwidth was isolated to SIP traffic at 100 Mbps.

Pairs of UA nodes were used to represent benign SIP callers (UA-1) and callees (UA-2). These nodes ran instances of the SIP Proxy (SIPp) [10]: a SIP

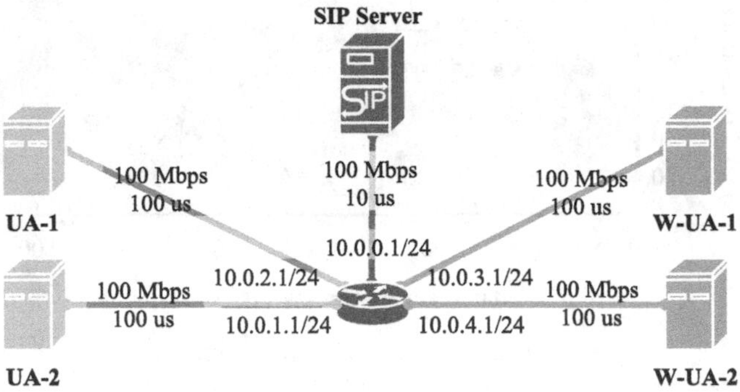


**Fig. 6.** SIP DDoS testbed used in our experiments. UA-1 and UA-2 are benign user agents. W-UA-1 and W-UA-2 are attack (weaponized) agents.

benchmarking tool to generate SIP caller/callee workloads. While we did not model the audio portion of the call, we leveraged the log-normal feature of SIPp to insert a random, lognormal distributed pause between call setup and hang up to simulate variability among call lengths. Our call length distribution was log-normal with a mean of 10.28 and variance of one ms equating to an average call length of 30 s. Each call consisted of an INVITE transaction followed by the variable pause, and then terminated with a BYE transaction. SIPp can initiate calls in parallel, allowing us to model many users from a single node.

Attacks were initiated from the W-UAs at caller W-UA-1 and callee W-UA-2. We staged attacks by repurposing SIPp as an attack tool, supplying it with scenario files that specify malicious caller/callee behaviors such as flooding requests or excessive duplication of responses. For example, a BYE flood attack equates to W-UA-1 initiating a number of spurious BYE transactions, each with a new call id to represent a new transaction. Because SIP does not associate a BYE with a prior INVITE, the BYE is accepted and transaction memory is wastefully reserved while the attack is in process. W-UA-2 colludes with W-UA-1 by purposefully not responding to the request, which adds to the time transaction memory is held at the server. Like the benign workload, we can tune the amplitude of SIPp to control the number of simultaneous attack calls.

The *Cogo* model for OpenSIPS was built from five benign observation collecting runs, totaling 8 h of benign measurements. During this observation run OpenSIPS was subjected to a benign load between the SIPp clients (UA-1, UA-2) and the SIP server. The clients initiated calls to the server. Call setup and call disconnect were specified using XML files input to SIPp and followed standard SIP call setup conventions for invite, ringing, bye, and appropriate response and status messages. Call hold used the SIPp log-normal distribution. The SIPp maximum calls per second rate was set to 10 and call limit to 200. This combination of SIPp settings produced a steady call rate of ∼7 calls every second. Several additional benign observation runs were made during which OpenSIPS was started and then terminated to ensure the observations captured startup

**Table 3.** Summary of OpenSIPS results. The number of benign call requests was 6,342.

| Item | Radmin | *Cogo* | Improvement |
|---|---|---|---|
| Training time (sec.) | 43,493 | **258** | ▼ 169× |
| Model size (MB) | **41** | 55 | ▲ 0.75× |
| FPs, FPR | 9, 0.1419% | **4, 0.0631%** | ▼ 2.25× |
| Bye flood detection delay (sec.) | ∞ | **6** | ▼ ∞ |
| Invite flood detection delay (sec.) | ∞ | **4** | ▼ ∞ |

and shutdown which from experience has shown considerable variability. The total size of the observation data was 515 MB. Processing these observations resulted in a model of 55 MB. Several test runs were made using the model and with it *Cogo* exhibited virtually zero false positives under a load with the same characteristics as that used for the observation runs.

**Detection Results.** Table 3 summarizes the results. *Cogo* reduced training time from about 12 h to only 4 min (greater than 169× reduction). The model size increased by a factor of only 0.75×, from 41 MB to 55 MB. In terms of accuracy, *Cogo* only had 4 FPs throughout the experiment. The four FPs all occurred at startup time of OpenSIPS. Radmin triggered 9 FPs also at startup time. The impact of BYE and INVITE floods on OpenSIPS, and the detection behavior of *Cogo* is shown in Fig. 7. The attacks were not detectable by Radmin since OpenSIPS uses a fixed size memory pool, therefore preventing memory exhaustion by the attack calls. In other words, without monitoring network I/O, it is impossible to early detect BYE and INVITE floods. *Cogo*, on the other hand, detected the attacks almost immediately, within less than six seconds after the attacks onset. Note that we did not implement any remediation policy for OpenSIPS; proper remediation requires a protocol-specific solution that times out or hangs up the attack calls.

### 5.3 Performance Overhead

*Cogo* effectively had a negligible overhead. We measured the throughput of Apache and OpenSIPS on the benign workloads with and without *Cogo*. Apache maintained a steady rate of 130 requests per second. We benchmarked Apache with HTTPerf and experienced a very marginal $0.2 \pm 0.3$ ms response time increase per request. The average response time increased from 10.3 ms to 10.5 ms. For OpenSIPS, it maintained a steady call rate of 200 calls per second. We experimented with call rates from 300 to 1000 calls per second and did not observe any degradation in throughput.

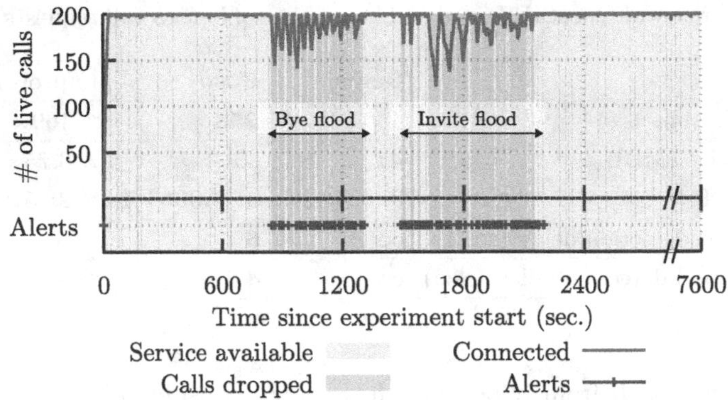


**Fig. 7.** *Cogo* detection of bye and invite floods against OpenSIPS.

# 6 Related Work

Modern operating systems have a number of threshold-based facilities to limit resource consumption (`ulimit`, `AppArmor` [3]). However, these limits are static upper bounds and disregard different consumption of different program segments for different inputs. This enables attackers to maximize the DoS time by crafting inputs that trigger prolonged resource consumption or starvation, such as Slow-rate attacks [21,23,30]. Several static and dynamic instrumentation tools exist for profiling, such as Valgrind [32] and Intel Pin [31]. However, the instrumentation overhead is often too high to enable their continuous usage, especially when detection of exhaustion is the goal [34,35]. Apostolico [18] presented a theoretic study for linear prediction using a Generalized Suffix Trees (GST). However, to the best of our knowledge, there is no implementation or a quantitative study of [18]. Our approach, builds a simpler model using a PFA construction that provided tight detection time and space guarantees instead of a GST.

In [14,30] there is a survey of different approaches for anomalous traffic detection which is not connected directly or indirectly to resource consumption at the application layer. Antunes et al. [17] proposed a system for testing servers for exhaustion vulnerabilities using fuzzed test cases from user-supplied specs of the server protocol. Groza et al. [27] formalized DoS attacks using a protocol-specific cost rules. Aiello et al. [16] formalized DoS resilience rules that protocols should meet but they are not feasible requirements in practice [37]. Chang et al. [20] proposed a static analysis system for identifying source code sites that may result in uncontrolled CPU time and stack consumption. The system employed taint analysis and control-dependency analysis to identify source code sites that can be influenced by untrusted input. Several similar approaches that required manual code annotation were also developed [28,38]. Closely related, Burnim et al. [19] used symbolic execution to generate inputs that exhibit worst case complexity.

*Cogo* substantially differs from those systems in that it does not require access to the source code or any side information and it covers network resources used by an application, not only CPU and memory. Elsabagh et al. [25] proposed Radmin, a system for early detection of application layer DoS attacks. This is the system we used as a starting point for *Cogo*. The system showed good accuracy and low overhead. However, it did not monitor network I/O, had a prohibitive quadratic training time, and could not monitor containerized processes or attach to a running process.

## 7 Conclusions

This paper presented *Cogo*, a practical and accurate system for early detection of DoS attacks at the application layer. Unlike prior solutions, *Cogo* builds a PFA model from the temporal and spatial resource usage information in linear time. *Cogo* monitors network state, supports containerized processes monitoring and attaching to running processes. *Cogo* detected real-world attacks on Apache and OpenSIPS, both are large-scale servers. It achieved high accuracy, early detection, and incurred negligible overhead. *Cogo* required less than 12 min of training time, incurred less than 0.0194% false positives rate, detected a wide range of attacks less than seven seconds into the attacks, and had a negligible response time overhead of only $0.2 \pm 0.3$ ms. *Cogo* is both scalable and accurate, suitable for large-scale deployment.

**Acknowledgments.** We thank the anonymous reviewers for their insightful comments and suggestions. This material is based upon work supported in part by the National Science Foundation (NSF) SaTC award 1421747, the National Institute of Standards and Technology (NIST) award 60NANB16D285, and the Defense Advanced Research Projects Agency (DARPA) contract no. HR0011-16-C-0061 in conjunction with Vencore Labs. Opinions, findings, conclusions, and recommendations expressed in this material are those of the authors and do not necessarily reflect the views of the NSF, NIST, DARPA or the US Government.

## References

1. myths of ddos attacks. http://blog.radware.com/security/2012/02/4-massive-myths-of-ddos/
2. The apache http server project. https://httpd.apache.org/
3. Apparmor. http://wiki.apparmor.net/index.php/Main_Page
4. Application layer DoS attack simulator. http://github.com/shekyan/slowhttptest
5. Are you ready for slow reading? https://blog.qualys.com/securitylabs/2012/01/05/slow-read
6. Availability overrides security. http://hrfuture.net/performance-and-productivity/availability-over-rides-cloud-security-concerns.php?Itemid=169
7. Httperf - http performance measurement tool. http://linux.die.net/man/1/httperf
8. Mobile users favor productivity over security. http://www.infoworld.com/article/2686762/security/mobile-users-favor-productivity-over-security-as-they-should.html
9. OpenSIPS: the new breed of communication engine. https://www.opensips.org/

10. Sipp: traffic generator proxy for the sip protocol. http://sipp.sourceforge.net/
11. Slow-Rate Attack. https://security.radware.com/ddos-knowledge-center/ddospedia/slow-rate-attack/
12. Slowloris - apache server vulnerabilities. https://security.radware.com/ddos-knowledge-center/ddospedia/slowloris/
13. When the lights went out: Ukraine cybersecurity threat briefing. https://www.boozallen.com/insights/2016/09/ukraine-cybersecurity-threat-briefing/
14. Denial of service attacks: A comprehensive guide to trends, techniques, and technologies. ADC Monthly Web Attacks Analysis 12 (2012)
15. Ahrenholz, J.: Comparison of core network emulation platforms. In: Military Communications Conference (2010)
16. Aiello, W., Bellovin, S.M., Blaze, M., Ioannidis, J., Reingold, O., Canetti, R., Keromytis, A.D.: Efficient, DoS-resistant, secure key exchange for internet protocols. In: 9th ACM Conference on Computer and Communications Security (2002)
17. Antunes, J., Neves, N.F., Veríssimo, P.J.: Detection and prediction of resource-exhaustion vulnerabilities. In: International Symposium on Software Reliability Engineering (2008)
18. Apostolico, A., Bejerano, G.: Optimal amnesic probabilistic automata. J. Comput. Biol. **7**(3–4), 381–393 (2000)
19. Burnim, J., Juvekar, S., Sen, K.: Wise: automated test generation for worst-case complexity. In: 31st International Conference on Software Engineering (2009)
20. Chang, R.M., et al.: Inputs of coma: static detection of denial-of-service vulnerabilities. In: 22nd Computer Security Foundations Symposium (2009)
21. Chee, W.O., Brennan, T.: Layer-7 ddos. (2010). https://www.owasp.org/images/4/43/Layer_7_DDOS.pdf
22. Choi, H.K., Limb, J.O.: A behavioral model of web traffic. In: 7th International Conference on Network Protocols (1999)
23. Crosby, S., Wallach, D.: Algorithmic dos. In: van Tilborg, H.C.A., Jajodia, S. (eds.) Encyclopedia of Cryptography and Security, pp. 32–33. Springer, USA (2011)
24. Desnoyers, M.: Using the linux kernel tracepoints. https://www.kernel.org/doc/Documentation/trace/tracepoints.txt
25. Elsabagh, M., Barbará, D., Fleck, D., Stavrou, A.: Radmin: early detection of application-level resource exhaustion and starvation attacks. In: 18th International Conference on Research in Attacks, Intrusions and Defenses (2015)
26. Gray, R.M., Neuhoff, D.L.: Quantization. IEEE Trans. Inform. Theory **44**(6), 2325–2383 (1998)
27. Groza, B., Minea, M.: Formal modelling and automatic detection of resource exhaustion attacks. In: Symposium on Information, Computer and Communications Security (2011)
28. Gulavani, B.S., Gulwani, S.: A numerical abstract domain based on expression abstraction and max operator with application in timing analysis. In: Computer Aided Verification, pp. 370–384 (2008)
29. Hilt, V., Eric, N., Charles, S., Ahmed, A.: Design considerations for session initiation protocol (SIP) overload control (2011). https://tools.ietf.org/html/rfc6357
30. Kostadinov, D.: Layer-7 ddos attacks: detection and mitig. InfoSec Institute (2013)
31. Luk, C.K., Cohn, R., Muth, R., Patil, H., Klauser, A., Lowney, G., Wallace, S., Reddi, V.J., Hazelwood, K.: Pin: building customized program analysis tools with dynamic instrumentation. In: Proceedings of the 2005 ACM SIGPLAN Conference on Programming Language Design and Implementation, PLDI 2005, pp. 190–200. ACM, New York (2005). http://doi.acm.org/10.1145/1065010.1065034

32. Nethercote, N., Seward, J.: Valgrind: a framework for heavyweight dynamic binary instrumentation. In: ACM Sigplan Notices, vol. 42, pp. 89–100. ACM (2007)
33. Rosenberg, J., et al.: SIP: Session initiation protocol (2002). https://www.ietf.org/rfc/rfc3261.txt
34. Ruiz-Alvarez, A., Hazelwood, K.: Evaluating the impact of dynamic binary translation systems on hardware cache performance. In: International Symposium on Workload Characterization (2008)
35. Uh, G.R., Cohn, R., Yadavalli, B., Peri, R., Ayyagari, R.: Analyzing dynamic binary instrumentation overhead. In: Workshop on Binary Instrumentation and Application (2007)
36. Ukkonen, E.: Online construction of suffix trees. Algorithmica **14**(3), 249–260 (1995)
37. Zargar, S.T., Joshi, J., Tipper, D.: A survey of defense mechanisms against distributed denial of service (ddos) flooding attacks. IEEE Commun. Surv. Tutorials **15**(4), 2046–2069 (2013)
38. Zheng, L., Myers, A.C.: End-to-end availability policies and noninterference. In: 18th IEEE Workshop Computer Security Foundations (2005)

# Exploring the Ecosystem of Malicious Domain Registrations in the .eu TLD

Thomas Vissers[1(✉)], Jan Spooren[1], Pieter Agten[1], Dirk Jumpertz[2], Peter Janssen[2], Marc Van Wesemael[2], Frank Piessens[1], Wouter Joosen[1], and Lieven Desmet[1]

[1] Imec-DistriNet, KU Leuven, Leuven, Belgium
{thomas.vissers,jan.spooren,pieter.agten,frank.piessens,wouter.joosen, lieven.desmet}@cs.kuleuven.be
[2] EURid VZW, Brussels, Belgium
{dirk.jumpertz,peter.janssen,marc.wesemael}@eurid.eu

**Abstract.** This study extensively scrutinizes 14 months of registration data to identify large-scale malicious campaigns present in the .eu TLD. We explore the ecosystem and modus operandi of elaborate cybercriminal entities that recurrently register large amounts of domains for one-shot, malicious use. Although these malicious domains are short-lived, by incorporating registrant information, we establish that at least 80.04% of them can be framed in to 20 larger campaigns with varying duration and intensity. We further report on insights in the operational aspects of this business and observe, amongst other findings, that their processes are only partially automated. Finally, we apply a post-factum clustering process to validate the campaign identification process and to automate the ecosystem analysis of malicious registrations in a TLD zone.

**Keywords:** Malicious domain names · Campaigns · DNS security

## 1 Introduction

The Domain Name System (DNS) is one of the key technologies that has allowed the web to expand to its current dimensions. Virtually all communication on the web requires the resolution of domain names to IP addresses. Malicious activities are no exception, and attackers constantly depend upon functioning domain names to execute their abusive operations. For instance, phishing attacks, distributing spam emails, botnet command and control (C&C) connections and malware distribution: these activities all require domain names to operate.

Widely-used domain blacklists are curated and used to stop malicious domain names[1] shortly after abusive activities have been observed and reported. As a

[1] We use the term *malicious domain name* whenever we refer to a domain name that is registered to be bound to a malicious service or activity.

**Electronic supplementary material** The online version of this chapter (doi:10.1007/978-3-319-66332-6_21) contains supplementary material, which is available to authorized users.


M. Dacier et al. (Eds.): RAID 2017, LNCS 10453, pp. 472–493, 2017.
DOI: 10.1007/978-3-319-66332-6_21

consequence, attackers changed to a hit-and-run strategy, in which malicious domain names are operational for only a very small time window after the initial registration, just for a single day in 60% of the cases [11]. Once domain names have fulfilled their purpose, attackers can simply abandon them and register a new set of domain names to ensure continuity of their criminal activities [24].

This strategy is economically viable to the attackers when the cost of registering a domain name is minimal. However, this approach requires repetitive and often automated domain name registrations. We refer to these series of malicious domain names registered by a single entity as *campaigns*. To obscure their actions, attackers often use fake registration details and need to switch between identities, registrars and resellers to avoid detection.

Moreover, we have observed that certain underground services pop up to facilitate the bulk domain registration process for abusive activities. For instance, on the darknet forum "AlphaBay", we found several instances of "Domain and Email Registration as a Service". In one example[2], cyber criminals register new domain names and create fresh, private email accounts that are sold to be used for illegal activities, such as carding.

The sheer volume of malicious domain names, as well as the fact that the registration process is being automated and monetized, illustrates the need for strong insights into the modus operandi of cybercriminals to produce effective countermeasures.

In this paper, we focus on the malicious campaign ecosystem by extensively leveraging the registrant and registration details, with the goal to better understand how miscreants operate to acquire a constant stream of domain names. We rigorously investigate 14 months of .eu domain registrations, a top 10 ccTLD [15] for the European Economic Area. Overall, the dataset of this study contains 824,121 new domain registrations; 2.53% of which have been flagged as malicious by blacklisting services.

Among others, the following conclusions can be drawn from this in-depth assessment:

1. While most malicious domains are short-lived, a large fraction of them can be attributed to a small set of malicious actors: 80.04% of the malicious registrations are part of just 20 long-running campaigns. We identified campaigns that were active for over a year, and campaigns that registered more than 2,000 blacklisted domains (Sect. 3).
2. The campaign identification process suggests that 18.23% of malicious domains does not end up on a blacklist (Sect. 3.3).
3. The malicious domain registration process is only partially automated: underground syndicates work along office hours, take holiday breaks and make human errors while registering domains (Sect. 4).
4. Ecosystem analysis can be automated and reproduced by leveraging clustering algorithms. In our experiment, the 30 largest clusters formed by agglomera-

[2] http://pwoah7foa6au2pul.onion/forum/index.php?threads/%E2%96%84-%E2%96%88-%E2%98%85-paperghost-%E2%98%85-%E2%96%88-%E2%96%84-fresh-non-hacked-private-email-logins-lower-your-fraud-detection-score-2.71566.

tive clustering encompass 91.48% of blacklisted campaign registrations. These clusters exhibit a clear mapping with manually identified campaigns (Sect. 5).

The remainder of this paper is structured as follows. First, in Sect. 2, we introduce the data set used in this research, along with initial insights. Next, we perform a large scale experiment to manually identify malicious campaigns (Sect. 3), followed by several analyses to gather more insights (Sect. 4). In Sect. 5, we follow up with a method to automate campaign identification. We discuss applications and limitations in Sect. 6, followed by a summary of related work in Sect. 7. Lastly, we conclude this study in Sect. 8.

## 2 Datasets and Initial Findings

In this section, we present the data used in this research and give initial insights based on a first, high-level analysis.

### 2.1 Registration Data

We analyzed 824,121 .eu domain registrations between April 1, 2015 and May 31, 2016. We inspected the following fields:

**Basic registration information** contains the domain name, the date and time of registration, and the registrar via which the registration happened.

**Contact information** of the registrant contains the company name, name, the language, email address, phone, fax, as well as postal address information. We decomposed two additional attributes from the email address: the email account and the email provider.

**Nameservers** or glue records that are responsible for resolving entries within the domain. We enriched the nameserver data with their geographical location by resolving the NS records and adding IP geolocation data.

### 2.2 Blacklists

To capture whether or not a domain was used in malicious activity, a set of public blacklists was queried on a daily basis. Each new domain is monitored daily during 1 month after registration. Afterwards, all domains were checked once more 4 months after the last registration in our dataset. The following blacklist services have been used:

**dbl.spamhaus.org blacklist** [21]. This Spamhaus blacklist is queried using their DNS API, and provides indicators for botnet C&C domains, malware domains, phishing domains, and spam domains.

**multi.surbl.org blacklist** [20]. SURBL features a combination of different lists, such as abuse, phishing, malware, etc. The combined SURBL list is queried over DNS.

**Google's Safe Browsing list** [7]. Google's Safe Browsing list is queried via a Web API, and provides indicators for malware domains, phishing domains, and domains hosting unwanted software, as described in [8].

### 2.3 Preliminary Insights

Given the data described above, we present a preliminary analysis to provide insights in the general trends and patterns of malicious registrations.

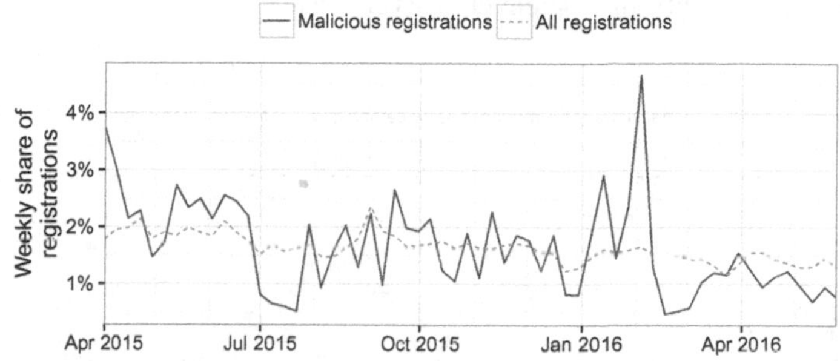


**Fig. 1.** Weekly share of malicious and all registrations over time.

Observing the 824,121 registrations that occurred between April 1, 2015 and May 31, 2016, we find that 2.53% end up on a blacklist. This corresponds to a total of 20,870 registrations used by cyber criminals in the given 14 month time span. Figure 1 shows the weekly share of both malicious and all registrations over this period. The differences in intensity of malicious registrations are moderately correlated with those of all registrations ($\rho = 0.54$). However, the variance of malicious registrations is clearly much larger. Most of the increased malicious activity, for instance at the start of February 2016, can be attributed to a single malicious campaign. These cases are discussed in depth in Sect. 3.

The selected blacklists return metadata that encode the reason(s) why a particular domain name was flagged. In our records, 93.68% of the blacklisted domains in the dataset is labelled for spam, 2.09% for malware infrastructure, 0.57% for unwanted software, and 3.22% for phishing activities.

Most domains appear on blacklists very shortly after their registration. More specifically, 72.93% of malicious domains were flagged within 5 days of delegation. 98.57% of malicious registrations are listed on a blacklist in their first month.

## 3 Campaign Identification Experiment

Typically, illegal online activities do not occur in an isolated or dispersed fashion [5,11]. Instead, malicious actors commonly set up campaigns that involve multiple, tightly related abusive strategies, techniques and targets. Through an in-depth, a posteriori analysis of the .eu dataset, we assessed whether such patterns can be identified between domain registrations and to what extent these registrations happen in bulk.

Ultimately, we manually identified 20 distinct campaigns responsible for the vast majority of malicious registrations. A campaign represents a series of registrations over time, with strong similarities in terms of registration data (e.g. the registrar, the registrant's address information, phone number or email address, and the set of nameservers). Moreover, a campaign can most probably be attributed to a single individual or organization. In this section, we first give a more thorough description on how these campaigns were identified, followed by some general insights into their characteristics.

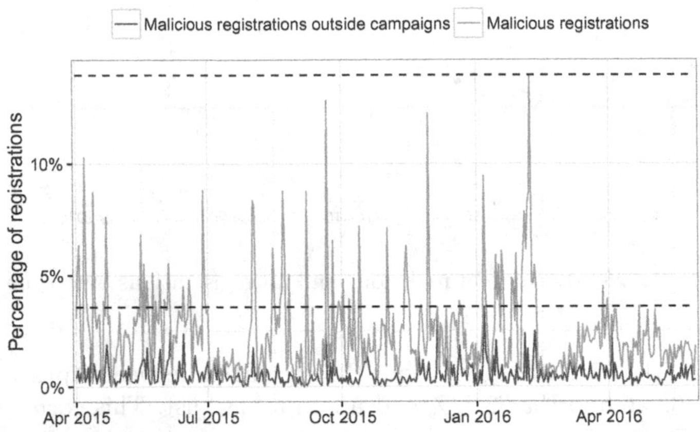


**Fig. 2.** Daily percentage of malicious registrations, including and excluding campaign registrations. The dotted lines represent the highest daily concentration of both sets.

### 3.1 Campaign Identification Process

As malicious registrations often occur in batches [10,11], high temporal concentrations can serve as a preliminary indicator of campaign activity. Figure 2 plots the relative amount of malicious registrations on each day. That graph can be used to identify the time periods in which the amount of malicious registrations was surging. If a campaign was responsible for a high concentration of malicious registrations, a substantial subset of registrations within that timeframe should be related to each other. Hence, all malicious registrations that occurred in that time span are examined to find common characteristics in the registration data. These can be recurring values or distinct patterns in the email address, the address info, the registrar, the registrant name, etc. To detect useful outliers, we visualized correlations between registration fields. For example, by plotting the email providers of the registrants versus the country listed in their street address (as shown in Fig. 3), multiple hotspots of malicious registrations can be found that contribute to one or more campaigns. These unique combinations and patterns form the basis of the manually assigned campaign selection criteria. To evaluate these, we apply them to the full dataset, i.e. on both benign and blacklisted registrations, over all 14 months. If the criteria match multiple active days and contain a substantial number of blacklisted domains, they are withheld as a new campaign. This process was repeated iteratively, reducing the number of malicious concentrations each time.

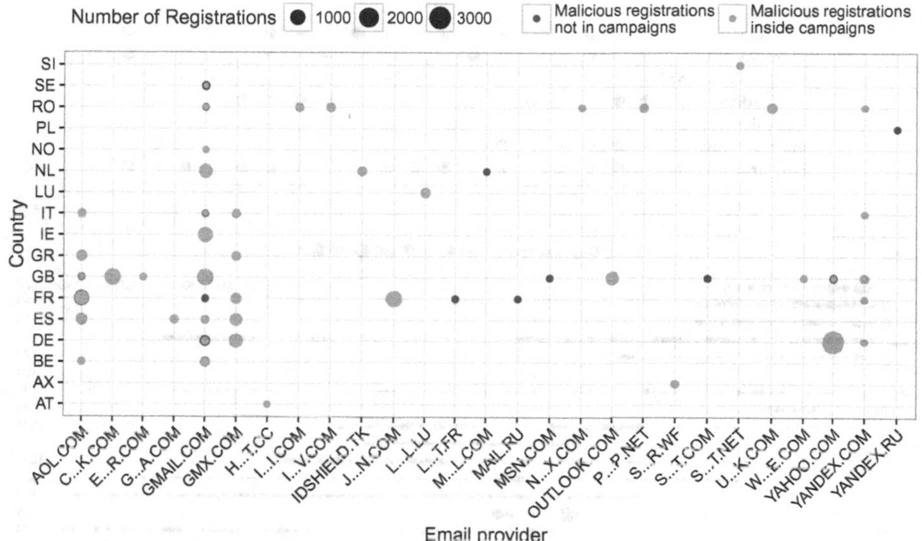


**Fig. 3.** Malicious registrations, grouped by email provider and country of the registrant. For visibility, combinations with less that 50 registrations are left out of the figure. Moreover, email providers with less than 50 distinct email addresses in the dataset have been obfuscated for privacy reasons.

Over the complete dataset, we identify 20 distinct campaigns. A variety of attributes of the registration details have been used to characterize a campaign, the specifics for each campaign are listed in Table 1.

### 3.2 General Campaign Observations

The activity of the 20 identified campaigns is depicted in Fig. 4. A first observation is that most of the campaigns are long-living: only one campaign runs for less than a month, while some campaigns run up to a year and more[3].

Secondly, campaigns strongly vary in their activity patterns. Some campaigns are active on almost a daily basis (e.g. campaign c_19), whereas others only have a few distinct active days throughout their lifetime (e.g. campaign c_07). Similarly, campaigns vary in concentration. An intense, six week campaign was for instance responsible for almost 2,000 new registrations (c_20), whereas one

[3] Note that some campaigns might be running even longer than 372 days, as they might have been active before the starting date of our dataset (campaigns c_01 - c_05) or they may still be active past the time span that is covered in our dataset.

**Table 1.** Attributes used to express the selection criteria of a campaign. ● represents a string match, and ☆ a regular expression pattern.

| | Campaign | | | | | | | | | | | | | | | | | | | |
|---|---|---|---|---|---|---|---|---|---|---|---|---|---|---|---|---|---|---|---|---|
| Criteria | 1 | 2 | 3 | 4 | 5 | 6 | 7 | 8 | 9 | 10 | 11 | 12 | 13 | 14 | 15 | 16 | 17 | 18 | 19 | 20 |
| domain name | – | – | – | – | ☆ | – | – | – | – | – | – | – | – | – | – | – | – | – | – | – |
| registrar | – | – | – | ● | – | – | – | – | ● | – | – | ● | – | – | ● | – | – | – | – | ● |
| nameservers | – | – | – | ☆ | – | – | – | ● | – | – | – | – | – | – | ☆ | – | – | – | – | ● |
| name | ☆ | – | – | – | – | – | – | – | – | – | – | – | – | – | – | – | – | – | – | – |
| address | – | ● | ● | ☆ | – | ● | – | – | – | – | – | – | ● | ● | ☆ | ● | – | – | – | – |
| organization | ☆ | – | – | – | – | – | – | – | – | – | – | – | – | – | – | – | – | – | – | – |
| email account | – | – | ☆ | ☆ | – | – | ● | – | – | – | – | ☆ | – | – | – | – | – | – | ● | – |
| email provider | ● | – | ● | ● | ● | – | ● | – | ● | ● | ● | – | – | – | ☆ | ● | – | ● | ● | ● |

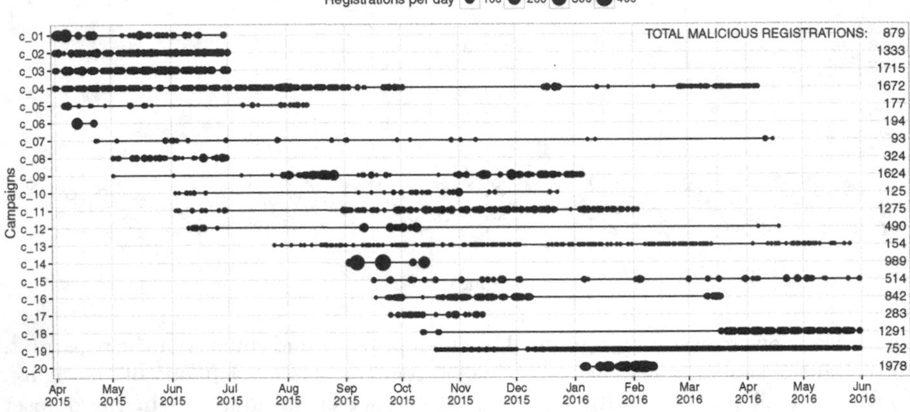


**Fig. 4.** Campaign duration and activity over time. The black lines represent the overall duration of the campaign, while the black dots indicate the number of malicious registrations on that day.

steady campaign ran over 10 months and produced only 154 malicious registrations (c_13).

A third observation is that campaigns contribute to a large fraction of malicious registrations found in the .eu registration data. Together, the 20 campaigns cover 16,704 domain registrations, that appeared on blacklists. This represents 80.04% of the 20,780 blacklisted registrations in our dataset.

Lastly, not all registrations identified as part of a campaign are flagged as malicious. In total, 19.30% of the campaign registrations we identified are not known as abusive domains by blacklisting services. A more in-depth analysis of these potential false positives is discussed in Sect. 3.3. Note that to avoid any bias, Fig. 4 only include registrations that appeared on blacklists, and thus represent a lower bound of campaign activity.

### 3.3 Validation of Campaign Selection Criteria

As briefly mentioned in the previous section, 19.30% of the registrations associated with malicious campaigns do not appear on blacklists. We expect that various reasons contribute to this mismatch:

1. **Incomplete coverage by blacklists.** As blacklists are not exhaustive oracles, we expect that certain domains in a campaign may simply not have been picked up by the specific set of blacklists used.
2. **Not abused.** It is possible that a number of campaign registrations simply has not been used for malicious purposes (yet).
3. **False positives.** Some of our campaign criteria might not be strict enough, introducing false positive matches.

Figure 5 depicts in red the percentage of registrations for each individual campaign that appears on a blacklist. There are three campaigns with less than 60% of their registrations blacklisted: c_05, c_11 and c_15. In the remainder of this section we validate the quality of the campaign selection criteria. We attempt to gauge the real false positive rate by inspecting domains belonging to campaigns, but do not appear on blacklists. A high false positive rate would imply that the selection criteria are imprecise and include a significant set of domains that were registered without any malicious intent. In contrast, a very high true positive rate implies that the selection criteria are substantially more exhaustive in defining domains with malicious intent compared to blacklisting services.

**Transitive Attribution.** To assess the prevalence of incomplete blacklists and not-active malicious domains, we examine the registrant data of false positives in order to find undeniable traces that connect them to malicious domains. We base this transitive attribution on phone numbers as these are uniquely assigned identifiers that were never used in our campaign selection criteria. Thus, if the registrant's phone number is identical to that of a blacklisted registration, we consider the domain name to be part of the malicious campaign and assume that it has either not been abused yet, or was not picked up by a blacklist. In total, 3,252 campaign domains are transitively considered as malicious. As shown in yellow in Fig. 5, 14 of the 20 identified campaigns are thereby completely validated.

A threat to using phone numbers to identify malicious registrants arises when an attacker retrieves the WHOIS information of a legitimate .eu domain and falsely uses it for his own registration. With three small experiments, we try to invalidate the presence of this scenario in the transitive attributed set. Firstly, we measure the time interval between the registration time of a transitively attributed domain and of the blacklisted domain that it was associated with. We find that for 2,058 domains, the malicious registration (with the same phone number) occurred within 60 s of the transitively attributed registration. We argue that it is virtually impossible for an attacker to observe a new registration (which is non-public information in the .eu zone), query its WHOIS data and subsequently make a similar registration in that time interval. In a second experiment, we argue that an attacker would not exploit a benign registrant's information if those contact details are already tainted. In that regard, we filter out 965 of the remaining domains that were registered after a prior registration with the same phone number was already blacklisted. Lastly, we consult a phone number verification tool [22] and identify invalid phone numbers for 189 of the 229 remaining domains. We presume that a malicious actor would not steal benign registrant details with an invalid phone number while attempting to mimic a legitimate registrant. In the end, we observe one of these three indicators for 3,212 (98.77%) of the transitively attributed domains and conclude that this attribution is justified.

**In-Depth Analysis of Campaign C_15.** After the transitive attribution step, still 30.6% of the registrations in campaign c_15 remain potential false positives. This set of domain names is further investigated.

Within campaign c_15, all domain names are composed of concatenated Dutch words (mostly 2 words, but sometimes up to 4). The same words are frequently reused, indicating that a limited dictionary was used to generate the domain names. The remaining 583 potential false positives domain names were split up by a native Dutch speaker in segments of existing words. 396 of these unflagged domain names turned out to be exclusively constructed out of Dutch words used in blacklisted domains of the campaign. As this is a very specific pattern, these domains have been labeled as *validated true positive*. The remaining domain names had either one word segment in common (172 domains) or no common word at all (15 domains). Thereafter, a new iteration of transitive attribution strategy was applied on that remaining set. Hereby, 147 registrations shared a phone number with the previously validated registrations, reducing the potential false positives to just 40 registrations.

Interstingly, we find that 95 out of the 98 registrant names that are used in c_15 can be generated with on of the Laravel Faker generator tool forks [16] using its nl-NL language option.

**Manual Analysis of the Remaining False Positives.** After the transitive attribution and the analysis of c_15, the residual potential false positives in all campaigns were further investigated manually, by querying DNS records, visiting websites, and searching on blacklists (e.g. *URLVoid* [23]) and search engines. Only two additional domains could be validated as true positives: one registration in campaign c_04 was identified as a phishing website by FortiGuard [6], and one registration in campaign c_15 sent out unsolicited to a temporary email account on email-fake.com.

**Summary of Validation.** Of the 20,698 campaign registrations, 16,704 domains (80.73%) were flagged by blacklisting services, 3,252 registrations (15.71%) were linked to malicious domains via transitive attribution, and 552 (2.67%) have been manually validated as registered with malicious intent.

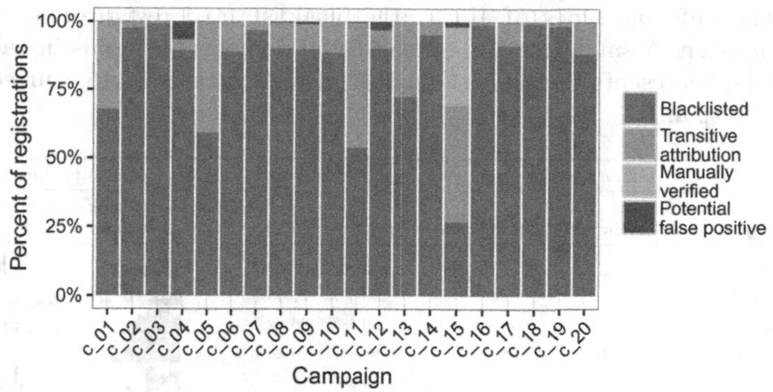


**Fig. 5.** Extended false positive analysis of each campaign. (Color figure online)

To conclude, the campaign selection criteria resulted in only 190 potential false positives (i.e. 0.92%). This is a strong indicator that the selection criteria are sufficiently accurate to perform a representative analysis and to give us the necessary insights into the malicious domain ecosystem.

## 4 Insights into Malicious Campaigns

In this section, we discuss several interesting observations regarding malicious campaigns, found during our assessment.

**Abuse Indicators and Categories.** Overall, the vast majority of blacklisted domains (93.68%) were associated with spam domains. As listed in Table 2, all campaigns follow this general distribution, except for c_19 where nearly 28% is linked to botnet C&C servers.

Spamhaus DBL and SURBL are the two abuse sources that cover the largest number of domains. While there is a considerable overlap, both are required to get an exhaustive coverage of all campaigns. In particular, c_1 and c_19 are exclusively flagged by just one of the two sources. Interestingly, Google Safe Browsing was not involved in flagging domains in any of the campaigns. Presumably, Safe Browsing focuses more on malware delivery, as opposed to malicious infrastructure.

**Cross-Campaign Characteristics.** Some interesting characteristics exist across multiple campaigns. For instance, c_03, c_04 and c_20 generate the registrant's email address from its name followed with a numerical suffix. Similarly, the registered domain names in c_05 and c_11 follow clear character patterns with numerical suffixes. Another returning peculiarity is the discrepancy between the registrant's street address and his country. c_07, c_9, c_13 and c_14 use valid street addresses located outside of Europe (US and Panama) in combination with a European country (Norway, Ireland and others). Presumably, this is to partly confuse the residential requirements for registering a .eu domain. In

**Table 2.** The different types of abuse, the blacklists and registration timing patterns per campaign. A small fraction of blacklisted domains has a missing abuse type. The max. burst represents the highest number of registrations that occurred within a 60-second time span.

| | Abuse types | | | | | Blacklist sources | | | Registration timing patterns | | |
|---|---|---|---|---|---|---|---|---|---|---|---|
| Campaign | Spam | Botnet | Malware | Phishing | Unwanted | Spamhaus | SURBL | Google SB | Day of week (Mon-Sun) | Hour of day (00-23h) | Max. burst |
| c_01 | 100.00% | | | | | | 100.00% | | | | 99 |
| c_02 | 100.00% | | | | | 100.00% | 27.53% | | | | 59 |
| c_03 | 100.00% | | | | | 99.48% | 86.82% | | | | 51 |
| c_04 | 99.88% | | 0.12% | 1.38% | | 99.64% | 76.26% | | | | 28 |
| c_05 | 83.05% | | | | | 12.99% | 77.97% | | | | 9 |
| c_06 | 100.00% | | | | | 87.63% | 12.37% | | | | 3 |
| c_07 | 91.40% | | | | | 91.40% | 1.08% | | | | 10 |
| c_08 | 100.00% | | | | | 100.00% | 3.70% | | | | 19 |
| c_09 | 99.63% | | 0.12% | 1.97% | | 99.26% | 28.45% | | | | 46 |
| c_10 | 99.20% | | | 1.60% | | 78.40% | 90.40% | | | | 48 |
| c_11 | 85.18% | | 0.08% | | | 16.00% | 77.02% | | | | 59 |
| c_12 | 99.59% | | | 0.20% | | 99.39% | 74.29% | | | | 23 |
| c_13 | 96.75% | | | | | 81.82% | 19.48% | | | | 1 |
| c_14 | 100.00% | | | | | 84.43% | 86.05% | | | | 132 |
| c_15 | 97.28% | | | | | 73.35% | 33.46% | | | | 13 |
| c_16 | 100.00% | | | 0.12% | | 100.00% | 43.71% | | | | 8 |
| c_17 | 100.00% | | | | | 100.00% | 8.83% | | | | 18 |
| c_18 | 99.85% | | | 0.15% | | 99.77% | 28.04% | | | | 10 |
| c_19 | 72.07% | 27.93% | | | | 100.00% | | | | | 5 |
| c_20 | 99.29% | | 0.96% | | | 99.14% | 7.58% | | | | 19 |
| All malicious | 93.68% | 1.27% | 0.85% | 3.22% | 0.57% | 81.07% | 50.04% | 1.81% | | | |

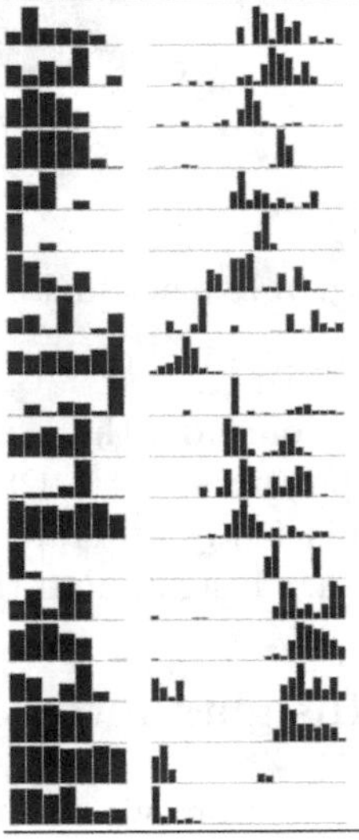

the case of c_10, a fixed street address is listed throughout the campaign while 10 different countries are combined with it.

**Registration Process is Not Fully Automated.** While performing the in-depth analysis of the malicious domain registrations, we found multiple indications that the malicious registration process in (at least some of) the campaigns is not fully automated: syndicates work along office hours and make human errors while registering domains.

*Office hours and holiday breaks.* As expected, the overall registrations in the .eu zone follow a weekly pattern. Figure 6 demonstrates this by zooming into 1 month of registrations. During weekends, a significantly smaller amount of registrations occurs than during the week. On average, week days have 2.34 times more registrations than weekend days. For blacklisted registrations, the difference is even more prominent. During weekend days, 3.85 times less malicious registrations occur as compared to weekdays. Moreover, several weekend days have no blacklisted registrations at all. Table 2 displays this behavior separately for each campaign.

As already mentioned in Sect. 2, the distribution over time of malicious registrations is much more fluctuating than those of all registrations (Fig. 1). Interestingly, the longer drops in malicious registration activity coincide with holiday periods. The most significant one starts at the first week of July and continues for several weeks, concurring with the summer holidays. The other major periods of recess correspond to Labour day weekend (May 1), the Christmas holidays (last week of December) and the beginning of Lent or Carnival (mid-February).

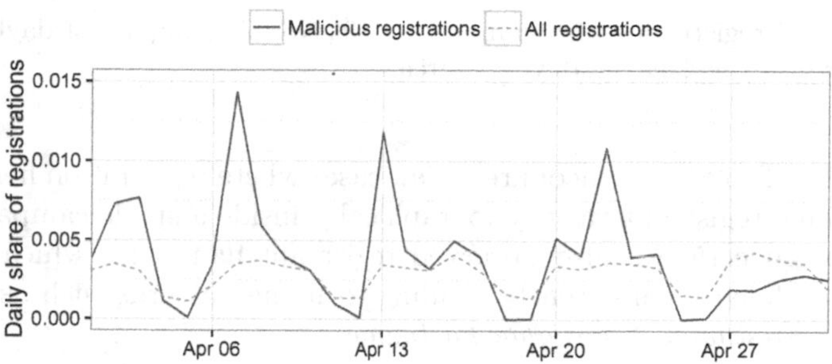


**Fig. 6.** Daily share of all and malicious registrations between April 1, 2015 and April 20, 2015. A clear weekly pattern is measured for both.

There are multiple hypotheses to explain these registration patterns:

1. Malicious actors might deliberately mimic normal registration patterns to avoid detection.
2. There might be a lower demand for new malicious domains during holidays, when potential victims are less active online.
3. Cybercriminal activities could be managed as any other business and are therefore equally susceptible to vacation periods.

To substantiate the latter hypothesis, we also zoomed in into the variation in registration time per campaign. Interestingly, as shown in Table 2 displays this separately for each campaign, we identified that some of the campaigns clearly align with a typical day at the office. For instance, in campaign c_11 and c_18 syndicates are working 8 to 10 h a day, and the daily pattern of c_11 even suggests that there is sufficient time to take a lunch break. In contrast, the daily registration pattern of campaign c_19, further illustrated in Fig. 7, hints at a more automated process. The vast majority of registrations are made daily at midnight and 1 PM. Furthermore, campaigns such as c_14 are registering at a rate up to 132 new domains per minute, suggesting underlying automation.

*Minor inconsistencies in the data.* We observe a number of inconsistencies in several registration details of certain campaigns. These inconsistencies could be the consequence of small errors or typos, suggesting that some of the data has been manually entered into scripts or registration forms, or that different input validation rules have been applied by registrars or resellers.

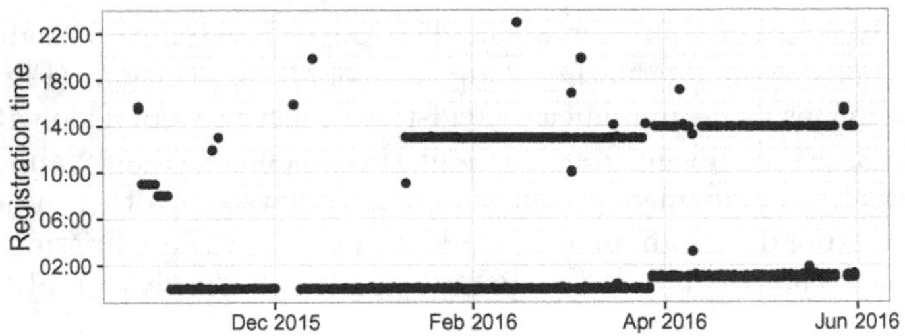


**Fig. 7.** Times of registrations for campaign c_19. Note the impact of daylight saving time starting from the last Sunday of March.

As listed in Table 3, we encounter a few cases where registration fields belonging to the same registrant vary typographically inside a single campaign.

In campaign c_15, we also observed registrant names for which the name field has been filled inconsistently, leading to name patterns such as *Lastname Lastname* or *Firstname Firstname Lastname.*

**Table 3.** Minor inconsistencies found in the registration details campaign domains. Some registration details have been obfuscated for privacy reasons.

| Attribute | Inconsistencies | |
|---|---|---|
| c_04 street | P.O BOX 3...4 | P.O BOX 3...4, |
| c_11 city | AIX EN PROVENCE | AIX-EN-PROVENCE |
| c_11 street | 1... ROUTE D AVIGNON | 1... ROUTE D'AVIGNON |
| c_16 street | 947 C...R | 9457 C...R |

**Adaptive Registration Strategies.** Several campaigns alter their strategies throughout their lifetime. For instance, five campaigns have registered domains via multiple registrars: c_01, c_03, c_11, c_12 and c_16. Figure 8 illustrates how campaign c_11 sequentially changes between 4 registrars over the entire duration of the campaign. Malicious actors might change registrars for economic reasons (cheaper domain registrations) or to evade detection. Alternatively, the change in registrar can be triggered by an intermediate reseller that changes registrar.

Table 4 lists for each campaign the amount of adaptive registration details that were used throughout its lifespan. While five campaigns use just a single phone number and email address, the large majority leverage multiple registration details. The email providers that are categorized as "Campaign" indicate that a domain name that was registered as part of the campaign, was later used as the email provider for a new registration.

As primary indicators of evasion sophistication, we list two metrics. Firstly, we give the maximum number of domains for which a campaign has reused a single phone number or email address. Secondly, we measure the longest period during which a registrant's phone or email address has been reused. c_15, c_12 and c_8 demonstrate the highest sophistication in terms of minimizing the reuse of registrant details. However, c_15 uses many different self-registered email providers and only reuses details sparsely over a long period. In other words, they leverage a more elaborate strategy than c_12 and c_8, where registrant details seem to be automatically generated in a hit-and-run fashion The success of c_15's strategy is supported by its low blacklist presence. In contrast, c_2, c_11 and c_18 deploy exhibit more simple and high-volume strategies.

**Table 4.** The amount of registrars, phone numbers, email addresses and types of email providers used per campaign.

| | Campaign | | | | | | | | | | | | | | | | | | | |
|---|---|---|---|---|---|---|---|---|---|---|---|---|---|---|---|---|---|---|---|---|
| | 1 | 2 | 3 | 4 | 5 | 6 | 7 | 8 | 9 | 10 | 11 | 12 | 13 | 14 | 15 | 16 | 17 | 18 | 19 | 20 |
| Nb of registrars | 3 | 1 | 2 | 1 | 1 | 1 | 1 | 1 | 1 | 1 | 4 | 2 | 1 | 1 | 1 | 3 | 1 | 1 | 1 | 1 |
| Nb of phones | 4 | 3 | 19 | 54 | 1 | 2 | 1 | 29 | 14 | 1 | 2 | 29 | 1 | 1 | 97 | 8 | 1 | 4 | 1 | 13 |
| Max domains per phone | 338 | 1026 | 385 | 169 | 177 | 158 | 93 | 20 | 590 | 125 | 1220 | 24 | 154 | 989 | 16 | 372 | 283 | 1265 | 752 | 237 |
| Max phone usage (days) | 90 | 71 | 69 | 276 | 129 | 1 | 359 | 2 | 155 | 204 | 246 | 15 | 307 | 41 | 232 | 147 | 50 | 75 | 226 | 35 |
| Nb of email addresses | 6 | 18 | 71 | 54 | 177 | 2 | 1 | 29 | 13 | 1 | 2 | 29 | 29 | 1 | 98 | 8 | 1 | 4 | 1 | 14 |
| Max domains per email | 263 | 103 | 68 | 169 | 1 | 158 | 93 | 20 | 590 | 125 | 1240 | 24 | 126 | 989 | 16 | 373 | 283 | 1265 | 752 | 237 |
| Max email usage (days) | 50 | 8 | 14 | 267 | – | 1 | 359 | 2 | 155 | 204 | 157 | 15 | 255 | 41 | 232 | 147 | 50 | 75 | 226 | 35 |
| Email Providers: Public | – | 1 | 1 | 2 | – | – | – | 6 | 1 | – | – | 1 | – | 1 | – | 3 | 1 | 1 | 1 | 1 |
| Email Providers: Private | 5 | – | – | – | – | 2 | 1 | – | – | 1 | 1 | – | 1 | – | – | – | – | – | – | – |
| Email Providers: Campaign | – | – | – | – | – | – | – | – | – | – | – | – | 28 | – | 98 | – | – | – | – | – |
| Email Providers: WHOIS privacy | – | – | – | – | 1 | – | – | – | – | – | – | – | – | – | – | – | – | – | – | – |

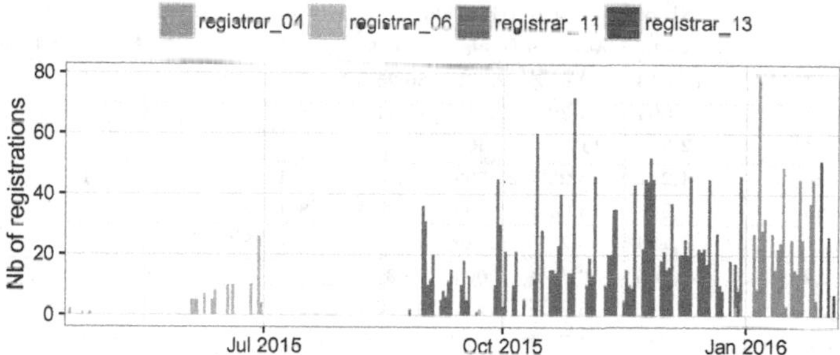


**Fig. 8.** Registrations per day and per registrar of campaign c_11.

**Related Campaigns.** By searching for overlaps between campaigns in their registrants' details, as well as temporal characteristics (simultaneous or chained activity), we have identified that several campaigns are likely related to each other:

- c_02 and c_03 have registrants with the same phone number
- c_08 and c_12 have registrants with the same phone number, email and address
- c_16 and c_18 have registrants with the same address

Similarly, the abrupt ending of campaigns c_01, c_02 and c_03 suggest that these campaigns might be of the same actor, or depend on the same reseller or registrar that ended their service.

**Most Active Malicious Actors.** Table 5 gives the highest represented malicious registrars, registrants and email providers in our dataset. Most surprisingly, 49.6% of all the malicious domain names are registered with one single registrar. Furthermore, it used by half of all the campaigns we identified. We argue that this registrar is either very *flexible* in accepting registrations, or has the most interesting price setting for bulk registrants. Note that this registrar only accounts for 2.27% of all benign registrations. This observation confirms earlier findings in [11, 13] that a handful of registrars accounts for the majority of spammer domains.

The most used malicious email providers are all popular public webmail providers. The situation is different compared to the registrars as gmail.com has the largest share of malicious registrations but also well-represented in benign registrations. In contrast, aol.com and yahoo.com do have a large fraction of malicious registrations.

Over 3,000 malicious registrations can be attributed to just 3 registrants who are predominantly malicious. Related to the reasoning in Sect. 3.3, we suspect that non-blacklisted registrations of these registrants are likely malicious as well.

**Table 5.** Top 3 most malicious registrars, email providers and registrants. For each entry, we list their contribution to all malicious and benign registrations, their toxicity and the campaigns that are associated with them. The toxicity expresses the percentage of malicious registrations within that entity.

| | Nb of malicious | Contribution Malicious | Benign | Toxicity | Associated campaigns |
|---|---|---|---|---|---|
| 1. registrar_5 | 10,353 | 49.61% | 2.27% | 36.25% | 1 2 3 4 9 10 12 13 14 17 |
| 2. registrar_3 | 3,004 | 14.39% | 2.64% | 12.41% | 3 7 8 12 16 18 |
| 3. registrar_7 | 2,327 | 11.15% | 0.46% | 38.67% | 20 |
| 1. gmail.com | 4,221 | 20.23% | 24.79% | 2.08% | 4 14 19 |
| 2. yahoo.com | 3,348 | 16.04% | 1.49% | 21.85% | 2 3 4 8 20 |
| 3. aol.com | 2,134 | 10.23% | 0.31% | 46.28% | 8 9 |
| 1. m...s@c...k.com | 1,265 | 6.06% | 0.00% | 99.37% | 18 |
| 2. abuse@j...n.com | 1,240 | 5.94% | 0.12% | 54.89% | 11 |
| 3. n...t@gmail.com | 989 | 4.74% | 0.01% | 95.37% | 14 |

## 5 Automating Campaign Identification

In the previous section, we discussed a large-scale experiment in which we manually identified large campaigns from a corpus of malicious registrations. The criteria that defined these campaigns were mainly recurring registrant and nameserver details. In this section, we use that knowledge to automate the campaign identification process by using a clustering algorithm. The results serve to both validate the manual experiment, as well as to demonstrate the capabilities of automatic campaign identification to aid ecosystem analyses in TLDs.

### 5.1 Clustering Process

**Algorithm.** *Agglomerative clustering* is chosen as the basis to perform automatic campaign identification. It is a hierarchical clustering algorithm that works by iteratively merging the two clusters that are closest to each other [12]. We adopt the complete linkage criterion to determine the distance between clusters. Using this criterion, the distance is equal to that of the most dissimilar instances of both clusters, promoting a high density. There are two main reasons for opting for agglomerative clustering.

1. The algorithm does not require a predetermined number of clusters, allowing us to statistically evaluate the optimal number of clusters afterwards.
2. Given the results from Sect. 3, we presume that about 80% of malicious domains can be grouped into clusters. Agglomerative clustering allows the remaining independent domains to have their own singleton cluster, without necessarily polluting the large clusters.

**Feature Set.** For each of the 20,870 blacklisted registrations, we extract 13 features. There are two general **registration features**, *domain length* and *registrar*. Next, we have ten **registrant features**: *name, street, city, region, country, zip code, phone number, email account* and *email provider*. Lastly, two **nameserver features** were included, the *nameserver domain names* and their *geographical location*.

Agglomerative clustering uses the Euclidean distance measure to calculate the distance between two instances. However, except for *domain length* and *address score*, all features in our set are categorical, not numeric. In order to accommodate these features, we apply one-hot encoding [18]: for each possible category in our set, a new binary feature is created. Each instance that carried that value will receive a value of 1 in the new binary encoded feature, all others are set to 0. Naturally, one-hot encoding dramatically increases the number of features, more specifically from 13 to 30,843.

**Cutoff Selection.** Agglomerative clustering has no predefined stopping criteria and merges clusters until only one remains. Using the campaign labels from the manual analysis in Sect. 3, we calculate the *V-measure* after each merging step to statistically express the mapping between clusters and campaigns. The V-measure is the harmonic mean of the *homogeneity* and *completeness score* [19]. The former is a metric that represents how homogeneous each cluster is in terms of campaign labels, the latter measures whether the instances of a certain label are all assigned to the same cluster[4]. The highest V-measure is observed at a cutoff of 432 clusters, where the homogeneity is 0.90 and the completeness score 0.86.

[4] For instances without campaign labels, the registrant's phone numbers are set as their label.

### 5.2 Results

In the selected model, very large clusters have formed. Namely, 80% of domains reside in the 39 largest clusters, while a long tail of 227 clusters consisting out of only 5 registrations or less. In other words, the clustering algorithm forms a Pareto distribution similar to the manual campaign identification in Sect. 4. Furthermore, the top 30 clusters represent 91.48% of blacklisted registrations that reside within the 20 manually identified campaigns.

Using Fig. 9, we analyze the top 30 largest clusters and their correlation to the campaign labels from the manual analysis. The clustering algorithm largely aligns with the manual campaign identification, with most clusters mapping to a single campaign. The notable exceptions being the two largest clusters. The first cluster encompasses 2,052 domains of both c_02 and c_03. This is in line with our previous speculation (Sect. 4) that c_02 and c_03 are related given their synchronized ending and the fact that they share registrants with the same phone number. The same is true for the second cluster, as both c_16 and c_18 clearly share registrants with the same address.

Cluster 16 is the only automatically identified cluster that solely exists out of domains without campaign labels. When inspecting those domains, we find that this cluster is likely related to or part of c_20. More specifically, their active days align and the same registrar is used for all registrations in both sets, as shown in the bottom part of Fig. 10.

Several clusters also contain a small amount of instances without a campaign label. We distinguish two cases: instances that closely align to a campaign, but were not selected because of too narrow selection criteria; and instances that have no campaign affinity, but are most probably merged because the clustering algorithm has executed too many merges. The former are labeled as (Related) in Fig. 9, the latter as (Unrelated).

18 of the 20 manually identified campaigns are represented in the top 30 clusters. The smallest identified campaign, c_07, is not found in this subset of clusters because it is simply too small. Cluster 30 contains 110 domains, more than c_07 encompasses as a whole. However, we find that c_07 is completely and homogeneously represented by the 35th cluster. The second campaign that is missing is c_15. As mentioned in Sect. 3.3, this campaign was selected by a unique and complex address formatting pattern. Since the clustering algorithm only performs binary matches on these fields, it is less effective at detecting these more advanced similarities. As shown in the top part of Fig. 10, c_15 is spread out over 18 clusters, that essentially represent 18 different registrants that are reused throughout the campaign. The affinity between those clusters is clear when considering their active days.

In conclusion, the manual and automatic campaign identification results align to a large extent. We find that, when performing automatic detection using clustering, we achieve a more exhaustive identification of clear similarities as opposed to manual identification (e.g. cluster 16). However, the automatic approach has difficulties to detect more advanced similarity patterns (e.g. c_15). In future work, more sophisticated techniques, such as n-grams, can be integrated into the clustering algorithm to detect more advanced similarity patterns.

In general, the outcome of the clustering algorithm both validates the approach of the manual analysis, as well as demonstrates the capabilities of automatic and reproducible campaign identification using registrant and nameserver details.

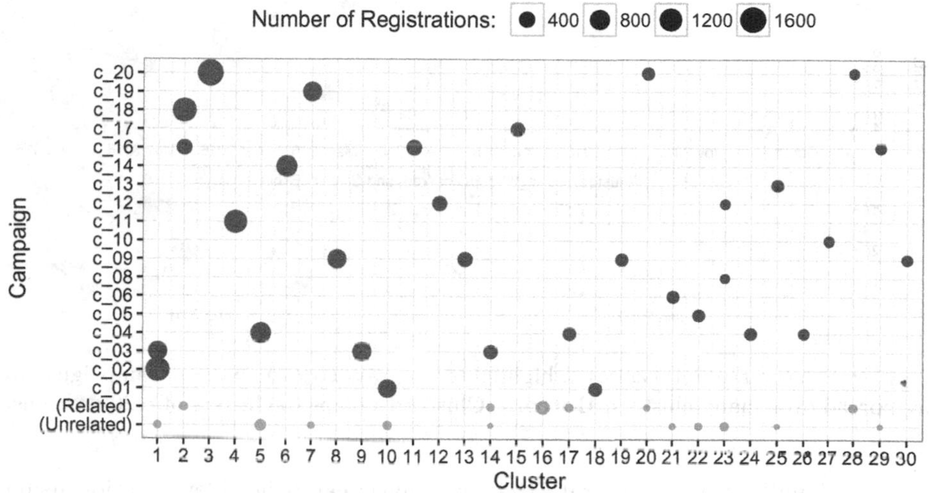


**Fig. 9.** Mapping of the top 30 clusters to campaign instances. The bottom two rows represent domains without a campaign label: the (Related) row groups the registrations that closely align with campaigns, the (Unrelated) groups registrations without campaign affinity. The clusters are ranked from large to small.

## 6 Discussion and Limitations

In this section, we want to discuss the relevance and applications, as well as the limitations of our study.

**Applications.** Given the exploratory nature of this research, we anticipate several applications and next steps.

The relevance of this work is not limited to .eu domains. Presumably, malicious actors do not restrict their potential to a single TLD. Furthermore, bulk registrations can be made across multiple TLDs using the same registrar. Therefore, the findings and methods described in this paper can most likely be applied to other or across TLDs. To reproduce this study, access to registrant and nameserver details of registrations is required. This data can generally be obtained by downloading zone files and WHOIS data.

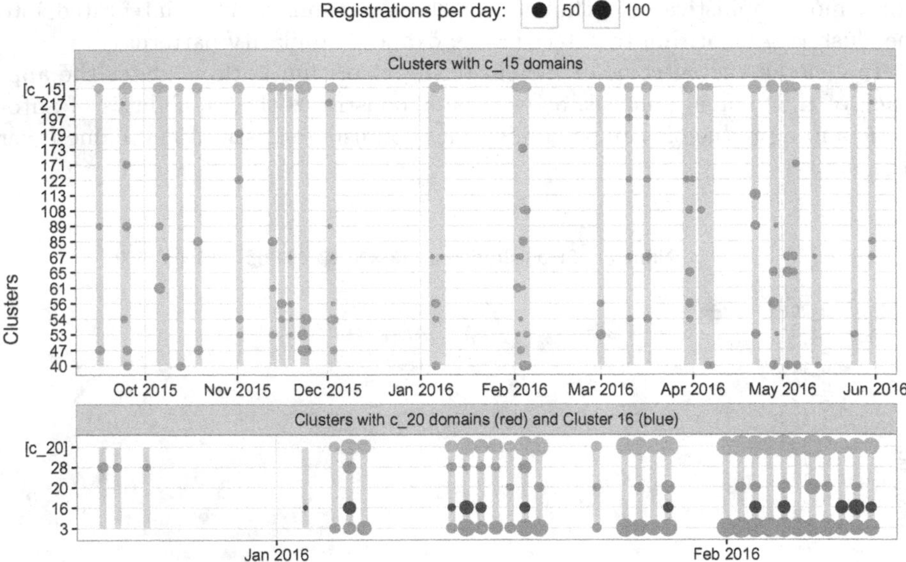


**Fig. 10.** Related temporal activity, highlighted in gray. **Top**: Domains of campaign c_15 are spread over many clusters. **Bottom**: Cluster 16 maps to clusters of c_20 domains.

Additionally, we demonstrate that automatic campaign identification using clustering is a feasible strategy. Moreover, 18.38% of registrations in the identified campaigns are not present on blacklists. This entices interesting opportunities to extend the coverage of blacklists. Although the proposed system relies on a post-factum analysis, it could create opportunities to stop ongoing campaigns.

**Limitations.** We note four limitations and potential validity threats.

Firstly, the main subjects of this research are domain names that are registered with malicious intent. However, backlists also contain legitimate registrations that have been compromised later on. We argue that the prevalence of these cases is minimal, since 98.57% of blacklisted registrations were already flagged within the first 30 days of registration. Furthermore, compromised benign domains would appear as outliers in our data and could thus hardly pollute campaign analyses.

Secondly, both the manual and automatic identification rely on patterns in the registration data. Malicious actors can leverage this dependency by constantly using different registration data and patterns. However, the cost for attackers would increase to achieve this higher level of circumvention. Furthermore, it is hard not to exhibit any pattern when performing bulk registrations (same registrars, time patterns, fake identity generating tools,...).

Additionally, several registrars offer anonymization services to their customers, obscuring the registrant contact information to the registry. Evidently, this diminishes the ability to differentiate between registrations and conceals information that can be used to identify domains registered by the same entity. In the case of .eu, the use of such obfuscation services is not allowed by the registry's terms and conditions. During our analysis, we find that such services were only deployed by c_05 which could have impacted this campaign.

Finally, our research is based on a set of publicly available blacklists that are, at least to some extent, incomplete. A more complete ground truth would likely improve the performance of our approach.

## 7 Related Work

Prior to our research, Hao et al. [11] studied the domain registration behavior of spammers. They reported that most spam domains are very short-lived. More specifically, 60% of these domains were active for only a single day. Spammers are registering many "single-shot" domains to minimize interference by blacklists. To counter this strategy, the authors explore various features on which spam domains exhibit distinctive behavior. For instance, in contrast with benign registrations, they find that malicious domains are more often registered in batches. Recently, Hao et al. implemented many features discussed in that prior work to create a machine learning-based predictor capable of detecting malicious domains at time-of-registration [10]. The three most dominant features of their classifier are authoritative nameservers, trigrams in domain names and the IP addresses of nameservers.

While both papers approach malicious domains as a two-class problem (benign vs. malicious registrations), many of their features essentially depend on returning characteristics of different underlying malicious campaigns. In this work, we are the first to shift the focus to the campaigns itself, exploring their modus operandi and different identifying characteristics.

A method related to ours was proposed by Felegyhzi et al. [5], who investigated the feasibility of proactive domain blacklisting, by inferring other malicious registrations from known-bad domains through shared nameservers and identical registration times. The proposed system shortens the time required to blacklist malicious domains, while providing important insights regarding the similarities of registrations within campaigns. Additionally, Cova et al. [4] identified different rogue antivirus campaigns by looking at the hosting infrastructure and registration details (including the registrant's email) of different domains.

Related studies concentrate on DNS traffic of newly registered domains to characterize malicious behaviour [1–3,9,14]. These systems mainly focus on the initial operational DNS patterns of domain names.

Other important efforts regarding malicious domains come from the study of domain generation algorithms (DGAs). Recent work by Plohmann et al. [17] demonstrates the increasing importance of understanding DGAs to thwart C&C communication. Using reimplementations of these algorithms, the authors execute forward generation of domain lists, which enables proactive identification of C&C domains.

## 8 Conclusion

In this study, we analyzed the maliciously-flagged .eu registrations over a 14-month period. This paper is the first to extensively dissect the underbelly of malicious registrations using registrant details to identify its operational components, namely campaigns. We explored the ecosystem and modus operandi of elaborate malicious actors that register massive amounts of domains for short-lived, malicious use.

By searching for shared characteristics, we established that at least 80.04% of all malicious registrations can be attributed to 20 campaigns with varying duration and intensity. Moreover, the coverage of blacklists can be extended by 19.30%, using the information from the campaign identification. After a rigorous evaluation, we are able to confirm that the vast majority of these previously undetected registrations are genuinely related to malicious activity; at most 0.92% are false positive registrations.

Our study demonstrates the potential to leverage the registrant details and other registration characteristics to identify large campaigns. Aided by an automatic identification process, this insight can be used to easily track and interfere with massive, long-running campaigns and to preemptively extend blacklists with malicious domains that have yet to be actively used by a cybercriminal.

**Acknowledgements.** We thank the reviewers for their valuable feedback. We would also like to express our gratitude to the PC chairs and in particular our shepherd, for supporting us in improving the paper.

## References

1. Antonakakis, M., Perdisci, R., Dagon, D., Lee, W., Feamster, N.: Building a dynamic reputation system for DNS. In: Proceedings of the 19th USENIX Conference on Security, p. 18 (2010)
2. Antonakakis, M., Perdisci, R., Lee, W., Vasiloglou II., N., Dagon, D.: Detecting malware domains at the upper DNS hierarchy. In: Proceedings of the 20th USENIX Conference on Security, p. 27
3. Bilge, L., Sen, S., Balzarotti, D., Kirda, E., Kruegel, C.: Exposure: a passive DNS analysis service to detect and report malicious domains. ACM Trans. Inf. Syst. Secur. (TISSEC) **16**(4), 14 (2014)
4. Cova, M., Leita, C., Thonnard, O., Keromytis, A.D., Dacier, M.: An analysis of rogue AV campaigns. In: Jha, S., Sommer, R., Kreibich, C. (eds.) RAID 2010. LNCS, vol. 6307, pp. 442–463. Springer, Heidelberg (2010). doi:10.1007/978-3-642-15512-3_23
5. Felegyhazi, M., Kreibich, C., Paxson, V.: On the potential of proactive domain blacklisting. In: Proceedings of the 3rd USENIX Conference on Large-Scale Exploits and Emergent Threats: Botnets, Spyware, Worms, and More, p. 6 (2010)
6. FortiGuard Center: Antispam - IP & Signature Lookup (2017). https://www.fortiguard.com/more/antispam
7. Google: Google Safe Browsing (2016). https://developers.google.com/safe-browsing/

8. Google: Unwanted Software Policy (2016). https://www.google.com/about/company/unwanted-software-policy.html
9. Hao, S., Feamster, N., Pandrangi, R.: Monitoring the initial DNS behavior of malicious domains. In: Proceedings of the 2011 ACM SIGCOMM Conference on Internet Measurement Conference, pp. 269–278. ACM (2011)
10. Hao, S., Kantchelian, A., Miller, B., Paxson, V., Feamster, N.: Predator: Proactive recognition and elimination of domain abuse at time-of-registration
11. Hao, S., Thomas, M., Paxson, V., Feamster, N., Kreibich, C., Grier, C., Hollenbeck, S.: Understanding the domain registration behavior of spammers. In: Proceedings of the 2013 Conference on Internet Measurement Conference, pp. 63–76 (2013)
12. Hastie, T., Tibshirani, R., Friedman, J.: The Elements of Statistical Learning. Springer Series in Statistics. Springer, New York (2001)
13. Levchenko, K., Pitsillidis, A., Chachra, N., Enright, B., Félegyházi, M., Grier, C., Halvorson, T., Kanich, C., Kreibich, C., Liu, H., McCoy, D., Weaver, N., Paxson, V., Voelker, G.M., Savage, S.: Click trajectories: end-to-end analysis of the spam value chain. In: Proceedings of the 2011 IEEE Symposium on Security and Privacy, SP 2011, pp. 431–446. IEEE Computer Society, Washington, DC (2011). http://dx.doi.org/10.1109/SP.2011.24
14. Moura, G.C., Müller, M., Wullink, M., Hesselman, C.: nDEWS: a new domains early warning system for TLDs. In: NOMS 2016–2016 IEEE/IFIP Network Operations and Management Symposium, pp. 1061–1066. IEEE (2016)
15. Myles, P.: DomainWire Global TLD Report 2016/2. https://www.centr.org/library/statistics-report/domainwire-global-tld-report-2016-2.html
16. Pattanai: Faker is a PHP library that generates fake data for you. https://github.com/teepluss/laravel-faker
17. Plohmann, D., Yakdan, K., Klatt, M., Bader, J., Gerhards-Padilla, E.: A comprehensive measurement study of domain generating malware. In: 25th USENIX Security Symposium, pp. 263–278 (2016)
18. Scikit-learn developers: Encoding categorical features (2017). http://scikit-learn.org/stable/modules/preprocessing.html
19. Scikit-learn developers: Homogeneity, completeness and V-measure (2017). http://scikit-learn.org/stable/modules/clustering.html
20. SURBL: SURBL - URI Reputation Data (2016). http://www.surbl.org
21. The Spamhaus Project Ltd: The Domain Block List (2016). https://www.spamhaus.org/dbl/
22. Twilio: Lookup (2017). https://www.twilio.com/lookup
23. URL Void: Website Reputation Checker Tool (2016). http://www.urlvoid.com/
24. Vixie, P.: Domain name abuse: how cheap new domain names fuel the eCrime economy. Presentation at RSA Conference 2015 (2015)

[illegible]

# Author Index

Printed in the United States
By Bookmasters